Public
Personnel
Systems

Public Personnel Systems

by
Robert D. Lee, Jr.
The Pennsylvania State University

University Park Press
Baltimore

UNIVERSITY PARK PRESS
International Publishers in Science, Medicine, and Education
233 East Redwood Street
Baltimore, Maryland 21202

Typeset by American Graphic Arts Corporation

Manufactured in the United States by the Maple Press Company

Library of Congress Cataloging in Publication Data

Lee, Robert D.
  Public personnel systems.

  Bibliography: p.
  Includes index.
  1. Civil service—United States.   2. Civil service
—United States—States.   3. Local officials and
employees—United States.   4. Personnel management—
United States.   I. Title.
JK765.L43   353.006   79-12468
ISBN 0-8391-1452-4

Contents

Figures

Tables

Preface

This is a general book on public personnel systems. The book surveys the emergence of these systems, their current status, and possible future directions. Special attention is given to whether each aspect of personnel administration contributes to or deters from effective and efficient government operations.

Personnel administration is examined within a systems context. The components of the system are considered along with the relationships among those components. The book discusses whether the components of personnel systems are well integrated with each other and whether personnel systems are integrated within the broader governmental system, including within an intergovernmental framework.

The book blends the new with the old. Traditional topics, such as recruiting, testing, and selecting, are considered. In recent decades, however, there have been new forces that have influenced public personnel systems. These forces include the rise of public-sector collective bargaining and equal employment opportunity for minorities and women. One bias of the book is its emphasis on the role of judicial decisions in personnel systems. In recent years courts have become major instruments for determining what may and may not be done in personnel administration. The reader should be careful, however, not to assume that judicial decisions constitute the "whole story." Neither laws nor judicial opinions by themselves account for the operations of personnel systems. For instance, while employment discrimination based on race and sex is clearly prohibited, such discrimination continues today in some places in government.

A balanced discussion of personnel systems has been attempted. Both outright condemnation and unqualified endorsement of existing systems have been avoided. The reason for this approach is not timidity on the part of the author. Instead, the problem lies in the competing values that public personnel systems are expected to serve. One recurrent theme throughout the book, for example, is the appropriate balance between what government should rightfully expect of its workers and what workers should rightfully expect of government, juxtaposed with what citizens should expect from the governmental system. Many of the issues of the book are discussed in pro and con terms, with the reader having to judge which set of arguments is more persuasive. Choosing one side over the other depends upon the relative weights a reader assigns to various values. As is discussed in the last chapter, society has been unable to reach consensus on the relative importance of many values that impinge on public personnel systems.

The discussion also is balanced, in that it reviews state, local, and federal personnel systems. Emphasis on state and local systems is appropriate, especially considering the dramatic growth in the number of state and local employees in recent decades. The federal civil service reforms approved in 1978 are presented, but much of the discussion necessarily focuses upon the federal experience prior to those reforms. While the specific changes approved in 1978 are explained, the effects of those changes will not be known for several years. *Great variation exists among these levels of governments and within them. Therefore, the reader should avoid overgeneralizations. What exists in any one government does not necessarily exist in other governments.*

Personnel systems are treated in a broad context. The discussion is not limited to those activities performed by personnel administrators. The reason for this is that an understanding of human behavior in government requires looking beyond traditional personnel functions. Therefore, there are discussions of motivation theory along with specific techniques, such as flexitime, management by objectives, and organization development.

The first two chapters serve as an overall introduction. The first chapter, "Introduction," differentiates public personnel from private personnel and discusses how personnel systems are part of the larger governmental system. Chapter 2, "Patronage and the Merit Principle," explains how and why personnel systems emerged and the organizational arrangements that have developed for furthering the merit principle.

The next five chapters are sequenced according to major personnel processes. Chapter 3, "Organizational Design, Job Design, and Position Classification," shows how bureaucracies can be structured and how jobs are established within bureaucratic units. The chapter concentrates upon determining what work is to be done in each job and the categorization of jobs into classes and series. Next, the assigning of pay to groups of jobs and individual jobs is discussed in Chapter 4, "Pay and Employee Benefits." The chapter also is concerned with employee benefits as a form of compensation. With positions having been defined and pay assigned to them, attention turns to "Recruitment, Examination, and Selection" in Chapter 5; emphasis is given to the validity of testing programs. Chapter 6, "Probation and Performance Evaluation" discusses what happens to individuals after they become public workers. Chapter 7, "Careers and Career Development," focuses upon promotion procedure and training as a vehicle for career development; career executives are of special concern in the chapter.

The second half of the book deals with special problems associated with personnel systems. Chapters 8 and 9 concentrate upon employee rights. "Employee Rights and Responsibilities," Chapter 8, discusses such critical matters as employee ethical responsibilities, loyalty and security problems, political rights of workers, and rights in adverse action proceedings. Chapter 9, "Equal Rights and Affirmative Action," identifies the numerous ways by which people have been discriminated against and the individual and collective remedies that have emerged. The chapter emphasizes judicial interpretations of equal opportunity in employment.

Chapter 10, "Personnel Planning and Economic Policy," draws upon the earlier discusssion of personnel processes and indicates how personnel planning can be conducted. Constraints on planning are discussed, especially the frequent lack of coordination between personnel and budgetary processes. The chapter considers personnel systems within an intergovernmental context and how public employment is used as a vehicle for economic stimulation.

The next two chapters deal with topics that usually are not considered the responsibility of personnel administrators but rather that of line administrators. Chapter 11, "Motivation Theory," discusses why people behave as they do from the perspective of theories relating to individual motivation. Chapter 12, "Motivation in Daily Operations," reviews the opportunities and limitations of applying motivation theories. Daily management problems provide frequent obstacles to motivation.

Labor management problems are reserved for the last substantive chapter in the book, although this significant subject is kept before the reader throughout the book. At this point, however, Chapter 13 pulls together those earlier discussions, explains the processes of collective negotiations, and discusses the implications for governmental operations.

Chapter 14, "Critique," looks to the future. With the earlier chapters having cited numerous strengths and weaknesses of contemporary personnel systems, this chapter considers to what extent substantial changes are needed and whether appropriate changes are likely to occur. Of special concern is the need for a newly stated set of internally consistent concepts that can help guide the future development of public personnel systems.

This book is intended for a wide audience. For those contemplating careers in government, the material provides a general background on how personnel functions are carried out at all levels of government and how personnel systems affect the lives of public employees. A sensitivity to the techniques and issues associated with personnel administration is essential for all government employees. Another audience consists of those who have a career objective of being personnel administrators; the book can serve as a starting point in the study of personnel administration. Another audience consists of current government workers in both personnel and nonpersonnel jobs; the discussion can serve as a review of some familiar issues as well as an update on current trends in personnel. Ideally, all readers will gain from this book an increased awareness of the immense importance of personnel systems in government.

Acknowledgments

Many people helped along the way. Robert T. Daland of the University of North Carolina, Chapel Hill; Sally Greenberg of the U.S. Office of Personnel Management; and Frederick C. Mosher of the University of Virginia provided comments on most of the manuscript. Their suggestions were extremely valuable. Ms. Greenberg deserves special thanks not only for her extensive substantive suggestions, but for taking time to watch for errors in detail; I am most appreciative of her assistance. Staff members to the Chairman of the U.S. Civil Service Commission provided exceedingly helpful advice on the draft chapters. Others who provided comments on portions of the manuscript include Frank J. Landy and John M. Stevens of The Pennsylvania State University; Kurt H. Decker of the Commonwealth of Pennsylvania; and Virginia Lauer of the U.S. Equal Employment Opportunity Commission.

I also am thankful for the support I received from the Institute of Public Administration of The Pennsylvania State University. The Institute's Director, Robert J. Mowitz, provided encouragement in this effort and helped provide the needed support to prepare the manuscript. Graduate assistant Dennis B. Phifer helped in the research. Gail Dillon typed some of the first chapters to be written and then Debbie Putt assumed responsibility for typing the remaining chapters plus making the seemingly endless corrections in the process of revising and editing.

Finally I wish to thank Maurice Ramsey, professor emeritus of Wayne State University, who has served as one of my mentors for about two decades. Although he was not involved with preparation of the manuscript itself, his insights into the field of public administration have had a major influence on my thoughts and therefore on this book.

The people I have mentioned here have contributed immensely, but this note of appreciation does not imply their endorsement of the book nor the endorsement of their respective organizational affiliations. The final product is ultimately my responsibility.

To my mother, father, and grandmother

Public
Personnel
Systems

Chapter 1

Introduction

A government is not just what exists on the printed pages of a constitution and in statute books. Although these documents are extremely important in setting the framework for what a government does, documents by themselves do nothing. People must make decisions about what government should and should not do. People must make decisions about how government services are to be provided, and people, not laws and regulations, provide those services. Citizens benefit not from the dollars spent on public programs but from the services provided by public workers.

This is a book about people in government, but not all government personnel are considered. Generally beyond the scope of this book are legislatures and their staffs, courts and their staffs, and chief executives. The focus here is upon career personnel and, to a lesser extent, noncareer personnel who work for the executive branches of the federal, state, and local governments. The concern is with the methods by which human resources are managed in governments.

This chapter has three sections. The first differentiates public personnel systems for those in the private sector. The second section considers the growth of public bureaucracies and the magnitude of personnel in government. The third section discusses the characteristics of systems and how personnel systems are parts of larger systems.

PUBLIC AND PRIVATE SECTOR COMPARISONS

Both government and industry hire millions of workers, but the two are different in their basic missions and the ways by which human resources are managed. One basic difference in missions is that the private sector is profit-oriented, whereas the public sector is not. Profits result from selling goods and services at prices that are higher than costs. Costs are minimized in order to maximize profits. Industry, therefore, has an incentive to hire only those people who are needed. Industry avoids overhiring and has an incentive to hire those individuals who will be productive. Private-sector employees whose productivity declines tend to be demoted or dismissed, although so-called "deadwood" is to be found in both sectors. Government, of course, is concerned with providing quality services with as few resources as possible, but government lacks the profit incentive that encourages keeping personnel costs low.

Competition is another aspect of a market economy based on the profit motive. A corporation attempts to keep prices and production costs low in order to have a competitive advantage over other firms. If personnel costs push prices upward, the firm's sales will fall and so will profits. On the other hand, government in most instances operates as a monopoly rather than as part of a competitive market economy. A city fire department has a monopoly on its service, so that consumers do not have a choice about quality and cost. An additional feature is that government has the option of raising tax rates and borrowing extensively to offset higher operating costs. While a corporation might be forced out of business if personnel costs rose excessively, government is not under such a constraint. Rapidly rising expenditures coupled with tax increases can result in taxpayer revolts and can lead to bankruptcy, as in the case of New York City in the 1970s; nevertheless, governments are not threatened with extinction.

The public sector is labor intensive. Industry uses raw materials and machines that turn those materials into finished goods. Government, in contrast, typically provides services and not products, and in most instances those services must be provided by people rather than by machines. Industry frequently has a choice between people and machines. If the cost of labor increases, industry will replace expensive workers with less expensive machines. The profit incentive encourages such shifts in personnel utilization. Much of what government does, on the other hand, defies mechanization. Mail-sorting machines, for example, may be able to replace some workers, but people are still required for mail delivery. Similarly, there are limits on the ability to substitute machines for teachers, road-repair workers, and fire fighters.

In some respects, society probably expects more of government workers than it does of private workers. High ethical standards are expected of public employees. While some private-sector practices may be shrugged off as "that's just business," those same practices in government would arouse public outcry. Government workers serving the commonweal are expected to avoid conflicts of interest in which special interests and personal benefits might be furthered at the expense of the public interest. On the other hand, the public probably believes that private-sector employees are more efficient and productive than government workers. Neither generalization invariably holds true.

Managers in the private sector may have greater freedom in personnel matters than public managers. A corporation has considerable flexibility in how it hires and fires people. Public administrators, in comparison, frequently feel bound by bureaucratic red tape concerning personnel actions. This distinction between the two sectors, however, should not be overdrawn. State and federal laws affect many private-sector personnel matters. Private-sector occupational safety, pension system laws, unemployment compensation, equal employment opportunity, and labor relations are regulated by government. Indeed, government sets rules by which industry must operate.

Authority is more structured in the private sector than in the public sector. In a corporation an employee is rarely uncertain about who is the boss. Authority in government is more dispersed. Not only are there sometimes conflicting lines of authority within the executive branch, but there are also great uncertainties over the relative powers of the executive and legislative branches vis-à-vis public employees. Workers are expected to be responsive to both their administrative superiors and to legislators. Public employees may find themselves in positions where they are responsible for implementing a statute having strong legislative support, but which is basically opposed by the political leadership within the executive branch.

Another contrast is that the executive branch of government is led by amateurs/politicians with short tenure, while the private sector has experienced executives. A departmental secretary is appointed by and serves at the pleasure of the chief executive. Continuity of leadership in departments and major agencies is rare in any large government. Politically appointed executives obtain positions in part because of their roles in partisan politics, whereas private-sector executives are more likely to be chosen because of their technical and managerial capabilities. This is not intended to suggest that politically appointed managers are incompetent and that private-sector managers are always well qualified, but rather to indicate that different sets of criteria are applied in selecting executives in the two sectors.

One other distinguishing feature is the single purpose of personnel in the private sector compared with the multiple purposes they serve in the public sector. Industry uses people to make products and deliver services. Government uses people for these functions but for other reasons as well. Government jobs have been used to reward the politically faithful; patronage has been a common characteristic of all governments. Government employment is used to aid veterans, who are favored in being hired and promoted. Government employment is used to stimulate the economy; unemployed people are hired by governments as a device for increasing consumer spending. Public employment sometimes is a disguised form of welfare. Government jobs also have been handed out by regional quota systems. Until 1978 the federal government set quotas on the mix of its workers in the Washington, D.C. area. By setting limits on the number of people hired from each state, it was thought that the bureaucracy would be more representative of the population.[1]

In addition to contrasts, there are similarities between government and the private sector. One characteristic that the two sectors share is a wide range in the nature of jobs. Both have jobs that greatly affect the general citizenry. There also are many intrinsically dull jobs in both government and industry. The latter has the assembly line, where people often seem to be appendages of machines. Government has paperwork. Workers may complain about the tedium of forms processing, and yet those forms are what provide their jobs.

Both sectors have units that range from small to large. There are "mom and pop" stores and "mom and pop" local governments. The private sector has giants, such as General Dynamics, General Electric, and General Motors, and the public sector has giant city governments, such as those of Los Angeles, Philadelphia, and Detroit. State governments range from comparatively small to large employers. The federal government is the largest single employer in the country.

MAGNITUDE AND GROWTH OF PUBLIC BUREAUCRACIES

Government employment has grown from a miniscule size to one that constitutes a major segment of the labor market.[2] Today, one out of every six jobs in the country is a government job. Under the Articles of Confederation the government had few employees, but with the adoption of the Constitution in 1789, an executive branch was created from which the present giant bureaucracy eventually emerged. Growth originally was slow. As late as 1816 there were fewer than 5,000 full- and part-time civilian employees in the federal service. Following the Civil War, greater growth was recorded. In 1871 there were over 50,00 federal employees,

---

[1] Subcommittee on Civil Service and General Services, Senate Committee on Governmental Affairs, *Repeal of Apportionment Requirement: Hearings*, 95th Cong., 1st sess. (Washington: Government Printing Office, 1977).

[2] The data for this section are from the following Census Bureau publications: *Governmental Units in 1977*, preliminary report (1977); *Historical Statistics on Governmental Finances and Employment* (1974); *Historical Statistics of the United States: Colonial Times to 1970* (1975); *Government Organization* (1973); *Governmental Finances in 1975–76* (1977); *Public Employment in 1977* (1978); and *Annual Report of Employment of Geographic Area* [in 1976] (1978).

and by 1881 this number had doubled to 100,000. The fastest growing period was from the Depression through World War II. In 1931 there were still only 610,000 employees, but by 1945, the peak of the war-time economy, the federal civilian work force had climbed to nearly 4 million. Within a year, this was reduced to less than 3 million.

Although the federal budget has grown dramatically since World War II, rising from $35 billion in 1947 to $460 billion in 1978, federal employment has remained relatively constant. Figure 1.1 shows that federal civilian employment has remained between 2 and 3 million; only once during this period, in 1950, has the federal work force dropped below 2 million. The Civil Service Reform Act of 1978 limited employment through 1981 to the level that existed in 1977, which was about 2.8 million.

State and local employment, on the other hand, has shown dramatic growth. State employment just after World War II was equal to about half of federal employment, but state employees now outnumber federal employees (in 1977, 3.5 million compared with 2.8 million federal workers, see Figure 1.1). Local government employment has shown even more marked growth, rising from less than 3 million in 1947 to close to 9.1 million today. Local government employees after World War II accounted for slightly less than half of the public work force, whereas now they account for about 60 percent. The federal share of the public labor force has slipped from 34 percent down to less than 20 percent.

Altogether there are more than 15 million full- and part-time government workers in the United States. Following World War II there were about 400 government workers for every 10,000 people in the country. That number has now risen to approximately 700.

These workers, of course, are geographically dispersed. Not all federal workers are in the Washington, D.C. area nor do all state workers work in their state capitals. Less than 15 percent of federal employees work in the Washington, D.C. metropolitan area. California, alone, has about 300,000 federal civilian employees. The federal government has ten regions with a city in each designated as the regional headquarters for major federal agencies; Denver, for example, has been designated for the states of Colorado, Montana, North and South Dakota, Utah, and Wyoming. In addition to these regional cities, many other cities have federal installations, the most common being post offices. State employees are similarly dispersed. A state such as Illinois needs to have offices in Chicago, Peoria, and Rockford, as well as in Springfield.

Personnel are the most expensive components of a government's operating budget. When the money the federal government gives to state and local government is excluded, federal personnel costs are about a

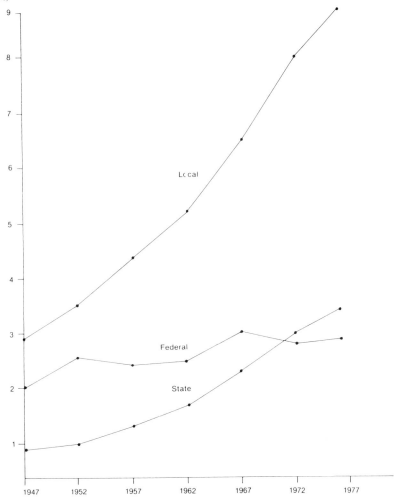

Number of
employees
(full- and part-time)
(in millions)

Local

Federal

State

1947   1952   1957   1962   1967   1972   1977

Figure 1.1.   Federal, state, and local employment, 1947–1977. Sources: Census Bureau, *Historical Statistics on Governmental Finances and Employment* (Washington: Government Printing Office, 1974), p. 59, and Census Bureau, *Public Employment in 1977* (Washington: Government Printing Office, 1978), p. 12.

quarter of direct federal expenditures. When insurance funds, especially
social security, also are excluded, personnel costs amount to about 45
percent of direct federal expenditures. In other words, nearly half of
direct federal outlays are for personnel. The figures at the state and local
levels are comparable (38 and 51 percent of outlays exclusive of
intergovernmental and trust expenditures).

Governments specialize in the services they provide, and this is
reflected in their use of personnel. Table 1.1 shows the functional distribution of employees for the three main levels of government. More
than half of all local employees are in education, as are more than 40
percent of the state workers. These figures reflect the importance of local
school districts and state-operated colleges and universities. The other
major function for states is health and hospitals (18 percent of employment). Other local functions are small in comparison with education.
Although crime is a major problem today, only 6 percent of local
employment is committed to police protection. Federal civilian employment is concentrated in two fields—international relations, including
defense, and mail service. About 60 percent of federal workers are in
these two fields.

Local employment has been increasing at a time when the number of
local governments has been decreasing (Figure 1.2). Local governments
have declined from more than 140,000 in 1942 to about 80,000 today.
This loss of approximately 60,000 governments is explained largely
through state-mandated school district consolidation; the number of dis-

Table 1.1. Percent distribution of employment by level of government and
function, 1977

Function	Total	Federal (civilian)	State	Local
National defense and international relations	6	35	0	0
Postal service	4	23	0	0
Education	42	1	43	55
Highways	4	*	8	4
Health and hospitals	10	9	18	7
Police protection	5	2	2	6
Natural resources	3	9	5	*
Financial administration	3	4	3	2
General control	4	2	3	4
Other	19	15	21	22
Total	100	100	100	100

Source: Census Bureau, *Public Employment in 1977* (Washington: Government Printing
Office, 1978), pp. 7 and 9.

* Less than 1.0 percent.

tricts dropped from 109,000 in 1942 to 15,000 in 1977. Today relatively small changes are occurring in the number of local governments. The number of counties, cities, townships, and school districts is largely stable, although the number of special districts is increasing slightly.

Employment is unevenly distributed among the various types of local government. As can be seen from Table 1.2, school districts account for nearly half of all local employment, followed by municipalities, which account for close to 30 percent. Special districts, while being the most numerous type of local government, hire only 4 percent of all local government personnel. Counties have the largest average work force (558 employees) and school districts have the second largest (268 employees). The high figure for counties is partially explained by many counties operating schools and some operating community colleges. About a quarter of county government employment is in education.

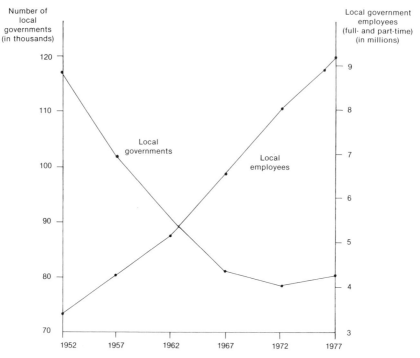

Figure 1.2. Number of local governments and local employees, 1952–1977. Sources: Census Bureau, *Historical Statistics on Governmental Finances and Employment* (Washington: Government Printing Office, 1974), p. 59; Census Bureau, *Public Employment in 1977* (Washington: Government Printing Office, 1978), p. 12; Census Bureau, *Governmental Organization* (Washington: Government Printing Office, 1973), p. 23; and Census Bureau, *Governmental Units in 1977*, preliminary report, (Washington: Government Printing Office, 1977), p. 1.

Table 1.2.   Local government units and employees, 1977

	Number of governments	Full- and part-time employees		Average number of employees
		Number (000)	Percent	
Counties	3,042	1696	19	558
Municipalities	18,856	2487	27	132
Townships	16,822	415	5	25
School districts	15,260	4094	45	268
Special districts	26,140	399	4	15
Total	80,120	9091	100	113

Sources: Census Bureau, *Public Employment in 1977* (Washington: Government Printing Office, 1978), p. 11, and Census Bureau, *Governmental Units in 1977*, preliminary report, (Washington: Government Printing Office, 1977), p. 1.

These average figures should be interpreted with care, because they can obscure the great variation in size among governments of the same type. While cities have an average of about 130 employees, some cities are far above that figure and others are far below. The City of Los Angeles, for example, has about 45,000 employees, a figure that is greater than the population of most cities in the country. These variations must be kept in mind for they greatly influence the nature of specific public personnel systems. Small jurisdictions will tend to have less formalized personnel procedures than large jurisdictions have.

PERSONNEL SYSTEMS

Identifying what is a public personnel system is difficult. If people make government run and this book is a study of people in government, then seemingly all aspects of government are germane to the discussion. The discussion needs to be more focused, however, and this can be accomplished using the concept of a system, which can be defined simply as a "set of units with relationships among them."[3] A social system is composed of organizations, individuals, the values held by these individuals, and the relationships among these units and values. A system can be thought of as a network typically consisting of many different parts with messages flowing among the parts. Systems have boundaries that distinguish them from other systems; these can be considered as subsystems, which are parts of larger systems. Personnel systems, then, can be viewed as components or subsystems of the larger governmental/political system.

---

[3] James G. Miller, "Living Systems: Basic Concepts," *Behavioral Science*, 10 (1965):200.

One way of defining a personnel system is to limit it to personnel-related agencies. Job-testing agencies, training bureaus, boards that hear appeals from employees who are being dismissed, and other similar units would constitute the system. A related approach would be to set boundaries to the system by limiting it to what personnel administrators do. Among other things, they recruit and test people for public jobs and are involved in promotions and disciplinary actions. This has been described as a "maintenance" system or a subsystem that is not directly related to the main function of the organization.[4] In other words, personnel systems can be seen as facilitating the continuation of the organization through supplying needed workers, but that process in itself is only ancillary to the main goals and objectives of the organization. Personnel systems can be viewed as serving facilitative functions and not immediately serving such ends as combating crime, mental illness, or illiteracy.

The focus of this book, however, is broader, in that it is concerned more generally with how employees perform in government and are treated by government. Managers necessarily are included. Disciplinary actions against workers, for example, are initiated not by personnel agencies but by line managers. Motivating workers to perform efficiently and effectively is less the responsibility of personnel administrators than of line managers, who work closely with their subordinates on a daily basis. The personnel system must be defined to include line managers because they influence behavior in organizations. Later chapters consider alternative motivation theories and their potential for application by government managers.

Individual government workers surely must be considered part of personnel systems. Involved here are difficult value issues about the rights of individuals who choose to work for government. On the one hand, they do not relinquish their citizenship when accepting government jobs, and one can argue that these workers should retain all personal freedoms. On the other hand, the claim can be made that government has a right to insist upon certain standards of conduct. Conflict between individual and government rights is particularly acute in matters of free speech, political participation by government workers, and demands for collective bargaining and the right to strike.

Unions that represent groups of workers in collective bargaining constitute another important set of elements of public personnel systems. Unions are usually organized on a national basis, and their national policies affect state and local personnel systems as well as the federal

---

[4] Daniel Katz and Robert L. Kahn, *The Social Psychology of Organizations* (New York: Wiley and Sons, 1966), pp. 39–47.

system. Collective bargaining in the public sector gained considerable ground in the 1960s and 1970s, and major problems remain about how to integrate that process with the other components of personnel systems.

Politically appointed executives need to be included as well as career executives. A critical interface exists between career employees who have obtained their positions on the basis of merit and political executives who have obtained their positions through partisan activities. Political executives frequently are amateurs, having less substantive knowledge about their agencies' programs than their subordinates have. These executives have neither broad public support nor continuous, strong support from their chief executive. Personnel systems often seem to frustrate the political executive from taking whatever actions are considered essential.[5]

The boundary of a personnel system must be extended even further to include the chief executive and aspects of the judicial and legislative branches of government. Legislative bodies must be considered, at least in terms of the laws that have established parameters for personnel actions. Such laws, for example, set standards for the dismissal of incompetent workers. Chief executives also must be included, since they issue executive orders that establish ground rules for many forms of personnel activities. For example, collective bargaining in the federal government was established by a Presidential executive order. Courts— both state and federal—are part of the personnel system in that they interpret constitutional provisions and statutes that affect government workers.

Intergovernmental relationships are another aspect of personnel systems. Local governments have been created by their respective state governments and must follow their state's statutes. State and local governments are required to adhere to the provisions of the U.S. Constitution and pertinent national laws. Local personnel systems are not independent, but rather are subjected to extensive controls by the federal and state governments. In recent years one of the greatest influences on state and local personnel systems has been the federal court system.

There are many nonprofit organizations that influence the character of public personnel systems. Universities train many of the people who serve in governments, and standards of conduct are conveyed in varying degrees in instructional programs. The National Association of Schools of Public Affairs and Administration represents higher education programs that are major providers of administrators for government. People with business training also make careers in government, and business schools are part of the American Association of Collegiate Schools of

---

[5] Hugh Heclo, *A Government of Strangers: Executive Politics in Washington* (Washington: Brookings Institution, 1977).

Business. Professional associations that are especially concerned with personnel include the International Personnel Management Association and the National Civil Service League. The American Society for Public Administration is concerned with furthering professionalism in government management. In addition, there are more specialized professional groups, such as the National Association of State Budget Officers. The Council of State Governments, the National League of Cities, the International City Management Association, and the National Association of Counties are concerned with improved management practices, including personnel practices, for their respective constituencies. Besides these organizations, many others from time to time are concerned with aspects of personnel systems. Veterans' organizations, civil rights groups, and other associations have been important lobbyists concerning state and federal laws affecting public personnel.

The general citizenry also is part of public personnel systems. Citizens make demands upon the bureaucracy, and a frequent complaint has been that government workers are insensitive to the needs of the citizens they serve. A particularly difficult problem is balancing citizen rights with the rights of government workers who also are citizens. For instance, to what extent should workers be insulated from citizen and client pressures, especially insulated from liability suits?

Public personnel systems should be viewed as dynamic processes involving group efforts to win acceptance of their values. Superseding all other values in the effort to reform personnel systems has been the merit principle, which maintains that personnel decisions should be based on criteria relating to how well an individual performs a job. The next chapter explores that principle in conjunction with the reform effort to oust patronage from government personnel systems. Many of the proponents of the merit principle have advocated that it is incompatible with other values, such as preference for veterans, minorities, and women, and the rights of workers to organize and bargain collectively. These conflicts over values are cast in terms of such issues as who should set personnel policies, what those policies should be, who should execute those policies, and how the policies should be translated into daily operations.

There is no single public personnel system; instead there are many. Any one government may have several personnel systems, in that different groups of workers are influenced by different agencies. Some units within a government may have authority for recruiting and selecting their own employees, while other units must fill positions through a central personnel agency, such as a civil service commission. While fragmentation may best describe what exists, at the same time all personnel systems—federal, state, and local—are related to each other. Changes made in one system are felt in other systems. Because of the numerous systems in existence and the numerous parts that constitute these systems, the student of public personnel must be careful not to become myopic. The next chapter helps to clarify the relationship between personnel functions and agencies. That chapter and those that follow, however, should not be considered as independent discussions but rather as being integrally related to each other. Chapters in a book are intended to organize the discussion to provide clarity, but given the multiplicity of people, organizational units, and values associated with public personnel systems, chapter discussions cannot be airtight compartments.

SUMMARY

Important distinctions exist between public- and private-sector personnel systems. The profit motive in the private sector encourages the minimization of personnel costs, but government does not operate under such an incentive. Competition in the private sector also encourages efficient and effective use of personnel. Government is labor intensive and has fewer opportunities to mechanize operations than does industry. Higher ethical standards are imposed on public workers. Private-sector managers may have greater freedom in making personnel decisions. Lines of authority are distinct in the private sector, whereas public-sector workers are subject to conflicting channels of authority. Unlike the private sector, the public sector uses personnel for reasons unrelated to the provision of services; these factors include patronage, aid to special groups, such as veterans, and economic stimulation.

Government employment is a major segment of today's economy. The number of federal employees has grown from virtually nothing in the 1780s to nearly 3 million today. Since World War II, federal employment has been largely unchanged, while state and local employment has grown rapidly. Personnel costs account for about half of direct outlays, exclusive of insurance trust fund expenditures. Federal employment is concentrated in defense and mail service, while state and local employment is heavily committed to education. Local employment has been increasing during a period when the number of local governments has been decreasing. Among local governments, counties have the largest average work force, followed by school districts and cities.

Personnel systems are part of the larger governmental system. A personnel system is not restricted to personnel agencies but must include the employees affected and their supervisors. Legislative bodies, chief executives, courts, and the general citizenry are important components. Intergovernmental relations, labor organizations, and various professional and governmental associations also are part of public personnel systems. At stake are major value issues, especially how the merit principle should be applied in personnel decisions.

Chapter 2

Patronage and the Merit Principle

The practice of appointing friends or political associates to public jobs has been characteristic of governments in the United States. Although this practice of patronage has been under strong attack for more than a century and the reform effort to eliminate it has been successful in many respects, vestiges of the practice remain. The merit principle has been advocated as the appropriate alternative to patronage. As the following discussion shows, a concise definition of merit does not exist, but for the moment merit can be considered as making personnel decisions based upon the qualifications or capabilities of individuals rather than on their political allegiances or friendships.

This chapter discusses the rise of political patronage and the attempts that have been made to eliminate it. The first section provides an historical perspective on patronage practices and reforms. The second section discusses alternative organizational arrangements that have been used in furthering the merit principle.

PATRONAGE AND REFORM IN HISTORICAL PERSPECTIVE

One approach to the history of government appointments is to suggest that there were three main periods. The first period, extending from the Presidency of George Washington through that of John Quincy Adams, was characterized by appointments to government being based largely on the qualifications of individuals. Beginning in 1829 with the administration of Andrew Jackson, the patronage or spoils system flourished. The third period commenced in 1883 with the passage of the Pendleton Act, which reaffirmed the principle of merit and created the U.S. Civil Service Commission.[1]

Such an interpretation is technically correct but overly simplistic in that it ignores the vast changes that have occurred since the adoption of the Constitution. A review of American history, of course, is beyond the scope of this book, but one should recognize that the rise and fall of patronage occurred within the context of major societal and governmental changes. Events of the first era, which lasted until 1829, included substantial growth in the territory of the country (especially through the Louisiana Purchase), the War of 1812, and the increasing use of slaves. By 1830 there were more than 2 million Negroes in the country, constituting 18 percent of the population.[2] The period from 1829 to 1883 included westward movement of the population, the end of slavery, the introduction of railroads, extensive industrialization, and a large influx of immigrants to the country.

The years following the Declaration of Independence were truly formative ones for government. A major issue was what should be the relative powers of the national government and the states. The initial decision, incorporated in the Articles of Confederation, was to have strong states and a weak national government. A U.S. Congress was created under the Articles but there was no executive branch to implement the legislation adopted by the Congress. Change in this distribution of powers was not made until 1789, when the Constitution was adopted, and in the interim states experimented with new governmental forms. State constitutions were written that provided for the separation of

---

[1] Important volumes on civil service reform, aside from those cited separately throughout this section, include the following: *The Civil Service in Modern Government: A Study of the Merit System* (New York: National Civil Service Reform League, 1936); Luther Gulick, ed., "Improved Personnel in the Public Service," *Annals*, 189 (1937): entire issue, especially see Carl J. Friedrich, "The Rise and Decline of the Spoils Tradition," and William Turn, "In Defense of Patronage"; Ari Hoogenboom, *Outlawing the Spoils: A History of the Civil Service Reform Movement, 1865-1883* (Urbana: University of Illinois Press, 1961); Frederick C. Mosher, *Democracy and the Public Service* (New York: Oxford University Press, 1968); Carl E. Prince, *The Federalists and the Origins of the U.S. Civil Service* (New York: New York University Press, 1977); Carl Schurz, *The Spoils System* (Philadelphia: Altemus, 1896); M. Barris Taylor (U.S. Civil Service Commission), *History of the Federal Civil Service: 1789 to the Present* (Washington: Government Printing Office, 1941); Martin Tolchin and Susan Tolchin, *To the Victor: Political Patronage from the Clubhouse to the White House* (New York: Random House, 1971); Leonard D. White, *The Federalists: A Study in Administrative History* (New York: Macmillan, 1948); Leonard D. White, *The Jacksonians: A Study in Administrative History, 1829-1861* (New York: Macmillan, 1954); Leonard D. White, *The Jeffersonians: A Study in Administrative History, 1801-1829* (New York: Macmillan, 1951); Leonard D. White, *The Republican Era: 1869-1901, A Study in Administrative History* (New York: Macmillan, 1958).

[2] Census Bureau, *Historical Statistics of the United States: Colonial Times to 1970* (Washington: Government Printing Office, 1975), p. 14.

powers among legislative, executive, and judicial branches; these documents included a bill of rights to protect the citizenry against abuses that had been prevalent during colonial rule.

One common requirement in early state constitutions was rotation in office. Provisions were made for fixed terms of office with limitations on being re-elected. That practice continues today, with many governors being allowed to serve only two consecutive terms (the same is true for Presidents). The original justification for rotation was that it provided a means of educating people in the operations of government. In time, rotation came to be justified in terms of preventing the rise of a king; tyrannical government could not emerge since office holders were required periodically to relinquish their positions.[3]

Information about the application of the rotation principle to appointed state officers is only sketchy. There are no accurate records for this early period that show how many people worked for the state governments or local governments. It seems likely, however, that the type of patronage that eventually emerged in the mid-1800s could not have existed earlier because there were relatively few government jobs to be filled.

With the adoption of the Constitution in 1789, attention was focused upon the method of appointing officials of the new executive branch. The Constitution grants Congress, and not the President, the power to decide how "lesser officers" are to be appointed, namely whether they are to be appointed by the President, the courts, or department heads.[4] George Washington was well aware that, as first President of the United States, he could establish a pattern to be followed by his successors. He used the standard of "fitness of character" in making appointments. "Fitness," however, did not mean technical competence, but rather was related to one's personal integrity and social standing. In other words, Washington sought honest individuals from the elite of society. Throughout this period prior to 1829, persons appointed to high government positions usually were wealthy, had considerable land holdings, and were far better educated than the general public. Another characteristic was that they often were related to one another. Nepotism, the appointment of one's relatives to government positions, was common throughout the period, even under Jefferson, who officially deplored the practice.[5]

One of the most important developments of the pre-patronage

[3] Carl R. Fish, *The Civil Service and the Patronage* (New York: Longmans, Green, 1905), pp. 79–85.

[4] U.S. Constitution, Article II, Section 2.

[5] Sidney H. Aronson, *Status and Kinship in the Higher Civil Service* (Cambridge, Mass.: Harvard University Press, 1964), pp. 11–12 and 140–157.

period was the emergence of national political parties. Parties did not exist when Washington was first elected, and many thought parties were a European institution that should be avoided in the new government. Nevertheless, parties had emerged when Washington was elected for a second term. He and his successor, John Adams, were of the Federalist party, which was deposed in the election of 1800 by Thomas Jefferson, who was a Democratic-Republican. Upon taking office, Jefferson found that most government positions were held by Federalists, and he announced that he would use the appointment power to bring "balance" to the composition of the federal executive branch. For this reason, Jefferson sometimes is considered the "father" of political patronage, but that is probably an inappropriate label in that he did not engage in patronage on a wide scale.

The controversy over John Adams' "midnight appointments" is less important to the history of patronage than it is to constitutional history. When Jefferson became President, he found that Adams had appointed persons to judgeships in the last hours of his administration. The necessary paperwork had not been completed, and Jefferson's Secretary of State, James Madison, refused to execute the appointments. The case was brought directly to the Supreme Court in *Marbury* v. *Madison*.[6] The Court, led by John Marshall, who was one of Jefferson's opponents, feared that the Jefferson administration would ignore a ruling in behalf of the office seeker, yet siding with the new administration would seem to suggest the Court was impotent. The solution was that the Court ruled it had no power to handle the case. The Constitution specifies what cases can be brought directly before the Supreme Court, and the Court held that Congress had unconstitutionally expanded the Court's original jurisdiction by passing the Judiciary Act of 1789. The case established the power of judicial review, setting the Court as the main interpreter of the Constitution. This power now allows the Court to overrule the actions of Congress, the President, and state governments.

Open use of political patronage was introduced in 1829 by President Andrew Jackson. In his first inaugural address, he said:

> The recent demonstration of public sentiment inscribes on the list of Executive duties, in characters too legible to be overlooked, the task of *reform*, which will require particularly the correction of those abuses that have brought the patronage of the Federal Government into conflict with the freedom of elections, and the counteraction of those causes which have disturbed the rightful course of appointment and have placed or continued power in unfaithful or incompetent hands.
>
> In the performance of a task thus generally delineated I shall endeavor to select men whose diligence and talents will insure in their respective sta-

---

[6] *Marbury* v. *Madison*, 1 Cr. 137 (1803).

tions able and faithful cooperation, depending for the advancement of the public service more on the integrity and zeal of the public officers than on their numbers.[7]

One era had closed and another had begun. Turnover of federal workers in the Jackson administration was not as great as might have been expected, but widespread firings and replacements by the politically favored were characteristic of subsequent administrations. "Polk [1845–49] removed more incumbents than any of the 10 Presidents who preceded him."[8] Patronage became equally prominent at the state and local levels.

Democratization must be credited or blamed for the rise of patronage. The size of the electorate greatly expanded and so did the rate of voter participation in elections. The 1824 election of John Quincy Adams was decided by 356,000 voters, or only 27 percent of the electorate. The 1840 election of William H. Harrison, in contrast, was decided by 2.4 million voters, constituting 80 percent of the electorate. In the sixteen years between 1824 and 1840, the electorate increased from 1.3 million to 3 million, a growth of 126 percent, and the growth in the number of persons voting was 575 percent. These increases cannot be accounted for in terms of population growth. The white male population, the electorate of that era, grew only 82 percent between 1820 and 1840. What had occurred was the lowering of barriers to voting, such as being required to own property and to pay poll taxes. Persons previously disenfranchised not only could vote but did vote. From 1840 to the close of the century, between 70 and 80 percent of the electorate voted in presidential elections.[9]

The introduction of mass voting necessitated strong party organization to win elections. From the parties' perspectives, voters needed to be informed about which candidates and parties could best serve their interests. Many voters could not read newspapers because of illiteracy or inability to read English. Party workers, therefore, were required to disseminate information. This periodic, labor-intensive activity created a pool of individuals who sought government jobs as a reward for their efforts. Jackson did not invent patronage but instead had it thrust upon him.

Political patronage as practiced in the 1800s had both advantages and disadvantages. On the negative side, patronage resulted in high

---

[7] Andrew Jackson, First Inaugural Address (1829) in *Inaugural Addresses of the Presidents of the United States* (Washington: Government Printing Office, 1965), p. 57.

[8] Civil Service Commission, *Biography of an Ideal: A History of the Federal Civil Service* (Washington: Government Printing Office, 1973), p. 24.

[9] Discussion based on data from Census Bureau, *Historical Statistics of the United States*, pp. 14, 1072, and 1074.

turnover of personnel, thereby making government inefficient because of constant staff changes. Inefficiency also stemmed from deliberate featherbedding, in which two political associates were hired when only one worker was really needed. On the other hand, turnover can be seen as a protection against elitist government and the rise of a monarchy. The patronage system provided an important route of upward mobility for people from the lower class. The system also provided a simple mechanism for removing so-called "deadwood."

Patronage has been attacked for resulting in incompetent people running government. People received government jobs because of political ties, despite their lack of the skills and knowledge required by the jobs. This argument would be persuasive if it were applied to the type of work carried out by today's government, but it is not fully so when applied to the government in the 1800s. Nontechnical jobs largely characterized that early period, and the proponents of patronage could readily contend that virtually anyone could carry out the duties of most jobs. Patronage, at least at the federal level, seems to have been restricted to these nontechnical jobs; agencies involved in technical work, such as the Patent Office, were largely insulated from patronage.[10]

Patronage has been condemned for what it does to employees. Workers who prefer to stay out of politics are required to contribute part of their wages to the party in power and are required to campaign for the re-election of politicians. Low morale results from such political pressures. Also, career development supposedly is precluded. in that workers are removed from office whenever a new political party wins control of the government. This line of attack, however, should not be overextended. Patronage as practiced in the 1800s was rotational—one group of workers was dismissed with a change in administration but later was reinstated as the party out of power regained control through the electoral process. Career workers existed in government under the patronage system.

One of the strongest set of arguments in support of patronage is that it made the bureaucracy responsive to political leadership and helped to coordinate the executive and legislative branches of government. Patronage was used by chief executives to obtain legislative approval of proposed policies and programs. A mayor, for example, could win legislative votes by appointing the friends of city council members. Patronage encouraged government workers to be responsive to the demands of the chief executive. In the words of President Jackson, "faithful cooperation" from workers was likely when they knew they could be dismissed.

    [10] David H. Rosenbloom, *Federal Service and the Constitution: The Development of the Public Employment Relationship* (Ithaca, N.Y.: Cornell University Press, 1971), pp. 53–55.

Political patronage, however, did not make the bureaucracy as responsive as proponents of the system have suggested. Executives, by appointing political friends of legislators, in many instances appointed people who were not in agreement with them. A governor who appointed political friends of state legislators accepted into the administration people who had political views differing from his own. In order to win an election a person needed the support of all factions or wings of his political party, and once he was elected, he was obligated to appoint people from all wings of the party.

Another criticism of patronage is that it was excessively time consuming. Chief executives complained that they were too busy with appointments and dismissals, leaving little time for policy considerations. President Harrison died during his fourth week in office, and "the opinion of many historians is that the real cause was the spoils system."[11] President Lincoln complained of the many people who sought jobs from him. "Once, when Lincoln was suffering from an attack of smallpox, he asked an assistant to invite the jobseekers in, for at last he had something he could give to all of them."[12]

Reform was piecemeal at the federal level and was accomplished by small steps. In 1853 an amendment was added to an appropriations bill requiring "pass examinations" for selecting clerical workers. Although the process was frequently abused and ignored, the law is important because it initiated the examination process in the federal government. Nearly twenty years later, in 1871, an amendment to another appropriations bill was passed that allowed the President to set rules concerning personnel actions. Using this authority, President Ulysses Grant appointed a civil service commission that drafted regulations that would have greatly reduced the role of patronage, but the commission went out of existence in 1875, when Congress refused to appropriate money for the new system. However, pressure for reform continued to mount and became particularly intensive after the assassination of President James Garfield by a disgruntled jobseeker in 1881. In January, 1883, Congress passed the civil service reform law, entitled "A Bill to Regulate and Improve the Civil Service of the United States," and better known as the Pendleton Act, named after Senator George H. Pendleton (D, Ohio).[13] President Chester Arthur signed the bill.[14]

---

[11] Civil Service Commission, *Biography of an Ideal*, p. 22.

[12] Donald R. Harvey, *The Civil Service Commission* (New York: Praeger, 1970), p. 6.

[13] A Bill to Reguluate and Improve the Civil Service of the United States, 22 Stat. 403 (1883).

[14] Congressional Research Service, compiled for Subcommittee on Manpower and Civil Service, House Committee on Post Office and Civil Service, *History of the Civil Service Merit Systems of the United States and Selected Foreign Countries*, 94th Cong., 2d sess. (Washington: Government Printing Office, 1976), pp. 87–173.

The main features of the new law included competitive examination requirements, security from dismissal for political reasons, and protection from being coerced into political activities. A bipartisan Civil Service Commission was created to oversee the process. (The structure of personnel systems is discussed in the next section.) Coverage was limited under the new law. Initially only about 10 percent of all workers were protected. Clerical workers in Washington and workers in large post offices and customhouses were covered.

State and local governments followed the federal government's lead. In 1883 New York passed a law similar to the Pendleton Act. Massachusetts acted the next year. From 1884 until 1905, little reform took place at the state level. Then, several states took action to reduce or eliminate patronage: Wisconsin and Illinois in 1905, Colorado in 1907, New Jersey in 1908, and Illinois again in 1911.[15]

Civil service reform must be viewed in the context of broader governmental reform.[16] Many people had been repelled not only by favoritism in appointing government workers but by widespread corruption at all levels of government. Scandals were common. Lucrative government contracts and franchises were awarded to favored corporations. Looting from the public treasury was extensive. The press played an important role in bringing these scandals to the attention of the public.[17] Much of the corruption was tolerable as long as budgets operated in the black, but by the late 1800s and into the early 1900s, jurisdictions began to experience tighter financial situations. Budget surpluses turned to budget deficits.

Structural reforms were introduced at the local level beginning in the late 1800s and at the state level starting around 1910. One thrust of these reforms was to concentrate powers in the hands of the chief execu-

---

[15] John M. Mathews, *Principles of American State Administration* (New York: Appleton, 1927), p. 195.

[16] For discussions of the reform movement in state and local governments, see the following: Charles R. Adrian and Charles Press, *Governing Urban America*, 5th ed. (New York: McGraw-Hill, 1977); A. E. Buck, *The Reorganization of State Governments in the United States* (New York: National Municipal League and Columbia University Press, 1938); Richard S. Childs, *Civic Victories: The Story of an Unfinished Revolution* (New York: Harper and Brothers, 1952); Thomas C. Devlin, *Municipal Reform in the United States* (New York: Putnam's Sons, 1896); Ernest S. Griffith, *History of American City Government: The Colonial Period* (New York: DaCapo, 1972); William L. Riordon, *Plunkitt of Tammany Hall* (New York: Dutton, 1963); Martin H. Schiesl, *The Politics of Efficiency: Municipal Administration and Reform in America, 1800–1920* (Berkeley: University of California Press, 1977); Bruce M. Stave, ed., *Urban Bosses, Machines, and Progressive Reformers* (Lexington, Mass.: Heath, 1972); Jon C. Teaford, *The Municipal Revolution in America: Origins of Modern Urban Government, 1650–1825* (Chicago: University of Chicago Press, 1975).

[17] Lincoln Steffens, *The Shame of the Cities* (New York: McClure, Phillips, 1904).

tive and to hold that person answerable for the administration of government.[18] The movement toward a short ballot was one such approach; city charters were rewritten to allow for the election of only a few administrative officers, instead of many. Under the strong-mayor form of government, the mayor is responsible for appointing department heads. Should those officers engage in dishonest or unethical activities, the mayor is accountable and presumably would be voted out of office. Nonpartisan elections were another reform that was expected to eliminate corrupt party influences from municipal government. The council-manager form of government was introduced with the hope of bringing professional management to city government.

Financial reforms were part of this movement. Budget offices were established, usually under the direction of the chief executive. Restrictions were imposed on accounting for expenditures. Competitive bidding was mandatory for large government contracts. Audit agencies, independent of the executive, were created to watch for corruption.

The leaders of this reform movement were not average citizens. The civil service reformers were Protestant, often from old families, and ranged from the economically comfortable to the wealthy. "They were lawyers, editors, clergymen, professors, and mercantile and financial, rather than industrial, businessmen."[19] When the Grant civil service commission was disbanded in 1875, the opponents of patronage formed the New York Civil Service Reform Association, which later became the National Civil Service Reform League, an active lobbyist for reform at all levels of government. The individuals involved had little to gain personally from reform but saw their mission as cleaning up government in order to free the common citizen.[20]

There were forces other than reformers that helped end the period of spoils. One major factor was that ending patronage was good politics. Many of the members of Congress who voted for the Pendleton Act in early 1883 were lame ducks, having been defeated in the November, 1882, election. President Arthur was Republican, and the Senate was basically in the hands of Republicans. The House of Representatives, as a result of the 1882 election, was scheduled to change from Republican to Democratic control. Therefore, it was good politics to "freeze" into office the Republican workers, and also the Republicans would be able to campaign in 1884 as reformers. In the Senate debate on the Pendleton

---

[18] One exception to the reforms concentrating powers in the executive was the commission plan for cities, in which each elected commissioner operated one of the city's departments.

[19] Rosenbloom, *Federal Service and the Constitution*, p. 72.

[20] Paul P. Van Riper, *History of the United States Civil Service* (Evanston, Ill.: Row, Peterson, 1958), pp. 78–86.

Act, there was a brief effort to change the bill's name to "A Bill to Per-
petuate in Office the Republicans Who Now Hold the Patronage of the
Government."[21]

The merit principle has been used by legislative bodies and chief
executives for their political advantage. Where a chief executive has the
power to bring positions under merit coverage by issuing executive
orders, this power has been used when an administration leaves office,
thereby blanketing-in political appointees. Congress has used the alternative of legislation. Passage of the Hatch Acts of 1939 and 1940 (see
Chapter 8), which restrict government workers from participating in
politics, was in part politically motivated; these acts blocked President
Franklin Roosevelt from mobilizing government workers to oppose
members of Congress who had not cooperated with the administration.[22]
Many years later, members of the Nixon administration complained
about the extensive use of freezing or blanketing-in political appointees.
Of the 115,000 jobs in the Department of Health, Education, and
Welfare, only 47 were not protected by the merit system.[23]

Several other forces can be identified as encouraging the demise of
patronage. A rapidly expanding private economy with well-paying jobs
made government jobs less attractive. Workers in the private sector not
only were paid better but were not required to kick back part of their
salaries to the political party (the practice of macing). Various pieces of
social legislation limited the role of political machines as agencies for
helping the needy. Government jobs became increasingly specialized,
making it impractical to hire the politically faithful when they were
unskilled.[24] In recent years, unions have played an important role in
reducing patronage; organized labor, in protecting its membership, op-
poses dismissals for political reasons (see Chapter 13).

The U.S. Supreme Court is a new factor in the controversy over
patronage. In *Elrod* v. *Burns* (1976), the Court dealt with the issue of
whether an incoming Democratic sheriff could remove non–civil service

---

[21] Congressional Research Service, *History of Civil Service Merit Systems of the
United States and Selected Foreign Countries*, pp. 164–173.

[22] Herbert Kaufman, "The Growth of the Federal Personnel System," in Wallace S.
Sayre, ed., *The Federal Government Service* (Englewood Cliffs, N.J.: Prentice-Hall, 1965),
pp. 54–55. For discussions of the impact of World War II on patronage and merit, see
Gladys M. Kammerer, *Impact of War on Federal Personnel Administration, 1939–1945*
(Lexington: University of Kentucky Press, 1951), and Leonard D. White, ed., *Civil Service
in Wartime* (Chicago: University of Chicago Press, 1945).

[23] Subcommittee on Manpower and Civil Service, House Committee on Post Office
and Civil Service, *Final Report on Violations and Abuses of Merit Principles in Federal
Employment Together with Minority Views*, 94th Cong., 2d sess. (Washington: Government Printing Office, 1976), p. 579.

[24] Frank J. Sorauf, "The Silent Revolution in Patronage," *Public Administration Review*, 20 (1960):28–34.

workers appointed by the previous Republican sheriff.[25] Five judges, a bare majority of the Court, decided in favor of the workers, but there was no majority opinion, leaving in doubt whether the ruling might be overturned in a future case. Three of the judges in the majority wrote an opinion based upon the First and Fourteenth Amendments to the Constitution. The first Amendment provides for the freedom of speech and implicitly the freedom of belief, and the Fourteenth Amendment protects these rights from actions of states and, indirectly, their local governments. The opinion held that patronage restricted freedom of belief and that requiring government workers to contribute to a political party would have the effect of starving the opposition party. The opinion found that there was no evidence that keeping the Republican workers in their jobs would result in subversion of the new administration or would result in reduced efficiency and effectiveness. The view was that political considerations in removing and appointing government workers should be restricted to policy-making positions.

The dissenting opinions in the case were strong. One view was that the case involved an issue that should be decided by each state, and that if such an issue arose in the federal government, Congress and not the court system should handle the problem. Chief Justice Burger labeled the Court's ruling as "a classic example of trivializing constitutional adjudication." The dissenters observed that patronage was "as old as the Republic" and had "contributed significantly to the democratization of American politics." The judges noted an earlier state supreme court ruling in favor of patronage: "Those who, figuratively speaking, live by the political sword must be prepared to die by the political sword."[26]

Today, merit coverage is extensive at the federal level. More than 90 percent of all federal jobs are under a merit system. About 60 percent are under the competitive system of the Office of Personnel Management, and more than 20 percent are under the Postal Service system. An additional 8 percent are in separate systems, such as the Tennessee Valley Authority and the Foreign Service of the State Department.[27]

The Office of Personnel Management has the authority to exempt positions from coverage on a case-by-case basis. Schedule A, B, and C exemptions are made under Civil Service Rule VI. Schedule A and B positions involve work that is neither confidential nor policy-making,

---

[25] *Elrod v. Burns,* 427 U.S. 347 (1976).

[26] *American Federation of State, County, and Municipal Employees* v. *Shapp,* 443 Pa. 527, 280 A. 2d 375 (1971). This case is an example of a union attempting to protect its workers from political dismissals.

[27] *Management of Civilian Personnel in the Federal Government: The Present Situation and Proposals for Improvements* (Washington: General Accounting Office, 1977), p. 27.

whereas Schedule C jobs are either confidential or policy-making. Schedule A jobs pertain to cases where an examination would be impractical, such as hiring rehabilitated drug addicts to assist in a drug rehabilitation project. Schedule B jobs relate to cases where a competitive examination would be impractical but a noncompetitive examination is required. Schedule C positions are openly political or may be jobs involving close work with political officials (clerical and chauffeur jobs). Other exemptions are made under Civil Service Rule VIII, covering jobs outside of the U.S. and held by noncitizens. Schedule A and Rule VIII account for the vast majority of exemptions.

Considerable variation in merit coverage exists at the state and local levels. Variations exist not only in the number of employees covered but in the numerous aspects of coverage, such as testing and protection from dismissals that are politically motivated. A recent survey of large cities and counties found that competitive examinations for entry-level positions were used in 79 percent of the cities but only 35 percent of the counties.[28] Some local personnel systems may be nominally merit but practically political; gaps exist between what protections employees officially have and what they really have. Some jurisdictions protect almost all of their employees from patronage pressures. The City of Flint, Michigan, for example, has only four non–civil service positions, and only two of 17,000 workers in the Massachusetts Department of Mental Health hold non–civil service jobs.[29]

MERIT AND ORGANIZATIONAL RESPONSIBILITIES

A definition of the merit concept has been avoided until this point in the discussion. Now the problem must be addressed. Merit is not the same as civil service. In one sense, "civil service" refers to all appointed civilian workers in government, whether or not they are protected by the merit principle. "Civil service" in everyday discussion, however, tends to be used to refer to merit-protected employees, particularly those who come under the protection of a civil service commission. In other words, the concept of merit tends to be confused with the organizational responsibility for promoting the concept. This confusion stems from the fact that civil service commissions were created in response to patronage. Further confusion is added by a tendency to think of merit as the opposite of patronage, yet the two are not simple antonyms. Patronage is non-merit

[28] Civil Service Commission, *A Graphic Presentation of Public Personnel Systems in 172 Large Cities and Counties* (Washington: Government Printing Office, 1976).

[29] Neil R. Peirce, "State-Local Report: Civil Service Systems Experience 'Quiet Revolution,'" *National Journal*, 7 (1975):1647.

in that persons may be appointed to positions for reasons other than their capabilities; political loyalty is one of the main considerations under patronage. However, the two terms are not opposites in the sense that one results in the hiring of competent workers and the other in incompetent workers. Given today's political system, patronage or political appointees need to be capable in fulfilling the duties of their positions, since incompetence is likely to have unfavorable political ramifications. Appointing "hacks" is unlikely to be in the best political interest of a chief executive. Since passage of the Pendleton Act of 1883 and similar state and local actions, the field of personnel administration has been groping for a definition of merit that is distinct from being simply the antithesis of patronage.[30]

In 1978 Congress passed the Civil Service Reform Act, which greatly altered the federal personnel system. The law identified nine principles of merit:

1. Recruitment should be from qualified individuals from appropriate sources in an endeavor to achieve a work force from all segments of society, and selection and advancement should be determined solely on the basis of relative ability, knowledge, and skills, after fair and open competition which assures that all receive equal opportunity.

2. All employees and applicants for employment should receive fair and equitable treatment in all aspects of personnel management without regard to political affiliation, race, color, religion, national origin, sex, marital status, age, or handicapping condition, and with proper regard for their privacy and constitutional rights.

---

[30] Advisory Council on Intergovernmental Personnel Policy, for Subcommittee on Intergovernmental Relations, Senate Committee on Government Operations, *More Effective Public Service*, 93d Cong., 2d sess. (Washington: Government Printing Office, 1974); Hollis B. Bach, "The Merit Track in Local Government: Abused and Diffused," *Public Personnel Management*, 6 (1977): 116–120; Civil Service Commission, for House Committee on Post Office and Civil Service, *A Self-Inquiry into Merit Staffing*, 94th Cong., 2d sess. (Washington: Government Printing Office, 1976); W. Donald Heisel, "Administering the Personnel Function," in Winston W. Crouch, ed., *Local Government Personnel Administration* (Washington: International City Management Association, 1976), pp. 21–41; House Committee on Post Office and Civil Service, *Civil Service Reform: Hearings*, 95th Cong., 2d sess. (Washington: Government Printing Office, 1978); Florence Isbell, "Carter's Civil Service Reform: 35 Percent Ifs, Buts, and Maybes," *Civil Liberties Review*, 5 (May/June, 1978): 16–22; *Management of Civilian Personnel in the Federal Government;* F. Arnold McDermott, "Merit Systems Under Fire," *Public Personnel Management*, 5 (1976): 225–233; Chester A. Newland, "Public Personnel Administration: Legalistic Reforms vs. Effectiveness, Efficiency, and Economy," *Public Administration Review*, 36 (1976): 529–537; *Revitalizing the Federal Personnel System* (New York: Committee for Economic Development, 1978); Bernard Rosen for House Committee on Post Office, *The Merit System in the United States Civil Service*, 94th Cong., 1st sess. (Washington: Government Printing Office, 1975); E. S. Savas and Sigmund G. Ginsburg, "The Civil Service: A Meritless System?" *Public Interest*, No. 32 (1973): 70–85; David T. Stanley, "Symposium on the Merit Principle Today," *Public Administration Review*, 34 (1974): 425–452; and Robert G. Vaughn, *The Spoiled System: A Call for Civil Service Reform* (New York: Charterhouse, 1975).

3. Equal pay should be provided for work of equal value, with appropriate consideration of both national and local rates paid by employers in the private sector, and appropriate incentives and recognition should be provided for excellence in performance.
4. All employees should maintain high standards of integrity, conduct, and concern for the public interest.
5. The Federal work force should be used efficiently and effectively.
6. Employees should be retained on the basis of the adequacy of their performance, inadequate performance should be corrected, and employees should be separated who cannot or will not improve their performance to meet required standards.
7. Employees should be provided effective education and training in cases in which such an education and training would result in better organizational and individual performance.
8. Employees should be—
   A. protected against arbitrary action, personal favoritism, or coercion for partisan political purposes, and
   B. prohibited from using their official authority or influence for the purpose of interfering with or affecting the result of an election or a nomination for election.
9. Employees should be protected against reprisal for the lawful disclosure of information which the employees reasonably believe evidences—
   A. a violation of any law, rule, or regulation, or
   B. mismanagement, a gross waste of funds, an abuse to authority, or a substantial and specific danger to public health or safety.[31]

The law not only provides this list of principles, but also provides a list of prohibited personnel practices that basically restates the principles in a negative sense.

When the wording of the nine merit principles is compared with the principles enunciated in an earlier law, one can see changes in philosophy about how personnel systems should operate. The Intergovernmental Personnel Act of 1970 had six principles.[32] Both laws emphasize recruiting qualified workers, but the 1978 law includes recruiting from "all segments of society," reflecting the value that the bureaucracy be representative of society. Both laws support equal pay for equal work, but the new one emphasizes the use of pay as an incentive and recognition for "excellence in performance." The two laws adhere to the principles of training workers and removing incompetent workers. Non-discrimination provisions are in both laws, with the 1978 law extending coverage to marital status, age, and handicap. The laws are opposed to partisan influences on merit employees.

Three additional principles are included in the 1978 reform legisla-

---

[31] Civil Service Reform Act, 92 Stat. 1111 (1978). See Personnel Management Project, *Final Staff Report* and *Appendices to Final Staff Report* (Washington: Government Printing Office, 1977).

[32] Intergovernmental Personnel Act of 1970, 84 Stat. 1909 (1971).

tion. One principle, in part a response to Watergate and other scandals, holds that employees are to have "high standards of integrity, conduct, and concern for the public interest." Second, personnel should not be penalized for disclosing information about violations of law, mismanagement, and abuses of authority; in other words, "whistle blowers" in government are to be protected.

The third principle is that personnel are to be used efficiently and effectively. This concept is positive, in contrast to the negative aspects of merit, such as preventing partisan and other non-job-related considerations from being used in personnel decisions. The efficiency and effectiveness provision reflects a growing concern that personnel systems are replete with red tape that hinders rather than encourages effective administration; personnel administration has been seen as "the triumph of techniques over purpose."[33] The people who work full-time in personnel administration constitute a small fraction of the public work force, yet sometimes it seems that personnel administrators have tied the hands of line administrators. In 1978 the U.S. Civil Service Commission had about 7,000 employees, or a ratio of 1 to every 400 civilian workers. It should be recognized, however, that these figures do not begin to reflect the total personnel administration work force; thousands of federal workers are employed by personnel units within line agencies. At the state and local levels, personnel administration also is a comparatively small activity as gauged by the number of workers and expenditures. In large cities and counties, there is one personnel administration employee for every 200 other employees. State government and large cities spend only about $50 per employee per annum in administering their personnel systems.[34]

Criticism of merit systems may be camouflage for a more severe problem in government. Merit systems may simply provide a convenient rationale for managerial ineffectiveness. The chairman of the Municipal Manpower Commission of the 1960s has said:

> We found in over 600 interviews that in many cases the blame for the inability to make any progress programmatically was placed by management on the civil service system, when in fact the management did not know where it wanted to go, what it wanted to do, and as a result what kind of people it wanted. So it tended to make the system the scapegoat.[35]

---

[33] Wallace S. Sayre, "The Triumph of Techniques over Purpose," *Public Administration Review*, 8 (1948):134–137.

[34] Civil Service Commission, *A Graphic Presentation of Public Personnel Systems in 172 Large Cities and Counties* and Civil Service Commission, *1976 Annual Statistical Report on State and Local Personnel Systems* (Washington: Government Printing Office, 1977).

[35] Allen E. Pritchard, Jr., as quoted in Peirce, "State-Local Report: Civil Service Systems Experience 'Quiet Revolution'" p. 1675.

What becomes obvious is that the merit principle or principles impinge on all aspects of personnel administration. Personnel actions are decisions affecting individuals. These decisions include determining the score of an employment examination, selecting someone for a job, deciding who will attend a training program, and removing an incompetent employee. Besides these types of actions, the merit concept prescribes how workers are to perform regarding integrity, efficiency, effectiveness, and like concerns. As will be seen in subsequent chapters, however, the merit principle frequently is difficult to apply to specific situations. Sweeping generalities are used to define the merit principle, but the world of personnel administration is detailed, not general. Public personnel systems each day produce specific decisions that affect the lives of government workers, people who would like to become government workers, and the general citizenry.

Assigning organizational responsibility for the various aspects of personnel administration has been a controversial subject ever since the reform movement began in the 1800s.[36] Much of the problem stems from the fact that personnel administration involves legislative, administrative, and judicial responsibilities. The preparation of administrative rules and regulations to interpret civil service laws is a legislative process. Administrative activities are involved in such matters as administering civil service tests and selecting workers for jobs. Another aspect of administration involves enforcement activities that ensure that regulations are followed in personnel actions. Judicial activities include the interpretation of regulations and reaching decisions on whether particular actions have conformed with those regulations. The judicial function, for instance, involves reviewing appeals of employees who claim they have been dismissed in violation of merit standards.

How these legislative, administrative, and judicial functions are carried out vis-à-vis the chief executive has been a fundamental issue. As mentioned in the preceding section, the government reform movement of

---

[36] For a brief review of various reports recommending changes in personnel administration, see Congressional Research Service, *History of Civil Service Merit Systems of the United States and Selected Foreign Countries*, pp. 465–492. In addition to the volumes cited throughout this section, also see Commission on Organization of the Executive Branch of the Government, *Personnel Management* and *Task Force Report on Federal Personnel*, First Hoover Commission (Washington: Government Printing Office, 1949); Commission on Organization of the Executive Branch of the Government, *Personnel and Civil Service* and *Task Force Report on Personnel and Civil Service*, Second Hoover Commission (Washington: Government Printing Office, 1955); Commission of Inquiry on Public Service Personnel, *Better Government Personnel* (New York: McGraw-Hill, 1935); Conference Committee on the Merit System, *The Merit System in Government* (New York: National Municipal League, 1926); and Carl J. Friedrich et al., *Problems of the American Public Service* (New York: McGraw-Hill, 1935).

the late 1800s and early 1900s was aimed largely at strengthening the chief executive in order to be able to hold one individual accountable, but the personnel reform effort is a major exception. Rather than strengthening the power of the President, governor, or mayor, early personnel reformers attempted to limit that power. The device chosen was a civil service commission, usually consisting of three to seven individuals appointed by the executive with the advice and consent of the legislative body. At the federal level, the three-member Commission was appointed by the President with the approval of the Senate. Civil service commissions usually are bipartisan; only a bare majority of the commissioners may be from one political party. Commissioners' terms of office overlap and usually are for a period longer than that of the executive's term of office. For example, a governor may have a four-year term and the commissioners have six-year terms; this also was the case at the federal level.[37] The civil service commission, then, was designed to be largely independent of the chief executive in the hope that such an organizational configuration would prevent political considerations from entering into personnel matters. In this traditional merit system structure, the civil service commission serves as the policy-making body and oversees the operations of the personnel system. Daily operations are the responsibility of an executive director who is a career employee, selected by the merit process, and who reports directly to the commission as a whole.

Does such an arrangement protect against political influences, and are there disadvantages of this structure? The answer to the first question is "not necessarily" and to the second, "yes." The National Civil Service League in 1970 made this harsh judgment of independent civil service commissions: "The claim that these commissions are insulating the system against pressures is often unfounded. Experience in many jurisdictions has shown that the deliberations of so-called independent commissions frequently reflect political expediency rather than the requirements of good public personnel administration."[38] The Nixon administration demonstrated an ability to circumvent the merit principle. An unofficial "Federal Political Personnel Manual" was prepared to suggest to political appointees methods for ousting career employees and replacing them with people loyal to the Nixon administration. In effect, depart-

---

[37] For the composition of state civil service commissions and related personnel agencies, see the current edition of *The Book of the States* (Lexington, Ky.: Council of State Government, biennial).

[38] *A Model Public Personnel Administration Law* (Washington: National Civil Service League, 1970), p. 5.

ments were told to find jobs for individuals, with the assumption that some civil service rules would need to be "bent" to accomplish the task.[39]

An independent commission can hamper the chief executive in taking positive actions toward personnel management, since authority resides in the commission. A situation can develop in which the chief executive must plead with the commission to adopt personnel regulations and procedures that affect the personnel for whom the executive is ultimately responsible. A common criticism has been that civil service commissions assume a largely negative role, instituting bureaucratic red tape to prevent a resurgence of patronage. The National Civil Service League has made this criticism:

> Such commissions are often much more concerned with keeping people out of the public service than in developing new techniques to attract persons into public employment. The roadblocks that these commissions have managed to erect have, in numerous instances, managed to frustrate thoroughly and to cut the effectiveness of some of our most competent and responsible administrators.[40]

President Carter voiced a similar sense of frustration: "The system has serious defects. It has become a bureaucratic maze which neglects merit, tolerates poor performance, permits abuse of legitimate employee rights, and mires every personnel action in red tape, delay, and confusion."[41]

Another weakness of the traditional commission structure is that it makes no provision for strong leadership in personnel management. While the civil service commission has a chairman, that individual basically has powers no greater than those of the other commissioners. The executive director of the commission is equally limited in performing a leadership function in that that individual must answer to the commission. What can result is a languishing system that seems to have little sense of purpose other than the overriding concern to keep spoilsmen out of personnel matters. Procedures are apt to become ends.

An alternative to the traditional model is what existed in the federal government until the reforms of 1978. Commissioners could be removed by the President without regard to their terms of appointment. An incoming President could designate the Commissioners so that he need not be compelled to work with a Commission selected by the previous

---

[39] "Federal Political Personnel Manual," in Subcommittee on Manpower and Civil Service, *Final Report on Violations and Abuses of Merit Principles*, pp. 573–811. See Frederick C. Mosher et al., *Watergate: Implications for Responsible Government* (New York: Basic Books, 1974).

[40] *A Model Public Personnel Administration Law*, p. 5.

[41] Jimmy Carter, *Message from the President of the United States: Civil Service Reform*, 95th Cong., 2d sess., H. Doc. 95–299 (Washington: Government Printing Office, 1978), p. 1.

President. The chairman, moreover, was not just one of three individuals but instead was the "chief executive and administrative officer of the Commission." The chairman selected the executive director on a merit (competitive) basis in consultation with the other commissioners. Much greater power was provided to the President than was his under the traditional model. The President had power to prescribe what would be done in the competitive service and the Commission was required by law to aid the President.[42] This type of structure brings the merit system under greater control by the chief executive while retaining the relative independence of the commission in acting as a watchdog over the personnel system. A criticism, on the other hand, is that the chairman and the other commissioners to a lesser extent assume the role of advisor to the chief executive, which is a policy-making function, while they simultaneously perform administrative and judicial functions. This blending of powers can lead to abuses, and for that reason a common prescription has been to separate functions, particularly judicial functions, from others.

The debate over the desirability of having an autonomous civil service commission or one more closely linked with the chief executive has continued since the 1800s, but during that time additional considerations have been added. One factor is the rise of budgetary processes and budget agencies, a reform that has strengthened the chief executive's powers.[43] Beginning about 1910, governments began to establish budget offices that were directly answerable to the chief executive. At the federal level, this occurred with passage of the Budget and Accounting Act of 1921; that legislation not only created the Bureau of the Budget—reconstituted in 1970 as the Office of Management and Budget—but also established the General Accounting Office as an agency of Congress responsible for auditing the accounts of federal agencies.

Tensions exist between budget and personnel offices. Part of the problem is historical, in that budgeting is openly political and the personnel movement is deliberately apolitical. The tradition of budget offices is that they serve the needs of the elected executive, whereas personnel offices serve the cause of merit. Issues arise in that the budget office and line managers may be eager to move quickly on a given problem and feel frustrated by having to abide by civil service regulations. Organizational turf is at stake. A personnel agency will tend to claim all personnel matters within its jurisdiction, as will a budget office claim all financial matters. The two tend to conflict, therefore, in the matter of personnel costs.

---

[42] 5 U.S.C. § 1101.

[43] See Robert D. Lee, Jr., and Ronald W. Johnson, *Public Budgeting Systems*, 2d ed. (Baltimore: University Park Press, 1977).

One area over which budget offices have gained control is proposed legis-lation. When agencies wish to propose legislation, it must be cleared through the budget office. The purpose of this clearinghouse function is to avoid having administrative units support legislation that would require budget expenditures contrary to the chief executive's wishes.

Salary levels and hiring workers are other personnel areas in which budget offices play important roles. Given the importance of personnel costs in every government's budget, there obviously is concern that pay rates not be set excessively high. Total personnel expenditures also can be controlled by the number of people hired. This process is known as com-plement control, meaning that an agency must obtain budget office ap-proval to fill a vacancy or to create a new job or position.[44] How these matters are handled is discussed more thoroughly in subsequent chapters, but the point here is that budget offices have become powerful adminis-trative agencies, and, until recently, there has been little rethinking of the relative roles of personnel and budgeting.

In addition to the rise of budgeting, there have been two other themes or principles that have emerged to complicate the issue of organi-zational responsibilities for personnel functions. These are equal employ-ment opportunity and collective bargaining. Proponents of merit have readily accepted the notion that women, minorities, and other groups should not be discriminated against but they have had difficulty accept-ing affirmative action that might lead to giving preference in hiring to women because of their sex and to minorities because of their skin color (see Chapter 9). Similarly, merit proponents have had difficulty accept-ing the idea that some aspects of personnel administration are subject to negotiations between management and organized labor (see Chapter 13).

A consequence of budgeting, collective bargaining, and equal em-ployment opportunity is that the personnel systems involve many agencies and not just a civil service commission. The diagram in Figure 2.1 shows how the federal personnel system was structured prior to the 1978 reform legislation. As can be seen in the diagram, the Office of Management and Budget is part of the Executive Office of the President and is normally in close communication with the President. The Civil Service Commission had responsibility for setting policy and performed a judicial function in employee appeals; employee grievances were handled by the Federal Employee Appeals Authority and Appeals Review Board, which were directly answerable to the Commission as a whole (see Chapter 8). Other personnel functions were carried out by CSC staff

---

[44] *Personnel Restrictions and Cutbacks in Executive Agencies: Need for Caution* (Washington: General Accounting Office, 1978) and *Personnel Ceilings—A Barrier to Effective Manpower Management* (Washington: General Accounting Office, 1977).

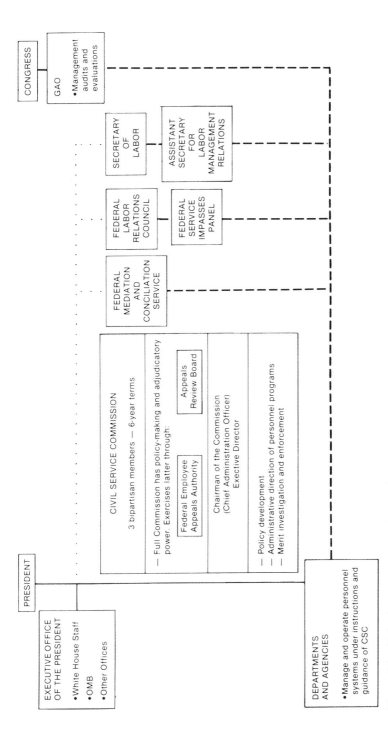

Figure 2.1. Federal government organization for personnel management prior to 1978 reforms. Source: Modified from Personnel Management Project, *Final Staff Report* (Washington: Government Printing Office, 1977), pp. 179 and 243.

35

under the direction of the Chairman and the executive director. Those other functions included testing, training, personnel planning, equal opportunity, and the like. The federal system was substantially decentralized so that personnel offices in line agencies carried out much of the work.

Several units were involved in labor relations (see Chapter 13). The Federal Labor Relations Council was a part-time body consisting of the chairman of the CSC, the Director of the OMB, and the Secretary of Labor. The Council set labor-management policy. The Assistant Secretary of Labor for Labor-Management Relations was responsible for administering the collective bargaining process. When labor and management could not reach an agreement through collective negotiations, the independent Federal Mediation and Conciliation Service could intervene. If the deadlock between the two sides continued, the Federal Service Impasses Panel, under the direction of the Council, had authority to resolve the conflict.

The General Accounting Office (GAO), an arm of Congress, also was and is part of the federal personnel system. The GAO in recent years has expanded greatly its audit function beyond traditional financial matters. The agency evaluates governmental programs and their use of personnel, and frequently issues reports dealing with personnel administration. Although in many instances the GAO is unable to order changes, its recommendations carry much weight.

Change in this complex system was accomplished in 1978 by President Carter using his reorganization power and by Congress passing the Civil Service Reform Act. The reorganization is based on the concept that the Chief Executive should have increased responsibilities in personnel administration while an independent body serves judicial and watchdog functions. The structure is similar to what was recommended by the 1937 President's Committee on Administrative Management headed by Louis Brownlow.[45] The Municipal Manpower Commission of 1962 had proposed a similar structure for cities.[46] The Model Public Personnel Administration Law of 1970 prepared by the National Civil Service League was based largely on the same idea.[47]

The new configuration, adopted in 1978 and implemented in 1979, is shown in Figure 2.2. The Civil Service Commission was abolished and its

[45] President's Committee on Administrative Management, *Report* (Washington: Government Printing Office, 1937) and Floyd W. Reeves and Paul T. David for the President's Committee on Administrative Management, *Personnel Administration in the Federal Service* (Washington: Government Printing Office, 1937).

[46] Municipal Manpower Commission, *Governmental Manpower for Tomorrow's Cities* (New York: McGraw-Hill, 1962).

[47] *A Model Public Personnel Administration Law.*

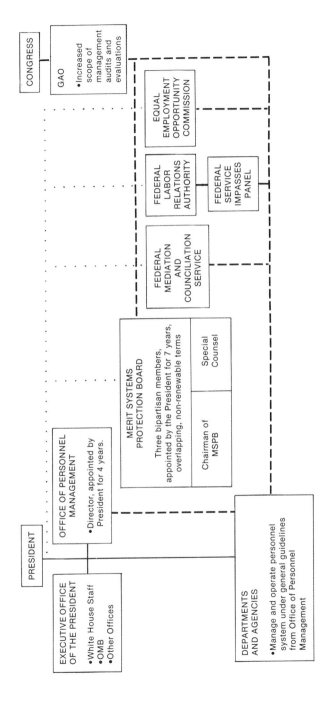

Figure 2.2. Current federal government organization for personnel management. Source: Modified from Personnel Management Project, *Final Staff Report* (Washington: Government Printing Office, 1977), p. 244, and based upon Civil Service Reform Act of 1978.

functions reassigned to the Office of Personnel Management (OPM) and the Merit Systems Protection Board (MSPB). The OPM is directly answerable to the President but is not part of the Executive Office of the President. The Director of the OPM is appointed by the President for a four-year term with the advice and consent of the Senate. The Director is responsible for advising the President on personnel administration. The Office of Personnel Management, under the supervision of the Director, issues rules and regulations pertaining to personnel procedures to be followed by departments and agencies. The Office has an oversight function for ensuring that departments and agencies adhere to merit principles and regulations.

The Merit Systems Protection Board consists of three members appointed by the President for seven-year overlapping terms with the advice and consent of the Senate. No more than two board members may be from the same political party. Independence of the board members from the President is strengthened by restricting their removal "only for inefficiency, neglect of duty, or malfeasance in office." The President appoints one of the board members as Chairman with Senate approval; the Chairman is the "chief executive and administrative officer of the Board." The Special Counsel of the MSPB is appointed by the President for a five-year term with the advice and consent of the Senate. The Special Counsel also "may be removed by the President only for inefficiency, neglect of duty, or malfeasance in office." The Special Counsel must be an attorney.

Labor-management relations, which prior to 1978 had been regulated by Presidential Executive Orders, were prescribed by the Civil Service Reform Act. The Federal Labor Relations Council was replaced by the Federal Labor Relations Authority (FLRA), consisting of three members appointed by the President to overlapping terms of five years. Like the MSPB, no more than two of the FLRA members may be from the same political party, and appointment to the Authority requires Senate approval. Authority members have the same protections from removal as the members of the Merit Systems Protection Board. The General Counsel of the Authority is appointed by the President for a five-year term with Senate approval and serves at the pleasure of the President. The General Counsel is the chief administrative officer of the Authority. As in the earlier system, the Federal Mediation and Conciliation Service can assist in resolving impasses in negotiations, and such impasses may be resolved by the Federal Service Impasses Panel (FSIP), which is a unit within the Authority. The Panel consists of at least seven members who are appointed by the President and can be freely removed by him. One of the main changes made in 1978 was the elimination of many duties previously administered by the Assistant Secretary of Labor.

Other changes pertained to equal employment opportunity. The Equal Employment Opportunity Commission, which was created in 1964, was provided an expanded role in the federal personnel system. Those changes are discussed in Chapter 9.

The law gives the General Accounting Office expanded responsibilities in the personnel field. The GAO is required to submit to Congress an annual report on the Office of Personnel Management and the Merit Systems Protection Board. The law specifically charges the GAO with considering whether the OPM is abiding by the merit system principles. The GAO also is responsible for assessing procedures used to appraise worker performance.

The changes made regarding labor-management relations and equal employment opportunity were far less controversial than the break-up of the Civil Service Commission into the Office of Personnel Management and the Merit Systems Protection Board. Alan K. Campbell, Chairman of the Civil Service Commission at the time and the first Director of the Office of Personnel Management, emphasized the need for change given perceived widespread public dissatisfaction with the existing federal bureaucracy as well as federal managers' dissatisfaction.[48] At the core of the issue was the familiar fear of political encroachment into personnel affairs. Proponents of the reorganization claimed that the then existing system was incapable of preventing partisan considerations and sometimes encouraged abuses. The red tape that blocked efficiency was seen as an invitation to managers to find shortcuts that might be contrary to merit. The proponents maintained that the political system had matured to the point that reversion to patronage was unlikely. Others, with the abuses of Watergate in mind, were not completely convinced that the concept of merit was sufficiently established to entrust personnel administration to a personnel director who was directly answerable to the President.

Safeguards against nonmerit are built into the reformed federal personnel system. As noted earlier, the new law not only identifies merit principles but also includes a list of prohibited practices. The Director of

---

[48] Alan K. Campbell, "Civil Service Reform: A New Commitment," *Public Administration Review*, 38 (1978):99–103; Alan K. Campbell, "Revitalizing the Civil Service," *National Civic Review*, 67 (1978):76–79; Alan K. Campbell, "Revitalizing the Federal Personnel System," *Public Personnel Management*, 7 (1978):59–64; Alan K. Campbell, "Running out of Esteem?" *Civil Service Journal*, 18 (January–March, 1978):4–10; Alan K. Campbell, "What's Right with Federal Employees," *Civil Service Journal*, 18 (April–June, 1978):6–12.

the Office of Personnel Management, the Merit Systems Protection Board, the Special Counsel, and the General Accounting Office all have roles in furthering merit in the personnel system. The MSPB is authorized to conduct personnel studies and may have access to agency personnel records. The law provides, "Any member of the Board, the Special Counsel, and any administrative law judge . . . may issue subpoenas requiring the attendence and testimony of witnesses and the production of documentary or other evidence." The MSPB may invalidate OPM rules and regulations that do not conform with merit. The Special Counsel can act as an ombudsman for employees seeking to reverse unwarranted adverse actions taken against them. When Counsel is convinced that a prohibited personnel practice or practices have occurred, the Counsel may file a complaint against an individual employee and/or the agency before the MSPB that has the authority to order corrective action.

The safeguards that have been established have created some potential for administrative and judicial controversy. The Director of the OPM has the authority to request a court of appeals to review MSPB decisions; it is possible that controversies between these two units could become substantial and involve extensive litigation. Additionally, controversies could emerge between the MSPB and the Special Counsel. Although the Counsel is officially part of the Board, the Counsel is appointed independently and is protected from removal. President Carter's Reorganization Plan, which provided for the new organizational structure, and the bills originally introduced in the House and Senate were silent on the matter of removing the Special Counsel.[49] The House of Representatives bill was amended to stipulate that the Counsel must receive notice and a hearing before being removed; while that provision was not included in the final version, the law does limit removal to "inefficiency, neglect of duty, or malfeasance."

Given that the terms of office of the MSPB members and the Special Counsel are longer than that for the President and given the overlapping terms of these various officers, it is conceivable that at some time substantially different views might exist among the individuals holding these important positions. For instance, the Special Counsel might be particularly active in bringing before the Board complaints that it considered inconsequential. Moreover, the Special Counsel has the right to intervene in any case before the Board, even though the Board might prefer to handle the case on its own. By providing for the relative independence of the Special Counsel, Congress may have created the

---

[49] Reorganization Plan No. 2 of 1978, *U.S. Code Congressional and Administrative News*, No. 5 (1978):1387–1395; H. R. 11280; and S. 2640.

potential for a situation similar to what developed between the National Labor Relations Board and its General Counsel following passage of the Taft-Hartley Act in 1947. In that instance, the General Counsel not only brought cases to the NLRB that it did not care to consider but also sought judicial review of NLRB decisions in hope of their being overturned.[50] The Civil Service Reform Act, however, does not grant the Special Counsel authority to seek judicial review of Board decisions.

One other organizational aspect of the federal system that warrants attention is the extent to which personnel functions are delegated to departments and agencies. The 1978 legislation permits the Director to "delegate, in whole or in part, any function vested in or delegated to the Director." The main restrictions are that competitive exams for administrative law judges and for positions common among federal agencies must be administered by the OPM. Also, the Office must prescribe rules and regulations for personnel functions conducted by departments and agencies. This authority to delegate functions is seen as an opportunity for eliminating much of the red tape that develops when systems are centralized and for providing agency flexibility that will encourage more efficient and effective operations. Skeptics are concerned that decentralization beyond what already existed prior to the reforms may lead to unintended or deliberate abuses of the merit principle.

If the federal structure is complex, the situation is no less complex at the state and local levels. Agencies to be found at these levels include civil service commissions, central personnel offices under the chief executive, units responsible for administering collective bargaining, other units responsible for representing management in the bargaining process, agencies responsible for patronage and political appointments, and units responsible for furthering the principle of equal employment opportunity. State and local systems even may be considered more complex than the federal system because of intergovernmental relations. State governments, since they impose various standards on local personnel operations, are part of local systems. Federal agencies are part of both state and local systems. Federal agencies in making grants to those governments require them to have a merit system and to be an equal opportunity employer. As will be seen in the following chapters, federal courts also have assumed prominent roles in state and local personnel systems.

---

[50] Ronald L. Gabriel, "The Role of the NLRB General Counsel," *Labor Law Journal*, 26 (1975):79–87; Kenneth McGuiness, "Effect of the Discretionary Power of the General Counsel on the Development of the Law," *George Washington Law Review*, 29 (1960):385–398; and Ernest J. White, "The NLRB and the General Counsel Revisited," *Labor Law Journal*, 10 (1959):255–264.

SUMMARY

The rise of political patronage is understandable when it is seen in perspective with the major societal changes that were occurring. In the early years of this country, appointments to government positions were based largely on individual qualifications, which tended to produce an elitist system. With the development of political parties and a rapidly expanding electorate, government jobs became attractive means for rewarding persons who had been effective campaigners.

Patronage had both strengths and weaknesses. Inefficiency may have increased with the appointment of political friends with minimal qualifications, but government of the early 1800s was comparatively nontechnical, and many jobs could be filled with unskilled workers. Patronage may have discouraged career development, although it is known that many workers rotated in and out of office as the parties rotated in power. Coordination between the executive and legislative branches may have been furthered by patronage, and that system may have encouraged the bureaucracy to be responsive to political leadership. On the other hand, chief executives complained about the excessive time they had to devote to patronage matters.

Civil service reform occurred in the context of a larger governmental reform movement. At the local level, strong-mayor and council-manager systems developed. Short ballots and nonpartisan elections were introduced, along with restrictions on financial matters, including the development of budget processes.

Patronage declined because of legislation and other forces. Blanketing-in employees under a merit system was politically expedient. Economic growth made government jobs less attractive. Patronage was more difficult to use as jobs became increasingly technical. In recent years unions have been important contributors to the demise of patronage.

Merit is not simply the opposite of patronage, and the merit principle is applicable to all personnel actions. Merit involves dealing with people on the basis of their knowledge, skills, and other capabilities rather than extraneous or non-job-related characteristics. Personnel administration involves legislative, administrative, and judicial activities, and a persistent problem has been finding appropriate organizational locations for these activities, particularly in relationship to the powers of the chief executive. The traditional model was to have a civil service commission that was insulated from the chief executive. That system has not guaranteed the elimination of political influences and has been criticized for blocking effective management.

Public personnel systems have become increasingly complex with the emergence of new values and governmental functions. Budget offices have been created, and these units have acquired important powers in personnel administration. More recently, equal employment opportunity and collective bargaining have become important concerns.

In 1978, the federal government undertook a major restructuring of its personnel system. The Civil Service Commission was eliminated and its functions assigned to the new Office of Personnel Management, Merit Systems Protection Board, and the Special Counsel. The process for labor-management relations was written into the Civil Service Reform Act, which provides for a Federal Labor Relations Authority to administer that system. The reconfiguration is designed to increase the leadership and administrative responsibility of the President through the Director of the OPM while furthering the concept of merit and protecting against partisan and other non-job-related influences.

This chapter has presented the values and cast of characters found in public personnel systems. Subsequent chapters consider the interplay between the values and characters in relation to specific personnel functions.

Chapter 3

Organizational Design, Job Design, and Position Classification

Given that a personnel system is part of a larger governmental system, personnel administration is inevitably associated with and limited by larger considerations. These larger considerations obviously include the objectives or purposes of governmental programs; governmental programs are established to meet societal needs and demands, with personnel administration being expected to facilitate meeting those needs and demands. Similarly, personnel administration is often limited by decisions about how services will be provided.

This chapter has three sections. The first focuses upon organizational and job design. The discussion considers limitations imposed by the structure of organizations and efforts that have been made in designing individual jobs. The second section considers how jobs or positions are grouped into classes, a process usually justified on the grounds that it furthers the objective of equal pay for equal work. The third section reviews some of the operational problems encountered in the use of position classification.

ORGANIZATIONAL AND JOB DESIGN

"Top down" and "bottom up" are terms commonly used in the design of organizations and programs. The issue involved is whether one should begin at the top or bottom in designing an organization. The top-down approach involves starting at the top of the organization and determining what units to create and in turn determining what subunits to create. For example, if one were reviewing the possibility of creating a state department on environment and energy, the question first asked would be "What responsibilities are to be assigned to the department?" and from that would follow the question "What bureaus should be created within the department?" The next step would be to determine the offices, divisions, or sections for each bureau. Next would be identification of the jobs or positions to be established within each of the lowest organizational units of the department. The final step would allocate specific tasks to each position, including how those tasks were to be performed and the sequencing of those tasks.

The bottom-up method is the opposite of the top-down method. The purposes or objectives of the organization are assumed and initial attention is focused upon designing individual jobs. Once these are defined, they are clustered into organizational units that in turn are clustered into larger units, such as bureaus.

The major weakness of the bottom-up approach is its premise. An assumption is made that the work to be performed is readily understood and that there is a known relationship between the performance of tasks and the achievement of objectives. In designing a job, an analyst may seek the most efficient method of processing a form, with an assumption that form processing is essential for meeting the objectives of the total organization. The danger of such an approach is suboptimization, in which work may be performed efficiently but the work is nonproductive in meeting objectives. Probably the "pure" form of the bottom-up approach is rarely used, but later in this section the discussion focuses upon the extensive efforts regarding job design.

The top-down approach, which is more popular in the design of organizational structure, has one major danger. There may be a tendency to focus upon structure without considering purpose. Organizational charts are common in all larger organizations—both private and public. Boxes are drawn showing what units report to what higher level unit. Shuffling the boxes from time to time is a popular sport. A common response to problems is to reorganize; when a department is not achieving what is expected of it or seems to be haphazardly operated, there may be a tendency to move boxes around on the chart; two boxes may be merged while another box is divided into two new ones.

Much energy, time, and tax dollars can be consumed by reorganization. New working relationships must be developed between managers and their employees. Substantial costs result from having to print new stationery, issue new personnel and function directories, and physically move furniture and equipment from one set of offices to another. Frequent reorganizations are likely to produce chaos: employees do not know from time to time who their supervisors are, few people seem to know who is responsible for what, and citizens seeking information or some other assistance from the department become bewildered and angered. In other words, reorganization is not a panacea, although reorganization can serve a useful purpose when used judiciously.

A related problem common in government is that organizations tend to be created in response to new problems. Instead of assigning responsibility to deal with a newly emergent problem to an existing organizational unit, the decision process may create a new organizational unit. Both chief executives and legislatures use this technique, in part because they wish to dramatize their concern for whatever the problem happens to be. At the federal level, special-purpose, narrowly focused commissions abound outside of the regular operating departments. Problems in coordination almost inevitably result. Organizational units frequently may seem to be operating at cross-purposes.

Numerous issues arise about the appropriate rules to follow in the design of organizations. These issues, although beyond the scope of this book, can be briefly identified. How many levels in the hierarchy should be used? Should there be only bureaus within a department or should bureaus be further subdivided? What is the appropriate span of control—that is, the number of persons reporting to a superior? For example, should five, ten, or more department heads report to a mayor? How should the staff functions of personnel, budgeting, and planning be located within the governmental structure? For larger jurisdictions, such as state governments and the federal government, how should functions within a department be related to geography? Should there be regional offices, and if so, how are they to relate to units at departmental headquarters? How is work to flow from one unit to another within a department and between departments? To what extent will centralization or decentralization policies be pursued? What authority will organizational subunits have and what authority will be retained by higher units in the department? What will be the relative roles of specialists and generalists within the department?

Issues of these types are typically not the direct concerns of the personnel administrator. The issues are resolved for better or for worse by others. Organizational structure or design may be largely mandated by the legislative body. City governments may be required by state law to have specified departments, even though some other configuration may be more appropriate for a given municipality. Cities with home-rule charters may determine their own departmental configurations, but they too may be restricted by their charters, which may impose organizational structure. Changing the structure included in a home-rule charter would require voter approval.

Flexibility in changing organizational structure may be available to a chief executive. Presidents have had limited authority to reorganize agencies subject to veto by either the House of Representatives or the Senate. Some governors also have this type of authority.

However, personnel units may be largely outside of the reorganization process. A "blue ribbon" committee composed of distinguished persons from the private sector and former government officials may be created to make recommendations about organizations. A private consulting firm may be used for the same purpose. Sometimes a central staff unit other than personnel may have an ongoing responsibility in this area. The unit may be responsible for so-called organization-and-management studies, which include analysis of work flow as well as organizational design.

Personnel systems, then, are greatly limited. A personnel organization typically must work with an agency organizational structure that has been imposed by others. The personnel office may be required to focus upon individual jobs when the problems of a department are more its structure and the programs that are administered.

While organizational design is likely to be beyond the scope of the personnel office, job design may be partially its responsibility. Job design involves the arranging of tasks or work to be performed by an individual. The efficiency criterion is paramount here. The job should be designed to minimize resource consumption and to maximize the outputs of work. Work is to be designed simply, since more complex approaches to the same task consume more worker time and are therefore more expensive. Tasks are to be defined in detail, and all workers performing the same tasks are to perform that task using the same procedures. Standardization of operations is to be imposed once an efficient method of performing a task has been identified. If each worker were permitted to operate as he or she saw fit, some would use less efficient procedures than others.

The school of scientific management is known for some of the most significant research conducted on job design. Observing that workers assigned identical duties often performed at differing rates and often below what management expected, participants in this school of thought concluded that a systematic approach to designing work could increase worker productivity. The term "scientific management" was used to emphasize that work should not be haphazardly organized and instead each aspect of work should be carefully studied to determine the "one best way." An assumption was made that a single ideal method existed for performing any given task. Therefore, scientific management sought through research to discover that one best way.

Frederick W. Taylor, beginning in the late 1800s, was able to make substantial accomplishments in improving the design of work. One of Taylor's most celebrated accomplishments was achieved in working with pig iron handlers at the Bethlehem Steel Company. These handlers were required to pick up pigs of iron weighing about 90 pounds and load them onto a railroad car. In a day, the average worker loaded between 12 and 13 tons, but Taylor developed a procedure which enabled a worker to load nearly 50 tons.[1]

Much of the work of Taylor and others focused upon avoiding fatigue. Workers who were fatigued were less able to perform at the expected level. In the iron handler case, Taylor prescribed when the worker was to lift and when he was to take a rest. By resting, the worker was able to prevent excessive fatigue. Similarly, Taylor studied the size of shovels and the "proper" load of coal per shovel in stoking furnaces. Few pounds per shovel load tended to waste much body movement, while a heavy shovel load required excessive exertion by the worker.[2]

Frank B. Gilbreth and Lillian M. Gilbreth also made great improvements in designing jobs. In one instance, bricklayers were able to increase the number of bricks laid in an hour from only 120 to 350. The Gilbreths and others focused upon the motions used by workers and the time required to perform each movement. In other words, scientific management introduced motion and time studies. "Therbligs" were developed by Frank Gilbreth to categorize the types of hand movements used in work.[3] Each of the 17 types of therbligs involves a specific function, for example, grasp, position, use, assemble, and search for a part. Work, then, can be defined by sequencing therbligs into the most efficient pattern. At a more detailed level, work can be specified for each hand and all other parts of the body, including eye movements. The following is a portion of the specifications for operating a lathe, "pick up part and move to machine, place medium part in chuck, tighten independent chuck 18-inch lathe, tighten chuck with pipe on wrench, true up part on chuck, pick up aligning bar from floor."[4]

Scientific management developed a detailed set of guidelines or principles in defining work. Work, for instance, was to involve the use of both hands, since one would be working at only 50 percent capacity when one hand was idle. Similarly, work should begin and end for both hands at the same time. Movements by both hands should be similar and hand movements should be rhythmical and not jerky or involving abrupt changes in movements.

---

[1] Frederick W. Taylor, *The Principles of Scientific Management* (New York: Harper and Row, 1911), pp. 42–48.

[2] Taylor, *The Principles of Scientific Management*, pp. 64–67.

[3] The term is a play on the Gilbreth name.

[4] Stewart M. Lowry, Harold B. Maynard, and G. J. Stegemerten, *Time and Motion Study* (New York: McGraw-Hill, 1940), p. 388, as quoted in James G. March and Herbert A. Simon, *Organizations* (New York: Wiley, 1958), p. 14.

Today, job design through motion and time studies is a highly developed science or art. Elaborate experiments are conducted in which different approaches to performing a task are assessed. Not only are stop watches used in evaluating alternative approaches to work, but so are movie cameras, which record both the time consumed and the motions used.

Body motions are now only one set of considerations in designing a job. While researchers continue to be concerned with efficient use of the body in work, they are also concerned with the tools and the arrangements of the workplace, the process or steps in the work, the design of the product being made, and the selection of the raw materials used in the product.[5] Instead of simply making adjustments in the motions of the worker, changes may be made in the design of a product, thereby eliminating the need for some movements. If a product is redesigned to eliminate a given component, savings are gained in body movements that previously were required in handling that component. All of this is still based upon the original premise of one best way: "There are usually numerous ways to perform any task, but with the knowledge obtainable at any one time, one method is usually superior to the others."[6]

The sophistication of job-design research in the private sector has not been matched in the public sector. While industries have used motion and time studies extensively, the practice has been far less common in government. One reason has been resistance by government workers. Successful lobbying by workers has yielded legislation in some cases that prohibited the use of stop watches in government facilities. A standard fear on the part of employees has been that such studies are intended to increase production in government by making employees work increasingly harder with no increase in pay.

Even without such legal restrictions on job-design research, the technique may have less direct application in government than in business. Such research has been particularly useful in situations involving the production of goods, whether they be radios, automobiles, or waterbeds. Government, on the other hand, produces few goods and instead concentrates upon services. The latter are not tangible and are therefore more difficult to examine in terms of quality. A radio factory can easily count the number of radios produced and determine the quality of this product. A school district, however, has no simple yardstick for measur-

---

[5] Marvin E. Mundel, *Motion and Time Study: Principles and Practices*, 4th ed. (Englewood Cliffs, N.J.: Prentice-Hall, 1970), p. 38. See also Benjamin W. Niebel, *Motion and Time Study*, 6th ed. (Homewood, Ill.: Irwin, 1976).

[6] Mundel, *Motion and Time Study: Principles and Practices*, p. 24.

ing service. As a result, there will always be great controversy over what is quality education.

This is not to suggest that motion and time studies have no role in government. Indeed, where repetitive work exists in government as in industry, job design can be valuable. Probably more routinization is to be found at the local government level, where routine housekeeping chores are common. Municipalities perform routine services, such as providing water and sewer services, cleaning and plowing streets, collecting and disposing of garbage, and extinguishing fires. Research has been conducted on how to staff a garbage truck, on what is the appropriate combination of personnel for a given type of truck. Job design can be helpful in prescribing how many fire personnel and in what ways these personnel should be used in fighting a fire. Work specifications can be set for each fireman upon arrival at the scene of a fire. Similarly, many aspects of clerical work can be routinized at all levels of government.

Where job design may face limitations is in the less repetitive or more innovative positions. While it is possible to prescribe for clerical secretaries on how to arrange their desks, where to store bond paper and carbon paper, and how best to insert paper into a typewriter, it is less obvious how to prescribe procedures for managers and other employees who are expected to cope with problems for which solutions are not known.

In both government and industry, the applicability of job-design research may be limited by the nature of workers. Scientific management to a large extent considers the individual much like a machine or as an appendage to a machine. By defining each step of a job, little initiative or imagination is expected of the individual; it is as if computer programs were written for a group of robots. As is seen in Chapters 11 and 12, extensive research on worker motivation suggests that workers may be more productive when given greater freedom in organizing their work. If one accepts various motivation theories, the search for "one best way" is unwarranted, since a job design that is appropriate for one worker would not necessarily be appropriate for others.

This is not to suggest that job design is antithetical to the needs of workers. Taylor and others saw scientific management as being compatible with the interests of both workers and management. Not only would management obtain benefits in increased worker productivity but so would workers. Employees would increase their earnings and, in Taylor's terminology, would increase their self-respect by becoming "high-priced men." The "surplus" achieved through greater productivity would be distributed to both labor and management. Taylor envisioned a "mental revolution" in the ways people thought about work, and he should not be regarded simply as one who wanted to turn people into gears in a giant machine.[7]

POSITION CLASSIFICATION

While job design concentrates upon structuring the work situation, position classification accepts the work situation as a given. Position classification entails the examination of work performed in various jobs and then the grouping of similar jobs or positions into classes.

Although there are many reasons for the use of position classification, the paramount reason is that it can be used to treat employees equitably. Position classification itself is not a pay plan (see Chapter 4), but the classification plan is used in constructing the pay plan. In other words, by classifying positions, all persons performing similar or identical work are paid the same amount. The common phrase is "equal pay for equal work." Regardless of differences in education, social background, or political "connections," two people performing the same type of job are entitled to the same pay. Similarly, position classification allows for treating differently positions that diverge in skill requirements or level of responsibility. Managers, therefore, will be classified separately from clerical workers.

Position classification is also justified on the grounds that it facilitates testing, career development, and employee evaluation.[8] Testing programs can be devised for classes of jobs that cross agency lines. Equity is served by qualifying those who have the required skills and disqualifying all others. Without position classification, there presumably would be no fair way of developing tests. Position classification further advances the equity principle by ordering or ranking positions so that employees know in advance what career opportunities exist. By specifying work requirements, position classification allows for assessing employee performance. Is the employee working at the expected rate and level of competency?

---

[7] Frederick W. Taylor, *Taylor's Testimony before the Special House Committee* (New York: Harper and Row, no date), p. 27.

[8] Gary Craver, "Survey of Job Evaluation Practices in State and County Governments," *Public Personnel Management,* 6 (1977):121–131; John F. Fisher, "Job Evaluation Through Point Rating," *Public Personnel Review,* 5 (1944):19–26; Harold Suskin, "Job Evaluation—It's More than a Tool for Setting Pay Rates," *Public Personnel Review,* 31 (1970):283–289; Harold Suskin, ed., *Job Evaluation and Pay Administration in the Public Sector* (Chicago: International Personnel Management Association, 1977); and Civil Service Commission, *Job Analysis for Improved Job-Related Employee Development* (Washington: Government Printing Office, 1976).

The how's and why's of the emergence of position classification are varied. One account of its emergence is that in the early 1900s (accounts vary between 1905 and 1910) the Chicago Civil Service adopted position classification, and the idea quickly spread in part because of that city's central geographic location in the U.S.[9] While Chicago apparently deserves substantial recognition for its early undertaking of position classification, the emergence of this idea, however, stems from several different sources.

One such source was the scientific management school (and Taylorism in private enterprise). An outgrowth of job design was classifying like positions into groups. E. O. Griffenhagen, a private consultant located in Chicago, worked with private corporations in classifying positions. Griffenhagen began working with the Commonwealth Edison Company in Chicago and went on to aid banks, insurance companies, and other firms.[10] A type of cross-fertilization took place as both private enterprises and governments adopted position-classification systems.

Where they diverged, however, was that corporations tended to restrict classification plans to manual labor and clerical positions while higher level positions were left unclassified. Governments, on the other hand, tended to apply position classification to most or all positions. The presumed justification for lack of full usage of position classification in industry was that higher level positions involved more varied work, making classification difficult, and that variations in work performance should be reflected in worker wages and salaries. The disadvantage is that, without some standardization of positions and pay, secrecy and distrust may arise. A worker does not want his pay rate revealed to fellow workers on the assumption that the rate he is receiving is better than what others are receiving. Yet even though all workers may think they

---

[9] Ismar Baruch, *Position-Classification in the Public Service* (Chicago: Civil Service Assembly, 1941), p. 8. See also Clyde L. King, "Pennsylvania Classified Her Employees," *National Municipal Review*, 13 (January, 1924):15–19; Richard H. Lansburgh, "Classification of Positions and Salaries in the Service of the State of Pennsylvania," *Annals*, 113 (May, 1924):261–268; Lewis Meriam, "The Uses of a Personnel Classification in the Public Service," *Annals*, 113 (May, 1924):215–220; Charles P. Messick, "Development and Administration of Classification and Compensation Plans in New Jersey," *Annals*, 113 (May, 1924):247–253; Fred Telford, "The Classification and Salary Standardization Movement in the Public Service," *Annals*, 113 (May, 1924):206–215; Fred Telford, "Methods of Developing and Administrating Classification and Compensation Plans in the Public Service," *Annals*, 113 (May, 1924):254–261.

[10] V. Seymour Wilson, "The Relationship between Scientific Management and Personnel Policy in North American Administrative Systems," *Public Administration*, 51 (1973):200; E. O. Griffenhagen, "Job Analysis for Position Classification," in W. J. Donald, ed., *Handbook of Business Administration* (New York: McGraw-Hill, 1931), pp. 1135–1144.

are faring better than others, they also might all think they are faring worse than others.[11]

Inequities in pay constitute another factor that led to usage of position classification. Indeed, that was one of the main stimulants in Chicago's adoption of such a system. Some workers were considered to be underpaid and others overpaid; when approving wage increases, there was no simple system for determining what positions should be awarded what wage increases.

Although such inequities had long existed, the problem at the federal level was worsened by World War I. During the war, personnel were added to the federal bureaucracy often at wage rates equal to or above rates being paid persons with considerable experience in government. This led to low morale and high turnover. Between 1917 and 1920, for example, one unit in the Bureau of Standards had 216 scientific employees and 110 of those left the federal service. Table 3.1 shows the ranges that existed for filing jobs; persons in junior filing positions were in some cases earning less than $720 per year, while others earned as much as $2,500. The variations tended to follow agency lines. Departments that expanded during the war tended to have higher average salaries than agencies that did not. In 1919 the average pay of a junior examiner in the Department of the Interior was $1,250, while the average pay for the same work in Treasury was $1,554, a 20 percent higher rate.[12]

Variations in job titles abounded, again making difficult or impossible any consistency in setting salaries and wages. Titles for a senior file and record clerk in the federal government included apprentice graphotype operator, assistant file clerk, bookkeeper, copyist, searcher, and even dictator, trouble chaser, special expert, and special agent.[13] In many cases, positions bearing dissimilar titles should have been treated the same because of the nature of the work performed, and, conversely, not all positions bearing similar or identical titles should have been treated the same because the work varied among the positions.

More generally, position classification became popular because it complemented a larger movement of reform in government. The economy and efficiency movement of the 1910s and 1920s brought many changes to government.[14] Budget surpluses vanished at all levels of

---

[11] George A. Graham, "Personnel Practices in Business and Governmental Organizations," in Carl J. Friedrich et al., *Problems of the American Public Service* (New York: McGraw-Hill, 1935), pp. 381–385.

[12] Congressional Joint Commission on Reclassification of Salaries, *Report*, 66th Cong., 2d sess., H. Doc. 686 (Washington: Government Printing Office, 1920), pp. 34–36.

[13] Congressional Joint Commission on Reclassification of Salaries, *Report*, pp. 46–47.

[14] William E. Mosher and J. Donald Kingsley, *Public Personnel Administration* (New York: Harper and Brothers, 1936), pp. 32–34, 354–355.

Table 3.1.   Range of salaries of federal file and record clerks, 1919

Rate of pay exclusive of bonus	Employees (13,449) in the filing and record "series" according to the preliminary tabulation, April 30, 1919					
	Under	Junior	Senior	Principal	Head	Chief
All rates	383	10,154	2,334	462	96	20
Under $720	92	27				
$720 but under $840	56	41	2			
$840 but under $900	24	26	5			
$900 but under $1,000	134	309	18	1		
$1,000 but under $1,100	43	999	123			
$1,100 but under $1,200	19	3,373	369	11		
$1,200 but under $1,320	15	4,935	1,208	112	1	
$1,320 but under $1,440		377	437	147	6	
$1,440 but under $1,560		50	63	43		
$1,560 but under $1,800		8	74	101	23	1
$1,800 but under $2,000		7	30	36	50	11
$2,000 but under $2,500		2	5	8	12	6
$2,500 but under $3,000				1	4	1
$3,000 but under $4,000				2		1

Source: Congressional Joint Commission on Reclassification of Salaries, *Report*, 66th Cong., 2d sess., H. Doc 686 (Washington: Government Printing Office, 1920), p. 33.

government, stimulating concern for better planning and management in government. Emphasis was given to bringing greater order to the ways in which government operated. The Taft Commission on Economy and Efficiency in 1912 issued its report recommending the use of a structured budget process.[15] During the 1910s many state and local governments adopted such systems, although it was not until 1921 that the Budget and Accounting Act was passed by Congress, creating the Bureau of the Budget (now Office of Management and Budget) and the General Accounting Office. A common slogan of the day was that government should be more businesslike, and so government officials and reformers turned to industry for possible innovations that might be adopted.

Position classification, then, blended well with the general reform movement. By classifying positions, government could suitably reward workers for the work they performed. Savings could be achieved by not overcompensating workers. Government could become more efficient by taking a systematic approach rather than a haphazard one as to how work was assigned to employees.

---

[15] William Howard Taft, *Economy and Efficiency in the Government Services*, H. Doc. 458 (Washington: Government Printing Office, 1912). See also Chapter 2, "Patronage and the Merit Principle," this volume, and Robert D. Lee, Jr., and Ronald W. Johnson, *Public Budgeting Systems*, 2d ed. (Baltimore: University Park Press, 1977), pp. 64–65.

Position classification has come to be recognized as one of the most fundamental aspects of public personnel systems. At the federal level, position classification was launched by the Classification Act of 1923 which applied only to workers in Washington, D.C. The Ramspeck Act of 1940 as well as some earlier legislation extended coverage to field personnel, and the Classification Act of 1949 replaced the 1923 legislation. In 1970 Congress passed the Job Evaluation Policy Act, which mandated a two-year study of classification practices. At the state level, as of the early 1970s, all but two states used some form of position classification for at least part of their staffs. Less is known about local governments, but it can be assumed that most—if not all—large cities use some form of position classification. Smaller local governments, however, may be more casual in their personnel operations and may have only the rudiments (if that) of a position classification system.[16]

A position-classification plan is an organization or categorization of job types according to the nature of work performed. A job in a given agency, then, is classified or assigned a classification found in the plan. The plan is in effect a set of abstractions, statements about "typical" jobs, with the actual jobs existing in government being grouped according to the typology. Positions differ in kind and in level. Classification systems normally take both of these into account. For example, on one dimension all clinical psychology positions would be grouped together; on the other dimension, all entry-level professional positions regardless of occupation could be considered alike. Typically, level similarities are known as "classes" and occupational similarities as "series."

The development of a position-classification plan begins with setting criteria for measuring work. Two positions cannot be compared unless standards exist for measuring their scope and content. Without such standards, the first position might be characterized in one way and the second in a different way, thereby presenting an "apples and oranges" problem. For example, one analyst might emphasize that a clerical secretary had to interact extensively with a wide range of persons both within and outside the organization, while another analyst considering a similar position would emphasize the extent of dictation and typing.

Usually, four to ten clusters of measures are identified. One set of such criteria could be as follows: "(1) difficulty of duties, (2) supervisory responsibility, (3) non-supervisory responsibility, and (4) requisite qualifi-

---

[16] Classification Act of 1923, 42 Stat. 1488; Rampseck Act of 1940, 55 Stat. 613; Classification Act of 1949, 63 Stat. 954; and Job Evaluation Policy Act of 1970, 84 Stat. 72. See Job Evaluation and Pay Review Task Force of the U.S. Civil Service Commission, *Interim Progress Report* (Washington: Government Printing Office, 1971), p. 56.

cations."[17] Another alternative is: "(1) subject matter, (2) difficulty and complexity of duties, (3) non-supervisory responsibilities, (4) supervisory and administrative responsibilities, and (5) qualification standards."[18] Five factors have been suggested for the federal government: "(1) job requirements, (2) difficulty of work, (3) responsibility, (4) personal relationships, and (5) other level factors."[19]

While there is no obvious ideal number of factors to use, what is important is to establish criteria within each factor so that measurement of positions may take place. If "job requirements" is to be used, what kinds of measures or standards might be applied? How is "job requirements" to be distinguished from other factors such as "responsibility." A beginning step is to describe in words the meaning of the factor, so that "job requirements" might be restricted to the subject matter of the job whereas responsibility would deal with the extent to which a person in a position was expected to act independently and/or to direct the activities of other workers.

Word descriptions of factors, however, are not the same as specified measures that could be used in classifying an individual position, but such measures cannot be readily set without taking into consideration the general types of positions in existence. For this reason, broad categories are determined. The federal government uses four levels: 1) executive; 2) administrative, professional, and technological (APT); 3) clerical, office machine operation, and technician; and 4) trades, crafts, and manual labor. Executives are considered separately with regard to levels but are part of the APT group with regard to occupation. State and local governments may use as few as four classes or they may use a dozen or more. Substantive classes can be identified, such as for education, health, agriculture, public safety and the like, in addition to general executive, administrative, clerical, and laborer classes.

The position-classification plan, then, is constructed on the basis of broadly to narrowly defined classes of positions, and within each class

---

[17] William G. Torpey, *Public Personnel Management* (New York: Van Nostrand, 1953), p. 44.

[18] Baruch, *Position-Classification in the Public Service*, p. 92.

[19] Job Evaluation and Pay Review Task Force to the United States Civil Service Commission, *Report: Volume II, Models of Evaluation Systems and Pay Structures* (Washington: Government Printing Office, 1972), p. xiii. The five factors were later disaggregated into nine: 1) knowledge required by the position, 2) supervisory controls, 3) guidelines, 4) complexity, 5) scope and effect, 6) personal contacts, 7) purpose of contacts, 8) physical demands, and 9) work environment. For the sake of brevity, the five factors are used throughout this discussion. See Charles H. Anderson and Daniel B. Corts, *Development of a Framework for Factor-Ranking Benchmark System of Job Evaluation* (Washington: Civil Service Commission, 1973), and Arch S. Ramsay, "The New Factor Evaluation System of Position Classification," *Civil Service Journal*, 16 (January–March, 1976):15–19.

criteria are applied to specific positions. Table 3.2 illustrates how the five factors mentioned above could be applied at the federal level. Criteria are deemed not applicable in some instances. Working conditions, such as whether a person must work outdoors in severe heat or cold, are important to manual laborers but not applicable to executives. The criteria can be geared specifically to the nature of the work, so that, for example, the creativity or initiative expected of clerical workers can be differentiated from that expected of administrative personnel.

Establishing measures for some factors is probably easier than for others. Within the area of "supervision," it is easy to determine the number of workers supervised by an administrator and the geographical dispersion of workers being supervised. Do all employees work within the same office, as in a bookkeeping department? Are the workers required to move throughout the jurisdiction, as police on patrol do? Are many of the workers permanently assigned to locales removed from the supervisor, as in the case of state regional welfare offices being supervised by the main office? The nature of the supervision, however, is more difficult to measure. Where employees must operate by a procedures manual that prescribes how to handle virtually every possible situation, the extent or intensity of supervision is not as great as when problems frequently arise requiring a supervisor to intervene.

Scales are used to reflect gradations in factors. One popular approach, developed by McCormick, Jeanneret, and Mecham, is the position analysis questionnaire (PAQ). Six major divisions are identified, for example, mental processes and work output. Within each division are several sections, such as decision-making and information-processing sections within the division for mental processes. Job elements are contained within each section; separate elements for compiling, coding, and analyzing information are included in the information processing section. A scale is used to rate the importance of each element to the job being analyzed. The range is from the element being not applicable or very minor to being extremely important to the job.[20]

One of the most technical and controversial aspects of position classification is the quantification of the factors to be used. Where such practices are used in government, a point system is applied. Points are

---

[20] Ernest J. McCormick, P. R. Jeanneret, and Robert C. Mecham, *Position Analysis Questionnaire* (West Lafeyette, Indiana: Purdue Research Foundation, Purdue University, 1969) and Ernest J. McCormick, Paul R. Jeanneret, and Robert C. Mecham, "A Study of Job Characteristics and Job Dimensions as Based on the Position Analysis Questionnaire," *Journal of Applied Psychology,* 56 (1972):347–368. For an alternative evaluation device, see Sidney A. Fine and Wretha W. Wiley, *An Introduction to Functional Job Analysis* (Kalamazoo, Mich.: Upjohn Institute for Employment Research, 1971) and Sidney A. Fine et al., *Functional Job Analysis: An Annotated Bibliography* (Kalamazoo, Mich.: Upjohn Institute for Employment Research, 1975).

assigned on the extent to which various factors are part of a given position; the greater the responsibilities of a position, the greater the points. This point-evaluation approach is in contrast with "factor comparison" in the private sector. Instead of points being assigned to each factor, dollars are used in the private sector. The total of the dollars for each factor is the wage or salary to be paid. In effect, a laborer might be paid $4,000 annually for the skill involved, $1,000 for working conditions, and $4,000 for such factors as physical and mental requirements and level of responsibility.[21] Government, on the other hand, would first classify positions by points and later would determine compensation through the preparation of a pay plan (see Chapter 4).

An example of the use of the point system is contained in Table 3.3. The table is for the State of Indiana in classifying clerical positions using the "personal relationships factor." Three types of persons are identified (persons within the unit, persons in other units within the same agency, and persons outside), along with three types of interpersonal relationships. As can be seen from the table, 15-point increments are used. It is here where criticism can arise. Are such increments appropriate or does the system at this juncture break down into arbitrariness? Why should not 12-point increments be used in some instances and 15-point increments in other cases?

The federal government uses a similar point system. In classifying a supervisory position, no points are awarded for a position supervising fewer than six workers, while 24 points are awarded to positions supervising 100 to 200 workers. Four points are assigned if the supervisory position involves constantly changing deadlines.[22] Why four points and not three or five points? Great potential exists for inappropriately assigning points to various factors and subfactors. The alternative—nonquantification—also has potential for arbitrariness. Without some guidelines for quantification, position classifiers may apply their own unique standards so that any one position might be classified differently depending upon who was doing the classifying.

Regardless of whether a point system is used to establish level or class, position-classification plans typically provide for series within each class. A series is a set of jobs that are similar in content but differ in level of factors or criteria applied. Each job in the series has the same basic title but usually has a numerical suffix reflecting the level of skill, knowledge, and the like. Agronomist positions in a state might range from Agronomist I for an entry level position to Agronomist V. It is this

---

[21] See J. Walker Morris, *Job Evaluation*, 3d ed. (Birmingham, England: Institute of Supervisory Management, 1968).

[22] Civil Service Commission, *Supervisory Grade-Evaluation Guide* (Washington: Government Printing Office, 1976), pp. 27–32.

Table 3.2. Relationships among evaluation factors in job evaluation systems

Master Factors	Executive (EES Factors)	Administrative-Professional-Technological (APTES Factors)	Clerical-Office Machine Operation-Technician (COMOT Factors)	Coordinated Federal Wage System (CFWS Factors)
A. Job requirements	I. Job requirements	I. Job requirements	I. Job requirements and difficulty of work	I. Skill and knowledge
1. Knowledge	X	X	X	X
2. Specialized training	X	X	X	X
3. Skills	X	X	X	X
B. Difficulty of work	II. Difficulty of work	II. Difficulty of work		II. Responsibility
1. Complexity	X	X	X	X
2. Mental demands	X	X	X	X
C. Responsibility	III. Responsibility	III. Responsibility	II. Responsibility	
1. Impact	X	X	X	X
2. Scope	X	X	X	X
3. Job controls	X	X	X	X
4. Supervision exercised	(Evaluated under Factor II)	N.A.	N.A.	N.A.

	IV. Personal relationships	IV. Personal relationships / V. Other level-determining factors	III. Personal relationships / IV. Physical effort and work environment	N.A. / III. Physical effort and / IV. Working conditions
D. Personal relationships				
1. Internal	X	X	X	N.A.
2. External	X	X	X	
E. Other level-determining factors (not elsewhere covered)	N.A.			
1. Environment		X	X	N.A.
2. Hazard		X	X	N.A.
3. Physical effort		X	X	X
4. Intensity of effort		X	X	X
5. Security requirements		X	X	X

Source: Job Evaluation and Pay Review Task Force to the United States Civil Service Commission, *Report: Volume II, Models of Evaluation Systems and Pay Structures* (Washington: Government Printing Office, 1972), p. xiii.

Note: This model is provided for illustrative purposes and does not indicate existing practice in the federal government.

Table 3.3.   Indiana guide chart for clerical/office machine operator/technician (COMOT). Factor III: Personal relationships

Nature of persons contacted in person or by phone Purpose and nature of required contacts	P. Contacts are with supervisor and with associates in the same organizational unit.	Q. Contacts are also with persons employed in other units of the same agency.	R. Contacts are also with persons employed by other agencies, or with the public, including patients or inmates.
10. Cooperative work relationships incidental to purpose of work (e.g., giving and receiving factual information about work).	15	30	45
11. Person-to-person work relationships with explanation or interpretation of what is required in order to render service, carry out policies and maintain coordination.		45	60
12. Person-to-person work relationships where non-routine, cooperative problem solving is involved, or where gaining concurrence or cooperation is required through discussion and persuasion.		60	75

Source: Philip M. Oliver. "Modernizing a State Job Evaluation and Pay Plan," *Public Personal Management*, 5 (1976): 172. Copyright: International Personnel Management Association. Reproduced by permission.

aspect of position classification that is said to enhance career development. The new employee, starting as an Agronomist I, can quickly determine what constitutes the promotion ladder.

There are several potential negative effects of inept series classifications. When a series is very narrowly defined and has only a few levels, an employee may quickly rise to the top level and have no further opportunities for advancement in that specialty. At that point, the employee must forego further advancement or seek to enter a different series. Since qualifying for other series often will require education and experience of specified types and duration, few opportunities may exist for changing series. Excessively narrow series definitions thwart career advancement. Narrow definitions often stem from values society places on various occupations. Clerical work, for example, has a generally low value, and opportunities for advancement through clerical series are limited. The complaint that employees are "pigeon holed" into narrowly defined series is common. New Jersey in 1973 had a class (not a series) for managerial positions, and within that class on the average there were only 1.5 employees per class title. Similarly, the "supervisory" class had only 8.5 employees per class title.[23]

Use of numerous levels within a series can be equally disadvantageous. Arbitrary distinctions emerge between each level of jobs within the series. In a city planning office there may be only a few practical distinctions in the jobs of Planner I, II, and III, yet real differences may exist in pay. The individual holding a Planner I position is likely to complain that he or she is doing the same work as all other planners in the office, yet is being paid far less.

Once a classification structure is established, it must be applied to the positions in the organization. Various techniques are used for classifying specific positions. A position classifier may conduct a desk audit in which the individual in the position is observed for a period of time—from a few hours to perhaps several days—to determine what work is being performed. From such an audit it can be learned how much time the worker spends alone and with peers, subordinates, and superiors. For a clerical position, it would be important to know whether the work was largely restricted to typing form letters or was more varied, including taking dictation, answering telephones, and operating office machines. Although the desk audit is a useful device, it is expensive and cannot be applied to all positions. Another drawback of the desk audit is that it presumes the classifier can appropriately interpret what work is being done simply by observing an employee. In actuality, the use of observa-

---

[23] Office of Fiscal Affairs, New Jersey State Legislature, *Administration of the New Jersey State Civil Service System* (Trenton: State of New Jersey, 1975), p. 82.

tion alone may not be enough to allow the classifier to grasp the types of problems being handled by the worker.

Other techniques rely upon the descriptions and judgments of persons knowledgeable about the position. The incumbent of the position, therefore, is asked to complete a form that asks questions about the position. "What machines and equipment do you use in your job?" "What percent of your time is spent using each of these machines?" "To what extent is your work reviewed by your supervisor?" Open-ended questions like these may also be submitted to the supervisor of the position being classified and to subordinates as well. One study of these alternative methods found that subordinates either overrated or underrated the supervisor's position. Incumbents tended to underrate their jobs, and supervisors tended to be closest in properly describing a subordinate position.[24] Still, all three types of descriptions may be used as a check against each other.

Job descriptions or specifications are prepared; such descriptions often are the bases for classifying specific positions. A job description for most jobs can be done in a page or two. Job-description formats all include the title of the job and a statement of the type of work performed. Often a statement of the knowledge and skill required to perform a job will be included. The job description may follow the format of the factors used in classifying a position; for example, a section would explain the interpersonal aspects of the job.

A common practice is to include minimum education and experience requirements of the position or group of positions. In theory, position classifiers derive the education and experience requirements from examining the work performed. The assumption is made that persons without the requisite background will not perform well, and, conversely, those with it will. This practice is defended as facilitating a fair examination process, screening out persons with inappropriate backgrounds.

The education criterion works best for highly technical jobs; not everyone can be a nuclear physicist or surgeon. The education requirement is less obvious for other jobs. Can only persons with master's degrees in social work be capable social workers? Can only persons with master's degrees in public administration, business administration, or education administration be competent administrators? Does the nature of a manual labor position really require a high school education or would a sixth grade education be sufficient? Education requirements that are arbitrarily set can establish barriers to employment or promotion. Such requirements can serve as a form of credentialism, i.e., they can

[24] Lawrence L. Epperson, "The Dynamics of Factor Comparison/Job Evaluation," *Public Personnel Management*, 4 (1975):38–48.

serve to protect from competition those individuals holding the credential. Of particular concern is that such standards can discriminate against minorities and benefit middle-class whites.

The experience requirement can be criticized on the same grounds. Simply because an individual has held a position for three years does not necessarily mean there has been much growth. He may have learned most of what there was to learn in the position in one year and then have spent the other two years simply performing the job. Yet a person with three years of experience might be eligible for promotion to higher level positions, whereas persons with only one year of experience would not be eligible.

OPERATIONAL PROBLEMS OF POSITION CLASSIFICATION

There are numerous problems that arise in the use of position classification on a daily basis.[25] One set of problems relates to keeping the position-classification plan current and keeping the classification of jobs current.

The position-classification plan is really a set of abstractions about the types of work performed in government. As government assumes new responsibilities or performs work differently in the pursuit of existing responsibilities, there is need for adjusting the position-classification plan to reflect those changes. A state government that assumes a new responsibility for approving or disapproving the installation of septic tanks for sewage disposal will create new positions requiring expertise in water pollution, soils, and related fields, but the classification plan may not reflect such a cluster of skills within any one type of job or group of jobs. Therefore it becomes necessary to alter the plan.

Line managers and professional organizations sometimes seek the creation of special classifications. Professional groups seek to aggrandize their own specialties in the classification system. In the example of septic tanks, there may be pressure for a new job series of Septic Tank Regulators when there already exists an adequate series called Water Quality Engineers. This may be done to overemphasize the technical knowledge required to deal with septic tanks so as to boost the pay level above that for Water Quality Engineers. If the plan is repeatedly allowed to be modified without genuine need, the plan becomes no plan at all.

The other side of the issue is whether positions are kept properly classified over time. Jobs change: what a given worker does is not necessarily the same as what was being done a year or two previously. A

---

[25] For a strong attack on position classification, see Jay M. Shafritz, *Position Classification: A Behavioral Analysis for the Public Service* (New York: Praeger, 1973).

filing clerk may have been assigned increasing duties as the amount of work increased in an office; over time, the clerk's job has been informally upgraded to a secretarial position. Since wages are tied to the position-classification plan and not to the work performed by a specific employee, inequity can result—the employee simply is not being adequately paid for the work performed.

Employees tend to request upgrading of their positions; obviously there will be few employees who recommend a downgrading of their jobs. This is the problem of classification inflation, or grade creep, and there are few incentives for managers to resist such inflation. The line manager, being constantly concerned with employee morale, may see upgrading the positions under him as a way of rewarding industrious employees and generally keeping employees happy. Higher level jobs will enlarge the organization's budget, which in turn may be seen as bringing greater prestige to the unit and its manager. Upgrading lower level positions may eventually serve as justification for upgrading the manager's position and pay, so that the manager may gain a monetary benefit by helping subordinates.

Although upgrading positions may be beneficial to managers, other aspects of position classification may seem to create problems for managers. They may well prefer extensive flexibility in dealing with personnel matters, but position classification thwarts such flexibility. Employees cannot be financially rewarded or penalized by their supervisor by a simple edict, since pay is structured according to the position-classification system. Where positions need to be reclassified, managers, at least from their perspective, are expected to wait patiently for the personnel system to make the appropriate changes. Red tape seems to abound, producing almost endless delays. Also, position classification is sometimes used as a weapon by subordinates against their supervisors. "It's not in my job specs" may be the rebuttal when a manager assigns new duties to an employee. Employees claim they are only responsible for those duties described in the position-classification plan. As public employees become increasingly organized and even militant, this refusal to accept duties from managers may increase. Managers may see themselves in a situation where they are expected to produce results but are not granted sufficient authority to deliver those results.

Still another issue is who should be responsible for classifying positions.[26] When the work is done by a central personnel department or civil service commission, complaints often arise over the time required in classifying and reclassifying jobs. There may be complaints that the

---

[26] For a discussion of how position classification is conducted at the local level, see Elizabeth Lanham, *Job Evaluation in Municipalities* (Austin: Bureau of Business Research, University of Texas, 1971).

central agency is not adequately aware of the unique characteristics of agencies and the jobs within them so that the resulting classifications are faulty, that jobs are misclassified when classification is done by outsiders.

Given the complaints about central classifiers and given the large classification workload in any sizable government, decentralization of position classification is common.[27] This is the case at the federal level and in many states. Each department has its own personnel unit responsible for classifying positions. The central personnel department or civil service commission sets standards for classification that are used by the department personnel offices. The decentralized approach may facilitate faster action. A potential disadvantage is that consistency from department to department may not be achieved. Under a decentralized system, for example, administrative assistant positions might be classified differently among the departments. Some observers have been concerned that decentralization may allow for abuses in which some employees with "connections" are able to have their jobs upgraded even though there is no justification for this. Well-defined classification standards and selective audits conducted by the central personnel unit can limit the extent of such abuses.[28]

There are private consulting firms specializing in personnel administration that can assist governments in developing position-classification plans and that may actually classify specific positions. These firms are particularly useful for smaller jurisdictions that do not have the internal capability for devising position classification plans or undertaking major revisions in an existing plan. A potential disadvantage is that a consulting firm may apply its own standardized system on all customer governments even though modifications are needed.

A final problem of position classification involves the appeals procedures available to employees. Complaints are especially likely to arise when positions are reclassified downward. When a position is classified downward, the incumbent usually is permitted to stay at the original salary level, but any new appointee to the position will be paid at a lower rate. Problems also occur when employees are denied an upgrading of their positions. In a large government, there can be several levels of appeals within a department, after which appeals can be made to a central personnel agency, such as a personnel department or civil service commission. If the employee or employees are still not satisfied, a legal suit may be possible.[29]

---

[27] See John F. Fisher, Harold H. Leich, and Robert E. Reynolds, *Decentralizing Position Classification* (Chicago: Public Personnel Association, 1964).

[28] See Gilbert A. Schulkind, "Monitoring Position Classification—Practical Problems and Possible Solutions," *Public Personnel Management*, 4 (1975):32–37.

[29] *Bookman* v. *United States*, 453 F. 2d 1263 and *Kavazanjian* v. *United States*, 399 F. Supp. 339 (1975).

SUMMARY

Organizational design is typically beyond the jurisdiction of personnel administrators, yet the design will greatly influence the structuring of work and the arrangement of jobs. Job design, in contrast, may be partially the responsibility of personnel administrators. Highly developed techniques are used to determine how work can be conducted to minimize worker fatigue and maximize work output. Having emerged from the scientific management school, however, job design may overlook worker motivation as an important contributor to productivity.

Position classification is one of several aspects of personnel administration intended to further the equitable treatment of employees. The position-classification movement was part of a more general governmental reform movement of the 1910s and 1920s. Clusters of factors or aspects of work are identified, and positions are arranged in a plan according to the types of work performed. A system often is used in which points are assigned to positions according to the work performed; the greater the demands of a position, the greater the number of points. Technical problems abound, such as the appropriate number of classes to use, when and when not to create a job series, how to obtain information for classifying a specific job, and how to determine the education and experience needed to perform a job.

Position-classification problems also persist in the daily operations of governments. Keeping both the position-classification plan and the classification of specific jobs current is difficult. Classification inflation pressures can destroy the rationale of a classification plan. Managers often feel thwarted by classifications. Central administration of position classification can produce consistency and an unbiased approach to administration, but it can also produce excessive delays and other red tape. Decentralization may aid in faster classification procedures but it can result in nonstandardization of positions from department to department.

Chapter 4

Pay and Employee Benefits

Compensation provided public employees is necessarily an important concern in government. The cost of pay and benefits is typically the largest single item of a government's operating budget, excluding transfer payments, such as welfare and Social Security benefits and intergovernmental grants. Compensation is equally important to the individuals employed by government; obviously, one's livelihood and standard of living are at stake when salaries and wages are set.

This chapter has two sections. The first concentrates upon pay for employees and the procedures used in determining pay levels. The second section focuses upon employee benefits, or so-called "fringes." While these two subjects are treated separately in the chapter, they must be considered together in understanding the total compensation that is provided employees.

PAY

There are no absolute standards that can be applied in setting pay levels.[1] From a government's perspective, pay must be sufficiently high to attract the necessary number of persons with requisite skills.[2] Neither the number nor the skill level is fixed, however, since jobs can be redesigned

---

[1] For extended discussions of pay administration, see Kenneth O. Warner and J. J. Donovan, eds., *Practical Guidelines to Public Pay Administration* (Chicago: Public Personnel Association: Volume 1, 1963 and Volume 2, 1965); Edwin McDermott, ed., *Modern Federal Civilian Pay Law* (Philadelphia: McDermott, 1969); and Harold Suskin, ed., *Job Evaluation and Pay Administration in the Public Sector* (Chicago: International Personnel Management Association, 1977).

[2] See James E. Annable, Jr., "A Theory of Wage Determination in Public Employment," *Quarterly Review of Economics and Business*, 14 (Winter, 1974):43–58.

to adjust the level of skill requirements and thereby alter the number of employees needed. A state mental hospital can adjust the relative mix of psychiatrists, psychologists, and counselors depending upon the availability of persons in these occupations and the salaries necessary to attract them. Pay is important in attracting personnel, since conscription, at least in modern times, has been restricted to the military; when the military draft was eliminated in the mid-1970s, concerns arose over the increasing costs necessary to attract military personnel and whether, even with such increased costs, the "right" personnel were being recruited.

In attracting employees, a government competes in the labor market. Not only does a government compete with industry, but it also competes with other governments. Individuals may be dedicated to working in government but are not necessarily dedicated to any one government. As a result, school districts compete with other school districts, cities with other cities, and states with other states. Competition also exists among levels. In any given locale there may be federal and state offices as well as city, school, and county offices, with all of these governments somewhat in competition with each other for personnel. The problem can be particularly acute for a relatively poor central city that is the host for the state capital.

At the opposite end of the spectrum from pay being high enough to attract workers is the need for pay to be low enough for government to be able to afford workers. It could be that, in order to attract any qualified mechanics to service police patrol vehicles, so high a wage level must be set that the government is effectively prevented from hiring a sufficient number of mechanics. If the mechanics example is weak, that of medical doctors surely is not. The incomes that MDs command in the private sector make it difficult for governments to afford large numbers of these persons. Also, as salaries are increased to compete with private-sector salaries, the costs of personnel increase; a not infrequent response to rising salaries is to reduce the number of workers. Police departments in some instances have been forced to reduce their staffs as wage rates have increased faster than available revenues.

There is no simple balance between government's obligation to its employees and its obligations to its clients and taxpayers. Much rhetoric has been heard about government having an obligation to treat its employees fairly, i.e., that good performance on the job is deserving of a good pay level. While few would take issue with such a position (although it may be overly paternalistic), there are competing legitimate claims of taxpayers for low taxes and of clients for good services. Raising compensation levels to be "fair" to employees can raise the ire of taxpayers. Raising salaries but cutting back on the number of employees can result in worker opposition and taxpayer dissatisfaction with reduced services.

Traditionally, government salaries were lower than those for equivalent positions in the private sector. The standard explanation for this was that government employees traded money for security and fringe benefits. Now, however, public salaries have increased substantially. In some jurisdictions, notably the federal government, the principle of full comparability with the private sector has been adopted.

Although figures vary greatly from source to source, it is safe to say that government compensation is now generally competitive with the private sector. One study found that, on the average, federal salaries were equal to 118 percent of private industry earnings in 1955 and that this had risen to 146 percent by 1973. In the same time period, state and local earnings had risen from below the private level (92 percent) to 106 percent.[3] This pattern, however, is by no means consistent for all job types. Wages for government blue-collar workers and lower level white-collar workers have been generally equal to or better than those for similar workers in the private sector. One study comparing federal jobs with private jobs found that a file clerk in government would be paid 109 percent of the wages of a similar clerk in industry but that a government senior chemist would be paid only 91 percent of the private-level salary.[4] Because of a consistent pattern for upper-level government positions to be less competitive in earnings with the private sector, there has been a longstanding concern about how government is to attract qualified professional, administrative, and technical personnel.

Males and females apparently differ in how well they are paid by the private and public sectors. A recent study has found that women consistently are paid more by government than by industry. This pattern increases by level of government; going from the local to the state and federal levels, women are paid increasingly more. Men, on the other hand, on the average earn less in local government than in industry, about the same or slightly less in state government, and more in the federal government.[5]

Salary levels, of course, vary among governments. As might be expected, larger jurisdictions tend to have higher pay levels.[6] Unionized

---

[3] Neal R. Peirce, "Federal-State Report/Public Worker Pay Emerges as Growing Issue," *National Journal*, 7 (1975):1199. See also David Lewin, "Aspects of Wage Determination in Local Government Employment," *Public Administration Review*, 34 (1974): 149–155; and *Recent Federal Personnel Cost Trends* (New York: Tax Foundation, 1974); *Federal Civilian Employment, Pay, and Benefits* (New York: Tax Foundation, 1969).

[4] Walter Fogel and David Lewin, "Wage Determination in the Public Sector," *Industrial and Labor Relations Review*, 27 (1974):429.

[5] Sharon P. Smith, "Government Wage Differentials by Sex," *Journal of Human Resources*, 11 (1976):185–199.

[6] See Linda Ganschinietz and Carol Berenson, "Salaries of County Officials for 1975," *Urban Data Service Report*, 8 (May, 1976):1–24 and *Pay Rates in the Public Service* (Chicago: International Personnel Management Association, 1977).

government workers tend to be paid more than nonunionized workers, although the "threat" of unionization may force the earnings of nonunionized workers to rise.[7] Central cities tend to pay more than suburbs. For example, the Dallas police chief in 1978 was paid $42,650, while suburban police chiefs on the average received only $17,380; these differences in wages reflect the variation among communities in the scope and difficulty of police work.[8]

The approaches to setting pay in government are diverse. During the height of the patronage era, salaries depended largely upon the political ties of job holders. As late as the 1920s, it was common for a government to have no systematic method by which pay rates were set. One study of state government in that period found four common practices: 1) state legislatures set salaries by statute, 2) department heads set salaries with the approval of the governor, 3) department heads set salaries without needing gubernatorial approval, and 4) a board or commission set salaries.[9] In many state governments and local governments as well, budget documents listed the names of employees and their compensation. The purpose of publicizing individuals' salaries was to avoid undue compensation being awarded some persons. Table 4.1 is an example from the State of Washington's budget for 1939–1941. Such publicity presumably tended to encourage equal pay for equal work. Today salaries of individual employees are rarely published, except for those of high-level officials, such as department heads and other cabinet-rank officers. In the federal service, however, salary information on any employee is available to the public on request.

Pay plans have generally replaced the less structured approach to pay determination. A pay plan consists of a number of grades and steps within grades that are integrated with the classification of jobs existing in the government. The merit principle is presumably served by providing equal pay for equal work. Since the nature of work varies from job to job, some translation is necessary so that eventually two seemingly dissimilar jobs may receive the same pay. The preceding chapter discussed the use of points in classifying positions. A comparison of two jobs may reveal that the first requires little technical knowledge and substantial interpersonal skills, while the demands of the second may be just the opposite. Under a point system the result may be that both jobs receive the same number of points and therefore the same pay. Accord-

---

[7] Ronald G. Ehrenberg and Gerald S. Goldstein, "A Model of Public Sector Wage Determination," *Journal of Urban Economics* 2 (1975):223–245.

[8] Stanley M. Wolfson, "Salaries of Municipal Officials for 1978," *Urban Data Service Report*, 10 (February, 1978):1–26.

[9] Clyde L. King, "How Shall Salaries of State Employees Be Fixed," *Annals*, 113 (May, 1924):202–206.

Table 4.1. Political science salaries and wages, University of Washington, 1938–1941 (monthly rate in dollars)

Occupation	Name of present employee	Salary		No. months employed or on duty	Amount ($) requested from state appropriations
		Present (May, 1938)	Requested		
Professor	Martin, C. E.	510.00	536.00	20	10,642.00
Professor	Cole, K.	360.00	389.00	20	7,693.00
Professor	Levy, E.		150.00	3	450.00
			158.00	17	2,686.00
Professor	Mander, L. A.	350.00	389.00	20	7,663.00
Professor	Wilson, F. G.	380.00	399.00	20	7,923.00
Associate Professor	Spellacy, E.	330.00	357.00	20	7,059.00
Associate Professor	None		342.00	21	7,182.00
Assistant Professor	Von Brevern, N.	260.00	284.00	20	5,608.00
Instructor	Biesen. C.	180.00		3	540.00
Research assistant	Epstein. J.	150.00	185.00	24	4,440.00
Research fellow	Jonas, F.	75.00		18	1,350.00
Research fellow	None		75.00	18	1,350.00
University fellows	Various			18	5,850.00
Graduate and Undergraduate assistants	Various			18	540.00
Secretary	Christensen, V.	100.00	105.00	24	2,460.00
Stenographer (half-time)	Clyde. E.	40.00	50.00	24	1,200.00
Secretary	Foster, D. G.	100.00	105.00	24	2,460.00
Total Political Science					77,096.00

Source: Governor's Budget Compiled for the Twenty-Sixth Legislature, for Biennium 1939–41 (Olympia: State of Washington, 1939), part 2, pp. 496–497.

ingly, budget and personnel analysts may receive the same pay, or a given type of clerical worker will be paid the same as a laborer, or a high-level clerical worker may earn the same as an administrative aide.

Under the pay plan, jobs are assigned to pay grades. At the federal level the main civilian set of pay grades is the General Schedule, ranging from the lowest grade, GS-1, to the so-called supergrades of GS-16 through 18; the GS system is for white-collar workers only. Separate systems are used for blue-collar workers, the uniformed services, foreign service officers, foreign service staff officers, and the Department of Medicine and Surgery of the Veterans Administration, among others. In addition there is an Executive Schedule, which has five grades and which covers cabinet officers down to directors of some large bureaus.

Congress has provided legislation that defines the differences between grades, although the language of the legislation is extremely broad and subject to varying interpretations. The description for GS-1 includes the statement that such positions involve "the simplest routine work," while GS-18 positions involve the execution of "frontier or unprecedented professional, scientific, technical, administrative, fiscal or other specialized programs of outstanding difficulty, responsibility, and national significance."[10]

It should be kept in mind that jobs are joined with the pay plan regardless of the individual employees involved. A federal worker might refer to herself as a GS-12 when in actuality she is not. She simply holds a position that has been assigned the pay grade of GS-12.

One issue in establishing a pay plan is the appropriate number of grades to include. As has been seen, the General Schedule for the federal government includes 18 grades, but some state and local governments use 40 or even more while others use far fewer. The advantage of using several pay grades is that differences in pay can be assigned according to differences in the demands of various jobs. A system that had only four grades by definition would require that all employees in the jurisdiction be placed in one of the four. This may be workable in a small local jurisdiction with few employees but it would present great problems in a large jurisdiction responsible for a variety of services and having employees with a wide range of skills. The disadvantage of numerous grades is that needless complexity may be introduced. Grades that require splitting hairs are of little use.

Since positions are assigned to pay grades, there is a natural preference among employees to have their positions reclassified upward and assigned to a higher paying grade level. Classification inflation or "grade creep" is a continuous problem in all jurisdictions. A study by the

---

[10] 5 U.S.C. §5104.

General Accounting Office found that the average GS rating in 1949 was 5.25, and that this had climbed to 7.87 in 1974.[11] Part of this increase can be explained by the federal government's greatly expanding its scientific responsibilities during this period, with a justified increase in grade levels. Nevertheless, unwarranted grade escalation was also a factor.

Pay steps within each grade are used in most pay plans. In other words, not all persons within the same pay grade will receive the same pay. As few as four steps can be used, and often as many as ten are used. Usually some standard percentage or dollar increase is employed from one step to another. As with grades themselves, there is no ideal number of steps, but a general rule of thumb has been that the highest step in any grade should be approximately 25 or 30 percent above the lowest step. The use of grades and steps can be seen in Table 4.2 for the federal government's General Schedule. Ten steps are used for the 18 grades, with the highest step in each grade being 30 percent above the lowest step and a constant dollar difference between steps being used within each grade. Another thing to note from the table is that pay grades overlap each other. The pay at the fourth to seventh step of each grade is about the same as the pay at the first step at the next higher grade.

Movement from one step to the next typically requires satisfactory performance on the job and a minimum period of time in each step (usually at least three months and often more). In the federal system, the minimum time is one year. The rationale for this approach is that the longer a worker holds a position, the more productive he or she becomes, and so the movement to the next step is a merit increase. Officially, step increases are not automatic; satisfactory job performance is required. In practice, however, step increases in many jurisdictions are virtually automatic for all employees.

The automaticity of these increases has been criticized as failing to provide an incentive to workers. It has been suggested that public employees can become lazy, sit back and relax, and yet the pay increases continue. An alternative would be to have a highly developed performance appraisal system that would be used to determine whether an employee would receive a raise and the amount of the raise. The difficulties of using such a system, however, are substantial because of the problems involved in performance appraisal itself (see Chapter 6).

While there may be some truth in the argument that automatic step increases provide few incentives, one should also question whether any system based upon steps can provide incentives. Research has indicated that wages are often not the main motivator for good job performance

---

[11] *Classification of Federal White-Collar Jobs Should be Better Controlled* (Washington: General Accounting Office, 1974), p. 4.

Table 4.2. U.S. General Schedule pay rates effective October 1, 1978

	1	2	3	4	5	6	7	8	9	10
GS-1	$6,561	$6,780	$6,999	$7,218	$7,437	$7,656	$7,875	$8,094	$8,313	$8,532
2	7,422	7,669	7,916	8,163	8,410	8,657	8,904	9,151	9,398	9,645
3	8,366	8,645	8,924	9,203	9,482	9,761	10,040	10,319	10,598	10,877
4	9,391	9,704	10,017	10,330	10,643	10,956	11,269	11,582	11,895	12,208
5	10,507	10,857	11,207	11,557	11,907	12,257	12,607	12,957	13,307	13,657
6	11,712	12,102	12,492	12,882	13,272	13,662	14,052	14,442	14,832	15,222
7	13,014	13,448	13,882	14,316	14,750	15,184	15,618	16,052	16,486	16,920
8	14,414	14,894	15,374	15,854	16,334	16,814	17,294	17,774	18,254	18,734
9	15,920	16,451	16,982	17,513	18,044	18,575	19,106	19,637	20,168	20,699
10	17,532	18,116	18,700	19,284	19,868	20,452	21,036	21,620	22,204	22,788
11	19,263	19,905	20,547	21,189	21,831	22,473	23,115	23,757	24,399	25,041
12	23,087	23,857	24,627	25,397	26,167	26,937	27,707	28,477	29,247	30,017
13	27,453	28,368	29,283	30,198	31,113	32,028	32,943	33,858	34,773	35,688
14	32,442	33,523	34,604	35,685	36,766	37,847	38,928	40,009	41,090	42,171
15	38,160	39,432	40,704	41,976	43,248	44,520	45,792	47,064	*48,336	*49,608
16	44,756	46,248	*47,740	*49,232	*50,724	*52,216	*53,708	*55,200	*56,692	
17	*52,429	*54,177	*55,925	*57,673	*59,421					
18	*61,449									

Source: Civil Service Commission, *Federal News Clip Sheet*, No. 191 (October, 1978).

* The cap on General Schedule salaries, as set by Congress, was $47,500 in 1978.

and nearly automatic ones practically never are (see Chapters 11 and 12). Moreover, step increases may be so small that they could hardly be expected to have any effect. Using Table 4.2, a GS-5 moving from step 1 to step 2 would receive a 3.3 percent increase, resulting in $350 extra per year, or a $29 monthly increase. Some of this increase would be consumed by federal, state, and local taxes and increased retirement contributions so that take-home pay would be less than the $29 figure. Given current price levels, such an increase is unlikely to serve as a strong incentive.

Step increases eventually are exhausted by an employee who remains in any grade, and at that point the only salary increase that the employee may receive is for general across-the-board increases for all employees, that is, changes in the pay table. The rationale for this is that eventually productivity improvement on the part of an employee reaches a plateau. The individual has learned basically all that is to be learned in that job and is not increasingly more productive than other employees of comparable rank. Reaching the final step may serve as an incentive to the employee to seek a more demanding position at a higher grade level. Some jurisdictions, however, mitigate this situation by providing longevity pay increases that are based solely upon length of service. Longevity increases are defended as rewarding employees who have been "faithful" to the jurisdiction, but they have been criticized for rewarding laziness and retaining "deadwood." From a purely rational standpoint, a jurisdiction may not need to provide longevity increases to retain long-term employees; the employee who is at the top step in a grade and has been with the jurisdiction for more than fifteen years is unlikely to resign.

How pay plans are adjusted over time varies greatly among jurisdictions. Collective bargaining at the state level, and especially at the local level, is used extensively in adjusting pay; the discussion of that process is reserved for Chapter 13. Salary increases at the state and local level also are often made simply in terms of the constraint of available revenues. Since these governments have substantial limits upon their ability to incur debt, they therefore must adjust salaries upward no higher than what can be paid for with expected revenues. It is not uncommon for jurisdictions in any given year to provide only token increases or even no increases because of expected shortfalls in revenues. A jurisdiction may be faced with the unpleasant choice of providing no salary increases and possibly losing employees because of this or providing increases but furloughing many employees because of the lack of funds.

At the federal level, much attention in recent years has been focused upon the method by which General Schedule salaries are set. The Federal Salary Reform Act of 1962 and the Federal Pay Comparability Act of 1970 firmly established the principle that white-collar federal workers should be compensated on a par with private workers. The method by which this is to be accomplished begins with the PATC survey conducted by the Bureau of Labor Statistics. This survey of professional, administration, technical, and clerical pay collects data from private employers on occupation types that are part of the General Schedule 1 through 15. The PATC survey results are provided to the President's "Agent"— collectively the Director of the Office of Management and Budget, the Director of the Office of Personnel Management, and the Secretary of Labor. The Agent is required to consult with the Federal Employees Pay Council, whose five members represent federal employee groups or unions. The Agent then provides advice on salary adjustments to the President. The Advisory Committee on Federal Pay, whose three members are appointed by the President from outside the federal government, provides advice to the President. He issues an executive order adjusting the General Schedule effective each year on October 1, the beginning of the federal fiscal year. Congress is not involved unless the President decides to give an adjustment below what the PATC survey indicated because of national emergency or economic conditions affecting the general welfare. The President took such action in 1978, approving a 5.5 percent increase for all grades instead of the payline calculation that would have resulted in an average increase of 8.4 percent. When this happened either chamber of Congress could have rejected the President's decision and required him to give the full PATC adjustment. The President's 1978 decision was not overturned.[12]

Much of the controversy about this process has focused upon technical aspects of the PATC survey. These technicalities are far from trivial, in that they greatly affect the pay of individuals and the total personnel costs of the government. One issue involves the employment size of a private employer; depending upon the particular industry, an employer must have 100 employees or 250 employees to be included in the survey. The reason for these cutoffs is that in smaller firms it is difficult to find jobs that are comparable to ones in the federal government. Critics of these cutoffs complain that, by excluding small employers, who typically pay lower salaries, the survey tends to yield an inflated view of private salaries and thereby produces excessively high federal salaries.

---

[12] Congressional Budget Office, *Capping Federal Pay: Alternative Pay Adjustments for Fiscal Year 1979* (Washington: Government Printing Office, 1978); Congressional Budget Office, *The Federal Government's Pay Systems: Adjustment Procedures and Impacts of Proposed Changes* (Washington: Government Printing Office, 1977); *Federal Compensation Comparability: Need for Congressional Action* (Washington: General Accounting Office, 1978); and William M. Smith, "Federal Pay Procedures and the Comparability Survey," *Monthly Labor Review*, 99 (August, 1976):27–31.

The result is not only higher costs to the federal government but increased federal competition with private employers in attracting qualified personnel.

Industry coverage is another issue. The PATC survey samples manufacturing and nonmanufacturing industries, such as transportation, wholesale and retail trade, and utilities. Controversy arises over the sampling of these industries regarding the types of personnel they employ. Arch A. Patton, Chairman of the 1973 Presidential Commission on Executive, Legislative, and Judicial Salaries, has bluntly stated that the government "is a big clerical operation with a lot of guys who administer a lot of people. This is almost exactly like an insurance company or big utility. These are the kinds of industries you ought to compare government jobs to—not General Motors, Boeing, and the like—except when you're comparing a few engineers, for example."[13]

Another issue involves the exclusion of state and local governments, as mandated by Congress in the 1962 legislation, and the exclusion of private nonprofit organizations. The original justification for this exclusion was that state and local employment was comparatively small and that emphasis should be given to the private sector, where wages were set competitively through collective bargaining. With the increasing growth of state and local employment and collective bargaining in these governments, these arguments for exclusion seem less persuasive. The President's Panel on Federal Compensation, appointed by President Gerald R. Ford and chaired by Vice President Nelson A. Rockefeller, recommended in 1975 that state, local, and private nonprofit employment should be included in the survey when needed "to obtain adequate samples and appropriate job matches."[14] The panel stopped short of recommending full inclusion. President Carter's Personnel Management Project, which was responsible for recommending revisions in federal personnel practices, recommended in 1977 that state and local governments be included in the survey.[15]

Occupational coverage constitutes another problem. Since the PATC survey is conducted annually, all occupations within the General Schedule cannot be surveyed in the private sector. The 1975 survey, for example, covered only 18 occupations and 74 levels of work, such as

---

[13] Arch A. Patton as quoted in Neal R. Peirce, "Steady Wage Gains for Federal Employees May Be a Thing of the Past," *National Journal*, 8 (1976):484.

[14] President's Panel on Federal Compensation, *Report* (Washington: Government Printing Office, 1975), p. 22. See also President's Panel on Federal Compensation, *Staff Report* (Washington: Government Printing Office, 1976), p. 84.

[15] Personnel Management Project, *Final Staff Report* (Washington: Government Printing Office, 1977), pp. 155–156.

Accountant I, II, and III; at the GS-1 level, the survey covered only two jobs—File Clerk I and Messenger.[16] The complaint has been that inappropriate jobs have been selected, which results in either underpayment or overpayment of workers.

Other issues involve the weighting of positions, the use of averaging salaries, and the elaborate computer programming used to determine the final results. "Paylines" are developed by the computer for the private sector and the General Schedule. This "dual payline" system is too complicated to explain here but suffice it to say that complaints have arisen over its adequacy. The process has been criticized by the Federal Employees Pay Council as being like a modern skyscraper built upon a clay foundation.[17]

One of the most difficult problems has involved relating the diversity of occupations to the 18 grades of the General Schedule using the paylines. In effect, a dual structure exists within the General Schedule. Clerical and technical jobs range from GS-1 through approximately GS-11 and promotions are made one grade at a time. Professional and administrative positions, on the other hand, begin at GS-5 and progress by two-grade intervals to GS-11, after which promotions are one grade at a time. The rationale for this is that lower level professional positions involve the equivalent of two grades, that is, that GS-7 for a professional is the equivalent of GS-7 and GS-8 for a clerical or technical worker. Problems arise when attempts are made to accommodate these two divergent groups within the same structure. Some occupational groups within the same grade may be underpaid while others are overpaid. GS-5 chemists, for example, typically are underpaid, while GS-5 secretaries are overpaid.[18] Both the Rockefeller Panel and President Carter's Personnel Management Project recommended separating the two groups into separate pay plans.

A related problem with the wide scope of occupations within the General Schedule is that the system does not recognize regional differences in pay. The argument for the uniform system is that employees who are covered can be expected to move from one location to another and that salaries should not fluctuate each time an employee moves. This mobility argument, however, applies mainly to professional and adminis-

---

[16] President's Panel, *Staff Report*, pp. 70–75.

[17] "Views and Recommendations of the Federal Employees Pay Council," in Senate Committee on Post Office and Civil Service, *Documentary History of Federal Pay Legislation, 1975*, 94th Cong., 2d sess. (Washington: Government Printing Office, 1976), p. 248.

[18] Joel Havemann and William J. Lanouette, "The Comparability Factor in Federal Employees' Pay," *National Journal*, 10 (1978):1552–1555. See also *Federal White-Collar Pay Systems Need Fundamental Changes* (Washington: General Accounting Office, 1975).

trative personnel and not to clerical and technical personnel, who are less mobile from region to region. The system results in overpaying and underpaying secretarial staff in comparison with regional, private pay structures. The President's Personnel Management Project recommended a combination of national pay structures for some occupations and regional structures for others, particularly for clerical workers.

Turning to blue-collar employees, wage surveys have been long used for these types of workers at the federal level, and one of the most important features of these surveys is that wages are dependent upon regional variations, unlike the white-collar salaries of the General Schedule. While a GS-9 will be paid the same salary whether he is located in Philadelphia or San Diego, a mechanic will be paid different comparable private-sector mechanic wages in these two locales. This prevailing rate system is under the direction of the Office of Personnel Management, which has designated about 140 geographic wage areas. The department with the largest number of blue-collar employees in an area is designated the "lead agency," which is responsible for conducting the wage survey in cooperation with a wage committee consisting of agency and labor representatives. The Federal Prevailing Rate Advisory Committee provides advice to the OPM on the overall operations of the system. A variety of complaints similar to those involving the PATC survey have been made against the prevailing rate system. Some analyses have indicated that the prevailing rate system as presently implemented tends to produce government wages that are above private wages.[19] Both the Ford and Carter administrations proposed major reforms in this system, but Congress took no action.

At the other end of the spectrum from blue-collar workers are executives. Compensation for public executives has never been comparable to the private sector and never will be. Six-figure incomes are common in the private sector but not the public sector. To some extent, low pay for top-level executives has been converted to a political virtue. Undoubtedly, citizens are wary of large salaries for government executives, especially if there is a belief that these officials do little and therefore deserve little compensation. As a result, people who leave private enterprise to become cabinet- or subcabinet-level officers often must take cuts in income. The compensation they receive is typically set by statute and is structured in terms of the compensation of the chief executive and the jurisdiction's legislators. In a state, cabinet officers' salaries would be kept below whatever salary is provided to the governor.

---

[19] *Improving the Pay Determination Process for Federal Blue-Collar Employees* (Washington: General Accounting Office, 1975); Fogel and Lewin, "Wage Determination in the Public Sector," pp. 410–431.

This ceiling on cabinet officers' salaries may have the effect of imposing ceilings on lower level officials. Since it would seem inappropriate for a department's assistant secretary to earn more than the secretary, ceilings are imposed on subcabinet salaries. Here, politics become important. Particularly in election years, politicians are reluctant to pass major salary increases. *Quid pro quos* must be developed whereby the legislators and executives both gain salary increases. The issue is so sensitive that several years may pass before legislation to raise these salaries is initiated, while the rest of the jurisdiction's employees receive annual increases.

The problem is illustrated at the federal level. The supergrades of the General Schedule and their equivalents in other federal pay plans are limited by the lowest grade of the Executive Schedule. That schedule was not adjusted by Congress between 1969 and 1975, thereby imposing a ceiling upon salaries for other government employees. Before the ceiling was lifted, most employees in the top four grades of the General Schedule were being paid identical salaries. Such salary compression had the effect of encouraging career employees to retire early and discouraged private-sector executives from accepting public positions. The problem was partially alleviated in 1975 when Congress passed the Executive Salary Cost-of-Living Adjustment Act, which provides for automatic annual changes. This has not solved the problem, however, since the Congress is apt to suspend the operation of this law, as it did in 1978.

An alternative approach to automatic adjustment of executive salaries has been the use of special compensation commissions. This method has been used by all levels of government. A commission is created, with representatives of the executive, legislative, and sometimes the judicial branch, to review compensation for high-level positions. The commission's recommendations either can require legislative approval through enactment into law or can become law unless rejected by either the executive or legislative branch. The commission method sometimes neutralizes many political concerns about public criticism for officials giving themselves raises, but this is not always the case. For example, executive salaries at the federal level were not changed between 1969 and 1975 because Congress and the President could not reach an agreement about the recommendations of the Commission on Executive, Legislative, and Judicial Salaries, and because Congress feared public reactions against Congressional pay increases.[20]

---

[20] *Critical Need for a Better System for Adjusting Top Executive, Legislative, and Judicial Salaries* (Washington: General Accounting Office, 1975). See also Commission on Executive, Legislative, and Judicial Salaries, *Report* (Washington: Government Printing Office, 1976), and Congressional Budget Office, *Executive Compensation in the Federal Government* (Washington: Government Printing Office, 1977).

The 1978 Civil Service Reform Act made two important changes in the methods by which federal pay is awarded. First, the legislation established a Senior Executive Service, which provides for a more flexible pay structure for specially designated supergrade positions and some Executive Schedule positions; that system is discussed in Chapter 7. The other change was provision for a "merit pay system," covering GS-13, 14, and 15 positions, to be implemented no later than October 1, 1981. The system eliminates step increases for these grades, and employees are to be awarded salary increases according to their performance. Criteria in judging performance include improvements in "efficiency, productivity, and quality of work or service, including any significant reduction in paperwork." Cash awards of up to $10,000 may be made to highly productive workers in the merit pay system, and an agency may make cash awards of up to $25,000 when approved by the OPM. The system is aimed at eliminating automaticity in pay increases and rewarding productive managers and supervisors.

Beyond wages and salaries there are several types of supplements to pay. Special compensation may be paid to employees who work evenings and night shifts. Overtime pay at time-and-a-half may be used, although some jurisdictions do not allow this.[21] Where overtime pay is not authorized, compensatory time is used; a worker who perhaps works late several evenings or comes in on a weekend will be entitled to the same amount of time off. Holiday pay is common among service areas that must operate throughout the year; fire, police, and hospital services are examples at the local level. Extra compensation is paid by the military for employees in combat, and the same practice is used for other hazardous duty in state and local governments. Some school districts have provided extra compensation to teachers in ghetto schools. Differential pay may be provided to federal workers overseas and in Alaska and Hawaii.[22] Special housing and clothing allowances also may be provided; clothing allowances are common for uniformed employees. Extra compensation for extra work may be given; the high school teacher who coaches the debate or soccer team after regular school hours may receive extra compensation.

Finally, it should be recognized that there are important intergovernmental and economic policy concerns with regard to pay. To attract qualified employees, governments must have wage scales comparable to the private sector and other governments. Organized labor

---

[21] During the 1975–1976 racial disturbances in Boston's schools, the highest paid city employee was a policeman who accumulated many hours of overtime.

[22] *Fundamental Changes Needed to Achieve a Uniform Government-Wide Overseas Benefits and Allowances System for U.S. Employees* (Washington: General Accounting Office, 1974); and *Policy of Paying Cost-of-Living Allowances to Federal Employees in Nonforeign Areas Should be Changed* (Washington: General Accounting Office, 1976).

sometimes has been successful in gaining wage increases by taking advantage of the layering of governments. Under collective bargaining, teacher unions could successfully negotiate salary increases in one school district after another, but there is a simpler and possibly more effective approach. If the union can persuade the state legislature to pass a minimum wage law for teachers above what generally is the existing wage rate, that law would have the effect of adjusting all teachers' salaries upward.

The same approach was taken at the federal level when in 1974 Congress amended the Fair Labor Standards Act by applying its provisions to state and local governments. Not only was the national minimum wage to be applied, but also state and local governments were expected to meet maximum hour standards. This feature particularly troubled municipalities regarding their fire personnel, who spend far more than forty hours a week on their jobs, although much of that time is spent sleeping in fire stations. The law, however, was overturned by the U.S. Supreme Court in 1976 in *National League of Cities* v. *Usery*.[23] The Court held that state and local governments should be allowed to handle such matters without interference on the part of the federal government. The Court said that the 1974 legislation would have impaired the states in functioning effectively within the federal system. The decision was applauded by spokesmen for state and local governments but severely criticized by organized labor.

As for economic policy, both the size of public employment and pay levels are important. The creation of public jobs to stimulate the economy is discussed later in Chapter 10. Here it should be noted that government pay rates are especially important during inflationary periods. Since public employment has become a major portion of the total job market, public employee wage increases can stimulate private wage increases, eventually resulting in higher costs for all goods and services. Also, public wages are thought to have important psychological effects on private wages. Particularly at the federal level, it is thought that holding wage increases to a minimum sets an example for private employment. Therefore, Presidents on occasion have reduced or blocked proposed federal employee salary increases even though data were available to justify such increases for comparability purposes.

While the federal government may not be able to impose general pay standards on state and local governments, restrictions can be

---

[23] *National League of Cities* v. *Usery*, 426 U.S. 833 (1976). See William J. Kilberg and Linda B. Fort, "*National League of Cities* v. *Usery:* Its Meaning and Impact," *George Washington Law Review*, 45 (1977):613–632, and Bernard Schwartz, "*National League of Cities* v. *Usery:* The Commerce Power and State Sovereignty Redivivus," *Fordham Law Review*, 46 (1978):1115–1134. In the 1960s, the Court did allow extension of the Fair Labor Standards Act to state hospitals and schools: *Maryland* v. *Wirtz*, 392 U.S. 183 (1968).

imposed in special situations involving economic policy. In *Fry* v. *United States* (1975), the Supreme Court dealt with the power of the federal government to limit wage increases for state government employees in Ohio.[24] The wage increases that would have gone into effect were higher than what had been approved by the Federal Pay Board. That Board, operating under the Economic Stabilization Act of 1970, sought to limit wage increases in order to reduce inflation. The Court ruled that while the employees were within a single state, the increase would have an impact on interstate commerce and that, therefore, the federal government was empowered to set ceilings on wage increases. The Court found this to be an emergency measure that did not infringe upon state sovereignty.

The discussion now turns to a review of other benefits provided to public workers.

EMPLOYEE BENEFITS

There is no such thing as a fringe benefit. Although people often speak of fringe benefits, these "fringes" are a form of compensation that employees consider as an integral part of their work relationship, and the fringes involve substantial dollar outlays by government. For lack of a better term, "employee benefits" is used here.

The preceding section discussed efforts to make pay in the public sector comparable to pay in the private sector. If comparability is the stated objective, however, then compensation and benefits need to be viewed as a whole. It is quite possible that salaries for some positions in the public sector are lower than salaries for comparable positions in the private sector but that this differential is more than offset when benefits are taken into account.[25] President Carter's Personnel Management Project recommended that federal pay comparability procedures include employee benefits in the calculations.

Attempting to achieve such total comparability is difficult because some benefits defy placing a price tag on them. One of the most important nonmonetary price tags of public employment is job security. Public employees are less likely to be furloughed, "Reductions in force," or RIFs, do occur in government but not nearly as frequently as in the private sector, where firms may be forced to reduce staff because products or services are not selling at expected levels. This means that in the typical career of a private-sector worker there will be intermittent

[24] *Fry* v. *United States*, 421 U.S. 542 (1975).

[25] Ross A Marcou, "Comparing Federal and Private Employee Benefits," *Civil Service Journal*, 19 (October/December, 1978):14-18, and *Need for a Comparability Policy for Both Pay and Benefits of Federal Civilian Employees* (Washington: General Accounting Office, 1975).

periods of unemployment during which income is reduced, while such periods may not be encountered by the government employee.

If private employees are laid off for no fault of their own, they are entitled to unemployment compensation, but this has not always been the case for public workers. In 1976 Congress amended the unemployment compensation law to require this benefit for state, city, and county workers effective in 1978. The law was of course supported by organized labor. State and local governments are challenging the legislation on the same grounds that were used in challenging the Fair Labor Standards amendments.[26]

Work hours and work days constitute another set of employee benefits. The twelve-hour day, six-day week have long disappeared from both the private and public sectors, although long hours may be expected of executives and other high-level officials in both sectors. The forty-hour workweek is generally standard, but in recent years some state and local jurisdictions have reduced the workweek below forty hours, often as part of collective bargaining agreements. Assuming no change in the amount of work to be done or the productivity of workers, shortening the work-week results in hiring additional personnel and higher personnel costs. It should also be noted that some jurisdictions alter the workweek over the course of the year; New York City and other cities have had a practice of having shorter operating hours during the summer months.

Coffee and lunch breaks also affect the total working day. At one extreme, one can have an 8:00 to 5:00 job with two ten-minute coffee breaks and an hour for lunch, or, as in the case of North Dakota, two fifteen-minute coffee breaks and 75 minutes for lunch.[27] Sometimes such breaks are required of employees, while in other situations a more flexible approach may be taken. An employee might work during lunch and then quit for the day an hour early.

Featherbedding exists in both the private and public sectors, and there are no reliable data that indicate where it is more prevalent. Simply defined, featherbedding is a situation in which there is not enough work to fill the time of employees. Sometimes this results from overstaffing, so that there are too many people to do the required work. This results in such absurd situations as a work crew of five people being dispatched to fill one small pothole in a city street. In other situations, the employees reduce their effective work hours by taking long lunch hours and rest breaks. It is not unusual to find employees who use the first half hour or

[26] Unemployment Compensation Act Amendments, 90 Stat. 2667 (1976). The act was upheld in *Los Angeles County v. Marshall*, 442 F. Supp. 1186 (1977).

[27] *Fringe Benefits in State Government Employment* (Lexington, Ky.: Council of State Governments, 1975), p. 38. See also *Fringe Benefits in State Government Employment* (Lexington, Ky.: Council of State Governments, 1972).

so of each day to "prepare" for work. For instance, some clerical workers may take considerable time in the morning getting out paper, sharpening pencils, watering plants in the office, and the like, with a comparable ritual taking place at the end of each day. Practices such as these reduce the length of the work day and may necessitate the hiring of additional employees.

Government is generally liberal in giving days off to its employees for holidays. As with industry, Christmas, New Year's Day, Thanksgiving, Memorial Day, Independence Day, and Labor Day are legal holidays for most government employees. Other holidays are also common in government but less common in the private sector. A recent survey by the Council of State Governments found that 19 states had Lincoln's birthday as a holiday, 30 states had Columbus Day, and 44 had Veteran's Day. About half of the states release employees for part or all of Good Friday, and about half of the states release their employees for each general election day.[28] Federal employees, on the other hand, do not get a holiday on Lincoln's birthday, Good Friday, or election day.

Vacations are liberal in government. Many years ago, granting a vacation was largely at the discretion of administrative officers; if an employee was considered to have worked hard, he or she might be given up to two weeks of paid vacation.[29] Today, provisions for vacations typically are embedded in statutes and administrative regulations. The method for calculating vacation or annual leave varies greatly among and sometimes within jurisdictions. When a person begins work, he or she is likely to have to work for six months before becoming eligible for a vacation. The length of the vacation may be a function of the years of service, so that the new employee may receive a two-week vacation (ten working days) and an employee with ten or more years of service may receive a three-week vacation (fifteen working days). The length of the annual leave is sometimes structured by position, with lower level positions having shorter vacations than higher level ones. According to the Council of State Governments survey, 13 states grant 12 days of annual leave and 11 states grant 15 days, the other states ranging from as little as five days for new employees (Iowa) to 29¼ days for senior employees (Alabama).[30] Vacation days, like the other factors discussed here, need to be considered when approaching the issue of comparability in compensation between the private and public sectors.

In addition to vacation days, leave is often granted for civic, military, and "personal" activities. Leave is granted for jury duty and

---

[28] *Fringe Benefits in State Government Employment*, (1975), pp. 16–22.

[29] R. Y. Stuart, "Vacation and Sick Leave in Government Service," *Annals*, 113 (May, 1924): 350–351.

[30] *Fringe Benefits in State Government Employment*, (1975), pp. 3–5.

summer training for military reserve personnel. "Personal leave days" are also included in some jurisdictions, which may or may not require an explanation for an absence, such as attending a funeral.

Sick leave is still another way in which the total workweek is reduced. Just as vacations are needed by employees to relax and become refreshed, sick leave is essential in that nearly all employees from time to time are too ill to work. Employees in government are typically entitled to ten to fifteen days of paid sick leave each year. Sometimes employees feign illness, call in sick, and stay home, thereby gaining some additional vacation days. Other employees remain on the job and accumulate both sick days and vacation days by taking the minimum time off. These accumulated days can be valuable in the case where an employee wants to take an extended vacation or is stricken by protracted illness.

Restrictions are often imposed on the number of days that may be accumulated. About half of the states limit accumulated vacation time to 30 days; if the employee earns more than that, he or she simply loses those days.[31] Accumulation of sick leave is less restricted, although about 20 states limit such accumulation to between 45 and 190 days. The federal system allows indefinite accumulation of sick days. Accumulated vacation and sick leave are important at the time of termination of employment. Depending on the jurisdiction, an employee may be paid for those days, may in effect quit early by being on vacation or officially ill the last weeks of employment, or may apply these days toward retirement benefits.

The various forms of leave and holidays are expensive to government. Estimates for 1974 federal expenditures show that $2.7 billion was spent on annual leave, $1.1 billion on sick leave, $1.1 billion on holidays, and $0.4 billion on civic and other leave, giving a total of $5.3 billion.[32] For that same year, all governments spent $2.8 billion on sick leave alone.[33]

Other important benefits include various forms of insurance, e.g., life insurance, health insurance, workmen's compensation, and disability insurance. Life insurance provides benefits to survivors in the case of the employee's death. Health insurance typically covers accidents as well as illnesses and disease. Workmen's compensation protects employees from accidents and illness on the job. Disability insurance protects the earning capacity of employees who become temporarily or permanently unable to work.

---

[31] *Fringe Benefits in State Government Employment*, (1975), pp. 11–13.

[32] *Need for a Comparability Policy*, p. 1.

[33] Bureau of the Census, *Statistical Abstract of the United States*, (Washington: Government Printing Office, 1976), p. 308.

Life insurance under governmental programs is usually group term insurance, as distinguished from whole life and other endowment policies in which premiums become a form of investment as well as providing financial protection in the event of death. The insurance program is handled by a private carrier or sometimes by a consortium of private carriers, as in the case of the federal government. The amount of coverage usually varies by compensation, with high-level employees being insured at a higher rate than low-level employees. Often insurance plans allow for employees to purchase additional insurance. Who pays for insurance varies by jurisdiction from all of it being paid by government to all of it being paid by the employee. According to the Council of State Governments survey, in ten states employees pay 100 percent, with the other states having joint sharing of the costs between employees and their governments.[34] The federal government pays a third of the insurance premium.

These term insurance plans can present problems to employees upon retirement. Life insurance usually expires upon resignation and sometimes upon retirement. In other cases, the amount of insurance drops drastically upon retirement. Persons in their sixties attempting to buy life insurance find it extremely expensive and sometimes are denied coverage by carriers. The federal government provides free life insurance to its retired employees. However, beginning at age 65, the amount of coverage is reduced 2 percent each month until the floor of 25 percent of the original coverage is reached. For the employee who retires early, the benefits are substantial from the standpoint of not having to pay insurance premiums; average retirement age in 1976 was 58. Nevertheless, complaints about the 2 percent monthly reduction have been common. Of course the need for such insurance in the later years of life is usually less than earlier, but the argument can be made that the current provisions reduce life insurance for the lowest-paid employees to the point of barely covering funeral expenses.[35]

Like life insurance, government health insurance plans are handled through private carriers, and commonly both government and its employees contribute. Blue Cross-Blue Shield is the most common insurer

---

[34] *Fringe Benefits in State Government Employment,* (1975), pp. 61–62.

[35] *Changes to the Federal Employees Group Life Insurance Program are Needed* (Washington: General Accounting Office, 1977); Subcommittee on Retirement and Employee Benefits, House Committee on Post Office and Civil Service, *Federal Employees' Group Life Insurance Program: Hearings,* 94th Cong, 1st sess. (Washington: Government Printing Office, 1975); and Subcommittee on Retirement and Employee Benefits, House Committee on Post Office and Civil Service, *Value of Federal Employees' Life Insurance After Retirement: Hearings,* 94th Cong., 1st sess. (Washington: Government Printing Office, 1975).

among state employees. In about half of the states, the government pays the entire insurance premium on the employee, and at the federal level the government pays up to 75 percent. When an employee wishes his or her dependents to be included in the plan, the employee may be expected to pay all of the premium for the dependents.

The cost of health insurance to government has been growing dramatically. This growth has been due to rising hospitalization and medical service costs, liberalization of coverage, and the assumption by government of a greater portion of the insurance bill. "For example, in fiscal year 1970, the [federal] Government contributions amounted to $233 million. In fiscal year 1977, they will reach $1.76 billion, 7.6 times what they were in 1970. In 1970, employee contributions were $666 million, and in 1977, $1.6 billion. Employee contributions during the same period of time increased 1.7 times."[36]

As has been stated throughout this section, comparing compensation between the private and public sectors requires consideration of both direct compensation and other employee benefits. However, it should be noted here that tax laws affect total compensation. There is, for example, a difference between employee A who receives a $12,000 salary and a given amount of life insurance and employee B who receives a total salary of $12,000 plus the sum required to purchase the same amount of insurance held by employee A. Employee B's full cash income is generally subject to federal income tax, while employee A does not pay tax on the "free" insurance. Employee A, therefore, is actually receiving higher compensation than employee B.

The capacity to earn a living obviously is endangered when an employee is injured or becomes ill. Health insurance will help cover medical expenses but it will not provide the income necessary for food, clothing, housing, and the like. Sick leave will allow the employee to maintain his income without working but only for a relatively short time. In response to more severe ailments, two types of income protection programs exist: workmen's compensation and disability insurance. When employees are injured at work or become ill because of a work situation,

---

[36] Thomas A. Tinsley, U.S. Civil Service Commission, in Subcommittee on Retirement and Employee Benefits, House Committee on Post Office and Civil Service, *Changes in Computation Formula Determining Federal Health Benefits Contribution: Hearing*, 94th Cong., 2d sess. (Washington: Government Printing Office, 1976), p. 2. See also Subcommittee on Retirement and Employee Benefits, House Committee on Post Office and Civil Service, *Increase in Government's Contribution Under Federal Employees Health Benefits Program: Hearings*, 94th Cong., 1st sess. (Washington: Government Printing Office, 1975); *More Civil Service Commission Supervision Needed to Control Insurance Costs for Federal Employees* (Washington: General Accounting Office, 1977); *Civil Service Needs to Improve Claims Review Process Under the Federal Employees Health Benefit Program* (Washington: General Accounting Office, 1978).

they become eligible for workmen's compensation.[37] The compensation is usually based on a percentage of wages, with employees often receiving two-thirds of their normal pay. Group disability insurance covers nonoccupational accidents, such as falling down stairs at one's home, or illnesses, such as a heart attack. Disability insurance is substantially less common than workmen's compensation in most jurisdictions.

If an employee becomes substantially disabled, he or she may be eligible for disability retirement. In virtually all cases the employee must have worked for the government for some minimum period of time before becoming eligible for such a retirement; at the federal level, the minimum is five years, a typical waiting period. This type of retirement program is expensive. In 1975 alone the federal government paid over $1 billion in disability retirements, and the number of persons receiving such retirements has been rising rapidly. "There were about 1,189 disability retirements per 100,000 [federal] employees in fiscal year 1975 compared to 412 per 100,000 employees in fiscal year 1955."[38] The most common reason for disability retirement was nervous disorders, followed by bone and joint ailments and then by cardiovascular problems.

Studies conducted by the General Accounting Office have raised several questions relating to the possibly over-generous nature of the federal government's disability program.[39] For example, an employee is declared eligible if he or she cannot perform any single task of the current job. Apparently, there has been minimal effort to redesign jobs so that employees can remain at work. It has also been possible for disabled, retired employees to obtain employment outside of government and obtain a higher income (combining disability retirement benefits with wages from the new job) than would have been earned had the individuals remained in the employ of the federal government. GAO, in studying a sample of persons on disability retirement, found that 20 percent of the persons had been given retirement benefits based upon insufficient information or information that did not warrant disability retirements. This finding, however, should be viewed tentatively, given the small sample of cases and legitimate differences of opinion about what constitutes a disability. Nevertheless, it does seem that a rather incongruous situation has emerged in which the federal government has become a spokesman for hiring the handicapped while at the same time it may be

---

[37] *Workmen's Compensation and Rehabilitation Law*, rev. ed. (Lexington, Ky.: Council of State Governments, 1974).

[38] *Civil Service Disability Retirement: Needed Improvements* (Washington: General Accounting Office, 1976), p. 2.

[39] *Civil Service Disability Retirement: Needed Improvements* and *Disability Provisions of Federal and District of Columbia Employee Retirement Systems Need Reform* (Washington: General Accounting Office, 1978).

retiring many of its own employees who, while handicapped, might be able to perform useful roles either in their own jobs that have been redesigned or in other jobs.

One of the most severe criticisms of the disability retirement program is that it is often used for nondisability reasons. The charge is that federal supervisors have "counseled" some of their employees into taking a disability retirement as a means of getting rid of "deadwood." Rather than attempting to fire incompetent or troublesome employees, a task that is both difficult and unpleasant, supervisors may encourage employees to retire early using the disability route. While physical disabilities are not easily faked, nervous disorders are more easily manufactured or exaggerated. The extensiveness of this practice is anyone's guess.

General retirement, as distinguished from disability, is still another benefit and is one of the most expensive and troublesome ones today.[40] Depending on one's view, retirements can be regarded as rewards by government to employees who have served faithfully for many years or as benefits earned by employees and not mere charitable contributions.[41] From a humane standpoint, it is undesirable to force an elderly employee to work simply because he or she cannot afford to be without a source of income. Not only would that be inhumane but it would necessarily mean retention of superannuated, less productive workers. Back in 1870, U.S. Senator Francis M. Cockrell (D, Missouri) advocated a federal retirement system to get rid of "the fossils infesting the departments and performing no real service."[42] Another early justification for public employee retirement systems was that wage and salary rates in government were so low that employees had little choice but to use all income for daily survival and could not save for their retirement. Perhaps the most persuasive reason for these retirement systems is that they encour-

---

[40] Thomas P. Bleakney, *Retirement Systems for Public Employees* (Homewood, Ill.: Irwin, 1972); Robert Tilove, *Public Employee Pension Funds* (New York: Columbia University Press, 1976); Philip M. Doyle, "Municipal Pension Plans: Provisions and Payments," *Monthly Labor Review*, 100 (November, 1977):24–31; *Federal Employee Retirement Systems* (New York: Tax Foundation, 1978); Anthony M. Mandolini and Gary W. Findlay, eds., *Public Employee Retirement Administration* (Chicago: Municipal Finance Officers Association, 1977); "Public Employee Pensions in Time of Fiscal Distress," *Harvard Law Review*, 90 (1977):992–1017; and *A Public Safety Employees Contractual System: An Alternative to Traditional Programs and to Tenure-Reducing Retirement* (Berkeley, Calif.: Institute for Local Self Government, 1977).

[41] The early view of pensions was that they constituted gifts from government and were not rights of employees. The U.S. Supreme Court in *U.S. ex rel Burnett* v. *Teller*, 107 U.S. 64 (1883) held: "No pensioner has a vested legal right to his pension. Pensions are the bounties of the Government, which Congress has the right to give, withhold, distribute or recall, at its discretion."

[42] Francis M. Cockrell as quoted in John T. Doyle, "The Federal Service Retirement Law," *Annals*, 113 (May, 1924).

age employees to remain with government and to develop careers. Without government retirement programs, workers would be more attracted to private-sector careers where retirement benefits are available.

Despite many early efforts to provide public retirement benefits, these programs were slow in being adopted. Although the federal government did provide various retirements to its employees early in the nation's history, not until 1920 did Congress adopt the first generally applicable retirement program—the Civil Service Retirement Law of 1920. Since that time the law has been amended many times, providing expanded coverage of employees and increased benefits. Military personnel are covered by separate legislation. Altogether there are ten major federal retirement programs, with the Civil Service Retirement System being the largest.

State and local governments have followed a similar route of gradually expanding the number of employees covered and increasing the benefits provided. There are about 2,300 of these state and local systems, with the vast majority being locally administered (92 percent). Most of the systems are small, having fewer than 100 members (about 1,400 systems in 1972). The smallness of these systems is a result of many jurisdictions having separate retirement systems for special types of workers; police and fire personnel, for example, often have retirement programs independent of each other and those of other municipal workers. Of the 2,300 retirement systems, about 1,500 are for police and/or fire department employees. On the other hand, there are 28 state retirement systems that not only cover a wide range of state employees but also cover a similarly wide range of local employees.[43]

Retirement benefit rates are usually based upon the employee's salary and years of service. The higher these are, the higher will be the benefits. Often "final average salary" is used in the calculation. This may be an average of the employee's last three to five years' salaries. The salary figure is multiplied times the years of service and then multiplied by a percentage, usually between 1 and 2 percent. Here is an example: 30 (years of service) × $12,000 (final average salary) × .02 (2 percent) = $7,200 annual retirement benefits per year. Of course great variations exist among jurisdictions. Some average the salaries of all years of service instead of just the last three years, while others average the three consecutive highest salaries, which need not be those of the last years of service. Some retirement plans give proportionately increasing amounts

---

[43] Bureau of the Census, *Employee Retirement Systems of State and Local Governments* (Washington: Government Printing Office, 1973), p. 9. See also H. H. Baish, "Retirement Systems and Morale in Public Service," *Annals*, 113 (May, 1924):338–350, and Norman Walzer and David Beveridge, "Municipal Employee Benefits: The Intergovernmental Dimension," *National Tax Journal*, 30 (1977):135–142.

as the number of years of service increase. Using the above example, 1.5 percent might be applied to the first ten years of service and 2.0 percent for the years beyond the initial ten years.

Vesting is an important aspect of most public retirement plans and is also common in private plans. Vesting allows employees to quit their jobs and receive retirement benefits when they would normally become eligible (such as at age 60 or 65). To become vested the employee normally must work for the government for some minimum number of years, with five and ten years being the most common standards. Upon quitting his job, the employee of course must leave his retirement contributions in the fund. The advantage to the employee is that not only will he be entitled to the benefits earned from his contributions but also the benefits from the government's contributions to the system.

Reciprocity in retirement plans is sometimes available for employees who change employers. Reciprocity has the effect of allowing the workers to take retirement "credit" with them when changing employers.[44] About two-thirds of the states have some form of reciprocal agreement.[45] These types of agreements have the effect of allowing workers to enhance their careers by changing jobs without jeopardizing their financial positions during retirement years. Of course, there is no problem of reciprocity when an employee moves from City A to City B or to the state government when all state and local employees are part of a single state retirement plan. Florida and Nevada have systems of this type.

The use of private, nonprofit retirement funds is another method used to enable employees to change from one public employer to another without jeopardizing retirement benefits. Teachers Insurance and Annuity Association (TIAA) is one example. A school district or university may provide for a retirement program through TIAA so that there is no problem should the teacher change jobs.

In response to inflation, which can erode retirement benefits, jurisdictions have provided methods for adjusting annuities upward after the employee has retired. This can be accomplished by linking benefits to the consumer price index, so that as prices rise, benefits also rise. Another method is to grant retirees the same annuity increase that is provided to current workers; if the workers receive an across-the-board 5 percent salary increase, then the retirees will receive a 5 percent increase.

---

[44] *Transferability of Public Employee Retirement Credits Among Units of Government* (Washington: Advisory Commission on Intergovernmental Relations, 1963).

[45] *Employee Pension Systems in State and Local Government* (New York: Tax Foundation, 1976). See also *State and Local Employee Pension Systems* (New York: Tax Foundation, 1969).

The consumer price index is used by the federal government for upward adjustments in annuities. This approach was enacted in 1962 and 1963 for civilian and military personnel. However, in 1969 the then existing legislation was amended to include what became known as the "1 percent kicker." To compensate for delays between the time prices increased and the time benefits increased, an additional 1 percent retirement benefit was added each time an adjustment was made. Given the continuous high inflation of the 1970s, the 1 percent kicker had the effect of improving benefits rather than merely keeping pace with the cost of living. According to the General Accounting Office, an employee who retired in October, 1969, and received a retirement of $10,000 would have needed to receive $15,615 by March, 1976, in order to have the same purchasing power. However, the 1 percent kicker would have provided that retiree a benefit of $17,174.[46] In 1976 Congress changed the procedures for calculating increased benefits and dropped the 1 percent kicker.

Where does the money come from to pay for retirement benefits? In most instances the employee and employer contribute approximately equal sums into the retirement fund. Between 5 and 10 percent of the employee's salary is commonly contributed by both the employee and employer. These monies are invested, so that contributions plus earnings on investments are expected to cover eventual benefits for the employee. Such systems are said to be actuarily sound.

State and local systems invest their retirement monies in a variety of ways. Of the approximately $100 billion these systems had in cash and securities in 1976, approximately half ($52 billion) was invested in corporate bonds and another quarter ($21 billion) was in corporate stocks.[47] The remainder of the funds' assets was in mortgages, federal securities, and other private and public investments. A troublesome aspect of these

---

[46] Cost-of-Living Adjustment Processes for Federal Annuities Need to be Changed (Washington: General Accounting Office, 1976), pp. 2–3. See also Gerald R. Ford, Overcompensation in Federal Retirement Systems: Message from the President, 94th Cong., 2d sess., H. Doc. 94-421 (Washington: Government Printing Office, 1976); Daniel N. Price, Automatic Increases in Federal Compensation Programs, 1964–75, Research and Statistics Note (Washington: Social Security Administration, 1975); and Subcommittee on Retirement and Employee Benefits, House Committee on Post Office and Civil Service, Amendments to Cost-of-Living Adjustments for Retired Federal Annuitants: Hearings, 94th Cong., 2d sess. (Washington: Government Printing Office, 1976) and Cost-of-Living Adjustments for New Federal Retirees: More Rational and Less Costly Processes are Needed (Washington: General Accounting Office, 1977).

[47] Finances of Selected Public Employee Retirement Systems (Washington: Bureau of the Census, 1976), p. 1. See Bureau of the Census, Finances of Employee Retirement Systems of State and Local Governments (Washington: Government Printing Office, issued annually).

investments has been investments in corporate stocks. Retirement funds in recent years have become active in stocks at a time when the stock market has been more volatile. Stock investments on occasion have not performed as hoped, thereby producing shortfalls in expected dividends. Some public retirement systems are legally barred from investing more than 25 percent of their funds in corporate stocks.[48]

The adequacy of the funding of public retirement systems has long been a concern. In the 1920s some envisioned a "day of reckoning" when the federal retirement system would not be able to meet its obligations to retirees.[49] Forty years later—in 1963—the Advisory Commission on Intergovernmental Relations concluded that many state and local systems were "operating on an unsound financial basis."[50] This concern increased in the 1970s.[51] Simply stated, employee and government contributions plus earnings on investments are not adequate to meet future obligations in most retirement systems.

Public employees have exerted great influence over their retirement benefits. Federal employees have lobbied effectively before Congress. State and local employees have used collective bargaining not only to raise salaries but to raise retirement benefits. In the bargaining process, the management side has sometimes preferred granting retirement increases to granting wage increases. The reason is simple: wage increases have a greater immediate impact on the jurisdiction's current budget than retirement increases. When the day of reckoning comes, the result is large outlays for retirement benefits. In 1976, federal, state, and local governments combined paid $24.6 billion in retirement benefits to former employees and survivors of former employees.[52]

---

[48] See "Third Annual Survey of Municipal Employee Retirement Systems: How the Cities Invest," *Pension World*, 12 (April, 1976):12–24; "Third Annual Survey of State Retirement Systems: Sizing Up Their Asset Packages," *Pension World*, 12 (August, 1976):14–30; *Accounting and Operating Handbook for Public Employee Retirement Systems* (Chicago: Municipal Finance Officers Association, 1966).

[49] Doyle, "The Federal Service Retirement Law," p. 337.

[50] *Transferability of Public Employee Retirement Credits*, p. 20.

[51] Troy R. Westmeyer and Wesley Westmeyer, "Public Pensions are Underfunded," *National Civic Review*, 65 (1976):408–409, and *Federal Retirement Systems: Unrecognized Costs, Inadequate Funding, Inconsistent Benefits* (Washington: General Accounting Office, 1977).

[52] Interprogram Studies Branch, Division of Retirement and Survivors Studies, *Benefits and Beneficiaries under Public Employee Retirement Systems, Calendar Year 1976*, Research and Statistics Note No. 8 (Washington: Social Security Administration, 1978), p. 1. See also Roy W. Bahl and Bernard Jump, "The Budgetary Implications of Rising Employee Retirements System Costs," *National Tax Journal*, 27 (1974):479–490 and Maurice Criz and David Kellerman, "Finances of State-Administered Public Employee Retirement Systems," *The Book of the States: 1978–1979* (Lexington, Ky.: Council of State Governments, 1978), pp. 175–184.

The ramifications of underfunding of retirement plans are debatable.[53] One line of argument is that full funding is needed far more in private plans, where, if funding is not adequate, retirees will not receive the promised level of benefits. Since governments, unlike any individual corporation, are not threatened with possibly being forced out of business, public systems can expect to have the continued support of government and therefore do not need to be fully funded. An alternative to full funding, then, is pay-as-you-go, in which current revenues are used to meet current retirement costs.

The other side of the argument is that public decision makers, if required to make full funding contributions when benefit increases are granted, would be more cautious in granting these benefits. From an economic standpoint, government should pay for resources when "consumed," and personnel services are consumed when individuals are employees and not retirees. Underfunding has the effect of postponing paying for current consumption. In other words, a hidden form of debt is being accumulated.[54] In the future local governments on a pay-as-you-go system may face severe problems trying to meet retirement costs along with needs for operating expenses and payments on the principal and interest on debt from bond issues.

Action has been taken to move retirement systems toward full funding and further action is being considered. In 1969 Congress passed legislation to accelerate the government's contributions. In 1974 Congress passed the Employee Retirement Income Security Act (ERISA), which requires actuarial funding for private pension plans. Public employee labor unions have expressed support for a similar law for state and local systems, while such proposed legislation is generally opposed by state and local governments. The National Governors' Conference in 1975, for example, adopted a policy statement that their governments' pension systems were solely their responsibility.[55] Whether this legislation would be upheld in the courts if passed is in doubt considering the 1976 Supreme Court decision, *National League of Cities* v. *Usery*. That decision, as explained above, affected fair labor standards and not retirement plans, but the main thrust of the decision was that the federal govern-

---

[53] Subcommittee on Retirement and Employee Benefits, House Committee on Post Office and Civil Service, *The Civil Service Retirement System: Hearings*, 94th Cong., 1st sess. (Washington: Government Printing Office, 1976).

[54] One analysis of this problem at the state level is *Long Term Debt and Unfunded Pension Liabilities of the Commonwealth of Pennsylvania* (Harrisburg: Office of the Budget, Commonwealth of Pennsylvania, 1976).

[55] Thomas P. Southwick, "Public Pension Plans: Federal Standards?," *Congressional Quarterly Weekly Report*, 34 (1976):1133–1135.

ment should not intervene in relationships between state and local government and their employees.

Benefits under a public retirement system are not necessarily the only retirement benefits for any given employee. An employee can qualify for more than one retirement program. Some retirement systems are structured to encourage early retirements. An employee can work for 20 years, earn a comfortable retirement, and then obtain a new position and earn a second retirement. Retired U.S. military personnel often find civilian employment in the federal government (a practice known as "double dipping") or they may work for state and local governments. As of 1975 there were 142,000 retired military personnel in the federal government, and they constituted 5 percent of the federal civilian work force.[56] The Civil Service Reform Act of 1978 provided that the combined pay and retirement benefits to new double dippers could not exceed the salary rate of level V of the Executive Schedule. At the state and local levels, employees may accrue better retirement benefits earning minimum benefits in two or more jurisdictions. To earn $10,000 in annual retirement benefits, for example, fewer years of work may be required to earn two $5,000 retirements from two jurisdictions than to earn one $10,000 retirement from one jurisdiction.

Social Security is still another factor. Integration with Social Security is discretionary on the part of state and local governments; there is a constitutional question about whether it could be made compulsory. As of 1977 about 72 percent of all state and local employees were covered under old-age, survivors, disability, and health insurance (OASDHI). Great variation exists, so that, for instance, less than half of all employees are covered in California, Illinois, and Louisiana, and all employees are covered in Pennsylvania, Mississippi, and New Jersey.[57] When Social Security is integrated with a jurisdiction's retirement plan, the assumption is that the two in combination will provide a "comfortable" retirement; neither plan will by itself.

These governments voluntarily join and may withdraw from Social Security. Overall the pattern has been for increasing coverage, but 1975 was the first year in which the number of state and local workers being withdrawn was greater than the number being added. As of 1976, 332

---

[56] Civil Service Commission, *Study of Retired Uniformed Services Personnel in the Federal Civilian Service* for the House Committee on Post Office and Civil Service, 95th Cong., 1st sess. (Washington: Government Printing Office, 1977), pp. 4–7. See *Special Retirement Policy for Federal Law Enforcement and Firefighter Personnel Needs Reevaluation* (Washington: General Accounting Office, 1977).

[57] Bertram Kestenbaum, *Estimates of Covered State and Local Government Employment, March 31, 1977*, Research and Statistics Note No. 7 (Washington: Social Security Administration, 1978).

governments, with 46,000 employees, had withdrawn, and another 236 governments, involving 430,000 workers, had applications for withdrawal pending. Included in the latter figures were 360,000 workers in New York City and 13,000 in the Alaska State Government.[58]

One reason for these withdrawals is the structure of both the retirement systems and Social Security. Specifically, retirement plans for police and fire personnel are often geared to 20 years of service, with compulsory retirement at age 50 or 55; early retirement of these workers is justified because of the type of work they perform. Upon retirement firemen and policemen can obtain other jobs, which will qualify them for minimum Social Security benefits. Minimum rates under OASDHI are intended to aid lower income workers so that benefits are not proportional to the number of years of work and the amount of contributions to Social Security. The result is a perhaps more than comfortable retirement for persons able to combine public retirement benefits with minimum Social Security benefits. Investment opportunities are another reason for withdrawing from Social Security. Some state and local jurisdictions and their employees have thought their contributions could be invested to yield higher benefits than would be provided under Social Security.

The withdrawal from Social Security is seen as disadvantageous to both the Social Security system and to some workers. OASDHI has funding problems similar to those of the retirement systems, and the state and local actions worsen the situation.[59] Moreover, some employees within any group being withdrawn from coverage may not have the same retirement benefits as others; these workers, particularly those in fields other than public safety, may be required to work longer for comparable public retirement benefits and do not have an opportunity to qualify for Social Security after retiring from the public service.

Legislation is under consideration to modify the existing provisions in Social Security. One possibility would be to make irreversible the decision to join Social Security. Once a jurisdiction entered the system, it could not withdraw. Another alternative would be to treat state and local employees not covered by Social Security as if they were self-employed; they would then become subject to Social Security. The law could be modified, freezing benefits at the level in existence when the jurisdiction

---

[58] Bertram Kestenbaum, *State and Local Government Employees Covered Under Social Security, 1972-73*, Research and Statistics Note No. 18 (Washington: Social Security Administration, 1976), p. 1.

[59] Robert S. Kaplan, *Financial Crisis in the Social Security System* (Washington: American Enterprise Institute for Public Policy Research, 1976); and Lawrence H. Thompson, "Toward the Rational Adjustment of Social Security Benefit Levels," *Policy Analysis*, 3 (1977):485–508.

withdraws. Since Social Security benefits are often upgraded, particularly to adjust for increases in the cost of living, a freeze would reduce the attractiveness of withdrawal.[60]

Finally it should be noted that there are many other benefits and forms of compensation that public employees enjoy. Free or low-cost education and training are often provided (see Chapter 7). Some employees may be provided with a government automobile. Travel opportunities exist for some workers; employees may be sent to various governmental installations and to attend conferences. Other compensation and/or benefits include free housing, uniforms, cash for suggestions, moving expenses, and other awards. An important benefit that is difficult to gauge is the increased salary a person can obtain in the private sector as a direct result of having worked in the public sector. While these benefits are important, it should be recognized that public employees rarely receive other benefits available to some private-sector employees. Government employees typically do not receive special bonuses, are not eligible for stock options, and are not paid on commission or piecework.

SUMMARY

Personnel compensation is typically the largest portion of any jurisdiction's operating budget. The pay plan, integrated with the position classification plan, provides a series of grades and steps within grades. Procedures are used that attempt to provide comparability in compensation between the private and public sectors; considerable controversy has been generated over the procedures used in determining compensation levels in the private sector for use in determining public compensation levels. Comparability has been largely achieved for low- and medium-level positions; in some instances, public pay may be greater than private pay for similar jobs. Where comparability has not been achieved and never will be is in executive level positions; for these jobs, private pay is considerably higher.

Public employees have numerous benefits other than pay. The forty-hour workweek with rest and lunch breaks is generally standard. Numerous holidays are provided, along with lengthy vacations and allowances for leave time due to illness. Life insurance, health insurance, workmen's compensation, and disability insurance often are provided.

---

[60] Subcommittee on Social Security, House Committee on Ways and Means, *Coverage and Termination of Coverage of Government and Nonprofit Organization Employees Under the Social Security System: Hearings*, 94th Cong., 2d sess. (Washington: Government Printing Office, 1976); Subcommittee on Social Security, House Committee on Ways and Means, *Decoupling the Social Security Benefit Structure: Hearings*, 94th Cong., 2d sess. (Washington: Government Printing Office, 1976).

Disability retirement is still another benefit; there is some concern that employees may abuse this benefit and that supervisors use the benefit as a method for getting rid of "deadwood."

General retirement benefits are increasng in cost and have stimulated fears that a crisis in funding will arise in the future. Benefits typically are based upon an employee's final average salary and years of service. Both employees and government contribute to retirement plans, with the funds being invested in corporate bonds and stocks. Annuities are often adjusted upward to compensate for rises in the cost of living. The result is that retirement plans are not actuarially sound; proposals for federal control over state and local plans to require actuarial funding have been made. Integration with or withdrawal from Social Security is another growing issue involving state and local retirement systems.

Achieving comparability between the private and public sectors requires considering both direct compensation and other benefits. As has been seen, the two groups of workers are often comparable in pay. Since it is extremely difficult to determine the real value of tangible and intangible benefits to public and private workers, a firm conclusion cannot be reached on the relative compensation levels of these two groups of workers.

Chapter 5

Recruitment, Examination, and Selection

Getting the "right" people into government obviously will have an impact on the quality of governmental services that are provided. Placing workers in jobs for which they are not qualified can be expected to produce disappointing results for both government and the individuals involved. A worker who is dismissed for failing to be able to perform his job may find it difficult to obtain another job. The need for an effective intake process in which the skills and knowledge of individuals are matched with the demands of jobs is hardly debatable, but the gap between aspiration and practice is often significant.

This chapter examines the process by which individuals are brought into public service. The first section considers methods of recruitment. The second section analyses the controversial field of civil service testing. The third reviews the procedures by which individuals are selected from among qualified applicants to become public servants. The discussion throughout the chapter concentrates upon entry rather than promotion and reassignment, which are discussed in Chapter 7. The discussion focuses here upon the techniques of recruitment, examination, and selection, whereas the discussion of personnel planning in Chapter 10 takes a broader perspective on the overall matching of individuals with public jobs.

RECRUITMENT

Recruitment in the public sector is often not well planned, in part because somewhat conflicting purposes are at stake. While all recruitment efforts are intended to obtain sufficient numbers of personnel, there are differing views on the extent to which personnel with high qualifications should be sought. One view is that government should seek only those persons with the best skills; to accomplish this would require an extensive recruiting program, which would bring large numbers of people under consideration for public employment. Since extensive recruiting is expensive, jurisdictions are often satisfied with somewhat less than the best; jurisdictions may settle for capable but not necessarily superior workers.[1] Another value that sometimes enters into the recruiting system is that public job opportunities should be available to a wide spectrum of persons as a democratizing aspect of the public service. Finding satisfactory or even superior personnel, then, is not all that is intended. The recruitment program, therefore, may be specifically aimed at minorities, and in some cases goals may be set to attain a representative mix of personnel.

Recruiting involves getting people to apply for public positions, and getting them to take that step may be largely dependent on the public sector's image in general and the jurisdiction's image in particular. People who think government work is dull, full of red tape, and pays little are unlikely to apply. If government is seen as being corrupt and/or ineffectual, job applicants may be few. If nonwhites think government deliberately discriminates against them, then they may not apply. On the other hand, recruitment is likely to be more successful if a government is perceived as a place in which employees perform interesting work, make real contributions to solving societal problems, have opportunities for developing productive careers, and enjoy substantial pay, benefits, and job security.

Current information is lacking on the image of public employment. In the early 1960s, much information was gathered, particularly concerning the federal government's image, but little research has been done in this area since that time.[2] One of the most important studies of this type found that when people employed in private jobs were asked how they would rate performing the same jobs for the federal government, most thought their private jobs would be better.[3] Persons with more positive attitudes had not completed high school, were unskilled and semiskilled,

---

[1] Of course, what constitutes a superior worker is highly debatable. Examination systems, discussed in the next section, may be unable to differentiate between persons with satisfactory skills and those with superior skills.

[2] W. Lloyd Warner et al., *The American Federal Executive* (New Haven: Yale University Press, 1963), and John J. Corson and R. Shale Paul, *Men Near the Top* (Baltimore: Johns Hopkins Press, 1966). See also Leonard D. White, "The Prestige Value of Public Employment," *American Political Science Review*, 26 (1932):910–914.

[3] Franklin P. Kilpatrick, Milton C. Cummings, Jr., and M. Kent Jennings, *The Image of the Federal Service* (Washington: Brookings Institution, 1964), p. 88.

had a low family income, and/or tended to be black. Students also were asked to compare potential private and federal government jobs. High school juniors and seniors rated federal jobs slightly higher than private jobs, but college seniors and graduate students rated private jobs higher. However, students who had A level grades tended to favor federal jobs.[4]

The scandals of the Nixon administration could have worsened the image of the federal government and state and local governments as well, but there is little information to substantiate or refute this suggestion. One survey did attempt to assess Watergate's impact on a small town.[5] The survey found that between 50 and 60 percent of the respondents thought federal employees were as honest or more honest than private, local government, or state employees. Two out of five respondents (38 percent) said Watergate had made them more negative toward federal officials. One-third (35 percent) said they were not surprised by what had happened—a rather cynical view of the integrity of federal officials.

Of particular concern has been the ability of government to recruit professional, administrative, and technical (PAT) workers. There often is an overabundance of unskilled or semiskilled applicants but a scarcity of highly trained individuals. Government typically is at a disadvantage in competing for medical doctors, attorneys, and engineers, considering the pay differentials between the private and public sectors. Moreover, professions often allow for nonbureaucratic work, so that a medical doctor may well prefer to have his own practice rather than having to cope with red tape as a governmental employee.

This concern for PAT employees has led to suggestions for careful personnel planning (see Chapter 10), but in recent years the problem seems to have diminished. The recession of the mid-1970s made public employment far more attractive to many persons than it previously was. Also, colleges and universities "overproduced" many types of graduates, and this surplus necessarily forced individuals to turn to the public sector for possible employment. The leading role taken by the federal government in many scientific fields (for example, space and medical research) has made it comparatively easy to recruit top talent in these areas.

The success or failure of recruitment also is a function of whether people are willing to relocate and/or change employers. Young people, especially unmarried young people, are more likely to be willing to move to another city to take a government job than are older persons with families and homes. Persons already employed in the private sector may be unwilling to forfeit their job seniority to take a public job; as is shown

---

[4] Kilpatrick et al., *The Image of the Federal Service*, p. 107.

[5] Robert D. Lee, Jr., "Watergate and the Image of the Federal Service Revisited," *Public Personnel Management*, 3 (1974):111–114.

in Chapter 4, retirement programs may discourage such a change. Pay may be an incentive to change jobs, but that can easily be to the disadvantage rather than the advantage of government.

The techniques of recruitment are varied. All jurisdictions issue public announcements of job vacancies and scheduled examinations. These advertisements may appear in the classified section of newspapers as well as in poster form in government buildings, community centers, and such places as municipal buses and subways. This shotgun approach is intended to reach a wide range of people, albeit that many will not be interested or not qualified to take the examination. A more directed approach is to advertise in newsletters and journals of professional associations, such as in the newsletter of the International City Management Association (ICMA).

Brochures and pamphlets covering general career opportunities are used. The federal Office of Personnel Management issues the *Federal Career Directory: A Guide for College Students*, which is intended to provide general information about job opportunities. Printed materials such as these are sent to libraries, high school counselors, and college placement offices.

Job information centers and telephone hot lines are used. The federal government has about 100 job information centers located throughout the country. Toll-free 800 numbers may be used, allowing a person to call at any time of the day for information on how to apply for a job. Mechanisms such as these have the advantage of providing a "personal touch," but they can be counterproductive if inquiries are given cold and abrupt treatment or elicit sketchy information.

Personnel or job banks constitute another recruitment device. Local governments, often having small personnel staffs, do not have the resources to develop elaborate recruitment strategies. On the other hand, there are many people who want local government employment but lack the resources to contact every local government for information on job opportunities. The personnel bank, then, serves as a matchmaker. Individuals fill out standard forms describing their education, experience, job interests, salary requirements, and similar job-related information. When a jurisdiction has a vacancy, it can contact the "bank" for resumes on people with the appropriate skills. The New England Municipal Center in Durham, New Hampshire serves this role for the New England states.[6] It should be understood that these personnel banks do not test applicants. Once the bank identifies possible candidates for a position, the jurisdiction decides in what ways these people will be screened.

---

[6] Since the bank contains information about individuals and not jobs, it is really a misnomer to call it a job bank; however, that term is often used. The Pennsylvania Local Government Job Bank at University Park, Pennsylvania performs a similar function in that state.

One of the most expensive forms of recruiting is in person. Recruiters interview interested applicants at job placement centers established at state and national professional conventions, such as at the annual meetings of the American Society for Public Administration. Recruiters are sent to college placement offices and to specific departments of colleges and universities. A city government may send recruiters to particular neighborhoods, such as to low-income/nonwhite neighborhoods. Whether the recruiter is trained in interpersonal relations can have a major effect on whether the interviewee will pursue a job with that jurisdiction.[7] Also, a common constraint on the recruiter is that he or she can only explain job opportunities. No commitments can be made because interested individuals must still pass civil service tests.

On the whole, government recruitment is haphazard. Although there are many recruiting techniques available, jurisdictions frequently do not carefully plan their recruiting strategies. It would seem that a separate strategy should be planned for each job type or at least job series, but funds to support such recruitment planning usually are unavailable. Despite the paucity of data on the subject, one can safely say that governments spend only a small amount on recruitment, in contrast with expenditures for other personnel functions, such as testing and position classification.[8] Failure to recruit extensively sometimes results in no qualified applicants being available for some types of jobs that become vacant. When that happens, line agencies may be forced to conduct their own recruiting to compensate for the inadequacies of the civil service commission's recruiting. The federal Office of Personnel Management has undertaken to make its recruitment program more effective. The system is called the Managed Approach to Recruitment (MAR—a perhaps unfortunate acronym).[9]

EXAMINATION

Testing or examining is an essential aspect of the merit principle.[10] According to that principle, people are to obtain government positions on

---

[7] Neal Schmitt and Bryan W. Coyle, "Applicant Decisions in the Employment Interview," *Journal of Applied Psychology*, 61 (1976):184–192.

[8] For a discussion of recruitment planning, see Alden L. Brock, "Planning the Recruitment Program," in J. J. Donovan, ed., *Recruitment and Selection in the Public Service* (Chicago: Public Personnel Association, 1968), pp. 84–99.

[9] Arch S. Ramsay, "Toward a Modernized Federal Examining System," *Civil Service Journal*, 17 (October/December, 1976):17–20.

[10] For an extended discussion of this process, see Grace H. Wright, *Public Sector Employment Selection* (Chicago: International Personnel Management Association, 1974). For applications in the field of education, see Dale L. Bolton, *Selection and Evaluation of Teachers* (Berkeley, Calif.: McCutchan, 1973) and Reed M. B. Adams, *The Application of a Special Approach to Teacher Selection and Appraisal* (New York: Vantage, 1967).

the basis of their capacity to perform certain job duties, and the examination process is designed to determine that capacity. This section considers the types of tests that are used, test validity, and test administration. It is essential to understand that the term "test" does not necessarily mean a set of questions that the candidates must answer. As will be seen, tests involve a wide variety of measurement devices.

Types of Tests

Testing is essentially a predictive process. A test is intended to screen out those persons who would not perform well on the job. The test preferably will not only screen out inappropriate individuals but will allow for differentiating gradations in skills among qualified applicants. A worker with a high score on an examination should not only perform satisfactorily but in a superior fashion.

In developing a testing program for a given type of job, job analyses are undertaken to identify what abilities, skills, and knowledge are required and at what levels. One such analysis of city police officers, for example, found that at least 17 different attributes were required, ranging from general police knowledge, such as understanding the law, to being able to deal with peers and the public, being able to care for and use equipment, being attentive to detail, and being able to make decisions.[11] Each of these in turn must be operationalized. The ability to make decisions is obviously too broad a concept to be a useful guide to testing an applicant for a police position. Should a police officer, confronted with a situation in which persons are being held hostage, be able to decide how to handle the situation or only know that his/her superior should be called into the case? The point is that the test should be geared to the type and extent of decision making required by the job.

Once characteristics have been defined, then it is possible to consider what techniques to use in testing the candidates. All testing programs begin with an application; a candidate provides basic information, such as name and address, and job-related information, such as education and experience. At the federal level, Standard Form 171 is used to collect much of this type of information, although a separate, more specific job application also may be required. The candidate describes experience related to each job held, including job title, pay, length of service in job, immediate supervisor, and a description of the work performed. Informa-

---

[11] W. W. Ronan, T. L. Talbert, and G. M. Mullet, "Prediction of Job Performance Dimensions: Police Officers," *Public Personnel Management*, 6 (1977):173–180. See also Eugene J. Rouleau and Burton F. Krain, "Using Job Analysis to Design Selection Procedures," *Public Personnel Management*, 4 (1975):300–304; and Ernest S. Primoff, *How to Prepare and Conduct Job Element Examinations* (Washington: Government Printing Office, 1975).

tion also is provided on education. Persons with college educations applying for entry-level jobs include information about the courses taken along with credit hours. The application is important in determining whether an individual meets minimal educational and experience requirements and can be used to screen out clearly unacceptable persons at the outset.

How critical formal education is to a given job is debatable. As is observed in Chapter 3, education may be a good predictor of performance in highly technical fields. However, "credentialism," the practice of delineating a specific education as a prerequisite for a certain job, can unfairly exclude some persons from employment. For federal jobs, the law specifically prohibits minimum education requirements, except for science, technology, and professional jobs, even then these requirements apply only when the Office of Personnel Management has ruled such education is necessary.[12]

The application also can be used in predicting whether the candidate has had the "right" mix of experience to be able to cope with the job. For example, one study found that, in recruiting counselors for working with alcoholics, counseling ability was not the only important skill. Counselors needed some experience in coping with bureaucratic red tape; whether applicants had such experience could be gleaned from job applications.[13]

Verification of information on the application is important. Applicants may have a tendency to overstate their education and experience. Verifying education is relatively simple; all that need be done is to require a formal transcript from the appropriate school or schools. A more difficult task is assessing job experience beyond simply verifying jobs held and employers. How varied was the work performed? How much judgment did the candidate have to exercise? If an applicant previously held a position of administrative aide, was she merely a clerical worker, a bookkeeper, or a trouble shooter for her supervisor? Similarly, in comparing two workers who have been administrative aides, one for one year and the other two years, should the assumption be made that two years is better?

Letters of recommendation and structured evaluation questionnaires can be used as part of the application process. Their usefulness is limited, because the information may be of doubtful reliability. Some letter writers tend to be extremely or excessively positive, while others attempt to be more objective and therefore write less glowing reports. Almost all references are positive, since candidates for jobs are unlikely to submit names of persons who would not write good recommendations.

---

[12] 5 U.S.C. § 3308.

[13] H. Paul Chalfant, LeRoy O. Martinson, and Daniel J. Crowe, "Prior Occupational Experience and Choice of Alcoholism Rehabilitation Counselors," *Community Mental Health Journal*, 11 (1975):402–409.

Confidentiality of reference information is an important factor. The Family Educational Rights and Privacy Act of 1974, better known as the Buckley Amendment, sought to protect individuals from persons who wrote unwarranted negative or derogatory reference letters. As a result of the legislation, letters of recommendation are available for inspection to the job applicant unless he or she waives this right. One experimental study found that letters marked "confidential" tended to be given greater credibility by evaluators than nonconfidential letters.[14] Material obtained from qualifications investigations also is subject to release to candidates under the Privacy Act, although identity of informants usually may be kept confidential.

Sometimes the application will be the only part of the testing program for a given set of jobs. Evaluators will determine points to be assigned to each type of experience and education and a total score will be calculated. This is called an unassembled examination because the applicants do not come together or assemble to take a test.

Assembled examinations are of two types—written tests and performance tests. Written examinations probably are the most commonly used measurement technique. The exact nature of a test for a particular purpose is again a function of what qualities are sought. For a trainee type of position, aptitude, learning capability, and other potential qualities are important. What the applicant knows actually may be less important than how well the applicant can be expected to learn. Closely associated with aptitude tests are intelligence tests. IQ tests, however, are often challenged as being weak predictors of job performance. An individual can be an excellent worker in many types of jobs even though his IQ is not particularly high.

Aptitude and personality tests attempt to gauge whether a person's emotional and mental "make-up" will be compatible with a given type of work. Personality tests may be able to identify those who would become bored with a routine job from others who perhaps might find that same type of work satisfying. In private enterprise, the assembly line is an example where high intelligence is not necessarily a positive attribute and where the ability to maintain a continuous routine is.

Other paper-and-pencil tests are more specifically geared to the substance of jobs. A common controversy about these tests is whether the questions are truly job-related. An accounting test that is specifically geared to the accounting system of a jurisdiction might be appropriate when the required depth of information is so extensive that an inexperienced person would need months of training before becoming a

---

[14] David R. Shaffer, "Who Shall be Hired: A Biasing Effect of the Buckley Amendment on Employment Practices?," *Journal of Applied Psychology*, 61 (1976):571–75. The study used college students as "evaluators" of job applications and not persons in personnel offices.

productive employee. On the other hand, such a test, if focusing upon trivial items peculiar to the jurisdiction's accounting system, gives unwarranted advantage to current employees and raises artificial barriers to outsiders.

How much job information or knowledge is expected is equally important. A forest ranger test might ask questions about tree diseases, insect classifications, animal species, and soil types, but unless such knowledge is needed on the job, these questions should not be included. Similarly, reading skill may be regarded as essential, but should the test concentrate upon reading speed, vocabulary, reading for detail, or reading for general comprehension?[15]

One frequent criticism of paper-and-pencil tests is that they are biased in terms of language skill achievements. A person may score low on an examination not because of lack of knowledge, skill, or capability but because of the language used in the test. If all that is necessary to perform a given job is a ninth grade reading capability, tests written at levels above ninth grade clearly are inappropriate. Today there are tests that test tests for reading level; among these are SMOG, Batel, and Flesch.[16]

One of the most important tests used at the federal level is the Professional and Administrative Career Examination (PACE), and it is a blend of some of the techniques discussed above. PACE is for professional and administrative jobs and covers positions at the GS-5 and GS-7 levels (see Chapter 4 for an explanation of GS ratings). PACE was introduced in 1974 to replace the Federal Service Entrance Examination (FSEE), which had been criticized as not being sufficiently job-related. PACE has several sections dealing with reading comprehension, the use of synonyms, logical sequencing, basic mathematics, and the like. A logical sequence question would expect a person to determine what symbol would be next in a series; for example, how would you complete the following: E, ɯ, Ǝ, _____? Portions of the test are related to aptitude, while others test achievement.

Written tests used in public personnel systems are usually "objective." Multiple-choice, true-false, matching, and fill-in-the-blank questions are used. These types of tests are not only relatively easy to score, they are also less subject to varying interpretations by test evaluators.

Some tests, on the other hand, are of the essay type, requiring examinees to write a paragraph or more about a given problem. A technique that is little used now but that may become popular is the future

---

[15] Lyle F. Schoenfeldt et al., "Content Validity Revisited: The Development of a Content-Oriented Test of Industrial Reading," *Journal of Applied Psychology*, 61 (1976):581–588.

[16] Steven L. Edgell, "Readability of Tests: Are Things Really That Bad?" *Public Personnel Management*, 4 (1975):311–316.

autobiography, which requires a person to discuss what he or she will be doing five or ten years from now. The future autobiography may be especially useful in selecting managers.[17]

Nonwritten tests can measure physical capabilities, skills, or aptitudes. An example of a physical aptitude test is the MacQuarrie Test of Mechanical Ability. It requires such things as "tracing with a pencil through gaps in straight lines" and "tapping three times in each of a number of circles with a pencil."[18] Although paper and a pencil are used in the test, the objective is to test motor skills. The MacQuarrie Test is useful for testing candidates for positions requiring the use of their hands in precise movements and is used more in industries, where products are made, than in government.

Government can use aptitude tests for jobs involving physical activities. Fire personnel, for example, need to be able to make hydrant connections, ascend ladders, lift equipment, walk through debris-laden buildings, and climb through windows. Therefore, tests are made to determine the ease with which candidates can achieve these tasks.[19] Physical achievement tests, as distinguished from the aptitude variety, include typing and other machine operation tests.[20]

Oral examinations are one of the most common forms of nonwritten examinations. It is important to understand that the oral examination is not the same as a job interview, which is discussed below. Job interviews are conducted by line supervisors and their staffs and can occur before or after a test has been given. In contrast, the oral examination is part of the formal testing program conducted by a civil service commission. This type of test is used to examine qualifications not easily measured by other types of tests. General oral communication skill is tested, along with abilities to think under pressure and to deal effectively with others in a face-to-face situation. The oral test allows for "probe" questions that seek to determine the candidate's depth and breadth of substantive knowledge. One question that might be asked at a personnel analyst oral examination could be: "If an administrator in one of the line agencies had requested an upgrading of the classification of a position, how would you deal with that administrator in re-evaluating the position?" This

---

[17] William L. Tullar, "The Future Autobiography as a Predictor of Sales Success," *Journal of Applied Psychology*, 61 (1976):371–373.

[18] Norman R. F. Maier, *Psychology in Industrial Organizations*, 4th ed. (Boston: Houghton Mifflin, 1973), p. 218.

[19] W. Considine et al., "Developing a Physical Performance Test Battery for Screening Chicago Fire Fighter Applicants," *Public Personnel Management*, 5 (1976):7–14 and Henry F. Hubbard, Thelma Hunt, and Robert D. Drause, "Job Related Strength and Agility Tests—A Methodology," *Public Personnel Management*, 4 (1975):305–310.

[20] For industrial applications, see Alan Jones and Peter Whittaker, *Testing Industrial Skills* (New York: Wiley, 1975).

question would allow exploration of interpersonal relations skills and substantive knowledge of position classification techniques.

The formats of orals vary greatly. Candidates may be examined individually or in groups; group interviews are useful in identifying interpersonal relations skills and leadership potential. In group orals the candidates are given a problem to work with and resolve within a specified time period. In individual orals, a standard set of questions is given to each examinee but probe questions will vary. The oral can be conducted by one person, but often a three-person examination board is used.

In the oral examination process it is difficult to maintain consistency of standards from one examinee to another and from one board to another. At the state level, two or more boards dealing with the same testing program might convene in the state capital or might be geographically dispersed. The board usually consists of substantive "experts," who, while knowing their field of work, such as law enforcement, often are not well trained in conducting tests. As a result, board members can be unintentionally unfair to some candidates. Also, some examiners are undoubtedly biased for or against the clothing, hairstyles, and mannerisms of candidates. Racial and sex biases are other common complaints.

Usually candidates are graded by oral examiners on scales, such as a 0 to 6 point scale. Unless these scales are behaviorally anchored, that is, have behavioral descriptions associated with each point on the scale, great inconsistencies can exist from one board member to another and among boards. Some boards, for example, may reserve the highest level for only the truly outstanding candidates. The result is the highest score is rarely if ever used, so that a scale of 0 to 6 becomes a scale of 0 to 5. Other boards, in contrast, may use the highest score more freely.[21]

Beyond these tests there are physical examinations and background investigations. Physical examinations are particularly important in jobs involving manual labor, such as sewer, water, and road maintenance jobs. The background investigation (BI) is used for sensitive positions, especially in the military and other national security jobs. BIs vary in their intensity; some involve extensive interviewing of the candidate's friends, former employers, relatives, and current and former neighbors.[22]

---

[21] This problem is analogous to performance evaluation scales; see Chapter 6 for a more detailed discussion. See James L. Moro, "Oral Interviews for Screening Social Worker Applicants," *Public Personnel Management*, 6 (1977):437–441 and James W. Sever, Robert W. Knippenberg, and Vincent J. Perfetto, "Minneconsin: A Behavior-Based Oral Test," *Public Personnel Management*, 6 (1977):427–436.

[22] *Proposals to Resolve Longstanding Problems in Investigations of Federal Employees* (Washington: General Accounting Office, 1977).

The background investigation should be distinguished from the qualifications investigation. The latter is concerned with whether a person has the necessary skills and knowledge for a position, whereas the BI is concerned with whether a person is loyal and not a security risk (see Chapter 8).

The examinations that have been discussed can be used in combination with each other. Table 5.1 reports the extent to which states and large cities use various types of tests for different types of job positions; the table is based upon data from a survey sponsored by the International Personnel Management Association.[23] As can be seen from the table, written tests are most common for professional/technical and clerical state jobs; all of the states use these tests for clerical positions, while only half use them for labor and trades positions. Oral tests are used at the state level mainly for professional and technical positions (71 percent, as compared with only 17 percent for clerical positions). Ratings of training and experience are common for professional/technical jobs (90 percent of the states), while performance tests are common for clerical jobs (81 percent). About a third of the states use background investigations and medical examinations for public safety workers.

Turning to the city portion of Table 5.1, written tests are common for all job types, ranging between 68 and 88 percent of the cities. Oral examinations are used more extensively at the city level, for clerical, labor, and public safety workers, than they are at the state level. Cities, like states, use performance tests for clerical workers, but cities use these tests substantially more for labor/trades jobs than do states (72 percent of cities, compared with only 24 percent of the states). Background investigations and medical examinations are more common at the city level for all types of positions. Not shown in the table is that 76 percent of the cities use agility tests, a form of physical aptitude test, for police and fire personnel.

When two or more techniques are to be used for a testing program, the "successive" hurdle approach is commonly applied. Candidates who do not clear one hurdle are not allowed to attempt the next one. This approach is economical, in that more expensive forms of testing are reserved for later hurdles, when the number of candidates is small. For instance, candidates might first be required to pass a review of their education and experience and a written test before being eligible to take an oral examination.

---

[23] Carmen D. Saso and Earl P. Tanis, *Selection and Certification of Eligibles* (Chicago: International Personnel Management Association, 1974). See this report for additional information on counties, small and medium size cities, public authorities, schools, and Canadian agencies.

Table 5.1.   Percentage of states and cities over 500,000 population using various types of tests by types of positions*

Type of test	States				Cities			
	Professional/ Technical	Clerical	Labor/ Trades	Police/ Fire	Professional/ Technical	Clerical	Labor/ Trades	Police/ Fire
Written	95	100	50	64	76	88	68	88
Oral	71	17	14	40	64	28	44	48
Training & Experience	90	40	71	10	92	52	80	28
Performance	19	81	24	7	16	84	72	28
Background	12	10	7	31	40	44	44	76
Medical	14	10	17	38	72	72	88	92

Source: Data compiled from Carmen D. Saso and Earl P. Tanis, *Selection and Certification of Eligibles* (Chicago: International Personnel Management Association, 1974), pp. 2 and 3.

* Note: Based upon responses from 42 states and 25 cities.

The hurdle approach can be illustrated by the testing program designed for police recruits in the City of Fort Collins, Colorado and developed in cooperation with the Colorado State University.[24] The testing program has three phases, the first being written examinations. This phase involves an intelligence test (Low Verbal Matrices Form 58) and a personality test (Minnesota Multiphasic Personality Inventory). Persons who successfully complete these tests enter the second phase, in which they are given an oral board examination, a situation test in which they act-out a possible street situation, a leadership group oral test, and an individual interview with a psychologist. Successful completion of the second phase leads to the final one, which involves a background investigation, polygraph test, and medical examination.

Test Validity

The concept of test validity is complex, but its main thrust is that the test must measure what it is designed to measure.[25] It is obvious, of course, that a test used in the employment process must be designed to measure some characteristic required in the job to be filled. If, for instance, candidates for drivers of municipal buses were given typing tests, the test probably would not be valid for that particular job. While the test may differentiate among skills—some candidates would pass and some would fail—it would have no bearing on their capabilities as bus drivers. Validating a test provides guidance about what interpretations or inferences may be properly made about test scores.

The issues of validity and job relatedness have become particularly important in recent years since screening devices have tended to limit the access of some groups to public jobs. Although the discussion of discrimination is reserved for later, it should be recognized here that charges of discrimination have resulted in substantial efforts to make certain that tests are valid and job-related. A recent survey of state and local govern-

---

[24] James F. Gavin and John W. Hamilton, "Selecting Police Using Assessment Center Methodology," *Journal of Police Science and Administration*, 3 (1975):166–176.

[25] For an early discussion of test validity, see Albert S. Faught, "Employment Tests in the Public Service," *Annals*, 113 (May, 1924):311–321. A standard work on testing, now somewhat dated but still useful, is Robert M. Guion, *Personnel Testing* (New York: McGraw-Hill, 1965). See also Lee J. Cronbach, *Essentials of Psychological Testing*, 3d ed. (New York: Harper and Row, 1970); Robert M. Guion, "Content Validity: Three Years of Talk—What's the Action?," *Public Personnel Management*, 6 (1977):407–414; Lawrence R. O'Leary, "Objectivity and Job Relatedness: Can We Have Our Cake and Eat it Too?" *Public Personnel Management*, 5 (1976):423–433; John W. Menne, William McCarthy, and Joy Menne, "A Systems Approach to the Content Validity of Employee Selection Procedures," *Public Personnel Management*, 5 (1976):387–396; and Stephen Wollack, "Content Validity: Its Legal and Psychometric Basis," *Public Personnel Management*, 5 (1976):397–408.

ments found that about half of all responding agencies were trying to ensure the validity of their tests.[26] (See Chapter 9 for a discussion of legal provisions and court decisions pertaining to test validity.)

A superficial appearance of relevance is known as face validity. Some tests may appear to be valid but when they are carefully scrutinized are found not to be. Measurement experts do not attach any importance to face validity. Rather, they have devised several ways of determining the genuine utility of measuring devices.

Validity can be demonstrated in a number of ways. Content validity assesses whether the test measures subject matter needed in the target position and whether it appropriately samples the subject matter. In other words, the test covers a representative sample of tasks in the job. A personnel test that asked no questions about labor-management relations would not meet the content validity requirement (assuming that the personnel analyst had to deal with such relations). Even if a test covered all aspects of personnel, it would not necessarily be content valid, because there could be an overabundance of questions dealing with one aspect of the field while other aspects received little emphasis (i.e., it might over-emphasize collective bargaining and underemphasize position classification). Moreover, the questions might be pitched at the wrong level of expertise for the target population.

A problem with the content validity test is that there is no easy way for determining the appropriateness of the questions that sample a given field. Complicating the problem is the fact that several testing devices may be used. The sampling issue, then, arises not only for the mix of questions on a written examination but the mix between a written and oral examination plus any others, such as physical and performance examinations.

The typical content validity procedure is to use "experts," either those currently holding positions or outside experts, to define the area and level of expertise. In the case of the personnel test, personnel analysts in the jurisdiction might be used along with personnel "experts" from other jurisdictions and professors who teach personnel administration courses. These persons would be asked to review the content of the examination to determine whether appropriate questions had been included. Fairly rigorous methodologies have been developed to assemble the judgments of experts, but the methodologies cannot overcome the fact that the validity test rests upon composite judgments or opinions. Had a different set of experts been used in validating a test, the outcome could be substantially different.[27]

---

[26] Saso and Tanis, *Selection and Certification of Eligibles*, pp. 8–9.

[27] Guion, *Personnel Testing*, pp. 124–125.

Criterion-related validity is another alternative. This technique uses statistical analyses to determine the relationship between test scores and job performance. The test is valid if test scores are related to job performance; high job performers, for example, generally earn high test scores. Either concurrent or predictive validity may be used.[28] The concurrent validity approach involves administering the test to job incumbents and comparing their test scores with appraisals of their job performance. Predictive validity, on the other hand, compares test scores of new job appointees with their performance measured at some later date. Both approaches involve correlation analysis.

Criterion-related validity can be understood by studying Figure 5.1. The horizontal axis of the graph indicates test scores and the vertical axis measures job performance. Each dot on the graph represents an individual's score and job rating. A horizontal line has been arbitrarily drawn to represent the demarcation between high and low job performance. The diagonal line is a regression line based upon a least squares criterion. The vertical broken lines A, B, and C represent possible cutoff points on hiring. If only those with scores of A or better were hired, the test would virtually guarantee that all new hires would be high performers. If the cutoff were at the B level, however, some of the new hires would be low performers. The concept of probability is then employed: perhaps in the case of the B cutoff there would be a 70 percent probability that each new hire would be a high performer. At the C cutoff the probabilities worsen so much that it is possible that low performers might outnumber high performers. Taylor-Russell tables have been used for decades to assess the effects of various cutoff points.[29] The test in this example would be generally valid, because there is a relationship between test scores and performance. The degree of validity, however, is affected by the cutoff point that is used. Many measurement devices are valid at extreme high or low scores, but much less so in the middle range.

Although criterion-related validity seems an attractive solution to the problem of measuring validity, there are at least three problems in using it. First, only test scores for persons who were hired can be considered, since job performance can only be measured for those individuals. The validity measurement, then, cannot indicate how the persons who were rejected might have performed. It is conceivable that the test

---

[28] William C. Byham and Morton E. Spitzer, *The Law and Personnel Testing* (New York: American Management Association, 1971), pp. 116–117. Also see Frank L. Schmidt, John F. Hunter, and Vern W. Urry, "Statistical Power in Criterion-Related Validation Studies," *Journal of Applied Psychology*, 61 (1976):473–485.

[29] H. C. Taylor and J. T. Russell, "The Relationship of Validity Coefficients to the Practical Effectiveness of Tests in Selection: Discussion and Tables," *Journal of Applied Psychology*, 23 (1939):565–578.

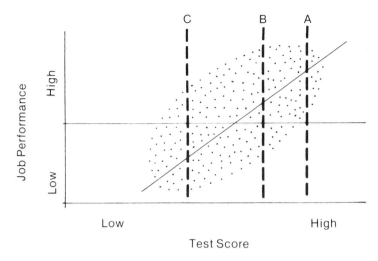

Figure 5.1.   Relationship between test scores and job performance.

screened out the potentially best workers. One method of overcoming this problem would be to randomly appoint a substantial sample of all applicants, and then compare performance with test results. Most governments would not be prepared to undertake such an experiment.

Second, measures of job performance are not necessarily valid or reliable themselves. As is seen in the next chapter, great inconsistencies exist among supervisors in rating their personnel. If the performance ratings are unsound, the rest of the criterion-related validity analysis will be unsound.

Third, different subgroups taking the same test may have different distribution patterns on test scores, that is, the test may be differentially valid for different groups. To check on the validity of the test, it must be analyzed separately for each subgroup. It is frequently impossible to assemble large enough subgroups to make criterion-related analyses. Because of these practical problems, criterion-related validity is rarely used in public personnel systems.

Besides the practical problem of gathering subgroup data for differential validity, there has been extensive debate over the appropriateness of differential validity. Part of the problem stems from a lack of agreement about what constitutes differential validity. One line of argument is that when differential validity is restricted to correlation coefficients, there may be little difference between subgroups and the alleged problem is only a "pseudoproblem." Rather than concentrating upon differential validity, it is said that the focus should be on differential prediction, namely how test results are used in predicting performance. The issue is highly technical and necessarily couched in statistical terminology.[30]

Construct validity is another alternative. A construct is a hypothetical concept. In personnel testing, the constructs usually are traits that are hypothetical in that they cannot be directly measured but nevertheless are presumed to exist. It may be extremely difficult to pin down definitions of these constructs. Such traits can be intelligence, industriousness, creativity, and aggressiveness to name a few. Construct validity, then, gauges the extent to which test scores vary with a given construct. For example, do scores on a given test increase with increases in creativity on the job? Often, construct validity considers how one test relates to previously existing tests that are accepted as measures of the construct. For instance, does the new test that purports to measure industriousness correlate with other tests of industriousness?

A problem of construct validity for personnel testing is that it is necessary to demonstrate that the traits being measured are job-related. Since the constructs themselves are difficult to define, it is extremely difficult to show that they are indeed required. Construct validity, therefore, requires the use of criterion-related validity as part of the overall strategy. Content validity also may be needed. As a result, construct validity is more difficult to undertake than either content or criterion-related validity.

Much confusion has existed over the specific steps to be used in any one of these validation strategies and whether one of the three was preferred. The issue is particularly acute when it relates to equal employment opportunity (see Chapter 9). In 1978, the major federal agencies concerned with employment discrimination agreed upon the Uniform Guidelines on Employee Selection Procedures.[31] The agencies were the Equal Employment Opportunity Commission, the Civil Service Commission (now, Office of Personnel Management), Department of Justice, Department of Labor, and Commission on Civil Rights. The guidelines

---

[30] See Philip Bobko and C. J. Bartlett, "Subgroup Validities: Differential Definitions and Differential Prediction," *Journal of Applied Psychology*, 63 (1978):12–14; John E. Hunter and Frank L. Schmidt, "Differential and Single-Group Validity of Employment Tests by Race: A Critical Analysis of Three Recent Studies," *Journal of Applied Psychology*, 62 (1978):1–11; Raymond A. Katzell and Frank J. Dyer, "Differential Validity Revived," *Journal of Applied Psychology*, 62 (1977):137–145; Raymond A. Katzell and Frank J. Dyer, "On Differential Validity and Bias," *Journal of Applied Psychology*, 63 (1978):19–21; Robert L. Linn, "Single-Group Validity, Differential Validity and Differential Prediction," *Journal of Applied Psychology*, 63 (1978):507–512; and Frank L. Schmidt, John G. Berner, and John E. Hunter, "Racial Differences in Validity of Employment Tests: Reality or Illusion," *Journal of Applied Psychology*, 58 (1973):5–9.

[31] "Uniform Guidelines on Employee Selection Procedures," 43 F.R. 38290 (1978). See also Bonnie Sandman and Faith Urban, "Employment Testing and the Law," *Labor Law Journal*, 27 (1976):38–54.

give major emphasis to content and criterion-related validity and warn of the "extensive and arduous effort" associated with construct validity; differential validity is not mentioned. The guidelines are consistent with the American Psychological Association's *Standards for Educational and Psychological Tests.*[32]

Test Administration

Test administration is usually the responsibility of civil service commissions, both in setting standards and in the actual conduct of examinations. Whereas functions like position classification may be the responsibility of a civil service commission or personnel department, with actual classification of jobs being delegated, the examination process usually has not been delegated. There have been significant exceptions to this, especially at the federal level with the reforms of 1978.

Examinations constitute one of the major workload fields for civil service commissions. Notices of scheduled examinations must be prepared and distributed. The commission must respond to each inquiry and application to take an examination. At the federal level, in 1976 the Civil Service Commission answered about 12 million job inquiries and processed 2 million job applications to fill 150,000–200,000 positions.[33] About 1,700 Commission employees were involved in this responsibility. The Civil Service Reform Act of 1978 permitted the Director of the Office of Personnel Management to delegate the testing function to line agencies, except for administrative law judge positions and those that are common among federal agencies.

In any testing program, tests must be prepared, and test preparation is a process that consumes much time. Once tests are administered they must be scored. If pigeonhole position classification is common (see Chapter 3), numerous different tests must be prepared. The greater the number of job series, normally the greater the number of tests that will need to be prepared. The use of a single entrance-level examination covering many series can greatly reduce the workload of test preparation. However, such tests may run into problems of job-relatedness. The survey by the International Personnel Management Association (IPMA) noted earlier found that about half of the states use these, while the vast majority of local governments surveyed do not.[34]

In designing the testing program for a job series, job analysis data, alternative types of tests, and potential costs are considered. In some

---

[32] *Standards for Educational and Psychological Tests* (Washington: American Psychological Association, 1974).

[33] Ramsay, "Toward a Modernized Federal Examining System," p. 17.

[34] Saso and Tanis, *Selection and Certification of Eligibles*, pp. 3–4.

cases, jurisdictions will use existing tests from external sources.[35] This approach greatly simplifies test development; the IPMA is one of the most important test vendors. A potential hazard of this approach is that the externally developed test may not be totally suitable for the jurisdiction, and again may run into job-relatedness problems.

Civil service personnel usually must work with agency personnel in designing a test program, and this can be a subject of tension between the two. With civil service presumably having expertise in testing and agency personnel having substantive expertise, a symbiotic relationship should but does not always develop. Consultation between the two may occur in the course of establishing content validity (see above); department personnel, particularly key supervisors, may be consulted. However, the commission staff, being concerned about the security of the test, often will be reluctant to allow department personnel to see test questions; there may be specific statutes, ordinances, or regulations that prohibit disclosure. The unfortunate situation can develop in which after the test has been given and information about the questions "leak" back to the supervisors, they conclude that many of the questions were not germane to the job content and could have had the effect of screening out excellent candidates.

The location for assembled examinations will depend on the type of jurisdiction. Local governments may have only one test site, while states may have several. The federal government uses approximately 1,000 examination locations. Wide dispersal of sites provides easy access to persons who wish to take civil service tests. However, a limitation is put on the types of tests that can be conducted. Written tests are easily conducted almost anywhere, whereas that is not the case with performance tests. Industry is moving toward greater use of so-called assessment centers. Some of these are just new names for the corporations' testing offices, but in other cases real changes have emerged. The assessment center consolidates much of the testing activity so that special, more costly facilities and techniques can be provided. If role-playing or some other type of group oral is to be used, the assessment center can provide special rooms, equipment, and materials for the test.[36]

An alternative that may hold some advantages over current practices is for jurisdictions to sponsor a joint testing facility and program.

---

[35] See Kenneth L. Wentworth, "Use of Commerical Tests" in Donovan, ed., *Recruitment and Selection in the Public Service*, pp. 154–162.

[36] See John P. Bucalo, Jr., "The Assessment Center—A More Specified Approach," *Human Resource Management*, 13 (Fall, 1974):2–13; James O. Mitchell, "Assessment Center Validity: A Longitudinal Study," *Journal of Applied Psychology*, 60 (1975): 573–579; and David Strausbaugh and Barry L. Wagman, "An Assessment Center Examination to Select Administrative Interns," *Public Personnel Management*, 6 (1977):263–268.

One such experiment has been the Utah Intergovernmental Personnel Agency Center. Funded under the federal Intergovernmental Personnel Act, the Center administers clerical type tests for the State of Utah, Salt Lake City and one other city, four counties, and three higher education institutions. This allows an applicant to take one test to become eligible for positions in ten different jurisdictions. The problem of developing standardized tests has been eliminated by the Center having gained approval to use tests of the federal Office of Personnel Management. The Center offers the potential for developing similar test programs in nonclerical fields.[37]

Timing as well as location considerations are important in testing programs. For many tests, if one does not apply to take it by a given date, there may be a wait of several months before the test is given again. Other tests are continuous; in many jurisdictions clerical tests are scheduled daily. When a large number of candidates have successfully completed a test and the number of associated job vacancies is expected to be small, the testing program may be closed for an indefinite period. There would seem to be little need for continuing to accept new examinees when there are thousands of already qualified persons and only a few jobs likely to become vacant. The frequency with which tests are given will also depend upon available resources. Again, pigeonhole classifications lead to excessive numbers of tests and available staff may be unable to provide frequent tests within each job series. When this occurs, the number of "real" eligibles dwindles as the list of eligibles ages; many persons on the list find employment elsewhere. When a test for a job series is offered frequently, limits may be imposed upon candidates' retaking the test. A person who hopes to raise his score may have to wait six months or more to retake the examination.

Another timing factor is the waiting periods between different portions of a testing program. The hurdle approach, explained earlier, may require an applicant to wait several weeks between filing an application and receiving a score on experience and training, and more weeks will pass before the applicant takes a written examination. Several more weeks may pass before the examinee may take the oral examination. The hurdle approach, therefore, can discourage many persons by lengthening the time required to become eligible for a public job.

Objective tests are, of course, the easiest to score. Many jurisdictions use optical scanners that "read" the answer sheets, score them, and provide raw and final scores. Computer programs are available for pro-

---

[37] Norman Hill, "Cooperative Recruitment Selection: An Evaluation of Utah's IPA Employment Service Center," *Public Administration Review*, 36 (1976):203–204; and William M. Timmins, "Utah's IPA Center—Report on Cooperative Recruitment and Selection," *Public Personnel Management*, 4 (1975):156–159.

viding item analyses, which compare responses to one question with overall test performance. These analyses allow for identifying weak questions, namely those that overall high-scoring examinees get wrong and that low-scoring examinees get right. The federal Office of Personnel Management operates a centralized written-test scoring system in Macon, Georgia. Area offices mail batches of answer sheets to the Center. The operation, begun in 1976, can provide test results within a few days, a substantial improvement over the previous six- to eight-week lag.[38]

Scoring an unassembled examination is necessarily more time consuming and has far greater potential for unreliable results. A reliable test device is one that can be applied several different times to the same individual with the same results. Unassembled test scoring, that is, rating of training and experience, is done by people, not machines, and this increases the chances of differences in judgments on the part of scorers. The General Accounting Office conducted a study of this process by taking a sample of applicants who had been rated eligible and having them rerated by the original regional Civil Service Commission office and by another CSC office. The reratings averaged 3.5 points from the original ratings within the original office and 5.5 points in the alternative office. "Sixty-two of the 302 applications [21 percent] originally rated eligible were rerated with scores that deviated 10 or more points from original scores, *or were rerated ineligible* [italics added]."[39] The differences in points is critical, given that this could greatly increase or decrease one's chances for obtaining a federal position. Since that study, the Commission has endeavored to maintain greater consistency (reliability) in the rating process, but this is an inherently difficult task.

At the federal level, there are several examinations that use a deferred rating system. The Mid-Level Examination, covering GS-9 through GS-12 positions, is one of these. Applications for this unassembled examination are simply entered into a computer without any scores being given. When the Commission is notified by an agency that it wishes to fill a vacancy, a computer search is run on selected qualifications; in that way eligible candidates are identified.

For other tests, weights will have been determined on the various portions of an examination, and then a final score will be calculated. Portions of the test may be weighted so that, for instance, the oral portion counts 40 percent and experience and training count 60 percent. The weighted score is then converted to a final score; the conversion, as often

[38] Ramsay, "Toward a Modernized Federal Examining System," p. 19.

[39] *Improvements Needed in Examining and Selecting Applicants for Federal Employment* (Washington: General Accounting Office, 1974).

required by law, adjusts all grades to some set range, such as 60 to 100, with 70 being the minimal passing score.[40] Therefore, a rating of 100 does not mean that all questions were correctly answered.

One of the most controversial aspects of the public service examination process has been veterans preference.[41] In 1865 Congress passed legislation giving preference to disabled veterans over others in appointment to positions. Ohio was the first state to adopt comparable legislation (1875), and by 1913 there were fourteen states with veterans preference legislation.[42] Congress rewrote the legislation in 1919 for World War I veterans and in 1944 passed the Veterans Preference Act.

How veterans preference applies to examinations has varied over time. In the 1930s, the U.S. Civil Service Commission conducted separate examinations for disabled veterans; those who passed were automatically placed at the top of eligibility lists even though numerous nonveterans may have scored much higher. Today, at all levels of government, the typical procedure is to require veterans to take the same test as all others, and if a veteran passes an examination, five points are added to his score (or ten points in the case of a disabled veteran).[43] Contrary to recommendations made by President Carter, in 1978 Congress not only retained the point preference system but strengthened preference for disabled veterans. Those with a 30 percent or more disability may be hired noncompetitively, meaning that they need not compete with others through a competitive testing program. Should the agency choose to pass over a disabled veteran and select someone else, the agency must provide a written reason for this action to the Office of Personnel Management. Another important feature of veterans preference legislation is that it does not apply only to veterans. At the federal level, preference also is extended to widows of veterans, mothers of veterans who lost their lives, wives of disabled veterans, and mothers of unwed disabled veterans.[44]

Veterans preference is defended on several grounds. It is seen as rewarding individuals for their patriotism and/or their willingness to risk

---

[40] For calculating this conversion, see Wright, *Public Sector Employment Selection*, pp. 112–114.

[41] See William E. Mosher and J. Donald Kingsley, *Public Personnel Administration* (New York: Harper and Brothers, 1936), pp. 193–211; and Stewart S. Manela, "Veterans' Preference in Public Employment: The History, Constitutionality, and Effect on Federal Personnel Practices of Veterans' Preference Legislation," *George Washington Law Review*, 44 (1976):623–641.

[42] John F. Miller, "Veteran Preference in the Public Service," in Carl J. Friedrich, et al., *Problems of the American Public Service* (New York: McGraw-Hill, 1935), pp. 243–334.

[43] For point benefits available by state, see Saso and Tanis, *Selection and Certification of Eligibles*, p. 21.

[44] 5 U.S.C. § 2108.

their lives in combat. Another justification has been that it helps compensate for the years of low pay received in the armed forces. Still another argument is that it helps veterans readjust to civilian life. That argument, however, fails to provide any justification for life-long veterans preference. Not only does a veteran receive five or ten points for his first public job but also he has this advantage every time he applies.

On the negative side, veterans preference distorts examination scores so that the most qualified people do not necessarily receive the highest score. Of course this presupposes that tests are sufficiently discriminating so that a person with a score of 95.8 can be expected to perform at a superior level to one with a score of 90.8. Advocates of preference would counter by claiming that veterans, having experienced what they did, are more mature or have other highly positive personality characteristics that make them better qualified than nonveterans. Veterans preference also can be criticized for treating public jobs as a form of welfare assistance. Rather than doing this, would it be preferable to provide a lifetime financial benefit to veterans, assuming that some form of extra compensation was considered appropriate? Still another criticism has been that veterans preference tends to discriminate against females. In rejecting this argument courts have reasoned that veterans preference applies to both sexes even though males are the primary beneficiaries. This may dispose of the matter legally, but it does not alter the fact that veterans preference operates to the disadvantage of the majority of women.

Debating the pros and cons of veterans preference is interesting but probably nonproductive. Political realities are such that preference could not be easily taken from those who have it, and such preference is likely to be extended to any future veterans. One possible means of overturning veterans preference would be the courts, but they generally have been unwilling to rule in that direction. Some state legislatures have modified preference provisions.

SELECTION

Once examinations have been taken and scored, eligibility lists are established. Persons are ranked by score, and, as was noted earlier, a score of 70 is often the cutoff for passing. Large jurisdictions usually establish lists by region. A state may have ten regional eligibility lists for each job series; such lists are needed because many applicants are willing to work only in a particular area within the state. Eligibility lists are often longest for the regions of the state capital and major metropolitan centers, while eligibility lists for the same types of jobs may be short or even nonexistent for small town and rural regions.

Separate lists may be maintained for different types of applicants. A promotion list may be used for current employees, with these persons having preference over "outsiders" (see Chapter 7). Persons previously employed by the jurisdiction may be on a separate list and receive preference over other "outsiders." This preference is often provided to employees laid off or employees who were temporarily disabled. A third list would be for persons not previously or currently employed by the jurisdiction. Some jurisdictions have all applicants compete with each other and rank them on a single list.

Usually names remain on a list for one or two years, after which the individuals must be re-examined or at least must reaffirm their interest in the job series and grade covered by the list. The jurisdiction's personnel director or head of the civil service commission frequently has the authority to determine the length of time that the list will be maintained. If a list is maintained only for one year, then the jurisdiction must have an active testing program in order to establish a new list. The reason for the time limit on eligibility lists is that the employment status of eligibles changes over time. An individual scoring high on two or more civil service tests may have accepted employment through one testing program, while her name remains on other lists, even though she is no longer interested in the jobs covered by them.

The selection process is triggered by an agency request of the civil service commission for a list of eligible candidates to fill a job vacancy. Before an agency may request this list, approval often must be obtained from the central personnel department, the central budget office, or a department of administration. Complement control is used to limit the number of governmental employees. When a jurisdiction is facing severe financial constraints, a rule may be imposed, such as requiring that for every four vacancies that occur only two or three may be filled.

Once the commission receives the agency's request, a list of eligible names is prepared.[45] This is known as the certification process. Often the list will be supplied to the agency within a couple of weeks, and the time period can be shorter when the process is computerized. The amount of information supplied by the commission to the agency on each candidate may be minimal, such as only name, examination score, and a few other essential pieces of information, or it may be extensive.

The employing agency usually will receive a list with only a few names on it rather than a complete list of all eligibles. The most common practice is the "rule of three," which limits the agency to hiring from the

---

[45] The discussion of certification is based largely on Saso and Tanis, *Selection and Certification of Eligibles*, pp. 10–23.

top three names on the list. The rule of three was formally established at the federal level by the Veterans Preference Act of 1944. The justification for this limitation is that agencies should be constrained by choosing among the top candidates and not be allowed to pass over these persons for less qualified individuals. The rule is severely criticized, on the other hand, because it assumes a precision in the measurement process far beyond what is realistically possible.

Of course jurisdictions vary on this practice. Minnesota, for example, uses a rule of ten. At the other extreme are Chicago, Detroit, Minneapolis, San Francisco, and the State of New Jersey, which use the rule of one, giving agencies a take-it-or-leave-it choice. Some jurisdictions, rather than using the top three or so names, use the top three scores. This can produce an eligibility list having dozens of names on it, since several people may have the same score. Michigan uses a flexible certification rule based upon the reliability of each testing program. When two or more agencies draw from the same eligibility list, a jurisdiction using the rule of three may certify the first three names to one agency and the next three to the second agency. Individuals in the first group of three will not be certified to another agency until the first agency has completed its review of them. In other jurisdictions, the top three names on the list may be sent simultaneously to two or more agencies.

Not only does veterans preference assist veterans in the examination process, but it also is beneficial in the selection process. At the federal level, for most examinations, disabled veterans are placed at the top of the eligible list regardless of their earned ratings; other veterans are placed on the list ahead of nonveterans with the same score. An agency that passes over a veteran to hire a nonveteran on the certification list must supply to the OPM a written statement explaining why this was done.[46] This requirement obviously has the effect of forcing agencies to give veterans careful consideration. Pennsylvania has absolute preference. In that state, if the third-ranked person on a list of three certified eligibles is a veteran, only that person may be hired.

Once the certification list has been received, the agency will conduct its own investigation of the candidates and will arrange for job interviews. Candidates' former teachers, professors, and employers may be contacted by telephone or letter. Candidates usually will be expected to pay their own expenses in coming to the job interview.

The job interview can be compared with the oral examination but usually is far more intensive and extensive. Whereas the oral examination

---

[46] 5 U.S.C. § 3318. The same preference applies to mothers/wives of disabled or deceased veterans.

format requires a standard set of questions, there is no such requirement for the interview. The oral examination may seem a routine process for the examiners, but the agency is likely to take the interview process far more seriously, since the person who is hired may remain in the agency for several years. The candidates can anticipate being exposed to a variety of situations in a full day of interviewing, ranging from rigorous "grilling" sessions conducted by one or more agency staff members to casual luncheons. When the certification list is long, two rounds of interviewing may occur. The first, using relatively short interviews, screens out the majority of candidates, and the second round interviews more intensively the remaining candidates.[47]

Considerable tension exists between the employing agency and the civil service commission over the selection process. The commission is continually concerned with potential abuses of the merit principle. Many jurisdictions have long histories of patronage or political cronyism, which personnelists fear can easily be reasserted. Undoubtedly, many agency managers would like to hire their friends but not necessarily only because they are friends but because they are considered to be well qualified. Also, agency managers frequently lack confidence in the testing program; they are not convinced that the top three people on an eligibility list are indeed the three most qualified. Sometimes an individual has been specially recruited by an agency only to find that he or she is not "within reach" on the eligibility list.

Various tactics are used by agencies to circumvent the rule of three or whatever number. One right the agency has is to hire no one. If all three certified individuals are unacceptable, the agency can leave the position unfilled. If other agencies are drawing from the same eligibility list, the first agency can wait until the unacceptable candidates at the top of the list have found employment in one of the other agencies. Other eligibles on the list then become "reachable." This practice, however, has two disadvantages. In the first place, the agency's workload may be of such magnitude that it cannot function well without a full complement. Second, a risk is taken that the vacancy left unfilled will be "collapsed" by some central unit, thereby prohibiting filling the vacancy in the future.

Other tactics are less above board and are proscribed by law and/or administrative regulations. The agency can encourage the certified eligi-

---

[47] There is an art to being a good interviewer and a good interviewee. For helpful suggestions, see Richard A. Fear, *The Evaluation Interview*, 2d ed. (New York: McGraw-Hill, 1973) and Theodore Hariton, *Interview!: The Executive's Guide to Selecting the Right Personnel* (New York: Hastings House, 1970). See also Frank J. Landy, "The Validity of the Interview in Police Officer Selection," *Journal of Applied Psychology*, 61 (1976):193-198 and Deborah Ann Kent and Terry Eisenberg, "The Selection and Promotion of Police Officers: A Selected Review of Recent Literature," *Police Chief*, 39 (February, 1972):20-29.

bles to decline a job offer. This can be accomplished by explaining to them that the job requires working nights and weekends, that one's office will be in a room no larger than a closet, that there will be virtually no opportunity for promotions, and that the agency's director is nothing less than an evil demon. Once the three eligibles have declined, the agency may request a new list of eligibles.

Another tactic is to ask for a reclassification of a position. The job might be reclassified as a politically sensitive one, not subject to the civil service examination process. An alternative would be to request the creation of a *new* job classification, which by definition would not have a standing eligibility list. Still another approach would be to ask for a reclassification where it was known that the eligibility list for that class had expired. In that case, the agency would be free to hire anyone as a "provisional." Once the civil service commission established a testing program for that job series, the provisional would be required to take the test. The advantages are that the provisional would have a better chance of scoring high since he would have been working on the job for a period of time, and that typically the provisional is only required to pass the test—not score the highest—in order to retain the job.

When other tactics fail, there is at least one more. In a jurisdiction having a rule of one and where the top person is considered by the agency to be a dullard at best, the agency may decide to hire that person. Once he is on the job, the individual's life is made as unpleasant as possible in hope that he will resign. If a resignation is not forthcoming, the individual may be dismissed relatively easily during the probation period, the subject of the next chapter. Once resignation or dismissal has removed that person, the agency is free to ask for a new certified candidate.

SUMMARY

Recruitment is one of the weakest functions performed in personnel systems. Part of the problem stems from conflicting or at least divergent values over the purpose of recruiting. Is government to seek the best or be satisfied with those who are simply qualified? To what extent should there be a commitment for recruiting from a wide range of persons, including a mix of races, income groups, and the sexes? Whether people apply for public employment will be partially dependent upon government's image, and that has not always been the best. The techniques of recruitment include newspaper advertising, job and examination announcements sent by mail and posted in public places, general brochures and pamphlets, information centers, hot lines, personnel banks, and individual recruiting. While the techniques are varied, recruitment is rarely planned systematically.

Examination strategies are based on job analyses. A standard application form is used on which candidates list their relevant education and experience. When candidates do not come together to take an examination, it is called an unassembled one. Written reference checks are used, although they are often difficult to assess. Written tests include intelligence, aptitude, personality tests and tests specifically geared to the substance of jobs. Most paper-and-pencil tests are objective, but some jurisdictions use essay tests. Physical aptitude tests (such as agility) and achievement tests (such as typing) also are used. Oral examinations are important for testing applicants for professional and administrative positions. The hurdle approach may be used when a testing program involves two or more separate measures.

Especially because of concern over possible discrimination, testing the validity of tests has become important. Content validity involves designing a testing program that samples the main aspects or subject matter of jobs. Criterion-related validity relates test scores with job performance. Construct validity involves identifying the traits needed to perform a job (for example, a leadership trait) and designing a testing program that examines candidates for those traits. A construct validity strategy will include criterion validity and may include content validity.

Test administration is usually the exclusive responsibility of a civil service commission. Examinations may be given in one central location or at several in the case of states and hundreds in the federal government. A joint testing center for state and local governments can reduce much of the cost of a testing program. Machine scoring is used for objective tests. Evaluation of experience and training is subject to varied interpretation and threatens test reliability. Veterans preference provides five or ten additional points to veterans' test scores. The practice has been widely criticized but is not likely to be abandoned.

Selection begins with the establishment of eligibility lists and the request of an agency for certification of eligibles. The rule of three is frequently used to limit agencies in their choice of employees. The practice is intended to encourage hiring on the basis of merit but is often criticized by line agencies as being too restrictive. Veterans preference applies in the selection process as well as the examination process. Job interviews tend to be more extensive and intensive than oral examinations. Agencies seeking freedom to hire individuals who think they are superior candidates use various tactics to circumvent civil service procedures. These tactics include deliberate discouraging of certified candidates, position reclassification, and hiring and then firing unacceptable candidates.

Chapter 6

Probation and Performance Evaluation

Once a government position has been offered and accepted, testing continues. During the initial weeks, months, or years, the individual will have a probationary status in which skills are tested on the job. The examination process may have been faulty in general or may have been in error in qualifying any one individual. The person may be well qualified from the standpoint of substantive knowledge but he may not be qualified in being able to perform a given job on a daily basis. For example, severe personality problems may prevent a person from working effectively with peers. Probation allows the worker to be tested on the job, during which time the worker will have limited job security. How the worker handles the job will be recorded through the performance evaluation process. The assessment of worker performance will be used for determining whether that individual will continue to be employed, and periodic performance evaluations will continue throughout the career of each person working in the government.

This chapter is an extension of the preceding ones, which discussed the design and classification of positions, the establishment of pay plans, and the processes of recruiting, examination, and selection. Now that a person has a job, what happens next? The first section of the chapter considers the probationary period and the second discusses performance evaluation.

PROBATION

Once appointed, the government worker will routinely be placed on probation, which may last several weeks to several years, as in the case of a college faculty member. At the federal level, an individual in effect may have two probationary statuses. If appointed as a career-conditional employee, the person must serve three years before qualifying as a career employee. During the first of those three years, the person has an official probationary status. Other persons who are appointed as career employees, as distinguished from career-conditional, must serve a one-year probation.[1] At all levels of government, periodic performance evaluations are completed by the worker's supervisor during the probationary period; these evaluations are the subject of the next section. The vast majority of workers successfully complete probation, but some are dismissed as not being suitable.

The probation experience is not the same for everyone. Some people enter at middle or senior levels of responsibilities. Others enter at more junior levels and come directly from high school, a baccalaureate program, or a professional graduate education program, such as public or business administration. From the first day on the job, these persons may be expected to perform as all other workers. Some may be assigned to work with experienced personnel, who act as coaches. Depending upon the agency, a team approach may be utilized at all times so that no new employee is ever expected to operate independently. Regardless of whether the coach or team approach is used, some form of orientation will occur. In a large government department, the central staff may provide several hours or days of orientation for all new departmental employees. This type of orientation is used to explain rules, regulations, procedures, and the like as well as to provide some familiarity with the names and faces of key personnel within the department. Also the new employee's supervisor provides some type of orientation, explaining duties and operating procedures and often warning against certain practices. The orientation of the supervisor and central staff can be at variance, with central staff emphasizing some matters and the supervisor discounting their importance.

Other new employees will go through what can be called a pre-probationary status. Some persons enter government through internships, which last one to two years. The internship may involve rotation from one position to another, and, in the case of a state or federal agency, from one geographical location to another. The purpose of the internship is for both the agency and the interns to assess their capabilities and interests. An intern may find that certain types of work within the agency are more interesting than others, and the agency may find the intern excels more in some types of work than in others. Another advantage is that the interns gain familiarity with the scope of the agency's responsi-

---

[1] *Federal Personnel Manual*, Chapter 315.

bilities and with the individuals involved; that familiarity is expected to facilitate intra-agency communication and work flow. Not all internships, however, are this systematic. Some persons in internship positions are not rotated among positions, are not rotated among units within a department, and receive virtually no training on the job. Instead, these interns are expected to perform basically like all other workers, although typically they are compensated at a substantially lower rate.

An alternative to the internship is to place the new employees in an intensive training program. Here all new employees are brought together for an extended period rather than being integrated with other employees. For example, in basic training in the military recruits are trained together, and after training are dispersed to various units. City and state police academies perform a similar function.[2] Some federal agencies that use non-uniformed personnel have somewhat analogous intake training programs.

Successful completion of the extended training program or internship is required for continuing in government service but it may not be a guarantee of continuing employment. The person who fails in the police academy obviously will not be retained, but success in the academy may provide no security, since there may have been more academy graduates than were needed by the police department. Assuming a job is provided at the end of the training or internship program, the individual then assumes a probationary status. The police rookie is a probationary employee.

The influences placed upon a probationary worker can be understood by using socialization theory, which is concerned with how "an organizational member learns the required behavior and supportive attitudes necessary to participate as a member of an organization."[3] Four stages can be identified in the socialization process: anticipatory socialization, accommodation, role management, and outcomes.[4] Anticipatory socialization entails the expectations individuals gain prior to obtaining employment. A student of social work may anticipate being able to work closely with impoverished families to help them resolve their problems, but once on the job, the social worker may find that such accomplishments are difficult to achieve because of unwillingness on the

---

[2] See Richard N. Harris, *The Police Academy: An Insider's View* (New York: Wiley, 1973).

[3] John Van Maanen, "Police Socialization: A Longitudinal Examination of Job Attitudes in an Urban Police Department," *Administrative Science Quarterly,* 20 (1975):207.

[4] The discussion is organized around these four stages as suggested by Daniel C. Feldman, "A Contingency Theory of Socialization," *Administrative Science Quarterly,* 21 (1976):433–450.

part of the poor to accept counseling; the social worker also may feel unable to provide the necessary counseling because of a large caseload and perceived excessive red-tape requirements of the bureaucracy. One study of graduates from a master's program in industrial administration found that, prior to joining a firm, the graduates had strong positive attitudes, but, once on the job, attitudes fell sharply in a year and still more in the next couple of years. The likely explanation is that the students' expectations about the firms were unrealistically high.[5]

Expectancy theory deals with the relationships between what an individual expects and what occurs and how the differences between expectations and reality influence behavior (see Chapter 11). One prescription that emerges is that expectations should approximate reality in order to avoid disillusionment and undesired behavior. Sometimes supervisors "oversell" jobs to candidates in the job interview. One experiment conducted by a telephone company illustrates the problem of overselling. Persons offered positions as telephone operators were normally required to view a movie about working for the telephone company. The standard film stressed the advantages of working for the company, but an experimental film that was introduced highlighted disadvantages as well as advantages. When the groups who watched the different movies were compared, it was found that there was no difference in the rate of persons who accepted the job offers. A difference, however, did develop later. Persons who viewed the experimental film had more realistic job expectations and thought less of quitting than other workers.[6]

Socialization, then, involves what the new employee anticipates coupled with perceptions of what occurs on the job. Accommodation is the process of learning about the job, the organization, and the people in it. Role management refers to the process of adapting; different roles may be played by one individual both within the organization and at home. Outcomes include satisfaction or dissatisfaction with the job, job motivation or the lack of it, and work productivity or its absence.[7]

There is no extensive descriptive literature about what usually happens to probationers during the first weeks or months on the job. For example, not much is known about the typical way or ways supervisors handle new employees. Some supervisors may assume a parental role, while others act more as friends. Some supervisors may be harsh when a

---

[5] Victor H. Vroom and Edward L. Deci, "The Stability of Post-Decision Dissonance: A Follow-Up Study of the Job Attitudes of Business School Graduates," *Organizational Behavior and Human Performance*, 6 (1971):36–49.

[6] John P. Wanous, "Effects of a Realistic Job Preview on Job Acceptance, Job Attitudes, and Job Survival," *Journal of Applied Psychology*, 58 (1973):327–332.

[7] For a detailed explanation of these terms, see Feldman, "A Contingency Theory of Socialization."

probationer makes an error, while others may be either positive by sympathetically explaining the problem or indifferent because of being engrossed in other agency matters. An extremely busy bureau chief will have little time to patiently explain procedures and correct problems involving a low-level clerical worker. Another aspect about which little is known is the extent to which supervisors use the occasion of a new person being appointed as an opportunity to reassign responsibilities among subordinates.

The probationer's co-workers also play important roles, but again there is no extensive literature that describes those roles or the interplay between them and the probationer. Some employees may regard the probationer as a potential threat and as a result are aloof or even hostile. Others may act as a friend, a big brother or sister, or as a parent. The probationer is thrust into a situation that has been evolving over time, a situation with all the complexities and nuances of any social order. Determining the organization's "pecking order" often is an initial task for the probationer. The person hired as a first-level professional will attempt to assess the relative influence or power of other professionals and also clerical workers. For example, how important is gaining favor or at least avoiding conflict with the boss's secretary?

Integration of these supervisory and co-worker influences is complicated by other factors, such as the substance of the job itself, and one's personal life. The new job may be a demanding one, involving long hours, including some evenings and weekends; these demands may come as a major shock to the person recently graduated from high school or college. The demands of the job can disrupt one's family routines. Moreover, the new job may have involved moving to a new city, resulting in the probationer and her or his family having to make a wide range of adjustments.

Role conflict and ambiguity can be consequences of the process. In the case of role conflict, competing demands are made on the individual. One's family may expect special attention to getting settled, and one's supervisor may expect dedication to the new position. Conflicting role expectations can easily emerge between supervisor and peers, with the supervisor expecting dedication and peers expecting less commitment to the job. Role conflict also develops between what one thinks is appropriate behavior and what behavior the organization seems to reward. One's profession may prescribe one type of behavior, while the organization prescribes another type. A study of police academy graduates found they perceived ". . . 'working especially hard' was linked to few, if any, of the system rewards."[8] Persons least motivated after graduating from the

---

[8] Van Maanen, "Police Socialization," p. 215.

police academy tended to receive better evaluations from supervising officers.

Ambiguity refers to an absence of clearly stated expectations. The supervisor may have given little direction about what types of behavior are considered appropriate or the supervisor may be mercurial, seemingly expecting one type of behavior one moment and a different type later. Such ambiguous situations obviously complicate the problem of developing behavior patterns that will meet with approval.[9]

The result of this myriad of forces will be varying behavior patterns. Some workers will become conforming and timid and others will become rebellious.[10] One study of psychiatric aides in a state mental hospital found that nonauthoritarian, nonrestrictive, and benevolent aides had a substantially higher rate of resignations than persons with the opposite characteristics.[11] The findings suggest that the socialization process is selective in the types of persons it encourages to continue with the organization. Another study, one dealing with workers in an Appalachian antipoverty program, found that new workers with no previous bureaucratic experience were less likely to resign when supervisors were understanding; the new workers who did not quit felt free to talk to their supervisors about their personal problems as well as job-related problems.[12]

How these influences affect job performance is not obvious. The discussion of motivation in Chapters 11 and 12 indicates that there are many influences on behavior besides the experience during probation. It is safe, however, to assume that the probationary experience can have lasting effects upon an individual's performance. Work habits—good or bad—may be firmly established during probation. One study of managers found that persons who had strong demands made on them during probation later tended to be more productive and successful (as measured by job status and pay) than other persons.[13]

If completion of probation is unsuccessful, resignation or dismissal is the possible outcome. No testing system can be expected to be able to select uniformly successful employees. For that reason, managers need

[9] See Robert T. Keller, "Role Conflict and Ambiguity: Correlates with Job Satisfaction and Values," *Personnel Psychology*, 28 (1975):57–64.

[10] See Edgar H. Schein, "Organizational Socialization and the Profession of Management," *Industrial Management Review*, 9 (Winter, 1968):1–16.

[11] Bernard B. Berk and Victor Goertzel, "Selection Versus Role Occupancy as Determinants of Role Related Attitudes Among Psychiatric Aides," *Journal of Health and Social Behavior*, 16 (1975):183–191.

[12] Robert Denhardt, "Bureaucratic Socialization and Organizational Accommodation," *Administrative Science Quarterly*, 13 (1968):441–450.

[13] David E. Berlew and Douglas T. Hall, "The Socialization of Managers: Effects of Expectations on Performance," *Administrative Science Quarterly*, 11(1966):207–223.

flexibility in determining whether a probationary employee should continue. Procedural rights are substantially more limited for probationary employees than for permanent ones.[14] At the federal level, a probationary employee first must be notified in writing that he is being considered for removal. The employee has a right to provide a written reply, which must be considered by the agency, but there is no right to an oral presentation. The final step is the formal notice of removal, which must include the reasons for the action.[15]

Both lack of use of the dismissal procedure and its abuse are problems in government. Some supervisors may delay taking the appropriate steps to remove an employee until that person automatically gains permanent standing at the end of the probationary period. This can result in the agency having to cope with an incompetent employee for many years. The delay may be because of other pressing demands on the supervisor's time or because of a desire to avoid an unpleasant situation. Dismissing a worker not only will affect that person but also can lead to low morale among other workers. Abuses, on the other hand, occur in the dismissal of employees because of race, sex, handicaps, and other extraneous matters. A personality clash between the supervisor and probationer can result in dismissal, even though the probationer is highly qualified. As was noted in the preceding chapter, supervisors sometimes accept persons at the top of eligibility lists and then encourage those persons to resign by making their jobs as unpleasant as possible.

Frequently, probationers may be dismissed for only vague reasons, and the right to appeal through administrative and judicial channels is greatly restricted. At the federal level, a probationary employee may be removed when "work performance or conduct . . . fails to demonstrate his fitness or his qualifications for continued employment" or when removal would "promote the efficiency" of the agency.[16] For instance, a federal poultry inspector was removed for "foul and abusive language."[17] A clerk typist working for the Equal Employment Opportunity Commission who openly admitted his homosexuality and was publicly involved in organizing activities for homosexuals was dismissed for "immoral and notoriously disgraceful conduct."[18]

Probationers have limited—if any—rights to work at their assigned jobs and demonstrate their competencies. In a New York State case, a probationer unsuccessfully claimed that the employing agency had not

---

[14] The issue of adverse action against permanent or tenured employees is discussed in Chapter 8.

[15] 5 U.S.C. § 3321 and 5 C.F.R. § 315.804.

[16] 5 C.F.R. § 315.804, 731.201.

[17] *Jaeger v. Freeman*, 410 F. 2d 528 (1969).

[18] *Singer v. U.S. Civil Service Commission*, 530 F. 2d 247 (1976).

allowed him to show his capabilities as a motor vehicle operator, the job for which he was hired; he had been assigned to work on a grounds crew instead of driving a bus.[19] A worker for the Federal Aviation Administration complained that during probation he was assigned to rewrite the Federal Aviation Procurement Manual, a duty for which he was not adequately prepared. He cited the FAA's Employee Performance Improvement Handbook, which said that supervisors were responsible for employee development and complained that he had received no guidance or training for redrafting the procurement manual. When the case came to court, the court held the personnel development section of the handbook did not "prescribe an iron rule to be applied alike to probationary and tenure employees."[20]

Judicial review of probationary employee dismissals is greatly limited. As one court has stated the matter, "Dismissal from federal employment is largely a matter of executive agency discretion. Particularly is this true during the probationary period. The scope of judicial review is narrow."[21] The courts generally have not required that probationers be given an opportunity to appear at an administrative hearing to rebut charges brought against them. One protection afforded probationary as well as tenured employees is that they cannot be dismissed for exercising a constitutional right; the First Amendment right to free speech has been particularly important in this respect (see Chapter 8).

Dismissal of probationers because of discrimination or the exercise of civil rights is also prohibited and reviewable by courts. The discrimination issue is considered in detail in Chapter 9, but here two cases can illustrate the types of problems involved. In a New York State case, a woman was hired as a probationary teacher with the stipulation that she complete a master's degree within five years. During the probationary period, she requested and was granted a five-year maternity leave but was denied a five-year extension on the master's degree requirement. The teacher was unsuccessful in court in alleging sex discrimination.[22] In another case, a probationary research assistant in the Equal Educational Opportunities Program of the U.S. Department of Health, Education, and Welfare alleged she had been dismissed because of her civil rights activities, especially because of her involvement in the Congress of Racial Equality (CORE). Dismissal for that reason would have violated the

---

[19] *De Salvo* v. *Kolb*, 387 N.Y.S. 2d 934 (1976). The court did note that DeSalvo had been assigned to grounds work after having had two accidents.

[20] *Donovan* v. *United States*, 433 F. 2d 522 (1970).

[21] *Toohey* v. *Nitze*, 429 F. 2d 1332 (1970).

[22] *New York City Board of Education* v. *New York State Human Rights Appeal Board*, 387 N.Y.S. 2d 873 (1976).

Constitution, but the woman was unable to prove in court that this had been the reason.[23] That particular case also illustrates how lengthy appeal procedures can be; although the probationer was dismissed in 1966, a final decision from a U.S. district court was not made until 1977. During the intervening eleven years, the case bounced among HEW, the Civil Service Commission, and the courts.

PERFORMANCE EVALUATION

Employee performance evaluations, appraisals, or efficiency ratings serve several purposes.[24] The reason that the topic is covered in this chapter is that one of the primary uses of performance evaluation is to determine whether an employee should be retained beyond the probationary period; a survey in the mid-1960s found this to be the most common use of evaluations in state, city, and county governments.[25] At the federal level, however, this is a comparatively minor function of performance evaluation. The second most common use of performance evaluation is for promotion purposes; persons with weak performance evaluations probably will not be promoted. More generally, evaluations can be used to judge employee potentials not only in terms of higher level positions through promotion but also in the assignment of duties among employees.[26] Evaluations also have been used for determining which employees will be laid off because of reductions in force (RIFs). Performance evaluations were used for this purpose by the federal government following World War II when the size of the bureaucracy was reduced sharply, and evaluations still carry some weight in RIF decisions.[27]

One of the more controversial uses of performance evaluation is for compensation purposes. Proponents suggest that employees should be financially rewarded for high performance. This practice has been less

---

[23] *Holden v. Mathews*, 554 F. 2d 1190 (1977).

[24] John P. Campbell et al., *Managerial Behavior, Performance and Effectiveness* (New York: McGraw-Hill, 1970); L. L. Cummings and Donald P. Schwab, *Performance in Organizations: Determinants and Appraisal* (Glenview, Ill.: Scott, Foresman, 1973); Richard Williams, James Walker, and Cline Fletcher, "International Review of Staff Appraisal Practices: Current Trends and Issues," *Public Personnel Management*, 6 (1977):5–12.

[25] Felix M. Lopez, Jr., *Evaluating Employee Performance* (Chicago: Public Personnel Association, 1968), p. 297.

[26] Marion S. Kellogg, *What To Do About Performance Appraisal* (New York: American Management Association, 1965), pp. 136–180.

[27] Commission on Organization of the Executive Branch of the Government (First Hoover Commission), *Personnel Management* (Washington: Government Printing Office, 1949), p. 33.

common in government than in industry, where flexible pay policies allow awarding extra compensation for high performance, although collective bargaining agreements may restrict some of that flexibility.

There are proposals that would base salary increases exclusively on performance ratings. If evaluations were based upon a point system, with high performing employees receiving high points and low employees the converse, then it would be possible to award wage increases based upon the point distribution. The jurisdiction might determine an average salary increase of 5 percent and set individual increases according to the standard deviation of evaluation points.[28]

There are conflicting views in both the private and public sectors on whether performance evaluations should be used in setting pay. On the positive side is the argument that wage increases can be used as incentives for improved worker productivity; according to proponents, employees will accept systems that provide differing levels of pay according to differing levels of job performance among workers.[29] This assumption was the basis for pay reforms made by Congress in 1978. Pay is linked with performance appraisal for persons in the Senior Executive Service, and no later than October 1, 1981, a similar system is to be used for GS-13s, 14s, and 15s (see Chapter 7). On the negative side, appraisal systems often have been criticized as being invalid, that is, not accurately gauging worker performance; to base compensation on invalid measures would produce the inequities of either over- or under-compensation. A more appropriate approach, according to this line of argument, is to base compensation on job evaluation rather than worker evaluation; pay should be set according to the work required by a job and not how well a worker performs.[30] If the worker does not perform as well as expected, then either his performance should be brought up to standards or he should be removed from the job.

It has been suggested that the use of performance evaluation in pay, promotion, and dismissal/retention decisions furthers the merit principle. Objective measures of worker performance are used to make important personnel decisions, instead of having the decisions be based upon political allegiances and cronyism. Morale of workers is supposedly

---

[28] Aaron Liberman et al., "Personal Evaluation—A Proposal for Employment Standards," *Public Personnel Management*, 4 (1975):248–258 and Aaron Liberman et al., "The Employee Service Review: Worker Perceptions of the System," *Public Personnel Management*, 6 (1977):84–92.

[29] L. L. Cummings, "A Field Experimental Study of the Effects of Two Performance Appraisal Systems," *Personnel Psychology*, 26 (1973):489–502.

[30] First Hoover Commission, *Personnel Management*, p. 33, and Nathan B. Winstanley, "The Use of Performance Appraisal in Compensation Administration," *Conference Board Record*, 12 (March, 1975):43–47.

improved, since workers understand that their contributions to government will be recognized and suitably rewarded.[31]

Another purpose of performance evaluation is to provide a basis for employee development.[32] By requiring supervisors to periodically assess the strengths and weaknesses of each subordinate, performance evaluation systems can serve as the basis for devising a strategy for assisting each employee to improve. Today, most evaluation systems require the supervisor to meet with each employee to discuss the evaluation; in some cases, workers must sign the rating form as proof that they have seen the document, not as evidence that they necessarily concur with the rating. The supervisor-subordinate meeting can be the occasion for planning improvements and for discussing why deficiencies in performance exist. From this perspective the supervisor serves as a coach or counselor. The result of the meeting may be an agreement that duties should be reassigned among workers or that an employee should be sent to a special training program.[33] This approach is credited with furthering not only the individual's self-growth through increased motivation but also with facilitating "organizational self-renewal."[34]

The primary argument against the coaching method is that it is sharply at variance with the other purposes of performance evaluation. The other purposes involve negative as well as positive incentives. Poor performance, if linked with pay decisions, results in little or no compensation increases. Poor performance also results in the denial of promotions and can lead to dismissal, either during the probationary period or later. In other words, the supervisor is required to assume the role of judge. Critics of the coaching method claim that a supervisor cannot successfully perform the roles of both judge and counselor.

Some private corporations have attempted to use both the judging and counseling aspects of performance evaluation by having supervisors use separate interviews with employees for these different purposes. In one interview, performance is reviewed along with plans for improving performance, and the other interview relates performance with salary decisions. The two interviews can be separated by two or more weeks. The results of these experiments have been mixed. The two-interview approach may be able to divorce the different roles, but that may be doubtful given expectancy theory (see above). If the counseling interview

[31] Arthur W. Procter, *Principles of Public Personnel Administration* (New York: Appleton, 1921), pp. 162–164.

[32] Douglas McGregor, "An Uneasy Look at Performance Appraisal," *Harvard Business Review*, 35 (May–June, 1957):89–94.

[33] Michael Beer and Robert A. Rich, "Employee Growth Through Performance Management," *Harvard Business Review*, 54 (July–August, 1976):59–66.

[34] Lopez, *Evaluating Employee Performance*, p. 54.

occurs first, the employee will anticipate the outcome of the second session on pay. The same type of anticipation will occur if the order of the interviews is reversed.[35]

Whether counseling and/or judging substantially improve worker behavior and especially performance is not really known. The evaluation process can serve as a vehicle for informing the employee how well he or she is doing. That is particularly important for probationers, so that, in the event of dismissal, they will not be surprised. Explaining deficiencies to probationers can provide an atmosphere of fairness and openness. Complaints over dismissal can be avoided in that way; employees cannot complain that they were unaware their work was substandard.

Existing evidence, however, suggests that performance evaluation tends to be more of a negative than a positive influence on behavior. In meeting with an employee the supervisor is likely to focus upon deficiencies, the intent being to identify how improvements can be made, but these comments are often interpreted by the subordinate as harsh criticisms. Even extensive praise by the supervisor may be largely ignored by the subordinate, who says to himself, "Yes, you said I am a good worker but. . . ." The employee may complain that he received only a good rating when an excellent rating would have been more appropriate. In other words, performance ratings can produce negative attitudes that have negative influences on behavior.[36]

Given the different purposes of performance evaluation and, as will be seen, the difficulties in devising evaluation systems, it should be no surprise that performance evaluation or appraisal has had an uneven history. Performance evaluation in the federal government dates back to the 1840s, when Congress required service reports from each department, but the requirement was soon ignored more than it was heeded. In the early 1900s performance appraisal became popular at all levels of government and in private enterprise, but the systems that were introduced tended to be abandoned over time. One observer in the 1930s wrote this: "Regardless of the nature of the form and the character of the organization, there is remarkable agreement in experience with rating systems. Most of the efforts to measure efficiency . . . have been failures."[37] Yet efforts to

[35] Herbert H. Meyer, Emanuel Kay, and John R. P. French, Jr., "Split Roles in Performance Appraisal," *Harvard Business Review*, 43 (January–February, 1965):123–129 and Cummings, "A Field Experimental Study of the Effects of Two Performance Appraisal Systems."

[36] Arie Shirom, "On Some Correlates of Combat Performance," *Administrative Science Quarterly*, 21 (1976):419–432.

[37] George A. Graham, "Personnel Practices in Business and Governmental Organizations," in Carl J. Friedrich et al., *Problems of the American Public Service* (New York: McGraw-Hill, 1935), p. 397. See also William E. Mosher and J. Donald Kingsley, *Public Personnel Administration* (New York: Harper and Brothers, 1936), pp. 428–430.

evaluate employees persist and will continue. A recent survey of private corporations and state governments found that more than 90 percent of the companies surveyed had evaluation systems for professional, administrative, and technical workers, and 80 percent of the states had state-wide appraisal systems.[38] Each federal agency is required to have an evaluation system.[39]

Performance evaluation, like position classification and the establishment of a pay plan, is necessarily based upon a set of assumptions about the work involved in any job. Just as job analysis is essential to the classification of positions, job analysis is essential to performance evaluation. Without an understanding of the work involved in a position, one cannot assess how well an individual is performing in that job. Therefore, any performance evaluation system created independent of job analysis is likely to be inappropriate.[40]

Performance appraisal includes three types of data: objective, personnel, and judgmental.[41] Objective data refer to the work accomplished by an employee. These might be the number of letters typed by a secretary, the number of traffic citations issued by a police officer, or the number of students taught by a school teacher. Personnel data include information on tardiness, absenteeism, and commendations and disciplinary actions; these data usually are to be found in a worker's personnel file. While both the objective and personnel data are valuable in assessing a worker's performance, these data do not provide a complete perspective on the individual. For that reason, judgmental data also are used. Judgmental data are the assessments of a rater about how well a worker performs. Rating systems, then, are basic tools of performance appraisal.

Virtually all rating systems rely upon the use of a form that lists items to be rated by supervisors. In some instances, the supervisor conducting the rating is expected to check only those items on the form that are applicable to the ratee. One of the most popular rating systems of this type, used extensively in the 1920s, was the Probst Service Report.[42]

---

[38] William H. Holley and Hubert S. Feild, "Performance Appraisal and the Law," *Labor Law Journal*, 26 (1975):423–430, and Hubert S. Feild and William H. Holley, "Performance Appraisal—An Analysis of State-wide Practices," *Public Personnel Management*, 4 (1975):145–150.

[39] 5 U.S.C. § 4301. See Mary S. Schinagl, *History of Efficiency Ratings in the Federal Government* (New York: Bookman Associates, 1966).

[40] See W. W. Ronan, T. L. Talbert, and G. M. Mullet, "Prediction of Job Performance Dimensions: Police Officers," *Public Personnel Management*, 6 (1977):173–180.

[41] The typology is from Robert M. Guion, *Personnel Testing* (New York: McGraw-Hill, 1965). See Frank J. Landy and Don A. Trumbo, *Psychology of Work Behavior* (Homewood, Ill.: Dorsey, 1976), pp. 105–111.

[42] See Lopez, *Evaluating Employee Performance*, p. 202.

The Probst municipal rating form included such items as "lazy," "too old for the work," "usually pleasant and cheerful," and "drink is one of principal failings."[43] The rater simply went down the list of more than seventy items, checking those that applied. Other systems have allowed for positive, negative, and neutral ratings. For example, the federal government in the 1930s used a plus for a positive evaluation, minus for a negative one, and a check for average. The rater would use one of these in assessing such items as "acceptability of work, thoroughness" and "amount of work accomplished."[44] The federal Performance Rating Act of 1950 required using the categories of "outstanding, satisfactory, and unsatisfactory" as overall evaluations of each employee.

The checklist or the three gradations of plus, minus, and check have the advantage of simplicity, but a complaint with them has been that they do not allow for distinguishing the variations in employee performance. As a result, scales have long been used. Figure 6.1 provides five sample scales. The first scale, using letters, was once common but has been largely abandoned. The second scale provides only the key words of "high, medium, and low," with twenty gradations to select among. The third uses a point system ranging from 0 to 25.[45] The fourth provides worker descriptions, ranging from exceptional, superior, and above average down to unsatisfactory. The last scale uses a percentage distribution, with 40 percent in the middle and smaller percentages above and below.

Criticism of these types of scales is common. The letter grade system is regarded as being too simplistic. Both that scale and the high-medium-low scale provide the rater with little guidance on what is meant by each gradation. Also, the twenty gradations on the latter scale may be overly detailed; what is the difference between one and two notches above middle? The point system has the same weakness. Sometimes the point system is used in combination with the word descriptor scale; a superior rating might be equivalent to between 20 and 25 points. The descriptor and percentage scales, however, do not indicate the standards being applied. Is one "superior" in comparison with current employees, all employees known by the rater, or some ideal standard? Similarly, on the percentage scale, what is meant by the middle 40 percent? It would be possible that the middle 40 percent might be considered by the rater to be unsatisfactory as well as all other employees rated below the middle.

These scales raise an issue far more fundamental than whether letter grades, percentages, and the like should be used. The issue is what is being measured by the scale. There are at least three possible groups of

---

[43] Probst Service Report form as reproduced in Mosher and Kingsley, *Public Personnel Administration*, p. 438.

[44] Schinagl, *History of Efficiency Ratings in the Federal Government*, pp. 50–51.

[45] See Aaron Liberman et al., "Personal Evaluation," pp. 248–258.

Scale

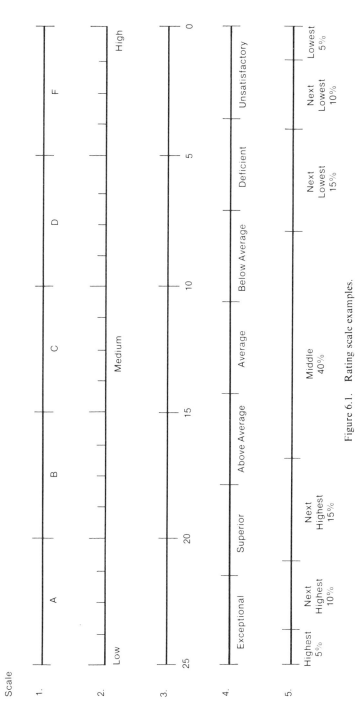

Figure 6.1. Rating scale examples.

147

items that can be rated. The first are traits, such as initiative, imagination, and loyalty (see Chapter 5). The second is behavior and/or performance. Behavior can be defined as the work being done and performance as the evaluation of the behavior.[46] The third is the result of the behavior or performance. To illustrate the differences among these three types, a worker might be highly motivated (trait), might work extra hours without compensation (behavior), and might rarely complete an assignment correctly or on time (result). Appraisal systems that rely on traits assume a linkage between the trait and the eventual result; an assumption may be made that loyalty to the organization will produce results. Trait ratings were once popular but now are considered a poor method of evaluating performance. The behavior/performance system assumes that a particular behavior will produce desired results. In some instances, the behavior is intrinsically desirable, for example, "always on the job when needed."

Most rating systems do not use the results orientation. Indeed, ratings by supervisors might be an inappropriate technique for gauging results. If one wanted to know whether an employee completed work on time, a records system would need to be maintained, and periodically a rating would be made of each individual's record. Such a system would work best for jobs in which employees worked independently of others and produced tangible items, perhaps in the case of a tool-and-die maker in industry. If the employee works with others, then the product made is a joint one and difficulties immediately arise over assessing the relative contributions of the workers. If an item was not produced on time, should the fault be assigned to worker A, B, or C? This type of problem is common in government. Moreover, it is easier to gauge performance when work is expected to yield tangible items, but government work typically involves providing a service rather than making tangible products. What, for example, would be the direct product of a day-shift prison guard as distinguished from other day-shift guards as well as evening and night guards?

The main thrust of performance evaluation has been in the area of attempting to describe what types of behavior are needed in each position, as distinguished from traits and performance results. The distinction between traits and behaviors, however, is not always obvious when applied to actual situations. The existing literature seems to be replete with internally conflicting examples of what should and should not be regarded as a trait. For instance, should "decisiveness," "cooperation,"

---

[46] John P. Campbell et al., "The Development and Evaluation of Behaviorally Based Rating Scales," *Journal of Applied Psychology*, 57 (1973):15. See also Cummings and Schwab, *Performance in Organizations: Determinants and Appraisal*.

and "adaptability" be considered traits or behaviors?[47] Is the behavior "handling stressful and emergency situations" little more than a more elaborate way of stating "adaptability," which can be considered a trait?[48] Indeed, a blending has resulted in which researchers have devised descriptions of behavior for traits such as initiative, attitude, and communication.[49]

Behaviorally anchored rating scales (BARS) provide work descriptions of behavior for various steps on a scale. The technique is related to the Probst rating system and the Thurstone psycholophysical test as adapted in the 1930s by Beyle and Kingsley. In more recent times Smith and Kendall have refined and popularized the approach as have Campbell, Dunnette, and others.[50]

A five-step process is used in developing BARS.[51] First, persons having experience with a given type of work are asked to describe real examples of effective and ineffective behavior; these are sometimes called critical incidents. In the second step, the researchers group the incidents under several headings, which will become the main dimensions of behavior around which scales will be devised. The third step is "retranslation," in which another group of experienced persons provide their judgments about whether the listed incidents are typical examples of positive and negative behavior. Agreement must be substantial for any item to be used; for instance, the researchers might require that at least 60 percent of the experts agree that the incident of "rarely argues with coworkers" is a measure of worker interpersonal behavior. The fourth step is to rank the incidents, often on a 7- or 9-point scale. This step is also done by a panel of experts, who need to agree on the point value in order for an item to be retained. If "rarely argues," for instance, is given a point rat-

---

[47] See Beer and Rich, "Employee Growth Through Performance Management," p. 63; Cheedle W. Millard, Fred Luthans, and Robert L. Otteman, "A New Breakthrough for Performance Appraisal," *Business Horizons*, 19 (August, 1976):66–73; and Hubert S. Feild and William H. Holley, "Traits in Performance Ratings—Their Importance in Public Employment," *Public Personnel Management*, 4 (1975):327–330.

[48] Walter C. Borman and Marvin D. Dunnette, "Behavior-Based Versus Trait-Oriented Performance Ratings: An Empirical Study," *Journal of Applied Psychology*, 60 (1975):561–565.

[49] Frank J. Landy et al., "Behaviorally Anchored Scales for Rating the Performance of Police Officers," *Journal of Applied Psychology*, 61 (1976):750–758.

[50] See Patricia C. Smith and L. M. Kendall, "Retranslation of Expectations: An Approach to the Construction of Unambiguous Anchors for Rating Scales," *Journal of Applied Psychology*, 47 (1963):149–155; John P. Campbell et al., *Managerial Behavior, Performance, and Effectiveness* (New York: McGraw-Hill, 1970); and Frank J. Landy and Robert M. Guion, "Development of Scales for the Measurement of Work Motivation," *Organizational Behavior and Human Performance*, 5 (1970):93–103.

[51] The discussion is based upon Donald P. Schwab and Herbert G. Heneman, III, "Behaviorally Anchored Rating Scales: A Review of the Literature," *Personnel Psychology*, 28 (1975):550–551.

ing of 2 by 30 percent of the experts and a rating of 6 by 40 percent, the item would be discarded. The last step is to select a subset of the tested incidents and develop the final instrument.

A behaviorally anchored rating scale for a supervisor of sales personnel is shown in Figure 6.2. The behaviors range from an example of the best behavior (item 9) to the worst (item 1). Item 5, reminding employees to wait on customers, presumably is a positive supervisory function, as are items 6, being courteous to employees, and 7, holding weekly staff training sessions and instructing staff about what is expected of them. If item 7 was chosen by a rater, there would be a presumption that items 5 and 6 also applied.

A potential weakness of BARS is that the scale may not be unidimensional, that is, two or more dimensions may be included on the same scale. Thoroughness and accuracy of work, for example, are not necessarily the same type of behavior. A clerical worker could be thorough in processing forms, i.e., ensuring that all blanks have been completed and that the correct number of copies of each form has been made, but the worker could be highly inaccurate in completing the forms. Another example would be a combined behavior of "planning and executing"; one could be an excellent planner and an unsatisfactory executor.[52] (Consider whether this type of problem exists in the BARS that is shown in Figure 6.2.)

Another set of problems with BARS involves the raters themselves. These problems are common to all rating systems and not just BARS. One such problem is rater leniency. Supervisors tend to be lenient in rating their subordinates, in part because of a willingness to give them the "benefit of the doubt," to encourage subordinates' efforts at self-improvement, and to avoid unpleasant situations. Since it is likely that a supervisor will be required to discuss the rating with each employee, he may not wish to have to explain or defend negative judgments. Another reason for leniency is that unsatisfactory performance ratings may reflect poorly on the supervisor himself. The frequent result is that few employees are ranked below the mid-range scale and most are rated high. The First Hoover Commission observed, "In two agencies examined, fewer than 3 in 1,000 employees were marked 'unsatisfactory' over a year."[53]

Some techniques have been instituted to make it impossible for managers to be excessively lenient. The percentage distribution technique allows the supervisor to place no more than a specified percentage of

---

[52] This "behavior" is from Borman and Dunnette, "Behavior-Based Versus Trait-Oriented Performance Ratings," p. 562.

[53] First Hoover Commission, *Personnel Management*, p. 32.

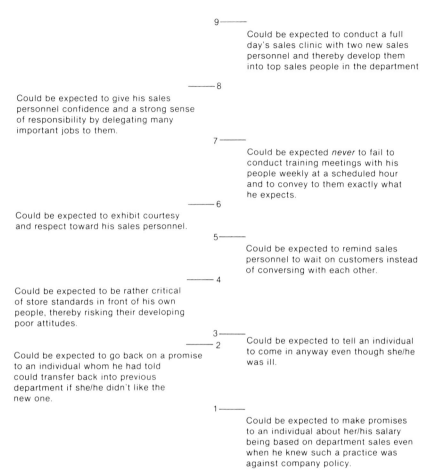

9 ———

    Could be expected to conduct a full day's sales clinic with two new sales personnel and thereby develop them into top sales people in the department

——— 8

Could be expected to give his sales personnel confidence and a strong sense of responsibility by delegating many important jobs to them.

7 ———

    Could be expected *never* to fail to conduct training meetings with his people weekly at a scheduled hour and to convey to them exactly what he expects.

——— 6

Could be expected to exhibit courtesy and respect toward his sales personnel.

5 ———

    Could be expected to remind sales personnel to wait on customers instead of conversing with each other.

——— 4

Could be expected to be rather critical of store standards in front of his own people, thereby risking their developing poor attitudes.

3 ———

——— 2

    Could be expected to tell an individual to come in anyway even though she/he was ill.

Could be expected to go back on a promise to an individual whom he had told could transfer back into previous department if she/he didn't like the new one.

1 ———

    Could be expected to make promises to an individual about her/his salary being based on department sales even when he knew such a practice was against company policy.

Figure 6.2.   Behaviorally anchored rating scale for supervisor of sales personnel. Source: John P. Campbell et al., "The Development and Evaluation of Behaviorally Based Rating Scales," *Journal of Applied Psychology*, 57 (1973):17. Copyright 1973 by the American Psychological Association. Reprinted by permission.

employees in a given category (see rating scale 5 in Figure 6.1). This forced distribution is relatively easy to administer when one overall rating is used for each employee but not when a dozen or more scales are used. Also, the percentage approach is arbitrary, assuming that it is possible to identify the top 5 percent of the workers and the like. The percentage approach is based upon the unwarranted assumption that workers are distributed according to the decreed distribution. It may be that the rating system allows for only 5 percent in the highest category, when in reality 10 percent of the workers are equally of the highest caliber.

An alternative is to use the person-to-person comparison method. The rater is expected to rank subordinates from highest to lowest. This can be done for the performance of employees considered as a whole or on the basis of traits or behaviors. For instance, employees might be ranked according to initiative and industriousness. A given worker might rank third on initiative but twentieth on industriousness. The ranking method has the disadvantage of being time consuming and arbitrary, especially in the mid-range. While it may be possible to identify one set of subordinates as being more cooperative than another set, the workers in the mid-range may seem equally cooperative, making it impossible to rank one higher than the others. Moreover, the rating is relative, not absolute. The very best worker might not be very good, or the worst one might be quite a good employee.

A related problem is what is commonly called the "halo effect." This refers to the tendency for employees to receive the same rating on all items being rated, such as an employee receiving all 7s on a 9-point scale for numerous different traits. Raters tend to have difficulty differentiating qualities in a worker. A supervisor who regards a worker as generally poor will give a negative rating on all items even though that worker may have significant strengths in some areas.

Other problems include what might be called the "human nature" of raters. Some raters have biases that result in discrimination against employees of a given sex, race, religion, or ethnicity.[54] Raters are likely to be affected by the recency of events.[55] If the day before a rating is made a worker makes a serious error on the job, the supervisor is likely to be harsh in making a rating. One study found that when a supervisor is particularly annoyed with the behavior of one subordinate, other subordinates are likely to receive higher ratings than would otherwise be the case.[56]

Still another problem is that rating systems may require judgments for which the supervisor has insufficient information. If may be that a rater is asked to assess the extent to which a subordinate consults peers in dealing with problems when the rater has not observed the ratee sufficiently to make any judgment. The rater may simply not complete this portion of the rating sheet, or, in some instances, rating forms provide a

[54] William J. Bigoness, "Effect of Applicant's Sex, Race, and Performance on Employers' Performance Ratings: Some Additional Findings," *Journal of Applied Psychology*, 61 (1976):80–84.

[55] Lopez, *Evaluating Employee Performance*, pp. 167–168.

[56] Ronald J. Grey and David Kipnis, "Untangling the Performance Appraisal Dilemma: The Influence of Perceived Organizational Context on Evaluative Processes," *Journal of Applied Psychology*, 61 (1976):329–335.

space to indicate "not observed." Serious errors can result if the rater decides to make a determination without having much information.[57]

One general prescription for problems associated with raters is that raters need to be trained in the rating process. Some advocate not merely rater training but also rater involvement in the development of the rating system itself.[58] One study found that a mere five-minute briefing of raters on the halo effect substantially reduced halo results. However, the study also found that when raters consciously attempted to avoid the halo effect, they tended to rate factors differently, so that there was less agreement or consistency among raters.[59] Another study concluded that extensive training involving videotapes and workshop critiques tended to reduce halo and leniency, but general group discussions with the raters did not achieve the same results.[60]

Training of raters should not be regarded as a panacea. Some raters, no matter how extensive their training is, may have difficulty in "social differentiation," which can be considered the opposite of the halo orientation. Even when a rater is shown that he tends to rate a person consistently on one scale after the other, the rater may be unable to compensate for that tendency. Should the rater consciously block his halo tendency, he can become arbitrary, making ratings dispersed simply for the sake of dispersion.[61]

Besides these problems involving raters, there are several other more general problems associated with performance evaluation. One problem

----

[57] One example is asking a school principal to determine whether a teacher "clearly stated the objectives of the course" to a class. Unless the principal attended the class, there would be no way of judging the matter. See William D. Wolansky, "A Multiple Approach to Faculty Evaluation," *Education*, 97 (1976):81–96.

[58] The standard interpretation is that raters are more likely to accept a system that they helped to develop. For a contrasting view, see Gary B. Brumback, *Personnel Administration and Public Personnel Review*, 1 (November–December, 1972):28–30.

[59] Walter C. Borman, "Effects of Instructions to Avoid Halo Error on Reliability and Validity of Performance Evaluation Ratings," *Journal of Applied Psychology*, 60 (1975):556–560, and Walter C. Borman, "Consistency of Rating Accuracy and Rating Errors in the Judgment of Human Performance," *Organizational Behavior and Human Performance*, 20 (1977):238–252. See also Wayne F. Cascio and Enzo R. Valenzi, "Behaviorally Anchored Rating Scales: Effects of Education and Job Experience of Raters and Ratees," *Journal of Applied Psychology*, 62 (1977):278–282, and Barry A. Friedman and Edwin T. Cornelius III, "Effect of Rater Participation in Scale Construction on the Psychometric Characteristics of Two Rating Scale Formats," *Journal of Applied Psychology*, 61 (1976):210–216.

[60] Gary P. Latham, Kenneth N. Wexley, and Elliott D. Pursell, "Training Managers to Minimize Rating Errors in the Observation of Behavior," *Journal of Applied Psychology*, 60 (1975):550–555.

[61] Abraham Pizam, "Social Differentiation—A New Psychological Barrier to Performance Appraisal," *Public Personnel Management*, 4 (1975):244–247.

involves the number of traits or behaviors to be assessed for each employee. For example, the rating form used by the Internal Revenue Service has had only nine traits for nonsupervisory personnel, while the Agriculture Stabilization and Conservation Service has used fifteen.[62] Some rating systems use a combination of rating scales and narrative comments. Not only does the rater check the appropriate location on each of a dozen or more scales, but also he provides short sentences or phrases describing the employees assets and weaknesses. Obviously, the longer the rating form, the more time will be required to complete it and the more likely will raters complain of needless paperwork.

Another issue involves whether persons other than the supervisor should be part of the rating process. Ratings by peers may be useful in providing a different perspective or second opinion.[63] Self-rating may be another method, encouraging workers to think more carefully about the different aspects of their activities on the job.[64] One of the most sensitive suggestions is the use of subordinates and clients to rate superiors. Here, intimidation is possible. Welfare clients may fear reprisals if it became known that they gave low ratings to their social workers, as would social workers fear reprisals for giving low ratings to their bosses. Nevertheless, subordinate and client ratings are sometimes used. A prominent example has been the use of faculty evaluations by students as one source of input in tenure and promotion decisions.[65]

Standardization versus decentralization is another issue. Some jurisdictions use a standard rating system for all employees throughout the government, while others allow agencies to develop their own rating

---

[62] Charles W. Langdom, "Evaluating Performance of Federal Employees," *Marquette Business Review*, 15 (1971):207.

[63] Jack R. Crisler and Oscar R. Barney, Jr., "A Comparison of Rehabilitation Counselor Effectiveness to Caseload Production—Supervisory and Peer Evaluations," *Journal of Applied Rehabilitation Counseling*, 7 (1976):114–118; R. G. Downey, F. F. Medland, and L. G. Gates, "Evaluation of a Peer Rating System for Predicting Subsequent Promotion of Senior Military Officers," *Journal of Applied Psychology*, 61 (1976): 206–209; and Craig E. Schneir, "Multiple Rater Groups and Performance Appraisal," *Public Personnel Management*, 6 (1977):13–20.

[64] Lloyd S. Baird, "Self and Superior Ratings of Performance: As Related to Self-Esteem and Satisfaction with Supervision," *Academy of Management Journal*, 20 (1977): 291–300; *Federal Employee Performance Rating Systems Need Fundamental Changes* (Washington: General Accounting Office, 1978); Robert E. Lefton et al., *Effective Motivation through Performance Appraisal* (New York: Wiley, 1977); Robert G. Pajer, "A Systems Approach to Results Oriented Performance Evaluation," *Personnel Administration and Public Personnel Review*, 1 (November–December, 1972):42–47; and Robert L. Taylor and Robert A. Zawacki, "Collaborative Goal Setting in Performance Appraisal: A Field Experiment," *Public Personnel Management*, 7 (1978):162–170.

[65] See also Martin M. Greller, "Subordinate Participation and Reactions to the Appraisal Interview," *Journal of Applied Psychology*, 60 (1975):544–549; and John Loveland and Arthur Whately, "Improving Public Administration School Effectiveness Through Upward Performance Evaluation," *Public Administration Review*, 37 (1977):77–80.

systems. As was noted above, federal law has required a rating about whether an employee was outstanding, satisfactory, or unsatisfactory but beyond that the agency could develop an elaborate rating system to meet its own needs.[66] The Civil Service Reform Act of 1978 eliminated the three standard categories and required each agency to develop its own appraisal system, with employees participating in setting performance standards. The law does specify general categories of overall ratings for the Senior Executive Service (see Chapter 7). State governments vary greatly, with some using a standard system for some jobs across departmental lines and others not.[67] It is probably inappropriate to expect that one standard evaluation system can be used for all positions in any large bureaucracy. The variety of jobs involved would seem to require tailoring the evaluation process.[68]

Whether there should be an overall rating for each employee and how that rating is to be derived constitute another issue. The argument for a single rating is that it condenses the evaluation into easily understandable terms—employee A is "satisfactory" and employee B is "outstanding." The argument against this is that human behavior is too complex to simplify into a single overall rating. Indeed, double talk may be the result, as in this example from the U.S. Navy: "The existence of a satisfactory performance rating will not in itself be considered to be evidence of an acceptable level of competence since an employee's performance may be satisfactory in a marginal way but not of a nature to warrant an increase of pay."[69] In other words, satisfactory performance may not be satisfactory for pay increase purposes.

As an alternative to the supervisor's providing a summary rating, a composite rating may be calculated by averaging the scores on the various scales of the rating sheet. It also is possible to assign weights to scales, so that, for example, behavior associated with knowledge about the nature of one's job might have greater weight than punctuality. In the early 1920s, New York City not only weighted factors but allowed raters to determine the weights within specified limits.[70] The greatest potential flaw of either an averaged or weighted total rating is that misjudgments may have been made in devising the system. Perhaps only 14 behaviors

---

[66] Guide for Improving Performance Evaluation (1977) in *Federal Personnel Manual*, Chapter 430, Appendix A. See also Priscilla Levinson and Mary Sugar, "Performance Evaluation and Rating," *Civil Service Journal*, 18 (July/September, 1977):28–31.

[67] See Feild and Holley, "Performance Appraisal—An Analysis of State-Wide Practices," pp. 145–150.

[68] See William J. Kearney, "The Value of Behaviorally Based Performance Appraisals," *Business Horizons*, 19 (June, 1976):75–83.

[69] U.S. Navy as quoted in Langdon, "Evaluating Performance of Federal Employees," p. 206.

[70] Procter, *Principles of Public Personnel Administration*, pp. 165–166.

of the 16 on a given rating sheet were "really" important or perhaps one of the most important behaviors was excluded from the sheet.

Given the potential for faulty overall ratings, they should be used with great caution if at all. One should not assume an employee with an average rating of 7.62 is superior to one with 7.48, or, for that matter, to one with a 6.0 average. Mosher and Kingsley, writing in the 1930s, said that the use of percentages, letter grades, and the like had been "thoroughly discredited," but, while that observation may have been correct, the practice continues.[71] One of the primary reasons is that often personnel decisions are binary—yes or no. There is a temptation to use overall ratings when critical personnel decisions, such as dismissals, promotions, and lay offs, are being made.

A final problem is evaluating the performance of managers and executives. These persons are more likely to make a lasting impact upon an organization than any one road-crew worker or clerical secretary, and, therefore, the need for performance evaluation can be assumed to be greater for managers than for other workers. Measuring the results of evaluations of managers is complicated, in that the direction and supervision they provide influence the work performed throughout the organization; the results of managerial work are the total outcomes of the organization. Given the difficulty in assessing the linkage between what a given manager does and the organization's productivity, most evaluation systems avoid a results-oriented rating system and concentrate upon traits and/or behaviors. Many jurisdictions may use the same types of scales for managers as subordinates but then provide additional scales pertaining to the managerial functions of supervising, budgeting, planning, and the like.[72]

The problem of management evaluation is most acute at the highest levels of administration, as in the case of city managers. These managers, serving at the pleasure of their respective city councils, are responsible for all government operations. Although the council is officially empowered to set policy, the city manager is frequently expected to recommend policy changes and is required to execute policies. Since the 1950s there has been increasing interest in council evaluations of their managers. Councils have expressed concern that they should not simply operate on faith that their managers are performing well. Managers, while feeling somewhat threatened by the prospect of undergoing evaluation by council, have indicated that periodic evaluations can further council-manager communications, can downplay the pressure on a

---

[71] Mosher and Kingsley, *Public Personnel Administration*, pp. 431–432.

[72] See Frederic R. Wickert and Dalton E. McFarland, eds., *Measuring Executive Effectiveness* (New York: Appleton-Century-Crofts, 1967).

manager to keep council members "happy" no matter what, and can minimize council-manager confrontations that directly or indirectly suggest the manager should be dismissed. However, devising appropriate criteria for gauging manager effectiveness remains a problem, and currently there are no such criteria that have gained wide acceptance.[73]

SUMMARY

Upon appointment to a government position, a new employee is placed in probationary status. Some persons, such as interns and police academy cadets, must first successfully complete a pre-probationary period. Probation can be viewed as the final step in a testing program in which workers are tested on the job. During the probationary period, which may extend from a few weeks to several years, the probationer is socialized into the organization. Expectations acquired prior to entering government can greatly influence whether the new worker successfully completes probation; unrealistic expectations can result in disillusionment. Role conflict and ambiguity can thwart successful socialization. In the event that a supervisor is not satisfied with the performance of a probationer, that worker can be dismissed with relative ease. Although an official reason or reasons for dismissal must be given, these are often vague, and the probationer has limited rights to administrative and judicial appeal. Violation of Constitutional rights and dismissals based upon discrimination are the primary areas for judicial review.

Performance evaluation is used not only in determining whether an employee successfully completes probation but also for other purposes throughout one's career. Evaluations are used for judging the potential of workers, making RIF decisions, deciding who should be promoted, and, to a limited extent, for determining pay increases. Another purpose, somewhat in conflict with the others, is the furthering of worker effectiveness through coaching or counseling. Today, most evaluation systems use scaling techniques that focus on traits and/or behaviors. Trait ratings, although popular, are not highly regarded by experts in performance appraisal. Behaviorally anchored rating scales (BARS) attempt to specify behaviors in order to provide clear standards for raters. Despite the extensive research that has been devoted to BARS, technical problems remain. More general problems, such as rater leniency and the halo effect, apply to all rating methods. Rater training may assist in minimizing some of these problems. Other questions involve the number of

---

[73] Christine Schwarz, "Council Evaluation: State of the Art," *Public Management*, 58 (May, 1976):2–7; see the rest of this issue for related articles. See also Lopez, *Evaluating Employee Performance*, pp. 261–283, and John P. Campbell et al., *Managerial Behavior, Performance, and Effectiveness* (New York: McGraw-Hill, 1970).

traits/behaviors to be rated, the use of peers and subordinates in the rating process, standardization versus decentralization of evaluation systems across departmental lines, the use of summary or overall ratings, and the difficulty of evaluating top-level managers. Although performance evaluation has had an uneven history and problems with its use abound, the evaluation of worker performance can be expected to continue.

Chapter 7

Careers and Career Development

Continuity in an organization is provided by members remaining with it over time. The problems that can result when such continuity is eliminated have been demonstrated in nations that underwent revolutions or abruptly shifted from colonial to independent status. Career public servants can maintain stability of services during political turmoil, as was the case in France following World War II. Careerists are essential in maintaining continuity from one political administration to another.

The subject of careers extends the time-frame involving the relationship between government and its workers. The preceding chapters considered matters such as how to attract people into government service and how to evaluate their performance, particularly during probation. The first section of this chapter focuses upon the concept of a career and career patterns in general, and the second concentrates on executive careers. The third section considers the role of education and training in career development.

CAREERS IN GOVERNMENT

Webster's Third New International Dictionary defines "career" as "a field for or pursuit of consecutive progressive achievement." Often implicit in the use of the term is an assumption of upward mobility in an organization, usually through a series of promotions. A common bias is that a career or at least a successful one involves advancement in job responsibilities. A related bias is that careers are for persons holding positions in the upper strata of an organization. Executives and professionals are said to have careers, whereas laborers have only jobs. Advancement, however, need not only be achieved by promotion. Advancement or growth can be accomplished in the same position held for many years and also in different jobs that have the same organizational rank or status. Moreover, careers are not only for executives, although this discussion emphasizes some of the special problems associated with executive career development.

Since government's first priority must be to meet societal needs through the efficient and effective delivery of services, the careers of workers must be less than first priority. The argument can be made that government needs careerists only at middle and higher levels in the bureaucracy or that only a small cadre of careerists located at all levels is essential. As in industry, many government jobs involve routine work where large numbers of career personnel are unnecessary. For these types of positions, high turnover rates may not be particularly troublesome, although daily shifts in personnel obviously would hamper efficient operations.

Governments generally take a middle ground between indifference and complete commitment to employee career development. If for no other reason, commitment to fostering career development is justified as humane; employees should be treated as individuals who need to develop their potential. However, governments usually are not involved in extensive career planning and development for each worker. While both formal and informal career counseling does occur, the responsibility for career planning rests largely with individual workers. Materials are provided to workers on how to plan careers, including advice on how to qualify for government training and how to apply for promotions.[1]

Managing one's own career involves difficult choices that must be made without complete information. In starting one's career, a person may have applied for positions with several different governments. Should the first job offer be accepted while other job applications are pending? If a person's career objective is to become a city manager, should one accept a position as an analyst in a city housing department or wait until an assistant manager position is offered by a city? Whatever the choice, the first job after completing one's education will influence future job opportunities. Experience in a city housing department will

[1] See *Career Planning Handbook* (Washington: Civil Service Commission, 1971) and Betsy McG. Cooley, *Career Counseling for Women in the Federal Government* (Washington: Government Printing Office, 1976). See also Verne Walter, "Self-Motivated Personal Career Planning: A Breakthrough in Human Resource Management," *Personnel Journal*, 55(1976):112–115+ and 162–167+.

tend to qualify the person for higher-level housing positions. If the first job is with a state, opportunities with that state usually will be greater than opportunities with other governments, because the worker will have more information about job openings and application procedures for his own jurisdiction.

Subsequent job decisions present similar problems of uncertainty. If a person is already an assistant city manager, should one accept an offer for assistant manager in a larger city, a job that involves greater responsibilities and pay, or should one pursue only city manager positions? Also, accepting a new position at higher pay can reduce real income, considering moving expenses and cost-of-living variations among cities, so that some advancement opportunities may not be particularly attractive.[2]

Procedures for promotion vary greatly among and within jurisdictions. Some state and local governments fill all positions through a standard examination process; persons already in government take the same examination as those not employed by the government. Other governments, including the federal government, give preference to promoting current employees. At the federal level, agencies develop their own promotion programs in conformance with policies established by the Office of Personnel Management. Some promotions are made on a "career" basis, by which people are promoted without competing with others; this is the case with foresters, Internal Revenue agents, and air traffic controllers. In other instances, depending upon the agency and the type of job involved, an examination may be given. Filling a vacancy begins with an announcement of the vacancy being made available to agency employees. They can apply for the position and submit information to update their personnel files concerning their qualifications. A panel, including a representative of the agency's personnel office, often is responsible for reviewing candidates' credentials, such as education, experience, and performance evaluations. The panel provides a ranked list of candidates to the person responsible for filling the position. Job interviews follow, and a person is subsequently selected.[3] Many variations on this procedure are possible. Sometimes vacancies are not posted, but all eligible employees are given consideration. Selection lists often are not ranked. Depending upon the jurisdiction, veterans preference may or may not be given in promotion actions.

---

[2] Barry B. Anderson, "Is a Grade Worth a Move?," *GAO Review*, 12 (Spring, 1977):65–71.

[3] See *Estes* v. *Spence*, 338 F. Supp. 319 (1972), as an example of this process, the ways in which violations of the process can occur, and the reluctance of courts to overturn agency promotion decisions.

When an appropriate person within an agency is not identified to fill a vacancy, the next step may be to open the position to persons in other agencies and then later to persons outside the government. The U.S. Office of Personnel Management operates the Federal Automated Career System (FACS), which until 1977–78 covered fields such as general administration, personnel, finance, and engineering at the GS-13 and 14 levels. This computerized skills inventory can be searched to identify possible job candidates from other federal agencies. The inventory has not been used extensively and has been cut back to cover mainly personnel occupations.

Given the uncertainties involved in job opportunities, most careers probably are not carefully planned. Instead, careers tend to evolve as employees are exposed to different types of work. Many government careerists did not initially plan to make government their career. A survey of federal GS-15 through GS-18 executives found that at the time these people entered the federal government more than a third either had no definite plans about a federal career or expected to stay for only a short period.[4] Another survey of federal employees, including federal executives, found the following to be the most common reasons why employees considered leaving the federal service: potential financial rewards outside of government, self-advancement and progress, and relations with supervisors.[5]

There are at least six different types of job mobility: intra-agency, interagency, interorganizational, geographic, occupational, and social-class mobility.[6] Intra-agency mobility, as its name suggests, involves movement from one job to another within an agency. The movement can be vertical, both up or down, and lateral, involving moving from one job to another having the same organizational status. Military personnel are one of the most intra-agency mobile types of government employees.[7] Interagency mobility refers to movement from one agency or department to another within the same government. A survey of state executives in the 1960s and a follow-up study in the 1970s found that approximately 40

[4] U.S. Civil Service Commission, "Characteristics of the Federal Executive," *Public Administration Review*, 30 (1970):176.

[5] Franklin P. Kilpatrick, Milton C. Cummings, Jr., and M. Kent Jennings, *The Image of the Federal Service* (Washington: Brookings Institution, 1964), p. 199. For a discussion of why executives leave government, see Thomas G. Cody, "Use Experience: Trying to Do the Job," *Government Executive*, 9 (May, 1977):26–35.

[6] For a general discussion of the types of mobility, see Paul P. Van Riper, "Basic Factors and Issues," *Public Administration Review*, 27 (1967):359–372. See also Marshall E. Dimock, "Mobility of Employment in the Public Service," *Public Administration Review*, 27 (1967):162–166 and Eugene B. McGregor, Jr., "Politics and the Career Mobility of Bureaucrats," *American Political Science Review*, 68 (1974):18–26.

[7] William F. Glueck, "Executive Mobility in Public Service and Business," *Public Personnel Review*, 31 (1970):95–101.

percent had served in two or more state agencies.[8] Similar interagency movement has been found among federal and municipal executives.[9]

Promotion opportunities within one's occupational field, whether within an agency or between agencies in a government, are limited by the number of available positions. Governments sometimes emphasize promotion opportunites for their workers when in fact there is little "room at the top."[10] The U.S. Civil Service Commission estimated in 1973 that for every 15 positions at the GS-15 level in the legal field, there was only one position in the supergrades, and the ratio was approximately 170 to one in the engineering field.[11]

The third type of mobility, interorganizational, includes movements between governments and between government and private corporations. Intergovernmental job changes can be at the same level, such as interlocal, and between levels, as in the case of state-local mobility. Some occupations may require intergovernmental mobility. City managers seeking positions of greater responsibility are forced to change employers, typically moving to larger cities. A recent survey of city managers found that a third had worked for two or three cities.[12] A study of state executives found that less than 15 percent had worked for other states, 10 percent had worked for the federal government, and about 5 percent or less had worked for a local government.[13] A survey of federal executives conducted in the 1960s found that nearly 90 percent had

---

[8] Deil S. Wright and Richard L. McAnaw, "American State Executives: Their Backgrounds and Careers," *State Government*, 38 (1965):152, and unpublished data from Deil S. Wright, American State Administrators Project, Institute for Research in Social Science, The University of North Carolina, 1975.

[9] W. Lloyd Warner et al., *The American Federal Executive* (New Haven, Conn.: Yale University Press, 1963), pp. 169–170 and Civil Service Commission, "Characteristics of the Federal Executive," p. 178. See Peter Allan, "Career Patterns of Top Executives in New York City Government," *Public Personnel Review*, 33 (1972):114–117.

[10] Elmer Staats, "Career Planning and Development: Which Way is Up?" *Public Administration Review*, 37 (1977):73–74.

[11] Civil Service Commission, *Executive Manpower in the Federal Services*, (Washington: Government Printing Office, 1973), p. 20.

[12] Laurie S. Frankel and Carol A. Pigeon, "Municipal Managers and Chief Administrative Officers: A Statistical Profile," *Urban Data Service Report*, 7 (February, 1975): 1–17. An earlier study indicated about 20 percent of municipal executives had moved from one city to another: Municipal Manpower Commission, *Governmental Manpower for Tomorrow's Cities* (New York: McGraw-Hill, 1962), p. 150. See also Timothy A. Almy, "Local-Cosmopolitanism and U.S. City Managers," *Urban Affairs Quarterly*, 10 (1975): 243–272 and Gene A. DeMarie, "Manager Mobility: What the ICMA Newsletter Can Tell You," *Public Management*, 59 (October, 1977):8–11.

[13] These percentages should not be added together, since a given executive may have worked for both another state and the federal government and would be included in each of the respective percentages. Data from Deil S. Wright, American State Administrators Project. See Deil S. Wright, Mary Wagner, and Richard McAnaw, "State Administrators" Their Changing Characteristics," *State Government*, 50 (1977):152–159.

worked continuously for the federal government, but more recent information indicates that 64 percent of the GS-15s and higher had at one time been employed in the private sector.[14]

Mobility between the public and private sectors often is associated with corporate interests in obtaining government contracts. Private firms hire government workers in order to enhance their pool of personnel qualifications, and undoubtedly there is an underlying assumption that former government employees will be able to "deliver" government contracts. The opposite flow also occurs, in which people move from industry to government.[15]

Interorganizational and interagency mobility have been the center of continuous controversy. Some personnel systems are structured to discourage or even prohibit these forms of mobility, requiring that a person enter at a low-level position to be eligible for higher positions. These restrictions are said to encourage career development and to guarantee that supervisors and managers are fully aware of operations at lower echelons. New York City in the 1920s basically prohibited both interagency and interorganizational mobility. A supporter of the system wrote, "Some of the most highly compensated men and women in this part of the service entered originally as office boys or typewriting copyists."[16]

The federal government makes both career and noncareer appointments, particularly at the top levels. The term "career" in this context refers to the method of appointment, not to length of government service. Noncareer appointments are often but not always "political" appointments. By their nature, they frequently are filled from outside the service. For career appointments, on the other hand, federal agencies first attempt to fill higher level positions through promotions. In 1975, 92 percent of vacant career executive positions were filled by persons already working for the respective agencies and another 5 percent were filled by personnel from other agencies. In other words, only 3 percent of the vacant executive positions were filled by outsiders.[17]

Several criticisms can be made of practices that discourage mobility. Government agencies can become walled-in empires that are not recep-

---

[14] David T. Stanley, *The Higher Civil Service* (Washington: Brookings Institution, 1964), p. 34, and Civil Service Commission, "Characteristics of the Federal Executive," p. 175.

[15] For a general discussion of private-public mobility, see Dan H. Fenn, Jr., "A View of the Practical Problems," *Public Administration Review*, 27 (1967):373–382.

[16] Thomas C. Murray, "Promotion in the Public Service," *Annals*, 113 (May, 1924):354.

[17] Civil Service Commission, *Executive Personnel in the Federal Service* (Washington: Government Printing Office, 1976), p. 16.

tive to new ideas nor even exposed to them. Such systems can deny agencies superior talent and force them to promote persons with mediocre skills. Barriers to persons outside of government can provide unwarranted opportunities to current employees.

The fourth type of mobility is geographic. This form of mobility often occurs in association with another type of mobility, as when workers change employers or make intra- and interagency position changes. About half of all federal supergrade personnel have at least once in their careers moved from one region to another.[18] Movement is common between the central office and regional offices of large state and federal agencies. However, there may be a reluctance to move because of the problems of finding new housing, making new friends, and the like. Employees additionally may be reluctant to move because of career considerations. Personnel in the central office of an agency may fear they will be overlooked for promotion if they move to a regional office. Available information indicates that about a third of high-level federal administrators prefer not to move.[19] A study of Pennsylavania professional, administrative, and technical workers found about half would be "very reluctant" to move.[20]

Occupational job changes are the fifth type of mobility.[21] These changes can be dramatic, as in the case when a nurse leaves the profession, returns to college, and develops a new career, perhaps in computer operations. These types of changes are likely to occur early in one's professional development, usually within the first ten years.[22] Position classification and qualifications standards greatly limit occupational mobility opportunities. An experienced personnel analyst who prefers to shift to budgetary work may not be able to meet the experience requirement for higher level budgeting positions and may be forced to accept an entry-level position in that field.

Perhaps the most common type of occupational change is into administration.[23] Frequently, the management shift is within a substan-

---

[18] Lloyd G. Nigro and Kenneth J. Meier, "Executive Mobility in the Federal Service: A Career Perspective," *Public Administration Review*, 35 (1975):292.

[19] Civil Service Commission, "Characteristics of the Federal Executive," p. 179.

[20] Robert D. Lee, Jr., Charles Crawford, and Kathleen Rabena, "A Profile of State APT Manpower Resources: Preliminary Findings," *Public Administration Review*, 30 (1970):607.

[21] See Fremont J. Lyden and Ernest G. Miller, "Why City Managers Leave the Profession: A Longitudinal Study in the Pacific Northwest," *Public Administration Review*, 36 (1976):175–181.

[22] See John J. Corson and R. Shale Paul, *Men Near the Top: Filling Key Posts in the Federal Service* (Baltimore: Johns Hopkins Press, 1966), p. 118.

[23] Stanley, *The Higher Civil Service*, pp. 31–32, and Nigro and Meier, "Executive Mobility in the Federal Service," p. 292.

tive field, for example, a nurse's becoming a hospital director of nursing or a social worker's becoming the administrator of a county social services agency. One study of federal executives found that, during their careers, 18 percent had risen from positions below GS-5.[24] Another study that compared federal executives with business executives found the former generally moved more slowly into management ranks. After fifteen years of experience, 82 percent of the business executives had already become executives, whereas the comparable figure for federal executives was only 47 percent.[25]

Social-class mobility is the sixth form of mobility.[26] Government employment has been an important route for persons to move from the working class to the middle class. A 1963 study of federal executives found that about one in five had fathers who were laborers.[27] Today, the working class is generally under-represented among government executives in comparison with the general population.[28]

The discussion of mobility should not leave the impression that government workers are continuously in the process of changing jobs. Between 1965 and 1969, two-thirds of federal civilian workers changed neither agency, occupation, nor geographical area. Lower-level workers were slightly more mobile than persons in the supergrades (40 percent of the GS-1 through 4 group changed, compared with 20 percent of the GS-16 through 18 group).[29]

At some point in one's career promotions cease, and a tongue-in-cheek but nevertheless plausible explanation is the Peter Principle.[30] Promotions are awarded to productive workers who are expected to be equally productive in positions of greater responsibility. Eventually a person is promoted to a position for which he or she is not well qualified and further promotions are not forthcoming. In other words, workers tend to be promoted until they reach their individual levels of incompetence.

At the end of a career is retirement, a subject that is attracting increasing attention. One concern is that employees are not psychologi-

---

[24] Stanley, *The Higher Civil Service*, p. 35.

[25] Warner, *The American Federal Executive*, p. 155. See also Corson, *Men Near the Top*, pp. 111–116.

[26] See Van Riper, "Basic Factors and Issues," pp. 362–363.

[27] Warner, *The American Federal Executive*, p. 29.

[28] Wright and McAnaw, "American State Executives," p. 150, and Lee, Crawford, and Rabena, "A Profile of State APT Manpower Resources," pp. 604–605.

[29] Thomas E. Scism, "Employee Mobility in the Federal Service: A Description of Some Recent Data," *Public Administration Review*, 34 (1974):249.

[30] Laurence J. Peter and Raymond Hull, *The Peter Principle: Why Things Always Go Wrong* (New York: Morrow, 1969).

cally prepared for retirement, which typically constitutes an abrupt change in lifestyle.[31] Although pre-retirement counseling often has been used to encourage early retirement for less productive workers, counseling is now being advocated to aid workers in adjusting to retirement life. This form of counseling is being used in industry and can be expected to become more extensive in government.

Another developing issue is the use of compulsory retirement. These measures have been introduced to force the superannuated to leave government but they often have debilitating effects upon persons who could continue to be productive workers. A counter-argument has been that forcing the elderly to retire opens opportunities for other workers to advance their careers and allows government to attract young persons into government careers. According to federal law, state and local governments may not have a compulsory retirement age below 70, and there is no compulsory retirement age for federal employees. Elderly federal workers may be forced to retire when they are unable to perform the duties of their jobs.

Many government workers simply do not retire when they officially retire. As noted in the discussion of retirement benefits in Chapter 4, military personnel and state and local police officers often find employment after retirement. The military uses an up-or-out system in which persons not promoted are forced to retire. Information is not available on the extent to which retired federal military and civilian workers find state and local government employment, but the numbers of persons with these career patterns is certainly substantial. Not only is the practice beneficial to the individuals involved, but it often provides state and local governments with exceptional talent that otherwise might not be affordable. Other retirees accept part-time or full-time employment with private corporations, particularly those dealing with government, or sometimes develop their own consulting agencies. The American Society for Public Administration provides a service that attempts to match retired government executives with temporary and part-time jobs. Many military retirees accept federal civilian jobs, where they are known as "double dippers." Other federal retirees often take part-time federal employment under contract.

CAREER EXECUTIVES

Although the terms executive, administrator, manager, and supervisor generally are used interchangeably in this book for convenience, at this

---

[31] For a general discussion of life-cycle patterns, see Gail Sheehy, *Passages: Predictable Crises of Adult Life* (New York: Dutton, 1976).

point it is necessary to distinguish "executive" from other types of administrative positions. An executive, like other administrators, is expected to supervise subordinates, but he also has an additional responsibility, participating in the policy-making process of a department or government. Given the nature of a system, all public workers influence policy, but executives can be said to have a primary policy function. Whereas subordinates may have prescribed procedures that delimit the area of their activities, executives are presumed to have greater latitude in molding governmental programs.[32]

At the highest level of the executive branch is a chief executive—President, governor, or mayor—under whom are political executives. These people serve at the pleasure of the chief executive and are expected to be personally and philosophically compatible with the chief executive. Department heads, deputy secretaries, and assistant secretaries are political executives.[33] Directly below these people in the organizational hierarchy are career executives, who generally remain in office regardless of changes in political administrations. Indeed, by their continuing in office through such changes, career executives help to provide continuity in government programs. These careerists, who are only a small fraction of all public workers, constitute the interface between partisans and the rest of the government bureaucracy. Career executives have been said to make perhaps 90 percent of the important decisions in government.[34]

One assumption frequently made is that government does not sufficiently utilize the executive talent available simply because of an inability to identify that talent. Potentially excellent executives are overlooked when critical positions are to be filled. In response, numerous efforts have been made to be more thorough in the search for outstanding personnel within the government. Some federal agencies have computerized their personnel files, which are searched when vacancies need to be filled. This type of effort dates back at least to 1940, when the U.S. Civil Service Commission established the Interdepartmental Placement Service, which used punchcards to record important data about nearly a

---

[32] Harlan Cleveland, *The Future Executive* (New York: Harper and Row, 1972); Yehezkel Dror, *Public Policymaking Reexamined* (San Francisco: Chandler, 1968), pp. 246–259; and Fritz M. Marx, "The Mind of the Career Man," *Public Administration Review*, 20 (1960):133–138.

[33] See Dean E. Mann with Jameson W. Doig, *The Assistant Secretaries: Problems and Processes of Appointment* (Washington: Brookings Institution, 1965) and Hugh Heclo, *A Government of Strangers: Executive Politics in Washington* (Washington: Brookings Institution, 1977).

[34] Jule M. Sugarman, Vice Chairman of the U.S. Civil Service Commission, as quoted in Timothy B. Clark, "Senior Executive Service: Reform from the Top," *National Journal*, 10 (1978):1546.

million federal employees.[35] The file was searched for referring names of persons to agencies but it fell into disuse during World War II. During the Eisenhower administration, the CSC established a manually operated executive inventory covering nearly 2,000 supergrade executives. That inventory was superseded in 1966 by a new computerized Executive Inventory, initially covering about 25,000 persons at GS-15 and above; GS-15 personnel were included since they would be the typical candidates for entering the supergrades. Under the Executive Assignment System, federal agencies have been required to ask for a search of the inventory before filling supergrade positions, unless special conditions permit a waiver.

Similar efforts have been underway at the state and local levels. In the 1960s Pennsylvania created a personnel inventory modeled after that of the U.S. Civil Service Commission, but coverage extended down to mid-range professional, administrative, and technical positions.[36] Also, California established a Career Executive Assignment Roster, although this computerized file has not been used for identifying potential candidates to fill executive vacancies.[37] During the 1970s, numerous state and local governments with federal grants provided under the Intergovernmental Personnel Act of 1970 established computer-based personnel files. Among these jurisdictions were the District of Columbia, Illinois, North Carolina, Toledo, and Wisconsin. Many of these projects were focused mainly upon gathering personnel data in a new mode, but the systems that were developed did offer the potential for computer searches to fill job vacanices.[38]

Executive rosters or inventories, separate from other personnel files, have been used to collect information otherwise not available.[39] Both the federal and Pennsylvania inventories were developed from data supplied

---

[35] W. P. Lehman, "The Interdepartmental Placement Service," *Personnel Administration*, 4 (November, 1941):1-7.

[36] The Pennsylvania system was developed jointly by the Commonwealth of Pennsylvania and the Institute of Public Administration of The Pennsylvania State University. William R. Monat, Arthur C. Eckerman, and Robert D. Lee, Jr., "Pennsylvania Cultivates the Capacity to Manage," *State Government*, 62 (1969):247-255, and Robert D. Lee, Jr., "New Directions in Manpower Administration: Problems in Establishing a State Executive Inventory," *Good Government*, 86 (Winter, 1969):9-12.

[37] John Birkenstock, Ronald Kurtz, and Steven Phillips, "Career Executive Assignments—Report on a California Innovation," *Public Personnel Management*, 4 (1975): 154-155.

[38] Private corporations have been major users of personnel inventories. See Samuel H. Cleff and Robert M. Hecht, "Computer Job/Man Matching at Blue-Collar Levels," *Personnel*, 48 (January–February, 1971):16-29, and Paul S. Greenlaw, "The Achievement Motive and PIDS," *Personnel Journal*, 51 (1972):658-661.

[39] For a discussion of central personnel data files, see A. Ray Demarest, "CPDF: Information for Decisionmaking," *Civil Service Journal*, 15 (October–December, 1974): 15-19.

through questionnaires completed by employees. This allowed for collecting information about special skills, such as statistical and language skills, as well as individual preferences, such as willingness to consider moving to a new geographical location and/or accepting a new government position. The skills and preference information available through inventories, while not being particularly helpful in identifying the so-called "hidden talent," has been useful in making better matches between job requirements and individuals.

Personnel procedures may greatly limit the extent to which personnel inventories can be used in filling job vacancies. In merit systems requiring open competitive examinations, only those persons who have scored high on an examination may be considered for appointment. Should an inventory identify an excellent candidate but one who has not taken the requisite test, that person could not be appointed. This factor precluded use of the Pennsylvania inventory in making job assignments.

Beyond personnel inventories are more fundamental proposals for reform; the British use of rank-in-person has received wide attention.[40] The British Administrative Class has been considered a "permanent brain trust" into which are recruited young persons who are expected to become career executives.[41] Two key features of the British system have been that it is based on recruitment at an early age and is closed to entry at higher level positions. The Administrative Class historically has consisted largely of graduates in history, classics, and humanities from Cambridge and Oxford Universities; these are persons expected to be generalists and they are not expected, prior to entry, to be trained in either a relevant substantive field or in administrative practices.[42] The rigorous examination process used for entry has concentrated upon reasoning powers and verbal skills rather than upon substantive knowledge. As one observer has written, "The quality of the candidates is so good and the examination so stiff that a person with less than a university honors degree has little chance of appointment. Thus, government service

---

[40] See Richard A. Chapman and A. Dunsire, eds., *Style in Administration: Readings in British Public Administration* (London: Allen and Unwin, 1971); H. E. Dale, *The Higher Civil Service of Great Britain* (New York: Oxford University Press, 1941); Herman Finer, *The British Civil Service* (London: Fabian Society and Allen and Unwin, 1937); and Harvey Walker, *Training Public Employees in Great Britain* (New York: McGraw-Hill, 1935).

[41] Herman M. Stout, *Public Service in Great Britain* (Chapel Hill: University of North Carolina Press, 1938), pp. 77–113.

[42] Between 1960 and 1964, 74 percent came from these academic fields and 83 percent of the total came from Oxford and Cambridge. C. H. Dodd, "Recruitment to the Administrative Class, 1960–64," *Public Administration*, 45 (1967):55–80, and J. F. Pickering, "Recruitment to the Administrative Class, 1960–64: Part 2," *Public Administration*, 45 (1967):169–199.

claims at the start some of the keenest intellects of every generation."[43] Leonard D. White in the 1930s said that "the whole world now admires" the British system.[44]

The Administrative Class and, more generally, a closed, career executive system have been severely criticized. In Britain, the Fulton Committee of 1968 characterized the Administrative Class as consisting of amateurs who preferred to move from one position to another, who delegated their responsibilities to the lower status Executive Class, and who tended to make decisions without seeking information and advice from knowledgeable subordinates.[45] Career public servants in other classes, especially the Executive Class, were generally denied opportunity to join the Administrative Class.

The main criticisms of the British system have been that it is elitist and is founded on the false assumption that generalists make good executives. By having a testing system that effectively screened out all but those people who had graduated from the most prestigious universities, the system worked to the disadvantage of the middle and working classes. People appointed to the Administrative Class supposedly developed a "crown prince" mentality concerning their role in government. Moreover, members of the Administrative Class were presumed to have general administrative skills that would qualify them for dealing with a wide range of problems. People could be periodically reassigned to wherever their talents were needed. Since rank was in the person, reassignment did not require matching a person's current position in terms of rank with a new position. The generalist concept, however, is criticized on the grounds that current problems in government are of a technical nature and require substantive expertise. Contemporary executives cannot suitably be transferred from one field to another, such as from education to defense.

Reforms were instituted in Britain as a result of the Fulton report. The previously existing Administrative, Executive, and Clerical Classes were consolidated into the Administrative Group that became part of the General Class. Other classes include the Scientific, Professional and Technology, and Training Classes. The objective to reduce some of the career barriers between the old Administrative and Executive Classes appears not to have been fully accomplished. Forty percent of the important positions of administrative trainee were expected to be filled by persons already working for government and 60 percent by recent

[43] Stout, *Public Service in Great Britain*, p. 86.

[44] White, *Government Career Service*, p. 8.

[45] Report of the Committee, Chairman Lord Fulton, *The Civil Service* (London: Her Majesty's Stationery Office, 1968).

college graduates. However, the new graduates have constituted 80 percent of this group. Also, two separate training tracks have been
established. The so-called "high flier" track results in faster promotions
and seems to be dominated by the new college graduates.[46]

Rank-in-person is used selectively in the United States. The U.S.
Foreign Service and the military are prominent examples. The Forest
Service and the National Park Service have systems that use the rank-in-
person concept to some extent.[47] The Foreign Service sometimes has
been criticized as elitist, drawing heavily from Ivy League universities for
its personnel; similarly, the military has been criticized for relying heavily
upon military academy graduates for filling high command posts.[48]
Police systems at the state and local levels use ranks, as do municipal fire
departments. An advantage of these systems, like the career executive
idea more generally, is that officers can be assigned to special positions
or problems irrespective of their ranks. This advantage, however, is not
unique to rank systems in that other merit systems allow for temporary
assignment of personnel to deal with special problems.[49]

Proposals to extend the rank-in-person concept to cover larger numbers of public workers have been common in the United States since the
1930s. In 1935 the Commission of Inquiry on Public Service Personnel
recommended the establishment of a generally closed career system in
which persons would be recruited for low-level positions and developed
into career executives; broad classes of positions were to allow flexibility
in job assignments.[50] The First Hoover Commission (1949), although not
specifically recommending a separate executive service, emphasized the
need for greater movement of personnel across departmental lines and
for identification of junior management positions to help structure execu-

---

[46] C. Painter, "The Civil Service: Post-Fulton Malaise," *Public Administration*, 53
(1975):427–441. See also Felix A. Nigro, "What Has Happened to Fulton?" *Public
Administration Review*, 33 (1973):185–187.

[47] Secretary of State's Public Committee on Personnel (Wriston Report), *Toward a
Stronger Foreign Service* (Washington: Government Printing Office, 1954); Committee on
Foreign Affairs Personnel (Herter Report), *Personnel for the New Diplomacy* (Wash-
ington: Carnegie Endowment for International Peace, 1962); Commission of the Organiza-
tion of the Government for the Conduct of Foreign Policy (Murphy Commission), *Report*
(Washington: Government Printing Office, 1975); Robert LaPorte, Jr., and Harry E. Jones,
"Reorganizing and Managing U.S. Foreign Affairs," *Public Administration Review*, 36
(1976):217–223; and Herbert Kaufman, *The Forest Ranger: A Study in Administrative
Behavior* (Baltimore: Johns Hopkins University Press, 1960).

[48] David R. Segal and Daniel H. Willick, "The Reinforcement of Traditional Career
Patterns in Agencies Under Stress," *Public Administration Review*, 28 (1968):30–38.

[49] Harold H. Leich, "Rank in Man or Job? Both!," *Public Administration Review*, 20
(1960):92–99.

[50] Commission of Inquiry on Public Service Personnel, *Better Government Personnel*
(New York: McGraw-Hill, 1935) and Leonard D. White, *Government Career Service*
(Chicago: University of Chicago Press, 1935).

tive career patterns.[51] The Second Hoover Commission (1955) recommended the creation of a Senior Civil Service; the proposal was debated extensively but not implemented because of opposition by Congress.[52] President Eisenhower by executive order created a Career Executive Board in 1957 to operate a Senior Civil Service; but in 1959, still in the developmental phase, it went out of existence after Congress refused to fund the board's operations.[53] In 1971, President Nixon recommended to Congress the establishment of a Federal Executive Service (FES); but the Nixon proposal was not accepted by Congress.[54]

Late entry and an open system have characterized the career executive proposals made in the United States in recent decades. The emphasis has been upon changing the way career executives are treated and not the routes by which they become executives. People would have opportunity to advance through promotions into executive status or could come from outside of government into executive positions. California and Minnesota have established career executive systems along these lines. Despite strong opposition from organized labor, in 1963 the California legislature established a Career Executive Assignment (CEA) system, which was

---

[51] Commission on Organization of the Executive Branch of the Government, (First Hoover Commission), *Personnel Management* (Washington: Government Printing Office, 1949). See also John J. Corson, *Executives for the Federal Service: A Program for Action in Time of Crisis* (New York: Columbia University Press, 1952), and Wallace S. Sayre, ed., *The Federal Government Service: Its Character, Prestige, and Problems* (New York: Columbia University, 1954).

[52] Commission on Organization of the Executive Branch of the Government (Second Hoover Commission), *Task Force Report on Personnel and Civil Service* (Washington: Government Printing Office, 1955). See Richard M. Paget, "Strengthening the Federal Career Executive," *Public Administration Review*, 17 (1957):91–96; Everett Reimer, "The Case Against the Senior Civil Service," *Personnel Administration*, 19 (March–April, 1956): 31–40; Paul P. Van Riper, "The Senior Civil Service and the Career System," *Public Administration Review*, 18 (1958):189–200; and Leonard D. White, "The Case for the Senior Civil Service," *Personnel Administration*, 19 (January–February, 1956):4–9.

[53] Mel H. Bolster, "The Strategic Deployment of Exceptional Talent: An Account of the Career Executive Roster's Short History," *Public Administration Review*, 27 (1967): 446–451. See also Marver H. Bernstein, *The Job of the Federal Executive* (Washington: Brookings Institution, 1958); Corson and Paul, *Men Near the Top* (Baltimore: Johns Hopkins Press, 1966); Paul T. David and Ross Pollock, *Executives for Government: Central Issues of Federal Personnel Administration* (Washington: Brookings Institution, 1957); Kilpatrick, Cummings, and Jennings, *The Image of the Federal Service;* David T. Stanley, *The Higher Civil Service; Improving Executive Management in the Federal Government* (New York: Committee for Economic Development, 1964); David T. Stanley, "Federal Executives and the Systems that Produce Them," *Personnel Administration*, 32 (May–June, 1969):29–33; David T. Stanley, Dean E. Mann, and Jameson W. Doig, *Men Who Govern: A Biographical Profile of Federal Political Executives* (Washington: Brookings Institution, 1967); and Warner, *The American Federal Executive.*

[54] Richard M. Nixon and U.S. Civil Service Commission, "The Federal Executive Service," *Public Administration Review*, 31 (1971): 235–252, and House Committee on Post Office and Civil Service, *The Federal Executive Service: Hearings*, 92nd Cong., 2d sess. (Washington: Government Printing Office, 1972).

designed only for career employees. Personnel enter the CEA and can be reassigned to positions as needed. In 1973 changes were introduced that provided increased pay to reflect the increased responsibilities of these executives. Traditional position classification has been abolished for executive positions, and executives who are found not to be performing as expected can be reassigned to their original positions.[55]

Action at the federal level came in 1978 with passage of the Civil Service Reform Act, which authorized the establishment of the Senior Executive Service (SES).[56] Positions at the GS-16, 17, and 18 levels are covered, along with levels IV and V of the Executive Schedule. Some exceptions exist, such as positions in government corporations, the General Accounting Office, and intelligence agencies, including the Federal Bureau of Investigation, the Central Intelligence Agency, the Defense Intelligence Agency, and the National Security Agency. Every two years, agencies submit to the Office of Personnel Management their proposed needs for SES employees; the OPM, in consultation with the Office of Management and Budget, authorizes positions for the agencies. Some positions are "career reserved," meaning that they may be filled only by career appointees. Noncareer appointees may constitute no more than 10 percent of the total Senior Executive Service. At least 70 percent of all positions must be filled by people who have a minimum of five years of current continuous service in the civil service immediately before being appointed to the SES.

General qualifications for appointment to the SES are set by the Office of Personnel Management, with more detailed qualifications set by each agency. Each agency has one or more "executive resources boards" responsible for reviewing candidates, and the OPM has one or more "qualifications review boards" responsible for certifying qualifications for initial appointment of career appointees into the Senior Executive Service. Career appointees serve a one-year probation and may be reassigned within their agencies upon fifteen days' written notice, except that the career appointee cannot be involuntarily reassigned within 120 days of the appointment of a new agency head or a new immediate supervisor.

---

[55] John F. Fisher and Robert J. Erickson, "California's Career Executive Assignment: Meeting the Challenge for Better Managers," *Public Personnel Review*, 25 (1964):82–86; Lloyd D. Musolf, "California's Career Executive Assignment: A Perilous But Necessary Voyage," *Public Personnel Review*, 25 (1964):87–89; Lloyd D. Musolf, "Separate Career Executive Systems: Egalitarianism and Neutrality," *Public Administration Review*, 31 (1971):409–419; and Birkenstock, Kurtz, and Phillips, "Career Executive Assignments," pp. 151–155.

[56] Civil Service Reform Act, 92 Stat. 1111, Title IV (1978). See Roger W. Jones, "Does 'Career Executive' Have a New Meaning?" *Civil Service Journal*, 19 (October/ December, 1978):6–12; Personnel Management Project, *Final Staff Report* (Washington: Government Printing Office, 1977), pp. 181–200; and Civil Service Commission, *Senior Executive Service* (Washington: Government Printing Office, 1978).

The Senior Executive Service stresses executive performance. Performance appraisals are based on such factors as improvements in efficiency, cost savings, reduction in paperwork, improvements in effectiveness of subordinates who are supervised by the executives, and meeting affirmative action goals. The 1978 legislation requires that summary appraisal ratings include "(1) one or more fully successful levels, (2) a minimally satisfactory level, and (3) an unsatisfactory level." An unsatisfactory rating can result in removal from the SES; two unsatisfactory ratings in a five-year period require removal. A person receiving less than the fully successful rating twice in any three-year period must be removed. Agency "performance review boards" are responsible for performance appraisal. Career appointees who are removed from the SES may have an informal hearing before a representative of the Merit Systems Protection Board. A career employee removed from the SES is entitled to a GS-15 position or above.

Rewards are an important component of the Senior Executive Service. Career appointees are eligible for sabbatical leaves for up to eleven months. All appointees are guaranteed a minimal pay rate equivalent to the base pay of GS-16. Up to half of the executives may be eligible for performance awards or bonuses of as much as 20 percent of their base pay. In addition, the President may award the rank of "meritorious executive" to up to 5 percent of the Senior Executive Service in any one year; this award, which one can receive only once every five years, provides a $10,000 cash payment. Even more prestigious is the rank of "distinguished executive," providing a cash bonus of $20,000; that award can be given to no more than 1 percent of the executives. Using 1978 pay rates, an executive theoretically could receive $80,000 in pay—combining the base pay with the 20 percent bonus and the $20,000 award—but the legislation places a cap on salaries, making them equal to cabinet secretary's pay, which was $66,000 at the time the legislation was passed.

Experience with the Senior Executive Service is too recent for any judgment to be made about its strengths and weaknesses. The intent is to help both political and career executives. Political executives have greater flexibility in assigning career personnel; management "teams" to implement administration policies can be more readily assembled than was the case before SES was adopted. Career executives are offered challenging assignments coupled with financial rewards; a career executive does not relinquish all job security upon becoming a member of the SES.

There is one concern about the Senior Executive Service that will linger. The debates over whether to establish the SES centered not on the old argument that the plan was elitist. The SES, unlike the British system, provides for late entry and is an open system. Debates, instead, centered upon whether the SES would result in politicizing this critical level of the bureaucracy. Having fresh in mind the Nixon administration's deliberate efforts to politicize personnel practices, some people are concerned that politicizing the bureaucracy is now much easier to accomplish. Civil Service Commission Chairman Alan K. Campbell has defended the SES as encouraging career executives to be more responsive to new directions that occur with changes in political administrations. Democratic theory holds that a public bureaucracy should be answerable to those who have been elected by the people and not just answerable to itself. At the same time, safeguards have been built into the system, such as the provisions limiting the number of noncareer appointees and the right of an executive to a hearing before being removed from the SES.

TRAINING AND EDUCATION

While government may be interested in providing training and education programs as part of an overall strategy for employee "growth" and career development, the fundamental purpose is to improve the work performance of employees in current and future jobs. Sometimes a distinction is made between training and education, with the former suggesting a close relationship between instruction and the job performed and the latter referring to a more general intellectual endeavor that may not have a simple, direct connection with the work performed. The distinction is probably most applicable to low-level positions, whereas the type of training needed by persons in higher positions blends into education. The argument can be made that education is the appropriate alternative for managers and executives.[57] For convenience, however, the terms "education" and "training" are used interchangeably in this discussion. A more general term is "development," which can include education and training but also may include other activities, such as patterned assignments. A person may be assigned different duties or temporarily assigned to different jobs in the interest not of mastering the particular tasks involved but more generally of enhancing his knowledge, skills, and abilities.

Training both prior to and after entry into government has become standard. As is seen in Chapters 3 and 5, minimum education requirements are often imposed by position-classification and testing systems. States often set standards for local governments. State governments specify educational requirements for a person to be certified as a school teacher and impose requirements for additional education in order to

---

[57] Frederick C. Mosher, *Democracy and the Public Service* (New York: Oxford University Press, 1968); Stephen K. Bailey, "Educational Planning: Purposes and Power," *Public Administration Review*, 31 (1971):345–352; Richard C. Collins, "Training and Education: Trends, Differences, and Issues," *Public Administration Review*, 33 (1973):508–516; and K. T. Beyers, ed., *Employee Training and Development in the Public Sector* (Chicago: International Personnel Management Association, 1974).

retain a teaching certificate. States also impose training requirements for municipal police. At the federal level, the Government Employees Training Act of 1958 has made training opportunities widely available to federal employees.

The objective of improving employee performance can be achieved through both substantive and process training. Substantive training can include such fields as health, defense, education, and transportation. Given changes in technology, employees can become out of date, so that training is used to update knowledge.[58] Process training, on the other hand, refers to the ways in which work is carried out; a training program might be conducted to explain to employees how to request data from a newly established information system or how to comply with the requirements of a new accounting system. The distinction between substance and process is often difficult to specify, and no rigid dichotomization should be attempted.[59]

One should also consider whether the purpose of training is general awareness or skill development. A training program for program analysts might instruct personnel in research design and statistical analysis, whereas another program for managers might concentrate upon making them only aware of research methodology and generally what types of statistical measures are suitable for what types of analytical problems; the objective of the program would not be to teach the managers how to conduct analyses.[60]

General awareness training programs in the management field often follow popular trends or fads. As various management techniques come into vogue, training programs are established to introduce these to government workers. Since the 1960s popular topics for training have included planning-programming-budgeting systems (PPBS), management by objectives (MBO), organizational development (OD), productivity improvement, and zero base budgeting (ZBB).

Some training programs have a psychological foundation (see Chapter 12). These behavior-oriented training programs tend to stress appreciation of the needs and attitudes of oneself and others. T-groups (the T is for "training") are used in which persons interact with each other, often for several days, attempting to gain a better understanding of why people behave as they do. Sensitivity training may be of a general type or

---

[58] Samuel S. Dubin, "Updating and Midcareer Development and Change," *Vocational Guidance Quarterly*, 23 (1974):152–158, and Gilbert B. Siegel, "Management Development and the Instability of Skills: A Strategy," *Public Personnel Review*, 30 (1969):15–20.

[59] For a discussion of personnel training needs, see Advisory Committee on Merit System Standards, *Progress in Intergovernmental Personnel Relations* (Washington: Government Printing Office, 1968), pp. 78–80.

[60] Robert J. Mowitz, "Training Model for State and Local Governmental Personnel," *Public Personnel Management*, 3 (1974):451–453.

directed at a specific problem.[61] For instance, a welfare agency might have its staff use role playing to gain a better understanding of how welfare clients react to agency personnel. Such training also may be focused upon internal problems, as with racial friction among agency personnel.[62] The training may be directed at assisting personnel in coping with the necessarily unpleasant aspects of their jobs, such as helping police officers to cope with enforcing unpopular laws and with being ridiculed by many citizens.[63] Assertiveness training has been used to teach workers to demand their own rights while not violating the rights of others.[64]

One of the most important forms of training is designed to prepare employees for broadened responsibilities and particularly for management responsibilities. Early in an Army career, for instance, the soldier may be sent to weapons school, such as an artillery school, but later he or she will be sent to schools that deal with battle strategies and even later to schools dealing with war strategies and global politics. Similarly, a criminal investigator in a municipal police department may be sent to a police management training program.[65] The need for midcareer training for managers and executives has been stressed repeatedly.[66]

Still another type of training focuses upon introducing a major change in the manner in which work is performed within an agency or an entire government. Training is on a sequential or phased basis, in which training sessions are held as each new step is initiated in the development and implementation of the change. Rather than being an awareness or skill type of training, this form is geared to reorienting the manner in which employees think and perform their work. An example is an

[61] See Robert T. Golembiewski and Arthur Blumberg, eds., *Sensitivity Training and the Laboratory Approach: Readings About Concepts and Applications*, 2d ed. (Itasca, Ill.: Peacock, 1973).

[62] John E. Teahan, "Role Playing and Group Experience to Facilitate Attitude and Value Changes Among Black and White Police Officers," *Journal of Social Issues*, 31, No. 1 (1975):35–45.

[63] Tom Denyer, Robert Callender, and Dennis L. Thompson, "The Policeman as Alienated Laborer," *Journal of Police Science and Administration*, 3 (1975): 251–258.

[64] Malcolm E. Shaw and Pearl Rutledge, "Assertiveness Training for Managers," *Training and Development Journal*, 30 (September, 1976):8–14. See also Robert J. Ringer, *Winning Through Intimidation* (New York: Fawcett World, 1976), and Michael Korda, *Power!* (New York: Random House, 1975).

[65] Richard P. Calhoon and Thomas H. Jerdee, "First-Level Supervisory Training Needs and Organizational Development," *Public Personnel Management*, 4 (1975): 196–200.

[66] Second Hoover Commission, *Task Force Report on Personnel and Civil Service*, pp. 63–80; Lawrence C. Howard, "Executive Development: An Inter-governmental Perspective," *Public Administration Review*, 33 (1973):101–110; Frederic V. Malek, "Mr. Executive Goes to Washington," *Harvard Business Review*, 50 (September–October, 1972): 63–68; and Frederic V. Malek, "The Development of Public Executives—Neglect and Reform," *Public Administration Review*, 34 (1974):230–233.

extended training effort to restructure the budgetary decision process in a government.[67]

Given that training is presumed to be critical in maintaining and improving government operations, government heavily subsidizes training programs. In 1972–73 nearly one million federal employees received training.[68] Employees sometimes may be expected to pay part of the cost of training, but often government pays the entire cost. Training programs of the federal Office of Personnel Management are operated much like a business, with agencies being charged for each person who is sent to a training program; this practice encourages the OPM to develop training courses that agencies consider important. States generally provide short training courses without charge to employees. About ten states pay tuition for any college courses taken by employees, with another 30 paying part or all of the tuition depending upon the courses and the jobs of employees.[69] Many state and local training programs have been funded through federal grants under the Intergovernmental Personnel Act of 1970.[70]

A standard prescription in training literature is that a needs assessment should be made before training programs are undertaken.[71] Training should be considered as only one possible option. Another option might be the provision of technical assistance to deal with a specific problem. State agencies often provide technical assistance to local governments, and the federal government provides some assistance to states and localities.[72] Private consulting firms are another source for technical assistance. Other options may be redesigning work flow, or an

---

[67] This type of training has been utilized by the Institute of Public Administration of The Pennsylvania State University in assisting municipalities to convert to program budgeting. Robert D. Lee, Jr., and Ronald W. Johnson, *Public Budgeting Systems*, 2d ed. (Baltimore: University Park Press, 1977), pp. 276–277, and Robert D. Lee, Jr., *A Program Budgeting System for Medium-Size Cities* (University Park: Institute of Public Administration, The Pennsylvania State University, 1977).

[68] Civil Service Commission, *Employee Training in the Federal Service* (Washington: Government Printing Office, 1975).

[69] *Fringe Benefits in State Government Employment* (Lexington, Ky.: Council of State Governments, 1975), pp. 118–119. Milwaukee Personnel Department Training Unit, "Tuition Reimbursement in Employee Productivity and OD: A Survey," *Public Personnel Management*, 6 (1977):166–172. For information about tuition plans in the private sector, see J. Roger O'Meara, *Combating Knowledge Obsolescence: Employee Tuition-Aid Plans* (New York: National Industrial Conference Board, 1970).

[70] Another source of federal funding is the Comprehensive Employment Training Act (CETA) of 1974 as amended in 1976. Although the act's title includes the word "training," the program is not discussed in this chapter, because CETA is directed more at providing temporary work experience to the unemployed than for training career employees. CETA is discussed in Chapter 10.

[71] William R. Tracey, *Designing Training and Development Systems* (New York: American Management Association, 1971).

[72] William J. Jorns and David G. Smith, "Developing Coordinated Technical Assistance and Training Programs," *Journal of Employment Counseling*, 13 (1976):39–47.

agency's structure, or staffing patterns. Rather than training employees to cope with problems, the problems may be resolved through redesign efforts.[73]

Training needs can be assessed by analyzing agency performance, observing interpersonal relations of staff members, and reviewing the training, education, and experience of the staff.[74] In practice, this type of comprehensive review is rare. A more common practice is to ask employees and their supervisors what types of training they think are needed. The federal executive inventory has done this, asking GS-15s through GS-18s whether they needed training in fields such as personnel administration, budgeting and fiscal management, contracting and procurement, and labor relations. The Pennsylvania executive inventory also asked these types of questions. A major problem of these surveys is that government workers may not be fully aware of what their training needs are, and therefore the results of these surveys should be carefully interpreted.

From the assessment of needs coupled with the objectives to be served, a training strategy can be devised. A curriculum emerges that specifies the extent of each type of training that is to be provided. One training program for senior police sergeants, for example, consisted of 27 hours of instruction related to the news media, 31 hours dealing with human behavior, and 39 hours on police-group relations.[75] The mode of the training and its extent will be governed by costs and expected results.[76]

Who is trained in any given training program is determined by the objectives and content of the training program. General orientation training for new employees would be obviously inappropriate for experienced workers. All departmental secretarial workers, both new and experienced, however, might jointly attend a training program involving new agency procedures. Programs aimed at reorienting attitudes of workers, such as dealing with racial friction among staff members, might include all members of a bureau or division, including secretarial, professional, and managerial personnel. Many training programs include personnel

---

[73] Douglas J. Brunnette, Robert E. Hoskisson, and Marion T. Bentley, "Systematic Approach to Training in the Utah Job Service," *Public Personnel Management*, 6 (1977):21–30.

[74] Daniel H. Nellis, "An Administrative Technique for Personnel Management and Training in Mental Health," *Public Administration Review*, 34 (1974):496–499, and Civil Service Commission, *An Application of a Systems Approach to Training: A Case Study*, rev. ed. (Washington: Government Printing Office, 1969).

[75] James M. Gardner and Arthur Veno, "A Community Psychology Approach to Police Training," *Professional Psychology*, 7 (1976):437–444.

[76] Chester Wright, "A Breakthrough in Planning Training Investments," *The Bureaucrat*, (Spring, 1972):95–105. The model presented by Wright was considered a "breakthrough" but later was not used by the U.S. Civil Service Commission.

from different agencies; this allows participants to compare practices across departmental lines. One complaint about these kinds of courses is that they may not be directly applicable to any one agency. A general course in personnel management, for example, may include many topics not relevant to some participants or may explain procedures not used by many agencies represented by the participants.

Time is another variable. Training ranges from a one-hour session to a year's internship or years of study in earning advanced academic degrees. An eight-hour training program can be held in one day or once a week for one hour over a period of two months. The intensive two- to five-day workshop is popular in government, particularly at the federal level. The Office of Personnel Management, for example, provides two-day courses on the Factor Evaluation System of Position Classification and on the Freedom of Information and Privacy Act; five-day sessions are offered on Managing Equal Employment Opportunity Programs and on Federalism and Decentralization of the Executive Branch. Costs per participant generally range between $150 and $300.

A wide variety of training providers exists. Within a large government, departments, as well as the government's civil service commission, may provide training programs. At the federal level, the Office of Personnel Management acts as a coordinator among agencies. There are standardized courses in such fields as supervision, mid-level management, and executive management that are offered by many departments. Departments also have special schools, such as the FBI Academy. The Defense Department operates the National Defense University (including the National War College and the Industrial College of the Armed Forces), the Armed Forces Staff College, and the Defense Systems Management School. Probably as much as 70 percent of all training in the federal government is conducted by agencies. Each regional office of the OPM provides additional courses. The OPM also has four residential seminar centers for higher-level personnel; these are located in Berkeley, California; Kingspoint, New York; Oakridge, Tennessee; and Wilmington, Delaware.[77]

The Federal Executive Institute (FEI) is the capstone residential training facility of the OPM. The FEI conducts programs for executives in the supergrades and some GS-15s as well as state and local officials of comparable status. The full-time faculty conducts a variety of programs, ranging in length from one day to several weeks. The FEI's major train-

---

[77] See Alice H. Blumer, "Using Technology for Training," *Civil Service Journal,* 17 (January/March, 1977):9–12; Civil Service Commission, *Agency Training Centers for Government Employees* (Washington: Government Printing Office, 1974); Civil Service Commission, *Off-campus Study Centers for Government Employees* (Washington: Government Printing Office, 1974); and *National Interagency Training Program* (Washington: Civil Service Commission, 1977).

ing programs are the Senior Executive Education Program (seven weeks) and the Executive Leadership and Management Program (three weeks). Since its establishment in 1968, the Institute has extended its offerings to include special programs for political executives and now provides instruction at locations other than its Charlottesville, Virginia center.[78]

Universities also provide important training services. Public administration programs not only are important in pre-entry training/education but also provide mid-career training. Government workers may be integrated with other students in regular degree programs or they may constitute a separate student body as either a special mid-career degree program or as a noncredit training program. The Education for Public Management Program of the federal government provides financial support for mid-career employees to obtain executive training at several major universities.[79] Some schools offer their programs only at their main campuses, whereas others operate at branch locations, such as the University of Southern California in Washington, D.C., or at government installations, as in the case of the University of Oklahoma, which offers courses at military bases throughout the world.[80] The University of

---

[78] Paul C. Buchanan, ed., *An Approach to Executive Development in Government: The Federal Executive Institute Experience* (Washington: National Academy of Public Administration, 1973) and Thomas P. Murphy, Donald E. Nuechterlein, and Ronald J. Stupak, eds., *The President's Program Directors: The Assistant Secretaries* (Charlottesville, Va.: Federal Executive Institute, Civil Service Commission, 1977). See also William B. Boise, "The French National School of Administration and the Education of Career Executives," *Public Personnel Review*, 30 (1969):31–35, and John Swettenham and David Kealy, *Serving the State: A History of the Professional Institute of the Public Service of Canada, 1920–1970* (Ottawa: Professional Institute of the Public Service of Canada, 1970).

[79] Civil Service Commission, *Education for Public Management: An Interagency Long-Term Training Program* (Washington: Government Printing Office, 1976).

[80] The variety of schools and modes of instruction prohibit cataloguing these in the available space. For information about public administration programs, contact the National Association of Schools of Public Affairs and Administration in Washington, D.C. For relevant literature on public service education consult the *Public Administration Review*, published by the American Society for Public Administration in Washington, D.C. For example, see "Symposium on Higher Education for Public Service," *Public Administration Review*, 27 (1967):292–356; James A. Medeiros, "The Professional Study of Public Administration," *Public Administration Review*, 34 (1974):254–260; and "Symposium on Education for Public Service," *Public Administration Review*, 35 (1975):173–190. Also, relevant articles may be found in selected issues of *Public Management*, published by the International City Management Association. Other relevant literature includes Richard L. Chapman and Frederic N. Cleaveland, *Meeting the Needs of Tomorrow's Public Service: Guidelines for Professional Education in Public Administration* (Washington: National Academy of Public Administration Foundation, 1973); Rowland Egger, "Civil Servants at Mid-Career: Management Training in American Universities," *Public Administration*, 54 (1976):83–98; Irving Swerdlow and Marcus Ingle, eds., *Public Administration Training for the Less Developed Countries* (Syracuse, N.Y.: Maxwell School of Citizenship and Public Affairs, Syracuse University, 1974); Stephen B. Sweeney with Thomas J. Davy and Lloyd M. Short, eds., *Education for Administrative Careers in Government* (Philadelphia: University of Pennsylvania Press, 1958).

North Carolina's Institute of Government is the most extensive university-based, in-service training facility in the United States for state and local officials. It has a full-time staff of about 40 trainers and annually trains 5,000 to 8,000 officials in courses and other sessions varying from a few hours to several weeks of work.

Other training programs are provided through affiliations of governments and government officials, and through private profit and nonprofit agencies.[81] The Council of State Governments, the National League of Cities, the International City Management Association, the Municipal Finance Officers Association, and the International Personnel Management Association sponsor training programs. Training programs can be operated on a multi-city basis (the South Jersey Training Consortium), on a multi-city basis crossing state lines (the New England Municipal Center in Durham, New Hampshire), and on a multi-level basis (the Neil Goedhard Valley Regional Training Center in Fresno, California, including city, county, state, and federal agencies).[82] The National Training and Development Service, a nonprofit agency located in Washington, D.C., provides a wide variety of training programs for state and local officials. Private corporations offer an abundance of training programs, either ones especially designed for a jurisdiction or standardized courses.

Other training is provided by experience on the job. Internships, either while a student or after completion of an academic degree, are common at all levels of government.[83] Rotation from one position to

---

[81] For information about available training programs, see *Government Training News* published in Florham Park, New Jersey.

[82] George R. Ariyoshi, "HIMAG: Hawaii's Answer to Management Development," *State Government*, 50 (1977):160–164; Brian W. Braley, "Public Service Training In Maine," *Public Management*, 56 (April, 1974):7–8; R. P. Everett and William Hall, "Regional Training Centers: A New Venture in Management Development and Intergovernmental Cooperation," *Public Personnel Review*, 32 (1971):143–147; Katherine C. Janka, "Municipal In-Service Training," *Municipal Year Book: 1976* (Washington: International City Management Association, 1976), pp. 185–199, and Carrol F. Pickens, "New Jersey/Training Consortium," *Public Management*, 57 (April, 1975):15–16. In the early 1930s there were some intergovernmental training centers for police personnel: William C. Beyer, "Municipal Civil Service in the United States," in Carl J. Friedrich et al., *Problems of the American Public Service* (New York: McGraw-Hill, 1935), pp. 160–161.

[83] Barbara R. DeShong, "Recruiting Effectiveness of a Texas Public Service Intern Program," *Public Personnel Management*, 4 (1975):331–338; Richard W. Gable, "A New Internship Program for the State of California," *Public Personnel Review*, 31 (1970): 250–253; "Internship: Field Experience," *Public Management*, 59 (January, 1977):2–18; Victor E. Ewing and John H. Galligan, "The Internship Through Intern's Eyes," *Public Management*, 53 (May, 1971):13–15; Jonathan A. Slesinger, *Personnel Adaptations in the Federal Junior Management Assistant Program* (Ann Arbor: Institute of Public Administration, University of Michigan, 1961); and Thomas P. Murphy, eds., *Government Management Internships and Executive Development* (Lexington, Mass.: Lexington Books, 1973). In August, 1977, President Jimmy Carter signed Executive Order 12008 creating the Presidential Management Intern Program.

another every few months is often a characteristic of internships and sometimes other entry-level positions.[84] Special job assignments are possible, such as university faculty working full-time for a government for a year or more; this has the dual advantages of providing faculty talent to the participating government and helping to make the faculty member a better informed teacher upon return to the university.[85] Developmental assignments are the fundamental tool in executive development in the federal service.

The federal government has been instrumental in encouraging the use of special assignments between governments and between government and the private sector. The President's Commission on Personnel Interchange, established by President Johnson in 1969, provides for exchange of personnel between the federal government and the private sector. The Intergovernmental Personnel Act (IPA) of 1970 provides for interchange between the federal government on the one hand and state and local governments on the other. As of 1976, approximately 1,500 federal staff members had been placed on such assignments, about half going to state governments. An equal number of state and local officials were assigned to federal agencies; about two-thirds of these personnel were from colleges and universities.[86] IPA funding for personnel interchanges as well as for training programs is part of a federal emphasis upon state and local "capacity building."[87]

The diversity of training providers and training modes has produced a largely uncoordinated training subsystem within the personnel field. While many observers have suggested the need for careful planning of training programs, little has been accomplished in integrating specific training efforts into an overall training design. The training field at the federal level has been described as "a vast, uncatalogued, uncoordinated series of conferences, seminars, meetings, training sessions, and, quite frankly, 'boondoggle' types of activities."[88] Certainly the same criticism applies at the state and local levels and the interconnections among the levels. The absence of any comprehensive approach to training is partially due to the absence of consensus about what constitutes quality training. Quality in the training field is an ambiguous commodity,

---

[84] Kendall J. Jenkins, "Rotation: New Experiences in Changing Times," *Public Personnel Review*, 33 (1972):123–127.

[85] Bernard Booms and Laura Kemp, "A Teaching Government," *Public Administration Review*, 35 (1975):289–290.

[86] *The IPA Intergovernmental Assignment Program* (Washington: Civil Service Commission, 1976).

[87] Study Committee on Policy Management Assistance, *Strengthening Public Management in the Intergovernmental System* (Washington: Government Printing Office, 1975).

[88] Bob L. Wynia, "Executive Development in the Federal Government," *Public Administration Review*, 32 (1972):316.

since comparatively few rigorous attempts are made to determine specific training objectives and to evaluate whether those objectives have been met.

Training effectiveness can be influenced by the instructor, the participants, their supervisors, and training materials, facilities, and techniques.[89] A common complaint of training courses conducted by professional trainers is that they know how to conduct a class but often lack depth of knowledge and experience in the courses' contents. The qualifications of persons from outside government also may be challenged for the same reason. Professors of public administration, professional psychologists, and others may be viewed by the trainees as not being adequately prepared.[90] Complaints of this type may sometimes be justified but they also may be a smoke screen for other influences upon the participants. Individuals often are sent to training programs without being consulted about whether they wish to attend. Sometimes the most expendable or the most deficient employees are the ones sent for training, and the resulting resentment by the trainees discourages effective training. In other situations, successful completion of a training course may be considered a requirement for promotion; some employees seek appointment to such a training course but view the course more as a troublesome hurdle than as an opportunity to learn.

The reactions of administrators to training and the overall mode of operations of agencies can reduce training effectiveness. For example, trainees may be instructed in how to use the team approach to work, but on return to their respective agencies they may find opposition to that approach voiced by both supervisors and peers.[91] It may be unrealistic to expect much change when perhaps only one person is trained out of a unit of 25 people. Indeed, a newly trained employee might be ill-advised to use what he learned if it was contrary to the preferences of the supervisor, since this could result in lower performance evaluations and could harm his chances of promotion.

Materials, facilities, and techniques can influence training effectiveness, although perhaps mainly in a negative sense. Inadequate materials and facilities can result in ineffective training, but adequate instructional support will not by itself produce benefits. As for instructional tech-

[89] Ruth D. Salinger, *Disincentives to Effective Employee Training and Development* (Washington: Civil Service Commission, 1973).

[90] James Hillgren and Paul Jacobs, "The Consulting Psychologist's Emerging Role in Law Enforcement," *Professional Psychology*, 7 (1976):256–266, and Joseph Zacker, "Is Opposition to Social Intervention Resistance or Coping?" *Professional Psychology*, 5 (1974):198–205.

[91] C. E. Teasley III and Leonard Wright, "The Effects of Training on Police Recruit Attitudes," *Journal of Police Science and Administration*, 1 (1973):241–248.

niques, there is no one best way. Lectures, group discussions, workshop sessions that have assigned tasks to accomplish, multi-media presentations, role playing, and the like can all be useful.[92]

Evaluation of training programs usually is done by testing participants and/or having participants complete a questionnaire at the end of a course.[93] Examinations often are given at the end of training programs, just as they are in regular college courses.[94] Also, participants are asked for their assessments of the training course, such as whether the course objectives were adequately explained by the instructor, whether the instructor's presentations were well integrated with assigned readings, and other similar questions.[95] This type of evaluation is necessarily subjective, and the extent to which an instructor is entertaining can greatly influence rater reactions. Participants may react favorably in part because they enjoyed the social interaction with each other; holding training courses at resort locations also can result in favorable ratings and have little to do with "real" training effectiveness. The federal Office of Personnel Management has developed "training value models" to attempt to arrive at more valid measures of training effectiveness.

The ultimate evaluation of training is whether employees perform differently after a training experience than they did before. To gauge this, one approach that is used is to ask the supervisors of trainees to assess changes in performance stemming from the training experience; the supervisors may be contacted several weeks or months after completion of the training program. A related approach is to compare personnel ratings of trained and untrained persons. Nevertheless, these types of

---

[92] Craig E. Schneier, "Training and Development Programs: What Learning Theory and Research Have to Offer," *Personnel Journal*, 53 (1974):288–293, and Civil Service Commission, *Instructional Systems and Technology: An Introduction to the Field and Its Use in Federal Training* (Washington: Government Printing Office, 1969).

[93] *Better Evaluation Needed for Federal Civilian Employee Training* (Washington: General Accounting Office, 1975); Civil Service Commission, *Training Evaluation: A Guide to Its Planning, Development, and Use in Agency Training Courses* (Washington: Government Printing Office, 1971); Christopher Gane, *Managing the Training Function: Using Instructional Technology and Systems Concepts* (Beverly Hills, Calif.: Davlin, 1972), pp. 158–75; James F. Guyot, "How Do We Know Which Training is Good Medicine for Managers?," *Public Administration Review*, 37 (1977):698–705; and William R. Tracey, *Evaluating Training and Development Systems* (New York: American Management Association, 1968).

[94] William G. Hayes and Eugene I. Williams, Jr., "Supervisory Training—An Index of Change," *Public Personnel Review*, 32 (1971):158–163.

[95] Brunnette, Hoskisson, and Bentley, "Systematic Approach to Training in the Utah Job Service," pp. 21–30, and Walter L. Patterson, Jr., Anthony F. McGann, and Raymond A. Marquardt, "A Practical Approach to the Analysis of TEOT Data," *Training and Development Journal*, 28 (December, 1974):32–36.

evaluations have one of the weaknesses of participants' rating of a training program, in that both types of evaluations are based upon opinion.

Objective evaluations are easiest to perform for training programs geared to routine work. Since that type of training program is intended to instruct employees in following a routine, variations from the routine can be considered a sign of lack of total training success. Many government jobs involve the processing of paper, such as procurement procedures or processing applications for welfare payments. By sampling the work product of trained and untrained employees, an assessment can be made about whether trained workers perform better than those not trained.

Objective evaluations are more difficult when training focuses upon nonroutine work and is especially difficult for managerial work. How is the effectiveness of a training program for first-line supervisors to be gauged? Even more difficult is assessing executive development programs. These often are not intended to have an immediately noticeable effect upon behavior. Proponents of such training claim that benefits are long-term, which defy objective measurement. To what extent, then, can the superior performance of an executive today be credited to a seven-week training program that was attended ten years ago?

Executive training, moreover, is challenged as to whether it can ever be effective except in a few special cases. Management courses tend to stress problem-solving skills but may be incapable of teaching how to identify and define problems and how to be imaginative in developing alternative solutions. Another alleged weakness is that only persons with specified personal characteristics can benefit from executive training. "Only those men who have a strong desire to influence the performance of others and who get genuine satisfaction from doing so can learn to manage effectively."[96]

Since measuring the value of training is difficult, training units often are at a disadvantage in competing for resources.[97] Training programs for which it can be shown that benefits outweigh costs are likely to be guaranteed funding, but these constitute a small minority of all training programs. To many persons, training is considered a luxury that can be drastically curtailed or eliminated during tight budget periods. While few would reject the principle that training is desirable, the absence of demonstrable results from training makes it a likely candidate for budget cuts.

---

[96] J. Sterling Livingston, "Myth of the Well-Educated Manager," *Harvard Business Review*, 49 (January–February, 1971):79–89.

[97] Charles J. Eichman, "In-Service Training: Correction's Stepchild?" *Public Personnel Review*, 30 (1969):21–24.

SUMMARY

Governments support the concept of career development for their employees but are less than fully committed to the concept. Employees are expected to be mainly responsible for their own career planning. Career advancement within a jurisdiction is affected by promotion procedures, with some jurisdictions using open competitive examinations for all persons and others providing advantages to current employees. Job mobility includes intra-agency, interagency, interorganizational, geographic, occupational, and social-class mobility. A series of issues is emerging concerning the last step in the career process—retirement.

Concerns for promoting careers for executives have led to the use of personnel inventories and to proposals for career executive systems separate from personnel systems for other government workers. Personnel inventories provide useful data but should not be expected to identify executive talent "hidden" in the bureaucracy. Rank-in-person systems are defended as allowing greater flexibility in assigning responsibilities to personnel and as fostering professionalism in administration. The federal government took a major step in this direction in 1978 by authorizing the establishment of the Senior Executive Service.

Training is extensive in government and is provided in many different forms. Variations exist in the type of training provided, the personnel included, the length of the instructional program, and the organizations that provide the training. While training programs are considered an important aspect of employee career development, they generally have not been integrated into a comprehensive design. Rigorous evaluation of training programs is rare, and executive development programs are probably the most difficult to evaluate. The general absence of evaluation efforts and the suspicion that training is often ineffective result in training being a weak competitor for scarce budget dollars.

Chapter 8

Employee Rights and Responsibilities

A common assumption throughout the history of the public service is that when people accept government jobs they relinquish some of the rights they would have as private citizens and assume responsibilities concerning their conduct that would not necessarily be expected of them as private citizens. That assumption has been challenged for decades and currently is under increasing attack on the grounds that government employees as individuals and as citizens should not be assigned second-class status in society. Yet, absolutes are difficult to prescribe. Employee rights must be considered in context with the needs of society in general and the needs of particular interests, such as the clients of governmental programs. Values are in competition with each other, thereby placing public employees in ambiguous positions concerning what type of behavior society expects of them.

This chapter highlights some of these competing pressures. The word "highlights" is used deliberately to indicate that the subject involves fundamental issues that could be thoroughly treated only in book-length form. The chapter's first section reviews some of the competing values concerning ethical conduct of employees. The second section focuses upon civil liberties and civil rights, as reflected in loyalty-security issues, freedom of speech for public workers, and the political activities of public personnel. The third section discusses approaches used in holding employees accountable for their actions.

ETHICAL STANDARDS AND AMBIGUITIES

Public employees are expected to be exemplars of moral or ethical conduct. Although the concept of ethics is difficult to define, it can be considered simply as differentiating between good and bad or between right and wrong behavior.[1] Justice Holmes in a famous 1892 Massachusetts case declared that a person "has no constitutional right to be a policeman" (*McAuliffe* v. *New Bedford*).[2] That pronouncement has been interpreted to mean that government may prescribe strict standards of conduct and greatly curtail the constitutional rights of public workers. Today Holmes' position is undergoing substantial revision. While most people demand a high standard of behavior from government employees, there is increasing pressure to afford public workers greater latitude in their own conduct. Increasing employee militancy is a partial reason for this trend. Employees as individuals and collectively through labor unions are insisting upon greater freedoms. This section considers ethical standards relating to behavior both on and off the job.

On-the-Job Conduct

One instance where ethical standards are relatively unambiguous is the prohibition against corruption in both the private and public sectors.[3] Although definitions of "corruption" vary widely, the concept generally involves some personal gain on the part of office holders (in the words of George Washington Plunkitt of New York's Tammany Hall, "I seen my opportunities and I took 'em'"[4]). Corruption can be limited to only one person, as in the case of a government worker who misappropriates government property by taking it home for personal use.[5] However, corruption usually implies more widespread and systematic activity, such as a group of workers who organize to steal supplies on a prolonged basis.

Frequently, the concept of corruption includes government workers in collusion with persons outside of government.[6] Contracting provides great opportunities for this form of corruption, as was evidenced at the federal level in 1978 in cases involving General Services Administration

---

[1] For general discussions of ethics, see Vernon J. Bourke, *History of Ethics* (Garden City, N.Y.: Doubleday, 1968); Harold D. Lasswell and Harlan Cleveland, eds., *The Ethic of Power: The Interplay of Religion, Philosophy and Politics* (New York: Harper and Brothers, 1962); and James A. Medeiros and David E. Schmitt, *Public Bureaucracy: Values and Perspectives* (North Scituate, Mass.: Duxbury, 1977).

[2] *McAuliffe* v. *New Bedford*, 155 Mass. 216, 29 N.E. 517 (1892).

[3] For a review of the literature on this subject, see Gerald E. Caiden and Naomi J. Caiden, "Administrative Corruption," *Public Administration Review*, 37 (1977):301–309.

[4] William L. Riordon, *Plunkitt of Tammany Hall* (New York: E. P. Dutton, 1963), p. 3.

[5] *Alsbury* v. *United States Postal Service*, 302 F. Supp. 71 (1975), is a case of a postal worker who took home a government air conditioner, tape recorder, and bookcase. *United States ex. rel.* v. *Hollander*, 420 F. Supp. 853 (1976) involved a Congressman who filed false travel vouchers.

[6] It should be understood that, despite ethical considerations, corruption can be a standard practice in a government, and unless one abides by that practice, he will be ineffective in accomplishing whatever is undertaken.

contracts. The result is that government usually spends more than would have been necessary had open competition existed. Another example of this type of corruption is in the area of inspections.[7] A major scandal of recent years involved Federal Housing Administration inspectors, who, in collusion with real estate and banking interests, approved substandard housing units for FHA loans; the result was that home buyers eventually defaulted on their mortgages, forcing the United States Department of Housing and Urban Development to become the largest single owner of slum housing in the country.

The personal gain of corruption usually has a monetary value.[8] Bribes and kickbacks on contracts are obvious examples. The payoffs of corruption can be "in kind," such as free trips to resort areas, or "gifts," such as vicuna coats in the Eisenhower administration and freezers in the Truman administration. The financial benefit may be in employment. The General Accounting Office (GAO), for example, found that a person who was on loan from a major oil firm to the Federal Energy Office had been given the responsibility of writing administrative regulations that would have major financial implications for his firm.[9] The "lure of future employment" is equally important.[10] Government administrators whose jobs involve dealing with private corporations may be tempted to make decisions that will enhance their job opportunities in those firms. The same type of behavior is exhibited between governments. A local government may lure a state official to accept a city job in hope that the result will be more favorable treatment by a state agency.

Corruption need not be exclusively monetary in nature. Watergate is one of the best examples.[11] The break-ins, dirty tricks in campaigning,

---

[7] *United States v. Kahan*, 415 U.S. 241 (1974), involved the acceptance of bribes by an inspector of the Immigration and Naturalization Service.

[8] J. Lincoln Steffens, *The Shame of the Cities* (New York: Hill and Wang, 1963) and Raymond Clapper, *Racketeering in Washington* (Boston: Page, 1933). Members of Congress periodically are implicated in alleged acceptance of bribes for favorable legislative action. See *United States v. Brewster*, 408 U.S. 501 (1972). In 1977, "Koreagate" became a major scandal in which Members of Congress allegedly accepted gifts from a Korean government representative in return for favorable voting on legislation affecting that country.

[9] Subcommittee on Energy and Environment, House Committee on Small Business, *Conflict of Interest Problems within the Presidential Executive Interchange Program: Hearings*, 94th Cong., 1st sess. (Washington: Government Printing Office, 1976). The Presidential Executive Interchange Program is designed to encourage private executives to take assignments with the federal government.

[10] Douglas, *Ethics in Government*, pp. 49–55.

[11] Hugh Heclo et al., "Watergate in Retrospect: The Forgotten Agenda," *Public Administration Review*, 36 (1976):306–310; Frederick C. Mosher et al., *Watergate: Implications for Responsible Government* (New York: Basic Books, 1974); Vermont Royster, "The Public Morality: Afterthoughts on Watergate," *American Scholar*, 43 (1974):249–259; and James L. Sundquist, "Reflections on Watergate: Lessons for Public Administration," *Public Administration Review*, 34 (1974):453–461.

cover-ups, and other abuses of the Nixon administration provided few immediate financial benefits to the principals involved; instead, the primary reward was remaining in power. While financial considerations certainly were at stake, the main motivator seems to have been to ensure the re-election of the President in 1972.

Statutes and ethics codes have been adopted by government to clarify for employees what activities should be avoided.[12] Typical prohibitions include "using public office for private gain," accepting gifts from private citizens or corporations with which the employee works, and having a direct or indirect financial interest in whatever the employee manages. The appearance of a conflict of interest is prohibited as well as an actual conflict of interest. An employee who resigns his government position may be barred from accepting a job from a corporation that received a contract with which the individual was involved. A former employee also may be prevented from representing a corporation or person before his former government employer.

Public officials and employees often must file financial disclosure statements. These requirements are common for elected and appointed officials. Persons holding positions that can influence the awarding of grants and contracts usually will be required to submit financial disclosure statements. The courts have upheld these requirements despite the complaint that they are an invasion of privacy.[13] A series of studies

---

[12] For United States policies, see "Bribery, Graft, and Conflicts of Interest," 18 U.S.C. § 201–224; "Standards of Ethical Conduct for Government Officers and Employees," Executive Order 11222, 18 U.S.C. § 201; and "Employee Responsibilities and Conduct," 5 C.F.R. § 735. See also Melvin G. Cooper, "The Alabama Ethics Act: Its Scope and Implementation," *National Civic Review*, 65 (1976):70–74; "Ethics in Local Government," *Public Management*, 57 (June, 1975):2–19; *Federal Prosecutions of Corrupt Public Officials, 1970–76* (Washington: Criminal Division, Department of Justice, 1977); George A. Graham, "Ethical Guidelines for Public Administrators: Observations on Rules of the Game," *Public Administration Review*, 34 (1974):90–92; Kenneth Kernaghan, *Ethical Conduct: Guidelines for Government Employees* (Toronto: Institute of Public Administration of Canada, 1975); S. Stanley Kreutzer, "Protecting the Public Service: A National Ethics Commission," *National Civic Review*, 64 (1975):339–342; "Nevada Ethics Law Overturned for Vagueness," *National Civic Review*, 65 (1976): 345–346; David Reich, "Ethics: Present Situation, Administration Proposals," *Civil Service Journal*, 18 (January/March, 1978):24–26; John A. Rohr, "The Study of Ethics in the P.A. Curriculum," *Public Administration Review*, 36 (1976):398–406; and Susan Wakefield, "Ethics and the Public Service: A Case for Individual Responsibility," *Public Administration Review*, 36 (1976):661–666.

[13] For an example of a city case, see *O'Brien v. DiGrazia*, 544 F. 2d. 543 (1976). See also *Ethics: State Conflict of Interest/Financial Disclosure Legislation, 1972–75* (Lexington, Ky.: Council of State Governments, 1975); Graham E. Johnson, "Ethics and Financial Disclosure: What Makes a Strong Law?" *National Civic Review*, 65 (1976): 553–556; Louis M. Kohlmeier, *Conflicts of Interest: State of Local Pension Fund Asset Management* (New York: Twentieth Century Fund, 1976); and Alan E. Staines, "A Model for Controlling Public Corruption through Financial Disclosure and Standards of Conduct," *Notre Dame Lawyer*, 51 (1976):636–705.

recently conducted by the General Accounting Office found major failures in complying with federal conflict-of-interest standards. Many employees who should have filed statements had not; others had submitted statements showing corporate stock holdings that should not have been owned. The GAO suggested the problem was of such magnitude to warrant the establishment of an executive office of ethics.[14] In response to these and other criticisms, Congress in 1978 passed financial disclosure legislation that applied to top officials of all three branches of the federal government. The legislation also provides for a "cooling off" period, requiring a one- or two-year wait before some former government employees may contact their former agencies.

Another kind of corruption is wasteful use of government resources. Agencies sometimes seek to aggrandize their operations to the point of consuming resources far beyond what is needed. Depending upon one's views, the defense establishment may have been particulary guilty of consuming tax dollars far beyond what is needed to deter and defend against potential aggressor nations.[15] Another form of wasteful use of resources is the lack of concern some employees show for government property; these workers have little sense of wrongdoing when they abuse government property, since it seems to belong to no one.

Problems in assuring ethical behavior stem from several sources. One common view is that humans are morally frail and easily succumb to temptation. James Madison in the *Federalist Papers* wrote:

> If angels were to govern men, neither external nor internal controls on government would be necessary. In framing a government which is to be administered by men over men, the great difficulty lies in this: you must first enable the government to control the governed; and in the next place oblige it to control itself.[16]

The assumption is that people left unchecked will abuse authority by harming the general citizenry and by favoring themselves and their associates. Of course, not everyone subscribes to this view of the inherent corruptness of the human race. The discussion of motivation in Chapter 11 presents a more positive view of human behavior.

---

[14] *Action Needed to Make the Executive Branch Financial Disclosure System Effective* (Washington: General Accounting Office, 1977); *Financial Disclosure for High Level Executive Officials: The Current System and the New Commitment* (Washington: General Accounting Office, 1977); and Subcommittee on Employee Ethics and Utilization, House Committee on Post Office and Civil Service, *Ethics and Financial Disclosure: Hearings*, 95th Cong., 1st sess., (Washington: Government Printing Office, 1977).

[15] See William Proxmire, *Report from Wasteland: America's Military-Industrial Complex* (New York: Praeger, 1970).

[16] James Madison, Federalist Paper No. 51, in Alexander Hamilton, James Madison, and John Jay, *The Federalist Papers* (New York: New American Library of World Literature, 1961), p. 322.

Ethical behavior is difficult to enforce because of the government's large size and complexity. The stakes are high in big government. When major highway construction or defense contracts are to be awarded, millions and billions of dollars are involved, and certainly some individuals will be inclined to use bribery as a means of winning such contracts. Size is also important in that government bureaucracies become difficult to oversee. It is impossible to watch over the behavior of each of the approximately 3 million civilian workers in the federal government. Smallness, however, does not ensure ethical purity. One view has been that ". . . the very intimacy between citizen and local government invites some corruption of government."[17] Competing special interests in large jurisdictions may cancel each other, whereas one special interest may come to dominate a small local government.

Associated with bigness is complexity. As society has grown in both size and complexity, so have governmental operations. This complexity has necessarily forced policy-making bodies, such as city councils, state legislatures, and Congress, to delegate authority to the executive branch. Delegation involves discretionary authority in making decisions within the policy framework established by laws.[18] Discretion at the local level, for example, includes deciding the extensiveness of street cleaning and snow removal in various neighborhoods, such as in middle class and poor neighborhoods, or at the state level discretion includes deciding who will receive welfare benefits. The corruption stemming from discretion can be deliberate, in terms of intentionally favoring some individuals, groups, or corporations over others. An equally important type of corruption and one frequently overlooked is the unintentional capricious or arbitrary action that administrators take in exercising discretion. The concept of fairness includes treating equals equally, whereas arbitrary action involves treating them unequally. The Internal Revenue Service, for example, has been criticized as failing to be consistent in dealing with taxpayers. These are not examples of venal corruption, but they still are a form of corruption.

Changes in societal values constitute another factor that complicates maintaining moral standards in government. Behavior that is considered acceptable or at least tolerable today may not be acceptable tomorrow, and the converse also is true. Post-Watergate morality has been seen as imposing stricter standards on public servants than were imposed earlier. On the other hand, societal standards concerning the sex lives of government workers have been somewhat relaxed in recent years. Extra-marital

---

[17] Paul H. Appleby, *Morality and Administration in Democratic Government* (Baton Rouge: Louisiana State University Press, 1952), pp. 58–59.

[18] See Rohr, "The Study of Ethics in the P.A. Curriculum," pp. 398–399.

sexual relations that once would have been grounds for immediate dismissal are often accepted or tolerated.

A frequently heard expression is that society expects higher ethical standards of public workers than it expects of private-sector workers. Giving special discounts to friends is accepted practice in business, while favoritism is taboo in government. Bert Lance, President Carter's first Director of the Office of Management and Budget, was forced to resign largely because of his previous business dealings, which were considered of questionable ethical rectitude for a person who had responsibility for managing the financial operations of the federal government. A small business owner sometimes may use a company vehicle for personal purposes and may even have employees make repairs on his residence. Again, that behavior would not be acceptable in the public sector.

This double standard, however, should not be overemphasized. Corporate ethics is a major concern in the private sector, as was evidenced by the scandals of the mid-1970s associated with the apparently widespread practice of corporate influence-buying in international trade.[19] What are different are the relative powers of the two sectors. Corporations indeed are powerful in determining what products appear on the market and what prices are charged. Still, the consumer does have some choice; this is not true in the public sector, which exercises coercive powers. Unethical public administrators can exercise the powers of government to compel citizen obedience.

Public servants are expected to adhere to several ethical standards, each of which may seem innocuous but when applied to specific situations may be in competition with each other and pose dilemmas in determining an appropriate course of action.[20] Public servants are expected to treat equals equally, to be professionals, to give government a fair day's work, to be efficient and effective. Each profession has its own set of

---

[19] For discussions of business ethics, see Neil Jacoby, Peter Nehemkis, and Richard Eells, *Bribery and Extortion in World Business* (Riverside, N.J.: Free Press, 1977); Blair J. Kolasa, *Responsibility in Business* (Englewood Cliffs, N.J.: Prentice-Hall, 1972); and Edgar H. Schein, "The Problem of Moral Education for the Business Manager," *Industrial Management Review*, 8 (Fall, 1966):3–14.

[20] Stephen K. Bailey, "Ethics and the Public Service," in Roscoe C. Martin, ed., *Public Administration and Democracy: Essays in Honor of Paul H. Appleby* (Syracuse, N.Y.: Syracuse University Press, 1965), pp. 283–298 and in *Public Administration Review*, 44 (1964):234–243; Clarence N. Callender and James C. Charlesworth, eds., "Ethical Standards in American Public Life," *Annals*, 280 (1952):1–157; Herbert Emmerich, "A Scandal in Utopia," *Public Administration Review*, 12 (1952):1–9; Wayne A. R. Leys, *Ethics for Policy Decisions: The Art of Asking Deliberative Questions* (New York: Greenwood, 1968); Frederick C. Mosher, *Democracy and the Public Service* (New York: Oxford University Press, 1968), pp. 209–215; and Thomas P. Murphy, "Ethical Dilemmas for Urban Administrators," *Urbanism Past and Present* (University of Wisconsin-Milwaukee), No. 4 (Summer, 1977):33–40.

standards about what is "good" practice. Professionals consider themselves as experts in their respective fields, and the application of that expertise is expected to further the public interest.

The dilemmas that can arise in pursuing professionalism can be seen in terms of client relations. Social workers may have professional standards regarding family counseling that cannot be met because of excessive caseloads. High caseloads can result in treating people as numbers and not as people. Government, then, can become cold and indifferent to human problems.[21] What is the proper course of action for the social worker? Should the worker provide substandard counseling to all families, selectively provide counseling to some families while largely ignoring others, publicly complain of the caseload, or resign in protest? Similar problems are involved in the following examples. Should therapists in a mental hospital be required to treat patients who in the professionals' judgment cannot benefit from treatment? Should teachers be expected to give passing grades to students who have not mastered the subject matter because the school district does not want a high dropout rate? What should police officers do when they think courts are excessively lenient in sentencing persons convicted of narcotics trafficking? Is there any single, obvious ethical course of action to take in these instances?

The value of allowing for citizen participation easily can conflict with the value of professionalism.[22] On the one hand, professionals in government consider themselves the embodiment of expertise and think they should be given relative freedom in applying that expertise. On the other hand, in a democratic society citizens should not only have access to government but also be involved in policy deliberations. Local school officials continuously confront this problem. Those officials having undergone professional training can be said to know what types of education are needed for children, yet citizen and parental pressures are strong in demanding a voice about school curriculum. For example, what should be the relative roles of school board members, administrators, teachers, students, parents, and citizens in determining the extent to which sex education should be taught in the schools? The administrators and teachers are likely to consider all of the others as amateurs, not suitably

---

[21] Paul H. Douglas, *Ethics in Government* (Cambridge, Mass.: Harvard University Press, 1952), pp. 28–29.

[22] A study of federal executives found that as many as a third held some anti-democratic views. For example, 27 percent agreed with the following statement: "To bring about great changes for the benefit of mankind often requires cruelty and even ruthlessness." Bob L. Wynia, "Federal Bureaucrat's Attitudes Toward a Democratic Ideology," *Public Administration Review*, 34 (1974):156–162.

informed in dealing with these kinds of issues. A professionally dominated agency or government can deny the general public the opportunity for democratic direction and decision making.[23]

Government workers are said to be public servants, but what does that mean? There is no operational definition of this concept, and, without such a definition, individual workers easily can rationalize almost any behavior as being in the public interest. Police officers and prison guards may consider that brutality furthers the value of public safety. State highway officials acting in the public interest may disregard the problems of families forced to vacate their residences because of freeway construction.[24]

Loyalty to a political administration is another competing value. Woodrow Wilson in an 1887 essay proposed a science of administration in which bureaucrats would exercise their professionalism while remaining politically neutral.[25] The preceding chapter discussed career executive systems in which high-level career administrators are permitted to become extensively involved in policy making yet are expected to remain flexible to changing directions in policy with changes in partisan administrations.[26] The potential for conflict is obvious between the values of unquestioning obedience and professionalism.[27] Should professionals in the Department of Defense be expected to accept administration policies that are considered to jeopardize national security? At the local level, "good" politics may require curtailing municipal expenditures for sewage treatment, but "good" sanitary engineering may dictate higher outlays. Administrators simultaneously are expected to follow orders and provide leadership, to be subservient and exercise initiative. Failure to take initiative can be considered "passive immorality," but taking initiative can be considered as politicizing administration and being disloyal.[28]

---

[23] Mosher, *Democracy and the Public Service*, p. 212.

[24] Rowland Egger, "Responsibility in Administration: An Exploratory Essay," in Martin, ed., *Public Administration and Democracy*, pp. 311–314, and Eugene P. Dvorin and Robert H. Simmons, *From Amoral to Humane Bureaucracy* (San Francisco: Canfield, 1972).

[25] Woodrow Wilson, "The Study of Administration," *Political Science Quarterly*, 2 (1887):197–222 and reprinted in *Political Science Quarterly*, 56 (1941):481–506.

[26] For a discussion of the British experience in ethical standards for career administration, see F. J. Tickner, "Ethical Guidelines for Administrators: Comparison with Whitehall," *Public Administration Review*, 34 (1974):587–592.

[27] Victor A. Thompson, "Bureaucracy in a Democratic Society," in Martin, ed., *Public Administration and Democracy*, pp. 206–209.

[28] George A. Graham, *Morality in American Politics* (New York: Random House, 1952), pp. 193–198.

Off-the-Job Conduct

Expectations about government employee behavior cover matters off the job as well as on the job.[29] A once common requirement at the local level was that female employees remain unmarried as a condition for retaining their jobs. The justification was that married women belong at home and should not be permitted to deny jobs to males who needed to support their families. A sometimes enforced rule, especially for school teachers, has been that employees should not be seen frequenting public drinking establishments. Church attendance, if not a requirement, often has been considered a highly recommended practice for public workers.

Sometimes the restrictions that are imposed are seemingly mundane, yet can have major effects on personnel. One example is the length of hair or, for men, the wearing of beards and mustaches. In 1976, the United States Supreme Court upheld the power of a local government to impose regulations on haircuts and the like for police officers.[30] The Court reasoned that short haircuts helped make police officers recognizable to the public and helped build esprit de corps among the officers. In reaching its decision, the Court argued that the objecting officers as employees and not as private citizens had the burden to prove their constitutional rights were being violated. In other words, the presumption was that the government operated within constitutional limits until employees could prove the contrary. Major complaints also have arisen in the military over hair-length restrictions.

Alcohol and drug abuse can be grounds for denying a person employment and for dismissing an employee, since alcohol and drug usage can markedly reduce worker performance. Sometimes the reduced performance may only reduce the efficiency of an agency, but in other circumstances there may be more far-reaching effects. Fire fighters who use drugs may inadvertently kill themselves or their co-workers on the job. Alcoholic bus drivers endanger their passengers as well as themselves. Police officers who use narcotics are unlikely to be effective in policing drug traffic and may well be "on the take."

Applicants for public jobs and current government workers are treated differently concerning alcohol and drug abuse. Applicants are subject to physical examinations that can detect excessive alcohol and drug usage. Polygraph tests have been used, but that practice has been challenged as an invasion of privacy. Regardless of the detection measure employed, excessive alcohol or drug usage normally disqualifies applicants, especially those applying for public safety jobs. On the other hand,

---

[29] See W. D. Heisel and Richard M. Gladstone, "Off-the-Job Conduct as a Disciplinary Problem," *Public Personnel Review*, 29 (1968):23–28.

[30] *Kelley v. Johnson*, 425 U.S. 238 (1976).

employees are treated more positively. Governments at all levels have established programs that attempt to provide early warning of individuals who may become addicted. Counseling often is provided free of charge. Dismissal is avoided until treatment and counseling efforts are considered to have failed and the worker's performance has become consistently unsatisfactory. Of course, not all governments have such humane approaches, and within any government wide variations may exist.[31]

Governments also screen applicants concerning criminal offenses. From a criminal justice viewpoint, rehabilitation of ex-offenders is often dependent upon their ability to secure employment, and practices barring the hiring of ex-offenders thwart rehabilitation. For that reason, the federal government has a program for helping ex-offenders obtain jobs in the government. An individual's criminal record is to be evaluated in relation to the job for which he or she is being considered. This procedure presumably allows for the hiring of many ex-offenders. In practice, however, the ex-offenders program has helped little. A 1976 study found that federal agencies and the Civil Service Commission had given little emphasis to hiring ex-offenders.[32]

Where one lives is another aspect of private life that government may control. Statutes and ordinances that require employees to reside within the jurisdiction employing them are justified on several grounds. Municipal employees by living within their city supposedly gain understanding of the mores and problems of the community. In jurisdictions that require applicants for jobs to be residents, would-be "interlopers" are denied jobs. One assumption is that employees residing within the jurisdiction will spend their incomes there, thereby stimulating local business. By requiring public safety workers to live within the jurisdiction, fast response to emergencies during off-duty hours is facilitated.

Racial considerations are involved in residency requirements. As nonwhites have increased in numbers in central cities and whites have moved to suburban communities, there has been increasing pressure to adopt residency requirements. Proponents contend that, without these requirements, a city's population could be predominantly nonwhite while

---

[31] For discussions of the implementation of the Alcoholic Rehabilitation Act of 1971 in the federal government, see John M. Stevens, *Managerial Commitment, Policy Receptivity, and Policy Implementation in Public Sector Organizations* (Buffalo: Ph.D. Dissertation, State University of New York at Buffalo, 1976); *Most Agency Programs for Employees with Alcohol-Related Problems Still Ineffective* (Washington: General Accounting Office, 1977; and House Committee on Government Operations, *Federal Employee Alcoholism Programs: Hearings*, 94th Cong., 2d sess. (Washington: Government Printing Office, 1976). See also Frank A. Malinoski, "Employee Drug Abuse in Municipal Government," *Public Personnel Management*, 4 (1975):59–62.

[32] *Civil Service Commission Actions and Procedures Do Not Help Ex-Offenders Get Jobs With the Federal Government* (Washington: General Accounting Office, 1976).

the government's work force was predominantly white. The issue has produced tensions between white and nonwhite employees.

Not all jurisdictions have residency requirements. The issue obviously is moot at the federal level and largely moot at the state level. Some states, however, do exercise control over residency for their local governments. Indiana, for instance, requires all police officers and fire fighters to live within the county of the city that hires them; the State specifically exempts school teachers from residency restrictions. California has prohibited residency requirements for its cities and counties. A survey of the fifty largest cities in the country found that about half had some residency requirements, although often these were limited to public safety workers.[33] Restrictions are most common in the north central states and least common in the west.[34]

Despite efforts to overturn residency requirements, they have been upheld by the judicial system. In 1976 in *McCarthy* v. *Philadelphia Civil Service Commission*, the United States Supreme Court upheld that City's residency requirement that was used to dismiss a firefighter who had moved to a suburb in New Jersey.[35] McCarthy unsuccessfully contended that his constitutional right to the freedom of travel had been violated by the residency requirement. While the right to travel has been recognized in other court cases, the Court found no such right for government workers as pertaining to restrictions on residency.[36]

Government imposes standards on employees' sex lives, although the standards vary greatly from one jurisdiction to another. The morals of "a little old lady from Dubuque" is sometimes expected.[37] The law is unsettled about what types of restrictions are permissible. For example, in 1975 a federal court upheld the dismissal of an unwed school teacher for having a man spend the night in her home, while another court disallowed the dismissal of another unwed school teacher for becoming pregnant.[38] Restrictions on sexual behavior generally must be shown to

[33] "Municipal Employee Residency Requirements and Equal Protection," *Yale Law Journal*, 84 (1975):1684–1704.

[34] James R. Mandish and Laurie S. Frankel, "Personnel Practices in the Municipal Police Service: 1976," *Urban Data Service*, 8 (December, 1976):1–14. See also Michael Hacker, "Locked in the City: Residency Requirements for Municipal Employees," *Industrial and Labor Relations Forum*, 11 (1975):200–223.

[35] *McCarthy* v. *Philadelphia Civil Service Commission*, 424 U.S. 645 (1976).

[36] See *Shapiro* v. *Thompson*, 394 U.S. 618 (1969); *Detroit Police Officers Association* v. *City of Detroit*, 385 Mich. 519, 190 N.W. 2d 97 (1971); *Dunn* v. *Blumstein*, 405 U.S. 331 (1972); *Detroit Police Officers Association* v. *City of Detroit*, 391 Mich. 44, 214 N.W. 2d 803 (1974); and *Memorial Hospital* v. *Maricopa County*, 415 U.S. 250 (1974).

[37] Lawrence Speiser on Subcommittee on Retirement and Employee Benefits, House Committee on Post Office and Civil Service, *Right to Privacy of Federal Employees*, 93d Cong., 1st and 2d sess. (Washington: Government Printing Office, 1974), p. 38.

[38] *Sullivan* v. *Meade County Independent School District No. 101*, 387 F. Supp. 1237 (1975) and *Andrews* v. *Drew Municipal Separate School District*, 507 F. 2d 611 (1975).

be job related. Therefore, a federal court disallowed the Internal Revenue Service from firing some of its agents who had rented a "shack pad" for off-duty use.[39] Another stipulation is that standards must not be so vague that employees cannot determine what behavior is acceptable. This vagueness standard, however, did not protect a schoolteacher who each night turned on the outside lights of his home and performed "unnatural" acts on a mannequin on his lawn.[40]

Inquiries into employees' sex lives and other investigations can threaten the constitutional right to privacy.[41] Personality tests ask questions that easily can be considered beyond the appropriate area of governmental inquiry. The Minnesota Multiphasic Personality Inventory is one such test, asking people the extent to which the following statements reflect their attitudes: "I am happy most of the time. I get mad easily and then get over it soon. I believe in the second coming of Christ. I wish I were not bothered by thoughts about sex."[42] An extreme example of the extensive detail that can be involved in governmental inquiry into private matters are the questions that were asked of a Defense Department worker who openly admitted being a homosexual: "Do you have any recollection when you had your first homosexual experience? What did it consist of? With how many partners did you have homosexual experiences at college? As for your relationship, could you define, or could you explain the type of relationship you had, that is, the mechanics or tactics or technique?"[43] At what point should a government employee's private life be truly private and beyond governmental inquiry?

CIVIL RIGHTS

The United States Constitution prescribes civil rights for all citizens, and since its adoption in 1789 there has been continuing debate over what limits should be placed upon those freedoms. It is recognized that rights are rarely absolute. Unfettered freedom of speech could be disastrous, as

[39] *Major* v. *Hampton*, 413 F. Supp. 66 (1976).

[40] *Wishart* v. *McDonald*, 500 F. 2d 1110 (1974). See also Richard H. C. Clay, "The Dismissal of Public School Teachers for Aberrant Behavior," *Kentucky Law Journal*, 64 (1975–76):911–36.

[41] *Griswold* v. *Connecticut*, 381 U.S. 11 (1966), is a landmark case establishing the right to privacy. The case dealt with a private citizen and not a government employee. See "Application of the Constitutional Privacy Right to Exclusions and Dismissal from Public Employment," *Duke Law Journal*, 1973 (1973), 1037–1062.

[42] Minnesota Multiphasic Personality Inventory as quoted in Lawrence H. Mirel, "The Limits of Governmental Inquiry into the Private Lives of Government Employees," *Boston University Law Review*, 46 (1966):18.

[43] Lawrence Speiser in Subcommittee on Retirement and Employee Benefits, *Rights to Privacy of Federal Employees: Hearings*, p. 30. Even more explicit questions were asked the government employee but they have been omitted here to avoid offending sensitive readers.

in the case of a person "falsely shouting fire in a theater and causing a panic."[44] The problem, however, is more complicated when applied to public employees, who are expected to assume responsibilities when accepting government positions.[45] This section explores three aspects of the problem—the rights of employees vis-à-vis loyalty and security issues, exercise by employees of their constitutional right to free speech, and the right to participate in the political process.

Loyalty and Security

Loyalty-security regulations have been used since the Revolutionary War, but these have become a standard aspect of the public service only since the 1930s.[46] The House Un-American Activities Committee, chaired by Martin Dies (D, Texas), held hearings in the 1930s and 1940s alleging that disloyalty within the federal bureaucracy was widespread, and Senator Joseph McCarthy (R, Wisconsin) assumed the same type of role in the 1950s.[47] The concern over ferreting out subversives was equally common at the state and local levels. States passed laws against treason, rebellion and insurrection, sedition, criminal syndicalism, criminal anarchy, displaying communist flags, and sabotage. Several states even passed laws against the wearing of disguises in public.[48] All levels of government demanded loyalty of both private citizens and government employees.

The reasons for the anti-communist movement of the 1950s are numerous. There was a sincere concern that communists, under the presumed direction of the Soviet Union, were attempting to create unrest within the United States, were directing sabotage activities, and were

---

[44] *Schenck v. United States*, 249 U.S. 47 (1919).

[45] For a discussion of this issue as it applies to private corporation employees, see David W. Ewing, *Freedom Inside the Organization: Bringing Civil Liberties to the Workplace* (New York: Dutton, 1977).

[46] For extended discussions of loyalty-security programs affecting both private citizens and public employees, see Appleby, *Morality and Administration*, pp. 176–199; Alan Barth, *The Loyalty of Free Men* (New York: Viking, 1951); Eleanor Bontecou, *The Federal Loyalty-Security Program* (Ithaca, N.Y.: Cornell University Press, 1953); Commission on Government Security, *Report* (Washington: Government Printing Office, 1957); Robert E. Cushman, "The Purge of Federal Employees Accused of Disloyalty," *Public Administration Review*, 3 (1943):297–316; Walter Gellhorn, *Security, Loyalty, and Science* (Ithaca, N.Y.: Cornell University Press, 1950); Mark R. Joelson, "The Dismissal of Civil Servants in the Interests of National Security," *Public Law*, (1963): 51–75; David H. Rosenbloom, *Federal Service and the Constitution: The Development of the Public Employment Relationship* (Ithaca, N.Y.: Cornell University Press, 1971), pp. 144–197; and Nathaniel Weyl, *The Battle Against Disloyalty* (New York: Crowell, 1951).

[47] Joe McCarthy, *McCarthyism: The Fight for America* (New York: Devin-Adair, 1952).

[48] Walter Gellhorn, ed., *The States and Subversion* (Ithaca, N.Y.: Cornell University Press, 1952).

attempting to steal secrets about nuclear weapons technology, military strategies, and the like. Political considerations also were at stake, with those out of power challenging those in power as being too lenient with subversives. The 1952 Republican party platform attacked the Truman administration: "'By the appeasement of Communists at home and abroad it has permitted communists and fellow travelers to serve in many key agencies and to infiltrate our American Life.'"[49]

Laws were passed and executive orders were issued by chief executives that curtailed the activities of those who sought the violent overthrow of the government. The Hatch Act of 1939 barred federal workers from "membership in any political party or organization which advocates the overthrow of our constitutional form of government." In 1943 President Franklin D. Roosevelt issued Executive Order 9300, controlling the subversive activities of federal employees. In 1947 President Harry S. Truman issued Executive Order 9835, which established procedures for the government's loyalty program. In 1950 Congress passed the Subversive Activities Control Act, and in 1953 President Dwight D. Eisenhower issued Executive Order 10450, replacing Truman's E. O. 9835. The Eisenhower order, which has been amended several times since its issuance, remains the governing policy of the federal government as concerns loyalty and security matters. State-level Little Hatch Acts also have loyalty provisions.

Loyalty and security are not synonyms. Loyalty refers to being faithful to the existing form of government and not seeking its overthrow through violent means. A person can be loyal and yet endanger national security. A loyal employee who has friends who are subversives may inadvertently leak government secrets. Executive Order 10450 provides for dismissing an employee who may be subject to "coercion, influence or pressure." An employee with relatives in a communist-dominated country might be blackmailed into leaking government secrets under threat that the lives of those relatives are endangered. Similarly, a person who keeps secret his homosexuality may become subject to blackmail. Alcoholics and drug addicts may be security risks in that they may divulge secret information when under the influence. Executive Order 10450 proscribes "any criminal, infamous, dishonest, immoral, or notoriously disgraceful conduct, habitual use of intoxicants to excess, drug addiction or sexual perversion."[50]

Loyalty and security procedures differ. Loyalty programs typically apply to all government employees, whereas security programs apply

---

[49] Republican Party Platform as quoted in Rosenbloom, *Federal Service and the Constitution*, p. 147.

[50] Executive Order 10450 as amended in 5 U.S.C. § 7311.

only to sensitive positions. Sensitive positions involve the handling of information related to national security and can include clerical as well as higher level positions. Loyalty programs often require the employee to take or sign an oath affirming allegiance to the government. A relatively superficial investigation of the person's background may be made, such as a routine check of FBI files. Forms may be sent to the person's former employers asking whether there is any reason to believe the person is disloyal. The person's loyalty is presumed unless negative information is reported.

Security, on the other hand, involves more extensive and continuous investigation of the individual. At the federal level, a full-field investigation is required of persons being considered for sensitive positions. Federal investigators personally interview the job candidate's current and former employers, friends, teachers, and neighbors. Once appointed, the individual may be periodically reviewed, and each time he or she is promoted and/or assigned different responsibilities another investigation will be undertaken. As of 1974, the cost of one full-field investigation by the United States Civil Service Commission was $675.[51]

While these distinctions between loyalty and security exist, they produce confusion. A person may be dismissed as a security risk because 1) he is disloyal, 2) he may be subject to blackmail, or 3) he did not report all relevant activities in completing the necessary paperwork for a security clearance. In the latter instance, an oversight on the part of the worker may be construed as a deliberate attempt to withhold information.[52] The result is that persons dismissed through security proceedings often are considered to be disloyal. The repercussions are life-long, in some cases denying a person the ability to pursue his occupation in either government or the private sector.

Loyalty-security programs have been challenged as violating various constitutional provisions. Article I of the Constitution prohibits Congress from passing bills of attainder, which are legislative acts that find persons guilty without a trial. Also prohibited are ex post facto laws that change the legal status of actions after they have been committed. In 1946 the Supreme Court ruled that Congress had passed a bill of attainder by including in an appropriation bill a provision prohibiting paying the salaries of three specified employees who were believed to be disloyal.[53] However, the Court in 1951 upheld the right of the City of Los Angeles

[51] Robert J. Drummond (U.S. Civil Service Commission) in Subcommittee on Retirement and Employee Benefits, *Right to Privacy of Federal Employees: Hearings*, p. 79. Also see *Proposals to Resolve Longstanding Problems in Investigation of Federal Employees* (Washington: General Accounting Office, 1977).

[52] *Harrison v. McNamara*, 228 F. Supp. 406 (1964), affirmed in 380 U.S. 261 (1964).

[53] *United States v. Lovett*, 328 U.S. 303 (1946).

to require employees to sign an oath to the effect that for the preceding five years they had not been members of any group advocating the violent overthrow of the government. The Court disagreed with the contention that this was an ex post facto law:

> We think that a municipal employer is not disabled because it is an agency of the State from inquiring of its employees as to matters that may prove relevant to their fitness and suitability for the public service. Past conduct may well relate to present fitness; past loyalty may have a reasonable relationship to present and future trust.[54]

The First Amendment to the Constitution guarantees the freedom of speech and the right to assemble peaceably. This amendment and the other initial amendments to the Constitution that make up the Bill of Rights have been largely applied to state and local governments through the Fourteenth Amendment: "No State shall make or enforce any law which shall abridge the privileges or immunities of citizens of the United States." Loyalty and security programs at all levels of government have been challenged as infringing upon employees' rights to speak freely and to associate with persons of their own choosing.

Courts have attempted to differentiate between thought and action and to differentiate among types of actions. Although there may be an absolute right to think the government should be overthrown, there is no absolute right to advocate its overthrow. Nevertheless, loyalty programs have to some extent invaded the freedom of thought. Loyalty review boards, for instance, have interrogated employees about their ownership of books written by Lenin and Marx.[55] In 1959 a case was brought before the Supreme Court involving the dismissal of a federal employee because, among other matters, he had "subscribed to the USSR Information Bulletin and had purchased copies of the Daily Worker and New Masses."[56] The dismissal was reversed by the Court on the grounds that due process protections had not been afforded the employee.

Adler v. *Board of Education of City of New York* (1952) illustrates the problem of preserving freedom of speech and association while protecting society from subversion.[57] In that case, the Supreme Court reviewed New York State's Feinberg Law as applied by New York City

---

[54] *Garner* v. *Board of Public Works of City of Los Angeles*, 341 U.S. 716 (1951). See also *Dennis* v. *United States*, 341 U.S. 494 (1951); *Joint Anti-Fascist Refugee Committee* v. *McGrath*, 341 U.S. 123 (1951); *Yates* v. *United States*, 354 U.S. 298 (1957); *Barenblatt* v. *United States*, 360 U.S. 109 (1959); and *Communist Party* v. *Subversive Activities Control Board*, 367 U.S. 1 (1961)

[55] See Adam Yarmolinsky, *Case Studies in Personnel Security* (Washington: Bureau of National Affairs, 1955), pp. 74–75.

[56] *Vitarelli* v. *Seaton*, 359 U.S. 535 (1959).

[57] *Adler* v. *Board of Education of City of New York*, 342 U.S. 485 (1952).

to its school teachers. No person could be a teacher who speaks, writes, or "deliberately advocates, advises or teaches that the government . . . should be overthrown or overturned by force, violence or any unlawful means." Moreover, a list of organizations that advocated such overthrow was compiled, and membership in any of these organizations was to "constitute prima facie evidence for disqualification" for a government position. The Court upheld the law as protecting children from subversive influences. No abridgement of free speech or association was found: "If they [the teachers] do not choose to work on such terms, they are at liberty to retain their beliefs and associations and go elsewhere. Has the State thus deprived them of any right to free speech or assembly? We think not." In making this ruling, the Court enunciated the "privilege doctrine," namely that holding public office is a privilege and a public employee's rights may be limited.

The three justices who dissented in the *Adler* case argued that the Feinberg Law violated free speech and thought. "This is another of those rapidly multiplying legislative enactments which make it dangerous—this time for school teachers—to think or say anything except what a transient majority happen to approve at the moment." The law was considered to find one guilty for membership. Excessive powers were placed in the hands of dismissing officials. "Public officials with such powers are not public servants; they are public masters."

Since the *Adler* decision, the Court has moved in the direction of greater First Amendment protections for public employees. Shortly after Adler, in *Wieman* v. *Updegraff* (1952) the Court ruled against an Oklahoma loyalty oath on the grounds that it penalized workers for membership when "membership may be innocent."[58] In that case, the Court largely rejected the privilege doctrine and held that employees had "substantial interest," given the far-reaching consequences of being dismissed for loyalty-security reasons. In 1966 the court took a similar position when an Arizona school teacher challenged a loyalty oath.[59] The Court held that the oath violated the freedom of association; belonging to an organization that advocated the violent overthrow of the government did not necessarily mean the person advocated such overthrow.[60]

---

[58] *Wieman* v. *Updegraff*, 344 U.S. 183 (1952).

[59] *Elfbrandt* v. *Russell*, 384 U.S. 11 (1966).

[60] In *Haskett* v. *Washington*, 294 F. Supp. 912 (1968), a district court held against a loyalty oath that prohibited membership in subversive organizations. The court noted that membership may be passive and inert. In *Stewart* v. *Washington*, 301 F. Supp. 610 (1969), a district court held that a statute unconstitutionally applied to general advocacy of overthrow and not overthrow by force or violence and applied regardless of whether the overthrow was only in the distant future. For an account of the 1949–52 loyalty oath controversy at the University of California, see David P. Gardner, *The California Oath Controversy* (Berkeley: University of California Press, 1967).

The protection from being a witness against oneself or self-incrimination is part of the Fifth Amendment. A landmark case involving this right is *Slochower v. Board of Higher Education of the City of New York* (1956).[61] That City's Charter provided for the automatic dismissal of any employee who used his protection against self-incrimination in answering questions about his official conduct. Slochower used that Fifth Amendment right, not before representatives of New York City, but before a United States Senate committee, and because of that was dismissed from the faculty of Brooklyn College. The Supreme Court ruled against this action, maintaining that no "sinister meaning" should be imputed from the exercise of one's constitutional rights. "The privilege against self-incrimination would be reduced to a hollow mockery if its exercise could be taken as equivalent either to a confession of guilt or a conclusive presumption of perjury."[62]

The Fifth Amendment not only protects against self-incrimination but also against being "deprived of life, liberty, or property without due process of law." The same protection is afforded to citizens against state governments, as provided in the Fourteenth Amendment. Additionally, in criminal cases the Sixth Amendment provides the right of a person to know the "nature and cause of accusation" and to "be confronted with the witnesses against him." Among the varied aspects of due process are the presentation of specific charges against a person, the presentation of evidence that substantiates those charges, the right to cross-examine evidence and witnesses and to present additional evidence and witnesses, representation by counsel, the impartiality or objectivity of the person or persons responsible for reaching a decision, the adherence to procedures prescribed by law and administrative regulation, and review of action by an appellate body (usually a court). The courts have applied these protections to varying degrees in cases involving the dismissal of public employees for loyalty-security reasons.

Due process considerations affect private workers as well as public ones. In 1959 the Supreme Court ruled against the denial of a security clearance for an aeronautical engineer employed by a private corporation because he had not been granted a hearing, which would have given him the safeguards of confrontation and cross-examination (*Greene v. McElroy*).[63] The denial of the clearance had had the effect of preventing

---

[61] *Slochower v. Board of Higher Education of City of New York*, 350 U.S. 551 (1956). See also *Sweezy v. New Hampshire*, 354 U.S. 234 (1957) and *Watkins v. United States*, 354 U.S. 178 (1957).

[62] In other cases, the Court has provided similar protection for employees testifying before grand juries. *Gardner v. Broderick*, 392 U.S. 273 (1968) and *Uniformed Sanitation Men's Association v. Commissioner*, 392 U.S. 280 (1968).

[63] *Greene v. McElroy*, 360 U.S. 474 (1959).

the engineer from pursuing his occupation, since without the clearance he would be unable to work at most private firms needing his specialty. Two years later, however, in *Cafeteria and Restaurant Workers Union v. McElroy*, the Court held that such a hearing was not required for a restaurant worker who was privately employed but whose job was on a military installation.[64] The Court ruled: "The Fifth Amendment does not require a trial-type hearing in every conceivable case of government impairment of private interest." Four of the Court's nine justices dissented: "The Court holds that petitioner has a right not to have her identification badge taken away for an 'arbitrary' reason, but no right to be told in detail what the reason is, or to defend her own innocence, in order to show, perhaps, that the true reason for deprivation was one forbidden by the Constitution."

Vagueness violates due process and the First Amendment. If laws and regulations are written in such ways that employees are unable to determine what activities are proscribed, then they cannot suitably determine the appropriate course of behavior without accepting the risk that their actions will be grounds for dismissal. The Supreme Court has struck down some loyalty oaths as being unconstitutionally vague (see *Keyishian v. Board of Regents of the University of the State of New York*, 1967).[65] Similarly, due process usually precludes vague charges being made against a person. However, the courts have been willing to accept relatively loosely stated loyalty charges for the basis of dismissal.

In *Bailey v. Richardson* a United States appellate court upheld disloyalty proceedings against a woman, and the Supreme Court in a per curiam opinion affirmed (1950).[66] Bailey, after having been furloughed because of a reduction in force, was denied reinstatement to a federal position because there were "reasonable grounds" for believing she was disloyal. The charges against her lacked specificity, as was acknowledged by the appellate court. She was not allowed to cross-examine her accusers nor even told who they were. While she was afforded an oral hearing, the only witnesses were herself and those persons she used in her own defense. The appellate court ruled that this procedure had not violated due process in that the government had a need to avoid revealing the methods used in detecting disloyalty. The court agreed that this seemed like "the Nazi judicial process" but concluded "an applicant for

---

[64] *Cafeteria and Restaurant Workers Union v. McElroy*, 367 U.S. 886 (1961).

[65] *Keyishian v. Board of Regents of the University of the State of New York*, 385 U.S. 589 (1967). See also *Baggett v. Bullitt*, 377 U. S. 360 (1964), involving a Washington State loyalty oath, and *Whitehill v. Elkins*, 389 U.S. 54 (1967) involving a Maryland teachers' oath.

[66] *Bailey v. Richardson*, 182 F. 2d 46 (1950), affirmed 341 U.S. 918 (1950).

office has no constitutional right to a hearing or a specification of the reasons why he is not appointed."

The Supreme Court has held the executive branch responsible for adhering to its own rules of the game in loyalty-security proceedings as part of the due process requirement. One such case involved the dismissal of a foreign service officer in the State Department.[67] The Secretary of State had been empowered to use "absolute discretion" in loyalty-security cases, a power that greatly limited due process requirements. However, the Court found that since the Secretary had issued administrative regulations prescribing procedures for handling these cases, the power of "absolute discretion" could not be exercised. Given that the established procedures had not been followed in dismissing the employee, the due process requirement had not been met.

Two Supreme Court cases of the 1950s involved alternative proceedings that could be taken against employees. *Cole* v. *Young* (1956) involved the dismissal of a federal food and drug inspector for having "a close association with individuals reliably reported to be Communists."[68] This dismissal was unreviewable according to the 1950 subversive control legislation, but Cole claimed the proceedings were reviewable by the Civil Service Commission under the Veterans Preference Act. The Court agreed with Cole, thereby substantially extending due process requirements in his case, in particular requiring determination first be made that his position could affect "national security."[69]

Three years later in *Vitarelli* v. *Seaton*, the Court dealt with the dismissal choices available to the Secretary of Interior.[70] As a Schedule A appointee, Vitarelli could be dismissed without any reason being given or he could be dismissed for loyalty-security reasons. The Secretary chose the second route but later altered the proceedings to dismissal as a Schedule A appointee. The Supreme Court held that having commenced dismissal for loyalty-security reasons, the Secretary was bound to follow the procedures established by him in departmental regulations. Since those procedures had not been followed, Vitarelli was ordered to be reinstated. Four of the nine justices partially dissented, claiming this requirement gave "governmental action the empty meaning of confetti throwing."

The *Vitarelli* case also is important in that it helped to establish

---

[67] *Service* v. *Dulles*, 354 U.S. 363 (1957). See also *Peters* v. *Hobby*, 349 U.S. 331 (1955).

[68] *Cole* v. *Young*, 351 U.S. 536 (1956).

[69] The Court restricted the term of "national security" to mean national safety and not simply national welfare.

[70] *Vitarelli* v. *Seaton*, 359 U.S. 535 (1959).

limits upon the scope of inquiry into the private lives of employees. In an administrative hearing, Vitarelli was asked numerous questions about his educational, social, and political beliefs. The questions included: "Do you know what Black Mountain Transcendentalism is? I was wondering whether you had ever heard of Consumers Union? Do I interpret your statement correctly that maybe Negroes and Jews were denied some of their constitutional rights at present?" The Court held these and other questions violated the administrative regulation requiring questions to be relevant.

While the *Vitarelli* case may seem to have broadened the protections available to public employees, there is a catch. Unfavorable material can be compiled in employee files that later may have a detrimental effect. A 1972 federal appellate court case illustrates the problem.[71] An employee in the Federal Housing Administration was changed from a nonsensitive classification to a sensitive one, thereby requiring a security clearance. The report on the full field investigation stated that two of his friends had homosexual "mannerisms," and the implication was that he was a homosexual. His position then was changed back to a nonsensitive one. The employee sued, claiming that he had been denied a security clearance and that the references to homosexuality should be removed from his file. The court disagreed, finding that he had not been denied a security clearance but that the position had been merely reclassified. The court said he had no right to ask for a change in his record since he had not been harmed in any way, whereas denial of a security clearance would have been harm.

Although the furor over loyalty-security programs has long subsided, reaching a balanced perspective on the efforts to ensure employee loyalty and protect national security remains a difficult task. It is easy to condemn what transpired in the 1940s and 1950s. These efforts to ensure loyalty and security seem to have been largely unsuccessful in surfacing subversives. Careers of many loyal persons both in and out of government were destroyed, and those dismissed under loyalty-security proceedings continue to find difficulty in practicing their chosen occupations. What could be seen as totally unconstrained witch-hunts had the effect of intimidating public employees, forcing them to subscribe to orthodox views rather than encouraging them to use their intellects. One observer summed up the situation in this way:

> You should not discuss the admission of Red China to the U.N.; you should not advocate interracial equality; you should not mix with people unless you know them very well; if you want to read the *Nation* you should not take it to the office; if you bring it to the office, you should explain in considerable

---

[71] *Finley v. Hampton*, 473 F. 2d 180 (1972).

detail why you have it with you; you should take certain books off your private bookshelves. . . .[72]

Loyalty-security programs undoubtedly have discouraged many highly qualified, loyal citizens from applying for government positions and encouraged many government workers to resign in disgust.

In contrast with this negative view, probably few would deny government the power to protect itself from disloyalty and carelessness of its own employees. The idea of subversion from within directed by governments from abroad gains some credence given international events. When governments are overthrown and replaced by communist regimes, it is understandable for some people to suspect that government in this country may be under similar attack from within. The late Senator McCarthy may be condemned as a tub-thumper. He, however, did not single-handedly create a mood of distrust, since that already existed and has been a continuing strain throughout the nation's history.

Loyalty-security issues should not be thought of as largely in the past. Government employees still are required to sign loyalty oaths. Security checks and full-field investigations still are made. The legal bases and administrative machinery for these activities remain in place and could be "cranked up" should there be a resurgent concern that numerous subversives held important governmental positions. As has been seen, the courts have curtailed government in dismissing suspected employees and have sought to protect the civil freedoms of employees. Yet the possibility remains of a renewed effort to ferret out disloyal employees and other security risks.

Freedom of Speech

Issues over employees exercising their constitutional right to free speech arise not only in loyalty-security cases. Employees may be unquestionably loyal and present no risk to security but, as will be seen, may choose to speak on matters that become the center of controversy. In the United States, government employees generally have the freedom to resign their positions and then freely criticize their former agencies and the individuals involved. A common practice has been for disgruntled employees to resign in protest, and then to speak publicly against the government and to publish highly critical articles and books.[73] This practice is in contrast with the British system, in which the Official

---

[72] Marie Jahoda, "Morale in the Federal Civil Service," in Thorsten Sellen, ed., "Internal Security and Civil Rights," *Annals*, 300 (1955):111.

[73] Edward Weisband and Thomas M. Franck, *Resignation in Protest: Political and Ethical Choices between Loyalty to Team and Loyalty to Conscience in American Public Life* (New York: Grossman, 1975).

Secrets Act precludes current *and* former employees from divulging information about government agencies.

One major exception to this practice in the United States relates to national security. A former employee involved in military and other national security matters does not have the privilege of divulging government information. One of the most celebrated cases of this type involves Victor Marchetti, who resigned from the Central Intelligence Agency in 1969. Marchetti is under a court injunction requiring that all of his proposed speeches and publications about the CIA be submitted to that agency. The CIA has the authority to censor all material that Marchetti obtained while an agency employee. The injunction remains in effect for his lifetime.[74]

Resigning in protest is not a feasible alternative for many government workers. If an employee is not independently wealthy or does not have a job offer from another employer, resigning obviously will present financial obstacles. Even if finances are of no concern, an employee might be generally satisfied with her position and prefer not to resign. Therefore, the critical issue here is what speech rights can be exercised by employees without losing their jobs?

There are different types and purposes of speech. Speech may be internal to the agency, involving a confrontation between an employee and his supervisor or an employee criticizing the agency before a group of other employees. Courts have held that some degree of courtesy should be required. An employee is not free to speak to a superior in such terms as "bastard, you're a son of a bitch, you have such a little regimented mind."[75] Reckless, intemperate, insulting, and vituperative speech is not protected.[76]

Speech involving persons external to an agency usually is in the form of "whistle blowing," when employees seek to embarrass superiors and hopefully instigate changes in agency policies and practices.[77] The speech may be covert, such as a state employee privately telephoning a legislator, or overt, such as writing a letter to a newspaper's editor or even holding a press conference. Whistle blowing is usually considered to be

---

[74] *United States* v. *Marchetti*, 466 F. 2d 1309 (1972), and Anthony Lewis, "In the Censor's Grip," *New York Times* (November 10, 1977).

[75] *Starsky* v. *Williams*, 353 F. Supp. 900 (1972).

[76] *Pietrunti* v. *Board of Education* 319 A. 2d 262 (1974), and Kenneth Walters, "Employee Freedom of Speech," *Industrial Relations*, 15 (1976):26–43.

[77] Harry Grossman, "Public Employment and Free Speech: Can They Be Reconciled?" *Administrative Law Review*, 24 (1972):109–119; Mitchell J. Lindauer, "Government Employee Disclosures of Agency Wrongdoing: Protecting the Right to Blow the Whistle," *University of Chicago Law Review*, 42 (1975):530–561; and Henry V. Nickel, "The First Ammendment and Public Employees: An Emerging Constitutional Right to be a Policeman?" *George Washington Law Review*, 37 (1968):409–424.

intentional but it can be unintentional. For example, Dr. Jacqueline Verrett of the Food and Drug Administration did not intend or expect a furor to develop when she consented to be interviewed about the use of cyclamates as artificial sweeteners in foods and beverages. That interview ultimately resulted in halting the use of cyclamates.[78]

In intentional cases of whistle blowing, a conflict exists between administrative loyalty and loyalty to a "higher cause." The merit principle includes the idea that employees should loyally serve political administrations and not create problems by leaking information to administration opponents. The merit principle, however, also includes the idea that employees should serve the public interest, and it is likely that every administration conducts some activities that some people can consider not to be in the best interests of society.

Whistle blowing requires courage, since a person can lose his job in the process, but whistle blowers should not automatically be accorded the status of hero. In acting on his own initiative the whistle blower has appointed himself a judge of what should be brought to the public's attention. The whistle blower frequently is not in possession of the full facts, and sometimes he is motivated more by malice than by serving the public interest. Were every employee to act in this manner, government bureaucracies would become chaotic. Yet unqualified condemnation of whistle blowing is equally inappropriate, since the practice has brought to public attention important situations that otherwise would have been kept secret. Without an anonymous leaker, the public probably would not have learned about the government-sponsored study that allowed many syphilitic black persons go for decades without medical treatment.[79] Without a whistle blower, the public probably would not have learned of the secret files the Army was maintaining on private citizens.[80]

Free speech can be individual or collective. Whistle blowers often act as loners. In contrast, there have been some instances in which groups of employees have complained of government action. During the Vietnam War, some federal employees organized protest groups that issued newsletters and other publications against the War. Workers in the Department of Health, Education, and Welfare and in other departments participated in anti-war parades and other demonstrations. It should be noted, however, that these employees were exercising their speech rights

---

[78] Jacqueline Verrett, "Dr. Jacqueline Verrett," in Ralph Nader, Peter J. Petkas, and Kate Blackwell, eds., *Whistle Blowing: The Report of the Conference on Professional Responsibility* (New York: Grossman, 1972): pp. 90–97.

[79] Alan M. Katz, "Government Information Leaks and the First Amendment," *California Law Review*, 64 (1976):108–145.

[80] Christopher Pyle and Ralph Stein, "Christopher Pyle and Ralph Stein," in Nader, Petkas, and Blackwell, eds., *Whistle Blowing*, pp. 126–134.

without using classified information. HEW employees had access only to information generally available to the public. A different situation would have existed had Department of Defense employees been involved.[81]

The courts have moved in the direction of protecting the speech rights of public employees. One of the most important cases is *Pickering v. Board of Education*, decided by the United States Supreme Court in 1968.[82] Pickering, a school teacher in Illinois, wrote a letter to a newspaper criticizing how a series of bond issue proposals had been handled by the school system. He was dismissed for falsely impugning the "motives, honesty, integrity, truthfulness, responsibility, and competence" of the school board and administration. The Court, recognizing a need for public discussion on school issues, held that the school board's pronouncements on the need for voter approval of the bond issue should not be considered "conclusive."

> In sum, we hold that, in a case such as this, absent proof of false statements knowingly or recklessly made by him, a teacher's exercise of his right to speak on issues of public importance may not furnish the basis for his dismissal from public employment.[83]

As was discussed above, vagueness is a threat to the constitutional exercise of one's rights. If laws and the administrative regulations that are based upon them are vague, then employees may not know what speech is permissible and what is proscribed. The Supreme Court dealt with this problem in the case of *Arnett v. Kennedy* (1974).[84] Kennedy, an employee of the United States Office of Economic Opportunity, publicly claimed that his agency had bribed a local Community Action Agency (CAA) by promising to award a grant if the CAA followed specified practices. He was dismissed for "recklessly false and defamatory statements," in accordance with the Lloyd-La Follette Act, which provides for dismissal "only for such cause as will promote the efficiency" of the agency. Kennedy claimed the law was unconstitutionally vague, that he could not have known what types of speech were prohibited.

---

[81] See Cary Hershey, *Protest in the Public Service* (Lexington, Mass.: Heath, 1973), and David H. Rosenbloom, "Some Political Implications of the Drift Toward a Liberation of Federal Employees," *Public Administration Review*, 31 (1971):420–426.

[82] *Pickering* v. *Board of Education of Township High School District 205*, 391 U.S. 563 (1968).

[83] *Pickering* v. *Board of Education*. Four years later, two cases were decided by the Court that related to the freedom of speech issue: *Board of Regents of State Colleges* v. *Roth*, 408 U.S. 564 (1972), and *Perry* v. *Sinderman*, 408 U.S. 593 (1972). These cases are discussed in the last section of this chapter.

[84] *Arnett* v. *Kennedy*, 416 U.S. 134 (1974). See also Philip L. Martin, "The Improper Discharge of a Federal Employee by a Constitutionally Permissible Process: The OEO Case," *Administrative Law Review*, 28 (1976): 27–39.

Six of the Court's nine justices sided against Kennedy on the vagueness issue. The case is unusual in that the justices were unable to adopt a majority opinion. The concurring opinions generally held that Kennedy should have known what speech was permissible given that the law had been in effect since 1912. Justice William O. Douglas wrote a stirring dissent:

> The federal bureaucracy controls a vast conglomerate of people who walk more and more submissively to the dictates of their superiors . . . A pleasant manner, promotion of staff harmony, servility to the cadre, and promptness, civility and submissiveness are what count. The result is a great levelling of employees. They hear the beat of only one drum and march to it.[85]

Employees who have not completed a probationary period have limited protections in dismissal proceedings, but one right is the freedom of speech. This was made clear in the 1977 United States Supreme Court case of *Mt. Healthy City School District Board of Education* v. *Doyle*.[86] Doyle, an untenured school teacher, had done several things that displeased school officials, such as swearing at students and arguing with school cafeteria employees in front of students. Doyle called a local radio station to complain about a proposed dress code for the school district, and the board dismissed him, citing these incidents, including the telephone call. The Court held that he could not be dismissed for contacting the radio station, that this was a constitutionally protected form of speech. The Court noted that, as an untenured employee, Doyle could have been dismissed without any reason being provided. The school board, however, did not have the power to fire an employee for an unconstitutional reason.[87]

Agency reaction to whistle blowers and other outspoken employees may not be so direct as outright dismissal. Firing someone may not be an option if that someone has covertly leaked information. In response, stricter security measures over the control of information may be imposed. Where information leaks have been frequent, attempts will be made to uncover the persons involved. The Nixon administration "plumbers" used extreme measures in plugging leaks. Columnists,

---

[85] *Arnett* v. *Kennedy*, 416 U.S. 203 (1974). This case also is important in terms of procedural due process and is discussed in the last section of this chapter.

[86] *Mt. Healthy City School District Board of Education* v. *Doyle*, 429 U.S. 274 (1977); and "The Nonpartisan Freedom of Expression of Public Employees," *Michigan Law Review*, 76 (1977):365–404.

[87] The Court's decision did not reinstate Doyle. The Court remanded the case to a district court to determine whether the school board would have dismissed him for reasons other than the telephone call. It is possible that a government is barred from dismissing an employee for statements made in public but that those same statements made in private can be grounds for dismissal; see *Givhan* v. *Western Line Consolidated School District*, 555 F. 2d 1309 (1977), cert. granted 98 S. Ct. 1575 (1978).

notably Jack Anderson, were put under surveillance in order to uncover who was releasing information to the press.

If the whistle blower is no longer a government employee, dismissal is obviously precluded. The tactic, then, may be to undermine his credibility, as was the case of Daniel Ellsberg, who released the secret Pentagon Papers concerning the Vietnam War.[88] His psychiatrist's office was illegally entered, apparently in the hope that information could be obtained to discredit him.

In other instances, reorganization and a reduction in force (RIF) can be used to oust the employee who has met with agency disapproval. This approach certainly seems to have been used against A. Ernest Fitzgerald, an Air Force employee. In the late 1960s he released information to Congress about cost overruns on the Air Force transport C-5A being built by Lockheed Aircraft Corporation. Shortly thereafter, Fitzgerald's job was eliminated. Through a series of administrative and court proceedings, however, he was able to require the Air Force to reinstate him in a position of comparable grade, but the process was a long and expensive one. By 1977, he had run up sizable legal fees in fighting these battles, and in that year a federal district court held the government was not responsible for reimbursing him for these costs, even though the government was originally responsible for this drawn-out affair.[89] Fitzgerald's victory may seem to be an empty one.

The federal Civil Service Reform Act of 1978 includes protection for whistle blowers. This provision was recommended by President Carter. Reprisals may not be taken against whistle blowers who reveal violations of the law, waste of funds, or abuse of authority, providing that in releasing such information the whistle blower has not violated a law or executive order concerning classified material. The special counsel to the Merit Systems Protection Board has responsibility for enforcing this protection afforded to whistle blowers.

Political Activities

Government employee involvement in many types of political activities has been prohibited for generations. Have those prohibitions unjustly denied employees their constitutional rights? Do such prohibitions make political eunuchs of public workers? Is it possible to relax legal provisions

---

[88] Gerald Gold, Allan M. Siegal, and Samuel Abt, eds., *The Pentagon Papers: as Published by the New York Times* (New York: Bantam, 1971).

[89] *Fitzgerald v. United States Civil Service Commission*, 554 F. 2d 1186 (1977). See A. Ernest Fitzgerald, "A. Ernest Fitzgerald," in Nader, Petkas, Blackwell, eds., *Whistle Blowing*, pp. 39–54. See also A. Ernest Fitzgerald, *The High Priests of Waste* (New York: Norton, 1972).

to allow for increased political activities on the part of government employees and simultaneously preserve the merit concept?[90]

In 1802 President Thomas Jefferson issued a circular providing for the political neutrality of federal employees, and since that time federal workers have been limited in exercising their political rights. The Pendleton Act of 1883 is commonly cited as formally establishing the merit principle in the federal government, and with that law the Civil Service Commission established procedures for restricting political activities. The reform effort was further strengthened in 1907 when President Theodore Roosevelt issued Executive Order 642. The Civil Service Commission, operating under that order, had by 1939 dealt with approximately 3,000 cases of alleged involvement of federal workers in proscribed political activities. In that year Congress passed the Hatch Political Activities Act, further detailing what forms of political activity were prohibited; the legislation also adopted as policy the 3,000 rulings of the Civil Service Commission.[91] The following year Congress extended coverage to state and local employees who were substantially funded with federal monies.[92]

The Hatch Act prohibitions on political activities are wide ranging. Employees cannot "take an active part in political management or in political campaigns" or interfere with or affect an election. Money for political purposes can be neither received nor given between federal employees. An employee cannot "coerce the political action" of others. An employee cannot be forced to provide "political service" and cannot be dismissed for refusing to aid a campaign.

---

[90] John R. Bolton, *The Hatch Act: A Civil Libertarian Defense* (Washington: American Enterprise Institute for Public Policy Research, 1976); Richard Christopherson, *Regulating Political Activites of Public Employees* (Chicago: Civil Service Assembly, 1954); Glen S. Howard, "Patronage Dismissals: Constitutional Limits and Political Justifications," *University of Chicago Law Review*, 41 (1974):297–328; Roger W. Jones, "The Merit System, Politics, and Political Maturity: A Federal View," *Public Personnel Review*, 25 (1964):28–34; Kenneth Kernaghan, "Politics, Policy and Public Servants: Political Neutrality Revisited," *Canadian Public Administration*, 19 (1976):432–456; Philip L. Martin, "The Hatch Act: The Current Movement for Reform," *Public Personnel Management*, 3 (1974):180–184; Dalmust H. Nelson, "Political Expression under the Hatch Act and the Problem of Statutory Ambiguity," *Midwest Journal of Political Science*, 2 (1958):76–88; Henry Rose, "A Critical Look at the Hatch Act," *Harvard Law Review*, 75 (1962): 510–526; C. R. Santos, "The Political Neutrality of the Civil Service Re-examined," *Public Personnel Review*, 30 (1969):9–14; Martin and Susan Tolchin, *To the Victor . . . . Political Patronage from the Clubhouse to the White House* (New York: Random House, 1971); Civil Service Commission, *Employment Rights and Responsibilities of Non-career Executive Appointees* (Washington: Government Printing Office, 1976); and Robert G. Vaughn, "Restrictions on the Political Activities of Public Employees: The Hatch Act and Beyond," *George Washington Law Review*, 44 (1976):516–553.

[91] Hatch Political Activities Act, 53 Stat. 1147 (1939).

[92] Hatch Political Activities Act, 54 Stat. 767 (1940).

The law does not prohibit all political activity. Government workers retain their right to vote. An employee has the right "to express his opinion on political subjects and candidates." An employee may participate in nonpartisan elections, even by being a candidate for office. Federal employees may participate in partisan elections in those communities designated by the Office of Personnel Management. These for the most part are in the Washington, D.C. area, but some communities in Alaska, Georgia, Washington, and a few other states are included.

The Election Campaign Act of 1974 greatly reduced federal restrictions on political activities of state and local employees by deleting the prohibition against political management and political campaigning. As far as federal law is concerned, these workers may participate extensively in partisan activities, with the major exception that they cannot run for political office. Whether this change has had any effect is unknown, since state and local employees still must abide by the prohibitions contained in the so-called Little Hatch Acts of the states.

How these rights mesh with the prohibitions has been clarified to some extent through administrative regulations.[93] Federal employees may publicly state their views on political candidates but they cannot state those views before a political convention or rally. They may act as election judges or clerks but not as poll watchers for a political party. They may attend a political convention but not as delegates or alternates. While they may not make a financial contribution to other federal employees, they may contribute to political parties. Wearing campaign buttons and displaying political posters is acceptable but driving voters to the polls is not. Signing a partisan nominating petition is permitted but circulating a petition for others to sign is not.

Violating the law results in dismissal. The Hatch Act provides for removal unless the Office of Personnel Management decides on a lesser penalty. The minimum penalty is thirty days suspension without pay. Employees must be notified in writing of the charges against them and are entitled to an oral hearing, where they may be represented by an attorney. State and local employees charged with violating the Hatch Act have similar rights. Although the OPM cannot directly remove state and local violators, it can force their removal. If a state or local government fails to remove an employee found guilty by the OPM, that government will be denied the equivalent of the employee's salary for two years out of whatever federal program is providing financial support.[94]

---

[93] 5 C.F.R. § 733 for federal employees and 5 C.F.R. § 151 for state and local employees.

[94] See Harry W. Reynolds, Jr., "Merit Controls, the Hatch Acts, and Personnel Standards in Intergovernmental Relations," *Annals*, 359 (1965):81–93.

Table 8.1. Percentage responses of federal employees about what political activities they think they "can" and "cannot" do under present Hatch Act rules*

Activity	Can	Cannot	Not Sure
Make a speech at a rally held by a political party	15.8	69.4	14.6
Put a political sticker on his own car	63.0	24.4	12.5
Hold office in a political party organization	8.5	80.6	10.7
Run for state or national political office	8.9	81.0	9.6
Write a letter to his senator or his congressman	96.0	1.5	2.2
Drive people to the polls on election day	45.0	40.5	14.2
Run for a school board position where people are not candidates of either major political party	66.5	15.8	17.3
Become actively involved in local issues, such as civil rights and taxes	49.5	32.6	17.3
Participate in voter registration drives	48.1	35.6	16.0
Distribute campaign materials for a party or candidate	18.6	71.2	10.1

Source: Commission on Political Activity of Government Personnel, *Findings and Recommendations*, (Washington: Government Printing Office, 1967), p. 20.

* A box indicates the correct answer to the question.

Given the severity of the penalties involved and the importance of political rights as provided by the First Amendment to the Constitution, it is important that government workers understand what they may and may not do. A study conducted in the mid-1960s for the Federal Commission on Political Activity of Government Personnel found that employees do not have thorough knowledge of the Hatch Act. About 85 percent of the federal employees surveyed had some knowledge of the Hatch Act, but, conversely, between one and two of every ten workers were unaware that they could be dismissed for engaging in politics. Table 8.1 lists various types of political activities as well as whether they are prohibited or permitted and whether employees thought these activities were prohibited or permitted. Not one of the workers correctly answered all ten questions! A majority answered seven of the ten questions correctly, but only 40 percent realized that driving voters to the polls was illegal and only 36 percent realized helping in voter registration efforts was illegal. Employees with less education, in low-grade levels, and with few years of government service were less knowledgeable about the law than employees with more education, in higher government jobs, and with many years of government service.[95]

The Hatch Act and the Little Hatch Acts have been challenged as being unconstitutional because they limit First Amendment rights, because they violate state rights, and because they are excessively vague.

---

[95] Commission on Political Activity of Government Personnel, *Research* (Washington: Government Printing Office, 1967), p. 24.

In 1947 the United States Supreme Court dealt with the first of these issues in *United Public Workers of America* v. *Mitchell*.[96] The case involved twelve federal employees, but the Court only dealt with one of them, a low-level Mint worker. The Court held that Congress had a right to prohibit political activities. In the Court's view an individual's rights must be balanced "against the supposed evil of political partisanship by classified employees." Were the Mint worker allowed to participate in politics, he might then be subjected to reprisals such as being denied a promotion should he not consent to such participation.

Also in 1947, the Court reviewed the constitutionality of the Hatch Act as it pertained to the states. In *Oklahoma* v. *United States Civil Service Commission* the issue was whether the federal government could force the dismissal of a state official, in this instance a member of the Oklahoma State Highway Commission.[97] The Court ruled affirmatively, reasoning that Congress had a right to attach conditions to the receipt of federal grants. The states were not compelled to accept federal monies, but if they did accept these grants, compliance with Hatch was mandatory.

These cases did not finalize the law. *United Public Workers* v. *Mitchell* was decided by a 4-to-3 vote, and many observers speculated that the Court at a later time might be willing to overturn that decision. In 1973, however, the Court reaffirmed its position. *United States Civil Service Commission* v. *National Association of Letter Carriers* tested the vagueness issue.[98] The six-justice majority held that the prohibitions "are set out in terms that the ordinary person exercising ordinary common sense can sufficiently understand and comply with, without sacrifice to the public interest." The Court noted that, when in doubt over what activities were permissible, an employee could contact the Civil Service Commission for advice. The three-member minority, in contrast, criticized Hatch as being "pregnant with ambiguity." Government workers were expected to comprehend the 3,000 rulings prior to the passage of Hatch as well as the hundreds of rulings passed since 1939.[99] The effect was seen to be a "chilling" influence upon the exercise of one's constitutional rights, resulting in a "self-imposed censorship" by workers.

---

[96] *United Public Workers of America* v. *Mitchell*, 330 U.S. 75 (1947). See also *Ex parte Curtis*, 106 U.S. 371 (1882) and *United States* v. *Wurzbach*, 280 U.S. 396 (1930).

[97] *Oklahoma* v. *United States Civil Service Commission*, 330 U.S. 127 (1947).

[98] *United States Civil Service Commission* v. *National Association of Letter Carriers*, 413 U.S. 548 (1973). See "The Hatch Act Reaffirmed: Demise of Overbreadth Review?" *Fordham Law Review*, 42 (1973):161–177 and Philip L. Martin, "The Hatch Act in Court: Some Recent Developments," *Public Administration Review*, 33 (1973):443–447.

[99] James W. Irwin (U.S. Civil Service Commission), *Hatch Act Decisions (Political Activity Cases) of the United States Civil Service Commission* (Washington: Government Printing Office, 1949).

Decided on the same day as the *Letter Carriers* case was *Broadrick v. Oklahoma*.[100] The Court upheld that state's Little Hatch Act as not being excessively broad. Justice Douglas, in dissenting, wrote, "A bureaucracy that is alert, vigilant, and alive is more efficient than one that is quiet and submissive."

Prohibitions against participation in politics have been held constitutional, but Congress and state legislatures could adopt new legislation allowing for greater participation. Although the survey mentioned above is more than ten years old, the results offer some insights into what might happen if prohibitions were relaxed. About half of the federal employees thought more political participation should be allowed, while the other half thought the law should remain unchanged. When asked whether they would become more active if the law permitted it, 60 percent answered they would probably not change and only 8 percent said they would become "a lot more active." Only 17 percent thought allowing for political activity would reduce efficiency in government, but about half thought it would affect "promotion decisions and job assignments."[101] Secondary analysis of the data has found that, in the event greater participation would be permitted, men would be more likely to exercise their rights than women, persons with more than a high school education would be more active, and blacks would be more likely to increase their activity than would whites.[102]

The 1967 Commission on Political Activity of Government Personnel criticized the Hatch Act for its vagueness and issued several recommendations. The Commission suggested changing the law to prohibit only those activities that are "a serious threat to the public service." The distinction between partisan and nonpartisan elective offices should be abolished, since in the Commission's view there are no truly nonpartisan elections. The practice of allowing federal employees to participate in local politics in some communities and not in others should be abolished. State governments should be encouraged to develop their own systems for complying with federal standards involving political activities.[103] The

---

[100] *Broadrick v. Oklahoma*, 413 U.S. 601 (1973). John D. Hvizdos, "State Regulation of Partisan Political Activities of Public Employees," *Ohio State Law Journal*, 34 (1973):949–957.

[101] Commission on Political Activity, *Research*, pp. 20–21.

[102] Jeffrey C. Rinehart and E. Lee Bernick, "Political Attitudes and Behavior Patterns of Federal Civil Servants," *Public Administration Review*, 35 (1975):603–611. See also Gary M. Halter, "The Effects of the Hatch Act on the Political Participation of Federal Employees," *Midwest Journal of Political Science*, 16 (1972):723–729.

[103] Commission on Political Activity of Government Personnel, *Findings and Recommendations* (Washington: Government Printing Office, 1967) and *Hearings* (Washington: Government Printing Office (1968). See also Charles O. Jones, "Reevaluating the Hatch Act: A Report on the Commission on Political Activity of Government Personnel," *Public Administration Review*, 29 (1969):249–254.

Commission's report generated extensive debate but no change in legislation.

By the mid-1970s, however, a concerted effort to relax the restrictions on political activities was able to move Congress into passing the Federal Employees Political Activities Act of 1976 (HR 8617), but the legislation was vetoed by President Gerald R. Ford.[104] The law would have retained prohibitions on using one's office to affect an election, soliciting campaign contributions from fellow employees, and political campaigning while on duty and in government buildings. What was controversial was the provision that encouraged employees "to fully exercise . . . their rights of voluntary participation in the political processes." Not only could employees participate in campaign activities, but also they could run for political office. Employees who were candidates would be expected to use their annual leave while they were candidates. The main exception was that persons holding sensitive positions could not engage in politics; this included workers in the Internal Revenue Service, the Justice Department, and the Central Intelligence Agency. The law would have created a three-member Board on Political Activities of Federal Employees, consisting of employees appointed by the President with the advice and consent of the Senate. The board would hear cases of alleged violation brought to it by an investigative staff of the Civil Service Commission.

The 1976 legislation was criticized for opening the federal bureaucracy to political abuse. Employees who previously could have turned down requests for campaign assistance on the grounds that they were "Hatched" would now be pressured into campaign activities. According to President Ford, "We would be endangering the entire concept of employee independence and freedom from coercion."[105] Other criticisms were that Congress would have the right to disapprove administrative regulations issued to implement the law and that enforcement powers would be assigned to the Board on Political Activities rather than the Civil Service Commission.

---

[104] Neal R. Peirce and Jerry Hagstrom, "Is It Time to Hatch Federal Workers from Their Nonpartisan Shells?" *National Journal*, 9 (1977): 585–587; Senate Committee on Post Office and Civil Service, *Documentary Background to the Federal Employees' Political Activities Act of 1975*, 94th Cong., 1st sess. (Washington: Government Printing Office, 1975); Senate Committee on Post Office and Civil Service, *Federal Employees' Political Activities: Hearings*, 94th Cong., 1st sess. (Washington: Government Printing Office, 1975); and Subcommittee on Employee Political Rights and Intergovernmental Programs, House Committee on Post Office and Civil Service, *The Federal Employees' Political Activities Act of 1976: Documentary Background and Legislative History* (Washington: Government Printing Office, 1976).

[105] Gerald R. Ford, *Veto of Hatch Act Repeal: Message from the President of the United States* (Washington: Government Printing Office, 1976).

In 1977, liberalizing the Hatch Act was again undertaken, with the encouragement of President Carter. The House of Representatives passed a new bill by a wide margin, but it met stiff opposition in the Senate, which took no action. Supporting revision of the law were the AFL-CIO, the American Civil Liberties Union, Americans for Democratic Action, and the National Association for the Advancement of Colored People. These groups supported change on the grounds of liberating employees to exercise their constitutional rights. On the other hand, there were those, such as Common Cause, who were concerned that relaxing standards would produce a politically corrupt bureaucracy. Memories of the abuses of the Nixon administration were fresh. An unofficial "Federal Political Personnel Manual" had been prepared and was designed to show how to politicize the bureaucracy despite the Hatch and Pendleton Acts.[106] Supporters of Hatch were understandably fearful that a future President intent on using the bureaucracy for political purposes could not be controlled should Hatch restrictions be relaxed.

EMPLOYEE ACCOUNTABILITY

Employees are held accountable for their actions both directly to the public and internally through disciplinary or adverse actions. This section first considers the routes available to citizens in general and clients in particular for holding public officials accountable. The second part of this section concentrates upon adverse actions and the protections that are afforded public workers accused of misconduct and ineffective work performance.

Direct Accountability

Secrecy in government is understandable in that few people wish to have their failures or mistakes made public. Even when there is nothing to hide or cover up, public administrators may prefer to work outside of the public spotlight, because their activities then can be conducted in relative

---

[106] Subcommittee on Manpower and Civil Service, House Committee on Post Office and Civil Service, *Violations and Abuses of Merit Principles in Federal Employment: Hearings*, 94th Cong., 1st sess. (Washington: Government Printing Office, 1975); Subcommittee on Manpower and Civil Service, House Committee on Post Office and Civil Service, *Final Report on Violations and Abuses of Merit Principles in Federal Employment Together with Minority Views*, 94th Cong., 2d sess. (Washington: Government Printing Office, 1976); and Subcommittee on Political Rights and Intergovernmental Programs, House Committee on Post Office and Civil Service, *Investigation into Possible Violation of Political Rights of Federal Employees: Hearings*, 94th Cong., 2d sess. (Washington: Government Printing Office, 1976).

tranquility, thereby promoting efficient operations.[107] Openness in government, however, helps hold government directly accountable to the citizenry and reduces the need for such practices as whistle blowing.

Legislation has been passed to counteract tendencies toward secrecy in government. The Federal Freedom of Information Act (FOIA) of 1966, amended in 1974 and 1976, took the affirmative stance that, whenever possible, citizens should have access to public records.[108] The Privacy Act of 1974 allowed citizens to have access to records on themselves maintained by federal agencies.[109] The 1976 Government in the Sunshine Act opened many federal agency meetings to the public.[110] Many states have laws comparable to the FOIA and Sunshine Act. Through these mechanisms, citizens can learn about what transpires within government agencies and in turn hold officials answerable for those actions.

---

[107] Morton H. Halperin and Daniel N. Hoffman, "Top Secret—National Security and the Right to Know," *Dissent*, 24 (1977):241–247; Francis E. Rourke, *Secrecy and Publicity: Dilemmas of Democracy* (Baltimore: Johns Hopkins Press, 1961); and Francis E. Rourke, ed., "Administrative Secrecy: A Comparative Perspective," *Public Administration Review*, 35 (1975):1–42; and Morton H. Halperin and Daniel N. Hoffman, "Secrecy and the Right to Know," *Law and Contemporary Problems*, 40 (Summer, 1976):132–165.

[108] Freedom of Information Act of 1966, 80 Stat. 383, 5 U.S.C. § 552. See Robert R. Belair, "Less Government Secrecy and More Personal Privacy?: Experience with the Freedom of Information and Privacy Acts," *Civil Liberties Review*, 4 (May/June, 1977): 10–18; Robert M. Blum, "Developments Under the Freedom of Information Act—1976," *Duke Law Journal*, 1977 (1977):532–564; Hugh A. Bone, "Washington's Open Government: A Look at Initiative 276," *National Civic Review*, 65 (1976):437–445; Walter B. Connolly and John C. Fox, "Employer Rights and Access to Documents Under the Freedom of Information Act," *Fordham Law Review*, 46 (1977):203–240; David B. Montgomery, Anne H. Peters, and Charles B. Weinberg, "The Freedom of Information Act: Strategic Opportunities and Threats," *Sloan Management Review*, 19 (Winter, 1978):1–13; Robert L. Saloschin, "The Freedom of Information Act: A Governmental Perspective," *Public Administration Review*, 35 (1975):10–14; Gregory L. Waples, "The Freedom of Information Act: A Seven-Year Assessment," *Columbia Law Review*, 74 (1974):895–959; and Ann C. Wilson, "Freedom of Information," *Civil Service Journal*, 18 (January/March, 1978):32–33.

[109] Privacy Act of 1974, 88 Stat. 1896, 5 U.S.C. § 552a. *Annual Report of the President on the Privacy Act of 1974* (Washington: Government Printing Office, issued annually); Kenneth A. Kovach, "A Retrospective Look at the Privacy and Freedom of Information Acts," *Labor Law Journal*, 27 (1976):548–563; *Lawsuits Against the Government Relating to a Bill to Amend the Privacy Act of 1974* (Washington: General Accounting Office, 1977); David M. O'Brien, "Privacy and the Right of Access: Purposes and Paradoxes of Information Control," *Administrative Law Review*, 30 (1978):45–92; "The Privacy Act," *Civil Service Journal*, 16 (July-September, 1975):1–6; and "Privacy and the FOIA," *Administrative Law Review*, 27 (1975): 275–294.

[110] Government in the Sunshine Act, 90 Stat. 1241, 5 U.S.C. § 552b. Benita S. Baird, "The Government in the Sunshine Act—An Overview," *Duke Law Journal*, 1977 (1977):565–592; Jerry W. Markham, "Sunshine on the Administrative Process: Wherein Lies the Shade?" *Administrative Law Review*, 28 (1976):463–482; Robert W. Sloat, "Government in the Sunshine Act: A Danger of Overexposure," *Harvard Journal on Legislation*, 14 (1977):620–650; and "Government in the Sunshine Act: Opening Federal Agency Meetings," *American Law Review* 26 (1976):154–207.

Another approach has been the establishment of government ombudsman offices. These offices, based upon a concept initially introduced in Scandinavian countries, serve as a mediator between government agencies and citizens. When a citizen has a complaint about the action of an agency and its workers, the ombudsman investigates the complaint and seeks to mediate the problem. Although seldom having any enforcement powers, the ombudsman can bring pressure upon the agency to correct a situation.[111]

In the 1960s and 1970s citizens and clients have increasingly used direct confrontation with government officials. Public demonstrations were used extensively in the 1960s, such as in the case of picketing and sit-ins over school desegregation and the Vietnam War. Prison inmates not only have gone on hunger strikes and conducted prison riots but also have negotiated procedures to be used in resolving grievances over prison management practices. In establishing their rights as clients, prisoners have reduced the extent to which prison officials may act unilaterally.

Courtroom confrontations have become a particularly popular approach to holding government officials responsible for their actions. This has been made possible by court liberalization of the requirements for "standing." In order to file suit, one must first demonstrate direct involvement or standing in the situation. In 1973, for example, the United States Supreme Court held that a student group concerned with the environment had standing in a case involving railroad freight rates; the reasoning was that increased rates would encourage manufacturers to use nonreturnable bottles and other unrecycled materials and that this would increase the potential for littering and thereby harm the environment.[112]

Courts frequently have decided in favor of agency clients who allege that government has violated their rights. For instance, the Supreme Court has held that, as part of the freedom of expression, high school

---

[111] Stanley V. Anderson, ed., *Ombudsmen for American Government?* (Englewood Cliffs, N.J.: Prentice-Hall, Inc., 1968); Charles T. Burnbridge, "Problems of Transferring the Ombudsman Plan," *International Review of Administrative Sciences*, 40 (1974): 103–108; Paul Dolan, "Creating State Ombudsmen: A Growing Movement," *National Civic Review*, 63 (1974):250–254; William B. Gwynn, "Obstacles within the Office of Economic Opportunity to the Evaluation of Experimental Ombudsmen," *Public Administration* (London), 54 (1976):177–197; Vance Hartke, "Ombudsman: Mediator Between the Citizen and His Government," *California Western Law Review*, 10 (1974):325–358; John E. Moore and Alan T. Wyner, "Responses of Law Enforcement Agencies to External Grievance Mechanisms: The Experience of Two American Ombudsman Offices," *American Politics Quarterly*, 3 (1975):60–80; Albert Rosenthal, "The Ombudsman—Swedish "Grievance Man,"" *Public Administration Review*, 24 (1964):226–230; Donald C. Rowat, "Ombudsman for North America," *Public Administration Review*, 24 (1964):230–233; and Kent M. Weeks, *Ombudsmen Around the World: A Comparative Chart*, 2d ed. (Berkeley, Calif.: Institute of Governmental Studies, University of California, 1978).

[112] *United States* v. *Students Challenging Regulatory Agency Procedures* (*SCRAP*), 412 U.S. 669 (1973).

students had a right to wear black armbands in school to protest the Vietnam War and that school officials had violated the Constitution by prohibiting such armbands.[113] Although there is no constitutional right to an education, the courts have held that states have created a property right to education and that education cannot be denied students through suspension from school without adherence to due process standard.[114] A state government may not halt payments to a welfare recipient without first providing that person an opportunity to defend himself in an administrative hearing where adverse witnesses may be cross-examined.[115] Although the Court has not ruled in favor of prison inmates demanding due process when being transferred from one state prison to another or allowing inmate "unions" to hold meetings and distribute literature within a prison, the fact that such cases have been brought to the Supreme Court is an indication of increasing client militancy and of an increasing willingness on the part of the judicial system to hear such cases.[116]

One barrier to suits against government is the concept of sovereignty, which presumes that government is all-powerful and can do no wrong. In practice, of course, wrongful acts are sometimes committed by government officials and in the process citizens are harmed. In 1946, Congress passed the Tort Claims Act, which allowed for cases in tort against the government. As a result the government has been held accountable for such things as allowing a lighthouse light to burn out, resulting in a barge running aground and damaging its cargo.[117] In another case, the government was found negligent in its supervision of the private manufacture of live polio vaccine; a person had contracted polio from vaccine that had not been properly processed.[118]

Federal employees were generally immune from suits that alleged violations of Constitutional rights until the 1978 Supreme Court case of *Butz v. Economou*.[119] In that case, the Secretary of Agriculture was

---

[113] *Tinker v. Des Moines Independent Community School District*, 393 U.S. 503 (1968).

[114] *Goss v. Lopez*, 419 U.S. 565 (1975).

[115] *Goldberg v. Kelly*, 397 U.S. 254 (1970). See also *Edelman v. Jordan*, 415 U.S. 651 (1974); and *Mathews v. Eldridge*, 424 U.S. 319 (1976).

[116] *Meachun v. Fano*, 427 U.S. 215 (1976); *Montanye v. Haymes*, 427 U.S. 236 (1976); and *Jones v. North Carolina Prisoners' Labor Union*, 430 U.S. 927 (1977). See also *Morrissey v. Brewer*, 408 U.S. 471 (1972); and *Managers Need Comprehensive System for Assessing Effectiveness and Operation of Inmate Grievance Mechanisms* (Washington: General Accounting Office, 1977).

[117] Tort Claims Act, 28 U.S.C. § 1291. *Indian Towing Co. v. United States*, 350 U.S. 61 (1955).

[118] See *Griffin v. United States*, 351 F. Supp. 10 (1972) and 353 F. Supp. 324 (1973), and James J. Sullivan and Rodger L. Tate, "The Federal Seal of Approval: Government Liability for Negligent Inspection," *Georgetown Law Journal*, 62 (1974):937–961.

[119] *Butz v. Economou*, 98 S. Ct. 2894 (1978).

alleged to have inflicted $32 million of property damage on a businessman by circulating false statements among the press and the public. The court ruled that only when an executive exercised discretion should he be granted immunity, and that the immunity granted would normally be qualified, and not absolute.

Suits against state and local governments have been more difficult than suits against the federal government, because states generally do not have legislation comparable to the Tort Claims Act. The concept of sovereign immunity has protected state and local governments from suits. In recent years, however, some states have greatly limited the application of this concept, but, in the meantime, citizens have taken an alternative legal route—suits against state and local officials as individuals. Whereas in any given state a person might not be able to sue a local or state government in one of the state's courts, it is possible to sue the individuals involved in a federal court. Cases of officer tort liability are possible under the Civil Rights Act of 1871, which makes liable "every person, who under color of any statute, ordinance, regulation, custom, or usage, of any State or Territory" deprives one of "any rights, privileges, or immunities" guaranteed by the Constitution. Cases under this act are called Section 1983 cases, because the pertinent language is in Section 1983 of Title 42 of the United States Code. A landmark Section 1983 case is *Monroe v. Pape* (1961).[120] In that case, Chicago city policemen were held liable for violating the rights of citizens, although the City of Chicago was not held liable. The policemen had entered a home, forced people to stand naked in the living room while the house was searched, and denied them the right of seeing an attorney when they were brought to jail.

In 1974, the Supreme Court dealt with the liability of Ohio officials in the killing of Kent State University students by National Guardsmen (*Scheur v. Rhodes*).[121] Absolute immunity from suits was claimed by the Ohio governor and other state officials, but the Court held there could only be limited immunity, and that would be granted when there was substantial discretion involved in handling a situation and when the officials had acted in "good faith." Since discretion is more extensive at higher levels of government than at lower levels, it would appear that executives may be granted limited immunity, whereas lower level public employees may be held liable.

---

[120] *Monroe v. Pape*, 365 U.S. 167 (1961). See also *Bivens v. Six Unknown Named Agents of Federal Bureau of Narcotics*, 403 U.S. 388 (1971).

[121] *Scheur v. Rhodes*, 416 U.S. 232 (1974). Steven E. Bernstein, "Civil Rights—State Executive Officials Afforded a Qualified Immunity from Liability in Suits Maintained under Section 1983," *Villanova Law Review*, 20 (1975):1057–1068.

The following year, in *Wood* v. *Strickland,* the Court dealt with a suit against school officials who had suspended students for having alcoholic beverages at a school function.[122] The students claimed that the suspension proceedings had violated their constitutional rights as protected under Section 1983. The Court seemed to take a narrower approach to immunity in this case than it did in *Scheur* v. *Rhodes.* Whereas the earlier case seemed to permit immunity if one did not realize at the time that an action would violate someone's rights, *Wood* v. *Strickland* seems to suggest that officials have a responsibility to know what is and is not constitutional, that ignorance of the law is not an acceptable defense. ". . . An act violating a student's constitutional rights can be no more justified by ignorance or disregard of settled, undisputable law . . . than by the presence of actual malice."[123]

In 1976 two Section 1983 cases were decided in favor of granting immunity. In *Rizzo* v. *Goode,* involving a suit against the Mayor of Philadelphia for supposedly failing to properly handle misconduct in the police department, conduct that allegedly violated the constitutional rights of citizens, the Supreme Court ruled that the district court originally hearing the case should not have "injected itself . . . into the internal disciplinary affairs" of the city.[124] *Imbler* v. *Pachtman* involved a person convicted of murder who had served nine years in prison before being paroled.[125] Imbler sued the prosecutor, Pachtman, for using false and misleading information in the court trial. The Court held the prosecutor had absolute immunity from Section 1983 suits, because "qualifying a prosecutor's immunity would disserve the broader public interest."

What is the public interest in these cases? Certainly, they seem to present dilemmas. Government officials need to be restricted so that abuses cannot go undetected. On the other hand, officer tort liability suits can reduce public officials to timid creatures fearful of both taking and not taking action. Section 1983 convictions generally have not resulted in major financial settlements, with one exception being a Georgia mayor who was assessed $35,000 damages and $15,000 punitive damages for issuing a "shoot-to-kill" order.[126] While such court-imposed fines

---

[122] *Wood* v. *Strickland,* 420 U.S. 308 (1975).

[123] See also *United States* v. *Park,* 421 U.S. 658 (1975). In that case the Court held the President of Acme Markets personally liable for allowing food to be exposed to rodents. At the time, the corporation had 36,000 employees, 874 stores, and 12 warehouses.

[124] *Rizzo* v. *Goode,* 423 U.S. 362 (1976).

[125] *Imbler* v. *Pachtman,* 424 U.S. 409 (1976).

[126] Charles R. McManis, "Personal Liability of State Officials," *State Government,* 49 (1976):86–92. See also Marshall E. Dimock, "Public Administration and Administrative Law," *American Political Science Review,* 26 (1932): pp. 875–920, and Charles S. Rhyne, William S. Rhyne, and Stephen P. Elmendorf, *Tort Liability and Immunity of Municipal Officials* (Washington: National Institute of Municipal Law Officers, 1976).

may be rare, they may have a chilling effect upon public employee action, just as unrestrained public employees can have a chilling effect upon citizens exercising their constitutional rights. One response is that jurisdictions are subscribing to liability insurance for their employees.[127] A more positive approach might be for states to allow for tort cases against themselves and their local governments, thereby reducing the need for officer liability suits.[128]

In 1978 the Supreme Court opened the door to suits in federal courts against local governments that previously were thought to be immune. *City of Lafayette* v. *Louisiana Power and Light Company* involved municipally operated electric utilities.[129] The City claimed it could not be sued by the private utility for having violated federal antitrust laws. The Court ruled that the City was a "person" as defined in those laws and, therefore, the City was not immune. *Monell* v. *Department of Social Services of the City of New York* involved compulsory, nonpaid leaves of absence for pregnancy.[130] The Supreme Court overturned the *Monroe* v. *Pape* decision by holding that New York City was a "person" under Section 1983. The ruling was restricted to situations where the "custom" of a jurisdiction has been to deny citizen rights and explicitly excluded were suits against a government for torts committed by individual employees.

Adverse Actions

Adverse actions, involving demotion, suspension, reassignment, and removal, are disciplinary in nature.[131] The purpose is to correct a situation

---

[127] Nester Roos, "Public Official Liability: 1976," *Urban Data Service Report*, 9 (May, 1977):1-4.

[128] Peter G. Brown, *Personal Liability of Public Officials, Sovereign Immunity, and Compensation for Loss* (Columbus, Ohio: Academy for Contemporary Problems, 1977).

[129] *City of Lafayette* v. *Louisiana Power and Light Company*, 98 S. Ct. 1123 (1978).

[130] *Monell* v. *Department of Social Services of the City of New York*, 98 S. Ct. 2018 (1978).

[131] Joseph Adler and Robert Doherty, eds., *Employment Security in the Public Sector: A Symposium* (Ithaca, NY: Institute of Public Employment, Cornell University, 1974); Arch Dotson, "The Emerging Doctrine of Privilege in Public Employment," *Public Administration Review*, 15 (1955):77-88; Carl F. Goodman, "Public Employment and the Supreme Court's 1976-77 Term," *Public Personnel Management*, 6 (1977):283-293; Thomas K. Houston, "Due Process and Public Employment in Perspective: Arbitrary Dismissals of Non-Civil Service Employees," *UCLA Law Review*, 19 (1972):1052-1083; Mark R. Joelson, "Legal Problems in the Dismissal of Civil Servants in the United States, Britain, and France," *American Journal of Comparative Law*, 12 (1963):149-171; Richard C. Johnson and Richard G. Stoll, Jr., "Judicial Review of Federal Employee Dismissals and Other Adverse Actions," *Cornell Law Review*, 57 (1972):178-197; David H. Rosenbloom, "Public Personnel Administration and the Constitution: An Emergent Approach," *Public Administration Review*, 35 (1975):52-59; William E. Slack and Mark G. Weisshaar, "Reduction in Force: A Guide for the Uninitiated," *George Washington*

in which an employee is incompetent or has violated established agency policies and practices. Before discussing the procedures used in disciplining employees and the rights afforded them, it should be noted that employees have legal rights in nondisciplinary situations. In managing an agency, officials may need to reassign personnel, including geographically relocating personnel; depending upon the jurisdiction, an employee may have appeal rights concerning not only whether the new assignment carries the same grade and pay as the original position but also whether the levels of responsibility are "truly" comparable between the two positions.[132] Many nondisciplinary cases arise over position reclassifications, most frequently where positions are being downgraded. In some cases, employees have used appeal proceedings to attempt to force an upgrading of their positions.

Adverse actions are governed by procedures established by statute, administrative regulations, and executive orders.[133] At the federal level, the Lloyd-LaFollette Act of 1912 has been the primary legislation; it provided that an employee "may be removed or suspended without pay only for such cause as will promote the efficiency of the service."[134] In passing the Veterans Preference Act of 1944, Congress granted special appeal rights to veterans in adverse actions. Presidential Executive Orders have been used to require agencies to establish adverse action procedures for all employees and to provide for a system of appeals. President Nixon's Executive Order 11787, issued in 1974, has been the main governing order. The 1978 Civil Service Reform Act substantially revised the

---

Law Review, 44 (1976):642–676; Clyde W. Summers, "Individual Protection Against Unjust Dismissal: Time for a Statute," Virginia Law Review, 62 (1976):481–532; Joseph C. Ullman and James P. Begin, "The Structure and Scope of Appeals and Procedures for Public Employees," Industrial and Labor Relations Review, 23 (1970):323–334; Robert G. Vaughn, The Spoiled System: A Call for Civil Service Reform (New York: Charterhouse, 1975), pp. 59–111; June Weisberger, Job Security and Public Employees, 2d ed. (Ithaca, N.Y.: Institute of Public Employment, Cornell University, 1973); June Weisberger, Recent Developments in Job Security: Layoffs and Discipline in the Public Sector (Ithaca, N.Y.: Institute of Public Employment, Cornell University, 1976); "The Due Process Rights of Public Employees," New York University Law Review, 50 (1975):310–365; "S.1035—Congress in the Vanguard: The Establishment of Rights for Federal Employees," George Washington Law Review, 37 (1968):101–131; "Substantive Due Process: The Extent of Public Employees' Protection from Arbitrary Dismissal," University of Pennsylvania Law Review, 122 (1974):1647–1663.

[132] Leefer v. Administrator, National Aeronautics and Space Administration, 543 F. 2d 209 (1976).

[133] See the following landmark cases on the powers of the President and Congress in cases of dismissal: United States v. Perkins, 116 U.S. 483 (1886); Myers v. United States, 272 U.S. 52 (1926); Humphrey's Executor v. United States, 295 U.S. 602 (1935); and Wiener v. United States, 357 U.S. 349 (1958).

[134] Lloyd-LaFollette Act, 5 U.S.C. § 7501. See "Adverse Action by Agencies," 5 C.F.R. § 752.

processes involved, but retained the fundamental principle of allowing for adverse actions only when that would "promote the efficiency of the service."

The steps in the federal appeal process are presented in Figure 8.1. This process does not apply to minor disciplinary actions, such as being suspended without pay for fourteen days or less, or to reductions in force

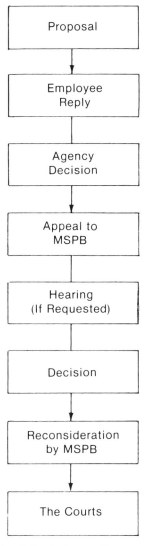

Figure 8.1.   Federal adverse action appeal system.

(RIFs) or to reductions in rank. In the last instance, a person could not appeal when her title or duties were changed but her grade and pay were not changed. When an employee is to be removed, suspended for more than fourteen days, or reduced in grade or pay, the process begins with thirty days' written notice of the proposed action being provided to the employee. The worker has a right to respond to the proposal both orally and in writing; the law permits agencies (but does not require them) to provide a formal hearing at this step in the process. The employee may have an attorney in the oral session.

The next step is to appeal to the Merit Systems Protection Board (MSPB). The Board may hear the case itself, or, more likely, it may assign the case to an administrative law judge or other MSPB employee skilled in hearing procedures. At this point, the employee has a right to a formal hearing and may have an attorney to assist in the case. The agency decision is to be upheld unless it is shown that in cases of alleged unacceptable work performance there was not "substantial evidence" to support the charge. In cases other than unacceptable performance, there must be a "preponderance of the evidence." The agency's action is to be overturned if it is shown that the agency did not follow its own procedures and in doing so harmed the employee in the case. The Director of the Office of Personnel Management may intervene in those cases where in his opinion "an erroneous decision would have a substantial impact on any civil service law, rule, or regulation." Following the decision of the administrative law judge, the MSPB may reconsider the case either on its own initiative or at the request of the employee, the agency, or the Director of the OPM. If a decision is made in favor of the employee, the agency may be required to pay the employee's attorney fees. If the decision is against the employee, he may appeal the case to a circuit court of appeals or, in the matter of pay, to the Court of Claims.[135]

The appeals process produces a considerable workload. In 1976, the U.S. Civil Service Commission dealt with 13,000 appeals on demotion,

---

[135] Connie Gargan, "Easy Access to the Appeals Information System," *Civil Service Journal*, 17 (January–March, 1977):23–24; Paul Mahoney, "Another Step: Implementation, Employee Appeals," *Civil Service Journal*, 15 (July–September, 1974):1–5; Richard A. Merill, "Procedures for Adverse Actions Against Federal Employees," *Virginia Law Review*, 59 (1973):196–278; John Murtha and Tom Kell, "For Faster, Fairer Appeals," *Civil Service Journal*, 13 (April–June, 1973):4–9; Personnel Management Project, *Final Staff Report* (Washington: Government Printing Office, 1977), pp. 49–80; Bernard Rosen, *The Merit System in the United States Civil Service* prepared for House Committee on Post Office and Civil Service, 94th Cong., 1st sess. (Washington: Government Printing Office, 1975), pp. 52–54; and Subcommittee on Manpower and Civil Service, House Committee on Post Office and Civil Service, *Proposed Changes in Adverse Action and Appeals Systems: Hearings*, 93d Cong., 1st sess. (Washington: Government Printing Office, 1973).

4,500 removal cases, and 200 suspensions.[136] The typical employee who appealed was male (82 percent of the cases), was in his mid-40s, and had 15 years of government service.[137]

Several appeal systems can exist in any large government. Some agencies may have personnel systems independent of the jurisdiction's civil service commission and, therefore, may have independent appeal systems. Collective bargaining in government provides additional appeal routes. A state employee who has been notified of a proposed adverse action may have a choice of using the state civil service commission procedure or one established by a collective bargaining agreement. If the employee thinks his "chances" are better with the union grievance procedures, obviously that route will be taken. Should he be unsuccessful in the collective bargaining appeal route, he still may have the option of shifting to the civil service procedure. Since employees covered by a collective bargaining agreement may have dual appeal systems, these workers may have greater protection than other employees.[138] The 1978 federal reform legislation attempted to resolve this problem by excluding several matters from labor-negotiated grievance procedures; excluded are cases involving removal and suspension, benefits (such as retirement, life insurance, and health insurance), and cases dealing with examination, certification, and appointment.

Another area in which alternative appeals procedures sometimes exist is with regard to alleged discrimination. Employees may be able to appeal their cases to the jurisdiction's civil service commission and to the agency responsible for enforcing equal employment opportunity. How such cases are handled at the federal level is discussed in the next chapter.

Pay usually is at stake in appeals proceedings. Removal obviously results in loss of income. Appeals in nondisciplinary cases frequently arise over the downgrading of positions. Grade creep or inflation can become a serious problem, and when a government seeks to correct the situation, many employees will be downgraded (see Chapters 3 and 4). A large increase in appeals related to downgrading occurred in 1976 in the

---

[136] Data supplied by the United States Civil Service Commission.

[137] *Design and Administration of the Adverse Action and Appeal Systems Need to be Improved* (Washington: General Accounting Office, 1974) p. 53.

[138] Robert J. Donahue, "Disciplinary Actions in New York State Service—A Radical Change," *Public Personnel Management*, 4 (1975):110–112; Eugene B. Granof and Stephen A. Moe, "Grievance Arbitration in the U.S. Postal Service," *Arbitration Journal*, 29 (1974):1–14; *Grievance Systems Should Provide All Federal Employees an Equal Opportunity for Redress* (Washington: General Accounting Office, 1978); and Joseph Krislov and Robert M. Peters, "Grievance Arbitration in State and Local Government: A Survey," *Arbitration Journal*, 25 (1970):196–205.

federal government when it undertook to reclassify many positions. The Civil Service Reform Act allows employees to continue to receive their current salaries for two years after their positions are downgraded; if these employees leave those positions, the new appointees receive the lower pay.[139] When employees successfully appeal adverse actions, they receive back pay. The federal Back Pay Act is for this purpose and cannot be used in cases where an employee's position is found to be graded lower than it should be.[140]

Courts have been active in delineating the rights of employees who are subjected to disciplinary actions. The earlier discussion of loyalty-security, free speech, and political activities indicated some of the protections the courts have afforded employees as well as many of the limitations placed on employees. One of the major hurdles for employees seeking judicial redress has been proving that some legal right is at stake. Aside from the First Amendment cases discussed above, the due process clause of the Fifth Amendment pertaining to the national government and the Fourteenth Amendment pertaining to the states has been the primary avenue for seeking judicial review. That clause, however, does not guarantee due process in all instances but rather is restricted to situations that deprive one of life, liberty, or property. Since one's life obviously is not threatened by being dismissed from government employment, the reasoning necessarily hinges upon deprivation of liberty and property.

Two cases decided in 1972 by the United States Supreme Court illustrate this problem of defining liberty and property. *Perry* v. *Sindermann* involved a junior college professor who had been employed for ten years by the college and then was dismissed without explanation and without an opportunity to defend himself in a hearing.[141] The Court ruled that although the professor technically was nontenured, the college had a de facto tenure system that had the effect of providing the professor with a property right. Due process, including a hearing, was required in such a dismissal.

Board of Regents v. *Roth* also dealt with the dismissal of a nontenured faculty member but it had a different outcome.[142] The Court ruled that neither an explanation for the professor's nonreappointment

---

[139] Subcommittee on Investigations, House Committee on Post Office and Civil Service, *Downgrading in the Federal Service*, 95th Cong., 1st sess. (Washington: Government Printing Office, 1977).

[140] *United States* v. *Testan and Zarrilli*, 424 U.S. 392 (1976).

[141] *Perry* v. *Sindermann*, 408 U.S. 593 (1972).

[142] *Board of Regents of State Colleges* v. *Roth*, 408 U.S. 564 (1972).

nor a hearing was required. The Court ruled that without having tenure, there could be no property interest and that Roth had not proved his liberty had been denied. Roth was free to seek employment elsewhere. In the view of the Court, had the university in its dismissal stigmatized the faculty member, such as finding him incompetent, then his freedom to seek new employment might have been deprived. The three dissenting justices contended that all dismissals have a stigmatizing effect.

The Court again dealt with this liberty and property issue in 1976 in *Bishop* v. *Wood*.[143] A municipal policeman was dismissed after successfully serving a probationary period and becoming classified as a permanent employee. In interpreting the city regulations that governed dismissal of permanent employees, the Court held that permanent employees in actuality had no right to be retained; the Court in effect ruled that permanent employees did not have a property right. The policeman, therefore, could not claim due process had been denied when he was not granted a hearing. Moreover, the Court suggested that courts should not be extensively involved in these kinds of issues:

> The federal court is not the appropriate forum in which to review the multitude of personnel decisions that are made by public agencies. We must accept the harsh fact that numerous individual mistakes are inevitable in the day-to-day administration of our affairs . . . The Due Process clause of the Fourteenth Amendment is not a guarantee against incorrect or ill-advised personnel decisions.[144]

The dissent in the case reasoned that since the policeman had been dismissed for "causing low morale" and for "conduct unsuited to an officer," the dismissal constituted a "badge of infamy" that infringed upon property and liberty rights.[145]

Stigmatization may last for years after a person leaves government employment, as was evidenced in the 1977 Supreme Court case of *Codd* v. *Velger*.[146] A former New York City policeman applied for a position with the Penn Central Railroad and in order to obtain the position had to agree to have his city personnel file shown to the railroad. He was denied

---

[143] *Bishop* v. *Wood*, 426 U.S. 321 (1976).

[144] For a strong criticism of court intervention into matters previously avoided by courts, see Raoul Berger, *Government by Judiciary: The Transformation of the Fourteenth Amendment* (Cambridge: Harvard University Press, 1977).

[145] For a case in which a federal employee sued a private corporation for maliciously making false charges against him and which adversely affected his employment, see *Stern* v. *United States Gypsum, Inc.*, 547 F.2d 1329 (1977), cert. denied by United States Supreme Court, 1977.

[146] *Codd* v. *Velger*, 429 U.S. 624 (1977).

the job when the railroad learned that when working for New York he allegedly had put a gun to his head as though he were about to commit suicide. He claimed that he should have received a hearing by New York City when it dismissed him, since the allegation had a stigmatizing effect and that the allegation should be removed from his personnel file. The Court disagreed, basing its position on the failure of the former policeman to claim the accusation was false.

The timing of when a hearing takes place and when an adverse action is implemented is important. If an employee is removed and the hearing is conducted at a later date, that situation can place a severe financial burden on a possibly falsely accused employee; of course, if the charge is not upheld in the hearing, the employee will be entitled to back pay. On the other hand, if an employee cannot be removed until after a hearing, an incompetent employee not only might be kept on the payroll but also might cause extensive confusion and inefficiency in the agency.[147] The Supreme Court has held that a federal employee need not be kept on the payroll throughout a possibly protracted appeal process in the courts unless irreparable injury can be shown; loss of income is not considered irreparable injury, since the Back Pay Act would eventually provide for compensation should the employee win on appeal.[148]

The administrative process in adverse action does not have all of the trappings of courtroom proceedings, but basic standards of due process or perhaps simply "fair play" have emerged. As noted earlier, one requirement is that agencies abide by their own rules, although that requirement is not a rigid one.[149] Hearsay evidence, which might not be admissible in a court, frequently is admissible in an administrative hearing. For example, a court upheld the dismissal of an Internal Revenue Service agent under the Lloyd-LaFollette Act based upon newspaper accounts that he had fatally shot a woman, even though he was later acquitted of murder.[150]

Administrative hearings should not be biased against the employee. In a dismissal proceeding against an investigator in the United States Bureau of Narcotics and Dangerous Drugs, the officer who was to judge the case and the prosecutor in the case flew together to where the case was to be heard, stayed in the same hotel, rode in the same automobile to

[147] For divergent views on this issue, see *Shelton* v. *Equal Employment Opportunity Commission*, 357 F. Supp. 3 (1973), affirmed 416 U.S. 976 (1973); *Arnett* v. *Kennedy*, 416 U.S. 134 (1974); *Kennedy* v. *Robb and Gannon*, 547 F.2d 408 (1976); and *Giles* v. *United States*, 553 F.2d 647 (1977).

[148] *Sampson* v. *Murray*, 415 U.S. 61 (1974).

[149] See *Bates* v. *Sponberg*, 547 F.2d 325 (1976).

[150] *Wathen* v. *United States*, 527 F.2d 1191 (1975), cert. denied 429 U.S. 821 (1976).

the hearing, and privately discussed the case on several occasions.[151] This practice was held to be biased against the employee.

The opportunity to cross-examine witnesses is important to due process. A local policeman's dismissal, for example, was overturned by a court because, after a hearing was conducted, the city civil service commission accepted accusatory affidavits from other police officers without informing the employee of these materials.[152]

An employee entitled to a formal hearing commonly may have legal counsel, but this is at the employee's and not the government's expense. Having an attorney present can provide important safeguards for the worker but it also can tend to produce unnecessarily rigid, legalistic procedures. Whether the right to counsel should be extended to all interrogations of employees is debatable. On routine matters, such as a supervisor asking an employee why he was late to work, should an attorney be present to represent the employee?[153]

As part of the due process requirement, the dismissal must be based upon some reason, and the action cannot be arbitrary. A federal court did not side with a civilian employee of the Army who was dismissed because of having been convicted of possessing narcotics; the employee contended that the action was arbitrary, since possession of narcotics had not affected his work performance.[154] In contrast, an agency may be required to show motive as the basis for dismissal. The Internal Revenue Service, for example, expects its employees to be above reproach in income tax matters, and therefore has disciplined employees for failing to file their income tax returns or failing to file them on time. Adverse actions against two female IRS clerks were overturned by a court

---

[151] *Brown v. United States*, 377 F. Supp. 530 (1974). See also *Hortonville Joint School District v. Hortonville Education Association*, 426 U.S. 482 (1976); this case is discussed in Chapter 13.

[152] *Richardson v. Pasadena, Texas*, 513 S. W. 2d 1 (1974).

[153] *Extent of Use and Application of Fitness-For-Duty Examinations by Federal Agencies* (Washington: General Accounting Office, 1977); Subcommittee on Civil Service, House Committee on Post Office and Civil Service, *Federal Employee Administrative Hearing Rights Guarantee Act: Hearing*, 95th Cong., 1st sess. (Washington: Government Printing Office, 1977); Subcommittee on Civil Service, House Committee on Post Office and Civil Service, *Right to Representation: Hearing*, 95th Cong., 1st sess. (Washington: Government Printing Office, 1977); Subcommittee on Compensation and Employee Benefits, House Committee on Post Office and Civil Service, *Use of Physical and Psychiatric Examinations to Determine Fitness for Duty: Hearings*, 95th Cong., 2d sess. (Washington: Government Printing Office, 1978); and Subcommittee on Retirement and Employee Benefits, House Committee on Post Office and Civil Service, *Right to Counsel During Interrogations: Hearings*, 94th Cong., 1st sess. (Washington: Government Printing Office, 1975).

[154] *Young v. Hampton*, 420 F.Supp. 1358 (1976). See also *Umholtz v. Tulsa, Oklahoma*, 565 P.2d 15 (1977).

because the agency had not shown willful intent.[155] The employees had not deliberately violated the tax law but rather had depended upon their husbands to file the income tax returns, and the husbands had forgotten to do so.

Agency failure to meet the due process standards does not reinstate employees who have been dismissed. If a court holds the procedure was biased, that an unacceptable level of hearsay evidence was used, or that the employee was not permitted to cross-examine witnesses, he does not regain his job. Instead, a new hearing is conducted, and there is a good chance the employee will be dismissed a second time.

Criticisms of adverse action proceedings abound. Greater safeguards for employees supposedly have limited the authority of managers to manage. Employees are not dismissed as early as they should be because managers must build a case that will withstand court review. In the disciplinary hearing, the employee's supervisor often seems to be the one accused rather than the employee. Other employees in the agency "watch to see whether the supervisor or the employee will triumph. This sort of a struggle does not help the organization, the employee, or the supervisor."[156] Both employees and managers complain that adverse proceedings are excessively time-consuming. The delays are partially the result of court insistence on protecting employees by giving them due process.

SUMMARY

Efforts have been made to balance the rights of government and its employees. No longer is it assumed that government may prescribe whatever behavior it chooses for its workers; public servants do not automatically relinquish their rights as citizens when they are hired by government. At the same time, absolute rights cannot be granted employees, since that would seriously handicap the government in serving the citizenry. The concept of balancing government and employee rights sounds good as a general principle, but, as has been seen, applying that concept to specific situations is difficult.

Government demands high ethical standards of its employees. Corruption and conflicts of interest are grounds for dismissal. Dilemmas develop over such matters as whether employees should follow the dictates of their chosen profession in the delivery of services or should

---

[155] *Boyce and Dixon* v. *United States*, 543 F.2d 1290 (1976).

[156] Commission on Organization of the Executive Branch of the Government (Second Hoover Commission), *Task Force Report on Personnel and Civil Service* (Washington: Government Printing Office, 1955), p. 96. See also *Design and Administration of the Adverse Action and Appeals Systems Need to be Improved*, p. 29.

remain loyal to a political administration, even though the administration's actions run counter to professional standards. Employees are expected to serve the public interest and execute statutes, but often considerable discretion or judgment must be exercised, allowing each worker to decide to some extent what is in the public interest. Not only does government establish standards for employee conduct on the job, but standards also are set for off-the-job conduct. Employees may be required to live within the jurisdiction that they serve. Alcoholics and former criminal offenders are unlikely to be hired, and employees who become alcoholics or are convicted of crimes may be dismissed. The sex lives of employees also are subject to some government restrictions.

The presumed right of government to protect itself from employees who would subvert it either by leaking national security information or by advocating its violent overthrow has come into direct conflict with the rights of government workers as citizens. Loyalty and security charges have destroyed the careers of many former public employees. The freedoms of speech and peaceful assembly as guaranteed in the First Amendment have been used selectively to protect public workers, but the judicial system has been unwilling to provide blanket protections. The due process clause has provided additional protections for employees dismissed for loyalty or security reasons. The "red scares" of the 1950s have vanished but loyalty oaths and security regulations remain in force.

Public workers have considerable free-speech rights. Whistle blowing is common, both for employees who choose to remain in government and for those who resign in protest. Whistle blowing helps to keep government accountable but it can lead to each employee acting on his own. Laws and regulations pertaining to limits on speech are expected to be clear so that employees know what speech is prohibited, but a lingering question is whether existing statutes are sufficiently clear. When an employee exercises his constitutional right to free speech, he may be technically protected from dismissal, but other means, such as RIFs, can be used to seek his ouster.

Unresolved is the issue of whether public employees should be permitted to participate in political activities. The Hatch Act and its counterparts at the state level have been defended as providing for political neutrality in government administration and for protecting workers from attempts to coerce them into partisan activities. The courts have not found these laws to violate First Amendment rights or to be unconstitutionally vague. The federal government may impose political restrictions on state and local employees who are funded substantially by the federal government. While these limitations on public servants are constitutional, existing legislation could be rewritten to allow for greater involvement of public employees in the political process.

Several methods are used to hold civil servants directly answerable to the citizenry. Laws require the release of government information and meetings on policy and regulations to be held in public. Ombudsman offices help mediate problems between citizens and government agencies. Through legislation the federal government has allowed for liability suits against itself, but this is far less common at the state and local levels. In response, citizens have filed Section 1983 suits against individual government officials, holding them personally liable for their actions.

Employees have protections when their superiors attempt to demote, suspend, reassign, or remove them. Appeal procedures are provided by statutes, executive orders, and administrative regulations. The courts have moved away from the concept of government employment being a privilege and have recognized that property and liberty rights may be at stake in adverse actions. When such rights are involved, due process standards must be observed, including having an oral hearing, having an attorney to represent the employee, having an opportunity to cross-examine witnesses, and the like. The procedures used are extremely time-consuming, and, depending on one's point of view, do not adequately protect employees, severely handicap the ability of public managers to manage, or both.

The issues in this chapter are of immense importance. In order to facilitate the discussion, the chapter is divided into sections and subsections, but these should not be considered to be independent of each other. All of the issues relate to the rights of employees and their employers. What is in the best interests of society: protecting government's ability to function or protecting the rights of government's employees? The desirable approach would be to protect both, but achieving that objective is difficult.

Chapter 9

Equal Rights and Affirmative Action

Discrimination in government employment has existed for a long time. "In 1802 Postmaster General Gideon Granger warned that if Negroes were allowed to carry the mail, it would pose a threat to security because they might coordinate insurrectionary activities and acquire subversive ideas. For example, they might learn 'that a man's rights do not depend on his color.'"[1] As recently as 1913, regulations barred married women from the postal service.[2] The "liberals" of the day who advocated hiring blacks and women often based their positions on being able to pay them less than other workers, thereby increasing government efficiency.[3] People have been discriminated against on the basis of their race, sex, marital status, ethnicity, age, and religion. The physically handicapped, mentally retarded, mentally ill, obese, and homosexuals also face discrimination barriers.

This chapter pursues the same theme as the previous one, namely what rights people have in obtaining government jobs, in developing careers in government, and in not being discharged. The concern is with the right to be treated the same as other persons with like skills rather

[1] David H. Rosenbloom, *Federal Service and the Constitution: The Development of the Public Employment Relationship* (Ithaca, N.Y.: Cornell University Press, 1971), p. 124. See Samuel Krislov, *The Negro in Federal Employment: The Quest for Equal Opportunity* (Minneapolis: University of Minnesota Press, 1967).

[2] Rosenbloom, *Federal Service and the Constitution*, p. 129.

[3] See Lucille F. McMillin, *Women in the Federal Service*, 3d. ed. (Washington: Government Printing Office, 1941) and Paul P. Van Riper, *History of the United States Civil Service* (Evanston, Ill.: Row, Peterson, 1958), pp. 159–160.

than being discriminated against for a non-job-related reason. Although the possible bases for discrimination are infinite, the chapter concentrates largely upon discrimination based on sex and race. The first section discusses the distribution of minorities and women in government jobs. The second considers the legal remedies available to eliminate discrimination and the agencies that enforce relevant statutes. The third section concentrates upon various aspects of personnel administration and how discrimination affects these. The fourth discusses affirmative actions to increase the numbers of women and minorities in public employment.

MINORITIES AND WOMEN IN GOVERNMENT

The federal government and state and local governments are remarkably similar in the extent to which they employ minorities and women.[4] Table

---

[4] Data discussed in this section, unless otherwise indicated, have been compiled from the following sources: Civil Service Commission, *Educational Attainment of General Schedule Employees by Minority Group and Sex* (Washington: Government Printing Office, 1977); Civil Service Commission, *Minority Group Employment in the Federal Government* (Washington: Government Printing Office, 1971 and 1977); Civil Service Commission, *1976 Annual Report* (Washington: Government Printing Office, 1977); and Equal Employment Opportunity Commission, *Minorities and Women in State and Local Government, 1975*, vol. I (Washington: Government Printing Office, 1977). Data for 1975 are used throughout the discussion for consistency purposes, although more current data may be available on selected topics. Additional statistical analyses can be found in Frank K. Gibson and Samuel Yeager, "Trends in the Federal Employment of Blacks," *Public Personnel Management*, 4 (1975): 189–195; Peter Grabosky and David H. Rosenbloom, "Racial and Ethnic Integration in the Federal Service," *Social Science Quarterly*, 56 (1975):71–84; Grace Hall and Alan Saltzstein, "Equal Employment Opportunity for Minorities in Municipal Government," *Social Science Quarterly*, 57 (1977):864–872; and Civil Service Commission, *A Profile of Hispanic Employment, 1974–76* (Washington: Government Printing Office, 1978). Literature of general interest to this chapter includes the following: Civil Service Commission, *Equal Employment Opportunity Court Cases* (Washington: Government Printing Office, 1976); Commission on Civil Rights, *For All the People by All the People: A Report on Equal Opportunity in State and Local Government Employment* (Washington: Government Printing Office, 1969); Cleveland L. Dennard and Carl Akins, eds., "Minority Perspectives on Bureaucracy," *The Bureaucrat*, 2 (1973): 127–191; Nestas M. Gallas, ed., "Symposium on Women in Public Administration," *Public Administration Review*, 36 (1976):347–389; Nathan Glazer, *Affirmative Discrimination: Ethnic Inequality and Public Policy* (New York: Basic Books, 1975), pp. 33–76; Adam W. Herbert, ed., "Symposium on Minorities in Public Administration," *Public Administration Review*, 34 (1974):519–563; Lawrence C. Howard, "Civil Service Reform: A Minority and Woman's Perspective," *Public Administration Review*, 38 (1978):305–309; J. Donald Kingsley, *Representative Bureaucracy: An Interpretation of the British Civil Service* (Yellow Springs, Ohio: Antioch, 1944); Harry Kranz, *The Participatory Bureaucracy: Women and Minorities in a More Representative Public Service* (Lexington, Mass.: Heath, 1976); Samuel Krislov, *Representative Bureaucracy* (Englewood Cliffs, N.J.: Prentice-Hall, 1974); Helene S. Markoff, "The Federal Women's Program," *Public Administration Review*, 32 (1972):144–151; David H. Rosenbloom, *Federal Equal Employment Opportunity: Politics and Personnel Administration* (New York: Praeger, 1977); Catherine Samuels, *The Forgotten Five Million: Women in Public Employment* (New York: Women's Action Alliance, 1975); Mitchell Sherman, "Equal Employment Opportunity:

Table 9.1. Percentage distribution of minorities and women in federal and state and local positions, 1975

	Positions	
	Federal	State and Local
Minorities	21.0	20.4
Blacks	15.9	15.4
Hispanics	3.3	3.8
Native Americans	0.9	0.3
Asians	0.9	0.7
Women	35.3	37.5

Sources: Federal data from Civil Service Commission, *1976 Annual Report* (Washington: Government Printing Office, 1977): p. 40. State and local data from survey of 2,387 jurisdictions, Equal Employment Opportunity Commission, *Minorities and Women in State and Local Government, 1975*, vol. I (Washington: Government Printing Office, 1977): p. 9.

9.1 shows that in 1975 the work forces of these governments consisted of about 20 percent minorities and about 35 percent women. Geographical variations were great. Only about 5 percent of the federal employees in New England were minorities, and the comparable figure for the northwestern states of Idaho, Oregon, and Washington plus Alaska was 8 percent. In contrast, nearly a quarter of all federal employees were minorities in the Dallas federal region, consisting of Arkansas, Louisiana, New Mexico, Oklahoma, and Texas. Less than 1 percent of federal employees were minorities in the states of Maine and Vermont, whereas about a third were minorities in Arizona, the District of Columbia, Illinois, and Texas. New Mexico had the highest percentage of federal employees who were minorities (45 percent); 27 percent of the employees were Hispanics and 16 percent were Native Americans (American Indians). These variations are partially a reflection of the racial and ethnic composition of geographic areas. Only about 6 percent of federal workers in Wisconsin were blacks, but Wisconsin is a state in which blacks constitute only about 3 percent of the population, in comparison with a national average of 12 percent.

Legal Issues and Societal Consequences," *Public Personnel Management*, 7 (1978):127–134; Larry E. Short, "Equal Employment Opportunity as Perceived by Government Officials," *Public Personnel Management*, 2 (1973):118–124; Donald R. Stacy, "Applying Federal Employment Discrimination Laws to State and Municipal Employees," *Employee Relations Law Journal*, 3 (1977):94–108; Frank J. Thompson and Bonnie Browne, "Commitment to the Disadvantaged among Urban Administrators: The Case of Minority Hiring," *Urban Affairs Quarterly*, 13 (1978):355–378; and Frank J. Thompson, *Personnel Policy in the City: The Politics of Jobs in Oakland* (Berkeley: University of California Press, 1975), pp. 112–139.

Minorities and women tend to be concentrated in low-level positions at all levels of government. Among General Schedule or similar positions in the federal government, minorities held about 17 percent of the jobs in 1975. However, they held about half of the GS 1 positions and about a third of the GS 2 and 3 positions. There is a steady decline in the percent of minorities ranging from GS 1 to GS 18, so that less than 5 percent of the supergrade jobs were held by minorities. Women were similarly over-represented in low positions and underrepresented in high positions; more than 70 percent of the GS 2 through 4 jobs were held by women, but less than 5 percent of the GS 14 through 18 jobs were held by women. Only two out of every 100 GS 17s and 18s were women.

The same pattern exists at the state and local levels. As of 1975, median salary for a white worker in states, counties, cities, townships, and special districts was $10,167, while for minorities it was $8,788; Asians were the only minority whose median salary was above that of whites ($12,271, compared with $10,167 for whites). Males earned higher incomes than females ($11,295, compared with $8,178). Approximately 8 percent of the highest paying state and local jobs ($25,000 or more) were held by women and about 9 percent were held by minorities. One out of every 10 jobs paying between $16,000 and $25,000 went to women, and the same was true for minorities.

Minorities and women are concentrated in some occupations. Table 9.2 shows the distribution of state and local minorities and women by occupation for 1975. It is not surprising that more than 80 percent of

Table 9.2. Percentage distribution of state and local minorities and women by occupation, 1975

	Minorities		Women	
Occupation	As percent of occupation	As percent of total	As percent of occupation	As percent of total
Officials and Administrators	8.3	2.0	18.9	2.5
Professionals	12.8	11.1	39.8	18.7
Technicians	15.2	7.2	32.2	8.3
Protective Service Workers	12.2	8.0	5.9	2.1
Paraprofessionals	34.6	15.4	66.9	16.3
Office and Clerical	19.6	18.7	83.8	43.4
Skilled Craft Workers	16.0	6.6	5.1	1.1
Service-Maintenance	36.6	31.0	16.4	7.6
Average	20.4		37.5	
Total		100.0		100.0

Source: Equal Employment Opportunity Commission, *Minorities and Women in State and Local Government, 1975*, vol. I (Washington: Government Printing Office, 1977): pp. 1–9, and 177. Data based upon 2,387 jurisdictions.

Table 9.3. Percentage distribution of state and local minorities and women by functional area, 1975

| Function | Minorities | | Women | |
	As percent of function	As percent of total	As percent of function	As percent of total
Financial Administration	13.6	8.2	51.5	16.8
Streets and Highways	12.5	7.4	8.4	2.7
Public Welfare	26.2	9.8	72.9	14.8
Police Protection	11.0	5.9	14.0	4.1
Fire Protection	6.7	1.4	1.6	0.2
Natural Resources	17.2	4.4	19.8	2.8
Hospitals and Sanitariums	29.6	25.5	70.2	32.9
Health	21.8	5.9	63.7	9.5
Housing	42.7	3.6	26.9	1.2
Community Development	18.8	0.8	32.3	0.8
Corrections	20.7	4.4	27.9	3.2
Utilities and Transportation	26.8	9.8	12.1	2.4
Sanitation and Sewage	40.1	7.2	3.4	0.3
Employment Security	18.6	1.9	56.7	3.2
Other	18.5	3.7	45.9	5.0
Total		100.0		100.0

Source: Equal Employment Opportunity Commission, *Minorities and Women in State and Local Government, 1975*, vol. I (Washington: Government Printing Office, 1977): pp. 12–176. Data based upon 2,387 jurisdictions.

clerical jobs were held by women, and these clerical jobs accounted for more than 40 percent of all state and local jobs held by women. Paraprofessional jobs were another major area of female concentration. Paraprofessionals include library assistants, homemaker aides, and child support workers. Minorities, in comparison, were concentrated in service-maintenance jobs. More than a third of these jobs were held by minorities, and those jobs accounted for about a third of all jobs held by minorities. Minorities fared about the same as women in administrative jobs; only 2 percent of state and local minorities and women held official and administrator positions. Nearly 20 percent of all administrators are women, compared with only 8 percent being minorities.

Concentrations of minorities and women are found in certain departments and functional areas. Table 9.3 shows that in 1975 half or more of state and local workers were female in the functions of financial administration, public welfare, hospitals and sanitariums, health, and employment security. More than 60 percent of all jobs held by women were in the areas of financial administration, welfare, and hospitals. Minorities did not hold a majority of the jobs in any functional area but did hold over 40 percent of the jobs in the housing and sanitation/sewage fields. Approximately a quarter of all jobs held by minorities were in hospitals.

Great variation among federal departments also is common. In 1975, a majority (54 percent) of the staff of the Government Printing Office, which is responsible for the publication and distribution of federal documents, consisted of minorities. The Civil Service Commission had 31 percent minorities, while the Department of Agriculture had 10 percent minorities. The Tennessee Valley Authority had only 7 percent minorities, and about three-quarters of these minority workers were in jobs equivalent to GS 5 or below.

These patterns for minorities and women are in part a reflection of education. If a state department of agriculture needs to hire an agronomist, it must select among individuals with the appropriate education, and neither women nor minorities have tended to concentrate in agronomy. Similarly, only a small fraction of graduates from civil engineering are women, and therefore a state department of highways will have difficulty in hiring women. ". . . Nearly half of all degrees received by women in 1972 were in education, the health professions, and library science—over 65 percent of the degrees were received by women."[5] As for minorities, fewer go to college than whites, which means the latter have an advantage in winning high-level positions, but that pattern is changing. Minority college enrollments grew by 44 percent between 1968 and 1972.[6]

OUTLAWING DISCRIMINATION

Discrimination has been outlawed through a variety of means. Courts have interpreted state and federal constitutional provisions as protecting against discrimination. State and federal statutes have furthered the antidiscrimination cause. Presidents and governors have issued executive orders for the same purpose. As is seen in this section, each of these legal routes has differing effects. Some are sweeping, protecting numerous groups from discrimination, while other routes are limited to one classification, such as protecting against sex discrimination.

The United States Constitution can provide protection against discrimination through the Fifth and Fourteenth Amendments. Both amendments include the due process clause, and it is possible to contend

[5] *Problems in the Federal Employee Equal Employment Opportunity Program Need to be Resolved* (Washington: General Accounting Office, 1977), p. 32.

[6] *Problems in the Federal Employee Equal Employment Opportunity Program Need to be Resolved*, p. 32.

that without having been granted due process one has been denied a property right, as in the case of not receiving equal pay. The Fourteenth Amendment, which applies to the states, has the additional guarantee of equal protection of the laws.

The chance of winning a suit under the Fourteenth Amendment is partially dependent upon what type of test the courts choose in determining whether a given practice is discriminatory. The "rationality" test holds that if a policy is found to have some rational basis or purpose it will be held constitutional even though the policy has an adverse effect upon some groups. The "strict scrutiny" test is more probative and is more likely to overturn a given practice as discriminatory. This test, however, is limited to what the courts call "suspect classes," namely groups that have had "a history of purposeful unequal treatment." A policy that had adverse effects upon blacks, therefore, would likely be subject to the strict scrutiny test, while a policy adverse to older employees would not.[7]

Another difficulty with using the Fifth and Fourteenth Amendments in discrimination cases is that they place a heavy burden of proof upon a person challenging a government's action. In *Washington v. Davis* (1976), the Supreme Court held that simply showing that a government's practice negatively affected blacks was insufficient proof that they were the victims of discrimination.[8] When claiming discrimination under the Fifth Amendment, intent to discriminate must be shown. In *Washington v. Davis* the Court concluded that, although blacks were adversely affected by the process used to select Washington, D.C., police officers, there had been no contention that the city had intentionally discriminated against blacks and that, in fact, the government had actively recruited them.

Because of the difficulties in winning a suit under the Fourteenth Amendment, other legal routes are used, including Sections 1981–83 of Title 42 of the United States Code. Those sections are part of the Civil Rights Acts passed by Congress following the Civil War. Sections 1981 and 1982 protect only against racial discrimination and, therefore, cannot be used in cases involving sex, age, and ethnic discrimination. Section 1983, which is not restricted to race, protects against state officials who "under color of any statute, ordinance, regulation, custom, or usage" deprive one of "rights, privileges, or immunities" (see discussion of § 1983 in Chapter 8). All of these provisions have the drawback that they

---

[7] See *Massachusetts Board of Retirement v. Murgia*, 427 U.S. 307 (1976). The case is discussed in the next section of this chapter.

[8] *Washington v. Davis*, 426 U.S. 229 (1976).

may not be used in any federal employment cases involving discrimination (*Brown* v. *General Services Administration*, 1976).[9]

The Civil Rights Act of 1964 was a landmark in the effort to eliminate discrimination. That law established the Equal Employment Opportunity Commission (EEOC), and Title VII empowered the Commission to prosecute cases of discrimination in private employment. The law also reaffirmed the policy of nondiscrimination in federal employment. In 1965 President Johnson issued Executive Order 11246 prohibiting discrimination involving federal contracts, and the order included a provision against discrimination in federal employment. The order was amended in 1967 by Executive Order 11375, extending coverage to discrimination based on sex. In 1969 President Nixon issued Executive Order 11478, "Equal Employment Opportunity in the Federal Government." Encouraged by Title VII and the executive orders, persons who claimed they had been discriminated against in federal employment attempted to bring suit in federal courts but were repeatedly turned away; courts held that such suits were precluded, since Congress had not yielded sovereign immunity.[10] A Catch-22 situation had arisen in that it was illegal for the federal government to discriminate and yet no one could sue the government for having discriminated.

The situation was changed in 1972 by the Equal Employment Opportunity Act. This legislation extended coverage of Title VII to the federal, state, and local governments. The law protects against discrimination based on race, color, sex, religion, and national origin; although the coverage is broad, it does not protect against discrimination based on age or handicap. As is seen in the following discussion, the 1972 legislative changes led to much controversy. Implementation of the law was said to be ineffective and state and local governments were subjected to conflicting pressures from various federal agencies pursuing equal opportunity.

Important changes in the federal government's approach to equal employment opportunity were approved in 1978. President Carter's Reorganization Plan No. 1 reassigned equal employment responsibilities among federal agencies. That plan was clarified in part by Executive

---

[9] *Brown* v. *General Services Administration*, 425 U.S. 820 (1976). See Roy L. Brooks, "Use of the Civil Rights Act of 1866 and 1871 to Redress Employment Discrimination," *Cornell Law Review*, 62 (1977):258–288; *Bowers* v. *Campbell*, 505 F. 2d 1155 (1974); and *Penn* v. *Schlesinger*, 497 F. 2d 970 (1974).

[10] *Beale* v. *Blount*, 461 F. 2d 1133 (1972) and *Ogletree* v. *McNamara*, 449 F. 2d 93 (1971). Sovereign immunity is discussed in Chapter 8. See "Racial Discrimination in the Federal Service," *George Washington Law Review*, 38 (1969):265–304, and Charles F. Abernathy, "Sovereign Immunity in a Constitutional Government: The Federal Employment Discrimination Cases," *Harvard Civil Rights-Civil Liberties Review*, 10 (1975): 322–368.

Order 12067, pertaining to equal opportunity in federal employment; Executive Order 12068, pertaining to the powers of the Department of Justice as they applied to state and local governments; and Executive Order 12086, relating to the Office of Federal Contract Compliance Programs in the Labor Department. Also, the Civil Service Reform Act of 1978 contains antidiscrimination provisions; the law prohibits discrimination based on "political affiliation, race, color, religion, national origin, sex, marital status, age, or handicapping condition." The important changes made by the reorganization plan, the executive orders, and the new law were intended to resolve many of the problems that had been evident since passage of the Equal Employment Opportunity Act of 1972. The immediate result of these changes, nevertheless, was considerable uncertainty about how specific provisions would be implemented. The discussion that follows necessarily focuses upon the experience prior to the 1978 changes.[11]

Procedures have been established for processing complaints against federal agencies that allegedly have discriminated in violation of Title VII.[12] Prior to the 1978 changes, a person alleging discrimination, whether he was already a federal employee or one seeking a federal job, was required first to contact the equal employment opportunity (EEO) counselor of the agency where the offense occurred. The counselor investigated the charge, but if no action was taken, the person claiming discrimination could file a formal complaint. If the agency was unable to reach an informal solution to the problem, the complaining person could demand a formal decision and have a hearing before an examiner. Should the agency decision be negative, the individual could file suit in a United States district court or could appeal the decision to the Appeals Review Board of the Civil Service Commission. In the latter instance, a negative ruling could be appealed in district court.

There were many problems with this procedure. One complaint was that EEO counselors often were located in their agency personnel offices, giving the impression that the counselors were apologists or defenders of the agency rather than advocates of equal opportunity. Another complaint was that EEO staff were not sufficiently trained in personnel

---

[11] Reorganization Plan No. 1 of 1978, 43 F.R. 19807 (1978); Executive Order 12067, 43 F.R. 28967 (1978); Executive Order 12068, 43 F.R. 28971 (1978); Executive Order 12086, 43 F.R. 46501 (1978); and Civil Service Reform Act, 92 Stat. 1111 (1978). See *A Compilation of Federal Laws and Executive Orders for Nondiscrimination and Equal Opportunity Programs* (Washington: General Accounting Office, 1978).

[12] Commission on Civil Rights, *The Federal Civil Rights Enforcement Effort, 1974: To Eliminate Employment Discrimination* (Washington: Government Printing Office, 1975), pp. 1–137; and Commission on Civil Rights, *The Federal Civil Rights Enforcement Effort, 1977: To Eliminate Employment Discrimination (A Sequel)* (Washington: Government Printing Office, 1977), pp. 1–60.

administration and therefore could not provide effective assistance in protecting against discrimination. Still another contention was that complainants often were not informed of their rights, such as having their names kept secret while the EEO staff investigated.[13]

Noting in his reorganization message to Congress that the Civil Service Commission had been "lethargic in enforcing fair employment," President Carter recommended that the CSC's responsibilities be transferred to the Equal Employment Opportunity Commission.[14] The administrative process for investigating discrimination charges would be shifted to the EEOC, while persons claiming discrimination would retain the right to appeal unfavorable decisions in court. This shift was supported on the grounds that the EEOC would be more assertive in guaranteeing equal opportunity and would not have mixed loyalties, i.e., support of equal opportunity versus support for agency personnel actions. The reorganization would provide for consistency in that the federal government would be brought under the same set of standards used for state and local governments.

One potential problem with the Carter plan was that two parallel investigation and hearing processes would exist, one for discrimination cases and one for other personnel matters. For example, a black woman denied a promotion could appeal the decision through the process of the Merit Systems Protection Board.[15] That same woman also could allege discrimination and seek redress through the EEOC.

The Civil Service Reform Act provided a mechansim for dealing with this problem. Cases exclusively involving alleged discrimination may be appealed to the EEOC. In so-called "mixed cases" involving discrimination and an action that is subject to appeal before the MSPB (see Chapter 8), the appeal route is through the Board and not the Commission. Should the individual not be satisfied with the Board's decision, the case may be appealed to either a court of appeals or the Equal Employment Opportunity Commission. In the latter instance, the EEOC

---

[13] *System for Processing Individual Equal Employment Opportunity Discrimination Complaints: Improvements Needed* (Washington: General Accounting Office, 1977). See also Wendy T. Kirby, "The United States as Prevailing Defendant in Title VII Actions: Attorneys' Fees and Costs," *Georgetown Law Journal*, 66 (1978):899–929; Paul Mahoney, "Equal Opportunity," *Civil Service Journal*, 15 (July–September, 1974):4–5; Charles R. McManis, "Racial Discrimination in Government Employment: A Problem of Remedies for Unclean Federal Hands," *Georgetown Law Journal*, 63 (1975):1203–1244; and Robert G. Vaughn, *The Spoiled System: A Call for Civil Service Reform* (New York: Charterhouse, 1975), pp. 28–111.

[14] *Message from the President of the United States: Reorganization Plan No. 1 of 1978*, 95th Cong., 2d sess., H. Doc. 95-295 (Washington: Government Printing Office, 1978).

[15] See Chapters 2 and 3.

may concur in the Board's decision or issue a different opinion in the event it thinks the Board misinterpreted the law. If the Commission and the Board are in disagreement, the case is submitted to a Special Panel consisting of a representative from each agency and a Chairman who is appointed by the President with the Senate's advice and consent. The Chairman serves a six-year term and "may be removed by the President only for inefficiency, neglect of duty, or malfeasance." Decisions of the Special Panel may be appealed in court.

Federal officials accused of discrimination are in an ambiguous position. In one perspective, these officials are well protected and perhaps overly protected. Discrimination suits are against the agency and not against the employee who allegedly discriminated. Moreover, even when an official has been found to have discriminated, he or she is only rarely severely disciplined. The common practice is to issue a letter of reprimand, a copy of which is placed in the employee's personnel file. This practice has been defended on the grounds that the accusation of discrimination and the ensuing investigation constitute sufficient punishment. While these practices may seem lenient, the official involved is at a particular disadvantage. Since the agency and not the individual is being accused, the employee has less opportunity to defend herself or himself. For example, the employee has no right to participate in the agency hearing in the case unless called as a witness.[16]

The mandated appeals process has been criticized as being both time-consuming and overly rigid. In *Brown v. General Services Administration* (1976), involving alleged racial discrimination in promotion decisions, the Supreme Court disallowed a Title VII suit simply because it had been filed twelve days too late. That case is particularly important, because the Court held that the 1972 legislation that extended Title VII to cover the federal government constituted the exclusive route for federal discrimination cases. In other words, if an individual fails to meet one of the prescribed deadlines in the process, the entire case will be lost. One other issue concerning the appeals process has been the extent to which courts should review federal discrimination charges. If a trial de novo were required, then the court would hear all evidence in the case as though it were new, whereas a more limited approach would involve simply reviewing the records in the case. The argument against the trial de novo approach was that complainants would get the equivalent of two trials or chances to prove their cases, namely a formal hearing and then a

---

[16] *System for Processing Individual Equal Employment Opportunity Discrimination Complaints*, pp. 28–29 and 45–46; and Glenn E. Schweitzer, "The Rights of Federal Employees Named as Alleged Discriminatory Officials," *Public Administration Review*, 37 (1977):58–63.

full court trial. The argument in favor was that the administrative hearing could be biased and therefore a person should be granted a court trial. The Supreme Court resolved the issue in *Chandler* v. *Roudebush* (1976), holding that a trial de novo was required.[17] The Civil Service Reform Act guarantees this right to a trial de novo.

The Equal Employment Opportunity Act of 1972 also was extended to state and local governments. If a person thinks she has been discriminated against by a state or local government, she can complain to the Equal Employment Opportunity Commission. The Commission will refer the case to a state or local equal opportunity commission, such as a state human relations commission. If the matter is not resolved, the EEOC may initiate its own investigation. In the event the Commission concludes there is little grounds for complaint, the Commission can close the case, but it can also issue a letter to the individual involved permitting the filing of a private civil suit in a federal court. If the EEOC concludes that there are grounds for a suit, it refers the matter to the Justice Department, with the recommendation to file the suit.

The major criticisms of this process are that it is excessively cumbersome and that coordination among empowered agencies often is lacking. A person who feels he has been discriminated against is likely to be frustrated by the seemingly endless steps in the process. State and local EEO agencies have been criticized for relying upon the EEOC to investigate; in defense, these agencies have claimed they do not have sufficient staff to investigate the cases that arise, although that problem has lessened because of federal financial assistance for this activity. One of the most important areas of criticism has been the relationship between the EEOC and the Department of Justice (DOJ). EEOC has complained that DOJ is slow in prosecuting, while Justice has complained that EEOC frequently does an inadequate job in investigating cases.[18]

---

[17] *Chandler* v. *Roudebush*, 425 U.S. 840 (1976). See *Sperling* v. *United States*, 515 F. 2d 465 (1975); *Hackley* v. *Roudebush*, 520 F. 2d 108 (1975); and William A. Denman, "Judicial Review of Federal Employee Discrimination Complaints," *Catholic University Law Review*, 25 (1976):299–319.

[18] *The Equal Employment Opportunity Commission Has Made Limited Progress in Eliminating Employment Discrimination* (Washington: General Accounting Office, 1976); and Commission on Civil Rights, *The Federal Civil Rights Enforcement Effort, 1977*, pp. 282–286. See also E. Richard Larson, "Remedies for Racial Discrimination in State and Local Government Employment: A Survey and Analysis," *Columbia Human Rights Law Review*, 5 (1973):335–382; Donald L. Kohansky, "The Coverage of Appointees of State and Local Elected Officials Under the Equal Employment Opportunity Act of 1972 and Congressional Power to Enforce the Fourteenth Amendment," *Georgetown Law Journal*, 65 (1977):809–836; Harry Grossman, "The Equal Employment Opportunity Act of 1972: Its Implications for the State and Local Government Manager," *Public Personnel Management*, 2 (1973):370–379; Jean J. Couturier and Stephen E. Dunn, "Federal Colonization of State and Local Governments," *State Government*, 50 (1977):65–71.

A disadvantage in processing individual discrimination complaints is that only one abuse may be resolved. A person who successfully alleges discrimination in a job interview or his performance appraisal may be the only one who receives redress. Therefore, it is possible that the extensive energy required to correct a case of discrimination may have a negligible overall impact. An alternative is to allow for class action administrative proceedings and legal suits where large groups of persons allege discrimination. This has been used, for example, by blacks claiming that a civil service test discriminated against them. The result can be a court order to halt the use of the test, thereby affecting many people.

Another alternative to the individual discrimination complaint process is for the government to file a "pattern or practice" case alleging that discrimination within a jurisdiction is widespread. These types of cases involve elaborate analyses of statistics used to demonstrate that women, blacks, or other minorities have been the subject of systematic discrimination. When these cases involved private employers, they were the responsibility of the EEOC as provided in the 1972 legislation. Confusion developed about which agency had authority for pattern or practice cases involving state and local governments. The Justice Department asserted that EEOC had authority over private employers but not state and local employers, but some of DOJ's cases were dismissed by courts that found this authority to be in the hands of the EEOC.[19] This situation was resolved in 1978 by President Carter's Reorganization Plan No. 1 and Executive Order 12068. Pattern or practice cases involving state and local governments were assigned to the Department of Justice.

Antidiscrimination legislation does not end with the Civil Rights Act and Equal Employment Opportunity Act. The Equal Pay Act of 1963 prohibits sex discrimination on pay; and in 1974 that protection was extended to cover public employees.[20] Until the Carter reorganization, the Civil Service Commission enforced equal pay in federal cases, while the Department of Labor handled state and local cases. These powers have been reassigned to the Equal Employment Opportunity Commission.

The Age Discrimination in Employment Act (ADEA) was passed in 1967 to cover private-sector employees and was extended in 1974 to

---

[19] *United States* v. *Pima County Community College District*, 409 F. Supp. 1061 (1976).

[20] Equal Pay Act amending Fair Labor Standards Act, 29 U.S.C. § 203 and § 206(d). For pertinent laws concerning sex discrimination, see U.S. Commission on Civil Rights, *A Guide to Federal Laws and Regulations Prohibiting Sex Discrimination* (Washington: Government Printing Office, 1976).

cover public employees.[21] As amended in 1978 the legislation protects persons between the ages of 40 and 70; the 1978 legislation also eliminated a compulsory retirement age for federal employees. As with the Equal Pay Act, age discrimination in federal government employment was handled by the Civil Service Commission and in state and local employment by the Department of Labor. Under the Carter plan, EEOC has been given enforcement responsibilities.

Handicapped persons are protected under the Rehabilitation Act of 1973, but the language of the legislation is less directive than that in the Civil Rights Act and Equal Employment Opportunity Act.[22] The Civil Service Commission has had responsibility for encouraging the employment of the handicapped in the federal government. The Department of Health, Education, and Welfare, working with the CSC and other agencies, has been empowered to encourage the hiring of the handicapped in state and local governments. The Carter reorganization assigned to the EEOC the responsibility for protecting the handicapped in federal employment.

In addition to the legislation already cited, state and local governments are expected to meet antidiscrimination requirements imposed through federal grant and contract programs. The Intergovernmental Personnel Act of 1970, administered by the Office of Personnel Management, requires recipient agencies to have merit systems, which include protections against discrimination. This brings the OPM into direct oversight of state and local governments. The legislation was amended by the Civil Service Reform Act. The law requires merit systems and prohibits discrimination, but a clause that was added requires that standards should "minimize Federal intervention in State and local personnel administration."

The Office of Federal Contract Compliance Programs (OFCCP) in the Department of Labor, as provided in Executive Order 11246 as amended, has the responsibility for enforcing equal opportunity involving federal contracts, including contracts with state and local governments.[23] Contract compliance enforcement had been decentralized among federal

---

[21] Age Discrimination in Employment Act, 81 Stat. 602 (1967) and Age Discrimination in Employment Act Amendments of 1978, 92 Stat. 189 (1978). "The Age of Discrimination in Employment Act of 1967," *Harvard Law Review*, 90 (1976):380–441; and Marc Rosenblum, *The Next Steps in Combating Age Discrimination in Employment: With Special Reference to Mandatory Retirement Policy*, prepared for Special Senate Committee on Aging, 95th Cong, 1st sess. (Washington: Government Printing Office, 1977).

[22] Rehabilitation Act, 29 U.S.C. § 791. See also Antidiscrimination in Employment, 5 U.S.C. § 7153.

[23] See William A. Wright, "Equal Treatment of the Handicapped by Federal Contractors," *Emory Law Journal*, 26 (1977):65–106.

agencies, resulting in agencies sometimes having overlapping powers and conflicting policies. This procedure was changed by Executive Order 12086, which amended E.O. 11246 and provided for direct administration by the OFCCP.

Another important example is the State and Local Fiscal Assistance Act, better known as general revenue sharing. Passed by Congress in 1972, the legislation was renewed in 1976 with important nondiscrimination provisions being added. The original legislation required recipient governments to report the functional area in which revenue-sharing money was used; each area that was reported by jurisdiction became subject to an antidiscrimination provision. The 1976 legislation established a presumption that *all* aspects of a state or local government are influenced by revenue-sharing monies, even if a city, for example, might claim the money was being used exclusively for police services. Since nearly 40,000 state, county, city, and township governments are receiving these funds, the legislation has broad impact. The Office of Revenue Sharing in the Treasury Department administers the legislation, thereby bringing another federal agency into the antidiscrimination effort. ORS has withheld funds from governments accused of discriminating. Similar powers are provided to the Department of Housing and Urban Development in administering the Housing and Community Development Act of 1974. The Department of Health, Education, and Welfare also has important antidiscrimination powers, particularly over educational institutions.

Confusion at the state and local levels resulted from these diverse pieces of legislation. State and local officials complained that federal agencies often gave conflicting directives. EEOC, for instance, has been especially forceful in having these governments change procedures so as to encourage greater hiring of minorities and women, but these efforts often were challenged by the Civil Service Commission as violating the merit principle. President Carter's reorganization plan did not remove antidiscrimination enforcement powers from federal agencies that provide grants to state and local governments.

One mechanism that might have resolved these interagency difficulties vis-à-vis state and local governments was the Equal Employment Opportunity Coordinating Council (EEOCC). Its members included representatives of the Departments of Labor and Justice, the Civil Service Commission, the Equal Employment Opportunity Commission, and the United States Commission on Civil Rights. The last agency has no enforcement powers but rather is responsible for monitoring the overall process of protecting civil rights, including equal employment opportunity. The EEOCC was weak in that it did not include departments such as Treasury, HUD, and HEW and had no powers to compel member agencies to abide by standards reached by a majority of its members.

The Carter reorganization dissolved the EEOCC and assigned to the Equal Employment Opportunity Commission the responsibility for coordinating equal opportunity efforts in federal agencies. Executive Order 12067 provides a "leadership and coordination" role for the Equal Employment Opportunity Commission in federal employment. The Commission sets standards for equal opportunity that are to be followed by federal departments and agencies. Federal agencies are required to submit proposed EEO regulations to the Commission. Disagreements between the Commission and an agency may be referred to the Assistant to the President for Domestic Affairs and Policy in the Executive Office of the President. The Civil Service Reform Act, moreover, provides the EEOC with responsibility for establishing guidelines for recruiting minorities and for determining where "underrepresentation" exists in the federal government. The Office of Personnel Management is responsible for administering the minority recruitment program.

One remaining major legal uncertainty at the federal level is the proposed Equal Rights Amendment (ERA) to the Constitution. If approved by the requisite number of states, ERA would guarantee the following: "Equality of rights under the law shall not be denied or abridged by the United States or by any State on account of sex." Although the debates on ERA have been vociferous, no one knows how the amendment would be interpreted by the courts. It is unclear whether ERA would provide any additional protection to women in public employment. Some states have added such amendments to their constitutions, but these seem to have had negligible effect in employment matters.[24]

Besides all of the federal protections against discrimination, there are additional safeguards at the state level. State governments have antidiscrimination laws that apply to both state and local government employment. While these laws are similar to federal laws, specific provisions vary. It is possible to commit an act that does not violate federal law but that does violate a state law.

---

[24] Phyllis W. Beck, "Equal Rights Amendment: The Pennsylvania Experience," *Dickinson Law Review*, 81 (1977):395–416; Barbara A. Brown et al., "The Equal Rights Amendment: A Constitutional Basis for Equal Rights for Women," *Yale Law Journal*, 80 (1971):871–985; "The Continuing Controversy Over the Women's Equal Rights Amendment," *Congressional Digest*, 56 (1977):162–192; "Equal Rights for Women: A Symposium on the Proposed Constitutional Amendment," *Harvard Civil Rights-Civil Liberties Law Review*, 6 (1971):215–287; Margaret K. Krasik, "A Review of the Implementation of the Pennsylvania Equal Rights Amendment," *Duquesne Law Review*, 14 (1976):683–721; and Lisa Cronin Wohl, "White Gloves and Combat Boots: The Fight for ERA," *Civil Liberties Review*, 1 (Fall, 1974):77–86.

DISCRIMINATION IN VARIOUS
ASPECTS OF PERSONNEL ADMINISTRATION

Discrimination can occur in all aspects of personnel administration. This section considers discriminatory practices as they relate to selection, on-the-job activities, and terminations.

Selection and Discrimination

The concept of validity in the selection process of a jurisdiction is discussed in Chapter 5. A valid testing program is one that selects those employees who will be superior workers and rejects less qualified employees. The concern here is that testing programs can have the effect of discriminating against some groups of individuals. A landmark case is *Griggs* v. *Duke Power Company* (1971), in which the United States Supreme Court rejected the requirements of a high school diploma and a satisfactory intelligence test score as conditions for employment.[25] Although intent to discriminate by the corporation had not been shown, the Court held that the diploma and IQ test requirements were discriminatory against blacks and were in violation of Title VII of the Civil Rights Act. The Court noted that these requirements had been imposed without examining their validity.

It should be recalled that different approaches are applied by the courts in reviewing alleged discriminatory practices. Courts require the use of validity tests for civil service examinations in cases brought under Title VII but not necessarily under the Fifth and Fourteenth Amendments. In *Washington* v. *Davis* (discussed above), the Supreme Court did not require a validity test of the examination used to select police academy recruits. Since the case was brought under the Fifth Amendment, the Court was satisfied that there was a relationship between test scores and performance in the police academy rather than insisting on proof that the police examination was related to job performance.

Since the *Griggs* decision, differential validity has become a major concern.[26] The focus of differential validity tests is to determine whether

---

[25] *Griggs* v. *Duke Power Company*, 401 U.S. 424 (1971).

[26] Betty R. Anderson and Martha P. Rogers, eds., *Personnel Testing and Equal Employment Opportunity* (Washington: Government Printing Office, 1970); Roger P. Balog, "Employment Testing and Proof of Job-Relatedness: A Tale of Unreasonable Constraints," *Notre Dame Lawyer*, 52 (1976):95–108; William C. Byham and Morton E. Spitzer, *The Law and Personnel Testing* (New York: American Management Association, 1971), pp. 128–146; George Cooper and Richard B. Sobol, "Seniority and Testing under Fair Employment Laws: A General Approach to Objective Criteria of Hiring and Promotion," *Harvard Law Review*, 82 (1969):1958–1679; Sidney Gael, Donald L. Grant, and Richard J. Ritchie, "Employment Test Validation for Minority and Nonminority Telephone Operators," *Journal of Applied Psychology*, 60 (1975):411–419; Robert M. Guion, "Content Validity: Three Years of Talk—What's the Action?" *Public Personnel*

the selection process varies in its effects upon selected groups. For example, a test might be valid for both men and women, but to differing degrees; a test score of 90 for men could correlate higher or lower with job performance than a test score of 90 for women. The procedures involved in differential validity are complex and have been difficult to apply for lack of adequate numbers of test scores for subgroups.

One problem noted in Chapter 5 was that validity tests often must be based only upon those persons who passed a test and were employed. In an effort to identify the extent to which minorities and women are screened out through testing, the United States Civil Service Commission (now Office of Personnel Management) announced in late 1977 that it would begin collecting data on the race, sex, and ethnicity of persons taking many of the Commission's examinations, including the Foreign Service Officers Examination, the Professional and Administrative Career Examination (PACE), the Mid-Level Examination, and clerical examinations.[27] This information, of course, cannot answer the question of how well persons who failed an examination would have performed on the job. The information collected is to be confidential and is not to be used in hiring decisions. Some groups, such as the American Civil Liberties Union, have expressed concern that the good intentions behind this information collection process may result in furthering discrimination rather than in reducing it.

Considerable confusion has existed over the use of validity testing for antidiscrimination purposes in state and local government. As noted in the preceding section, federal agencies have various enforcement powers concerning these governments, and until 1978 these agencies were unable to reach agreement on a common set of standards. Between 1973 and 1976 the Equal Employment Opportunity Coordinating Council unsuccessfully attempted to reach a consensus view among its constituent agencies. The outcome was the Federal Executive Agency (FEA)

Management, 6 (1977):407–414; Raymond A. Katzell and Frank J. Dyer, "Differential Validity Revived," *Journal of Applied Psychology,* 62 (1977):137–145; Robert L. Linn, "Single-Group Validity, Differential Validity, and Differential Prediction," *Journal of Applied Psychology,* 63 (1978):507–512; David H. Rosenbloom and Carole Cassler Obuchowski, "Public Personnel Examinations and the Constitution: Emergent Trends," *Public Administration Review,* 37 (1977):9–18; Robert Sadacca and Joan Brackett, *The Validity and Discriminatory Impact of the Federal Service Entrance Examination* (Washington: Urban Institute, 1971); Bonnie Sandman and Faith Urban, "Employment Testing and the Law," *Labor Law Journal,* 27 (1976):38–54; Frank L. Schmidt, John E. Hunter, and Vern W. Urry, "Statistical Power in Criterion-Related Validation Studies," *Journal of Applied Psychology,* 61 (1976):473–485; and Elaine W. Shoben, "Probing the Discriminatory Effects of Employee Selection Procedures with Disparate Impact Analysis under Title VII," *Texas Law Review,* 56 (1977):1–45.

27 Helen J. Christrup, "The Truth about Collecting Race Information," *Civil Service Journal,* 18 (April/June, 1978):16–17.

Guidelines for Employee Selection Procedures adopted in 1976 by the Civil Service Commission and the Departments of Justice and Labor.[28] These guidelines could not be issued as an EEOCC document in that the Equal Employment Opportunity Commission and the Civil Rights Commission did not endorse them. Instead, EEOC continued with its own Guidelines on Employee Selection Procedures.[29] This left federal line agencies with a choice of which set of guidelines to apply. The Office of Revenue Sharing (ORS) in the Treasury Department, for example, chose the EEOC guidelines, while the Law Enforcement Assistance Administration (LEAA) adopted the FEA guidelines. This added to confusion at the state and local levels, since both sets of guidelines could be applied simultaneously to police departments.[30]

In 1978 a new set of guidelines was adopted, this time by the EEOC and the Civil Rights Commission as well as by the Civil Service Commission and the Departments of Justice and Labor. The Uniform Guidelines on Employee Selection Procedures eliminated the confusion that had existed between the two competing sets of guidelines.[31] The Uniform standards are similar to the FEA guidelines, allowing for the use of content, construct, and criterion validity. The "bottom line" approach to selection was adopted as part of the Uniform Guidelines. Employers had complained that they were expected to undertake expensive validation studies of each component of their selection process when that process as a whole—the bottom line—had no adverse impact. It could happen that the written test portion might have an adverse impact but that was compensated for by other portions of the testing and selection program. In adopting the bottom line principle, the participating federal agencies agreed not to prosecute such employers; prosecution would be pursued in cases where the bottom line was an adverse impact.

In state and local cases involving testing programs, the normal procedure is for the federal government to establish before a court a prima facie case of discrimination. This means that at least on the face of the matter, the testing program appears to discriminate. The prima facie situation is shown by reviewing the composition of the jurisdiction's personnel and particularly the extent to which the examination process screens out some groups more than others. The Uniform Guidelines

---

[28] "Federal Executive Agency Guidelines on Employee Selection Procedures," 41 F.R. 51734 (1976).

[29] 29 C.F.R. § 1607.

[30] Commission on Civil Rights, *The Federal Civil Rights Enforcement Effort—1977*, pp. 327–328.

[31] Uniform Guidelines on Employee Selection Procedures, 43 F.R. 38290 (1978). See *Problems with Federal Equal Employment Opportunity Guidelines on Employee Selection Procedures Need to Be Resolved* (Washington: General Accounting Office, 1978).

provide that an adverse impact is one in which the selection rate for a group is below 80 percent of the rate of the highest group. The jurisdiction then has the burden of showing that the test program is valid. In "pattern or practice" suits (discussed above) the jurisdiction might show that the disproportionately low percentage of blacks was not the result of the existing selection process but rather stemmed from discriminatory practices prior to 1972 when local governments were not subject to the provisions of Title VII.[32]

In addition to paper-and-pencil tests, other aspects of testing can be discriminatory. For example, requiring five years of experience in addition to serving an apprenticeship to qualify for a city bricklayer job has been held to be discriminatory.[33] Background investigations need to have explicit standards so that the investigations cannot be used for discriminatory purposes.[34] Establishing criteria for professional positions is especially difficult in that some subjectivity is often appropriate; for instance, there is no objective means for determining which of three candidates for a supervisory position is best qualified. Yet such subjectivity opens the door to discrimination.[35]

Height and weight requirements constitute a particularly sensitive issue in that they tend to adversely affect women and some racial and ethnic groups. The height and weight issue was brought before the United States Supreme Court in *Dothard* v. *Rawlinson* (1977), involving correctional officer jobs in Alabama penitentiaries.[36] A woman had been unable to qualify because of the minimum weight requirement of 120 pounds; the state also had a minimum height requirement of five feet and two inches. The Court held that the practice was discriminatory in that the combined height and weight requirement would exclude 40 percent of all adult women and only 1 percent of adult men. Alabama had been unable to show that the requirements were job related, and the Court suggested that if physical strength was required, then a strength test should be used rather than height and weight requirements.

---

[32] *Hazlewood School District* v. *United States*, 433 U.S. 299 (1977). See also John Klinefelter and James Thompkins, "Adverse Impact in Employment Selection," *Public Personnel Management*, 5 (1976):199–204.

[33] *Crockett* v. *Green*, 534 F. 2d 715 (1976).

[34] *United States* v. *Chicago*, 549 F. 2d 415 (1977).

[35] Amy B. Ginensky and Andrew R. Rogoff, "Subjective Employment Criteria and the Future of Title VII in Professional Jobs," *University of Detroit Journal of Urban Law*, 54 (1977):165–236.

[36] *Dothard* v. *Rawlinson*, 433 U.S. 321 (1977). *Rodriguez* v. *Taylor*, 428 F. Supp. 1118 (1976). *Carter* v. *Gallagher*, 452 F. 2d 315 (1971), cert. denied 406 U.S. 950 (1972), required that the Minnesota Veterans Preference Act "give way" to allow for the hiring of minorities.

However, the Court went on to base its decision on another aspect of the Civil Rights Act, namely the bona fide occupational qualification, or "bfoq." Alabama not only had a height and weight requirement but specifically disqualified women from holding correctional officer positions in male prisons. The law permits discrimination where a bfoq exists. The court decided that such discrimination was appropriate given the nature of the prisons. Sex offenders were part of the prison population. The prisoners were routinely required to remove all of their clothing for searches. Bathroom facilities provided no privacy. In the words of the Court, "The environment in Alabama's penitentiaries is a peculiarly inhospitable one for human beings of whatever sex." Therefore, the bfoq requirement was met, permitting only the hiring of males.

Another illustration of the bfoq standard involves age. In one case, a city refused to consider applicants for security guard positions who were 40 years of age or older. The city contended that age was a bfoq in that guards needed to be in good physical condition. A district court held that this was not a bfoq, in that guards who reached the age of 41 were allowed to remain on their jobs. The city could not claim that guards needed to be relatively young and at the same time allow its guards to remain on the job past age 40.[37]

Veterans preference is one aspect of personnel administration that is being attacked by proponents of equal opportunity. This common personnel practice negatively affects women.[38] For state and local governments the main line of attack on these practices has been the equal protection clause of the Fourteenth Amendment. Women have claimed they are being denied equal protection. In attacking veterans preference, courts have held that while there is no right to a public job, government has a responsibility to treat people equally once a job is created.[39] The defense is that preference aids veterans in readjusting to civilian life, that preference is due veterans who risked their lives in defending the country, and that women are eligible for the same preference as men.[40] The Supreme Court has not ruled directly on the issue other than to hold that *Washington* v. *Davis* is the controlling case; that approach, however, requires that to declare veterans preference unconstitutional the intent to

---

[37] *Rodriguez* v. *Taylor*, 428 F. Supp. 1118 (1976).

[38] *Carter* v. *Gallagher*, 452 F. 2d 315 (1971), cert. denied 406 U.S. 950 (1972), required Minnesota Veterans Preference Act "give way" to allow for the hiring of minorities.

[39] *Anthony* v. *Massachusetts*, 415 F. Supp. 485 (1976). *Conflicting Congressional Policies: Veterans' Preference and Apportionment vs. Equal Employment Opportunity* (Washington: General Accounting Office, 1977).

[40] *Branch* v. *DuBois*, 418 F. Supp. 1128 (1976) and *Feinerman* v. *Jones*, 356 F. Supp. 252 (1973).

discriminate must be shown.[41] The Carter administration proposed that lifetime preference be restricted to disabled veterans, that preference be limited to ten years for nondisabled veterans, and that no preference be granted retired military personnel seeking civilian federal employment. Congress did not accept these recommendations and even strengthened preference for disabled veterans (see Chapter 5).

Citizenship is another condition of employment that frequently has been imposed. In 1973 the United States Supreme Court held that New York State's requirement that only citizens could qualify for permanent positions violated the equal protection clause of the Fourteenth Amendment.[42] The state law was held to "sweep indiscriminately" without any "substantial state interest" being evident. From 1973, therefore, state and local governments were precluded from such discrimination, but the United States Civil Service Commission continued to enforce its regulation against hiring aliens for permanent federal positions. Federal prohibitions against hiring aliens were brought before the Supreme Court in 1976 in *Hampton* v. *Wong*.[43] In a 5 to 4 decision, the Court ruled against the Commission and pointed to the need to avoid a double standard for federal jobs in comparison with state and local jobs. The Court held that no "overriding national interest" had been shown to warrant discriminating against aliens. The Court's decision, however, was nullified by President Ford, who issued Executive Order 11935, prohibiting hiring aliens as being in the national interest. Therefore a double standard continued between the levels of government.[44]

In 1978 the Court seemed to partially reverse its earlier position prohibiting discrimination against aliens in state and local employment (*Foley* v. *Connelie*).[45] The Court held that the equal protection clause did not prevent New York State from barring aliens from its police force. Policy making was considered the exclusive responsibility of citizens. In the Court's view, police officers had a policy making function in that they exercised discretion in law enforcement.

A new issue that may be emerging involves state and local government preference in hiring their own residents. Some governments not

---

[41] *Massachusetts* v. *Feeney*, 415 F. Supp. 485 (1976), 429 U.S. 66 (1976), 98 S. Ct. 252 (1977), cert. granted by Supreme Court, October, 1978. See "Veterans' Public Employment Preference as Sex Discrimination," *Harvard Law Review*, 90 (1977): 805–814, and John H. Fleming and Charles A. Shanor, "Veterans' Preference in Public Employment: Unconstitutional Gender Discrimination?" *Emory Law Journal*, 26 (1977):13–64.

[42] *Sugarman* v. *Dougall*, 413 U.S. 634 (1973).

[43] *Hampton* v. *Wong*, 426 U.S. 88 (1976).

[44] Denny Chin, "Aliens' Right to Work: State and Federal Discrimination," *Fordham Law Review*, 45 (1977):835–859.

[45] *Foley* v. *Connelie*, 98 S. Ct. 1067 (1978).

only have a residency requirement for employees but also provide preference in hiring their own residents. While such preference has not been reviewed by the U.S. Supreme Court, the Court has reviewed a related practice concerning private employment. In *Hicklin* v. *Orbeck* (1978), the Court examined an Alaska law that required private employers that had natural gas and oil leases to give state residents preference in hiring.[46] The state law was held to violate the Constitution's privileges and immunities clause, which in simple terms requires states to give equal treatment to residents of other states.

One other subject of controversy in the selection process has been the rule of three (see Chapter 5). That practice can have a negative effect upon hiring minorities and women if they tend to score lower on civil service examinations than others, and with the addition of veterans preference points, they often do score lower. The Equal Employment Opportunity Commission has encouraged state and local governments to expand the rule of three or perhaps to select three candidates at random among all persons passing an examination; that practice would increase the chances of selecting minorities and women. The United States Civil Service Commission, however, in enforcing the merit principle argued that these practices to encourage minority hiring could violate the merit principle by resulting in the hiring of less qualified personnel. State and local governments became trapped by these competing positions.

This problem was reduced in 1976 when the Equal Employment Opportunity Coordinating Council reached agreement on a policy statement that encouraged practices "to assure that members of the [negatively] affected group who are qualified to perform the job are included within the pool of persons from which the selecting official makes the selection."[47] Although this language may seem vague, it has allowed for more flexible certification procedures that increase the chances of hiring minorities and women. Washington State has the rule of 3 + 3; an agency may request the top three candiates plus the top three minority candidates. The Carter civil service reform proposals of 1978 would have established a rule of seven and would have permitted the OPM to use even broader certification procedures, but Congress did not accept these recommendations.

Discrimination on the Job

Discrimination does not end with the selection process. Once on the job, a person may be subjected to numerous discriminatory practices. Some

---

[46] *Hicklin* v. *Orbeck*, 98 S. Ct. 2482 (1978).

[47] Policy Statement on Affirmative Action Programs for State and Local Government Agencies," 42 F.R. 38814 (1976).

of these are blatant. St. Louis fire stations, for instance, have had "supper clubs" where firemen cook their meals and from which black firemen have been excluded.[48] Other practices are somewhat more subtle, such as employees largely ignoring and thereby alienating minority workers. An employee may be typecast as the bureau's black or the bureau's official woman. Agency clients sometimes encourage this typecasting; black clients may openly expect more favorable treatment from a black employee than from a white one.[49]

Performance ratings and promotion practices are subject to discriminatory abuses. Some administrators responsible for rating employees undoubtedly take into account, positively or negatively, the sex or race of an employee, but trying to prove such discrimination is difficult.[50] Promotion decisions can easily be used to discriminate. A female employee may be passed over for promotion, with the job being given to a male, yet there is nothing in writing to suggest that sex has been the basis for the decision. Proving discrimination, therefore, is difficult since the mere appointment of a male to a vacant position does not by itself show discrimination based on sex. In individual discrimination cases, the employee attempts to show that others of lesser qualifications were promoted and that a practice had emerged blocking further promotions.[51]

Equal pay for equal work has been a major issue. In 1974 the Supreme Court dealt with the problem of different pay rates for shifts in private industry.[52] The day shift staffed by women was paid less than the evening shift staffed by men. Under New York State "protective" law, women had been prohibited from being hired for the night shift; when that law was changed, women were hired on the evening shift and received the same pay as men on that shift. Nevertheless, the Court held that the women on the day shift were being discriminated against in that they were not receiving the same pay as the evening shift.

---

[48] *Firefighters Institute for Racial Equality* v. *St. Louis*, 549 F. 2d 506 (1977).

[49] Adam W. Herbert, "The Minority Administrator: Problems, Prospects, and Challenges," *Public Administration Review*, 34 (1974):556–563.

[50] Larry D. Baker, Nicholas DiMarco, and W. E. Scott, Jr., "Effects of Supervisors' Sex and Level of Authoritarianism on Evaluation and Reinforcement of Blind and Sighted Workers," *Journal of Applied Psychology*, 60 (1975):28–38 and William J. Bigoness, "Effect of Applicants' Sex, Race, and Performance on Employers' Performance Ratings: Some Additional Findings," *Journal of Applied Psychology*, 61 (1976):80–84.

[51] *McNutt* v. *Hills*, 426 F. Supp. 990 (1977).

[52] *Corning Glass Works* v. *Brennan*, 417 U.S. 188 (1974). See also Arthur J. Corrazzini, "Equality of Employment Opportunity in the Federal White-Collar Civil Service," *Journal of Human Resources*, 7 (1972):424–445; James A. Long, "Employment Discrimination in the Federal Sector," *Journal of Human Resources*, 11 (1976):86–97; and Sharon P. Smith, "Government Wage Differential by Sex," *Journal of Human Resources*, 11 (1976):185–199.

Another aspect of pay discrimination is providing selected employees additional pay increments for no additional work. That occurred in a school district which provided an additional $300 increment to "head of household" teachers. Those increments were paid to males, and a United States district court held the payments violated the Equal Pay Act.[53]

Employee benefits are another area of discrimination. In *Frontiero v. Richardson* (1973), the Supreme Court dealt with medical benefits and housing allowances available to air force officers.[54] While men were automatically granted these benefits, married women were required to show that they provided over half of the financial support in their marriages. The Court ruled that this violated the due process clause of the Fifth Amendment.

One of the most controversial benefit issues is whether government should cover pregnancy expenses. The governing case is *General Electric Company v. Gilbert* (1976).[55] The company's benefit plan covered many non-job-related disabilities, with the important exception of pregnancies. The Supreme Court ruled that the company was not required to cover pregnancies and held that there was no evidence of discrimination. In the Court's view, the total benefit package at General Electric did not necessarily favor men and, indeed, some evidence existed showing that women benefited more than men.

Retirement benefits for men and women have been another area of controversy. The problem stems from the simple fact that women live longer than men. If the same dollar retirement benefits are paid each month to men and women, women on the average will receive greater total benefits in their lifetimes. In response to this, some jurisdictions have required female employees to make greater contributions to the retirement system, but in 1978 the Supreme Court found this practice to violate Title VII of the Civil Rights Act.[56]

---

[53] *Marshall v. A. and M. Consolidated Independent School District*, D.C. Tex Civil Action 74-H-1532 (1977).

[54] *Frontiero v. Richardson*, 411 U.S. 677 (1973).

[55] *General Electric Company v. Gilbert*, 429 U.S. 125 (1976). See Subcommittee on Labor, Senate Committee on Human Resources, *Discrimination on the Basis of Pregnancy, 1977: Hearings*, 95th Cong., 1st sess. (Washington: Government Printing Office, 1977), and Helen Hadjiyannakis, "Sex Discrimination: Employer's Failure to Provide Pregnancy Disability Benefits Does Not Violate Title VII," *Fordham Law Review*, 45 (1977):1202–1222.

[56] *City of Los Angeles, Department of Water and Power v. Manhart*, 98 S. Ct. 1370 (1978). Important sex discrimination cases involving Social Security include *Califano v. Goldfarb*, 430 U.S. 199 (1977) and *Califano v. Webster*, 430 U.S. 313 (1977).

Terminations and Discrimination

Discrimination complaints in terminations have involved dismissals, compulsory retirements, and layoffs. Dismissal cases have involved mental illness, religious beliefs, and homosexuality. For example, what protections from dismissal does an employee have who becomes partially disabled through mental illness? One case involved a female United States Treasury Department employee who was dismissed because she became "hysterical, throwing currency in the air, intermittently sobbing and laughing unnaturally." The department had assisted the employee in obtaining psychiatric help but it was left undecided whether the department had made "every reasonable effort" to retain the employee.[57]

In 1977 the United States Supreme Court dealt with the difficult problem of whether a collective bargaining agreement providing for seniority had a religious discriminatory effect (*Trans World Airlines* v. *Hardison*).[58] According to the union contract with TWA, the most senior employees had first choice on job and shift assignments. As a result, an employee with little seniority was required to work on Saturday even though that was the Sabbath for him. The union insisted that the company abide by the labor contract requiring junior employees to accept whatever shift was available, and the company refused to allow the employee to work only a four-day week (that is, having the regular two days off plus Saturday). The employee was dismissed, and he sued on the grounds of religious discrimination under Title VII of the Civil Rights Act. The Court ruled that the employee's dismissal had not been discriminatory. ". . . Absent a discriminatory purpose, the operation of a seniority system cannot be an unlawful employment practice even if the system has some discriminatory consequences." The Court went on to reason that had the airline made special arrangements for this employee, the action would have discriminated against all other employees.

Homosexuals generally cannot be dismissed or denied employment for their homosexuality per se but are removed when their homosexuality adversely affects their work.[59] The judicial system has been divided over the extent to which a homosexual employee may publicly express support for homosexuality. On the one hand, courts have recognized this public speech as being protected by the First Amendment; on the other hand, courts have held employees do not have the right to flaunt their

---

[57] *Doe* v. *Hampton*, 566 F. 2d 265 (1977).

[58] *Trans World Airlines* v. *Hardison*, 432 U.S. 63 (1977). See Benjamin W. Wolkinson, "Title VII and the Religious Employee: The Neglected Duty of Accommodation," *Arbitration Journal*, 30 (1975):89–113.

[59] *Society for Individual Rights* v. *Hampton*, 528 F. 2d. 905 (1977) and *Cruz-Casado* v. *United States*, 553 F. 2d 672 (1977).

homosexuality.[60] In instances of overt acts of homosexuality, the courts have required proof that those acts reduced the employee's work performance or, in the case of the Lloyd-LaFollette Act, were related to the efficiency of the agency.[61]

Some of the most difficult situations have involved homosexual school teachers. The concern has been that a homosexual teacher provides an inappropriate model for impressionable children. Homosexuals, however, have contended that their homosexuality does not interfere with their teaching performance. As an illustration of the problem, when school authorities learned that an eighth-grade teacher was a homosexual, he was transferred from a classroom position to a nonteaching job. At that point, he made public his homosexuality, and the school district dismissed him. A lower federal court decision, which was not overturned by the Supreme Court, held that a "homosexual teacher need not become a recluse, nor need he lie about himself."[62] However, "discretion and self-restraint" should be exercised in speaking in support of homosexuality. The conclusion was that the school board had acted properly in dismissing the teacher since he had failed to exercise such self-restraint.

Even more controversial was the case of a school teacher who was dismissed for being a homosexual and who had not publicized his homosexuality. The teacher had not performed overt homosexual acts and had been an outstanding teacher for a dozen years, yet he was dismissed when it was learned he was a homosexual. A state court held he was immoral and that that impaired his teaching ability. The United States Supreme Court declined to hear the case, thereby letting his dismissal stand.[63]

Age discrimination is prohibited, but mandatory retirement based on age is permissible, except in the federal civil service. Federal law generally has limited compulsory retirement to age 65 or above, until 1978 when the ceiling was raised to 70. That legislation is a landmark in helping older workers continue their careers but may work to the disadvantage of younger workers, women, and minorities. If senior level positions are held largely by older, white males, career advancement for others may be slower than when the compulsory retirement age was 65.

---

[60] Compare the cases of *Singer* v. *United States Civil Service Commission*, 530 F. 2d 247 (1976) and *Aumiller* v. *University of Delaware*, 434 F. Supp. 1273 (1977).

[61] *Norton* v. *Macy*, 417 F. 2d 1161 (1969) and *Board of Education of Long Beach Unified School District* v. *M.*, 566 P. 2d 602 (1977).

[62] *Acanfora* v. *Board of Education of Montgomery County*, 359 F. Supp. 843 (1973), cert. denied 419 U.S. 836 (1974).

[63] *Gaylord* v. *Tacoma School District*, 559 P. 2d 1340 (1977), cert. denied 98 S. Ct. 234 (1977).

The Age Discrimination in Employment Act (ADEA) of 1967 protects employees against being forced to take early retirement. An agency cannot deny older employees training opportunities and promotions in hope of forcing them to retire.[64]

Mandatory retirement before age 70 is permissible in some cases. If a retirement plan requiring early retirement was in effect prior to the ADEA, the plan may continue.[65] Moreover, compulsory early retirement is permissible when there is a rationale for such a policy. In *Massachusetts Board of Retirement v. Murgia* (1976), the Supreme Court reviewed that state's requirement for police officers to retire at age 50.[66] A state employee who had been forced to retire complained that he was denied equal protection of the law as guaranteed under the Fourteenth Amendment in that he was in as good physical condition as younger employees. The Court applied the rationality test, finding there was a relationship between age and physical condition and that state police needed to be in good physical condition. The Court, however, stressed that the state law requiring retirement at age 50 was not necessarily wise, suggesting that physical examinations and agility tests might be more appropriate for determining who should be required to retire.[67]

Sex discrimination in terminations in another issue. Military officers are required to advance in rank or be forced to resign their commissions. Should male and female officers have the same time period to gain promotions before being discharged? That issue was brought to the Supreme Court when a male naval officer claimed discrimination in that he was discharged after nine years of service, having been passed over twice for promotion, while female officers were allowed 13 years before being removed.[68] The Court ruled that the Navy's "up-or-out" policy did not discriminate, in that men and women performed different functions and that women needed a longer period of time to demonstrate their abilities and earn promotions.

Not only are pregnancy benefits an issue but so are forced leaves for pregnancies. The Supreme Court has ruled that the Fourteenth Amend-

---

[64] *Christie v. Marston*, 551 F. 2d 1080 (1977).

[65] *United Air Lines v. McMann*, 434 U.S. 192 (1977).

[66] *Massachusetts Board of Retirement v. Murgia*, 427 U.S. 307 (1976).

[67] Senate Special Committee on Aging, *The Next Steps in Combating Age Discrimination in Employment: With Special Reference to Mandatory Retirement Policy*, 95th Cong., 1st sess. (Washington: Government Printing Office, 1977), and Subcommittee on Compensation and Employee Benefits, House Committee on Post Office and Civil Service, *Elimination of Mandatory Retirement at Age 70: Hearings*, 95th Cong., 1st sess. (Washington: Government Printing Office, 1977).

[68] *Schlesinger v. Ballard*, 419 U.S. 498 (1975).

ment due process clause was violated when a school district required a pregnant teacher to take a leave without pay five months before the baby was due and did not allow her to return until the beginning of the school term after which the baby was three months old.[69]

Discrimination can occur in denying an employee reinstatement following a pregnancy absence. In a private corporation, pregnant women were required to take a leave but in doing so lost their accumulated job seniority. The returning woman could not bid on a vacant job but would be considered only if no present employee applied for the position. If the woman was able to obtain a permanent position following the pregnancy, she regained her seniority for pension and vacation purposes but not for bidding on future jobs. The Supreme Court ruled this practice to violate Title VII of the Civil Rights Act.[70]

Seniority systems, while deemed acceptable by the Civil Rights Act, can operate against efforts to eliminate discrimination. "Last hired, first fired" is a familiar slogan describing the plight of minorities. Because of discrimination, they often have been among the last to be hired, giving them the least seniority; the result is that when layoffs occur, minority workers are the first to go. Equal employment opportunity and affirmative action efforts have been directed toward increasing minority and female employment, but when a jurisdiction has seniority rules, often embedded in collective bargaining agreements, and layoffs are necessary, then those efforts can be negated. Labor unions seek to protect their members and prefer to use seniority in layoffs, but such a position gives the appearance of supporting discrimination. Although some attempts have been made to use racial quotas in layoffs to maintain minority and female employees, these practices have been considered a form of reverse discrimination.[71]

---

[69] *Cleveland Board of Education* v. *LaFleur*, 414 U.S. 632 (1974). See also *Monell* v. *Department of Social Services of the City of New York*, 98 S. Ct. 2018 (1978).

[70] *Nashville Gas Co.* v. *Satty*, 434 U.S. 136 (1977).

[71] Iris A. Burke and Oscar G. Chase, "Resolving the Seniority/Minority Layoffs Conflict: An Employer-Targeted Approach," *Harvard Civil Rights-Civil Liberties Law Review*, 13 (1978):81–116; *Chance* v. *Board of Examiners and Board of Education of New York City*, 534 F. 2d 993 (1976), cert. denied 431 U.S. 965 (1977); *Last Hired First Fired: Layoffs and Civil Rights* (Washington: U.S. Commission on Civil Rights, 1977); Ellen R. Joseph, "Last Hired, First Fired Seniority, Layoffs, and Title VII: Questions of Liability and Remedy," *Columbia Journal of Law and Social Problems*, 11 (1975):343–402; *Koch* v. *Yunich*, 533 F. 2d 80 (1976); Michael B. Preston, "Minority Employment and Collective Bargaining in the Public Sector," *Public Administration Review*, 37 (1977):511–515; David T. Stanley, "Trying to Avoid Layoffs," *Public Administration Review*, 37 (1977):515–517; John C. Thomas, "Budget-Cutting and Minority Employment in City Governments: Lessons from Cincinnati," *Public Personnel Management*, 7 (1978):155–161; and Gary M. Whalen and Richard S. Rubin, "Labor Relations and Affirmative Action: A Tug-of-War," *Public Personnel Management*, 6 (1977):149–155.

AFFIRMATIVE ACTION

Administrative and judicial actions against discriminatory practices may affect only one individual or a large group of people. A person who proves discrimination against himself in terms of pay might only win a court order correcting his situation. In other cases, the court decision might be broader in scope, requiring a revision of the jurisdiction's pay practices. The case mentioned earlier about "head of household" increments for teachers is an example of broad or collective relief. In other instances, a court may rule that a jurisdiction no longer may use a given civil service examination, thereby affecting a large number of people.[72]

Some collective relief is retroactive. In *Albemarle Paper Company v. Moody* (1975), the Supreme Court held that back pay could be used as a remedy for compensating for discrimination.[73] Persons paid less than others because of discrimination can receive financial compensation back to the effective date of the Civil Rights Act. The Supreme Court has held that retroactive retirement benefits are permissible where men have been discriminated against and that such orders for retroactive benefits may be imposed upon state and local governments.[74]

The previous section has already described how layoffs based on seniority work against actions to increase the number of minorities and women in government. One factor that can alleviate this problem is the granting of retroactive seniority. The Supreme Court has held that in cases where discrimination has been proved, blacks may receive seniority back to the date when they applied for a position.[75] If they are granted retroactive seniority, minorities and women are then not necessarily the most junior employees and will not be the first to be laid off.

Collective relief not only includes measures to eliminate discrimination but also positive measures to increase minority and female employment in government. Such positive actions result from court orders and from actions on the part of governmental employers. Affirmative action is defined as a "planned, aggressive, coherent, management program to provide for equal employment opportunity."[76]

---

[72] *Jones v. New York City Human Resources Administration*, 528 F. 2d 696 (1976) and *Castro v. Beecher*, 459 F. 2d 725 (1972).

[73] *Albemarle Paper Company v. Moody*, 422 U.S. 405 (1975).

[74] *Fitzpatrick v. Bitzer*, 427 U.S. 445 (1976).

[75] *Franks v. Bowman Transportation Company*, 424 U.S. 747 (1976); *International Brotherhood of Teamsters v. United States*, 431 U.S. 324 (1977); and *Gurmankin v. Costanza*, 411 F. Supp. 982 (1977).

[76] Civil Service Commission, *Guidelines for the Development of an Affirmative Action Plan* (Washington: Government Printing Office, 1975). See also Civil Service Commission, *Reviewing State and Local Affirmative Action Plans* (Washington: Government Printing Office, 1977); Commission on Civil Rights, *Statement on Affirmative Action* (Washington:

As with antidiscrimination efforts, responsibility for affirmative action is divided among organizations. In the federal government, each agency is responsible for developing an agencywide and regional equal employment opportunity or affirmative action plan.[77] Under Civil Service Commision Guidelines, each plan had four parts—introduction, a discussion of the accomplishments of the affirmative action effort, an assessment of existing problems, and a report on objectives and affirmative actions to be taken. Eight subjects are covered within these reports: 1) the organization and resources for equal employment opportunity, 2) the handling of discrimination complaints, 3) recruitment, 4) utilization of employee skills and training, 5) upward mobility, 6) the commitment of supervisory and management staff to EEO, 7) community outreach, and 8) evaluation of the EEO program.[78] The Civil Service Commission had responsibility for setting standards for these plans and for reviewing the plans prepared by departments and agencies. Under the Carter reorganization, standards are set by the Equal Employment Opportunity Commission and agency plans are submitted to it through the Office of Personnel Management. EEOC has authority to review agency actions taken according to their affirmative action plans.

The Civil Service Commission has had responsibility for reviewing state and local agency plans of those jurisdictions covered under the Intergovernmental Personnel Act. While the Commission reviewed these plans, it neither approved nor rejected these; that approach was based on the assumption that an informal process was more conducive to cooperation between the Commission and state and local governments. The reorganization of 1978 provided for the Equal Employment Opportunity Commission to review the antidiscrimination standards applied to state

Government Printing Office, 1977); Mary E. Eccles, *Race, Sex, and Government Jobs: A Study of Affirmative Action Programs in Federal Agencies* (Cambridge Mass.: John F. Kennedy School of Government, Harvard University, 1976); Dorothy Jongeward and Dru Scott, *Affirmative Action for Women: A Practical Guide* (Reading, Mass.: Addison-Wesley, 1973); James V. Koch and John F. Chizmar, *The Economics of Affirmative Action* (Lexington, Mass.: Heath, 1976); John T. Marlin, "City Affirmative Action Efforts," *Public Administration Review*, 37 (1977):508–511; Lloyd G. Nigro, ed., "Mini-Symposium on Affirmative Action in Public Employment," *Public Administration Review*, 34 (1974):234–246; Thomas Sowell, "Affirmative Action Reconsidered," *Public Interest*, No. 42 (1976):47–65; and State Advisory Committees to Commission on Civil Rights, *State Government Affirmative Action in Mid-America* (Washington: Government Printing Office, 1978).

[77] Robert W. Hutchison, Eugene Walton, and Joseph Brawner, "The Organization of Affirmative Action Programs in 49 U.S. Federal Agencies," *Public Personnel Management*, 3 (1974):289–294.

[78] Federal Personnel Manual Letter 713–740, "Equal Employment Opportunity Plans," 1977. See Equal Employment Opportunity Commission, *Affirmative Action and Equal Employment: A Guidebook for Employers* (Washington: Government Printing Office, 1973).

and local governments by the OPM. The plans developed by these juris-dictions also are subject to review by other federal agencies that provide grants. In addition, state and local governments must report annually to the EEOC on the characteristics of their employees. Form EEO-4 is required of all jurisdictions having 100 or more employees, and a sample of smaller jurisdictions is selected each year for completing the form. A separate EEO-4 must be completed for each of fifteen functions, such as streets and highways, public welfare, police protection and the like. Salary data are provided by sex, race, and ethnicity and by occupational groups, such as officials/administrators, professionals, and technicians.

While EEO or affirmative action plans vary in format among juris-dictions, they have a common overall design. They begin with a policy statement supporting affirmative action and proceed to identify existing problems. Characteristics of the jurisdiction's work force are compared with the immediate labor market. A problem would be identified if the jurisdiction's clerical staff was almost exclusively white when private-sec-tor clerical personnel consisted of large numbers of nonwhites and His-panics. Once problem areas are determined, the plan attempts to identify the causes of racial imbalance. All aspects of the personnel systems are considered, such as whether the testing program is screening out minorities or whether the performance appraisal system serves as a bar-rier to women seeking promotions. Exit interviews conducted when an employee resigns from a jurisdiction may be used to determine whether and why minorities and women choose to quit.

The methods used to implement affirmative action focus upon recruiting persons who have been underrepresented and then working to keep those people in government and helping them to develop careers. Recruiting literature is directed at minorities and women. Outreach recruiting is used, such as having recruiters visit colleges and universities whose student bodies are predominantly nonwhite and female. Recruiters meet with community groups whose members are largely black, oriental, Hispanic, or female.[79] Testing and selection procedures may be adjusted, such as replacing the rule of three with the rule of the top 25 percent of the list. Selective placement may be used, as in the case of the physically handicapped or mentally retarded; the requirement for passing the civil service test may be waived, allowing the person to prove himself or herself on the job on a provisional basis.[80]

---

[79] *Problems in the Federal Employee Equal Employment Opportunity Program Need to be Resolved*, pp. 76–82.

[80] *Employment Opportunities in the Federal Government for the Physically Handicapped* (Washington: Government Printing Office, 1974).

Differences exist among the different targeted groups for equal employment opportunity recruitment, although the danger of stereotyping individuals should be stressed. A barrier in recruiting women, especially middle-aged women, may be their reluctance to seek employment after not having worked for many years. Women also must overcome previous assumptions that their proper role was that of mother and homemaker. Women with school-age children commonly face the additional problem of being expected to work from 8:00 a.m. to 5:00 p.m. and yet feel they should be home when their children return from school in the afternoon. To reduce this problem in federal employment, Congress in 1978 passed the Federal Employees Part-Time Career Employment Act, which requires agencies to establish part-time positions rather than relying almost exclusively on full-time employees, and Congress provided for the use of flexitime (see Chapter 12). Blacks and Hispanics may have limited skills and education, which reduce their usefulness in jobs. Hispanics often have difficulty with English. Facilities pose problems, such as the absence of restrooms for women at military installations and the lack of wheelchair ramps and elevators for the physically handicapped.

Once minorities and women are recruited into government, affirmative action efforts concentrate upon developing careers for these people.[81] The effort often is called "upward mobility." Such efforts include career counseling aimed at making employees aware of promotion opportunities, inventorying their skills, and devising individualized plans for training to allow people to qualify for higher level positions. Training also is directed at supervisors and managers to help break down privately held prejudices against minorities and women.

Job restructuring is used to reduce promotion barriers.[82] As was discussed in Chapter 3, position classification systems often include many dead-end jobs. One aspect of restructuring is to eliminate or reduce education and experience requirements so that a greater number of people can qualify for positions. Restructuring, moreover, includes redesigning the work done in given positions to provide opportunities to learn skills for higher level jobs. A critical aspect of restructuring is to provide "bridges" that enable employees to move from one job series to another. Clerical workers might be exposed to work that would allow

---

[81] Civil Service Commission, *Career Counseling for Women in the Federal Government* (Washington: Government Printing Office, 1975).

[82] Civil Service Commission, *Upward Mobility Through Job Restructuring* (Washington: Government Printing Office, 1976); *Review of Upward Mobility Using Job Restructuring, Department of the Interior* (Washington: General Accounting Office, 1976); and Clement J. Berwitz, *The Job Analysis Approach to Affirmative Action* (New York: Wiley and Sons, 1975).

them to qualify for technician positions and with additional training the technicians could qualify for professional positions.

Restructuring positions is used for the physically handicapped. Clerical positions can be adjusted to accommodate the blind, such as acting as a public receptionist and answering telephone inquiries. Work is redistributed among employees, with the handicapped person working equally as hard as other workers. Deaf persons may be particularly well suited to noisy facilities, such as in a government printing office.[83]

Problems abound with job restructuring. The traditions associated with position classification tend to discourage broad-based job classifications that would allow for greater career opportunities. Any restructuring may be viewed with skepticism by those holding the positions. Will the change threaten one's security and is the job redesign merely a disguise for attempting to get more work out of the worker with no increase in pay? There necessarily are limits on the use of job restructuring. Unbridled restructuring can result in widespread upward reclassifications of positions so that there are more generals and colonels than corporals and privates.

Equal employment opportunity is not the sole purpose of upward mobility. That effort is intended to provide career opportunities for all employees, whereas affirmative action concentrates upon minorities and women. Upward mobility often is handled by administrative units largely independent of affirmative action units, and that can result in limited coordination between the two programs.[84] It is possible that upward mobility programs may have the effect of helping white males as much as women and minorities, so that the latter see no appreciable improvement in their relative status in government.

The greatest issue associated with affirmative action efforts involves the use of goals and quotas in the hiring of women and minorities. Goals commonly refer to targets or objectives, such as increasing the

---

[83] Civil Service Commission, *A Chain of Cooperation: Severely Physically Handicapped Employees in the Federal Service* (Washington: Government Printing Office, 1977); Civil Service Commission, *Employment of the Handicapped in State and Local Government: A Guide for General Program Implementation* (Washington: Government Printing Office, 1977); Civil Service Commission, *Handbook of Selective Placement in Federal Service Employment of the Physically Handicapped, the Mentally Restored, the Mentally Retarded, the Rehabilitated Offender* (Washington: Government Printing Office, 1975); *Employment Opportunities in the Federal Government for the Physically Handicapped;* Sar A. Levitan and Robert Taggert, *Jobs for the Disabled* (Baltimore: Johns Hopkins University Press, 1977); and *Profile: What States are Doing (and Can Do) to Hire the Handicapped* (Washington: Government Printing Office, 1975).

[84] *Upward Mobility Programs in the Federal Government Should be Made More Effective* (Washington: General Accounting Office, 1975), and *Report on Progress Made by Agencies in Implementing Upward Mobility Programs* (Washington: General Accounting Office, 1977).

percentage of nonwhites by X percent in a given group of government jobs within a specified number of years.[85] Quotas, in contrast, establish requirements for filling positions based upon race, sex, or ethnicity; a percentage of all new appointments is designated for these groups.

Proponents of quotas contend that real change will result only when quotas are used to force that change. If only goals are used, administrators will find reasons why they could not hire minorities and women. Each year the goals will not be met, and each year the pattern of past discrimination will be perpetuated. The need for quotas is said to be particularly acute given the merit system itself and the role of public-sector employment as compared with the private sector. As late as 1950 public-sector jobs accounted for only 11 percent of all jobs in the United States, but today the figure is 17 percent. Government, therefore, needs to redress previous wrongs, especially given its increased share of the total job market. Moreover, this increased share of the job market has been accompanied by a closing of the door to many job seekers through the use of merit systems. In an earlier day, when patronage was standard practice, large groups of minorities (particularly ethnic minorities) were assured government jobs as a way of winning votes. Entry into the system was easier than it is today, when one must earn a high score on a civil service examination to be considered for appointment. Those blacks and Hispanics who score comparatively low on the examination have little hope for winning a government job even though they might constitute a large segment of the electorate in a jurisdiction.

The argument for goals instead of quotas rests on the concepts of equality and merit. Quotas are antithetical to equality, since they give preference to some people and deny jobs to others. This is said to be reverse discrimination, which, if carried out by state and local governments, violates the Fourteenth Amendment's guarantee of equal protection of the laws. Quotas also are said to run counter to merit since they may have the effect of hiring incompetent or less competent workers when more competent ones are available. If jobs are reserved for blacks and yet no highly qualified blacks are available on civil service lists, should persons with inferior skills be hired or should the positions go unfilled? Critics of quota systems note that Title VII of the Civil Rights Act specifically states that preferential treatment in pursuit of affirmative action is not required:

> Nothing contained in this subchapter shall be interpreted to require any employer, employment agency, labor organization, or joint labor-manage-

[85] Civil Service Commission, *Goals and Timetables for Effective Affirmative Action: A Guide For State and Local Government* (Washington: Government Printing Office, 1976).

ment committee subject to this chapter to grant preferential treatment to any individual or to any group because of race, color, religion, sex, or national origin of any such individual or group.[86]

Today, a combination of goals and quotas is used. Goals are most common, but quotas have been imposed by courts to redress gross imbalances in the racial composition of governmental agencies. Local fire departments and state and local police departments have been subjected to quotas imposed by federal courts,[87] These cases have involved jurisdictions where there have been no or virtually no minorities on the staff; in other words, quotas have been reserved for extreme situations. The court orders have required, for example, that one minority must be hired for every two or three positions that are filled until the court is satisfied that sufficient progress has been made in achieving some racial balance. The jurisdiction is not required to hire anyone, but, if it chooses to hire, then the quota system must be followed.

Quotas imposed by executives and administrators are being attacked in courts as constituting reverse discrimination. A United States district court has held that Detroit violated the Constitution in attempting to increase the percentage of blacks in the city's police department.[88] In another district court case, Virginia Commonwealth University was found to have violated the Constitution because of reverse discrimination.[89] In selecting between a male and female job applicant with basically identical qualifications, the University openly admitted to having selected the woman in order to further affirmative action. The court held this violated the Fourteenth Amendment.

The United States Supreme Court has not dealt directly with the issue of quotas in public employment, but in 1978 the Court did rule on the use of quotas for college students.[90] In *Regents of the University of*

---

[86] 42 U.S.C. § 2000e-2.

[87] Anthony J. Balzer, "Quotas and the San Francisco Police: A Sergeant's Dilemma," *Public Administration Review*, 37 (1977):276–285; *Davis* v. *Los Angeles*, 566 F. 2d 1334 (1977), cert. granted 98 S. Ct. 3087 (1978); Carl F. Goodman, "Equal Employment Opportunity: Preferential Quotas and Unrepresented Third Parties," *George Washington Law Review*, 44 (1976):483–515; James M. Horne, "Use of Quotas to Remedy Discrimination by Public Employers," *Dickinson Law Review*, 80 (1976):843–852; *Kirkland* v. *New York State Department of Correctional Services*, 520 F. 2d 420 (1975), cert. denied 97 S. Ct. 73; Rosalind B. Marimont, Kennedy P. Maize, and Ernest Harley, "Using FAIR to Set Numerical EEO Goals," *Public Personnel Management*, 5 (1976):191–198; *Morrow* v. *Crisler*, 491 F. 2d 1053 (1974), cert. denied 419 U.S. 895; *NAACP* v. *Allen*, 493 F. 2d 614 (1974); *Oburn* v. *Shapp*, 521 F. 2d 142 (1972); and Roscoe W. Wisner, "The Kirkland Case: Its Implications for Personnel Selection," *Public Personnel Management*, 4 (1975):263–267.

[88] *Detroit Police Officers Association* v. *Young*, 446 F. Supp. 979 (1978).

[89] *Cramer* v. *Virginia Commonwealth University*, 415 F. Supp. 673 (1976).

[90] *Regents of the University of California* v. *Bakke*, 98 S. Ct. 2733 (1978). See Johan A. Scanlon, Jr., "Racially-Preferential Policies in Institutions of Higher Education: State

California v. *Bakke,* the Court dealt with whether quotas established for admitting minority students to the Davis Medical School had the effect of discriminating against whites. By the narrowest possible margin (5 to 4) the Court agreed that a quota system was a form of reverse discrimination, but in another part of the decision one of the justices joined those holding the minority view on quotas to make a new majority of 5 to 4 in favor of affirmative action. The Court decided, then, that while rigid quotas for admitting students are unconstitutional, race can be taken into account to ensure that minorities are admitted. The implications of the Court's ruling for public employment practices are uncertain.

With all of the efforts to eliminate discrimination and to increase minorities and women in positions of responsibility, one might expect substantial changes in the mix of the public work force. Have those changes materialized? Earlier in this chapter it was found that minorities and women tend to be overrepresented in low-level positions and underrepresented in high-level positions, but was this imbalance worse at an earlier time?

Changes between 1970 and 1975 in the federal General Schedule and similar jobs are presented in Table 9.4 Over all, minorities increased their share of GS jobs from 14 percent to 17 percent, for a gain of 3 percentage points. Women increased from 33 percent to 42 percent, for a gain of 9 points. These increases occurred during a period when total federal jobs were declining; the job cutbacks, therefore, did not negatively affect minority and female representation.

All of the minority groups increased their overall share of GS jobs and increased their share within each level of the General Schedule, with the exception of blacks in GS 1 and 4 positions, where the figures were unchanged. Blacks gained over all by nearly 2 percentage points, whereas Hispanics, Asians, and Native Americans gained by only a fraction of a percent.[91] Depending upon one's viewpoint, these data show little or great progress. Blacks can be said to have made only minimal progress: for

---

Action Limitations on 42 U.S.C. § 1983 Complaints," *Notre Dame Lawyer,* 52 (1977):882–924; and Lewis D. Solomon and Judith S. Heeter, "Affirmative Action in Higher Education: Towards A Rationale for Preference," *Notre Dame Lawyer,* 52 (1976):41–76. At the time of the Bakke decision, the Court agreed to hear *Davis* v. *Los Angeles,* 566 F. 2d 1334 (1978); lower court rulings had found the County had discriminated against Mexican Americans by imposing a height requirement for firefighters and had mandated a quota system as a remedy. See also *Furnco Construction Corporation* v. *Waters,* 98 S. Ct. 2943 (1978), involving hiring practices in the private sector, and *Weber* v. *Kaiser Aluminum and Chemical Corp.,* 563 F. 2d 216 (1977), cert. granted by Supreme Court (1978), involving racial quotas for training in the private sector.

[91] See Don Hellriegel and Larry Short, "Equal Employment Opportunity in the Federal Government: A Comparative Analysis," *Public Administration Review,* 32 (1972):851–858; and Winfield H. Rose and Tiang Ping Chia, "The Impact of the Equal Employment Opportunity Act of 1972 on Black Employment in the Federal Service: A Preliminary Analysis," *Public Administration Review,* 38 (1978):245–251.

Table 9.4   Percentage distribution of minorities and women in federal General Schedule and similar positions, 1970 and 1975

	All Minorities		Blacks		Hispanics		Native Americans		Asians		Women	
	1970	1975	1970	1975	1970	1975	1970	1975	1970	1975	1970	1975
GS 1–4	27.3	28.5	21.8	21.5	3.0	3.7	1.8	2.5	0.6	0.7	68.8	75.8
GS 5–8	17.2	22.0	13.5	17.1	2.2	3.0	0.7	1.0	0.8	0.9	35.0	59.1
GS 9–11	8.0	12.0	5.1	7.9	1.5	2.2	0.5	0.7	1.0	1.2	18.4	24.5
GS 12–13	4.5	7.2	2.7	4.3	0.8	1.3	0.2	0.4	0.9	1.1	6.1	8.1
GS 14–15	3.3	5.6	1.7	3.3	0.7	1.0	0.2	0.3	0.8	1.0	3.5	4.3
GS 16–18	2.0	4.5	1.4	3.1	0.3	0.7	0.1	0.2	0.2	0.5	1.6	2.7
Average	14.4	17.3	10.9	12.7	1.9	2.5	0.8	1.1	0.8	1.0	33.2	42.1

Sources: Minorities data from United States Civil Service Commission, *Minority Group Employment in the Federal Government* (Washington: Government Printing Office, 1971 and 1977): p. 7 and p. 40, respectively. Data on women from United States Civil Service Commission, *Study of Employment of Women in the Federal Government, 1970* (Washington: Government Printing Office, 1971): p. 17; and United States Civil Service Commission, *1976 Annual Report* (Washington: Government Printing Office, 1977): p. 43.

instance, they hold only 3 percent of the GS 16 through 18 positions. The counter argument is that the shift from somewhat more than 1 percent to 3 percent of these jobs is a 121 percent increase in five years. Similarly, other minorities recorded 100 percent gains in the supergrades. Asians, unlike other minorities, are proportionately distributed throughout the General Schedule, holding about 1 percent of all jobs at each grade level.

Different interpretations also are possible for changes in the status of women. On the positive side, they have increased their share of the jobs at all levels in the General Schedule, but they remain greatly under-represented in GS 12 positions and higher. Although they hold over 40 percent of all GS jobs, they hold only 8 percent of the GS 12–13 jobs, 4 percent of the GS 14–15 jobs, and 3 percent of the GS 16–18 jobs. Women hold 66 percent of the GS 1 through 8 positions, but only 16 percent of the GS 9 through 16 positions.[92] For some observers these figures raise a question about whether much progress has been made in eliminating discrimination.

Changes at the state and local level cannot be readily determined. Not until the 1972 Equal Employment Opportunity Act were these governments required to report on race, ethnicity, and sex. Since 1973 the Equal Employment Opportunity Commission has issued annual reports on state and local employees, but because these reports have not been consistent in their coverage, comparisons across years are precluded.

[92] See W. Lloyd Warner et al., "Women Executives in the Federal Government," *Public Personnel Review*, 23 (1962):227–234.

SUMMARY

The distribution of minorities and women in state and local governments and in the federal government are similar. Women constitute somewhat more than a third of the work force and minorities about a fifth. These workers tend to be clustered in low-paying positions. Minorities in state and local governments tend to get jobs as service-maintenance workers and paraprofessionals, while women are concentrated in clerical positions.

A variety of legal routes exists for reversing discriminatory practices. The Fifth and Fourteenth Amendments to the Constitution have been used, along with the post–Civil War Civil Rights Acts. The Civil Rights Act of 1964 as amended by the Equal Employment Opportunity Act of 1972 serves as the primary legal route in discrimination cases for state and local governments and today is the only legal route involving federal employment. Confusion has existed about the relative roles of the United States Civil Service Commission, the Equal Employment Opportunity Commission, and the Department of Justice in cases involving states and local governments. Further complicating the situation is that these governments fall under the jurisdiction of other federal agencies responsible for protecting against discrimination. The reorganization of 1978 clarified the roles of federal agencies, such as providing to the Justice Department responsibility for pattern or pratice cases involving state and local governments. The Equal Employment Opportunity Commission was assigned a leadership role in furthering equal opportunity in all levels of government.

Discrimination occurs in all aspects of public personnel administration. In the field of selection, one of the biggest issues has been the validity of tests as they pertain to race, sex, and ethnicity. Veterans preference has been alleged to be discriminatory, along with height and weight requirements. On the job, discrimination is evidenced in not providing equal pay for equal work. Employee benefits have been the subject of much controversy, especially in terms of whether benefit packages work in favor of one sex. Compulsory retirement has been unsuccessfully attacked as discriminating against older employees. Seniority systems, often included in collective bargaining agreements, are being challenged when used to lay off workers, since the effect can be to remove a disproportionate number of minorities and women.

Affirmative action plans are used to increase minority and female representation in government. Recruiting and testing procedures are changed. Upward mobility programs and job restructuring are used to encourage the promotion of minorities and women in government. The most controversial issue is whether goals or quotas should be used in seeking to increase minority and female employment. Whether affirmative action plans have had an appreciable effect upon the public work force is debatable. Some observers contend that progress is being achieved. Other observers attack affirmative action as a form of reverse discrimination, saying that if affirmative action does alter the racial and sex composition of the work force, then an injustice has been perpetrated. Other critics contend that despite the numerous court cases and the flurry of activity associated with affirmative action, little real change has occurred.

Chapter 10

Personnel Planning and Economic Policy

Planning for personnel is future-oriented, and comprehensive personnel planning encompasses all of the subjects that have been discussed in previous chapters. Problems arise in conducting and executing personnel planning because public employment not only is designed to provide services but in addition has become an integral component of efforts to influence economic trends. Public employment is used to counteract economic recessions.

This chapter has two sections. The first discusses personnel planning techniques and some of the impediments to utilizing this form of planning. The second section considers personnel systems within an intergovernmental context. Emphasis is given to federal grants to state and local governments and how grants that increase state and local employment are expected to further national economic policy.

PERSONNEL PLANNING

"Planning is the process of preparing a set of decisions for action in the future, directed at achieving goals by preferable means."[1] In general, four characteristics are found in most definitions of planning: 1) emphasis upon rationality in choice selection, 2) attention to goals and objectives of society and/or organizations, 3) focus upon deriving means for the attainment of these goals and objectives, and 4) orientation toward the future. Planning entails making a forecast of what will happen and devising strategies either for meeting that forecasted situation or for averting the forecasted situation.

---

[1] Yehezkel Dror, *Ventures in Policy Sciences* (New York: American Elsevier, 1971), p. 106.

Macro socioeconomic planning has not been accepted in the United States. Although society has been willing to accept considerable governmental intervention in the economy, there has been an unwillingness to grant powers to control the economy. In simple terms, that type of planning is viewed as totalitarian, and this simplistic view has been reinforced by dictatorial governments relying heavily upon national planning. Macro planning has been seen as a device by which tyrants restrict individual freedoms.[2]

While macro-level planning is not practiced, macro-level forecasting is. Not only are forecasts made of economic trends, but forecasts are made of labor or personnel requirements. The Bureau of Labor Statistics (BLS) in the United States Department of Labor makes forecasts of the availability of persons with certain types of skills and indicates expected shortages or surpluses. The BLS publishes the *Occupational Outlook Handbook* and the journal *Occupational Outlook Quarterly*. These materials can be useful for employers and for persons contemplating various occupations. Employers can prepare to confront problems in recruiting persons with needed skills where shortages are expected; individuals can avoid occupations where there already is an oversupply of personnel. The BLS uses the term "keen competition" for warning individuals that finding a job in a given field will be difficult.

Making these kinds of forecasts is extremely difficult, in that what will ultimately happen in the future will be the product of millions of decisions.[3] Since the United States does not have a centralized decision system determining which individuals will enter which fields, forecasts must be based upon judgments about what various segments of the society/economy are likely to do. For instance, one of the greatest forecasting problems in recent years has been predicting the extent to which women will enter the labor market. More women may choose to enter the market and others aleady employed may choose to remain in their jobs, whereas in an earlier time they might have resigned to become full-time homemakers. Being in the labor market, however, is not the same as being employed. A person is part of the labor market if he is employed or seeking employment. An interactive process exists: people look for employment, but if they are unsuccessful for an extended period, they

---

[2] See James Burnham, *The Managerial Revolution* (Bloomington: Indiana University Press, 1941) and Friedrich A. Hayek, *The Road to Serfdom* (Chicago: University of Chicago Press, 1944).

[3] See Roger H. Bezdek, "Alternate Manpower Forecasts for the Coming Decade: Second Guessing the U.S. Department of Labor," *Socio-Economic Planning Sciences*, 7 (1973):511–521; Marc Rosenblum, "The Great Labor Force Projection Debate: Implications for 1980," *American Economist*, 17 (Fall, 1973):122–129; and Sol Swerdloff, "Manpower Projections: Some Conceptual Problems and Research Needs," *Monthly Labor Review*, 89 (February, 1966):138–143.

stop their search and drop out of the market. Similarly, if the outlook improves, they are likely to re-enter the job market.

These forecasts also involve predictions of economic and technological changes. What industries can be expected to expand and what will be their personnel needs? Will there be a boom in small appliances, and what types of persons are needed to manufacture these items? Similarly, will there be technological changes reducing the need for some skills and increasing the need for others? Since World War II automation obviously has had great impact upon the mix of skills required by the labor market.

Educational institutions are important in influencing the occupational mix of the labor force, and, as with the economy, these institutions are not centrally controlled. Colleges and universities have difficulty in adjusting their output to meet demands. One of the best illustrations is the "production" of school teachers. While there has been an oversupply of teachers for many years and the demand for teachers can be expected to decline because of falling enrollments in elementary and secondary schools, higher education continues to graduate teachers for jobs that will never exist. Part of the justification for this overproduction is that individuals ought to have access to education regardless of market trends. Rather than having a controlled system that allows only a predetermined number of people to enter a field, the existing system allows individual freedom of choice, but, as a result, allows for shortages and surpluses in some occupations.

Colleges and universities are subject to labor market pressures and frequently attempt to respond to market demands. At a time when enrollments are threatened, these institutions seek to develop or enlarge programs that will attract students. The emergence of new public administration degree programs in the 1960s and 1970s is an example of schools responding to markets. Overproduction is an ever-present danger, again because there is no central control. Each institution, recognizing government's need for administrators, establishes its own program, resulting in far more people seeking government jobs than the total number of available jobs. While some state educational systems attempt to control the number of public administration students as well as other types of students in their public institutions, there is no central control of all public and private institutions in the country.

Forecasts are made not only for occupations but also for industries, including government.[4] In 1964 the United States Civil Service Com-

---
[4] See Ewan Clague, "Government Employment and Manpower Planning in the 1970s," *Public Personnel Review*, 31 (1970):279–282; Frederick J. Lawton, "Manpower in the 1960s: Federal Management Must Choose," *Civil Service Journal*, 1 (October-December, 1960):2–23; and "Working for the Federal Government," *Occupational Outlook Quarterly*, 21 (Winter, 1977), entire issue.

Table 10.1.   Projected and actual state and local government employment by function for 1975 (in thousands)

Function	1975	
	1967 Projection	Actual*
Education	5,400	4,952
Elementary and Secondary	3,930	3,823
Higher Education	1,400	1,040
Other	70	88
Highways	675	569
Health	1,350	1,131
Housing	75	93
Sanitation	320	201
Natural Resources	450	323**
Other	3,130	2,842
TOTAL	11,400	10,111

Sources: Howard V. Stambler, "State and Local Government Manpower in 1975," *Monthly Labor Review*, 90 (April, 1967): p. 14, and United States Bureau of the Census, *Public Employment in 1975* (Washington: Government Printing Office, 1976): p. 9.

   * Full-time equivalent employment.

   ** Includes parks and recreation.

mission published a report forecasting employment in the federal government through 1968, and many of the document's predictions were on target.[5] That was basically a five-year projection, which is much easier to make than a forecast for ten or more years into the future. Table 10.1 compares a 1967 forecast of state and local employment for 1975 with actual 1975 employment. (In fairness to the author of those data, it should be noted that he described these as "illustrative of the possible direction" of state and local employment and not as a forecast.[6]) The 1967 projection overestimated the growth in state and local employment by about 1.3 million. This error in projecting is readily understandable given the kinds of assumptions that had to be made. For example, the forecast had to make assumptions about the status of the Vietnam War and the national employment picture. The projection was based on the assumption that the war would be concluded by 1970, when it was not concluded until 1975. The projection assumed a 3 percent unemployment rate in 1975, when the rate actually was over 8 percent. Of course, there was no assumption built into the forecast that an energy crisis would begin in 1973.

   [5] Civil Service Commission, *Federal Workforce Outlook, Fiscal Years 1965–68* (Washington: Government Printing Office, 1964).

   [6] Howard V. Stambler, "State and Local Government Manpower in 1975," *Monthly Labor Review*, 90 (April, 1967):13.

In contrast to macro-level personnel forecasting, personnel planning within a jurisdiction can be defined as providing for "the right numbers and the right kinds of people at the right places and the right times."[7] The concern is to employ neither too many nor too few workers, either of which would reduce efficiency. The importance of avoiding overhiring is perhaps greater in the public sector than in the private sector, since the former relies heavily upon salaried workers. A private corporation that finds itself overstaffed can reduce personnel costs by cutting back on the number of hours worked by each employee. For the public jurisdiction, whose staff is largely salaried, reducing personnel costs may require the drastic action of furloughing workers.

Personnel planning begins with a forecast of personnel require-ments.[8] As can be seen in Figure 10.1, the forecast can be short-range (covering a year or two), intermediate, or long-range, such as a ten-year forecast. The short-range forecast can be more accurate than the others,

---

[7] James W. Walker, "Trends in Manpower Management Research," *Business Horizons*, 11 (August, 1968):37–46.

[8] For discussions of personnel planning, see Glenn A. Bassett, "Elements of Manpower Forecasting and Scheduling," *Human Resource Management*, 12 (Fall, 1973):35–40; Glenn A. Bassett, "Manpower Forecasting and Planning: Problems and Solutions," *Personnel*, 47 (September, 1970):8–16; Angela Bowey, *A Guide to Manpower Planning* (New York: Macmillan, 1974); Don R. Bryant, Michael J. Maggard, and Robert P. Taylor, "Man-power Planning Models and Techniques," *Business Horizons*, 16 (April, 1973):69–78; Elmer Burack and James W. Walker, eds., *Manpower Planning and Programming* (Boston: Allyn and Bacon, 1972); Civil Service Commission, *Decision Analysis Forecasting for Executive Manpower Planning* (Washington: Government Printing Office, 1974); Civil Service Commission, *Executive Personnel Planning Guidance* (Washington: Government Printing Office, 1977); Eli Ginzberg and James K. Anderson, *Manpower for Government: A Decade's Forecast* (Chicago: Public Personnel Association, 1958); Erich Hardt, "Man-power Planning," *Personnel Journal*, 46 (1967):157–161; R. J. Howard et al., "Making Sense of Manpower Planning," *Personnel Management*, 7 (October, 1975):37–39; W. N. Jessop, ed., *Manpower Planning: Operational Research and Personnel Research* (New York: American Elsevier, 1966); Frank A. Malinowski and Sheldon R. Hurovitz, "Person-nel Research in State Government," *Public Personnel Management*, 6 (1977):259–262; *Manpower Planning Guide* (Washington: U.S. Department of Labor, 1969); Gordon L. Nielsen and Allan R. Young, "Manpower Planning: A Markov Chain Application," *Public Personnel Management*, 2 (1973):133–143; Thomas H. Patten, Jr., *Manpower Planning and the Development of Human Resources* (New York: Wiley-Interscience, 1971); Paul A. Roberts, Lance W. Seberhagen, and Richard R. Cottrell, *Manpower Planning for the Public Service* (Chicago: Public Personnel Association, 1971); Paul A. Roberts, "Problems and Prospects of Manpower Planning: An Example," *Public Personnel Review*, 31 (1970):126–128; Gilbert B. Siegel, "A Conceptual Framework for Manpower Planning and Forecasting in Governmental Organization," in Gilbert B. Siegel, ed., *Human Resource Management in Public Organizations: A Systems Approach* (Los Angeles: University Publishers, 1973), pp. 657–669; Eric Vetter, *Manpower Planning for High Talent Personnel* (Ann Arbor: Bureau of Industrial Relations, University of Michigan, 1967); James W. Walker, "Forecasting Manpower Needs," *Harvard Business Review*, 47 (March–April, 1969):152–156; Wesley L. Weber, "Manpower Planning in Hierarchical Organizations: A Computer Simulation Approach," *Management Science*, 18 (1971):119–144; Walter S. Wikstrom, *Manpower Planning: Evolving Systems* (New York: Conference Board, 1971).

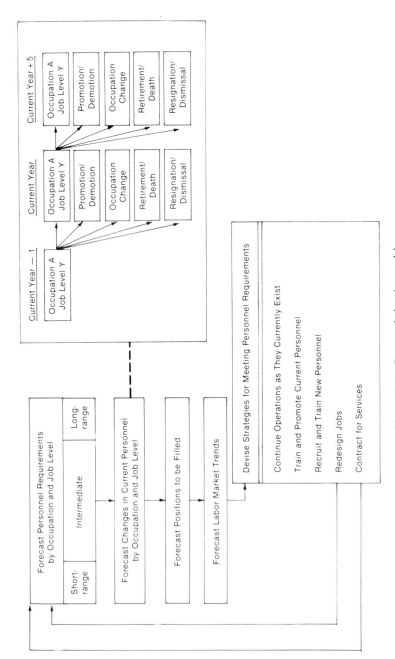

Figure 10.1. Personnel planning model.

since there are fewer uncertainties. One has a better chance of predicting what will happen tomorrow than what will happen ten or fifteen years in the future. A weakness of the short-range forecast is that options for response will be necessarily restricted, whereas a longer-range forecast provides greater lead time for devising and implementing response strategies. An important aspect of the needs forecast is to project on the basis of occupation and job level. The same specificity in forecasting is needed in the next step, namely an assessment of what will happen to current employees.

Position classification systems can be used as the structure for such forecasts, although alternative methods may prove more useful. Since under a merit system recruitment will be geared to the position classification plan, it is appropriate to forecast needs on the basis of the plan. A problem, however, is that position classification systems may fragment skills or not sufficiently highlight them. In the first instance, two positions involving similar work may be placed in different parts of the classification plan. Alternatively, the classification of a position might not adequately reflect the range of skills required. A labor economics analyst position, for example, might require knowledge of computer programming, but that skill might not be identified in the classification plan. Another aspect of the forecast should be whether positions involve managerial or supervisory roles. The federal executive inventory (see Chapter 7) gathers this type of information by asking participants to code their current and previous positions by occupational code and by level of responsibility. As many as three occupational codes can be used to describe one job, along with two functions, such as advisor or line manager.

Forecasting changes in current personnel is depicted in the inset to Figure 10.1 (upper right corner). Experience data are used to project future changes.[9] During any year, some employees will remain in their positions while others will be promoted (or in some cases demoted) or will change their occupations (perhaps moving from a clerical to an administrative aide position). Other employees will leave the jurisdiction, through either resignation, retirement, dismissal, or death. The personnel planner needs to assess whether past and current trends are likely to continue. The fact that a given set of jobs has had a high turnover rate may be because promotion opportunities have been unusually great or because opportunities in the private sector have been great. The question is whether those competing opportunities are likely to continue.

By comparing the forecasts of personnel requirements and expected

---

[9] See Fremont J. Lyden, "A Study of Turnover," *Public Administration Review*, 28 (1968):181–182.

changes in current personnel, a forecast can be derived for the net number of positions to be filled. That forecast then is compared with an assessment of the external labor market. Will there be sufficient numbers of people in the labor market who can be attracted to fill the vacant positions? Labor force projections by the BLS can be helpful. However, it is possible for sufficient numbers of people to be in the labor market but not be willing to accept government jobs. Engineers with job experience may prefer to work in private enterprise, where pay is higher than in government; as a consequence, the public jurisdiction may only be able to recruit inexperienced engineers who have recently completed college.

Once these forecasts are made, strategies can be devised. As is shown in Figure 10.1, a conclusion may be that there is no need to change current operations. If forecasts indicate that ample personnel will be available, then no new action is required. Should there be a projected gap between needed and available personnel, then a strategy might be adopted to increase training programs to upgrade the skills of current personnel, thereby filling positions through promotions.[10] Positions also can be filled through more extensive recruiting, possibly coupled with increased training for newly recruited employees. Where it seems doubtful that the needed personnel will be able to be recruited, an alternative is job redesign (see Chapters 3 and 9). If highly skilled personnel cannot be recruited in sufficient numbers, it may be possible to redesign work so that fewer of these people are needed. Still another alternative is to contract for services, alleviating altogether the need to hire personnel. For instance, if sufficient numbers of medical doctors cannot be recruited because of low salaries in government, a fee-for-service arrangement can be made with doctors in private practice. Both job redesign and contracting for service involve revising the forecast of needed personnel.

Comprehensive personnel planning, as has been described here, is not common in government. A survey in the early 1970s found that only 2 percent of the responding local governments reported they had developed a personnel planning system and none of the states reported they had such systems.[11] Partial planning systems were reported in 20 percent of the local governments and 33 percent of the states.

Comprehensive personnel planning probably is neither cost efficient nor feasible for most governments. To attempt such planning for an entire government requires considerable staff and probably extensive computer support. Much of the planning would be superfluous, in that many jobs would be automatically filled. One of the main justifications

---

[10] T. W. Bonham, Edward R. Clayton, and Lawrence J. Moore," A GERT Model to Meet Future Organizational Manpower Needs," *Personnel Journal*, 54 (1975):402–406.

[11] Personnel Office, *Manpower Planning: The State of the Art* (Washington: District of Columbia Government, 1973).

for personnel planning is that it devises strategies for coping with personnel shortages, but, if few shortages exist, then that benefit does not materialize.[12] For that reason, personnel planning probably should be restricted largely to professional, administrative, and technical (PAT) positions, disregarding clerical and laborer positions. Even with PAT positions, shortages may be minimal, as has been the case in the 1970s. However, some aggregate forecasting of all types of personnel is useful because of budgetary implications.

One of the severest weaknesses of personnel planning involves forecasting future personnel requirements. An approach that might be taken would be to make straight-line projections, so that if PAT positions have been increasing by 1 percent per year, the assumption would be that that pattern would continue in the future. Such an assumption obviously can be faulty, and therefore other apporaches are used. An alternative is to canvass administrators about what they expect their personnel needs will be. This requires time, which translates into additional costs both for personnel planners and administrators. In some cases the process has been even more elaborate, using the Delphi technique, in which first various experts make forecasts and then review each others' forecasts, ultimately making a consensus forecast.

If left to operate by themselves, personnel planning systems can result in putting the cart before the horse. Before planning for personnel, plans should be made for government programs. Program planning sets forth recommendations on how programs are to be modified in the future. Decision makers, then, are presented with alternative futures. Once a decision is made to modify a program or to retain it in its current format, future personnel needs can be derived.

In some governments program planning is being undertaken through what is known as program budgeting.[13] Some central budget offices require line agencies to project future growth/decline in programs based upon the concept of current commitment. The current commitment budget projects future workload and future costs with no improvement in services.[14] At the federal level, the President is required to submit a Cur-

---

[12] Municipal Manpower Commission, *Governmental Manpower for Tomorrow's Cities* (New York: McGraw-Hill, 1962).

[13] See Robert D. Lee, Jr., and Ronald W. Johnson, *Public Budgeting Systems*, 2d ed. (Baltimore: University Park Press, 1977); Robert J. Mowitz, *The Design and Implementation of Pennsylvania's Planning, Programming, Budgeting System* (Harrisburg: Commonwealth of Pennsylvania, 1970); and Chester P. Grossmuck, "Budgeting Personnel Requirements," in W. J. Donald and Leona Powell, eds., *Handbook of Business Administration* (New York: McGraw-Hill, 1931), pp. 1063–1072.

[14] For an example of workload and personnel forecasting, see Milton Drandell, "A Composite Forecasting Methodology for Manpower Planning Utilizing Objective and Subjective Criteria," *Academy of Management Journal*, 18 (1975):510–519.

rent Services Budget to Congress each November. Budget requests, then, are considered as proposals to change programmatic commitments. If those proposals are approved by the chief executive and legislative body, future personnel requirements can be derived. In Pennsylvania, the Budget Office has required agencies to project personnel needs as part of each proposal to change a program.

Linking program planning with personnel planning is difficult because of the differing data requirements of these forms of planning. The budget process cannot be expected to collect all data needed for personnel planning. Budget offices are concerned with aggregates, such as how many additional technical workers will be needed if a proposed program change is approved, and are less concerned with detailed personnel information. Personnel units, in contrast, are concerned with specific types of technical positions. Budget processes are already complicated, involving the preparation of numerous forms, and to add more forms requiring detailed information on personnel could add to the frustrations of line administrators.

A possible solution to this problem is to require aggregate personnel projections in program planning through the budget process and to provide detailed personnel planning only for selected areas. Rather than attempting to devise personnel plans for all types of positions throughout a government, personnel planners might focus upon known or anticipated problems. For example, a simple computer search of personnel files may identify some agencies having a large percentage of their staffs that are approaching retirement age. In that instance, turnover can be anticipated, and the personnel planner can assist in meeting the expected change. Similarly, personnel planning can be useful for agencies that are to be reorganized, where some personnel may find their positions have been collapsed; the personnel planner can help plan for finding jobs for those who are displaced. This limited type of planning is useful in cases where a new agency is to be created, where an agency is to be substantially increased in size, or where an agency is to be decentralized so that central office positions will be reduced in numbers while regional office positions are increased. Personnel planning, of course, can be useful for selected occupations where shortages are common.[15] The federal government has had chronic problems recruiting sufficient numbers of engineers, and state and local governments have had difficulty recruiting attorneys and medical personnel. Personnel planning can be helpful in analyzing why some agencies have high turnover rates.[16] Planning is use-

[15] Eugene J. Devine, *Analysis of Manpower Shortages in Local Government: Case Studies of Nurses, Policemen, and Teachers* (New York: Praeger, 1970).

[16] Eric G. Flamholtz, "Human Resources Accounting: Measuring Positional Replacement Costs," *Human Resource Management*, 12 (Spring, 1973):8–16.

ful for recruiting minorities and women as part of an affirmative action program.

Problems exist even with this limited type of personnel planning. Planning that focuses upon individual employees and how they will develop within an agency can result in the "crown-prince" or "heir apparent" syndrome. Also, line administrators will not necessarily welcome the assistance of personnel planners. An administrator in a line agency may feel under great pressure to cope with current problems and be unwilling or unable to contemplate future problems.[17] The personnel administrator may be viewed as not having any relevant expertise. A police chief might ask, what does a personnel planner know about law enforcement or traffic control? Planning also may be hampered by inadequate data bases and information systems.[18] Planning may be difficult to undertake because of financial constraints; if a jurisdiction's budget is tight, any increased funds are more likely to be provided for delivering services than for what may be viewed as the luxury of personnel planning. Those personnel plans that are devised may not be implemented because of budgetary constraints.[19] Sometimes agencies have new positions authorized, but later the budget office imposes a freeze on all hiring in order to cut costs.

INTERGOVERNMENTAL RELATIONS, ECONOMIC POLICY, AND MANPOWER PROGRAMS

The importance of federal aid to state and local governments is well known.[20] In 1975–76, states received 28 percent of their revenues from the federal government, and local governments received 8 percent.[21]

---

[17] J. B. Bartlett, "Problems in Manpower Planning," *Personnel Management* 5 (February, 1973):30–31+.

[18] Martin I. Taft and Arnold Reisman, "On a Computer-Aided Systems Approach to Personnel Administration, *Socio-Economic Planning Sciences*, 5 (1971):547–567; Robert D. Lee, Jr., and William M. Lucianovic, "Personnel Management Information Systems for State and Local Governments," *Public Personnel Management*, 4 (1975):84–89; John R. Hinrichs, "The Computer in Manpower Research," *Personnel Administration*, 33 (March-April, 1970):37–44; Albert C. Hyde and Jay M. Shafrtiz, "HRIS: Introduction to Tomorrow's System for Managing Human Resources," *Public Personnel Management*, 6 (1977):70–77.

[19] *Personnel Ceilings: A Barrier to Effective Manpower Management* (Washington: General Accounting Office, 1977).

[20] For a discussion of intergovernmental finance, see Lee and Johnson, *Public Budgeting Systems*, pp. 281–311. The Intergovernmental Personnel Act is not discussed in this chapter. See Chapter 3 for a discussion of intergovernmental personnel assignments funded under the IPA and Chapter 9 for a discussion of the IPA as influencing equal rights and affirmative action.

[21] Census Bureau, *Governmental Finances in 1975–76* (Washington: Government Printing Office, 1977), p. 19.

While the percentage for local governments may seem small, the importance of those federal dollars should not be underestimated. A 5 to 10 percent change, upward or downward, in any government's budget has measurable effects. Moreover, some jurisdictions are more dependent on federal aid than others, and that dependence may be increasing. In 1957 St. Louis received federal funds equal to less than 1 percent of its locally generated revenues, but by 1978 the figure had climbed to over 50 percent.[22] In that same time period, federal aid to Buffalo increased from being equal to 1 percent of locally generated revenues to equal 76 percent.

The increasing importance of federal aid has complicated all forms of planning at the state and local levels. A chronic problem for these governments has been not knowing whether and when federal monies will be made available. This problem is particularly acute concerning categorical or project grants. Under these grant programs, of which there were about 1,100 in 1976, a jurisdiction must apply to a federal agency and explain how federal funds would be used. The agency reviews the application, a process which may take many weeks, during which time the state or local government might be required to submit additional data to substantiate its request. The uncertainty that stems from this process necessarily affects personnel planning. If people are to be hired under the grant, they cannot be brought onto the payroll until the grant has been finally approved.

Other federal grant programs are more conducive to state and local planning. The State and Local Fiscal Assistance Act, passed in 1972 and renewed in 1976, established general revenue sharing (GRS), which distributes monies to about 38,000 states and general purpose local governments, including cities, townships, and counties.[23] The legislation sets a dollar amount to be distributed each year, and the monies are allocated according to a complex formula. The advantage of this system is that

---

[22] "Federal Initiatives and Impacts," *Intergovernmental Perspective*, 4 (Winter, 1978):9.

[23] State and Local Fiscal Assistance Act, 86 Stat. 919 (1974) and 90 Stat. 2341 (1976). Also, Advisory Commission on Intergovernmental Relations, *General Revenue Sharing: An ACIR Re-Evaluation*, (Washington: U.S. Government Printing Office, 1974); David A. Caputo, ed., "Symposium on General Revenue Sharing," *Public Administration Review*, 35 (1975):130–157; David A. Caputo and Richard L. Cole, *Urban Politics and Decentralization: The Case of General Revenue Sharing* (Lexington, Mass.: Heath, 1974); *Case Studies of Revenue Sharing in 26 Local Governments*, summary volume and 26 case studies (Washington: General Accounting Office, 1975); *General Revenue Sharing Research Utilization Project*, several volumes (Washington: National Science Foundation, 1975); F. Thomas Juster, ed., *The Economic and Political Impact of General Revenue Sharing* (Washington: Government Printing Office, 1976); *Making Civil Rights Sense out of Revenue Sharing Dollars* (Washington: U.S. Commission on Civil Rights, 1975); Richard P. Nathan et al., *Monitoring Revenue Sharing* (Washington: Brookings, 1975).

state and local governments can plan for the use of these funds, including whether some personnel will be hired with GRS funds. Rather than the monies being earmarked for specific types of projects or activities, general revenue sharing can be used to support virtually any service of the state or local government. Another advantage of GRS is that the jurisdiction does not apply for the funds but instead automatically receives checks from the Office of Revenue Sharing in the Treasury Department.

Between categorical grants and general revenue sharing are block grants.[24] These grants are more restrictive than GRS but less restrictive than categoricals. One example is the community development program, established by the Housing and Community Development Act of 1974.[25] That program provides considerable latitude to recipient governments in community development efforts. The legislation provides for distribution of funds on a formula basis, but unlike general revenue sharing, the jurisdiction must apply for the monies.

While all federal grant programs have bearing on state and local personnel systems, manpower grant programs are of particular relevance.[26] Different purposes are served by these programs. One purpose is to provide assistance to persons who are unemployed because of a declining economy. A related purpose is to provide purchasing power to the unemployed as a means of stimulating economic recovery. Still another purpose is to provide training and ancillary services that will increase the employability of persons with little or no skills. These purposes are different from those of other federal grant programs intended to assist in the provision of a service, such as grants for education or transportation.

Current federal manpower programs can be traced back to legislation of the 1920s, but for the most part the current programs emerged out of legislation from the 1960s.[27] The Area Redevelopment Act of

[24] Advisory Commission on Intergovernmental Relations, *Block Grants: A Comparative Analysis* (Washington: Government Printing Office, 1977).

[25] Housing and Community Development Act, 88 Stat. 633 (1974).

[26] The use of the word "manpower," is unavoidable given that it is standard in this field despite its sexual bias.

[27] Advisory Commission on Intergovernmental Relations, *Federal Grants: Their Effects on State-Local Expenditures, Employment Levels, Wage Rates* (Washington: Government Printing Office, 1977); Ewan Clague and Leo Kramer, *Manpower Policies and Programs: A Review, 1935-75* (Kalamazoo, Mich.: Upjohn Institute, 1976); James A. Craft, "New Directions for Public Service Employment in Manpower Programming," *Public Personnel Management*, 5 (1976):60–66; Everett Crawford, *Public Service Employment Programs: An Opportunity and a Challenge* (Washington: Center for Governmental Studies, 1971); Roger H. Davidson, *The Politics of Comprehensive Manpower Legislation* (Baltimore: Johns Hopkins University Press, 1972); Alan Gartner, Russell A. Nixon, and Frank Riessman, eds., *Public Service Employment: An Analysis of Its History, Problems,*

1961, the Manpower Development and Training Act of 1962, and the Economic Opportunity Act of 1964 were aimed at assisting the poor and unemployed.[28] The results of these acts and others was a substantial increase in federal expenditures for manpower programs, rising from $0.5 billion in 1961 to $3.5 billion in 1970. Complaints arose, however, over the seeming absence of planning and coordination of manpower programs, and in 1967 the Cooperative Area Manpower Planning System (CAMPS) was created. It involved a series of local, regional, and state committees intended to coordinate programs, but the result was disappointing. President Nixon in 1969 proposed a major overhaul of manpower legislation. Congress, not willing to accept the Nixon proposal, passed the Emergency Employment Act of 1971, which provided for the creation of transitional jobs in state and local governments; persons in those jobs were expected to find private jobs afterwards.[29]

A major revision of this legislation came in 1973 with the passage of the Comprehensive Employment and Training Act (CETA).[30] The Nixon

---

and Prospects (New York: Praeger, 1973); Richard D. Gustely, Municipal Public Employment and Public Expenditure (Lexington, Mass.: Lexington Books, 1974); Bennett Harrison, Public Employment and Urban Poverty (Washington: Urban Institute, 1975); Mark A. Haskell, The New Careers Concept: Potential for Public Employment of the Poor (New York: Praeger, 1969); William H. Leahy, "An Economic Perspective of Public Employment Programs," Review of Social Economy, 34 (1976):189–200; Richard Lehne, "Revenue Sources and Local Government Employment," Public Finance Quarterly, 3 (1975):400–410; Sar A. Levitan and Joyce K. Zickler, "Block Grants for Manpower Programs," Public Administration Review, 35 (1975):191–195; Sar A. Levitan and Joyce K. Zickler, The Quest for a Federal Manpower Partnership (Cambridge, Mass.: Harvard University Press, 1974); National Commission for Manpower Policy, Directions for a National Manpower Policy: A Collection of Policy Papers Prepared for Three Regional Conferences (Washington: Government Printing Office, 1976); National Commission for Manpower Policy, Proceedings of a Conference on Public Service Employment (Washington: Government Printing Office, 1975); A Public Service Employment Program: Effective Manpower Strategy (Washington: National Planning Association, 1974); Laurence S. Seidman, The Design of Federal Employment Programs (Lexington, Mass.: Lexington Books, 1975); Harold L. Sheppard, Bennett Harrison, and William J. Spring, eds., The Political Economy of Public Service Employment (Lexington, Mass.: Lexington Books, 1972); Special Revenue Sharing for Manpower Training and Employment Programs (Washington: American Enterprise Institute, 1971).

[28] Area Redevelopment Act, 75 Stat. 47 (1961); Manpower Development and Training Act, 76 Stat. 23 (1962); and Economic Opportunity Act, 78 Stat. 508 (1964).

[29] Emergency Employment Act, 85 Stat. 146 (1971).

[30] Comprehensive Employment and Training Act, 87 Stat. 857 (1973). See Advisory Commission on Intergovernmental Relations, A Comprehensive Employment and Training Act: Early Readings from a Hybrid Block Grant (Washington: Government Printing Office, 1977); Civil Service Commission, Guidelines for Evaluation of Employment Practices Under the Comprehensive Employment and Training Act (Washington: Government Printing Office, 1974); Congressional Budget Office, CETA Reauthorization Issues (Washington: Government Printing Office, 1978); Information on the Buildup in Public Service Jobs (Washington: General Accounting Office, 1978); William Mirengoff and

administration had attempted since 1969 to get Congress to approve a broad-based block grant manpower program, but CETA was a blend between block grants and categoricals. Title I of the Act established a block grant program allowing state and local discretion in the provision of on-the-job training, classroom training, work experience, counseling, and public service employment. Funds are awarded to about 450 prime sponsors, which are city and county governments having 100,000 population or more, consortia of local governments, and states. State governments serve those areas not covered by local prime sponsors. Most of the funds are allocated on the basis of a formula, which takes into account previous manpower funding, the percentage of persons unemployed, and the extent of low-income adult population.[31] Title II earmarks monies for public-service employment in jurisdictions with high unemployment.

The other major component of the legislation that is relevant to public personnel is Title VI, which was added in 1974 and which authorized additional public service jobs. While both Titles II and VI provided for the creation of government jobs, they had different purposes. Title II was viewed as a permanent measure to provide transitional employment for the unemployed; not only were persons expected to obtain financial help by being hired by government but also they were expected to learn skills that would increase their employability in the private sector. Title VI, in contrast, was viewed as a temporary economic stimulus. By putting the unemployed to work, their increased buying power would stimulate private-sector production of goods and services. CETA was renewed in 1976–77 and again in 1978, when the program was authorized to continue for another four years.

The growing importance of the public-service employment component of manpower programs can be seen in terms of dollars and jobs. Figure 10.2 shows federal outlays for manpower programs since 1964; outlays for public-service jobs have risen sharply—in 1978 they reached $8 billion. Nearly three-quarters of a million people were employed in

---

Lester Rindler, *The Comprehensive Employment and Training Act: Impact on People, Places, Programs* (Washington: National Academy of Sciences, 1976); National Commission for Manpower Policy, *An Employment Strategy for the United States: Next Steps* (Washington: Government Printing Office, 1976); Subcommittee on Manpower, Compensation, and Health and Safety, House Committee on Education and Labor, *Oversight Hearings on the Comprehensive Employment and Training Act*, 94th Cong., 2d sess. (Washington: Government Printing Office, 1976); Task Force on Human Resources, House Committee on the Budget, *Comprehensive Employment and Training Act: Hearings*, 95th Cong., 1st sess. (Washington: Government Printing Office, 1977); and Carl E. Van Horn, "Implementing CETA: The Federal Role," *Policy Analysis*, 4 (1978):159–183.

[31] *Progress and Problems in Allocating Funds Under Titles I and II—Comprehensive Employment and Training Act* (Washington: General Accounting Office, 1976).

Outlays

$ Billions $ Billions

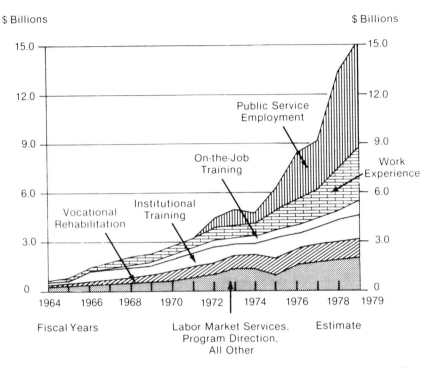

Figure 10.2. Federal outlays for manpower programs by type, 1964–1979. Source: Office of Management and Budget, *Special Analyses: Budget of the United States Government, Fiscal Year 1979* (Washington: Government Printing Office, 1978): p. 235.

1978 by state and local governments using CETA funds, but the 1978 renewal legislation approved by Congress provided for cutbacks in public-service jobs to somewhat below 700,000 jobs. With total state and local employment near 12 million, it is apparent that CETA has become an important part of the employment picture for these governments.

Given CETA's different objectives, its impacts must be considered from different perspectives: how has it influenced the unemployment rate, the participants in the program, and the state and local governments that received these funds? CETA has had a limited or perhaps negligible effect upon the nation's unemployment rate. There is no firm evidence that declines in unemployment have been associated with CETA public-service employment. In part this results from the size of the program. An estimate by the United States Labor Department was that, in 1974–75, $7 billion would have been needed to reduce unemployment by 1 percent when only $1.6 billion was available.[32]

One of the major contributing factors that has reduced CETA's impact on unemployment is what is called displacement or fiscal substitution. State and local governments generally are required to have balanced operating budgets; unlike the federal government, these governments are not permitted to engage in extensive deficit spending for current operations. Given this limitation, state and local governments tend to reduce their staffs during recessions because of declining revenues. Positions that become vacant are not filled and in some cases workers are furloughed. Under CETA, state and local dollars have been displaced and federal dollars have been substituted. Persons who otherwise might have been hired with state and local dollars are hired with federal dollars.[33]

Like its effect on the unemployment rate, CETA has not been an unqualified success in helping participants find permanent jobs in the private sector. As can be seen from Table 10.2, the public-service jobs under Titles II and VI serve a substantially different clientele than pre-CETA programs and Title I of CETA; Title II and VI clients also are different from the unemployed population. A greater percentage of the public-service jobs are given to males, workers between the ages of 22 and 44, persons with a high school education or more, whites, veterans, and people who are *not* economically disadvantaged. CETA workers generally have received no training in their government jobs but rather simply have been put to work. Therefore, no claim can be made that training in government jobs has markedly increased their employability, although any experience probably improves employability. The claim can be made, however, that the experience of working in government has increased their skills.

When one looks at the reasons for terminating employment under the public jobs programs, the results are not encouraging. According to the Labor Department, a positive termination is one where the worker has found a permanent job *or* has enrolled in school, joined the military,

---

[32] *More Benefits to Jobless Can Be Attained in Public Service Employment* (Washington: General Accounting Office, 1977), p. 7. See Michael Wiseman, "Public Employment as Fiscal Policy," *Brookings Papers on Economic Activity*, No. 1 (1976):67–114.

[33] Congressional Budget Office, *Public Employment and Training Assistance: Alternative Federal Approaches* (Washington: Government Printing Office, 1977), p. 27. Also see Alan Fechter, *Public Employment Programs* (Washington: American Enterprise Institute for Public Policy Research, 1975), pp. 12–19; Congressional Budget Office, *Employment and Training Programs* (Washington: Government Printing Office, 1976), pp. 47–58.

Table 10.2.   Characteristics of participants in CETA (1976) and other programs (1974) and of the unemployed population (1976) (percent)

Characteristic	Categorical Programs, Fiscal 1974	CETA 1976			U.S. Unemployed Population 1976
		Title I	Title II	Title VI	
TOTAL	100.0	100.0	100.0	100.0	100.0
Sex:					
Male	57.7	54.1	63.8	65.1	55.5
Female	42.3	45.9	36.2	34.9	44.5
Age:					
Under 22 yrs.	63.1	56.7	21.9	22.0	33.6
22 to 44 yrs.	30.5	36.5	64.0	64.1	46.6
45 yrs. and over	6.2	6.8	14.1	13.9	19.8
Education:					
8 yrs. and under	15.1	11.9	8.0	8.1	12.9
9 to 11 yrs.	51.1	42.9	17.9	17.1	28.7
12 yrs. and over	33.8	45.2	74.1	74.2	58.4
Economically disadvantaged	86.7	75.7	46.5	44.1	*
Race:					
White[1]	54.9	55.3	61.4	68.2	80.7
Black	37.0	37.1	26.5	23.0 ⎫	
American Indian	3.5	1.4[2]	1.3	1.0 ⎬	19.3
Other	4.6	6.2	10.8	7.0 ⎭	
Hispanic Origin	15.4	14.0	12.4	9.9	6.5
Limited English Speaking Ability	*	5.1[2]	4.3	3.5	*
Veterans:					
Special Vietnam Era ⎫	⎫ 15.3	⎧ 3.6	10.0	8.7	8.0
Other ⎭	⎭	⎩ 4.5	11.4	12.0	9.7

Source: United States Department of Labor, *Employment and Training Report of the President* (Washington: Government Printing Office, 1977): p. 49.

* Not available.

[1] Includes Hispanic-Origin Americans (Cubans, Puerto Ricans, Mexican Americans, and Latin Americans, as well as those who do not appear to belong to one of these groups but who have last names of Hispanic origin).

[2] Special programs for Indians and those with limited English-speaking ability are also part of Title III of CETA.

NOTE: Detail may not add to totals because of rounding.

or become a part of another manpower program. In 1975, for every 9 positive terminations under Title II, there were 7 nonpositive terminations, and under Title VI, the ratio was 5 to 6.[34] A study of twelve prime

---

[34] *More Benefits to Jobless Can Be Attained in Public Service Employment*, p. 27.

sponsors found that 42 percent of the positive terminations had not taken nonsubsidized jobs, that is, had not been integrated into the private economy.[35]

What has been the effect of CETA upon participating governments? State and local governments have been willing partners in the federal government's policy to use them to stimulate the economy and help the unemployed. The money came at a time when need was great for these governments. In many instances, CETA employees were used to avoid cutbacks in services or to restore cuts that had been made. What could be accomplished depended largely upon who were recruited as CETA employees. Common complaints have been that CETA workers often have no skills that can make them productive either in government or private employment and that they have poor work habits. It is not known to what extent CETA workers have been reliable in reporting on time for work and once on the job have been willing to work. Many CETA jobs undoubtedly have been of a make-work type. In other instances, CETA jobs have been created in agencies without expectations of any increases in production, thereby reducing the workload of regular employees and reducing government efficiency.

Another problem with CETA has been uncertainty about its con- tinuation. Each year Congress has debated whether to retain CETA and at what level to fund public-service jobs. When the uncertainties over CETA are combined with the uncertainties with categorical grants, state and local governments may be effectively precluded from program and personnel planning.

One of the most difficult problems for state and local governments under CETA has been how federally financed jobs are to be integrated with regular state and local jobs. Specifically, some jurisdictions have been forced to lay off their workers while at the same time they have had federal money to hire people. The temptation has been great simply to transfer employees from state and local payrolls to the CETA payroll. In 1976 Congress amended the legislation to allow no more than half of all previously existing CETA jobs that became vacant to be filled with laid- off government workers; newly created CETA positions were to be reserved for the "hard-core" unemployed.

In response to this problem of state and local governments being

---

[35] *More Benefits to Jobless Can Be Attained in Public Service Employment*, p. 28. See also Sar A. Levitan, "Does Public Job Creation Offer Any Hope?," *Conference Board Record*, 12 (August, 1975):58–64 and Charles R. Perry et al., *The Impact of Government Manpower Programs: In General, and on Minorities and Women* (Philadelphia: Industrial Research Unit, The Wharton School, University of Pennsylvania, 1975); and James A. Croft, "Transition in Public Service Employment: Concept and Measurement," *Labor Law Journal*, 26 (1975):417–422.

financially compelled to lay off workers, Congress in 1976 passed still another piece of legislation. The intent of Title II of the Public Works Act of 1976 was to avert layoffs in state and local governments at a time when unemployment is already high.[36] This is known as countercyclical or antirecession assistance. For the year beginning July, 1976, more than $1 billion was provided, and over $2 billion was provided for the following year. The funds were distributed by a formula based upon unemployment rates and general revenue sharing assistance, with one-third of the money provided to state governments and the balance to local governments. These funds averted layoffs in many jurisdictions, although there was evidence that the formula could be improved in targeting funds to jurisdictions in greatest need.[37] In 1978, the House of Representatives and Senate were unable to reach agreement on compromise legislation that would have renewed the program.

A far more sweeping piece of legislation that has been under consideration is the Full Employment and Balanced Growth Act, known as the Humphrey-Hawkins bill.[38] Although the various aspects of Humphrey-Hawkins extend well beyond the scope of public personnel, one component of the legislation as originally introduced is particularly relevant and controversial. The original 1975 version of the bill "declares and establishes the right of all adult Americans (sixteen years of age or older) able, willing, and seeking work to opportunities for useful paid employment at fair rates of compensation."[39] In effect, Humphrey-Hawkins would have guaranteed all adults a state or local government job when private jobs were unavailable. Proponents maintained that increased use of public-service jobs would be effective in stimulating economic recovery. Critics claimed that guaranteeing jobs for everyone would result in extraordinary rates of inflation and that many people would be permanently added to public payrolls. Supporters of Humphrey-Hawkins suggested that as the economy improved, people in

[36] Public Works Employment Act, 90 Stat. 2331 (1976).

[37] *Antirecession Assistance: An Evaluation* (Washington: General Accounting Office, 1977); *Antirecession Assistance is Helping But Distribution Formula Needs Reassessment* (Washington: General Accounting Office, 1977); and *Impact of Anti-Recession Assistance on 52 Governments: An Update* (Washington: General Accounting Office, 1978).

[38] Legislation was introduced by Senator Hubert H. Humphrey (D, Minn.) and Representative Augustus F. Hawkins (D, Cal.).

[39] Full Employment and Balanced Growth Act, H.R. 50, 95th Cong., 1st sess. (Washington: Government Printing Office, 1977), Section 102. See Subcommittee on Employment Opportunities, House Committee on Education and Labor, *The Full Employment and Balanced Growth Act of 1977; Authorization of Appropriations for CETA and the President's Economic Stimulus Proposals: Hearings*, 95th Cong., 1st sess. (Washington: Government Printing Office, 1977) and *Reducing Unemployment: The Humphrey-Hawkins and Kemp-McClure Bills* (Washington: American Enterprise Institute for Public Policy Research, 1976).

government jobs would quickly resign to accept better-paying private jobs. Opponents contended there are many unskilled people who would never be able to find private-sector jobs and who would become permanent, nonproductive, government employees.

A diluted version of Humphrey-Hawkins was passed by Congress in 1978. The legislation set a goal of reducing unemployment to 4 percent of the work force and inflation to an annual level of 3 percent by 1983. The impact of the legislation is expected to be negligible, since there was no provision for implementation and particularly no provision for creating state and local jobs for the unemployed. The 1978 legislation can be viewed as a statement of philosophy, a tribute to the late Senator Humphrey, and a tactical maneuver for Congressmen and Senators seeking re-election in 1978.

SUMMARY

Planning for the future may be a well accepted ideal, but personnel planning in government is not a well established practice. Personnel planning begins with forecasting future needs by occupation and job level and projecting what will happen to current personnel regarding promotions, transfers, and separations. Net personnel needs are compared with projected labor markets, and then strategies are devised to meet future personnel needs. Comprehensive personnel planning systems are probably too expensive for most jurisdictions. Planning perhaps should be restricted to occupations where shortages exist and to special situations, such as when agencies are expanding, declining, or decentralizing. Personnel planning would be greatly facilitated if more jurisdictions engaged in program planning that is linked with their budgetary systems.

State and local governments are dependent upon federal grant programs and are being used by the federal government to influence economic trends. Planning at the state and local levels has been handicapped by the numerous categorical grant programs but less by block grants and general revenue sharing. Manpower grants under the Comprehensive Employment and Training Act fund hundreds of thousands of state and local government jobs. These jobs have been created to provide an economic stimulus during recession and to provide training opportunities for the unemployed. Antirecession or countercyclical assistance has been provided to reduce the extent to which state and local governments furlough their employees during recessions. Finally, the Humphrey-Hawkins bill in its original form would have guaranteed state and local government jobs to workers who could not find private sector jobs; however, the bill that was passed in 1978 had no such provision.

Chapter 11

Motivation Theory

One of the greatest unknowns is why people behave the way they do. Understanding human behavior in organizations is critical, in that inappropriate policies can affect behavior to the detriment of workers, the organization, and especially the public. Motivation theories, then, attempt to explain the forces that influence worker behavior. It should be emphasized at the outset that, while each motivation theory may make some contribution to understanding human behavior, none definitively explains behavior.

Motivation is a component of public personnel systems, given that it pertains to how people work. An understanding of the alternative theories is important if for no other reason than that people in government operate as though one or more theories are valid; an understanding of behavior requires understanding the principles or theories that serve to guide individuals in their daily work. If the theories are valid, individuals can use these ideas to deal more effectively with their subordinates, peers, and superiors. While personnel administrators may play a small role in motivation, the main responsibility rests with managers and the workers, themselves. Motivation—or the lack of it—occurs on a daily basis throughout a government. The people in a central personnel agency will not have continuous and extensive contact with employees throughout the government. Personnel administrators, however, should be aware of contemporary motivation theories in order to consider their compatibility with specific personnel practices, such as position classification, pay, and promotion procedures.

This chapter and the one that follows sample some of the vast literature that attempts to explain human motivation in organizations, with this chapter concentrating upon theories of motivation and the next one

303

discussing the applications of theories.[1] This chapter emphasizes motivation as it relates to individuals, while the next chapter expands the focus to include group behavior. The first section of this chapter discusses some of the theories of human personality. The second examines what the literature calls content theories of motivation, namely theories that attempt to explain what common characteristics in humans motivate their behavior. The third section discusses process theories that suggest the methods by which workers become motivated.

DETERMINANTS OF PERSONALITY

When a person is hired by a government or any other organization, he brings to that organization something more than a physical body and a set of knowledge and skills. That additional ingredient is personality, which is a hypothetical construct. Although numerous alternative definitions exist, "personality" is defined here simply as the properties or traits of an individual. This section reviews both old and contemporary approaches to personality. While most of the theories in this section are not part of the mainstream of motivation, they are included to provide an appreciation of the wide range of concepts that exist. Indeed, many of these theories at best are at the periphery of current research efforts.

---

[1] Books that review motivation theory include: Robert C. Bolles, *Theory of Motivation* (New York: Harper and Row, 1967); C. N. Cofer and M. H. Appley, *Motivation: Theory and Research* (New York: Wiley and Sons, 1964); Saul W. Gellerman, *Motivation and Productivity* (New York: American Management Association, 1963); K. B. Madsen, *Theories of Motivation: A Comparative Study of Modern Theories of Motivation*, 4th ed. (Kent, Ohio: Kent State University Press, 1968); and Bernard Weiner, *Theories of Motivation: From Mechanism to Cognition* (Chicago: Markham, 1972). Textbooks on motivation and organizational behavior include: John P. Campbell et al., *Managerial Behavior, Performance, and Effectiveness* (New York: McGraw-Hill, 1970); Don Hellriegel and John W. Slocom, Jr., *Management: A Contingency Approach* (Reading, Mass.: Addison-Wesley, 1974); Frank J. Landy and Don A. Trumbo, *Psychology of Work Behavior* (Homewood, Ill.: Dorsey, 1976); David J. Lawless, *Effective Management: Social Psychological Approach* (Englewood Cliffs, N.J.: Prentice-Hall, 1972); Fred Luthans, *Organizational Behavior*, 2d ed. (New York: McGraw-Hill, 1977); Terence R. Mitchell, *People in Organizations: Understanding their Behavior* (New York: McGraw-Hill, 1978); and Lyman W. Porter, Edward E. Lawler III, and J. Richard Hackman, *Behavior in Organizations* (New York: McGraw-Hill, 1975). The *Annual Review of Psychology* is an excellent source for reviews of the literature; see Abraham K. Korman, Jeffrey H. Greenhaus, and Irwin J. Badin, "Personal Attitudes and Motivation," *Annual Review of Psychology*, 28 (1977):175–196; Edwin A. Locke, Personnel Attitudes and Motivation," *Annual Review of Psychology*, 26 (1975):457–480; and John B. Miner and H. Peter Dachler, "Personnel Attitudes and Motivation," *Annual Review of Psychology*, 24 (1973):379–402. See also Marvin D. Dunnette, ed., *Handbook of Industrial and Organizational Psychology* (Chicago: Rand McNally, 1976), especially John P. Campbell and Robert D. Pritchard, "Motivation Theory in Industrial and Organizational Psychology," pp. 63–130, and Edwin A. Locke, "The Nature and Causes of Job Satisfaction," pp. 1297–1349.

Defining motivation is as difficult as defining personality, in part because motivation theories start from different premises so that motivation does not have the same meaning for all researchers. Motivation, like personality, is a hypothetical construct and is presumed to account for behavior. The motivation within a person will influence what type of behavior will be initiated and the quality of that behavior. If an employee begins to work on a difficult project at 9:30 a.m., motivation will determine whether that employee is still working on the assignment at 10:30 and with what vigor.

Job satisfaction is not the same as motivation. Satisfaction and dissatisfaction are attitudes about jobs, and such attitudes influence approach-avoidance behavior. In other words, as an employee approaches work, he may avoid it because of dissatisfaction. A worker who is satisfied, on the other hand, eagerly comes to work. Satisfaction is important in having an employee come to work on time, while motivation influences behavior on the job.[2] This and the next chapter concentrate upon motivation, with job satisfaction receiving less attention but being integrated into the discussion.

The relative importance of heredity and the environment—nature versus nurture—is at the core of the debate over personality development. One view is that humans are malleable and that environmental influences determine personality. The argument is supported by comparing cultures; for example, women in one society may play submissive roles while in others they are equal to or dominant over men. Within a single society, the importance of the environment is evident. Mark Twain's *The Prince and the Pauper* is a fictional case study of the importance of the environment.

While few would deny that environment affects human development and behavior, others have suggested that there are innate physiological and psychological properties that influence behavior. The physiological requirement for sleep not only produces drowsiness but can produce irritable behavior. Hormonal changes also have important effects on behavior. Beyond these physiological matters are other properties assumed to be innate in humans. If these properties exist and constitute a predisposition toward some behaviors and against others, then it becomes important to understand these properties so that organizations do not attempt the impossible, namely do not expect a type of behavior from workers that is antithetical to the inherent properties of individuals.

Freud's psychoanalytic model of personality has had an immeasura-

---

[2] Landy and Trumbo, *Psychology of Work Behavior*, pp. 336–362.

ble impact on how human behavior is perceived.[3] Freud suggested that there are conflicting forces within each person, with each force attempting to assert control over behavior. The id, which is the most primitive of these forces, seeks pleasure in sexual relationships, comfort, and aggression. A critical aspect of the id is that the individual is unaware of this force since it is the unconscious. Freud's second force is the ego, which is the conscious and rational part of the personality. The ego keeps the id in check through the reality principle. Since in "reality" one cannot always be satisfying pleasure drives, the ego serves to postpone gratification. The ego is not a morality or ethical force, but rather a rational force. A woman may desire to hit her boss but the ego constrains her; hitting the boss could result in dismissal from the job. Freud's third aspect of personality is the superego, which is the conscience, representing values of right and wrong, which is largely unconscious, and which is learned rather than inherited. In the case of the woman desiring to hit her boss, the superego also may prevent such behavior because of a value that superiors are to be respected no matter how wrong they may be.

Associated with Freud were Jung and Adler, who later developed their own approaches to personality. Jung, like Freud, promoted the concept of instincts as determiners of behavior but placed less emphasis upon sex as a motivator.[4] Jung wrote of "archetypes" or model images that were passed from one generation to another through non-environmental means. Evolution from lower animals was thought not to have been complete in that there are properties of those animals within each individual.

---

[3] Sigmund Freud, *The Basic Writings of Sigmund Freud*, translated and edited with an introduction by A. A. Brill (New York: Modern Library, 1938). Sigmund Freud, *The Standard Edition of the Complete Psychological Works of Sigmund Freud*, translated by James Strachey in collaboration with Anna Freud (London: Hogarth, 1961); Sigmund Freud, *Civilization and its Discontents*, translated and edited by James Strachey (New York: Norton, 1962); Sigmund Freud, *Beyond the Pleasure Principle*, translated and edited by James Strachey (New York: Liveright, 1961); Sigmund Freud, *The Ego and the Id*, translated by Joan Riviere, edited by James Strachey (New York: Norton, 1962); Sigmund Freud, *Group Psychology and the Analysis of the Ego*, translated and edited by James Strachey (New York: Modern Library, 1950); Sigmund Freud, *The Future of an Illusion*, translated and edited by James Strachey (New York: Norton, 1975); Sigmund Freud, *The Freud/Jung Letters: The Correspondence between Sigmund Freud and C. G. Jung*, edited by William McGurie, translated by Ralph Manheim and R. F. C. Hull (Princeton, N.J.: Princeton University Press, 1974); Sigmund Freud, *Totem and Taboo, Some Points of Agreement between the Mental Lives of Savages and Neurotics* (New York: Norton, 1952); and Sigmund Freud, *The Interpretation of Dreams*, translated by A. A. Brill (New York: Modern Library, 1950).

[4] C. G. Jung, *The Collected Works of C. G. Jung*, edited by Herbert Read, Michael Fordham, and Gerhard Adler (Multivolume, publishers and dates vary); C. G. Jung, *The Integration of the Personality*, translated by Stanley Dell (London: Routledge and Kegan Paul, 1950); C. G. Jung, *Modern Man in Search of a Soul* (New York: Harcourt, Brace, and World, 1933); and C. G. Jung, *The Undiscovered Self*, translated by R. F. C. Hull (New York, American Library, 1958).

Adler de-emphasized the role of instincts but stressed the pleasure principle especially in terms of power.[5] According to Adler, having power over individuals was pleasurable. He also emphasized that cooperativeness was an important aspect of personality.

The theories of Freud, Jung, and Adler are rarely applied in their pure form to the study of organizational behavior, but many of the ideas of these psychologists are to be found in contemporary theories of motivation. Freud's id, ego, and super-ego concepts, as will be seen in Chapter 12, have been translated by Eric Berne into the roles of child, adult, and parent in a technique that is known as "transactional analysis."[6] The pleasure principle and the unconscious will be seen as important components of contemporary theories. Freud's concept of defense mechanisms also is important. He contended that when it is unsatisfied the desire for pleasure produces internal tensions that are transformed into behavior patterns. Repression is one such mechanism; if a desire cannot be gratified, the individual may repress that desire, so that in effect it seems not to exist.

These theories of Freud, Jung, and Adler suggest that to some extent human behavior is preset or determined, that in some situations an individual will not have any choice of behaviors. Instincts or innate drives trigger behavior. As the individual matures, the combination of instincts and acquired behavior patterns stemming from exposure to environmental conditions will greatly influence what that individual will do when confronted with a given situation. While these theories may seem largely deterministic, it is important to recognize that the three psychologists did allow for human choice in selecting behavior. Jung particularly introduced the concept of self-actualization, suggesting that as one grew older there was more conscious control over behavior. Jung did not provide an operational definition of self-actualization, but, as will be seen, contemporary theories rely heavily upon that concept.

Beyond the theories of these three giants of psychology is a seemingly infinite number of other theories, not all of which can be reviewed here. One such theory that periodically has been popular is that body type affects or reflects personality type. The major proponent of this

---

[5] Alfred Adler, *The Individual Psychology of Alfred Adler*, edited and annotated by Heinz L. Ansbacher and Rowena R. Ansbacher (New York: Basic Books, 1956); Alfred Adler, *Understanding Human Nature*, translated by Walter Béran Wolfe (New York: Greenberg, 1927); and Alfred Adler, *The Practice and Theory of Individual Psychology*, translated by P. Radin (New York: Harcourt, Brace, 1924).

[6] *Eric Berne, Games People Play: The Psychology of Human Relationships* (New York, Grove, 1967). For an application of Freudian psychology to political behavior, see Harold D. Lasswell, *Psychopathology and Politics* (Chicago: University of Chicago Press, 1930).

theory has been Sheldon, who identified three temperaments that corresponded with three body types.[7] The somatotypes of body types were 1) endomorphy, involving a rounded and fat body with small hands and feet; 2) mesomorphy, a body shape that is square, with the body having large bones and being muscular; and 3) ectomorphy, a body that is slight or fragile, with drooped shoulders and small face. Paralleling these three body types were three temperaments. The viscerotonia temperament, associated with endomorphy, involves seeking of physical comfort, the love of eating, and the person tends to be tolerant of others. The somatotonia, related to mesomorphy, is assertive, energetic, competitive, and aggressive. The cerebrotonia, paralleling ectomorphy, is an emotionally restrained person who enjoys privacy and contemplation. Sheldon did not suggest that body type determined personality, but that they were highly correlated. It follows, however, that if one has little control over one's body, one may have little control over one's personality, thereby suggesting that personality is somewhat predetermined. Today, Sheldon's ideas receive little attention in motivation literature.

A persistent strain of thought has been that humans are inherently evil and/or aggressive. The Biblical story of Adam and Eve can be interpreted as meaning that humans were pure of mind until that first bite of the apple, after which evil would always be a part of humans. More currently, experiments conducted by Milgram have suggested that people are readily willing to harm others.[8] The experiments involved subjects who were told they were participating in a study of punishment. An accomplice was strapped into an "electric chair" and the experimenter told the subject to administer electric shocks at increasing voltage whenever the accomplice made a mistake. The accomplice, of course, did not receive shocks and instead simply pretended to be in pain. In these experiments, Milgram found that nearly two-thirds of the subjects administered what they thought were severe shocks that could have been fatal. The studies demonstrate that people will follow instructions of an "authority figure" even though that could result in severe harm to others.

Evolution has been used in support of the aggression theory. Ardrey has suggested that, rather than evolving from herbivorous apes, humans

---

[7] William H. Sheldon, *The Varieties of Human Physique* (New York: Harper and Brothers, 1940), and William H. Sheldon, *The Varieties of Temperament* (New York: Harper and Brothers, 1942). More recently see Saburo Iwawaki and Richard M. Lerner, "Cross-cultural Analyses of Body Behavior Relations: III Developmental Intra- and Intercultural Factor Congruence in the Body Build Stereotypes of Japanese and American Males and Females," *Psychologia* 19 (1976):67–76; and Petrus F. Verdonik and Richard N. Walker, "Body Build and Behavior in Emotionally Disturbed Dutch Children," *Genetic Psychology Monographs*, 94 (1976):149–173.

[8] Stanley Milgram, "Some Conditions of Obedience and Disobedience to Authority," *Human Relations*, 18 (1965):57–76.

evolved from aggressive, carnivorous apes.[9] In order to obtain food, these apes bludgeoned other animals to death with stones or bones. If the aggression theory is valid, then it follows that such behavior is innate and always will arise in organizations.

Ardrey also has suggested that aggression frequently is focused upon protecting territory.[10] Drawing upon the behavior of lower animals and human evolution, Ardrey maintains that animals protect geographical areas from others of the same species. This imperative to protect territory is of such force that it can override concerns for personal and family safety. When this theory is applied to organizational behavior, individuals are seen as struggling with each other to protect their spheres of responsibility, and this behavior is the result of human evolutionary heritage. It should be noted, however, that Ardrey's aggression and territory theories are viewed with great skepticism.

The aggression theory has been criticized from two perspectives. One is that there are alternative explanations of aggression. Fromm has suggested that aggression results from childhood experiences; Hitler's aggressiveness, for instance, could be explained by the lack of warm relationships as a child, particularly relationships with his mother.[11] Another criticism of the innate aggression theory is that while humans may have evolved from killer apes, the purpose of the killing was not aggressive. Apes killed for food and not for pleasure.

Another line of inquiry has been whether society and organizations impose controls that are "unnatural" and therefore produce undesirable behavior. Morris has suggested that humans, having evolved from free apes, find themselves frustrated by societal controls.[12] He has compared human behavior with animal behavior in captivity. Animals in zoos exhibit atypical behavior, such as masturbation and homosexuality. Morris then draws the analogy that organizations are a form of captivity for humans and that captivity produces atypical human behavior.

One of the most persistent and controversial theories has been that intelligence varies among races. While this is not a theory of personality, the theory does suggest that human behavior will vary among races

---

[9] Robert Ardrey, *African Genesis: A Personal Investigation into the Animal Origins and Nature of Man* (New York: Atheneum, 1961). See also Desmond Morris, *The Naked Ape* (New York: Dell, 1972).

[10] Robert Ardrey, *The Territorial Imperative: A Personal Inquiry into the Animal Origins of Property and Nations* (New York: Atheneum, 1966).

[11] Erich Fromm, *The Anatomy of Human Destructiveness* (New York: Holt, Rinehart, and Winston, 1973). See also Alexander Alland, Jr., *The Human Imperative* (New York: Columbia University Press, 1972) and Robert Claiborne, *God or Beast: Evolution and Human Nature* (New York: Norton, 1974).

[12] Desmond Morris, *The Human Zoo* (New York, McGraw-Hill, 1969).

because of innate capabilities. In recent years, Arthur Jensen has been the chief proponent of the theory, arguing that blacks in the United States as a group are intellectually inferior to whites and Asians.[13] As would be expected, Jensen's idea has been strongly attacked by many people.

CONTENT THEORIES

Categorizing theories of motivation is artificial, in that existing theories greatly overlap with each other. In order to facilitate discussion, however, some categorization is necessary. One useful approach that has been widely accepted is to classify theories as to content or process.[14] Content theories pertain to the substance of motivation. What is it within people and their environment that serve as motivators? Process theories, on the other hand, pertain to the methods or processes by which individuals are motivated. This section discusses content theories, and the next considers process theories.

Content theory stems in part from Taylor. He viewed humans as inherently lazy and assumed they could be motivated by financial incentives. In designing jobs (see Chapter 3), Taylor sought to make workers more efficient and coupled increased efficiency with increased pay. Another aspect of content theory for Taylor was that human performance frequently was reduced by fatigue. Job design, then, was intended to improve work processes in order to avoid worker fatigue.[15]

In large part following Taylor's assumptions about fatigue, Mayo and a team of researchers undertook a series of studies that revolutionized the way worker motivation was percieved. Mayo and his staff conducted a series of experiments at the Western Electric Hawthorne plant in Chicago between 1927 and 1932. In the first experiment, lighting was adjusted to find an optimal level of illumination that would avoid fatigue. Efficiency rose as lighting was increased. However, later, when lighting was reduced to equal that of "ordinary moonlight," there was no

---

[13] Arthur R. Jensen, "How Much Can We Boost IQ and Scholastic Achievement," *Harvard Educational Review*, 39 (1969):1–123; Arthur R. Jensen, *Educability and Group Differences* (New York: Harper and Row, 1973); Arthur R. Jensen, *Educational Differences* (New York: Barnes and Noble, 1973); and Arthur R. Jensen, *Genetics and Education* (New York: Harper and Row, 1972).

[14] The content-process dichotomy was suggested by Campbell, *Managerial Behavior, Performance, and Effectiveness*, pp. 340–383.

[15] Research on fatigue is still conducted today. T. M. Nelson and C. J. Ladan, "Patterns and Correlates of Fatigue among Office Workers," *Journal of Occupational Psychology*, 49 (1976):65–74.

reduction in efficiency.[16] This finding led the researchers to conclude that social and psychological factors were important in influencing worker behavior.

Subsequent Hawthorne experiments involved rest breaks and wage incentive systems. The experiments adjusted the frequency and length of rest breaks as well as the length of the work day. Wage incentive systems were introduced so that, by adjusting their behavior, individual workers could increase their pay. Neither of these approaches seemed to have much influence on performance. Sometimes when the experimenters expected performance to decline because of changes they had introduced, performance increased. A conclusion that emerged was that performance sometimes increased because workers enjoyed being part of the experiment and not because of the experiment itself. Today this is known as the "Hawthorne effect."

The bank wiring study was one of the most important Hawthorne experiments. The study involved experimenters observing interpersonal relations while workers constructed telephone terminals. The conclusion was that workers acted not as isolated individuals but as part of informal work groups that determined the level of performance. Groups set standards for what was a fair day's work. A worker performing above that level was a "rate buster" and one performing below was a "chiseler."

The main content theme of the Hawthorne studies and the resulting human relations approach to motivation is that workers have a need to belong. Informal work groups satisfy that need, especially since managerial approaches tend to ignore the need. Advocates of human relations theory have concluded that informal work groups can affect performance both positively and negatively. The following chapter discusses some approaches to utilizing this body of theory for the betterment of workers and organizations.

The Hawthorne experiments have been both subjected to severe criticisms as well as lauded as a major breakthrough in motivation research. Judging the experiments by today's standards, the methodology has many flaws. For example, some of the outcomes may have been a result of the types of people recruited to participate in the experiments. Less willing participants might have performed much differently. Some of the experiments were not well controlled. Personnel changes while the

---

[16] F. J. Roethlisberger and William J. Dickson, *Management and the Worker* (Cambridge, Mass.: Harvard University Press, 1939), p. 17. The Roethlisberger and Dickson book is the main report on the Hawthorne experiments. See also T. N. Whitehead, *Leadership in a Free Society* (Cambridge, Mass.: Harvard University Press, 1937); George C. Homans, *Fatigue of Workers* (New York: Reinhold, 1941); and Gellerman, *Motivation and Productivity*, pp. 19–31.

experiments were in progress might have contributed to some of the results. Mayo and his researchers have been criticized for ignoring alternative explanations of performance and dogmatically concluding that groups were the primary determinant of performance. The Hawthorne studies have been criticized for ignoring the Depression and the rise of unions as possible influences on workers' motivations.[17]

A hierarchy of human needs, as suggested by Maslow, is another form of content theory.[18] Basing his theory on psychological clinical experience. Maslow proposed that human behavior was the result of unsatisfied needs; needs led to the search for gratification. Five sets of needs were proposed: 1) Physiological needs involve maintaining the body's normal balances of water, oxygen, salt, and the like (homeostasis). Deprivation of a needed item, such as water, will result in behavior to satisfy the need. 2) Safety needs include not only protection from physical dangers but also the sense of safety that comes with routine behavior. 3) Belongingness and love needs entail the sense of being part of a social group. 4) Esteem needs involve the desire to differentiate oneself from others. While belonging needs may have the effects of submerging one in a group, esteem needs make a person unique from others in the group. 5) The need for self-actualization entails self-fulfillment or maximizing one's potential.

According to Maslow, these five sets of needs are hierarchical, that is, one level precedes the other in importance. The term used to describe this is "prepotency." Physiological and safety needs must be satisfied before an individual can direct attention to belongingness needs. Although Maslow's theory has been extremely popular, research efforts have not substantiated the prepotency aspect of the theory. Cross-sectional studies have been conducted that compared workers at different levels in an organization, with the findings indicating that some groups of workers may emphasize some needs more than others.[19] Some studies have found that higher level needs seem to be motivators at a time when lower level needs have not been satisfied.[20]

---

[17] Henry A. Landsberger, *Hawthorne Revisited: Managment and the Worker, Its Critics, and Developments in Human Relations in Industry* (Ithaca, N.Y.: Cornell University, 1958), and Alex Carey, "The Hawthorne Studies: A Radical Criticism," *American Sociological Review*, 32 (1967):403–416.

[18] Abraham H. Maslow, *Motivation and Personality* (New York: Harper and Row, 1954); Abraham H. Maslow, "A Theory of Human Motivation," *Psychological Review*, 50 (1943):370–396; and Abraham H. Maslow, *Eupsychian Management: A Journal* (Homewood, Ill.: Irwin, 1965).

[19] Lyman W. Porter, "A Study of Perceived Need Satisfactions in Bottom and Middle Management Jobs," *Journal of Applied Psychology*, 45 (1961):1–10, and John P. Wanous and Abram Zwany, "A Cross-Sectional Test of Need Hierarchy Theory," *Organizational Behavior and Human Performance*, 18 (1977):78–97.

[20] J. C. Wofford, "The Motivational Bases of Job Satisfaction and Job Performance," *Personnel Psychology*, 24 (1971):501–518.

A variant of Maslow's theory is ERG theory, proposed by Alderfer.[21] He combined Maslow's physiological and safety needs into existence needs ("E"), combined love and esteem needs into relatedness ("R"), and relabeled the self-actualizing need as a growth need ("G"). Unlike Maslow, Alderfer does not contend these needs are hierarchical but rather suggests that two of the needs may be operating simultaneously. Both Maslow and Alderfer's theories are weak, in that the concepts of need and self-actualization/growth have not been made operational. It is unclear whether these needs are assumed to be psychological and/or physiological. It is not clear what is meant by a need being satisfied, that is, whether the need continues after being satisfied. Similarly, self-actualization is an elusive concept. How can one tell when an individual is being motivated by the need to self-actualize?[22]

Another proponent of self-actualization theory has been Argyris. Like Maslow and others, Argyris has suggested that people have "natural" development patterns. According to Argyris, people develop along seven continua, and these can be regarded as motivators. People tend to develop 1) from passivity to activity, 2) from dependence to independence, 3) from behaving in few ways to many ways, 4) from shallow to deep interests, 5) from having a short time perspective to a longer one, 6) from subordinates to equals and superordinates, and 7) from lack of awareness of self to control of self.[23] Like the other content theories, this one suggests these tendencies are inherent in individuals. It would follow, then, that organizations should recognize these needs—should attempt to

[21] Clayton P. Alderfer "An Empirical Test of a New Theory of Human Needs," *Organizational Behavior and Human Performance*, 4 (1969):142–175, and Clayton P. Alderfer, *Existence, Relatedness, and Growth: Human Needs in Organizational Settings* (New York: Free Press, 1972).

[22] David Guest, "Motivation After Maslow," *Personnel Management*, 8 (1976):29–32; Douglas T. Hall and Khalil E. Nougaim, "An Examination of Maslow's Need Hierarchy in an Organizational Setting," *Organizational Behavior and Human Performance*, 3 (1968):12–35; John S. Herrick, "Work Motives of Female Executives," *Public Personnel Management*, 2 (1973):380–387; Vance F. Mitchell and Pravin Moudgill, "Measurement of Maslow's Need Hierarchy," *Organizational Behavior and Human Performance*, 16 (1976):334–349; John W. Newstrom, William E. Reif, and Robert M. Monczka, "Motivating the Public Employee: Fact vs. Fiction," *Public Personnel Management*, 5 (1976):67–72; Gerald R. Salancik and Jeffrey Pfeffer, "An Examination of Need-Satisfaction Models of Job Attitudes," *Administrative Science Quarterly*, 22 (1977):427–456; and Mahmoud A. Wahba and Lawrence G. Bridwell, "Maslow Reconsidered: A Review of Research on the Need Hierarchy Theory," *Organizational Behavior and Human Performance*, 15 (1976):212–240.

[23] Chris Argyris, *Personality and Organization: The Conflict Between System and the Individual* (New York: Harper and Row, 1957), p. 50. See also Chris Argyris, "Some Limits of Rational Man Organizational Theory," *Public Administration Review*, 33 (1973):253–267; Herbert A. Simon, "Organizational Man: Rational or Self-Actualizing?" *Public Administration Review*, 33 (1973):346–353; and Chris Argyris, "Organizational Man: Rational *and* Self-Actualizing," *Public Administration Review*, 33 (1973):354–357.

assist employees to develop accordingly rather than presenting obstacles to such development.

Herzberg's two-factor theory offers still another explanation of worker motivation.[24] Herzberg has suggested that there is one set of factors that can motivate only in a negative sense in that they produce job dissatisfaction. When these factors are satisfied, they become neutral, much like Maslow's needs, which, when satisfied, no longer motivate behavior. Herzberg calls this first set hygiene factors. The second set are motivators and are particularly important as positive motivators. These include: 1) achievement, or the feeling of having accomplished a job, 2) recognition, or having someone praise or blame the worker for performance, 3) work itself, or a perception of the nature of the job, 4) responsibility, or having the duty for one's own work and possibly the work of others, and 5) advancement, or changing one's position in the hierarchy of the organization. A characteristic common to these motivators is that they all relate to work, that workers derive satisfaction from their work.

Hygiene factors, in contrast, can be dissatisfiers but not motivators. Herzberg includes as hygiene factors "supervision, interpersonal relations, physical working conditions, salary, company policies and administrative practices, benefits, and job security."[25] Perhaps most controversial in this list is the item of salary or pay. Financial incentives have long been thought of as prime motivators, yet Herzberg's research found pay not to be a motivator. If pay was perceived to be too low, dissatisfaction could result, but an adequate level of pay was a neutral factor. While there are many proponents of the two-factor theory, there is no consensus among researchers about the role of pay as a motivator. Many remain convinced that pay can serve as a positive incentive, while others suggest that pay should be used to recognize good work performance but not as an incentive device.[26]

The two-factor theory has been widely accepted but also has been subjected to severe attack. One issue has involved the methodology employed. Workers were asked to recall a time when they felt positively or negatively about their jobs. Then, through a series of questions, the researchers explored what series of events led to that positive or negative feeling. Responses were later coded by the researchers into the factors that have been mentioned. One is left with a question about how this coding was conducted, since Herzberg's factors seem to overlap. An altercation between a worker and his supervisor could involve the factors of

---

[24] Frederick Herzberg, Bernard Mausner, and Barbara B. Snyderman, *The Motivation to Work*, 2d ed. (New York: Wiley and Sons, 1964).

[25] Herzberg, Mausner, and Snyderman, *The Motivation to Work*, p. 113.

[26] See Edward E. Lawler III, *Pay and Organizational Effectiveness: A Psychological View* (New York: McGraw-Hill, 1971).

recognition, supervision, and interpersonal relations, the first of these being one of Herzberg's motivators and the other two being hygiene factors. The substance of that same argument between worker and supervisor could involve the factors of the work itself (a motivator) and physical working conditions (a hygiene factor).

Methodological issues concerning the Herzberg research also involve the role of those interviewed. In the original study, Herzberg used accountants and engineers rather than lower level workers, because professionals were better able to express their feelings. Critics have contended that if the two-factor theory is valid, perhaps it applies only to professionals and not to all workers.[27] Herzberg has rebutted the argument by citing independent research efforts that used similar methodology and that seemed to confirm his theory.[28] Another criticism is that human subjects may not know what motivates them and through psychological defense mechanisms may be prevented from providing accurate accounts of events that contributed to positive or negative attitudes about their jobs. A worker who is unable to admit his deficiencies may blame his supervisor for denying him a promotion.

The Herzberg methodology may have an element of self-fulfilling prophesy. By asking workers about how they felt, what events led to those feelings, and how those feelings affected performance, there seems to be assumed relationships among job satisfaction, motivation, and performance. Does being satisfied with a job mean that one will be motivated to work harder? The Herzberg methodology accepts at face value the responses of those interviewed without attempting to use objective measures of worker performance to see whether a relationship existed between what a worker did and how he said he felt at the time.

A prescription that emerges from virtually all of the content theories is that workers should be encouraged to develop, and this is to be accomplished through meaningful work situations. Intrinsic motivators are viewed as being more effective than extrinsic ones, such as pay and job security. The traditional view of the manager has been that of a severe taskmaster who must oversee workers lest they become lazy and nonproductive. McGregor has labeled this approach to management as Theory X.[29] Content theories, on the other hand, suggest that people are

---

[27] Victor H. Vroom, *Work and Motivation* (New York: Wiley and Sons, 1964), p. 128.

[28] Frederick Herzberg, *Work and the Nature of Man* (Cleveland: World Publishing, 1966). For applications of the Herzberg theory to the public sector, see Charles Dodson and Barbara Haskew, "Why Public Workers Stay," *Public Personnel Management*, 5 (1976):132–138, and Husain Mustafa and Ronald D. Sylvia, "A Factor-Analysis Approach to Job Satisfaction," *Public Personnel Management*, 4 (1975):165–172.

[29] Douglas McGregor, *The Human Side of Enterprise* (New York: McGraw-Hill, 1960).

better motivated by forces within them. People need and want to develop their capabilities, and organizations can help meet these human needs by providing work. Bureaucracy should be more humane, to encourage self-development, or, as McGregor puts it, should use Theory Y.[30]

PROCESS THEORIES

Process theories are nonsubstantive, in that they do not attempt to explain by what forces people are motivated. Whereas the content theories focused upon different types of needs as motivators, the process theories are concerned with the means by which people are motivated to act.

Stimulus-response theories are process theories. An assumption is made that a stimulus results in some form of behavior. Infants inherit this mechanism for basic bodily functions, so that hunger produces the response of crying and a full bladder produces the response of urination. As the infant develops, more elaborate stimulus-response patterns are developed and/or learned. Pavlov's experiments with conditioning a dog to salivate at the sound of a bell is an example of learned response patterns.[31] Thorndike developed what he called the "law of effect," which in brief terms holds that the probability of a response recurring will increase when a previous stimulus-response event has been pleasurable or satisfying.[32] Hull, building on Thorndike's theory, suggested that effort was a function of habit strength and drive. Habit strength refers to the probability of a response occurring because of previous pleasurable experience. Drives are needs, especially the primary needs of food, water, oxygen, and the like.[33] Many of the ideas of Pavlov, Hull, and Thorndike underlie contemporary process theories.

Field theory was developed at about the same time as drive theory. Lewin conceptualized the person as part of the environment, just as an

---

[30] See Eugene P. Dvorin and Robert H. Simmons, *From Amoral to Human Bureaucracy* (San Francisco: Canfield, 1972).

[31] Ivan Petrovich Pavlov, *Conditioned Reflexes: An Investigation of the Physiological Activity of the Cerebral Cortex*, translated and edited by G. V. Anrep, (London: Oxford University Press, 1927). See also Ivan Petrovich Pavlov, *Experimental Psychology and Other Essays* (New York: Philosophical Library, 1957); and Ivan Petrovich Pavlov, *Lectures on Conditioned Reflexes*, translated by W. Horsely Goutt, vols. 1 and 2 (New York: International Publishers, 1963).

[32] Edward L. Thorndike, *Animal Intelligence* (New York: Macmillan, 1911).

[33] Clark L. Hull, *Principles of Behavior* (New York: Appleton-Century-Crofts, 1943). See Clark L. Hull, *Essentials of Behavior* (New Haven, Conn.: Yale University Press, 1951); and Clark L. Hull, *A Behavioral System* (New Haven, Conn.: Yale University Press, 1952). See also Cofer and Appley, *Motivation: Theory and Research*, pp. 466–519, and Weiner, *Theories of Motivation: From Mechanism to Cognition*, pp. 11–91.

atom can be understood as part of its environment or field.[34] Emphasis was given to the forces within the environment that stimulate the individual to act. However, rather than using the stimulus-response model, Lewin used a cognitive model, seeing the individual as a thinking or perceiving organism. The individual acts in accordance with what he expects to happen. Whereas the stimulus-response theory emphasizes past experience, Lewin's expectancy theory focuses upon the future. Lewin's theory recognizes choice in behavior. The worker asks, "Should I do X or not?"[35]

The concept of expectancy has been coupled with that of instrumentality into what Vroom has called the V-I-E theory (Valence-Instrumentality-Expectancy).[36] When an individual considers a possible behavior, he questions whether it is likely to produce a desired outcome. The possible behavior is considered as an instrument for satisfaction. Valence refers to the strength with which one desires an outcome or wishes to avoid it; valence ranges from +1 to −1. A valence of zero means that the individual is indifferent about the outcome. Any single behavior can have two or more outcomes, each of which will have its own valence. A worker who persistently compliments his supervisor may expect this to result in a promotion (positive valence) but that same behavior might destroy friendships among the worker's peers (negative valence). As with the Thorndike theory, expectancy theory emphasizes probabilities: What are the probabilities of various possible outcomes occurring as a result of contemplated behavior?

[34] Kurt Lewin, *The Conceptual Representations and the Measurement of Psychological Forces* (Durham, N.C.: Duke University Press, 1938); Kurt Lewin, *Field Theory in Social Science: Selected Theoretical Papers*, edited by Dorwin Cartwright (New York: Harper, 1951); Kurt Lewin, *Principles of Topological Psychology*, translated by Fritz Heider and Grace M. Heider (New York: McGraw-Hall, 1966); and Kurt Lewin, *Resolving Social Conflicts: Selected Papers on Group Dynamics*, edited by Gertrud Weiss Lewin (New York: Harper, 1948).

[35] Madsen, *Theories of Motivation: A Comparative Study of Modern Theories of Motivation*, pp. 130–145; and Weiner, *Theories of Motivation*, pp. 92–168.

[36] Vroom, *Work and Motivation*. See also Anne Hoiberg and Newell H. Berry, "Expectations and Perceptions of Navy Life," *Organizational Behavior and Human Performance*, 21 (1978):130–145; Terence R. Mitchell, "Expectancy Models of Job Satisfaction, Occupational Preference and Effort: A Theoretical Methodological, and Empirical Appraisal," *Psychological Bulletin*, 81 (1974):1053–1077; Perry Moore, "Rewards and Public Employees' Attitudes Toward Client Service," *Public Personnel Managment*, 6 (1977):98–105; Donald F. Parker and Lee Dyer, "Expectancy Theory as a Within-Person Behavioral Choice Model: An Empirical Test of Some Conceptual and Methodological Refinements," *Organizational Behavior and Human Performance*, 17 (1976):97–117; John E. Sheridan, Max D. Richards, and John W. Slocum, "Comparative Analysis of Expectancy and Heuristic Models of Decision Behavior," *Journal of Applied Psychology*, 60 (1975):361–368; and John R. Turney and Stanley L. Cohen, "Influence of Work Content on Extrinsic Outcome Expectancy and Intrinsic Pleasure Predictions of Work Effort," *Organizational Behavior and Human Performance*, 17 (1976):311–327.

Porter and Lawler built upon the expectancy model in an attempt to explain worker performance. As was seen in the previous section, the content theories tend to assume job satisfaction affects performance; high satisfaction yields high performance. Porter and Lawler suggest the opposite is true. Performance or the accomplishment of tasks produces extrinsic and intrinsic rewards that lead to job satisfaction. The model also uses effort as a variable that influences performance in conjunction with role perceptions and abilities.[37]

Just as all other theories have been criticized, so has expectancy theory.[38] This theory is more difficult to apply than the need theory. With content theories, if one knows what needs are important to workers, then the organization can emphasize those needs. Expectancy theory, on the other hand, does not indicate what type of performance is likely to lead to satisfaction; the theory does not explain what expected rewards would energize the individual. Another criticism is that expectancy theory does not have a time perspective. It does not consider how values were acquired in the past, yet these values will influence an individual's decision about what rewards seem desirable. Neither does expectancy theory take into account the future time perspectives that vary among individuals. In selecting behavior, one worker may be concerned with only the immediate future, while another is concerned with how current behavior will produce rewards in five years. Another major criticism is that research often has been unable to confirm the model. Correlations between V-I-E data and measures of performance have been low.

Perhaps the most critical problem with expectancy theory is its reliance on hedonism, namely that individuals seek to maximize pleasure or minimize pain. Hedonism is deterministic, in that it suggests people are always motivated by a desire for pleasure. This cannot always be the case, since people often do things that are not pleasurable for them. Moreover, individuals may seek results that provide rewards but not the maximum possible rewards; this is known as "satisficing" behavior.[39] Without having to accept all facets of Freudian psychology, one can accept the concept of the unconscious, which influences behavior without the individual's awareness and without his being able to choose behavior solely on the basis of the pleasure principle. Finally, expectancy theory

---

[37] Lyman W. Porter and Edward E. Lawler III, *Managerial Attitudes and Performance* (Homewood, Ill.: Irwin, 1968).

[38] This critique of expectancy theory is based largely on a review of the literature by Locke, "Personnel Attitudes and Motivation," pp. 457–480.

[39] James G. March and Herbert A. Simon, *Organizations* (New York: Wiley and Sons, 1958).

considers pleasure and pain as opposite ends of the same spectrum, yet being motivated by a desire for pleasure and being motivated by a desire to avoid pain would seem to be substantively different.

Other process theories emphasize the function of human perception in influencing behavior; these theories, like expectancy theory, concentrate upon cognitive processes. At least four sets of theories are important here. Cognitive dissonance theory, developed by Festinger, posits that an individual cannot tolerate being confronted by two or more mutually exclusive alternatives and will seek to reduce the dissonance by choosing one alternative.[40] Once the decision is made and the behavior is carried out, the individual will avoid (repress) thoughts that the wrong decision was made. A worker who thinks that she has been unfairly criticized by her boss in front of her peers might perceive two choices, one of forgetting the event or the other of speaking out against the boss. Should the latter choice be selected and some adverse action is taken against her, according to the cognitive dissonance theory she will continue to believe that she made the right choice.

A second type of theory emphasizing perception involves the concept of exchange. The idea was developed primarily by Homans to explain group behavior, a subject that is discussed in the next chapter.[41] Homans conceptualized that groups formed when individuals made exchanges with each other. As people interact with each other, they exchange rewards and costs. A friendship may grow because the individuals involved here perceived favorable exchanges.

A third type of theory based upon perception is attribution theory. Developed by Heider, the theory explains behavior in terms of attributing motives to others.[42] If a manager comes back to the office after lunch and ignores others in the office, workers will generate reasons for that behavior. One worker may think the boss is simply engrossed in work, while another may think the behavior is typical in that the boss is perceived as a basically unfriendly person. The workers, then, will respond to the situation according to their differing attributions.

A fourth theory, which includes elements of the other three, is equity theory. According to this theory, proposed by Adams, an individual compares his effort on the job with the rewards of the job in relation to the

[40] Leon Festinger, *A Theory of Cognitive Dissonance* (Stanford, Calif.: Stanford University Press, 1957).

[41] George C. Homans, *The Human Group* (New York: Harcourt, Brace, and World, 1950).

[42] Fritz Heider, *The Psychology of Interpersonal Relations* (New York: Wiley and Sons, 1958), and Fritz Heider, "Attitudes and Cognitive Organization," *Journal of Psychology*, 21 (1946):107–112. See Weiner, *Theories of Motivation*, pp. 310–332.

effort and rewards of persons in comparable positions.[43] The theory focuses upon workers' perceptions of whether they are receiving equal pay for equal work. Although rewards may be other than financial, such as having a large, carpeted private office, the reward of pay has been the main focus of research on equity theory. Changes in behavior are motivated when workers perceive inequities. The perception of being underpaid results in the workers' decreasing the quality and/or quantity of work, while overpayment results in the opposite change in behavior. In some instances when inequities are perceived, behavior changes may not occur, because workers revise their standards to bring their perceptions into an equitable balance. A worker may initially think she is overpaid but upon further reflection concludes she is not, because she perceives herself to be performing duties not performed by others. While this rationalizing process is needed in the theory, it reduces the power of equity theory to predict performance.

Equity theory is based on the concept of balance, as is the related theory of cognitive consistency proposed by Korman.[44] He contended that people select behaviors that are consistent with their perceptions of themselves (self-esteem). If they perceive themselves to be capable workers, they will be motivated to perform well; low performance would be incompatible with high self-esteem. Organizations can influence self-perceptions. An organization that has rigid policies in effect tells its workers that they are inadequate and therefore must be controlled. The resulting low level of self-esteem will produce a low level of job performance. If a worker becomes increasingly effective in performance over

[43] J. Stacy Adams and Sara Freedman, "Equity Theory Revisited: Comments and Annotated Bibliography," *Advances in Experimental Social Psychology*, (1976):43–90; J. Stacy Adams, "Toward an Understanding of Inequity," *Journal of Abnormal Psychology*, 67 (1963):422–436; J. Stacy Adams, "Inequity in Social Exchange," in Leonard Berkowitz, ed., *Advances in Experimental Social Psychology*, Vol. 2, (New York: Academic Press, 1965), pp. 267–300. See Paul S. Goodman and Abraham Friedman, "An Explanation of Adams' Theory of Inequity," *Administrative Science Quarterly*, 16 (1971):271–288, and Charles S. Telly, Wendell L. French, and William G. Scott, "The Relationship of Inequity to Turnover Among Hourly Workers," *Administrative Science Quarterly*, 16 (1971):164–172; and Michael R. Carrell, "A Longitudinal Field Assessment of Employee Perceptions of Equitable Treatment," *Organizational Behavior and Human Performance*, 21 (1978):108–118.

[44] Abraham K. Korman, "Organizational Achievement, Aggression, and Creativity: Some Suggestions Toward an Integrated Theory," *Organizational Behavior and Human Performance*, 6 (1971):593–613; Abraham K. Korman, "Hypothesis of Work Behavior Revisited and an Extension," *Academy of Management Review*, 1 (January, 1976):50–63; Abraham K. Korman, "Toward a Hypothesis of Work Behavior," *Journal of Applied Psychology*, 54 (1970):31–41. See also Robert L. Dipboye, "A Critical Review of Korman's Self-Consistency Theory of Work Motivation and Occupational Choice," *Organizational Behavior and Human Performance*, 18 (1977):108–126; and J. H. Kerr Inkson, "Self-Esteem as a Moderator of the Relationship Between Job Performance and Job Satisfaction," *Journal of Applied Psychology*, 63 (1978):243–247.

time, this is largely because of internal attributions of outcomes; a reduction in effectiveness is likely to be caused by external attributions. Research findings have not fully confirmed the Korman theory.

The last theory to be considered here brings the discussion back to the stimulus-response theory described at the beginning of this section and to the nature-nurture controversy considered at the beginning of this chapter. The theory is behaviorism, or operant conditioning, as advanced by Skinner.[45] Skinnerian psychology, which has been well accepted and frequently criticized, is being used increasingly to explain behavior in organizations. One of the first to suggest the applicability of Skinnerian theory was Nord, who contended that the theories of Maslow and others had received a disproportionate amount of attention.[46] According to Skinner, behavior is shaped by the environment. However, he does not view animals and people as operating on the simple stimulus-response basis. The stimulus-response mechanism is based upon reflex motions in which the behavior is uncontrolled. A person does not consciously decide whether to kick his leg when tapped on the knee. "Classical" conditioning might be able to make the person involuntarily kick at the sound of a bell.

Operant conditioning, on the other hand, involves conditioning behavior to operate on the environment to produce a consequence. Rather than being a reflexive action, behavior is selected. Skinner experimented with animals and provided rewards when desired behavior was achieved. For example, a pigeon was conditioned to raise its head high and as a result to receive food. The food is a reinforcer of the behavior, and in this case is a positive reinforcer. Reinforcement also can be negative, although its effects may be more limited. An example of negative reinforcement is when a supervisor nags an employee for failing to complete an assigned task on time. A negative reinforcer may need to be actually present in order to prevent a behavior, whereas a positive reinforcer need only have a greater than zero probability of occurring. A person may be motivated to act even if the possibility of receiving a reward has low probability (gambling is a good example). Much of the research in this area has focused upon the frequency of rewards, such as providing the reward every fifth time that the correct behavior is elicited.

Critics of Skinnerian psychology see dangers in emphasizing extrinsic rewards at the expense of intrinsic ones. Whereas earlier the individual may have been willing to act for intrinsic satisfaction, he now

[45] B. F. Skinner, *Science and Human Behavior* (New York: Free Press, 1953), and B. F. Skinner, *Beyond Freedom and Dignity* (New York: Knopf, 1971).

[46] Walter R. Nord, "Beyond the Teaching Machine: The Neglected Area of Operant Conditioning in the Theory and Practice of Management," *Organizational Behavior and Human Performance*, 4 (1969):375–401.

needs an external reward. Workers may be willing to work past quitting time without extra compensation because their jobs are interesting. Once an overtime pay system is introduced, however, the workers may be unwilling to work even a minute past quitting time without extra pay. Another form of extrinsic reward is expressions of approval or praise. If workers are conditioned to expect praise, will their performance decline should praise no longer be given for a well-done job?[47]

The main line of attack on Skinnerian psychology is its emphasis upon behaviorism. "Modern Americans, especially of the managerial class, prefer to think of themselves and others as being self-actualizing creatures near the top of Maslow's need-hierarchy, rather than as animals being controlled and even 'manipulated' by their environment."[48] The contention is that humans are complex organisms and should not be compared with rats in a Skinnerian conditioning box. Skinnerian psychology, as with need theories, is criticized as being deterministic, i.e., that human behavior is determined by environment. Skinner has written that operant conditioning should not be confused with learning; the concept of learning those behaviors that produce rewards does not need to be used in explaining behavior. This argument disturbs those who see humans as thinking organisms who consciously select behaviors.

SUMMARY

There is an abundance of theories about human motivation. Some theories focus largely upon personality. The internal conflict theory of Freud continues to be an important influence upon how human personality is perceived. Other theories relate to human evolution, suggesting that aggressive behavior and defense of territory are innate qualities. Body type has been related to variations in personality.

Content theories attempt to explain behavior in terms of the types of forces that motivate people. Human relations theory has stressed the need for interpersonal relations. A hierarchy of needs, culminating in the need for self-actualization, has been one of the most popular theories in recent years; the theory suggests that humans are motivated by unmet needs that, when satisfied, lead to the arousal of other needs. Another popular approach has been the two-factor theory, suggesting that hygiene

---

[47] Edward L. Deci, "The Effects of Contingent and Noncontingent Rewards and Controls and Intrinsic Motivation," *Organizational Behavior and Human Performance*, 8 (1972):217–229; W. E. Scott, Jr., "The Effects of Extrinsic Rewards on 'Intrinsic Motivation'," *Organizational Behavior and Human Performance*, 15 (1975):117–129; and Simcha Ronen, "Personal Values: A Basis for Worker Motivational Set and Work Attitude," *Organizational Behavior and Human Performance*, 21 (1978):80–107.

[48] Nord, "Beyond the Teaching Machine," pp. 376–377.

factors can be dissatisfiers but not motivators; positive motivators involve satisfaction with work itself.

Process theories, being nonsubstantive, focus upon the methods by which people are motivated. Early concepts that serve as the foundation for contemporary process theories include stimulus-response theory, the law of effect, drive theory, and field theory. Especially popular has been expectancy theory, which suggests that behavior results from individuals calculating whether a possible behavior will be instrumental in providing a desired outcome. Cognitive dissonance stresses the desire of individuals to resolve problems by making a choice and then not reassessing the decision that has been made. Exchange theory sees human behavior as being based upon interactions; favorable interactions will increase the probability of more of these interactions. Attribution theory involves the process of attributing motives to others and then acting in response to those attributions. Equity theory is concerned with the relationship between effort and reward of one person in comparison with the same relationship for others. Cognitive consistency concentrates upon the balance between self-esteem and behavior. Behaviorism suggests that behavior is acquired by operating on the environment to produce a desired consequence.

None of the theories discussed here provides an all-encompassing approach to explaining human motivation, yet to some extent each of these theories has been propounded as the ultimate explanation. Frankly, the field of motivation has had an ample number of dogmatists. Social research in the last several decades has made remarkable strides in understanding human behavior, but there is still much to be learned. This will become apparent in the next chapter, which considers the limitations involved in applying motivation theories to real-world situations.

.

Chapter 12

Motivation in Daily Operations

Getting the right people for the right jobs *might* solve all motivational problems. If a job is intrinsically dull and the supervisor of that job is a tyrant, then a worker should be recruited who thrives on boring work and who is submissive. While there may be virtues in such an approach, it is impractical when applied to all positions. Instead, today there is much emphasis upon finding techniques that can motivate workers both for increasing their own satisfaction and for improving the productivity of the organization.

This chapter discusses techniques used in organizations to motivate workers. The techniques are based upon the theories discussed in the previous chapter. The first section concentrates upon procedures that provide for greater worker autonomy. The second one discusses work groups and leaders, especially leaders who are managers. In the third section, techniques emphasizing performance and organizational change are considered. The fourth section reviews some of the practical problems associated with applying motivation theory to daily management problems.

WORKER AUTONOMY

Many of the theories discussed in the preceding chapter either explicitly or implicitly suggest that worker motivation and/or job satisfaction improves as workers gain control over themselves. The prescription follows that work should be redirected to recognize employees as individuals rather than as robots that are programmed to perform tasks. Greater autonomy will provide workers with greater respect for themselves as capable individuals and greater respect for management and the organization. In turn, workers will become more creative in dealing with the problems of their job. Whereas a robot simply performs as it was programmed, "liberated" workers develop more efficient and effective means of performing tasks—at least that is the assumption.

McGregor's Theory Y is an example of the worker autonomy philosophy, while the traditional Theory X involves close supervision of workers. According to McGregor, "physical and mental work is as natural as play or rest"; employees are not inherently lazy. A worker will seek responsibility and will "exercise self-direction and self-control in the service of objectives to which he is committed."[1] Providing workers with greater autonomy, freedom, or self-control will encourage them to utilize their intellectual abilities more fully.

Increasing autonomy for employees requires rethinking of traditional roles of management. While the next section of this chapter considers alternative management or leadership styles, here it should be noted that one approach to motivation is to reduce the intensity of supervision. One such approach is to practice "management by exception." This technique sees the manager as dealing primarily with problems as they arise. Workers have great freedom to organize their work except when problems develop, at which time the manager intervenes. A requirement of management by exception is that considerable authority is delegated to lower levels in the bureaucracy. Lower level workers may take actions without having to obtain prior approval from their supervisors.

Since management by exception is only a style or conceptualization of how supervisory personnel should perform, it can be resisted by those in authority. Therefore some organizational changes can be made that will increase the likelihood of using management by exception. One alternative involves span of control, namely the number of personnel and the types of work performed under any given manager. Span of control has been a recurrent topic of discussion in the study of administration. An assumption has been that the span of control over personnel should be relatively narrow when each employee performs substantially different types of work.[2] If the supervisor had twenty employees all performing different work, adequate supervision cannot be provided. Today, if one chose to further the use of management by exception, an expanded span of control would be preferable. Such an approach would force the manager to delegate responsibilities to subordinates. Similarly, assistants to the administrator should be kept to a minimum. A bureau chief

---

[1] Douglas McGregor, *The Human Side of Enterprise* (New York: McGraw-Hill, 1960), pp. 47–48. See also Douglas M. McGregor, "The Human Side of Enterprise," *Management Review*, 46 (November, 1957):22–28+; and Arthur A. Thompson, "Employee Participation in Decision Making: The TVA Experience," *Public Personnel Review*, 28 (1967):82–88.

[2] See Luther Gulick and L. Urwick, *Papers on the Science of Administration* (New York: Institute of Public Administration, 1973).

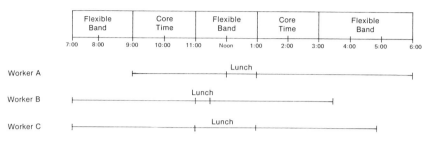

Figure 12.1.   Sample work schedules using flexitime.

without deputy chiefs or administrative aides will have limited time to supervise subordinates.

Flexitime

Adjusting working hours is seen as another method for increasing worker autonomy. Compressed work schedules involve four-day or, in some cases, three-day work weeks. Employees work usually about the same number of hours as in a five-day week; obviously, four ten-hour days are the same as five eight-hour days. A variant on this would be for workers to continue working eight-hour days but to alternate between four-day and six-day weeks, so that the average work week would remain forty hours long.[3] Compressed work schedules do not by themselves greatly increase worker freedom on the job. Such schedules obviously enhance freedom off the job, in that three-day weekends are provided, but workers are expected to arrive at work and to quit at specified times.

Flexible time, or flexitime, can be used with compressed schedules, but more often it is considered an alternative to them. Under most flexitime systems, workers are expected to work the same number of hours each day in a five-day week but flexibility is allowed as to when those hours are worked. Flexitime systems have core time periods when all employees are expected to be at work. Figure 12.1 shows core times between 9:00 and 11:00 a.m. and between 1:00 and 3:00 p.m. Flexible bands or "quiet times" occur before the morning core time and after the afternoon core time. Some flexitime systems have a set lunch break, such as noon to one, while others have a flexible band during the lunch period. Figure 12.1 shows three possible work schedules. Workers A and B might be husband and wife. Worker A begins work later in order to be home before their children go to school, while Worker B quits at 3:30 p.m. to be home about the time the children return from school. Worker C, in comparison, begins the day at 7:00 a.m. and does not quit until 5:00

---

[3] Alan L. Porter and Frederick A. Rossini, "Flexiweek," *Business Horizons,* 21 (April, 1978):45–51.

p.m., allowing for a two-hour midday break for shopping or possibly a doctor's appointment.

Flexitime plans vary in their flexibility. Not only may lunch periods be fixed or flexible, but so can the work day. Some systems require an eight-hour day, while others require an eight-hour day averaged over a week, two weeks, or in some cases two months. Where that flexibility exists, an employee who wanted a three-day weekend to take a trip could decide to work four ten-hour days in that week, as in the compressed work schedule. Some systems allow workers to decide each day when they will begin and quit work; an employee can choose each morning whether to sleep an extra hour and not report to work until later. Other systems require each employee to select a starting and quitting time to be followed for a month or perhaps indefinitely.

In Europe, where flexitime originated, it has become popular in both the private and public sectors, and European plans are generally more flexible than those in the United States. About 40 percent of Swiss workers have flexible working hours. Here in the United States, between 300,000 and 1 million non-federal employees have flexitime, and another 1.2 million have compressed schedules. As of 1977 close to 100 federal agencies, involving 140,000 employees, were experimenting with or were using flexible scheduling. Many thousands of New York City workers are on flexitime.[4]

Flexitime and compressed work schedules have both advantages and disadvantages. Because the total working day is stretched from eight hours to possibly eleven hours, workers frequently operate without immediate supervision, thereby increasing their control over their work; delegation of authority may be inevitable under such plans. This increased independence is said to improve morale and job satisfaction. Available evidence seems to indicate that employees like such arrangements; one study of 31 federal agencies found that morale and job satisfaction had been improved in 24 of the agencies experimenting with these systems.[5]

A possible retardant to improved morale is that more detailed record keeping on hours worked may be required under flexitime than under conventional arrangements. Employees may have to maintain time cards on the hours they work, in contrast with the system where everyone

---

[4] *Benefits from Flexible Work Schedules: Legal Limitations Remain* (Washington: General Accounting Office, 1977); *Contractors' Use of Altered Work Schedules for their Employees: How Is It Working?* (Washington: General Accounting Office, 1976); Robert J. Donahue, "Flex Time Systems in New York," *Public Personnel Management,* 4 (1975):212–215; Barbara L. Fiss, "Government Tests Flexitime," *Civil Service Journal,* 17 (January/March, 1977):1–4; and James Walker, Clive Fletcher, and Donald McLeod, "Flexible Working Hours in Two British Government Offices," *Public Personnel Management,* 4 (1975):216–222.

[5] *Benefits from Flexible Work Schedules,* p. 11.

begins and quits work at the same time and where records are not kept for specific hours. The time cards can be viewed as management's unwillingness to trust its employees. Another possible drawback is that supervision is not available when it is needed. If many employees report for work at 7:00 a.m. but the supervisor does not begin until 9:00 a.m., some work may be done in a way contrary to what the supervisor expected. By the same token, support staff sometimes are not at work when they are needed early or late in the normal working day.

A major claim in favor of flexitime and compressed scheduling is that they increase productivity.[6] In a four-day work week, each employee requires less start-up and shut-down time, so that time is utilized more effectively. Under flexitime, workers need not feel forced to work when they are psychologically or physically not ready to work. Attitudinal surveys have found that employees think their productivity increased, and there is some evidence using objective criteria (such as number of forms processed by clerical workers) to show that flexitime increased productivity.[7]

There is competing evidence to suggest that, when the work day is extended, productivity does not increase. Possible gains in productivity may be offset by worker fatigue.[8] Supervisors tend to be skeptical about the effects on productivity. There is suspicion that workers "goof off" when the boss is not around.[9] Additionally, supervisors tend to complain that key workers frequently are not available when needed. If a problem arises at 3:30 p.m., during the flexible band, action may have to be postponed until the next morning's core time. Proponents of flexitime contend the opposite, namely that key personnel will tend to stagger their schedules so that, rather than a supervisor's being available only from 8:00 a.m. to noon and 1:00 to 5:00 p.m., someone with the needed skills is available from 7:00 a.m. to 6:00 p.m. This also means more hours will be available for dealing with the public and agency clients. Although

[6] Thomas G. Cummings and Edmond S. Molloy, *Improving Productivity and the Quality of Work Life* (New York: Praeger, 1977), pp. 205–216; Richard I. Hartman and K. Mark Weaver, "Four Factors Influencing Conversion to a Four-Day Work Week," *Human Resource Management*, 16 (Spring, 1977):24–27; Janice N. Hedges, "Flexible Schedules: Problems and Issues," *Monthly Labor Review*, 100 (February, 1977):62–64; Richard J. Kühne and Courtney O. Blair, "Flexitime," *Business Horizons*, 21 (April, 1978):39–44; and Sol Swerdloff, *The Revised Workweek: Results of a Pilot Study of 16 Firms*, U.S. Bureau of Labor Statistics Bulletin 1846 (Washington: Government Printing Office, 1975).

[7] William H. Holley, Achilles A. Armenakis, and Hubert S. Feild, Jr., "Employee Reactions to a Flexitime Program: A Longitudinal Study," *Human Resource Management*, 15 (Winter, 1976):21–23; and Virginia E. Schein, "Impact of Flexible Working Hours on Productivity," *Journal of Applied Psychology*, 62 (1977):463–465.

[8] James G. Goodale and A. K. Aagaard, "Factors Relating to Varying Reactions to the 4-Day Workweek," *Journal of Applied Psychology*, 60 (1975):33–38.

[9] Oscar Mueller and Muriel Cole, "[Flexitime] Concept Wins Converts at Federal Agency," *Monthly Labor Review*, 100 (February, 1977):71–74.

worker productivity may be increased, some operating costs also may increase. Heating and lighting costs may increase, and additional personnel may be needed to staff telephone switchboards and operate other support services.

Flexible hours are said to reduce absenteeism and turnover and to improve employee recruitment. Some evidence suggests that absenteeism is reduced, but the relationship between turnover and flexitime is not known. If a worker becomes ill on the job, he can quit early under some flexitime plans and then make up the lost time in a day or two. This aspect of the plan, along with overtime, however, has caused problems with labor unions. If the worker makes up all lost time, sick leave is in effect denied. Similarly, should a worker who elects to work a ten-hour day be paid overtime rates for two of those hours? Some unions have insisted on such overtime pay. The federal government has been hampered in using flexitime by its own laws that govern the length of the work day and establish overtime pay requirements. This problem was reduced by passage of the Federal Employees Flexible and Compressed Work Schedules Act of 1978, which provides for a three-year experimental program in the use of flexitime.[10]

Another limitation of flexitime is that it is inappropriate when employees work as a team. When employees perform jobs largely independent of each other, there is little need for them all to be present at the same time; for routine processing of state income tax returns, for instance, some employees could work effectively between midnight and 9:00 a.m. In other situations, workers need to operate as a unit, as in the case of a road maintenance crew.

Changing the work schedules may improve worker satisfaction only marginally. The four-day week simply may please a worker because there is one less day a week when he must perform a dull and unpleasant job. A survey of private workers supports this view; the type of person most likely to favor the four-day week was "young, with a low job level, low tenure, and low income."[11] Neither compressed schedules nor flexitime makes fundamental changes in the work performed by each employee. Some observers, then, contend that more far-reaching changes are needed, with one set of proposals involving job enrichment and job enlargement.

[10] *Benefits from Flexible Work Schedules; Legal Limitations on Flexible and Compressed Work Schedules for Federal Employees* (Washington: General Accounting Office, 1974); U.S. Civil Service Commission, *Flexitime* (Washington: Government Printing Office, 1975).

[11] Randall B. Dunham and Donald Hawk, "The Four-Day/Forty-Hour Week: Who Wants It?" *Academy of Management Journal*, 20 (1977):644–655.

Job Enrichment

Job enlargement or enrichment is an old idea that regained prominence in the 1960s and 1970s. In simple terms, the process involves redesigning jobs to make them more interesting for workers. The assumption is that making work more interesting will increase job satisfaction, motivation, and performance. Enlargement means expanding the number of tasks to be performed in any one job in order to provide the worker with varied responsibilities. Most work involves routines and is cyclical. If the cycle is short, then the worker frequently repeats the same operations. If a worker begins and completes the processing of a form in one minute and begins another form the next minute, the cycle is short and the job is narrow rather than enlarged. The assumption is that this short cycle will result in worker boredom, dissatisfaction, poor performance, absenteeism, and possibly turnover. Job enlargement, on the other hand, provides the worker with greater autonomy and responsibility. In the case of processing a form, the worker may be assigned responsibility for reviewing not just part of the form but all of the form, and if the data from the form are to be entered into a computer, the worker may be given the responsibility for transposing data onto machine-readable worksheets. The worker may be given discretion about when each of these tasks is done. One worker might thoroughly process one form before beginning another, while another worker might handle them in batches at each step in the cycle.

The critics of this type of job enlargement contend that only "horizontal loading" has occurred; tasks of the same level of responsibility have been combined. The work is no more interesting than before. Therefore "vertical loading" is advocated in the name of job enrichment. Herzberg's two-factor theory is usually cited as the theoretical foundation for job enrichment. If the work is to be more satisfying, job redesign must concentrate on motivators. Herzberg contends that jobs should encourage employee growth by providing opportunities for increased knowledge, understanding, and creativity; employees should have an "opportunity to experience ambiguity in decision making" and "to individuate and seek real growth."[12] Enrichment involves having workers

---

[12] Frederick Herzberg, *Work and the Nature of Man* (Cleveland: World, 1966), p. 177. See also Kenneth O. Alexander, "On Work and Authority: Issues on Job Enlargement, Job Enrichment, Worker Participation and Shared Authority," *American Journal of Economics and Sociology*, 34 (1975):43–54; Chris Argyris, *Personality and Organization* (New York: Harper and Row, 1957), pp. 177–187; William F. Dowling, "Consensus Management at Graphic Controls," *Organizational Dynamics*, 5 (Winter, 1977):22–47; Robert C. Gallegos and Joseph G. Phelan, "Effects on Productivity and Morale of a Systems-Designed Job-Enrichment Program in Pacific Telephone," *Psychological Reports*, 40 (1977):283–290; Luis R. Gomez and Stephen J. Mussio, "An Application of Job Enrich-

learn why they perform certain tasks so that they are aware of the importance of their work. Administrative regulations should be relaxed, giving the worker freedom to experiment with alternative methods for doing the assigned job. Supervision should be less intensive, so that workers are their own supervisors. In job enrichment, some of the responsibilities of higher level positions are reassigned to lower level positions.

Techniques have been developed for gauging the motivational quality of existing jobs and potentially redesigned jobs. Turner and Lawrence developed the Requisite Task Attribute Index (RTA), which measures the attributes of 1) variety, 2) autonomy, 3) required interaction, 4) optional interaction, 5) knowledge and skill required, and 6) responsibility.[13] Building on that index and other models, Hackman and Oldham have developed the Job Characteristics Model of Work Motivation and the Motivating Potential Score (MPS).[14] The model is expressed by the following equation:

$$\text{MPS} = \left[\frac{\text{Skill Variety} + \text{Task Identity} + \text{Task Significance}}{3} \right] \times \text{Autonomy} \times \text{Feedback}$$

Variety, identity, and significance are seen as having an additive effect in determining whether the work is "meaningful." Variety involves the number of different activities performed; identity is the extent to which a "whole" or "identifiable" set of work is completed. Significance involves the effect of the work of a given job on others in or outside of the organization. Autonomy is having "responsibility for outcomes of the work" and feedback is obtaining information on the results of the work. Given the format of the equation, autonomy and feedback are extremely

---

ment in a Civil Service Setting: A Demonstration Study," *Public Personnel Management*, 4 (1975):49–54; Ted Mills, "Human Resources—Why the New Concern?" *Harvard Business Review*, 53 (March–April, 1975):120–134; W. J. Paul and K. B. Robertson, *Job Enrichment and Employee Motivation* (London: Gower, 1970); Peter P. Schoderbek and William E. Reif, *Job Enlargement: Key to Improved Performance* (Ann Arbor: Bureau of Industrial Relations, University of Michigan, 1969); Charles R. Walker, "The Problem of the Repetitive Job," *Harvard Business Review*, 28 (May, 1950):54–58; Roy W. Walters and Associates, *Job Enrichment for Results: Strategies for Successful Implementation* (Reading, Mass.: Addison-Wesley, 1975); and Roy W. Walters, "Job Enrichment Isn't Easy," *Personnel Administration/Public Personnel Review*, 1 (September–October, 1972):61–66.

[13] Arthur N. Turner and Paul R. Lawrence, *Industrial Jobs and the Worker* (Cambridge, Mass.: Graduate School of Business Administration, Harvard University, 1965).

[14] J. Richard Hackman and Greg R. Oldham, "Motivation Through the Design of Work: Test of a Theory," *Organizational Behavior and Human Performance*, 16 (1976):250–279. See also Denis D. Umstot, Cecil H. Bell, Jr., and Terrence R. Mitchell, "Effects of Job Enrichment and Task Goals on Satisfaction and Productivity: Implications for Job Design," *Journal of Applied Psychology*, 61 (1976):379–394.

important; a score of near zero on either of these items will yield a motivating potential score of near zero.

Job enrichment cannot be applied to all types of work. Some work may be essentially boring and yet the work needs to be performed. In such cases, substitution of machines for people may resolve the problem. Rotation of responsibilities also can be used. In any large government office building, for example, a great volume of mail comes in each day and must be sorted for distribution throughout the building. If the sorting and delivery of mail is considered to be uninteresting, one approach is to have office workers take turns in handling the mail so that no one worker has that assignment as a full-time responsibility. Another approach is to use teams to handle the work, with the team members deciding who will do what work and when. This approach has been used for mail sorting as well as other jobs.[15] Perhaps the team approach is the best that can be done in the private sector, where technology dictates some form of assembly line. In Sweden, Volvo automobiles are assembled by teams of workers who are not assigned to fixed positions, as in the more common assembly line. The team method, however, seems to conflict in part with the underlying theory of job enrichment. Placing some discretion in a team may increase autonomy for a group of workers but not necessarily for any single worker, yet job enrichment stresses the value of worker autonomy. In addition, the team approach stresses interpersonal relations, a hygiene factor, whereas job enrichment supposedly focuses upon motivators.

Efforts to enrich jobs have concentrated upon lower level positions and insufficient attention has been given to supervisory positions. If enrichment means vertical loading, it follows that supervisors necessarily lose some powers. Such changes obviously can be threatening, and, at the very least, require those in positions of authority to play different roles in managing their workers, roles that may be not only unfamiliar but also not preferred by the supervisors. The problem may be resolved by enriching managers' jobs as well as those of their subordinates. When it is applied throughout an organization, job enrichment becomes an equivalent of decentralization of authority. A mid-level manager yields some responsibility to lower levels and takes on additional responsibility from higher levels.[16]

Staff functions, particularly personnel and budgeting, can be used for enrichment purposes. Mid-level supervisors can be assigned responsi-

[15] Edwin A. Locke, David Sirota, and Alan D. Wolfson, "An Experimental Case Study of the Successes and Failures of Job Enrichment in a Government Agency," *Journal of Applied Psychology*, 61 (1976):701–711.

[16] See Clayton P. Alderfer, "An Empirical Test of a New Theory of Human Needs," *Organizational Behavior and Human Performance*, 4 (1969):142–175; and Robert N. Ford, *Motivation Through Work Itself* (New York: American Management Association, 1969).

bility for budgeting for their agencies and for operating within their budgetary ceilings. In the same manner, personnel matters can be decentralized so that lower level supervisors are assigned the responsibilities of selecting and disciplining employees. The result may be a reduction in staff size for personnel and budget offices.[17] The extent to which staff functions can be decentralized is dependent upon the desirability of consistency. To what extent should discretion in disciplining employees be delegated, since discretion can produce inconsistent or non-standardized actions? Extensive delegation of this responsibility could result in some managers being severe and others lenient in disciplining employees for any given instance of wrongdoing.

If job enrichment accomplishes what its proponents claim, then more work can be accomplished by the same number of employees. If more work is not needed, then a surplus of staff develops. Some reported job enrichment cases have resulted in surplus staff, although usually the workers have been reassigned to positions in other segments of the organization. Nevertheless, job enrichment holds the potential for layoffs, which can reduce employee morale and which does arouse labor union concern.

Another area of concern is how job enrichment relates to pay and promotion practices.[18] Using equity theory, an employee who, through job enrichment, becomes more productive but is not granted a pay increase will consider the situation inequitable and the result can be reduced performance, to bring effort and pay into balance. If pay increases are not awarded, then organized labor can contend that job enrichment is simply a management scheme to get more work out of each employee with no additional pay. For these reasons, enrichment programs may require pay increases, but that could result in an increase of total personnel costs. Not only must pay systems be adjusted but so must promotion systems, in order to recognize that a worker is performing at a higher level of responsibility. Promotional systems that rely heavily upon seniority may retard the effectiveness of job enrichment, yet it is these seniority rules that are particularly popular among labor unions, thereby creating one more reason for organized labor's opposition to or at least skepticism about job enrichment.

Although much of the job enrichment research and experimentation has found positive results in worker performance, job satisfaction has not always been increased. One possible explanation is that many workers

[17] Robert T. Golembiewski, *Men, Management, and Morality: Toward a New Organizational Ethic* (New York: McGraw-Hill, 1965), pp. 143–148.

[18] Edwin A. Locke, "Personnel Attitudes and Motivation," *Annual Review of Psychology*, 26 (1975):471–472; and Michael Beer and Edgar F. Huse, "A Systems Approach to Organization Development," *Journal of Applied Behavioral Science*, 8 (1972):79–101.

have become alienated, do not seek self-actualization on the job, and cannot find "work itself" to be interesting.[19] Another explanation is that job enrichment may encourage greater expectations, so that the level of satisfaction remains unchanged. This phenomemon has been found in studies with federal, state, and local government workers.[20] Workers may be moderately satisfied with their jobs. When provided with new challenges through job enrichment, moderately satisfied workers not only perform at a higher level but also have higher expectations about what they can accomplish and what responsibilities they think the organization should provide them. The outcome is that satisfaction remains at a moderate level.

The effects of job enrichment on individuals and interpersonal relations have not been well researched. "Role overload" can develop when workers' jobs are excessively enriched. Enrichment advocates ignore interpersonal relations, in that such relationships are considered only hygiene factors, but it is debatable whether that approach is warranted. Enrichment may create role ambiguities, so that workers are not told the full limits of their authority. This can be psychologically unsettling and can lead to interpersonal tensions, so that workers disagree about who has responsibility for what.[21] This ambiguity also is a reason for labor union opposition. Unions prefer to make responsibilities explicit through labor contracts, whereas job enrichment encourages fluidity.

There is one other unsettled aspect of job enrichment. Change in job responsibilities may have as great an influence on performance as enrichment. Again, enrichment research has shown positive effects on worker performance, but that does not mean enrichment is the only key to improving performance. Simply changing a person's duties without enlarging the job can have positive effects.[22]

GROUPS AND LEADERS

People are individuals but they are also part of social systems known as groups. While the preceding section concentrates upon liberating workers

---

[19] Charles L. Hulin and Milton R. Blood, "Job Enlargement, Individual Differences, and Worker Responses," *Psychological Bulletin*, 69 (1968):41–55; and Greg R. Oldham, J. Richard Hackman, and Jone L. Pearce, "Conditions Under Which Employees Respond Positively to Enriched Work," *Journal of Applied Psychology*, 61 (1976):395–403.

[20] Locke, Sirota, and Wolfson, "An Experimental Case Study of the Successes and Failures of Job Enrichment in a Government Agency," and Ralph Katz and John Van Maanen, "The Loci of Work Satisfaction: Job, Interaction, and Policy," *Human Relations*, 30 (1977):469–486.

[21] Abraham K. Korman, Jeffrey H. Greenhaus, and Irwin J. Badin, "Personnel Attitudes and Motivation," *Annual Review of Psychology*, 28 (1977):187–188.

[22] Ronald C. Bishop and James W. Hill, "Effects of Job Enlargement and Job Change on Contiguous but Nonmanipulated Jobs as a Function of Workers' Status," *Journal of Applied Psychology*, 55 (1971):175–181.

or giving them increased autonomy as a means of increasing their individualism, this section emphasizes how people behave in groups.[23] As will be seen, an important aspect of group behavior is the role performed by leaders.

Group Theory

A group can be defined as "a plurality of individuals who are in contact with one another, who take one another into account, and who are aware of some significant commonality."[24] Groups have a history or past and continue over time. A number of people in an elevator may interact briefly but they would not be considered a group. Groups vary in size, with the term "small" group usually being reserved for those with ten or fewer members. Most of the discussion here concentrates upon small groups.

A distinction is commonly made between formal and informal groups. An informal group is one that emerges out of interaction among people and has no official or formal designation; when workers interact on the job, they become an informal group. A formal group, in contrast, has prescribed members. Informal work groups can lead to the establishment of a labor union or grievance committee, which takes on the characteristics of a formal group. Also, organizations create formal groups known as committees. A characteristic of these committees is that the members usually have been chosen to participate by a person or persons in authority, whereas informal groups largely select their own members.

Formal and informal groups constitute dynamic subsystems in organizations. While any one group may continue over time, membership varies as people enter and leave the organization and as people change jobs within the organization. Groups have overlapping memberships. A person might be a member of several formal standing committees of an agency, a member of one or more interagency committees, and a member of numerous informal work groups. This field of group theory, then, sees the individual in a social system composed of a myriad of groups, in contrast with other theories that concentrate on the individual.

One possible explanation of why groups emerge is that people have an inherent need to be with others, and that organizations, themselves, fail to meet this need, thereby resulting in worker anomie and alienation.

---

[23] See Bertil Gardell, "Autonomy and Participation at Work," *Human Relations*, 30 (1976):515–533.

[24] Michael S. Olmsted, *The Small Group* (New York: Random House, 1959), p. 21. See also Michael Billig, *Social Psychology and Intergroup Relations* (New York: Academic, 1976), pp. 20–21, 308, 322; B. Aubrey Fisher, *Small Group Decision Making: Communication and the Group Process* (New York: McGraw-Hill, 1974), pp. 16–24; and Marvin E. Shaw, *Group Dynamics: The Psychology of Small Group Behavior*, 2d ed. (New York: McGraw-Hill, 1976), pp. 6–12.

In the 1840s Marx popularized such a view, claiming that industrialization had separated workers from the products of their work, alienating employees from their employers.[25] Mayo's school of human relations, based upon the findings of the Hawthorne studies, saw workers as isolated individuals who found a sense of belonging in neither old social institutions nor in industrial organizations. The report on the Hawthorne studies, however, did not go so far as to suggest that informal work groups always will arise. In one of the experiments a group did not develop, and the reason suggested was that individual autonomy coupled with an incentive pay system obviated some need for group formation.[26] This raises a question about whether worker autonomy techniques discussed in the preceding section would militate against group formation. Maslow's need hierarchy is another theory that is compatible with the belongingness stimulus for group formation; belongingness needs presumably arise after satisfaction of physiological and safety needs (see Chapter 11). Whyte's *Organization Man*, a best seller of the 1950s, portrayed organizations conveying to workers the need to belong, to be committed to a "social ethic" rather than an ethic based on individualism.[27]

A variant on the belongingness explanation of group formation is Fundamental Interpersonal Relations Orientation (FIRO) developed by Schutz.[28] Inclusion (the equivalent of belongingness), control, and affection are the main elements of the model. Groups develop and continue to the extent that members are compatible in terms of their needs to belong, their desire to be dominant or be dominated, and the need for affection or being liked by others.

A cluster of theories about group formation concentrates upon the interactive processes among individuals. Homans, who was associated with Mayo and the human relations school of thought, conceptualized groups in terms of four sets of variables. First, groups involve activities, whether those activities are work related or leisure oriented. Second, groups involve interaction among members. Third, groups have sentiments, or feelings, which may be happy, sad, and the like. Fourth, groups have norms, standards of what is considered proper and improper behavior.[29] Norms are discussed shortly, but at this point the main

---

[25] See W. J. Heisler, "Worker Alienation: 1900–1975," in W. J. Heisler and John W. Houck, eds., *A Matter of Dignity: Inquiries into the Humanization of Work* (Notre Dame, Ind.: University of Notre Dame Press, 1977), pp. 65–84.

[26] Fritz J. Roethlisberger and William J. Dickson, *Management and the Worker* (Cambridge, Mass.: Harvard University Press, 1939), pp. 155–156; Henry A. Landsberger, *Hawthorne Revisited* (Ithaca, N.Y.: Cornell University, 1958), pp. 61–62.

[27] William H. Whyte, *The Organization Man* (New York: Simon and Schuster, 1956).

[28] William C. Schutz, "What Makes Groups Productive?," *Human Relations*, 8 (1955):429–465; and William C. Schutz, *FIRO: A Three-Dimensional Theory of Interpersonal Behavior* (New York: Rinehart, 1958).

[29] George C. Homans, *The Human Group* (New York: Harcourt, Brace, 1950).

concern is that Homans stressed interactions. Groups emerge as people meet, speak, and work with each other and have positive feelings about those interactions. Field theory, developed by Lewin, takes a similar approach, emphasizing how people interact in spatial arrangements. Exchange theory is still another related approach that describes interaction as exchanges between people.[30] Smiles, compliments, derogatory comments, and physical punches are among the repertoire of exchanges. When exchanges are viewed favorably, the probability of additional exchanges increases and a group will be formed.

Groups have structures and communication networks. Not all members interact with each other equally frequently and in the same ways. Some members may speak to each other only periodically throughout the day, while others are in nearly continuous communication. The organizational structure prescribes various interactions, but informal networks of communication overlie the formal structure. Analyses of these networks usually begin with a focus upon two-person, or dyadic, relationships, and then linkages among the dyads are identified. The result of such analyses are social diagrams or sociograms, which schematically display the grapevine of a group or organization: A speaks with B, who in turn relays information to C and D, who together talk with E, and so forth.[31]

One aspect of a group's structure is the varied roles that people play. "A role consists of one or more recurrent activities which in combination produce the organizational output."[32] Group members develop expectations about how each other member is to behave, and these ideas are called expected roles. Some members may be submissive, while others are dominant or serve as leaders. Some may serve as mediators between aggressive members. Some may be major sources of new information for the group and others are major disseminators of that information. Some may be heavily task oriented and others stress humor and leisure aspects of group activities.[33] When a member deviates from an expected role, other members will experience uncertainty about how to respond to the aberrant behavior.

---

[30] John W. Thibaut and Harold H. Kelley, *The Social Psychology of Groups* (New York: Wiley and Sons, 1959).

[31] Alex Bavelas, "A Mathematical Model for Group Structures," *Applied Anthropology*, 7 (Summer, 1948):16–30; Arthur M. Cohen, Warren G. Bennis, and George H. Wolkon, "The Effects of Continued Practice on the Behaviors of Problem-Solving Groups," *Sociometry*, 24 (1961):416–431; Daniel Katz and Robert L. Kahn, *The Social Psychology of Organizations* (New York: Wiley and Sons, 1966), pp. 223–258; and Jacob L. Moreno, *Who Shall Survive?*, rev. ed. (New York: Beacon House, 1953).

[32] Katz and Kahn, *The Social Psychology of Organizations*, p. 179.

[33] Fisher, *Small Group Decision Making*, pp. 50–51; Kenneth D. Benne and Paul Sheats, "Functional Roles of Group Members," *Journal of Social Issues*, 4 (1948):41–49; Melville Dalton, *Men Who Manage* (New York: Wiley and Sons, 1959).

Roles can be portrayed in a dynamic manner through the use of Bales' Interaction Process Analysis (IPA).[34] Groups are conceptualized as problem-solving entities. Interactions, then, relate to how the group moves toward a decision in resolving a problem. Bales proposed twelve basic types of interactions, and his technique entails observing the frequency of these communications as the group moves toward a decision. The communications can be verbal or nonverbal, such as a smile or pounding on a desk. The communication types include asking for an opinion, showing solidarity with the group, and expressing agreement or passive acceptance. Researchers have attempted to use the Bales approach to distinguish different phases in the decision process.[35]

Groups have norms or rules about behavior that generally apply to all members. Norms simplify interaction, in that members know what is expected of them. Norms are restricted to behavior—verbal or nonverbal—and do not encompass thoughts. Only behavior that is perceived by the group to be important is controlled by norms, while less important matters are left to the discretion of each member. Norms are applied differently among the membership, with leaders usually being permitted greater deviation from the group norms.[36] One problem with the concept of norms is that a hollow explanation of behavior can develop: Group A behaves in one way because of its norms and Group B behaves differently because of a different set of norms.[37]

The concept of norms has led to concern that groups impose uniformity on their members and may diminish independent thinking. Laboratory experiments have demonstrated that a person sometimes will accept the group's position even though he knows that position to be false.[38] One interpretation, then, is that group decisions tend to be mediocre, but a conflicting view is that individuals acting as a group tend to take greater risks than when acting autonomously. The latter is exemplified by the lynch mob, where responsibility for an extreme action is diffused throughout the group. Janis has labeled the process "groupthink."[39]

---

[34] Robert F. Bales, *Interaction Process Analysis* (Cambridge, Mass.: Addison-Wesley, 1950).

[35] Fisher, *Small Group Decision Making*, pp. 140–145.

[36] Lyman W. Porter, Edward E. Lawler III, and J. Richard Hackman, *Behavior in Organizations* (New York: McGraw-Hill, 1975), pp. 392–393; and J. Richard Hackman, "Group Influences on Individuals," in Marvin D. Dunnette, ed., *Handbook of Industrial and Organizational Psychology* (Chicago: Rand McNally, 1976), pp. 1495–1496.

[37] Olmsted, *The Small Group*, p. 76.

[38] Solomon E. Asch, "Studies of Independence and Conformity: A Minority of One Against a Unanimous Majority," *Psychological Monographs*, 70, No. 9 (1956): 1–70.

[39] Irving L. Janis, *Victims of Groupthink* (Boston: Houghton Mifflin, 1972), and Irvin L. Janis, "Groupthink," *Psychology Today*, 5 (November, 1971):43–46+. See Dorwin Cartwright and Ronald Lippitt, "Group Dynamics and the Individual," *International Journal of Group Psychotherapy*, 7 (1957):86–102; and Shaw, *Group Dynamics*, pp. 70–77.

Group goals involve some desired future state, condition, or location. In work groups, these goals often are ambiguous or nonoperational. A goal of the group may be to operate with greater independence of management, but because the group does not subscribe to total independence, the group may have difficulty in determining its reaction to a new set of management directives. Each member brings to the group goals he or she would like the members to accept as group goals. In some cases these goals may be generally accepted, but that does not mean all members accept any one goal with the same intensity.[40]

The term "cohesiveness" is used to express the extent to which group members are pulled together, see themselves and behave as a unity, and remain as members of the group. Cohesiveness is sometimes viewed as a form of loyalty or simply the extent to which members like each other.[41] A broader conceptualization of cohesion is the extent to which members are in agreement on the roles, norms, and goals of the group. Members could like one another, but the group could disintegrate for lack of agreement on group goals.[42]

A group clearly affects the behavior of its members. A member may conform to the wishes of the group simply because he or she wishes to remain a member. Groups interpret new information for their members, such as whether the proposed agency reorganization will be beneficial to the members. Groups have ambient stimuli that affect all members; these stimuli include the individuals of the group and the various aspects of its surroundings.[43] This might be considered the general personality, sometimes called the syntality, of the group.[44] Simply being in the presence of other members will have the effect of "psychological arousal" when one thinks the others have the potential for evaluating performance or behavior.[45] This arousal will stimulate a person to be deliberative or more conscious in selecting behaviors.

---

[40] See Dorwin Cartwright and Alvin Zander, eds., *Group Dynamics: Research and Theory*, 3d. ed. (New York: Harper and Row, 1968).

[41] Rensis Likert, *New Patterns of Management* (New York: McGraw-Hill, 1961); pp. 29–34.

[42] See Peter M. Blau, *The Dynamics of Bureaucracy: A Study of Interpersonal Relations in Two Government Agencies* (Chicago: University of Chicago Press, 1955); Cartwright and Zander, *Group Dynamics;* Stanley E. Seashore, *Group Cohesiveness in the Industrial Work Group*, (Ann Arbor: Survey Research Center, Institute for Social Research, University of Michigan, 1954); Ivan D. Steiner, *Group Process and Productivity* (New York: Academic, 1972), pp. 161–163; and David B. Truman, *The Governmental Process: Political Interests and Public Opinion* (New York: Knopf, 1962).

[43] Hackman, "Group Influences on Individuals," pp. 1457–1458.

[44] Raymond B. Cattell, "Concepts and Methods in the Measurement of Group Syntality," *Psychological Review*, 55 (1948):48–63.

[45] Robert B. Zajonc, "The Requirements and Design of a Standard Group Task," *Journal of Experimental Social Psychology*, 1 (1965):71–88; Robert B. Zajonc, "Social Facilitation," *Science*, 149 (1965):269–274; and Robert B. Zajonc and Stephen M. Sales, "Social Facilitation of Dominant and Subordinate Responses," *Journal of Experimental Social Psychology*, 2 (1966):160–168.

Discretionary stimuli are selective in that they are directed at individual members in the group.[46] These stimuli can be thought of as the rewards and penalties meted out to individuals. Penalties—actual and threatened—are used to reduce the probability of deviant behavior. Skinner's operant conditioning stresses the importance of positive reinforcement. "The reinforcing consequences generated by the group easily exceed the sums of the consequences which could be achieved by the members acting separately. The total reinforcing effect is enormously increased."[47]

This influence of the group on an individual creates tension and anxiety when an individual is part of two or more groups that expect different types of behavior. One group may penalize the individual and another group might reward the individual for the same behavior. One's willingness to work during the lunch hour, for example, may be supported by one group and opposed by another. This situation is known as role conflict.

Effects of Leadership

One of the most important roles to be played in a group is that of leader, and much research has been devoted to leadership and power.[48] Both of these are relational concepts, namely how people relate to each other in a social context. "Power" usually is considered as the ability of one person to influence the behavior of another or to have control over another. Leadership often is seen as the ability to move a group toward its goals. A leader stimulates action by the group through the exercise of power, of which there are at least five types.[49] 1) Reward power involves the ability to dispense or withhold tangible and intangible things valued by a group member.[50] 2) Coercive power is the ability to compel a group member to behave in a way desired by the leader. 3) Referent power is based on the desire of a group member to behave like the leader (to model oneself

---

[46] Hackman, "Group Influences on Individuals," pp. 1473–1495.

[47] B. F. Skinner, *Science and Human Behavior* (New York: Free Press, 1953), p. 312.

[48] For reviews of leadership literature, see Victor H. Vroom, "Leadership," in Dunnette, ed., *Handbook of Industrial and Organizational Psychology*, pp. 1527–1551; Ralph M. Stogdill, *Handbook of Leadership* (New York: Free Press, 1974); and Jeffrey C. Barrow, "The Variables of Leadership: A Review and Conceptual Framework," *Academy of Management Review*, 2 (1977):231–251. See also Chris Argyris, *Increasing Leadership Effectiveness* (New York: Wiley and Sons, 1976); Alvin W. Gouldner, ed., *Studies in Leadership: Leadership and Democratic Action* (New York: Harper and Brothers, 1950); and Luigi Petrullo and Bernard M. Bass, eds., *Leadership and Interpersonal Behavior* (New York: Holt, Rinehart, and Winston, 1961).

[49] The typology is from John R. P. French, Jr., and Bertram H. Raven, "The Bases of Social Power," in Dorwin Cartwright, ed., *Studies in Social Power* (Ann Arbor: Institute for Social Research, University of Michigan, 1959).

[50] See T. L. Jacobs, *Leadership and Exchange in Formal Organizations* (Alexandria, Virginia: Human Resources Research Organization, 1971).

after the leader).[51] 4) Expert power comes with having knowledge unavailable to others; the leader is respected for technical competence.[52] 5) Legitimate power involves the acceptance by group members of the idea that a leader has a right to issue instructions and that the members have the obligation to follow those instructions.[53]

This last power, legitimate power, is equivalent or closely related to what others call "authority," and problems arise in the application of the concept to organizational behavior. In a government agency, a bureau chief has organizational authority to supervise employees to accomplish whatever tasks are expected of the unit. The chief is likely to have at least some legitimate power, in that subordinates accept the chief's role as a superior. At the same time, the informal work group may have its own leader, who is different from the bureau chief. An informal leader emerges who has not been selected by the organization. Michels has suggested an "iron law of oligarchy," namely that in any social setting one or a few individuals will emerge as having greater power.[54] The result can be dual leadership, in which there is an ascribed leader who holds a position designated as supervisor and an achieved leader, one who has emerged from the group as a leader. There is obvious potential for conflict between these leaders.[55]

If managers or supervisors are expected by the organization to perform leadership roles, a question arises about what specifically is to be done. Barnard, in his classic work *The Functions of the Executive*, saw the leader as providing technical and moral competence.[56] Barnard and others have emphasized that the leader is responsible for overseeing workers so that essential activities are completed; leadership is considered critical in meeting organizational goals. The leader also is responsible for overseeing interpersonal relationships, especially coordinating workers and resolving conflicts among them. Motivating

---

[51] See, for example, Howard M. Wiess, "Subordinate Imitation of Supervisor Behavior: The Role of Modeling in Organizational Socialization," *Organizational Behavior and Human Performance*, 19 (1977):89–105.

[52] See Victor A. Thompson, *Modern Organization: A General Theory* (New York: Knopf, 1961). Thompson suggests that managers are expected to be technically competent in an era when it is impossible for any one individual to be fully cognizant of highly technical subjects.

[53] See David M. Herold, "Two-Way Influence Process in Leader-Follower Dyads," *Academy of Management Journal*, 20 (1977):224–237.

[54] Robert Michels, *Political Parties: A Sociological Study of the Oligarchical Tendencies of Modern Democracy* (New York: Dover, 1959).

[55] Fisher, *Small Group Decision Making*, pp. 82–90; and Robert L. Peabody, *Organizational Authority: Superior-Subordinate Relationships in Three Public Service Organizations* (New York: Atherton, 1964).

[56] Chester I. Barnard, *The Functions of the Executive* (Cambridge, Mass.: Harvard University Press, 1938). See also William F. Whyte, *Streetcorner Society* (Chicago: University of Chicago Press, 1943) and Robert G. Lord, "Functional Leadership Behavior: Measurement and Relation to Social Power and Leadership Perception," *Administrative Science Quarterly*, 22 (1977):114–133.

workers to excel is assumed to be a major responsibility. One of the most important functions is to deal with the environment external to the work group. Groups have boundaries, and the leader deals with "boundary transactions."[57] Much of the leader's time is spent not with subordinates but rather with peers, superiors, and others external to the organization.[58] One of the most important aspects of this external function is obtaining resources (a budget) for the organizational unit. "The leader's job is to *test* the environment to find out which demands can become truly effective threats, to *change* the environment by finding allies and other sources of external support, and to *gird* his organization by creating the means and the will to withstand attacks."[59]

Since leadership is considered central to organizational effectiveness, research has concentrated upon finding what constitutes effective leadership. Trait theory was once popular, based on the idea that great leaders had common traits. Through the study of effective leaders, especially those who had influenced history, it was thought that common traits could be identified. Once these characteristics were identified, then managers could be selected "scientifically."

The trait approach has been abandoned in large part because of pioneering experimental research of the 1930s. Lippitt and White, under the direction of Lewin, experimented with alternative leadership styles in boys' groups.[60] The styles were autocratic, democratic, and laissez faire (freedom with little leadership direction or interest). Both morale and group performance were influenced by style; democratic leadership was particularly popular among the boys. The implication that was drawn from the research was that leadership style need not be inborn but could be selected to improve worker satisfaction and productivity.

During the 1940s and 1950s important leadership studies were conducted by researchers at Ohio State University and the University of Michigan.[61] Although important differences exist in their approaches to

---

[57] Gerald I. Susman, *Autonomy at Work: A Sociotechnical Analysis of Participative Management* (New York: Praeger, 1976).

[58] Morgan W. McCall, Jr., "Leadership Research: Choosing Gods and Devils on the Run," *Journal of Occupational Psychology*, 49 (1976):139–153.

[59] Philip Selznick, *Leadership in Administration: A Sociological Interpretation* (New York: Harper and Row, 1957), p. 145. See also Robert Dubin et al., *Leadership and Productivity* (Scranton, Pa.: Chandler, 1965).

[60] Kurt Lewin, Ronald Lippitt, and Ralph K. White, "Patterns of Aggressive Behavior in Experimentally Created 'Social Climates'," *Journal of Social Psychology*, 10 (1939):271–299; and Ronald Lippitt and Ralph K. White, "The 'Social Climate' of Children's Groups," in Roger G. Barker, Jacob S. Kounin, and Herbert F. Wright, eds., *Child Behavior and Development* (New York: McGraw-Hill, 1943), pp. 485–508.

[61] See Ralph M. Stogdill and Alvin E. Coons, eds., *Leader Behavior: Its Description and Measurement* (Columbus: Bureau of Business Research, Ohio State University, 1957), and Daniel Katz, Nathan Maccoby, and Nancy C. Morse, *Productivity, Supervision, and Morale in an Office Situation* (Ann Arbor: Survey Research Center, University of Michigan, 1950).

leadership, both groups focused upon two basic leadership styles. Leadership that concentrated attention upon organizing work and accomplishing tasks was labeled "initiating" at Ohio State and "job centered" at Michigan; "instrumental" also has been used to describe that leadership style. Leadership that showed concern for employee well-being was called "consideration" at Ohio State and "employee centered" at Michigan. The research of these groups and others who followed seemed to suggest that democratic, humane, or employee-concerned leadership increased worker satisfaction.

Likert, who directed much of the research at the University of Michigan, concluded that a new conceptualization of organizations was needed, along with a new approach to supervision.[62] Organizations should be seen as a series of hierarchical, overlapping groups. The supervisor/leader of one group was a subordinate/follower of a higher level group. The supervisor was seen as a "link pin" between groups. As for supervision, there were four styles, ranging from autocratic to employee-centered; the latter, called System 4, was seen as the most effective.

To some extent, democratic or participative leadership has become a dogma, but a lingering doubt remains about whether happy workers are necessarily productive workers.[63] An experimental study in the 1950s, for example, demonstrated that effective leaders are not always well liked by their subordinates.[64] Research today continues to show that democratic leadership is effective in some situations, but not in all. For instance, a study of professional employees found the initiating or somewhat autocratic style was a "pressure irritant" that tended to encourage employees to seek other employment.[65] Another recent study found that the consideration style is more beneficial in low-stress jobs than in high-stress jobs.[66] A study of police officers found that they preferred the initiating or structured style.[67]

One response to this uncertainty about the effectiveness of democratic leadership has been the "managerial grid" developed by Blake and

---

[62] Rensis Likert, *The Human Organization* (New York: McGraw-Hill, 1967) and Rensis Likert, *New Patterns of Management* (New York: McGraw-Hill, 1961).

[63] As an example of the faith in participative or democratic management, see William F. Dowling, "Consensus Management at Graphic Controls," *Organizational Dynamics*, 5 (Winter, 1977):22–47.

[64] Robert Bales, "The Equilibrium Problem in Small Groups," in Talcott Parsons, Robert F. Bales, and Edward A. Shils, eds., *Working Papers in the Theory of Action* (New York: Free Press, 1953).

[65] Robert H. Miles, "Leader Effectiveness in Small Bureaucracies," *Academy of Management Journal*, 20 (1977):238–250.

[66] Chester A. Schriesheim and Charles J. Murphy, "Relationships between Leader Behavior and Subordinate Satisfaction and Performance: A Test of Some Situational Moderators," *Journal of Applied Psychology*, 61 (1976):634–641.

[67] Arthur P. Brief, Ramon J. Aldag, and Richard A. Wallden, "Correlates of Supervisory Style among Policemen," *Criminal Justice and Behavior*, 3 (1976):263–271.

Mouton.[68] The grid is a matrix, with one axis ranging from low to high concern for production and the other axis from low to high concern for employees. Blake and Mouton were careful not to suggest that the high end of both scales, the so-called "9-9" style, was the ideal form of leadership, but "grid" training has typically attempted to instruct managers in being simultaneously concerned with the needs of the organization and the needs of employees.

Current approaches to leadership tend to stress its situational aspect, that one leadership style may be effective for one situation but not for others.[69] Research is concerned with identifying what styles are most effective in what situations. For example, it has been suggested that autocratic leadership may be most effective when employees do not seek self-actualization.[70] The situational concept is fundamental to Fiedler's contingency theory of leadership effectiveness.[71] The theory suggests that style depends upon the extent to which the leader has power, the tasks of the unit are unambiguous, and the leader and members have good relationships. Using these three sets of variables, eight combinations are derived, and Fiedler has suggested which style is most effective for each of the eight situations. For instance, when leader power is weak, the task is unstructured, and relations are good, then considerate or employee-centered style is appropriate; when power is strong, the task is unstructured, and relations are good, then structured leaderhip is needed. Research results have been mixed in substantiating Fiedler's theory.[72]

Vroom and Yetton have developed a normative model of leadership that attempts to provide explicit advice for managers on how to handle situations.[73] Without getting into the details of the model, it should be

---

[68] Robert R. Blake and Jane S. Mouton, "Managerial Facades," *Advanced Management Journal*, 31 (July, 1966):30–37; and Robert R. Blake and Jane S. Mouton, "An Overview of the Grid," *Training and Development Journal*, 29 (May, 1975):29–37.

[69] See Saul W. Gellerman, *Managers and Subordinates* (Hinsdale, Ill.: Dyrden, 1976); Arthur G. Jago and Victor H. Vroom, "Hierarchical Level and Leadership Style," *Organizational Behavior and Human Performance*, 18 (1977):131–145; and Terence R. Mitchell, James R. Larson, Jr., and Stephen G. Green, "Leader Behavior, Situational Moderators, and Group Performance: An Attributional Analysis," *Organizational Behavior and Human Performance*, 18 (1977):254–268.

[70] Chris Argyris, *Integrating the Individual and the Organization* (New York: Wiley and Sons, 1964).

[71] Fred E. Fiedler, *A Theory of Leadership Effectiveness* (New York: McGraw-Hill, 1967); Fred E. Fiedler, "Engineer the Job to Fit the Manager," *Harvard Business Review*, 43 (September–October, 1965):115–122.

[72] See Sally Coltrin and William F. Glueck, "The Effect of Leadership Roles on the Satisfaction and Productivity of University Research Professors," *Academy of Management Journal*, 20 (1977):101–116; Craig E. Schneier, "The Contingency Model of Leadership: An Extension to Emergent Leadership and Leader's Sex," *Organizational Behavior and Human Performance*, 21 (1978):220–239; and Robert P. Vecchio, "An Empirical Examination of the Validity of Fiedler's Model of Leadership Effectiveness," *Organizational Behavior and Human Performance*, 19 (1977):180–206.

[73] Victor H. Vroom and Philip W. Yetton, *Leadership and Decision-Making* (Pittsburgh: University of Pittsburgh Press, 1973).

noted that five different styles are included concerning the extent to which the manager should handle a situation with employee involvement. Like the Fiedler model, the normative model is concerned with whether the task is structured, but the Vroom-Yetton model also focuses on whether the manager has adequate information at hand without involving employees and whether employees have internalized the organization's goals.

A related contingency approach to leadership is path-goal theory.[74] Four different leadership styles are used by the theory: directive, supportive, participative, and achievement-oriented. Research has concentrated upon when a manager should use any of these styles. The theory assumes that a manager will use each style from time to time.

WORKER PERFORMANCE AND ORGANIZATIONAL CHANGE

Partially in response to criticisms that participative management may lose sight of organizational objectives, techniques have been developed that attempt to focus simultaneously upon worker needs and the needs of the organization. Leadership research has concentrated largely upon styles. Attempts have been made to identify which styles increase worker satisfaction and performance, but leadership styles are not the same as systematic management systems that can be implemented as agency policy. This section, therefore, considers more systematic approaches to managing. Management by objectives and organizational development are the main topics.

Management by Objectives

A basic premise of management by objectives, or MBO, is that managers should manage for results.[75] The beginning of MBO can be traced to the Dupont Company and General Motors following World War I.[76]

---

[74] Basil S. Georgopoulos, Gerald M. Mahoney, and Nyle W. Jones, "A Path-Goal Approach to Productivity," *Journal of Applied Psychology*, 41 (1957):345–353; Martin G. Evans, "The Effect of Supervisory Behavior on the Path-Goal Relationship," *Organizational Behavior and Human Performance*, 5 (1970):277–298; and Robert J. House, "A Path-Goal Theory of Leader Effectiveness," *Administrative Science Quarterly*, 16 (1971):321–338. See also Thomas C. Mawhinney and Jeffrey D. Ford, "The Path-Goal Theory of Leader Effectiveness: An Operant Interpretation," *Academy of Management Review*, 2 (1977):398–411; and Chester Schriesheim and Mary Ann Von Glinow, "The Path-Goal Theory of Leadership: A Theoretical and Empirical Analysis," *Academy of Management Journal*, 20 (1977):398–405.

[75] See Robert Hollman, "Applying MBO Research to Practice," *Human Resource Management*, 15 (Winter, 1976):28–36; John W. Humble, *Management by Objectives in Action* (New York: McGraw-Hill, 1970); Henry L. Tosi and Stephen Carroll, "Management by Objectives," *Personnel Administration*, 33 (July–August, 1970):44–48; and Fred Luthans, "How to Apply MBO," *Public Personnel Management*, 5 (1976):83–87.

[76] Peter F. Drucker, "What Results Should You Expect? A Users' Guide to MBO," *Public Administration Review*, 36 (1976):12.

Drucker in 1954 and McGregor in 1960 popularized the concept, followed by Odiorne in 1965.[77] By the 1970s, management by objectives had become a well-known concept in industry. In the federal government, MBO was introduced in the Department of Health, Education, and Welfare by Malek during the early years of the Nixon administration. Malek later became deputy director of the Office of Management and Budget, and in 1973 the system was promulgated for all major federal agencies.[78] That action had a ripple effect on state and local governments, which began efforts to use MBO.

There are several theoretical bases for management by objectives. One is that workers will tend to work harder when they have internalized the organization's goals. If a worker understands how a set of activities will lead toward goal attainment and the goal is perceived as legitimate, the worker will become motivated. Ryan has suggested that behavior is purposive; once workers have accepted goals, activity will continue until the goals are accomplished.[79] Locke has shown that, when difficult goals are suggested to people and they accept those goals, performance will tend to be higher than it would have been had less difficult goals been established.[80] Additionally, Locke has maintained that people will set goals for themselves if none are supplied by the organization. Management by objectives, sometimes called "goal-setting," therefore, attempts to use a process by which goals are established for workers.

MBO defies an explicit explanation of the process involved, because many variations exist. However, all such systems begin with the identification of goals and/or objectives. Some systems use these terms interchangeably, while others reserve the term "goal" for long-range desired

---

[77] Peter F. Drucker, *The Practice of Management* (New York: Harper and Brothers, 1954); Douglas McGregor, *The Human Side of Enterprise;* and George Odiorne, *Management by Objectives* (New York: Pitman, 1965).

[78] Rodney H. Brady, "MBO Goes to Work in the Public Sector," *Harvard Business Review*, 51 (March–April, 1973):65–74; Robert W. Fri, "How to Manage the Government for Results: The Rise of MBO," *Organizational Dynamics*, 2 (1974):19–33; John S. Jun, *Management by Objectives in Government: Theory and Practice* (Beverly Hills, Calif.: Sage, 1976); John S. Jun, ed., "Symposium on Management by Objectives in the Public Sector," *Public Administration Review*, 36 (1976):1–45; Fred V. Malek, "Managing for Results in the Federal Government," *Business Horizons*, 17 (April, 1974):23–28; Dale D. McConkey, "Applying Management by Objectives to Non-Profit Organizations," *SAM Advanced Management Journal*, 38 (January, 1973):10–20; and Edward J. Ryan, Jr., "Federal Government MBO: Another Managerial Fad?" *MSU Business Topics*, 24 (Autumn, 1976):35–43.

[79] Thomas A. Ryan, *Intentional Behavior* (New York: Roland, 1970).

[80] Edwin A. Locke, "Toward a Theory of Task Motivation and Incentives," *Organizational Behavior and Human Performance*, 3 (1968):157–189; Edwin A. Locke, Norman Cartledge, and Claramae S. Knerr, "Studies of the Relationship between Satisfaction, Goal-Setting, and Performance," *Organizational Behavior and Human Peformance*, 5 (1970):484–500; and Edwin A. Locke and Judith F. Bryan, "Performance Goals as Determinants of Level of Performance and Boredom," *Journal of Applied Psychology*, 51 (1967):120–130.

states and "objectives" for short-range measurable events. An operational MBO system establishes measurable results to be accomplished within a specified time period, often a year. The process encourages planning, since in setting goals/objectives one must consider what is feasible within the next twelve months. Individual worker autonomy or group autonomy can be increased when there is agreement on what is to be accomplished within that time period. Under MBO, work units have objectives, and these are factored into objectives for each employee. This allows individuals to know what is expected of them, thereby increasing role clarity.[81]

There are differing opinions about how objectives are to be established. The top-down approach has top-level management set overall objectives for each major unit, and these are factored into subobjectives for subunits and ultimately into objectives for individual workers. Such an approach is seen as being appropriate, given management's responsibility to manage.[82] The opposing view is that a top-down system can be detrimental in reducing worker autonomy, in blocking worker drives for self-actualization. The alternative is a bottom-up approach, in which objectives originally are proposed by employees to their supervisors, and then workers and supervisors negotiate an agreement on objectives. The process continues up the organizational hierarchy. MBO is seen as a form of decentralization, allowing considerable worker independence and encouraging the satisfaction of higher level needs as defined by Maslow.[83] Critics of that approach suggest that suboptimization is likely, namely that lower units will perform according to their needs and not the needs of the organization as a whole.

Regardless of whether a top-down or bottom-up approach is used, face-to-face interaction between supervisor and employee is stressed by MBO systems. In the top-down approach, the manager discusses with each employee what is expected to be accomplished in the coming year. It is assumed that the employee will gain a better understanding of his or her role and will internalize the organization's goals/objectives. The bottom-up approach emphasizes greater employee participation, presumably increasing the likelihood that employees will accept objectives that are beneficial to the organization. Available research seems to indicate that

---

[81] See Henry L. Tosi and Stephen J. Carroll, "Managerial Reaction to Management by Objectives," *Academy of Management Journal*, 11 (1968):415–426.

[82] Fred Luthans, *Organizational Behavior*, 2d ed. (New York: McGraw-Hill, 1977): p. 486. See discussion of top-down approach to organizational design in Chapter 3.

[83] John C. Aplin, Jr. and Peter P. Schoderbek, "MBO: Requisites for Success in the Public Sector," *Human Resource Management*, 15 (Summer, 1976):30–36; George S. Odiorne, "MBO in State Government," *Public Administration Review*, 36 (1976):28–33; Donald Timm et al., "Impact of Management by Objectives on Maslow's Need Hierarchy: An Empirical Study," *Psychological Reports*, 40 (1977):71–74.

participation in goal setting is most likely to enhance performance when employees have been accustomed to participation in general.[84]

An important element of management by objectives is feedback. Periodic reviews are made of performance. Employees who have not met their objectives are expected to explain why. Management is expected to help identify what problems each employee has in meeting objectives and help the employee overcome those problems through employee development plans that give special emphasis to training.[85] In many private corporations MBO is closely tied to performance appraisal.[86] Rather than evaluating workers on the basis of initiative, enthusiasm, or other traits, employees are evaluated in terms of whether they accomplish the tasks expected of them. Part of the feedback also involves decisions on pay and promotions.[87] The Scanlon plan, used in industry, provides financial rewards for productive workers and encourages employees to suggest changes that will increase productivity.[88] Under management by objectives, employees who can meet difficult objectives will have an advantage in gaining promotions. Once the performance in meeting objectives has been reviewed with the worker, the cycle is repeated. New objectives or targets are set, performance is monitored, and feedback is provided.

MBO systems have different orientations, depending upon the organizational locus of responsibility. Where management by objectives has been introduced through the personnel system, emphasis usually is upon the performance of individual workers. A complaint about this approach is that agency management largely ignores the process in making important decisions. The other orientation is to use MBO as a decision process, and that type of system usually is under the direct control of top management. Government has tended to use this approach, with MBO being handled by an agency head or possibly the agency or government budget office. Government MBO systems have placed less emphasis upon individual objectives and accomplishments and more emphasis on organizational unit performance.

---

[84] Edwin A. Locke, "Personnnel Attitudes and Motivation," *Annual Review of Psychology*, 26 (1975):467.

[85] Michael Beer and Robert A. Ruh, "Employee Growth Through Performance Management," *Harvard Business Review*, 54 (July–August, 1976):59–66.

[86] L. L. Cummings and Donald P. Schwab, *Performance in Organizations: Determinants and Appraisal* (Glenview, Ill.: Scott, Foresman, 1973).

[87] Stuart Murray and Tom Kuffel, "MBO and Performance Linked Compensation in the Public Sector," *Public Personnel Management*, 7 (1978):171–176; Robert L. Taylor and Robert A. Zawacki, "Collaborative Goal Setting in Performance Appraisal: A Field Experiment," *Public Personnel Management*, 7 (1978):162–170; and James Terborg and Howard E. Miller, "Motivation, Behavior, and Performance: A Closer Examination of Goal Setting and Monetary Incentives," *Journal of Applied Psychology*, 63 (1978):29–39.

[88] Cummings and Molloy, *Improving Productivity and the Quality of Working Life*, pp. 235–260; and Paul S. Goodman and Brian E. Moore, "Factors Affecting Acquisition of Beliefs about a New Reward System," *Human Relations*, 29 (1976):571–588.

Implementing management by objectives is more difficult in government than in private corporations.[89] Governments tend to have less freedom in personnel decisions. Government workers typically cannot be readily fired for failing to reach objectives, nor can promotions and salary increases be awarded simply because objectives have been met. (Greater flexibility in these areas was provided for the federal government by the civil service reforms of 1978.) Establishing explicit objectives is complicated because governmental objectives usually are less tangible.[90] Government lacks simple measures, such as increasing sales volume, the percentage of a market, or the return on investments. Unlike the private sector, government produces few tangible products, and government decision systems are more diffuse, so that it is difficult to obtain a fixed commitment to specified objectives.

One problem shared by government and industry is excessive paperwork. If objectives are made explicit under MBO, considerable paperwork will be generated. The complaint arises that employees are too busy filling in forms, so that little time is available for productive work. At the federal level, management by objectives was introduced in a way intended to avoid such paperwork. Agencies prepared only "presidential objectives" for review by the Office of Management and Budget. A criticism of that process, however, was that objectives became vague and lost all utility.

Whether management by objectives produces the intended results is uncertain. MBO in industry has received mixed reviews.[91] A survey of the nation's largest corporations found relatively few were using the system throughout their organizations.[92] The record of MBO in government probably has been even less encouraging, although no systematic analysis of MBO efforts is available. At the federal level, management by objectives has continued in some agencies during the Carter administration but has not been given high visibility. A quiet death has come to many state and local MBO efforts.

Management by objectives has been discussed here because it is based largely upon motivational theory, but there are other techniques

---

[89] John C. Aplin, Jr. and Peter P. Schoderbek, "How to Measure MBO," *Public Personnel Management*, 5 (1976):88–95.

[90] See *The Work Measure System of the Department of Housing and Urban Development Has Potential but Needs Further Work to Increase Its Reliability* (Washington: General Accounting Office, 1977).

[91] John M. Ivancevich, "Different Goal Setting Treatments and Their Effects on Performance and Job Satisfaction," *Academy of Management Journal*, 20 (1977):406–419; Locke, "Personal Attitudes and Motivation," pp. 465–468; and Henry Tosi et al., "How Real are Changes Induced by Management by Objectives?" *Administrative Science Quarterly*, 21 (1976):276–306.

[92] Fred E. Schuster and Alva F. Kindall, "Management by Objectives: Where We Stand—A Survey of the Fortune 500," *Human Resource Management*, 13 (Spring, 1974):8–11.

and management processes that should be mentioned since they also focus upon objectives or results. The difference is that these other techniques place less emphasis on employee motivation.[93] One of these techniques is program evaluation, which attempts to determine whether government programs accomplish what is expected of them; cost-benefit and cost-effectiveness analysis are specific techniques utilized in program evaluation.[94] Program budgeting, or what was called planning-programming budgeting (PPB) in the 1960s, uses the budget process to relate costs with program accomplishments; funds are allocated in terms of achieving desired objectives.[95] Zero base budgeting (ZBB), popular during the Carter administration, makes the assumption that programs should not necessarily continue over time; emphasis is upon identifying low-priority programs whose budgets can be reduced or entirely eliminated. 'Productivity' is another term that has been popular in the public sector.[96] Generally, productivity improvement efforts are aimed at providing increased levels of work and work output with no increase in the use of resources, particularly human resources. Some productivity improvement efforts are linked with wage incentive systems and because of that might be considered a form of Taylorism.[97] All of these techniques—program evaluation, program budgeting, zero base budgeting, and productivity—tend to de-emphasize the roles of individuals. In recent years, however, there has been a concern about whether productivity improvements can be achieved while improving the quality of working life (QWL).[98]

---

[93] For a discussion of the following techniques, see Robert D. Lee, Jr., and Ronald W. Johnson, *Public Budgeting Systems*, 2d ed. (Baltimore: University Park Press, 1977).

[94] Theodore H. Poister, *Public Program Analysis: Applied Research Methods* (Baltimore: University Park Press, 1978).

[95] Bruce H. De Woolfson, Jr., "Public Sector MBO and PPB: Cross Fertilization in Management Systems," *Public Administration Review*, 35 (1975):387–395.

[96] Walter L. Balk, ed., "Symposium on Productivity in Government," *Public Administration Review*, 38 (1978):1–50; Gilbert W. Fairholm, "Productivity Improvement," *State Government*, 50 (1977):170–178; Nancy S. Hayward, "The Productivity Challenge," *Public Administration Review*, 36 (1976):544–550; Joint Financial Management Improvement Program, *Productivity Programs in the Federal Government* (Washington: Government Printing Office, 1976); Chester A. Newland, ed., "Symposium on Productivity in Government," *Public Administration Review*, 32 (1972):739–850; and *The Status of Productivity Measurement in State Government: An Initial Examination* (Washington: Urban Institute, 1975).

[97] National Commission on Productivity and Work Quality, *Employee Incentives to Improve State and Local Government Productivity* (Washington: Government Printing Office, 1975); Paul D. Staudohar, "An Experiment in Increasing Productivity of Police Service Employees," *Public Administration Review*, 35 (1975):518–522; and Frederick C. Thayer, "Productivity: Taylorism Revisited (Round Three)," *Public Administration Review*, 32 (1972):833–840.

[98] The National Center for Productivity and Quality of Working Life served as a focal point for productivity research until it was phased out of existence in September, 1978.

Organization Development

Like management by objectives and job enrichment, organization development, or OD, is an approach to changing organizations.[99] It has been defined as a process aimed at "increasing the ability of the organization to do more effectively what it is mandated to do—perform its work."[100] It can be considered an intervention strategy whereby existing methods of operation are examined in order to find better or improved methods.[101] Organizational change is considered essential, given the need to respond to a continuously changing environment. An organization that is static will become antiquated, and so there is a need for continuous renewal. OD specialists, therefore, stress that a long-range commitment to ongoing change must be made.

The underlying premise of OD is that change comes about through a learning process. Lewin's field theory suggests that vectors push people in certain directions. Organization development maintains that vectors that encourage the individual to learn should be strengthened and those that discourage learning should be muted. The process is seen as "unfreezing" mind-sets, moving the individual to a new learning mind-set, and then "re-freezing" the vectors so that learning continues at an increased level.

---

[99] Richard Beckhard, *Organization Development: Strategies and Models* (Reading, Mass.: Addison-Wesley, 1969); Michael Beer, "The Technology of Organization Development," in Dunnette, ed., *Handbook of Industrial and Organizational Psychology*, pp. 937–993; Warren G. Bennis et al., eds., *The Planning Change*, 3d ed. (New York: Holt, Rinehart, and Winston, 1976); Warren G. Bennis, "Theory and Method in Applying Behavioral Science to Planned Organizational Change," *Journal of Applied Behavioral Science*, 1 (1965):337–360; Edward J. Giblin, "Organization Development: Public Sector Theory and Practice," *Public Personnel Management*, 5 (1976):108–119; Robert T. Golembiewski, *Renewing Organizations: The Laboratory Approach to Planned Change* (Itasca, Ill.: Peacock, 1972); Roger J. Goodman, "Change and the Public Personnel Manager," *Public Personnel Management*, 5 (1976):103–107; Roger J. Goodman, "Public Personnel Administration Requires an OD Effort," *Public Personnel Management*, 7 (1978):192–197; Katz and Kahn, *The Social Psychology of Organizations*, pp. 390–451; Larry Kirkhart and Neely Gardner, eds., "Symposium on Organization Development," *Public Administration Review*, 34 (1974):97–140; T. Roger Manley and Charles W. McNichols, "OD at a Major Government Research Laboratory," *Public Personnel Management*, 6 (1977):51–60; Newton Margulies, "Organizational Development and Changes in Organization Climate," *Public Personnel Management*, 2 (1973):84–92; Newton Margulies and Anthony P. Raia, *Organizational Development: Values, Process, and Technology* (New York: McGraw-Hill, 1972); Lloyd A. Rowe and William B. Boise, eds., *Organizational and Managerial Innovation: A Reader* (Pacific Palisades, Calif.: Goodyear, 1973); D. D. Warrick, "Applying OD to the Public Sector," *Public Personnel Management*, 5 (1976):186–190; Robert A. Zawacki and D. D. Warrick, eds., *Organization Development: Managing Change in the Public Sector* (Chicago: International Personnel Management Association, 1976).

[100] Edward J. Giblin, "Organization Development: Public Sector Theory and Practice," *Public Personnel Management*, 5 (1976):108.

[101] See Chris Argyris, *Intervention Theory and Method: A Behavior Science View* (Reading, Mass.: Addison-Wesley, 1970); Chris Argyris, *Organization and Innovation* (Homewood, Ill.: Irwin, 1965); and Evert Van DeVliert, "Inconsistencies in the Argyris Intervention Theory," *Journal of Applied Behavioral Science*, 13 (1977):557–564.

This may be considered a strategy to release creativity in employees.[102] Rogers, another important contributor to OD theory, stressed that individuals seek learning when they accept that concept or internalize it.[103] In other words, participation by employees is assumed to be essential for organizational change. In the 1940s Coch and French experimented with alternative approaches to change and came to the conclusion that worker resistance could be overcome through participation.[104]

Organizational development normally is considered to have emerged almost accidentally from the work of Lewin, Lippitt, Bradford, and Benne in a 1946 laboratory training session in Connecticut.[105] Lewin, who had established the Research Center for Group Dynamics at the Massachusetts Institute of Technology, was conducting a training program for community leaders and was approached by the participants for permission to attend a meeting of the training staff concerning their observations on how the group members were interacting. The participants were allowed to attend the meeting, and the result was seen as positive, namely that members received feedback on their performance. The following year, the National Training Laboratory (NTL) was established in Bethel, Maine, and since that time the laboratory training approach has gained great prominence. A similar movement emerged at about the same time in England at the Tavistock Institute.

Numerous techniques are associated, directly or indirectly, with organization development. Sensitivity training has been one of the most popular aspects of OD. Other techniques to be discussed here include transactional analysis, survey feedback, and team building.

The laboratory approach uses sensitivity training or encounter groups or T-groups (the T is for "training"). Individuals leave their normal work settings to spend a weekend or longer in residence at a

---

[102] Kurt Lewin, *Field Theory and Social Science* (New York: Harper and Brothers, 1951). See also Kurt W. Back, *Beyond Words: The Story of Sensitivity Training and the Encounter Movement* (Baltimore: Penquin, 1973), pp. 103–116; Frank Friedlander, "OD Reaches Adolescence: An Exploration of Its Underlying Values," *Journal of Applied Behavioral Science*, 12 (1976): 7–20; Neely Gardner, "Action Training and Research: Something Old and Something New," *Public Administration Review*, 34 (1974):106–115; Robert T. Golembiewski, "Organization Development in Public Agencies: Perspectives on Theory and Practice," *Public Administration Review*, 29 (1969):367–377; C. M. Hampden-Turner, "An Existential 'Learning Theory' and the Integration of T-Group Research," *Journal of Applied Behavioral Science*, 2 (1966):367–386; and Edgar H. Schein and Warren G. Bennis, *Personal and Organizational Change Through Group Methods: The Laboratory Approach* (New York: Wiley and Sons, 1965), pp. 269–337.

[103] Carl Rogers, *Client Centered Therapy* (New York: Houghton-Mifflin, 1951).

[104] Lester Coch and John R. P. French, Jr., "Overcoming Resistance to Change," *Human Relations*, 1 (1948):512–532, and Godfrey Gardner, "Worker's Participation: A Critical Evaluation of Coch and French," *Human Relations*, 30 (1977):1071–1078.

[105] See Warren G. Bennis, *Organization Development: Its Nature, Origins, and Prospects* (Reading, Mass.: Addison-Wesley, 1969); Back, *Beyond Words;* and Ned Levine and Cary L. Cooper, "T-Groups—Twenty Years On: A Prophecy," *Human Relations*, 29 (1976):1–23.

training center. Group size varies, but often there are about ten members in a group. In its "pure" form, sensitivity training is unstructured, unlike other forms of training where participants might be expected to learn specific bodies of knowledge. The absence of structure creates a social vacuum; people are together with no assigned tasks.[106] The vacuum, being uncomfortable to the group members, stimulates group discussion. Emphasis is given to becoming sensitive or aware of how one views oneself and how others view each other. Authenticity in interpersonal relations is stressed, so that members are encouraged to say what they think of each other.[107] The objective is not to get all group members to like each other but rather to learn to respect each other as individuals. OD specialists differentiate their work from group therapy. Whereas therapy focuses largely on the past, sensitivity training concentrates on the "here and now." In a T-group, Ms. A is encouraged to describe how she feels about Mr. B's behavior in the group.

While laboratory training does not strive for building friendships among the members of the group, supportive relationships are expected to emerge, and it is assumed that these will encourage creativity. Members are encouraged to give and receive feedback. Feedback should be immediate; a member should not wait an hour or more before saying that a comment made by another was annoying. The feedback should avoid value judgments of right and wrong and emphasize emotional reactions, such as anger or pleasure. The receiver of the feedback needs to learn to listen attentively.[108] From this type of feedback, members develop a sense of belonging and trust and learn to respect each other. This supportive atmosphere will encourage members to explore new ideas and feelings—the presumed key to learning.[109]

There are great variations among T-groups concerning the types of participants and the purposes of the training. Some sensitivity groups focus primarily upon the individual, seeking to "unleash" human potentials.[110] For these types of groups, participants normally do not know each other before beginning the session and normally pay their own

[106] Kenneth D. Benne, Leland P. Bradford, and Ronald Lippitt, "The Laboratory Method," in Leland P. Bradford, Jack R. Gibb, and Kenneth D. Benne, eds., *T-Group Theory and Laboratory Method: Innovation in Re-Education* (New York: Wiley and Sons, 1964), pp. 15–44.

[107] W. Warner Burke, "Changing Trends in Organization Development," in W. Warner Burke, ed., *Current Issues and Strategies in Organization Development* (New York: Human Sciences, 1977), pp. 26–29.

[108] Walter R. Mead, "Feedback: A 'How to' Primer for T-Group Participants," in Robert T. Golembiewski and Arthur Blumberg, eds., *Sensitivity Training and the Laboratory Approach: Readings about Concepts and Applications*, 3d ed., (Itasca, Ill.: Peacock, 1977), pp. 66–69.

[109] Argyris, *Organization and Innovation*.

[110] Techniques include Rolfing, bioenergetics, psychosynthesis, biofeedback, and transcendental meditation.

training fees. T-groups that are part of organization development, however, tend to stress developing interpersonal competencies in a group setting. A corporation may pay to have its mid-level managers attend a laboratory training program for the purpose of learning to deal more effectively with each other and with others in the organization.

Increasing emphasis is being given to "family group" sensitivity training in response to complaints that training one strata of workers may produce negligible results. If only junior-level supervisors, for instance, receive this training, they will have difficulty applying their new capabilities because the rest of the organization has been left unchanged. The family group is the work group, involving all of the personnel in a given organizational unit. OD specialists claim that focusing upon the family group will create a better organizational climate.

Besides having members simply talk with one another, sensitivity training can use other techniques. Members may act out a skit (role playing), and then discuss their views of what occurred. The group may be periodically broken into two-person groups where members interview each other. Members may be temporarily removed from their groups and reassigned to other ones. Physical contact among the members may be used as a means of breaking down psychological interpersonal barriers. So-called "trust falls" are used, where a member falls backward into the arms of another. Interspersed among the informal sessions may be more structured lectures on group behavior.[111]

The role of the trainer is pivotal in a sensitivity group. The trainer is seen as a change agent who is the catalyst for getting the members to abandon set ways and explore alternatives. The trainer can be largely nondirective; the feedback that is provided is largely of an inquiring nature. The trainer might ask a member why she said what she did or why she has said nothing. Other trainers take a more directive approach, perhaps telling one member that what he has said has hurt the feelings of others. OD consultants frequently contend that the success of their methodology is dependent upon having the trainer come from outside the organization. However, increasing use is being made of internal personnel. A consultant might be the primary trainer at the outset, but, as the group experience continues, the manager in a "family group" can assume the role of change agent.[112]

---

[111] Arthur H. Kuriloff, *Organizational Development for Survival* (New York: American Management Association, 1972), pp. 125–138; and Kenneth D. Benne, Leland P. Bradford, and Ronald Lippitt, "Designing the Laboratory," in Bradford, Gibb, and Benne, *T-Group Theory and Laboratory Method*, pp. 45–79.

[112] Burke, "Changing Trends in Organization Development"; Frank Friedlander and L. Dave Brown, "Organization Development," *Annual Review of Psychology*, 25 (1974):316; Norma B. Gluckstern and Ralph W. Packard, "The Internal-External Change-Agent Team: Bringing Change to a 'Closed Institution'," *Journal of Applied Behavioral Science*, 13 (1977):14–52; and David C. Lundgren and Catherine Schaeffer, "Feedback Processes in Sensitivity Training Groups," *Human Relations*, 29 (1976):763–782.

Transactional analysis (TA), while not specifically a part of organization development, is a technique that can be utilized. In *Games People Play* and *The Structure and Dynamics of Organizations and Groups*, Berne has translated Freudian psychology into a group framework.[113] Freud's id becomes Berne's child; the ego becomes a parent; and the superego becomes an adult. TA is concerned with how people relate to each other. The actions may be complementary, as in the case of Mr. A and Mr. B each acting as an adult. In other instances, Mr. A may act as parent and Mr. B as child. A seeming assumption of TA is that training should strive to have members relate to each other as adults, although Berne suggests that all of us at some time need to act as parents and children. Harris, using Berne's transactional analysis, has contended that as a child, one has a negative image of self ("I'm not OK") and a positive image of adults ("You're OK").[114] Training, then, should concentrate upon learning to accept oneself, resulting in the improved interpersonal relationship of "I'm OK, You're OK." What might be considered an offshoot of transactional analysis is assertiveness training, which is aimed at teaching people to demand their own rights and not to be submissive, while at the same time respecting the rights of others.[115]

Survey feedback is another technique of organization development but it is different from the laboratory approach of sensitivity training. Survey feedback begins with consultants obtaining information about the organization, usually by administering questionnaires to managers and employees. The questionnaire concentrates upon satisfaction/dissatisfaction with how the agency operates; the organizational climate is identified through this process. The consultants use work groups to feedback the information. In this process, problems are identified and solutions presumably emerge. "Fishbowling" may be used, in which Work Group 1 discusses its reactions to work Group 2 while that group watches; then Work Group 2 fishbowls before Work Group 1. In other

---

[113] Eric Berne, *Games People Play: The Psychology of Human Relationships* (New York: Grove, 1964) and Eric Berne, *The Structure and Dynamics of Organizations and Groups* (New York: Grove, 1963). See also Thomas C. Clary, "Motivation through Positive Stroking," *Public Personnel Management*, 2 (1973):113–117; Thomas C. Clary and Erica W. Clary, "Organizational Analysis with Results Using Transactional Analysis," *Training and Development Journal*, 30 (September, 1976):18–24; and James H. Morrison and John J. O'Hearne, *Practical Transactional Analysis in Management* (Reading, Mass.: Addison-Wesley, 1977).

[114] Thomas A. Harris, *I'm OK, You're OK: A Practical Guide to Transactional Analysis* (New York: Harper and Row, 1969).

[115] George R. Bach and Herb Goldberg, *Creative Aggression* (Garden City, N.Y.: Doubleday, 1974); James G. Hollandsworth, Jr., and Kathleen E. Wall, "Sex Differences in Assertive Behavior: An Empirical Investigation," *Journal of Counseling Psychology*, 24 (1977):217–222; Michael Korda, *Power!* (New York: Random House, 1975); Robert J. Ringer, *Winning Through Intimidation* (New York: Fawcett World, 1976); and Malcolm E. Shaw and Pearl Rutledge, "Assertiveness Training for Managers," *Training and Development Journal*, 30 (September, 1976):8–14.

words, the emphasis is on intergroup relations.[116] Fishbowling also can be used for improving relations between a work group and clients, as in the case of social workers and welfare clients.

Team-building in organization development stresses problem solving over interpersonal relations. Although team-building may use sensitivity training as part of the overall strategy, concentration is upon identifying and resolving problems of the organization. Survey feedback may be used to collect and critique data, but team-building takes the additional step of developing a plan of action for resolving the problems. Concentration is on how workers relate to each other as a team in carrying out the organizational unit's responsibilities.[117]

It must be asked whether organizational development accomplishes what it is supposed to accomplish and whether there are negative effects as well as positive ones. On the negative side, there has been continuous concern that OD is manipulative, that management may use it to the detriment of the individual. Sensitivity training has been seen as potentially dangerous in that the intensive peer pressures of the group can upset the mental stability of individuals; problems can arise that the trainers are not suited to handle and that can best be handled by persons trained in psychotherapy. Also, organization development, and particularly sensitivity training, has acquired a "kooky" reputation. A common criticism is that when OD stresses psychological aspects of behavior, there is a tendency to use "touchy-feely" training techniques that are of dubious utility.

Evaluation results have not been clear about whether or not OD is effective in bringing about organizational change.[118] The effectiveness of OD must be considered undetermined, because few thorough evaluations have been conducted. Persons completing sensitivity training may look favorably upon their cathartic experience, but there is justification to doubt whether that experience had an effect upon their work behavior.[119]

---

[116] Friedlander and Brown, "Organization Development," pp. 326–327; and Clayton P. Alderfer, "Organization Development," *Annual Review of Psychology*, 28 (1977):206–207.

[117] Alderfer, "Organization Development," pp. 205–206; Friedlander and Brown, "Organization Development," pp. 328–331; and William C. Giegold and Richard J. Dunsing, "Team Building in the Local Jurisdiction: Two Case Studies," *Public Administration Review*, 38 (1978):59–63.

[118] Alderfer, "Organization Development," pp. 210–220; Beer, "The Technology of Organization Development"; John P. Campbell and Marvin D. Dunnette, "Effectiveness of T-Group Experiences in Managerial Training and Development," *Psychological Bulletin*, 70 (1968):73–104; Jerome L. Franklin, "Characteristics of Successful and Unsuccessful Organization Development," *Journal of Applied Behavioral Science*, 12 (1976):471–492; Friedlander and Brown, "Organization Development," pp. 332–336; and Sam E. White and Terence R. Mitchell, "Organization Development: A Review of Research Content and Research Design," *Academy of Management Review*, 1 (1976):57–73.

[119] Daniel L. Kegan, "Perceived Effects of Sensitivity Training: Samples of Police Officers, College Students, and a Group Dynamics Class," *Small Group Behavior*, 7 (1976):131–146.

As has been seen, OD concentrates upon encouraging people to be creative or innovative, but it is not known whether innovative ideas can be absorbed by organizations. It is highly possible that the best ideas generated through OD are never used by agencies. Also, organization development literature is largely silent on the issue of power and authority. A person who may lose power through organizational change is likely to resist. Another weakness of organization development is that it has paid little attention to the role of labor unions, which surely have the potential of aiding or hindering OD efforts.[120] There is little firm evidence that organization development markedly helps organizations adapt to their environments.

LIMITATIONS ON MOTIVATION

The field of motivation and, more generally, the field of management have been characterized by fads. Management by objectives may be popular one year and something else may gain favor the next year. If the fad is short-lived and produces no appreciable results, harm can be done. Employees who have been subjected to one "new" technique after another only yawn at the announcement that the agency will begin implementing still another "new" process. On the other hand, the fads of the field may have some utility, even if it is only short-lived. It is possible that any change—whether it be flexitime, job enrichment, or fishbowling—is refreshing. It would follow, therefore, that introducing even a seemingly ludicrous change, such as having employees wear roller skates, may be as effective as more conventional motivation techniques.

Motivation theories and techniques generally share the weakness of having overlooked the role of labor unions. "Organization psychology as a field still has not recognized the fact that unions exist and have an influence on worker behavior."[121] The next chapter discusses labor-management relations, including the role of unions in decision-making and their influence on productivity.

The dimension of time is largely missing from motivation literature. Organizations have histories. The organization climate, of particular interest to OD specialists, does not just exist, but rather has emerged over a period of time. Changing that climate may be difficult. Workers are likely to keep the same behavior patterns even after an autocratic manager has been replaced by an employee-centered one.[122]

---

[120] Thomas A. Kochan and Lee Dyer, "A Model of Organizational Change in the Context of Union-Management Relations," *Journal of Applied Behavioral Science*, 12 (1976):59–78.

[121] Korman, Greenhaus, and Badin, "Personnel Attitudes and Motivation," p. 188.

[122] Graeme Salaman, "An Historical Discontinuity: From Charisma to Routinization," *Human Relations*, 30 (1977):373–388.

Theorists have sought general theories of motivation, but in doing so have tended to disregard the great variation among people. People are not a uniform mass, all being motivated by self-actualization and not being motivated by hygiene factors. Presthus has suggested that workers can be classified into three types: the upward mobiles, the indifferents, and the ambivalents.[123] While this may not be a perfect typology, it at least suggests that different individuals are motivated in different ways. Some workers may be incapable of being motivated. "They go but faintly to work . . . with one buttock."[124] Many individuals have interest patterns that cannot be satisfied vocationally. For instance, a person with mediocre artistic talent but intense interest cannot expect his interest to be supported in the labor market. In such a case, work is apt to be regarded solely as an economic necessity, with all motivation being channeled into a hobby. Workers bring their personal problems to work. One employee may be on the verge of a divorce, while another is losing the battle against alcoholism, and another is distraught over the death of a child. Another problem is raised by the employee who has an unrealistic view of his capacity, who is perennially seeking to take on responsibilities far beyond his grasp, and hence is chronically dissatisfied with any rational assignment of duties. The theories do not explain how motivation techniques are to work in these situations.

Among the most important concepts that current motivation theories overlook are the phases of adult life.[125] The 21-year-old has a considerably different view of the job and the agency than the 40- to 45-year-old worker. The younger worker may see his current job as only a stepping stone to better jobs and may have limited commitment to the agency. The older worker may have more commitment or may be unhappy because his career seems to have reached a dead end.

Are approaches to motivation cost-effective? The proponents of MBO, OD, and other techniques would suggest that their methods can be no less cost-effective than authoritarian approaches, but it is difficult to put a price tag on implementing motivation techniques. The use of sensitivity training is expensive, not because of consultant fees, but because of employee and managerial time required in the process. There is a lingering feeling that time might be better spent working than spent

---

[123] Robert Presthus, *The Organizational Society: An Analysis and a Theory* (New York: Vintage, 1962).

[124] Voltaire as quoted in Golembiewski, *Men, Management, and Morality: Toward a New Organizational Ethic*, p. 61.

[125] See Robert T. Golembiewski, "Mid-Life Transition and Mid-Career Crises: A Special Case for Individual Development," *Public Administration Review*, 38 (1978):215–222; Gail Sheehy, *Passages: Predictable Crises of Adult Life* (New York: Dutton, 1976); Douglas C. Kimmel, *Adulthood and Aging: An Interdisciplinary Developmental View* (New York: Wiley and Sons, 1974); and Merrill F. Elias et al., *Basic Processes in Adult Developmental Psychology* (St. Louis: Mosby, 1977).

in committee meetings. The agency that has committees layered upon other committees may be incapable of responding to the environment. Internal participation is achieved at the expense of being able to adapt to the external, real world.

Approaches to motivation have had difficulty in accommodating the idea that conflict in organizations can be functional. While most theorists will insist that conflict has utility, many of the prominent theories implicitly suggest that interpersonal and intergroup cooperation is the ideal toward which organizations should strive. However, conflict can have positive effects. Conflict can stimulate learning and creativity.[126]

Motivation theory can become its own trap when it attempts to explain all behavior. The person committed to job enrichment as a technique tends to look at every situation where worker performance is low as an opportunity for job redesign and enrichment. More generally, all performance problems tend to be seen as motivation problems, when there may be other possible explanations. Patching of potholes may be ineffective not because the road crews have low motivation but because of inferior patching materials.[127]

Motivation theories are difficult to apply in the public sector because of the constraints that exist. Laws specify what an agency can and cannot do regardless of whether some alternative might be more effective. Because of personnel and budget ceilings, a manager may be forced into assigning work to an employee who is not qualified to do the work; putting square pegs in round holes is not uncommon.[128] Rigid civil service systems hinder removing unproductive workers and providing financial incentives to productive workers. Public managers are busy people who have little time to contemplate how best to help each employee self-actualize. The manager is expected to be a boss and to see that work is done on time, yet motivation theory stresses that he should be a friend and encourage employee participation in decision-making. The manager is expected to be a manager, but should he or she be expected to be a psychologist as well?

There are also important ethical and value issues associated with approaches to motivation. The earlier Mayo approach has been criticized as being manipulative—techniques seemed to have been developed to be used by management in handling its marionette employees. Do contemporary approaches have the same underlying purposes? Proponents of

---

[126] Luthans, *Organizational Behavior*, pp. 384–402; Rensis Likert and Jane G. Likert, *New Ways of Managing Conflict* (New York: McGraw-Hill, 1976); and Kenneth Thomas, "Conflict and Conflict Management," Dunnette, ed. *Handbook of Industrial and Organizational Psychology*, pp. 889–935.

[127] Korman, Greenhaus, and Badin, "Personnel Attitudes and Motivation," p. 187.

[128] *Personnel Ceilings: A Barrier to Effective Manpower Management* (Washington: General Accounting Office, 1977).

management by objectives and other techniques defend these approaches as being humanizing, for the benefit of both workers and the organization.

The rights and responsibilities of employees and managers have not been well integrated with motivation theories. Public employees may be said to have a right to be treated humanely, but what rights do they have to participate in agency decision-making? It is possible to envision a system in which the employees make decisions at the expense of the citizenry, who pay for the decisions through taxes. If employees have rights to participate, do not citizens have similar rights?[129] What is the professional manager's role? Does the manager abdicate leadership responsibilities by encouragining employee participation? (Managers have been known to hide behind committees.)

This critique on the limitations of motivation should not be interpreted as an argument against all such theories and techniques. The appropriate interpretation is that the current state of the art is less than perfect but that certainly more is known today than was known in the 1920s or 1930s. Much is still to be learned about why people behave the way they do, why some people are creative and innovative while others are not, and why some organizations are receptive to change and others are not.

SUMMARY

Some techniques aimed at motivating workers stress worker autonomy. Flexitime has been advocated not only because it gives workers a choice about when they work but also because it releases them from close supervision. Managers are forced to delegate responsibilities, because some workers will be at their jobs when the managers are off duty. Flexitime is defended as increasing productivity, in that workers are not expected to work when they are physically or psychologically not prepared to work. Critics claim that without direct supervision workers may be less productive and that long working hours under compressed scheduling increase fatigue and reduce productivity.

Job enrichment also increases worker autonomy and gives each employee a greater range of responsibilities. By seeing how his work relates to the total effort of an organization, the worker may become more motivated and productive. Enriching jobs throughout an organization has the effect of decentralizing responsibilities. If job enrichment is to be used, pay and promotion practices need to be changed.

---

[129] D. Stephen Cupps, "Emerging Problems of Citizen Participation," *Public Administration Review*, 37 (1977):478–487; and Robert T. Golembiewski, "Mid-Life Transition and Mid-Career Crises."

While some motivation theories emphasize the individual, other theories stress the importance of groups and group leaders. At the core of group theories are dyadic relationships, in which two people relate to one another. Groups have structures and communication networks, and in informal work groups these networks may differ substantially from formal communication channels established by the organization. Members play different roles in the group, which establishes norms about behavior. Through the use of penalties and rewards, groups exert major influences upon members' behavior.

One of the most important roles in a group is that of leadership, and managers are often assumed to perform the role of leading their subordinates toward meeting the organization's goals. The trait approach to leadership has been abandoned, and research now concentrates upon effective styles for motivating workers. The prescription that has emerged is that supervisors should be concerned about the needs of their employees and not just the needs of the organization. The contingency approach suggests that different styles should be used, depending upon the situation at hand.

Management by objectives, or MBO, is a management technique that stresses the setting of goals and/or objectives with worker involvement. Participation is seen as encouraging workers to internalize or accept the goals of the organization. Through MBO, workers come to understand what is expected of them, and managers can manage on the basis of results. Techniques that share MBO's emphasis on accomplishments but that de-emphasize worker participation include program evaluation, program budgeting, zero base budgeting, and productivity improvement.

Organization development, or OD, seeks to help organizations adjust to their changing environments. Sensitivity training, T-groups, or encounter groups attempt to improve how people relate to each other. By becoming sensitive to others, people develop supportive relationships that encourage them to explore new ideas. Transactional analysis, although not a form of sensitivity training, can be used to gain insights into how two people relate to each other. Other variations of OD include survey feedback and team-building.

Although much has been learned about how and why people behave as they do in organizations, there still is much that is unknown. The theories and techniques discussed in this and the preceding chapter should not be considered as a set of panaceas. Criticisms of these theories and techniques include that they are often faddish, that they tend to ignore the role of unions, that they tend to de-emphasize the great variations among people, and that they tend to advocate cooperation and regard conflict as dysfunctional. Left unspecified is the extent to which public employees should be allowed to participate in decision-making vis-à-vis the responsibilities of public managers and the rights of the citizenry that they serve.

If the reader has carefully followed the discussion in this and the preceding chapter, a sense of confusion may have developed. This is unavoidable, because the field of motivation is itself confused. There is a myriad of theories of motivation and techniques for motivating employees, but currently there is no consensus about what works and what does not. Some degree of skepticism is warranted when one hears great claims that any one technique is superior to all others.

Chapter 13

Labor-Management Relations

The subject of labor-management relations has been placed near the end of this book not because of the subject's unimportance but because of its importance. The relationships between workers and their supervisors pervade all aspects of personnel administration, and therefore one cannot fully appreciate the scope of labor-management relations without understanding the scope of personnel administration. The emphasis here is on the relationship between employee organizations or unions and management and not on more general relationships between workers and their supervisors.[1]

[1] Works of general relevance to this chapter include Richard M. Ayres and Thomas L. Wheelen, eds., *Collective Bargaining in the Public Sector: Selected Readings in Law Enforcement* (Gaithersburg, Md.: International Association of Chiefs of Police, 1977); Committee on Employee Relations in the Public Service, *Employee Relations in the Public Service* (Chicago: Civil Service Assembly, 1942); Wilson R. Hart, *Collective Bargaining in the Federal Civil Service* (New York: Harper and Brothers, 1961); W. D. Heisel and J. D. Hallihan, *Questions and Answers on Public Employee Negotiation* (Chicago: Public Personnel Association, 1967); Michael H. Moskow, J. Joseph Loewenberg, and Edward C. Koziara, *Collective Bargaining in Public Employment* (New York: Random House, 1970); Murray B. Nesbitt, *Labor Relations in the Federal Government Service* (Washington: Bureau of National Affairs, 1976); Felix A. Nigro, *Management-Employee Relations in the Public Service* (Chicago: Public Personnel Association, 1969); Felix A. Nigro, ed., "Symposium on Collective Negotiations in the Public Service," *Public Administration Review*, 28 (1968):111–147; Felix A. Nigro, ed., "Symposium on Collective Bargaining in the Public Service: A Reappraisal," *Public Administration Review*, 32 (1972):97–126; Richard P. Schick and Jean J. Couturier, *The Public Interest in Government Labor Relations* (Cambridge, Mass.: Ballinger, 1977); Thomas Sedwick, ed., "Public Sector Labor Relations," *State Government*, 49 (1976):199–276; Sterling D. Spero, *The Labor Movement in a Government Industry: A Study of Employee Organization in the Postal Service* (New York: Macmillan, 1927); Sterling D. Spero, *Government as Employer* (New York: Remsen, 1948); David T. Stanley, *Managing Local Government Under Union Pressure* (Washington: Brookings Institution, 1972); Willem B. Vosloo, *Collective Bargaining in the United States Federal Civil Service* (Chicago: Public Personnel Association, 1966); Kenneth O. Warner, *Collective Bargaining in the Public Service: Theory and Practice* (Chicago: Public Personnel Association, 1967); Kenneth O. Warner and Mary L. Hennessy, *Public Management at the Bargaining Table* (Chicago: Public Personnel Association, 1967); Robert T. Woodworth and Richard B. Peterson, eds., *Collective Negotiation for Public and Professional Employees* (Glenview, Ill.: Scott, Foresman, 1969); Sam Zagoria, ed., *Public Workers and Public Unions* (Englewood Cliffs, N.J.: Prentice-Hall, 1972).

"Labor-management relations" is a broader term than "collective bargaining." The latter refers to employee unions negotiating agreements about the conditions of work. From the perspective of organized labor, collective bargaining includes negotiations over pay rates and the right of workers to strike when the two parties in the negotiations cannot reach an agreement. As will be seen, comparatively few public workers have such bargaining rights. For convenience purposes, however, the discussion uses the term "collective bargaining" to refer generally to negotiations regardless of whether pay is negotiable or whether workers may strike.

This chapter has three sections. The first examines the growth of public employee unions and the emergence of collective bargaining. The second section focuses upon collective bargaining processes. The last section discusses the impacts that public employee unions and collective bargaining have had on government administration.

THE EMERGENCE OF UNIONS AND COLLECTIVE BARGAINING

The concept of sovereignty has been a major impediment to the rise of public employee unions and public-sector collective bargaining. Just as sovereignty has been used to protect government from legal suits (see Chapter 8), sovereignty has been used to protect government from its employees. Under the concept of sovereignty, it is asserted that the government is omnipotent and can do no wrong. If government is all powerful, then by definition it cannot be forced to negotiate with its employees. Public workers as *servants* of the citizenry cannot assert a right to be treated by the government as a co-equal in bargaining. Three distinct but related issues are involved. One is whether public employees have a right to organize. Second is whether employee assocations or unions may bargain. Third is whether they may strike. The sovereignty issue has been asserted most strongly with regard to strikes, but for a long time it was used as well to defend against employees organizing and seeking negotiating rights.

At the federal level, employee unionism developed among blue-collar workers and in the postal system and has since spread throughout the government.[2] Laborers and mechanics in the 1830s organized in navy yards and federal arsenals. Postal workers, who organized in the 1880s and 1890s, focused their effort less upon collective bargaining rights and more upon influencing federal legislation in their behalf. "Gag" rules

---

[2] See A. Lawrence Chickering, ed., *Public Employee Unions: A Study of the Crisis in Public Sector Labor Relations* (Lexington, Mass.: Lexington Books, 1976), and Jack Stieber, *Public Employee Unionism: Structure, Growth, Policy* (Washington: Brookings Institution, 1973).

Table 13.1.   Union representation in the federal government, 1976

Union	Employees*
Exclusive Recognition under Executive Orders	
American Federation of Government Employees, AFL-CIO	678,447
National Federation of Federal Employees	133,549
National Treasury Employees Union	89,786
National Association of Government Employees	82,642
Metal Trades Council, AFL-CIO	58,453
International Association of Machinists and Aerospace Workers, AFL-CIO	33,492
Other	114,109
U.S. Postal Service	
American Postal Workers Union, AFL-CIO	298,168
National Association of Letter Carriers of America, AFL-CIO	188,890
National Rural Letter Carriers of America	52,013
National Association of Post Office Mail Handlers, Watchmen, Messengers, and Group Leaders, AFL-CIO	37,166
Other	2,662

Source: U.S. Civil Service Commission, *Union Recognition in the Federal Government* (Washington: Government Printing Office, 1977), pp. 25 and 661–663.

* Figures do not include employees represented by unions in Government Printing Office, Tennessee Valley Authority, or the District of Columbia.

followed from the executive branch, prohibiting employees from lobbying in Congress. These rules were overturned in 1912 by passage of the Lloyd-LaFollette Act, a measure strongly supported by the American Federation of Labor and its president, Samuel Gompers. That act permitted lobbying activities. The provision protecting against removal except for cause (see Chapter 8) was included in part to protect workers from being fired for union activities. (The Civil Service Reform Act of 1978 reaffirmed the right of employees and employee organizations to petition Congress.) From 1912 onward there were numerous efforts to reorient the federal government's position in labor-management relations, but no major change occurred until 1962, when President Kennedy issued Executive Order 10988. That order greatly expanded unionism in the federal government.

Today numerous unions represent federal workers, with about three-fourths of the employees in bargaining units being represented by an affiliate of the American Federation of Labor—Congress of Industrial Organizations (AFL-CIO).[3] Table 13.1 shows 1976 union representation

[3] For information on unions, see the current issue of the *Directory of National Unions and Employee Associations*, issued by the U.S. Bureau of Labor Statistics.

under Executive Orders and representation in the U.S. Postal Service, which by statute is under the jurisdiction of the National Labor Relations Board. The American Federation of Government Employees represents the largest number of federal workers, followed by the American Postal Workers Union and the National Association of Letter Carriers. These AFL-CIO unions are followed by the nonaffiliated National Federation of Federal Employees. Approximately 60 percent of the federal workers are organized in exclusive bargaining units. About half of the General Schedule positions and more than 80 percent of the trades and labor positions are covered by such agreements. Employees in exclusive units have risen from only 180,000 in 1963 to 1.9 million in 1976.[4] Unionism has become so widespread that some now think unionization of the armed forces is a possibility, although federal law prohibits uniformed military personnel from bargaining.[5]

Union representation and membership are not the same. A union has responsibility for representing all employees within a bargaining unit, even though some employees are not union members. Therefore, membership is almost always lower than the number of employees represented. Estimates of union membership in federal bargaining units range between 30 and 35 percent. In recent years, membership has been declining in federal unions. The American Federation of Government Employees, which represents about 680,000 workers, lost about 38,000 members between 1970 and 1978; its membership was about 266,000 in 1978. The reason most often suggested for declining membership is that federal collective negotiations are restricted to the point that many workers think joining a union will be of little advantage; specifically, unions cannot negotiate on the bread-and-butter topics of compensation and employee benefits.[6]

Unionization has become common in state and local governments too. Table 13.2 shows that half of all state and local workers are organized. School teachers are the most organized (64 percent in 1976) and state, county, and special districts the least organized (about 37 percent). The National Education Association (NEA) is the dominant

---

[4] Civil Service Commission, *Union Recognition in the Federal Government* (Washington: Government Printing Office, 1977).

[5] Kenneth A. Kovach, Ben F. Sands, and William W. Brooks, "Unions and the Military Services in the United States," *Labor Law Journal*, 29 (1978):87–94; *Information on Military Unionization and Organization* (Washington: General Accounting Office, 1977); and Subcommittee on Civil Service, House Committee on Post Office and Civil Service, *Prohibit Unionization of the Military: Hearings*, 95th Cong., 2d sess. (Washington: Government Printing Office, 1978).

[6] James W. Singer, "The Limited Power of Federal Worker Unions," *National Journal*, 10 (1978):1547–1551.

Table 13.2.   State and local organized full-time employees, 1976

Jurisdiction Type	Organized Employees	
	Number	Percent
State Governments	991,634	38
Local Governments	3,745,328	54
Counties	502,163	37
Municipalities	1,075,727	53
Townships	124,208	57
School Districts	1,924,195	64
Special Districts	119,035	37
Total	4,736,962	50

Sources: Census Bureau, *Public Employment in 1976* (Washington: Government Printing Office, 1977), p. 14; and Census Bureau and Labor-Management Services Administration, *Labor-Management Relations in State and Local Governments: 1976* (Washington: Government Printing Office, 1978), p. 1.

employee organization in school districts, followed by the American Federation of Teachers, an affiliate of the AFL-CIO. The American Federation of State, County, and Municipal Employees (AFSCME) is also an AFL-CIO union and has about 750,000 members. Within general purpose local government, firefighters are the most highly organized (72 percent), and the largest union representing them is the International Association of Fire Fighters (IAFF), an AFL-CIO union. Police officers (about 50 percent organized) are represented by the Fraternal Order of Police, the International Conference of Police Associations (police benevolent associations), AFSCME, the International Brotherhood of Teamsters, Chauffeurs, Warehousemen and Helpers Union, and the Service Employees International Union.[7]

Several factors account for the rise of public unions. Poor working conditions have been a major and persistent reason. In the 1890s, mail clerks were required to work in unsanitary and dangerous railroad mail cars, and the result was a high accident rate.[8] More recently, public workers have sought guaranteed rest breaks, and teachers have demanded time out of the classroom in order to prepare their lessons. Low pay has been a frequent reason; it was this that led to the famous Boston police strike of 1919. Some observers have suggested there is an almost inherent tendency to organize: "Whenever any sector of the labor

---

[7] Allen Z. Gammage and Stanley L. Sachs, *Police Unions* (Springfield, Ill.: Charles C Thomas, 1972).

[8] William E. Mosher and J. Donald Kingsley, *Public Personnel Administration* (New York: Harper and Brothers, 1936), p. 496.

force became sufficiently aware of its collective presence and power, it sooner or later organized to make itself seen and heard."[9]

The growth of unions and union militancy in the 1960s can be explained by additional factors.[10] Some groups of workers came to the conclusion they were not part of one big happy family. Teachers most notably wrestled with whether as professionals they should demand collective bargaining rights or whether bargaining was more appropriate for blue-collar workers. The NEA initially seemed opposed to collective bargaining, but shifted dramatically to meet the challenge of the AFT.[11] Police also became more militant in the 1960s, partially because of the evident public hostility against them.[12] Race was another reason. Blacks were concentrated in various departments of local governments, and the civil rights movement extended into their ranks.[13] The growth that had occurred in public employment following World War II presented new organizing opportunities for unions; with growth in unionism in the private sector at a standstill, organized labor turned to the public sector. Private-sector union membership grew by only 4 percent between 1968 and 1976, but public-sector membership grew by 40 percent.[14]

To cope with rising demands for collective bargaining and to avert strikes by public workers, governments turned to various devices for dealing with labor-management relations.[15] The approach taken at the federal level was to use an Executive Order rather than a statute to establish a labor-management process. In 1962 President Kennedy issued Executive Order 10988, which was a stimulus or legitimizing force for unionization at the state and local levels as well as within the federal government. The order was replaced by President Nixon in 1969 with Executive Order 11491, and that was amended by E.O. 11838, issued by President Ford.

President Carter recommended in 1978 that Congress replace the Executive Orders with a statute, and this was accomplished through Title

---

[9] Gus Tyler, "Why They Organize," *Public Administration Review*, 32 (1972):98.

[10] Rollin B. Posey, "The New Militancy of Public Employees," *Public Administration Review*, 28 (1968):111–117; and Lawrence D. Mankin, "Public Employee Organizations: The Quest for Legitimacy," *Public Personnel Management*, 6 (1977):334–340.

[11] T. M. Stinnett, Jack H. Kleinmann, and Martha L. Ware, *Professional Negotiation in Public Education* (New York: Macmillan, 1966).

[12] Hervey A. Juris and Peter Feuille, *Police Unionism* (Lexington, Mass.: Lexington Books, 1973).

[13] Harry H. Wellington and Ralph K. Winter, Jr., *The Unions and the Cities* (Washington: Brookings Institution, 1971), pp. 45–47.

[14] "Labor Union and Employee Association Membership," *U.S. Department of Labor News*, 77 –771 (1977).

[15] See Kurt L. Hanslowe, *The Emerging Law of Labor Relations in Public Employment* (Ithaca, N.Y.: School of Industrial and Labor Relations, Cornell University, 1967).

VII of the Civil Service Reform Act of 1978.[16] The AFL-CIO endorsed this change. A collective negotiation process established by statute was seen as providing permanent rights to workers, whereas under the previous system a President could unilaterally alter the collective bargaining process by issuing a new Executive Order. The legislation did not appreciably change employee union rights. Organizational responsibilities were altered both through the President's reorganization process and the reform legislation. The Federal Labor Relations Council was replaced by a Federal Labor Relations Authority, and most functions previously performed by the Assistant Secretary for Labor-Management Relations were transferred to the Authority (see discussion below).

At the state and local levels, labor-management relations are governed by a variety of measures. State statutes, attorney general opinions, and executive orders along with state court decisions set the framework for state and local labor-management relations. As employees have organized and demanded bargaining rights, states have shifted toward reliance on statutes. These vary as to whether they include local employees as well as state employees. Some statutes permit local governments to enter into collective bargaining agreements with employees, while other laws require collective bargaining if a majority of the employees request it. Some laws provide separate processes for school teachers and for public safety workers—police officers, prison guards, and firefighters. The administrative unit that oversees the process commonly is a labor relations board, but in some cases a civil service department may have responsibility or a separate state board may be established for a selected group of workers, such as teachers. As of 1976, 41 states reported having a labor relations policy for government workers.[17]

The diversity that exists among the states and their local governments has led to the suggestion that federal legislation is needed. Such legislation supposedly would reduce the confusion that exists within and among states. Expertise in labor-management relations could be transferred from jurisdiction to jurisdiction, whereas that is currently difficult because of the wide variations existing in state laws. Public employee unions, including AFSCME and the NEA, have supported national legislation as a means of providing workers with the rights they deserve. Even if the legislation is never passed, merely proposing such legislation has

---

[16] Civil Service Reform Act, 92 Stat. 1111 (1978), and "Reorganization Plan No. 2 of 1978," *Weekly Compilation of Presidential Documents*, 14 (1978):953–958.

[17] Census Bureau and Labor-Management Services Administration, *Labor-Management Relations in State and Local Governments: 1976* (Washington: Government Printing Office, 1978), p. 9. See also Department of Labor, *Summary of State Policy Regulations for Public Sector Labor Relations* (Washington: Government Printing Office, 1975).

had the effect of encouraging state and local officials to be more receptive to collective negotiations.[18]

Representatives of state and local governments have expressed misgivings about the proposed federal legislation for state and local employee-management relations. The Advisory Commission on Intergovernmental Relations in 1969 suggested an alternative to national legislation; each state could adopt with modifications the ACIR's model labor relations act.[19] The ACIR, however, was divided in that it provided two substantially different model laws. State constitutional rights supposedly would be violated by the passage of national legislation, and the National League of Cities court case dealing with fair labor standards would seem to substantiate that argument (see Chapter 4). The International City Management Association is "totally opposed to any extension of federal regulation of local government personnel policies. Proposals for federal regulation are not in the public interest, and in direct contrast to the concept of effective and responsive local government."[20] A national law would impose a uniformity that is considered undesirable, given the vast differences that exist in the characteristics of state and local governments.

It is uncertain whether federal legislation will be passed, but three options have been under consideration. One approach would be to remove the clause in the 1947 Taft-Hartley Act that specifically excludes state and local workers. Removal of the clause would have the effect of bringing these workers under the jurisdiction of the National Labor Relations Board, which currently oversees private labor relations and postal labor relations. A second option would be to create an agency that would be solely concerned with public labor relations; the presumed advantage of this approach would be that it would recognize the unique character of public employment. A third option would set minimal standards and allow each state to pass separate legislation in conformance with those standards.[21]

---

[18] Jerry Wurf, "Comment," in Thomas R. Colosi and Steven B. Rynecki, eds., *Federal Legislation for Public Sector Collective Bargaining* (Chicago: International Personnel Management Association, 1975), pp. 38–43.

[19] Advisory Commission on Intergovernmental Relations, *Labor-Management Policies for State and Local Government* (Washington: Government Printing Office, 1969).

[20] International City Management Association Executive Board, "Federal Regulation of Local Government Personnel," *Public Management*, 59 (June, 1977):5. See also John Matzer, Jr., "Proposals for Federal Regulation of Local Government Labor Relations," *Public Management*, 57 (February, 1975):10–12; and Richard V. Whalen, Jr., "Perspective on Federal Legislation," *Public Management*, 57 (February, 1975):13–14.

[21] Michael A. Mass and Anita F. Gottlieb, "Federally Legislated Collective Bargaining for State and Local Government: A Logical Imperative," *Employee Relations Law Journal*, 2 (1977):273–285; Dennis R. Nolan, "Public Sector Collective Bargaining: Defining the Federal Role," *Cornell Law Review*, 63 (1978):419–462.

COLLECTIVE BARGAINING PROCESSES

Although public jurisdictions differ greatly in how they handle labor-managment relations, there are processes that are common to collective negotiations. This section begins with a discussion of the steps that must be taken before bargaining can commence. Next, various aspects of the bargaining process are discussed. The section concludes with a review of procedures used when the two sides in the bargaining process cannot reach agreement.

Preliminary Steps

Before bargaining can begin, agreement must be rached about what group of employees will be in a bargaining unit. A union typically will request that specified jobs consititute a unit, but management may not agree. Therefore, some administrative agency is given power to determine the boundaries of the unit. At the federal level this was the responsibility of the Assistant Secretary of Labor for Labor-Management Relations until the 1978 reforms. Decisions of the Assistant Secretary could be appealed to the Federal Labor Relations Council (FLRC), chaired by the Chairman of the Civil Service Commission. The other members of the Council were the Secretary of Labor and the Director of the Office of Management and Budget. The Carter administration's reorganization replaced the FLRC with the Federal Labor Relations Authority, consisting of three members appointed by the President with the advice and consent of the Senate. The members have five-year terms, may not hold other positions in the government, and may be removed by the President only upon notice and hearing and only for "inefficiency, neglect of duty, or malfeasance in office." The Authority is responsible for interpreting the governing legislation, including the provisions for unit determination.[22] In states having labor-relations policies, unit determination for both state and local governments usually is the responsibility of the state labor relations board.

Great variations exist among governments as to the number of bargaining units and their size. Table 13.3 shows that in 1976 the federal government had recognized 3,567 units under Executive Order 11491. The Defense Department alone had nearly 1,700 bargaining units. Size varied, with the average unit having about 300 employees. Of the major agencies, Treasury had the highest average (nearly 700 employees per unit). On the other hand, there were some extremely small units. For example, two employees constituted a bargaining unit for HEW's Center for Disease Control Office in Hidalgo, Texas; and three nurses consti-

---

[22] Civil Service Reform Act of 1978. Also see Personnel Management Project, *Final Staff Report* (Washington: Government Printing Office, 1977), pp. 165–180.

Table 13.3.   Federal government exclusive recognition units by department, 1976

Departments*	Exclusive Unit	Average Size of Unit
Department of Defense	1676	377
Army (614)		
Navy (582)		
Air Force (250)		
Other (230)		
Veterans Administration	375	411
Health, Education, and Welfare	370	235
Interior	216	116
General Services Administration	164	155
Agriculture	152	179
Transportation	147	304
Treasury	141	689
Other	326	301
TOTAL	3,567	334

Source: U.S. Civil Service Commission, *Union Recognition in the Federal Government* (Washington: Government Printing Office, 1977), pp. 20–21.

* Excludes U.S. Postal Service.

tuted a unit in the Veterans Administration outpatient clinic in Brooklyn.[23]

Similar variations are found at the state and local levels. Table 13.4 shows that in 1976 there were over 25,000 such bargaining units, with an average of about 170 employees. State governments tend to have larger bargaining units (about 700 persons per unit in 1976) than either the federal government (330) or local governments (150). Among local governments, townships have the smallest average size (55 employees) and counties the largest (about 230 employees). Even though state bargaining units are considerably larger than local units, state governments tend to have numerous bargaining units, unlike local governments, which may have only four or five. A local government might have separate units for police officers, firefighters, labor and trades, and clerical employees.

The great differences among states on bargaining units is evident in Table 13.5. There were about nine states in 1976 with no bargaining units, while Minnesota and Washington were at the other extreme, with

---

[23] Civil Service Commission, *Union Recognition in the Federal Government*, pp. 431 and 572.

138 and 117 bargaining units, respectively. Kansas and Pennsylvania had about the same number of bargaining units (28 and 29, respectively), but the average size unit in Kansas was only 300 members, while in Pennsylvania the average was 3,300. New York State and California may be similar in population size, but not in terms of bargaining unit size. California's thirteen bargaining units covered only 4,517 employees in 1976 (average of 347 employees) while New York's nineteen units covered 166,585 employees (average of 8,768). Variations like these are used both to support and oppose possible federal legislation (see preceding section). On the one hand, proponents of the legislation claim that many states have denied workers their bargaining rights, and on the other, opponents claim that uniform legislation would not meet the diverse needs of the states.

Criteria for identifying the boundaries of a bargaining unit are established by statute or executive order, with the most important or common criterion being a "community of interest." This refers to employees having common concerns. Included are such factors as whether the workers interact with each other and perform similar tasks. One of the reasons for the multitude of federal bargaining units, therefore, is geography. There is little sense of community when agency employees work throughout the country or even the world; bargaining units, then, are established at regional or community levels. The Civil Service Reform Act also provides that the unit should "promote effective dealings with, and efficiency of the operations of the agency involved."

Table 13.4.   State and local government bargaining units, 1976

Jurisdiction Type	Number of Governments	Governments with Labor Relations Policy	Bargaining Units	
			Number	Average Size
State Governments	50	41	1,093	688
Local Governments	78,218	12,327	24,149	149
Counties	3,044	671	2,290	229
Municipalities	18,517	2,175	6,484	176
Townships	16,991	840	2,419	55
School Districts	15,781	7,987	12,081	140
Special Districts	23,885	654	875	123
TOTAL	78,268	12,368	25,242	172

Source: Census Bureau and Labor-Management Services Administration, *Labor-Management Relations in State and Local Governments: 1976* (Washington: Government Printing Office, 1978), pp. 2 and 10.

Table 13.5.   State government bargaining units* and size of units, 1976

Number of units	Average size of bargaining units		
	Under 400	400–799	800 or more
Less than 10			
	Arizona	Alabama	Florida
	Arkansas	Connecticut	Indiana
	Colorado	Missouri	Iowa
	Maine	New Mexico	Vermont
	Maryland	Tennessee	West Virginia
	Nevada		
	New Hampshire		
	North Carolina		
	North Dakota		
	South Dakota		
10–49			
	California	Alaska	Hawaii
	Delaware	Utah	New Jersey
	Kansas		New York
	Louisiana		Pennsylvania
	Nebraska		Wisconsin
	Ohio		
50 units or more			
	Minnesota	Illinois	Massachusetts
	Montana	Michigan	
	Rhode Island	Oregon	
	Washington		

Source: Census Bureau and Labor-Management Services Administration, *Labor-Management Relations in State and Local Governments: 1976* (Washington: Government Printing Office, 1978), pp. 33–58.

* There are no bargaining units in Georgia, Idaho, Kentucky, Mississippi, Oklahoma, South Carolina, Texas, Virginia, or Wyoming.

An aspect of effectiveness is whether a unit larger than what has been proposed would allow for greater expertise in the bargaining process. Efficiency might be increased with a larger bargaining unit, reducing the number of agreements to be negotiated.[24]

Other factors exclude certain types of employees from a unit. Supervisory personnel are not to be included with other workers. Professionals are not to be in the same unit as nonprofessionals unless the former agree to such a unit. The federal system includes these restrictions plus a prohibition on units consisting of workers who hold nonclerical personnel jobs or who hold intelligence positions related to national security.

---

[24] Civil Service Commission, *Representation Cases and Procedures* (Washington: Government Printing Office, 1977), pp. 32–34.

Another common restriction is that confidential employees are not to be included. Such confidential personnel might be administrative assistants, some clerical workers, and chauffeurs.

Recognizing that workers differ greatly on whether they support collective bargaining, labor unions sometimes favor small bargaining units. Labor representatives might not be able to win the support of all clerical workers but might be able to gain support from selected groups of clerical workers. If units can be established for those groups, then the union has an excellent chance of being able to engage in collective bargaining. Management, on the other hand, prefers not to have numerous units and, in some instances, not to have any collective negotiations. If a large unit can be established, then chances may be increased for the employees rejecting collective bargaining. The federal government and many states prohibit the establishment of a unit simply because employees in the proposed unit are organized.

While gaining approval of small units may seem an attractive strategy for unions in winning representation elections, the strategy can dilute the unions' capability in representing workers. Federal unions have had difficulty effectively representing small bargaining units that are geographically dispersed throughout the country. President Ford's Executive Order 11838 of 1975 encouraged the use of larger bargaining units, and this provision was incorporated in the 1978 reform legislation. When the union or unions representing two bargaining units agree to a consolidation and the agency also agrees, they may request consolidation approval of the Federal Labor Relations Authority. The consolidation can be accomplished without holding an election.

At the state and local levels, an alternative to fragmented bargaining units is multi-employer bargaining. Several local governments can bargain jointly with a union; communities in the Minneapolis-St. Paul area have used this approach. Hawaii combines state and local employees into bargaining units; that state has avoided the issue of unit determination by defining the units in a statute.[25] Multi-employer bargaining can be advantageous for a labor union in that it is not required to negotiate separate agreements with numerous jurisdictions. Both management and labor can afford better expertise under multi-employer bargaining. From management's perspective, such bargaining eliminates union "whiplashing," whereby the union wins a major settlement in one jurisdiction and then uses that agreement as leverage in negotiating similar settlements

---

[25] *Case Study of the Hawaii Public Employment Relations Act* (Washington: General Accounting Office, 1974); and Jack E. Klauser, "Multi-Employer Bargaining in the Public Sector of Hawaii," *Journal of Collective Negotiations in the Public Sector*, 6 (1977):73–79.

with other jurisdictions. A disadvantage is that individual jurisdictions lose direct control over the bargaining process.[26]

Rejection or approval of collective bargaining is accomplished by secret ballot. A union must petition for an election and must show that it has substantial support of the employees involved. At the federal level, a union must show that at least 30 percent of the workers want collective bargaining. Depending on the jurisdiction, once an election is called, other unions may be placed on the ballot, providing they too can show some support from the workers. The employees have the choice of voting for one of the unions or for no representation. If neither a union nor the "no representation" choice wins a majority vote, a runoff election is held for the two most popular choices. The election process was handled at the federal level by the Assistant Secretary of Labor and is now handled by the FLRA. State and local elections usually are conducted by state labor relations boards. For a union to participate in an election at the federal level, it must submit financial and other information to the Assistant Secretary of Labor for Labor-Management Relations, who is responsible for certifying that the union is "free from corrupt influences and influences opposed to basic democratic principles." A union must not have officers who are communists or members of other totalitarian movements.

Unfair labor practices can occur in all aspects of labor-management relations, but these practices arise particularly in the period prior to an election. An unfair labor practice simply is some action that violates the rights of workers, management, or unions. Employees have a right to information about unions, and unions have rights in soliciting employee support. Management has the right to be able to manage. Issues develop over where and when unions may talk with employees and distribute literature. Managers have an obligation not to intimidate employees—either directly or implicitly. A worker may not be dismissed for participating in union activities, and management may not imply that an employee will be denied a promotion because of union involvement.

Charges of unfair labor practices are filed with the administrative unit responsible for supervising the election. At the federal level, the General Counsel of the FLRA is responsible for investigating charges of unfair labor practices against both management and unions; the Counsel serves as prosecutor in such cases brought before the FLRA. Remedies may be granted when an unfair practice has been found to have occurred.

---

[26] Richard Pegnetter, *Multiemployer Bargaining in the Public Sector: Purposes and Experiences* (Chicago: International Personnel Management Association, 1975), and Roger Mansfield, "The Advent of Public Sector Multi-employer Bargaining," *Personnel Journal*, 54 (1975):290–294.

Management can be ordered to reinstate a person dismissed for union participation, and the individual will receive back pay. A union can be ordered to stop soliciting employees during regular working hours. Many unfair practice charges are never really pursued but rather are part of election strategies. Unions and management may each claim the other is engaging in unfair practices as a means of persuading employees to vote one way or the other.[27]

The Bargaining Process

Once a bargaining unit has been determined and a union elected to represent the workers, bargaining can commence. A key aspect is that the union becomes the exclusive representative for the workers, and unions are careful to protect that exclusivity. One case of exclusivity that came before the U.S. Supreme Court involved a Wisconsin school board that permitted a nonunion teacher to speak against a union-supported measure at one of the board's public meetings.[28] The issue of the case was whether the board had entered into negotiations with someone other than the union. The Court held that to bar the board from hearing the nonunion teacher would violate the teacher's First Amendment right of free speech.

On one side of the bargaining table will be union representatives, but who sits on the other side? Labor-management relations in the public sector involve more than labor and management. The process must in some way acknowledge the powers of the legislative branch. The legislative body cannot be ignored when a labor settlement involves money, since the executive branch has no independent spending powers. A mayor might negotiate an agreement that included a salary increase, but the city council could refuse to provide the necessary funds for the increase. Therefore, sometimes a settlement negotiated between the executive branch and a union must be submitted to the legislative body for ratification. The Hawaii legislature, for example, must approve cost items before they can be implemented.[29] All union contracts in Wisconsin must be submitted to that state's legislature for approval.[30] At the federal level, the Comptroller General, who heads the General Accounting Office and

[27] *Questions and Answers on Unfair Labor Practices* (Bloomington: Midwest Center for Public Sector Labor Relations, Indiana University, 1977); Charles C. Mulcahy, *County Labor Relations Casebook* (Washington: National Association of Counties, 1975), pp. 6-11; and Civil Service Commission, *Unfair Labor Practices* (Washington: Government Printing Office, 1976).

[28] *City of Madison, Joint School District No. 8 v. Wisconsin*, 429 U.S. 167 (1976).

[29] *Case Study of the Hawaii Public Employment Relations Act*, p. 14.

[30] Richard J. Carlson and Thomas Sedwick, *State Employee Labor Relations* (Lexington, Ky.: Council of State Governments, 1977), pp. 17-18.

who is an agent of Congress, has the authority to nullify some provisions in labor agreements. Legislatures, of course, are not solely a negative force that can reject negotiated agreements. Unions historically have scored end-runs around the executive by gaining from the legislative body what could not be obtained from the executive.[31]

A bargaining team usually represents the government. At the federal level, bargaining is decentralized so that agency managers have choices about who will serve on the team. One rule of thumb applying to all levels of government is that the manager of the unit should not be on the team, since that may encourage confrontation situations.[32] At the state level, a labor-relations unit may be established as the government's agent in bargaining; this unit takes an advocacy role, unlike the employee relations board that sides neither with management nor unions. The advantage of having a central agency responsible for representing management is that expertise can be developed along with a consistent policy across bargaining units. A possible disadvantage is that the central agency may not be in tune with the daily problems of line managers and as a result not effectively represent their needs in the negotiations. The bargaining team needs to have personnel expertise, budgetary expertise to understand the financial implications of various proposals, and legal expertise to interpret the language of any proposed agreement.

When the two sides sit down at the bargaining table, labor may have "meet and confer" rights, the right to negotiate a contract, or a combination of these two. "Meet and confer" involves discussion of various aspects of work but does not mean an agreement must be reached between the two sides. In some instances, where only meet and confer rights are granted, there may be no exclusivity for organized labor; representatives from two or more unions may collectively speak for the employees. Meet and confer rights can result in a written letter of understanding but only if management agrees to this practice. A letter of understanding, unlike a contract, is nonbinding.

Sometimes, one group of employees has negotiation rights leading to a contract, while other groups have only meet and confer rights. Supervisors often are granted only meet and confer rights, although their subordinates may have negotiation rights. The justification for limiting supervisors' rights is that to allow them to bargain would create conflicts of interest. For example, supervisory officers in a police department may tend to side with employees regarding wage increases but side with

---

[31] Wellington and Winter, *The Unions and the Cities*, pp. 121–136.

[32] Civil Service Commission, *Negotiations* (Washington: Government Printing Office, 1975), pp. 2–10.

management regarding enforcement of administrative regulations.[33] Nevertheless, some jurisdictions have allowed supervisors—as distinguished from higher level executives or managers—to bargain. Hawaii, Massachusetts, Michigan, Minnesota, and New York have granted such rights to supervisors.[34] School administrators in about twenty states have bargaining rights.[35]

The scope of bargaining is the extent to which various topics are subject to collective negotiations.[36] There are three categories of topics that relate to scope: 1) mandatory, 2) permissible, and 3) prohibited. In other words, state statutes and the federal Civil Service Reform Act prescribe some topics as mandatory; if management refuses to bargain on these, a union may seek relief from the unit responsible for administering the bargaining process. Other subjects are permissible, meaning that either side may refuse to bargain. Prohibited items are those excluded from the bargaining process even though labor and management may be willing to negotiate on these items.

These three types of provisions are found in the federal Civil Service Reform Act. The mandatory provision provides for negotiations on conditions of employment, which are defined as "personnel policies, practices, and matters . . . affecting working conditions." Permissible items are "the numbers, types, and grades of employees or positions assigned to any organizational subdivision, work project, or tour of duty." The two sides may agree to bargain on the "technology, methods, and means of performing work."

Prohibited items in the federal law relate to the rights of managers. Management must retain the right

1. to determine the mission, budget, organization, number of employees, and internal security practices of the agency; and
2. in accordance with applicable laws—

---

[33] Hoyt N. Wheeler and Thomas A. Kochan, "Unions and Public Sector Supervisors: The Case of Fire Fighters," *Monthly Labor Review*, 100 (December, 1977):44–48.

[34] Stephen L. Hayford and Anthony V. Sinicropi, "Bargaining Rights Status of Public Sector Supervisors," *Industrial Relations*, 15 (1976):44–61.

[35] Bruce S. Cooper, "Federal Actions and Bargaining for Public Supervisors: Basis for an Argument," *Public Personnel Management*, 6 (1977):341–352.

[36] Walter J. Gershenfeld, J. Joseph Loewenberg, and Bernard Ingster, eds., *Scope of Public-Sector Bargaining* (Lexington, Mass.: Lexington Books, 1977); Jerry Lelchook and Herbert J. Lahne (U.S. Department of Labor), *Collective Bargaining in Public Employment and the Merit System* (Washington: Government Printing Office, 1973), pp. 65–80; Nesbitt, *Labor Relations in the Federal Government Service*, pp. 186–208; Robert M. Tobias, "The Scope of Bargaining in the Federal Sector: Collective Bargaining or Collective Consultation," *George Washington Law Review*, 44 (1976):554–575; and Wellington, *The Unions and the Cities*, pp. 137–153.

(a) to hire, assign, direct, lay off, and retain employees in the agency, or to suspend, remove, reduce in grade or pay, or take other disciplinary action against such employees;

(b) to assign work, to make determinations with respect to contracting out, and to determine the personnel by which agency operations shall be conducted;

(c) with respect to filling positions, to make selections for appointments from—

(i) among properly ranked and certified candidates for promotion; or

(ii) any other appropriate source; and

(d) to take whatever actions may be necessary to carry out the agency mission during emergencies.

In addition, the law provides that the agreements cannot be contrary to laws or any government-wide rule or regulation, which has the effect of greatly restricting the scope of bargaining. Pay rates, since they are governed by statute, are beyond the scope of federal negotiations.

The Federal Labor Relations Authority interprets these provisions when issues arise. For instance, union proposals dealing with work shifts can be found to be nonnegotiable because they infringe upon management rights.[37] Occupational health and safety have constituted another area of controversy. Safety might seem to be a mandatory item, but specific safety provisions can be interpreted as prohibited if they relate to budgets or only as permissible if they relate to technology or the means of performing work. Despite these problems, unions have successfully negotiated extensive agreements relating to occupational health and safety. One such agreement under the former Executive Order specified that as the temperature rose, workers were to receive longer and more frequent rest periods, and that workers with heart conditions would not perform manual labor at temperatures above 85 degrees.[38] Negotiated agreements have been reached on such diverse subjects as "employee counseling, excused time for training, transfer, past practice provisions, union rights under the grievance procedure, suggestions and awards, technological displacement, labor relations training, pay policies, office service for the union, and environmental pay."[39]

Similar provisions on scope of bargaining are to be found at the

---

[37] Federal Labor Relations Council, *Report: 1970–76* (Washington: Government Printing Office, 1977), pp. 46–54.

[38] Nesbitt, *Labor Relations in the Federal Government Service*, pp. 202–203. See also Louis Aronon, "Collective Bargaining in the Federal Service: A Balanced Approach," *George Washington Law Review*, 44 (1976):576–603.

[39] Robert E. Hampton, "Progress and Problems in the Federal LMR Program," *Civil Service Journal*, 17 (October–December, 1976):9.

state level. Pennsylvania law for state and local governments (excluding public safety workers) provides for bargaining on "wages, hours, and conditions of employment."[40] A management-rights clause provides that employers need not bargain in "such areas of discretion or policy as the functions and programs of the public employer, standards of services, its overall budget, utilization of technology, the organizational structure and selection and direction of personnel." This provision was tested as it pertained to 21 different items in school negotiations; the court held non-negotiable such items as teachers chaperoning at athletic activities, maximum class size, maximum number of hours of teaching each week, or the availability of adequate instructional materials.[41] Items that are not negotiable, however, are subject to meet and confer provisions. Another area for negotiations are grievance procedures, including possible grievance arbitration. This subject is discussed in the last section of the chapter.

Provisions for union security have been a major area of controversy in public-sector bargaining. An employee cannot be required to join a union, but the union as the exclusive representative is required to work in behalf of all employees. Since union survival is dependent on dues collected, unions have sought negotiated agreements that prevent "free rides" by non-union employees. An agency shop agreement requires non-union workers to pay the union, usually an amount equal to membership dues. Although the agency shop is permitted in some state and local governments, it is not permitted at the federal level.

An agency shop agreement for Detroit schools was reviewed in 1977 by the Supreme Court as to whether the agreement violated the constitutional rights of teachers.[42] In accordance with Michigan law, the union had negotiated an agency shop clause, and some teachers objected that they were being compelled to fund political and ideological activities of the union. The teachers claimed that the union contract violated their rights of free speech and association as guaranteed under the First and Fourteenth Amendments (see Chapter 8 for a discussion of these Amendments). The Court ruled unanimously that these funds could only be used in conjunction with labor-relations matters, such as the bargaining process itself, contract administration, and grievance procedures.

---

[40] Pennsylvania Public Employee Relations Act, Act 195 of 1970. See J. Joseph Loewenberg and James W. Klingler, "The Scope of Bargaining in the Public Sector in Pennsylvania," in Gershenfeld, Loewenberg, and Ingster, *Scope of Public-Sector Bargaining*, pp. 97–115.

[41] *State College Education Association* v. *Pennsylvania Labor Relations Board*, 9 Pa. Cmwlth 229, 306 A. 2d 404 (1973).

[42] *Abood* v. *Detroit Board of Education*, 431 U.S. 209 (1977). See Kurt L. Hanslowe, *Union Security in Public Employment* (Ithaca, N.Y.: New York State School of Industrial and Labor Relations, Cornell University, 1978).

The "checkoff" is another method for providing union security.[43] Under the checkoff system, union dues are automatically deducted from payroll checks; this procedure eliminates the need for the union to collect dues. If the checkoff is agreed upon by labor and management, a charge is normally made for administrative costs. In the federal service, the standard charge was two cents per deduction, until the 1978 reform legislation, which provides for deductions at no cost to a union having exclusive representation.[44] The Supreme Court has held that, where an agency shop does not exist, a city cannot be required to collect dues from the union's members.[45] The Court agreed that a reasonable standard was used for making deductions; they were to be made only when they affected all members of a department. The city had refused to collect dues because the union's members constituted only 65 percent of the city's firefighters.

While the scope of bargaining greatly influences the outcome of the process, the abilities of the negotiators also are influential. Negotiators on both sides need to have done their "homework" before negotiations begin, need to have bargaining skills, and need to develop strategies for the negotiations. An important aspect of doing one's homework is knowing what agreements have been negotiated elsewhere. A union representing clerical workers will collect information to show that salary scales are low in comparison with other jurisdictions and with private enterprise. The computerized federal Labor Agreement Information Retrieval System (LAIRS) can be used for researching negotiated agreements, arbitration awards, and administrative decisions pertaining to collective bargaining. The system provides information to labor organizations as well as to management.[46]

Bargaining is not strictly a rational process, and negotiators need to know how to cope with the histrionics that develop. Unions sometimes can be expected to make unrealistic demands, in part simply to satisfy their constituents. Union negotiators need to be able to report back to their members how the union confronted management. Both sides need training in the bargaining process. Knowing when to make demands, how to make demands, and when to make concessions is important.[47]

---

[43] Nesbitt, *Labor Relations in the Federal Government Service*, pp. 206–216.

[44] Federal Labor Relations Council, *Report*, p. 61.

[45] *City of Charlotte* v. *Local 660, International Association of Firefighters*, 426 U.S. 283 (1976).

[46] Ronald A. Leahy, "Labor Relations Information Delivery in the Public Sector," *Civil Service Journal*, 17 (April–June, 1977):25–27.

[47] Morris Sackman, "Make Your Own Simulations to Train Public Managers in Collective Bargaining," *Public Personnel Management*, 4 (1975):231–237; and Kenneth L. Steen et al., "Labor Relations Training: Are We Meeting the Needs?" *Public Personnel Management*, 6 (1977):300–312.

Both sides need to assess what they want in the agreement and should anticipate each other's proposals. This can be called "collective bargaining by objectives," in which one identifies what is desired in the agreement and assesses the likelihood of winning each item.[48] In anticipating the other side's proposals, one needs to be prepared with counter offers; this is an essential aspect of good-faith bargaining. If bargaining over wages is mandatory, management is not permitted to sit back and simply reject every demand made by organized labor; management must offer an alternative wage settlement.

The strategy devised will include some low-priority demands that can be used as bargaining chips. A police union might yield on its demands for improved overtime provisions and uniform allowances in return for a large wage increase. Management may try to persuade the union to accept a low wage increase for substantially increased retirement benefits; the advantage of this is that the immediate impact on the budget will be less with retirement increases than with wage increases (see discussion of pension problems in Chapter 4). Winning a two-year contract instead of a one-year contract may be an important objective of management; but to win that concession management will need to offer an attractive package.

Organized labor and management have had to become skilled in budgeting. When labor makes a demand with financial implications, management needs to be able to determine the likely costs.[49] For example, what will be the cost of providing an additional paid holiday? What will be the future impacts on the budget if a major health benefits plan is approved? Organized labor can anticipate management's claiming to be too poor to afford what has been proposed. At this point, the labor negotiators need to be able to show that surpluses exist in the budget. One technique that has been used is to create surpluses. If a state teachers union effectively lobbies for increases in state aid to school districts, school management throughout the state may be unable to argue persuasively that they cannot meet labor's demands for salary increases.

When public-sector, collective negotiations became prominent in the 1960s, wage increases were justified by unions largely as a means of "catching up" with salary scales in the private sector, but today parity has been largely reached and there is increasing emphasis upon produc-

---

[48] Reed C. Richardson, *Collective Bargaining by Objectives: A Positive Approach* (Englewood Cliffs, N.J.: Prentice-Hall, 1977).

[49] Preston O. Stanley, "Cost Determination in Federal Collective Bargaining," *Public Personnel Management*, 5 (1976):335–342; and W. D. Heisel and Gordon S. Skinner, *Costing Union Demands* (Chicago: International Personnel Management Association, 1976).

tivity bargaining.[50] Management's position is that it cannot afford large wage increases unless workers become more productive. Some of the bargaining that has occurred can be seen as management reasserting its right to manage. Previous labor contracts may have tied management's hands in being able to direct workers. Various rules about work and minimum sizes of work crews that have been placed in bargaining agreements obviously curtail management flexibility and can be impediments to productivity improvement.[51]

For some state and local governments productivity bargaining has focused on wage incentive plans; if productivity is increased, then the financial savings can be used for salary increases or bonuses. New York City negotiated a productivity agreement providing wage increases for Medicare and Medicaid claims processors; the result was that collections increased much more than the cost of the wage increases. Detroit has had a shared savings formula for sanitation workers; the system was geared to the number of hours of labor required to collect a ton of refuse, with savings being shared by the City and the workers.[52] The City of Orange, California, negotiated a contract providing for wage increases for police officers when the rate of rapes, robberies, burglaries, and car thefts decreased.[53]

Productivity bargaining linked with wage increases has several fundamental problems. One is the issue of how to measure productivity.[54] In the private sector, where products are manufactured, productivity is more readily measured than in the public sector, which provides services.

---

[50] Walter L. Balk, ed., "Symposium on Productivity in Government," *Public Administration Review*, 38 (1978):1–50; John M. Capozzola, "Productivity Bargaining: Problems and Prospects," *National Civic Review*, 65 (1976):176–186; Raymond D. Horton, "Productivity and Productivity Bargaining in Government: A Critical Analysis," *Public Administration Review*, 36 (1976):407–414; Chester A. Newland et al., *MBO and Productivity Bargaining in the Public Sector* (Chicago: International Personnel Management Association, 1974); Ralph R. Smith, "Productivity Bargaining: Pattern for the Future?" *Employee Relations Law Journal*, 2 (1977):313–322; and Shin-ichi Takezawa, *Productivity, Quality of Working Life and Labour-Management Relations* (Tokyo: Asian Productivity Organization, 1976).

[51] Sam Zagoria, "Productivity in Bargaining," *State Government*, 49 (1976):248–251.

[52] National Commission on Productivity and Work Quality, *Employee Incentives to Improve State and Local Government Productivity* (Washington: Government Printing Office, 1975), pp. 79 and 82–86.

[53] Paul D. Staudohar, "An Experiment in Increasing Productivity of Police Service Employees," *Public Administration Review*, 35 (1975):518–522. See also Raymond D. Horton, "Productivity and Productivity Bargaining in Government: A Critical Analysis," *Public Administration Review*, 36 (1976):407–414.

[54] Harry P. Hatry and Donald M. Fisk, *Improving Productivity and Productivity Measurement in Local Governments*, prepared for National Commission on Productivity (Washington: Government Printing Office, 1971).

How can productivity be measured for workers in a city building permits office or an office in a state department of education that works with local school districts on curriculum development? Another problem is that productivity agreements commonly have treated all workers equally, regardless of whether some have become more productive than others. Such agreements may provide little incentive to government's better employees. Another problem with productivity bargaining is that it may be seen by organized labor as simply a way of making workers work harder and harder. Wage incentive systems tied to productivity also can be challenged as focusing on hygiene factors (see Chapter 11). It is conceivable that productivity gains are to be made more through increased motivation than by wage incentive arrangements in labor contracts. The relative absence of sustained use of productivity bargaining raises doubts about its success and future. Individual experiments with such bargaining have been short-lived, with an experiment receiving wide publicity but then being abandoned a year or so later.

In addition to productivity bargaining and other strategies, one other major influence on how negotiations are carried out is what will happen should the two sides not reach an agreement. Part of the bargaining process involves establishing a record or position that will be advantageous should an impasse occur. Impasse procedures are the next subject of this section. Assuming for the moment, however, that an agreement is reached, the negotiated settlement is submitted to the workers for their approval. Rejection of the agreement sends the negotiators back to the bargaining table.

Impasse Procedures

When the two sides cannot reach an agreement on a contract, an impasse occurs. The general rule of organized labor is "no contract—no work" and a strike ensues. In the public sector, however, strikes are usually prohibited. The courts have held that government may prohibit strikes, although there cannot be a prohibition on asserting the right to strike since that would violate the First Amendment's guarantee of free speech.[55]

The penalty for striking can be severe. Employees may be suspended or permanently removed from their positions. Union officials can be jailed, and the unions can be fined for striking. The courts have upheld these measures, although some procedural protections are provided to

---

[55] *National Association of Letter Carriers* v. *Blount*, 305 F. Supp. 546 (1969), appeal dismissed 400 U.S. 801 (1970) and *United Federation of Postal Clerks* v. *Blount*, 325 F. Supp. 879 (1971), affirmed 404 U.S. 802 (1971).

Table 13.6.   State and local government work stoppages by type of government, 1976

Jurisdiction type	Number of stoppages	Average duration in days	Average days of idleness*
State governments	27	11	4,610
Local governments	350	9	4,370
Counties	40	9	4,088
Municipalities	121	6	4,335
Townships	9	11	141
School districts	155	10	4,122
Special districts	25	12	8,046
Total	377	9	4,387

Source: Census Bureau and Labor-Management Services Administration, *Labor-Management Relations in State and Local Governments: 1976* (Washington: Government Printing Office, 1978).

    * Number of employees × number of days.

employees. The Supreme Court dealt with such a situation in 1976 in the *Hortonville* case.[56] Teachers in a Wisconsin school district went on strike in violation of the state's employee relations law. The school board then held a hearing and dismissed the teachers. The teachers claimed in court that their Fourteenth Amendment due process rights had been violated, in that the board had been biased. The Court agreed with the teachers that they were entitled to an impartial hearing but held that there was no evidence that the board had been biased. In explaining its position, the Court noted that while board members had made public statements opposing the strike, these statements could not be construed to mean that the board members were unwilling to change their views; the board had not necessarily come to a decision to dismiss the teachers prior to holding the hearing.

Despite the prohibition against strikes, they still occur and with considerable frequency. Until the mid-1960s public employee strikes were rare, but since then they have become commonplace in many jurisdictions. Table 13.6 shows work stoppages in 1976 in state and local governments. Of the 377 strikes, nearly half were in school districts and 121 were in cities. The average length of the strikes was nine days. The impact of the strikes varied depending upon the number of employees involved. The "typical" strike involved nearly 4,400 person-days of work that were lost. Teacher strikes were the most prevalent (146), followed by strikes of other workers in education (98). Highway workers were the next most frequent group to strike (65).

    [56] *Hortonville Joint School District #1* v. *Hortonville Education Association*, 426 U.S. 482 (1976).

As would be expected, great variations on the frequency of strikes exists among state and local governments. In the two-year period from October, 1974, to October, 1976, there were 867 state and local stoppages, but 22 states had less than five stoppages. No strikes occurred in the Dakotas, Nevada, Virginia, and Wyoming. At the other extreme, there were nine states with twenty or more strikes. California, Illinois, Michigan, New York, Ohio, and Pennsylvania each had 50 or more strikes in the two-year period. Pennsylvania had the most with 193 stoppages.[57]

Strikes are viewed as problems. During a strike, services to the citizenry in general and to agency clients are disrupted. Workers must survive without pay. Future labor-management relations may be harmed because of negative attitudes generated by a strike. For these reasons, procedures have been established to resolve impasses and thereby avert strikes. Third-party intervention is the typical approach that is taken. A third party other than labor and management attempts to resolve the conflict.

Mediation is the first step in impasse resolution procedures. The mediator is a neutral who performs the role of diplomat, seeking to find areas of agreement between the parties and to develop compromise positions on the key issues. Mediation is an essentially weak process in that the mediator does not have authority to compel the parties to agree to anything. For the federal government, this function is handled by the Federal Mediation and Conciliation Service (FMCS), an independent agency of the government. The FMCS also provides mediation services to private labor disputes and state and local disputes.[58] State governments have mediation agencies with varying responsibilities. Some states use the same agency for both public and private labor impasses, while others have separate agencies. Mediation offices may be invited to intervene by either labor or management or they may intervene on their own initiative.

In the event that mediation fails to bring the parties together, the next step is likely to be factfinding.[59] For state and local governments, a

---

[57] Census Bureau and Labor-Management Services Administration, *Labor-Management Relations in State and Local Governments: 1976*, p. 111. See also James Perry, "Strikes in State Government Employment," *State Government*, 49 (1976):257–262.

[58] Jerome H. Ross, "Federal-State Cooperation in Labor Mediations," *State Government*, 49 (1976):254–256; and Jerome H. Ross, "Federal Mediation in the Public Sector," *Monthly Labor Review*, 99 (February, 1976):41–45.

[59] Robert E. Doherty, "On Factfinding: A One-Eyed Man Lost Among the Eagles," *Public Personnel Management*, 5 (1976):363–367; Benjamin W. Wolkinson and Jack Stieber, "Michigan Fact-Finding Experience in Public Sector Disputes," *Arbitration Journal*, 32 (1976):225–247; and *Questions and Answers on Factfinding* (Bloomington: School of Public and Environmental Affairs, Indiana University, 1978).

state labor relations board usually has the power to determine whether a case should be submitted to factfinding. If factfinding is to be used, the board may submit a list of individuals to the two parties; a factfinder is chosen through the process of elimination, by which labor and management alternately strike names from the list until only one name remains. At the federal level, when mediation has not led to an agreement, labor and management may agree to binding arbitration (discussed below) or either side may request the Federal Service Impasses Panel (FSIP) to intervene. The seven-member FSIP is a unit within the Federal Labor Relations Authority and has considerable freedom in selecting a procedure that will resolve an impasse; one choice that the Panel has is to use factfinding.

Factfinding is more formal than mediation. The two sides submit lists of issues to the factfinder, who determines which issues to hear. The factfinder can only consider topics that are within the scope of mandatory bargaining. The factfinder holds a hearing at which labor and management present evidence on each of the issues. Witnesses are called to testify and may be cross-examined. Later, the factfinder issues a report, making recommendations on each of the issues. These are only recommendations in that neither side is required to accept them. The factfinder's report is submitted first only to labor and management in the hope that the recommendations will be accepted. If they are not accepted, the report is made public as a means of bringing pressure on the two parties to accept the suggested agreement.

Several criteria are used by factfinders. The criteria are established by executive order and/or statute. On the issue of wages, one criterion is comparability. Are workers being paid considerably less than similar workers in other jurisdictions and in the private sector? (Wages, of course, are not the subject of factfinding at the federal level since this is a nonbargainable item.) Changes in the cost of living are considered. The ability of the jurisdiction to pay higher wages is considered, and in the hearing, labor will attempt to show that money is not an obstacle to higher wages. The effectiveness and efficiency of operations are other criteria, as well as the general welfare of the public.

The willingness of labor and management to accept the factfinder's report is dependent on their assessment of the likelihood of being successful at the next step in the impasse procedure. Where strikes are prohibited, that next step often is interest arbitration (to be distinguished from grievance arbitration, discussed in the next section).[60] Binding arbi-

[60] Tim Bornstein, "Interest Arbitration in Public Employment: An Arbitrator Views the Process," *Labor Law Journal,* 29 (1978):77–86; Mollie H. Bowers, "Legislated Arbitration: Legality, Enforceability, and Face-Saving," *Public Personnel Management,* 3 (1974):270–278; Robert E. Dunham, "Interest Arbitration in Non-Federal Public Employ-

tration is the settlement of a dispute by the decision of a neutral third party. Seventeen states require this procedure for police and fire impasses, where strikes are considered not to be in the public interest.[61] A single arbitrator may be used, selected in the same manner as a fact-finder, or a three-member arbitraton panel may be used. In the latter instance, each side selects a registered arbitrator and those two select a third panel member. At the federal level, the Federal Service Impasses Panel has arbitration-type authority. The Civil Service Reform Act grants the FSIP authority to "take whatever action is necessary" to settle an impasse.[62] The procedure of arbitration is similar to factfinding, including the holding of a trial-type hearing, but the important difference is that the arbitration award is binding rather than only a recommendation.

Interest arbitration is a controversial subject in at least two respects. One criticism is that decision authority is granted to an individual or individuals not directly involved. From organized labor's perspective, the arbitrators may be largely insensitive to the workers' needs. From management's perspective, the arbitrators may make policy and yet are not accountable to the jurisdiction's constituents.[63] At one time management may have preferred arbitration to the alternative of a strike, and labor may have preferred the right to strike. Today, the opposite could be true. Organized labor has accepted interest arbitration as an alternative to striking.[64] On the other hand, management may sometimes prefer having to endure a strike rather than being forced to accept an arbitration award.[65] Management might well prefer a fire fighters strike rather than an arbitration settlement involving a large salary increase, because that increase will involve not only higher costs for fire services but will be used as precedent in negotiating with unions representing other bargaining units. Arbitrators' decisions can have the effect of forcing cities to raise taxes.

---

ment," *Arbitration Journal*, 31 (1976):45–57; Henry B. Frazier III, "Labor Arbitration in the Federal Service," *George Washington Law Review*, 45 (1977):712–756; Benjamin Jones, "Public Employee Labor Arbitration and the Delegation of Governmental Powers," *State Government*, 51 (1978):109–114; C. Richard Miserendion, "Arbitration in the Federal Service: The Regulation of Remedies," *Arbitration Journal*, 30 (1975):129–145; and Betty S. Murphy, "Interest Arbitration," *Public Personnel Management*, 6 (1977):295–299.

[61] Carlson and Sedwick, *State Employee Labor Relations*, pp. 31–32.

[62] Anthony F. Ingrassia, "State Report on Federal Labor-Management Relations," *Civil Service Journal*, 18 (July–September, 1977):41.

[63] Joseph R. Grodin, "Political Aspects of Public Sector Interest Arbitration," *California Law Review*, 64 (1976):678–701.

[64] Jerry Wurf, "Binding Arbitration: The View of a Public Union," *Employee Relations Law Journal*, 2 (1976):48–56.

[65] Tim Bornstein, "Perspectives on Change in Local Government Collective Bargaining," *Labor Law Journal*, 28 (1977):431–444.

The other main criticism of interest arbitration is that it discourages the two sides from reaching a compromise agreement. If binding arbitration is the final step in the impasse procedure, both sides in negotiating will be concerned with establishing a record for eventual use in arbitration. For example, labor's initial demand in negotiations may have been a 10 percent salary increase and management's offer was 4 percent; a midpoint compromise at 7 percent might seem appropriate. However, if in the negotiations labor reduced its demand to 8 percent while management raised its offer to only 4.5 percent, then, when the case goes to arbitration, the award could be a compromise figure considerably below 7 percent. In other words, compulsory arbitraton encourages the union and management to take extreme positions and discourages them from compromising.

One variation of interest arbitration intended to alleviate this problem is final-offer arbitration.[66] Under this procedure, the arbitration panel may not fashion its own agreement but must choose between the last offers made by management and labor. With each side knowing that the arbitrators must choose one position or the other, there will be pressure to make reasonable offers rather than taking extreme positions that are unlikely to be accepted by the panel.

The right to strike is the primary alternative to interest arbitration. Alaska, Hawaii, Minnesota, Montana, Oregon, and Pennsylvania allow strikes among some state and local employees. The usual requirement is that a strike is not permissible until mediation and factfinding have failed; even at that point, the two sides may agree to interest arbitration rather than having a strike occur. Once the strike is initiated, it can continue indefinitely until labor and management reach an agreement or until management wins a court injunction sending employees back to work. Such an injunction in Pennsylvania can be issued when a "strike creates a clear and present danger or threat to the health, safety, or welfare of the public." Other states that allow strikes have similar provisions.[67] If employees ignore the court order, the government may fire them, and the court may fine and imprison union leaders as well as fine the union.

---

[66] Peter Feuille, "Final-Offer Arbitration and Negotiating Incentives," *Arbitration Journal*, 32 (1977):203–220; Peter Feuille, *Final Offer Arbitration: Concepts, Developments, Techniques* (Chicago: International Personnel Management Association, 1975); Peter Feuille and Gary Long, "The Public Administrator and Final Offer Arbitration," *Public Administration Review*, 34 (1974):575–583; and Lawrence T. Holden, Jr., "Final-Offer Arbitration in Massachusetts: One Year Later," *Arbitration Journal*, 31 (1976):26–35.

[67] Marvin J. Levine and Joy J. Luna, "A Comparison of Impasse Procedures in the Public and Private Sectors: The Hawaii State Teacher's Experience," *Public Personnel Management*, 7 (1978):108–118.

A court-ordered injuction against a strike, however, does not bring about a settlement. The employees are ordered to work without a union contract. One suggestion for resolving the impasse at this point is to allow courts broad discretion, including the power to order interest arbitration.[68] That type of impasse procedure would follow the steps of mediation, factfinding, strike, and injunction, coupled with interest arbitration.

The right to strike has become a moot issue, at least at the state and local levels. At the federal level, employees have refrained from striking, with the notable exception of the postal strike of 1970. State and local employees have been less willing to abide by anti-strike laws. These laws have little effect, since they are difficult to enforce. Passing a law against strikes cannot compel employees to work. Some state laws have provided that striking employees are automatically dismissed from their jobs, but such a provision is largely unworkable. A school district would be chaotic if it seriously tried to replace all striking teachers with new teachers. It is for these reasons that several states have granted the right to strike, and other states can be expected to take that same route.

MANAGING UNDER COLLECTIVE BARGAINING

With the advent of collective bargaining, the ways in which government operates necessarily have changed. Collective negotiations leading to a written agreement between labor and management change the rules that govern how activities are carried out on a daily basis. This section considers the effects of collective bargaining on daily operations and more generally the impacts of collective bargaining.

Contract Administration

Once a collective bargaining agreement has been reached, management has the obligation of implementation. An exception is in the case of arbitration awards, where management may appeal to a court on the grounds that the award violated management rights guaranteed by the governing statute or executive order. Some of the more immediate implementation responsibilities include adjusting payroll records to meet the new wage and salary requirements and making any changes in withholding for health insurance benefits, retirement benefits, or union dues.

Major problems have arisen at the state and local levels over govern-

---

[68] Governor's Study Commission on Public Employee Relations, *Report* (Harrisburg: Commonwealth of Pennsylvania, 1978), pp. 27–32.

ment's ability to meet the financial costs of the labor settlement. In some cases, management may agree to a wage settlement in order to avoid a strike, but then the problem of finding needed funds arises. In other cases, interest arbitration awards pose the same problem of high wage increases, with no apparent source of funding for them. Some adjustments can be made in budgets, such as postponing proposed expenditures on equipment and large capital items, but often these adjustments cannot release sufficient funds to meet higher labor costs. At that point, the argument is made that the government is unable to pay, although in reality a government is rarely unable to pay but only unwilling to take steps that would enable it to pay. Tax increases usually are an option in meeting higher wage scales.

When governments confront such situations, the alternatives taken usually involve attempts to avoid the higher costs. A freeze may be placed on all new hiring in order to reduce payroll requirements. In some cases, freezes are imposed on wage increases in contradiction of the labor contract, but these freezes have been overturned by courts, which have insisted that government prove beyond doubt its inability to pay. Another approach is to temporarily furlough employees, for perhaps thirty days, on a staggered basis; this approach has the effect of paying employees about the same pay as in the prior year. Permanently laying off some workers is another tactic. All of these methods of minimizing personnel costs, however, can be challenged by unions as unfair labor practices. A union does not want to be in the position of bargaining for higher salaries at the cost of employees losing their jobs.[69]

The meaning of clauses in labor-management contracts frequently is subject to different possible interpretations. Sometimes clauses are hastily drafted in the midst of negotiations, and questions later arise about what those clauses mean. In other instances, clauses may be left intentionally vague, in part because the two sides are eager to reach an agreement and do not want a relatively minor issue to result in an impasse. Ambiguous language also may result when neither side is sure what it wants to win on a given item; the assumption is made that the language will gain clarity as issues arise while operating under the contract.

To resolve issues of contract interpretation, most agreements include an arbitration procedure; in most cases, the arbitration decision is bind-

---

[69] Albert G. Lauber, Jr., "Executory Labor Contracts and Municipal Bankruptcy," *Yale Law Journal*, 85 (1976):957–974; and Charles C. Mulcahy and Marion C. Smith, *Problems and Solutions Resulting from Inability to Pay in the Public Sector* (Washington: International Personnel Management Association, 1978).

ing, although some systems use an advisory approach.[70] Arbitraton used to interpret a contract is known as grievance or rights arbitration, in distinction from interest arbitration (discussed above). The grievance procedure, itself, is a negotiable item. Activating the grievance procedure normally is the prerogative of employees, not management; should management think employees are violating the contract, disciplinary proceedings may be initiated or unfair labor practices may be charged before the labor relations board.

The scope of possible grievances is great. Workers paid on an hourly basis may complain that overtime is not being paid as specified in the contract. There may be complaints that the administration is not adhering to sick-leave provisions. Workers may complain about inadequate safety equipment. One particularly difficult area is the disciplining of employees. Where an employee feels he is being unfairly charged with failing to meet his job requirements, he may have the choice of initiating the adverse action appeals procedures administered by the personnel agency (see Chapter 8) or the grievance procedure provided in the labor contract. Employees choose whichever procedure they think will work to their advantage. Unions prefer employees to use the negotiated route, since it provides the unions an opportunity to demonstrate their effectiveness in helping workers. Personnel administrators have argued that employees should not be required to use the negotiated procedure, given that some employees probably are opposed to collective bargaining even though they are in a collective bargaining unit.

The federal Civil Service Reform Act not only permits grievance procedures but also requires that they be included in negotiated agreements. The procedure must be "fair and simple" and provide for "expeditious processing." A union having exclusive representation has a right to participate in the grievance process, and an employee has a right

[70] Mollie H. Bowers, *Contract Administration in the Public Sector* (Chicago: International Personnel Management Association, 1976); Francis D. Ferris, "Contract Interpretation: A Bread-and-Butter Talent," *Public Personnel Management*, 4 (1975):223–230; Eugene B. Granof and Stephen A. Moe, "Grievance Arbitration in the U.S. Postal Service," *Arbitration Journal*, 29 (1974):1–14; *Grievance Arbitration in the Federal Service: Principles, Practices, and Precedents* (Washington: Civil Service Commission, 1977); Joseph Krislov and Robert M. Peters, "Grievance Arbitration in State and Local Governments: A Survey," *Arbitration Journal*, 25 (1970):196–205; James E. Martin, "Grievance Procedures in the Federal Service: The Continuing Problem," *Public Personnel Management*, 7 (1978):221–229: Gerald M. Pops, *Emergence of the Public Sector Arbitrator* (Lexington, Mass.: Lexington Books, 1976); Robert Sebris, Jr., "Formal or Informal: What Are the Union's Rights?" *Public Personnel Management*, 6 (1977):156–165; Federal Labor Relations Council, *Report*, p. 32; and Susan L. Williams, "Accommodation of Jurisdiction Over Federal Labor Disputes," *George Washington Law Review*, 44 (1976): 604–622.

to present his own case in the process. The final step in the grievance procedure is binding arbitration, which can be invoked by either the union or management. Several items are excluded from the grievance procedure:

1. Any claimed violation . . . relating to prohibited political activities;
2. Retirement, life insurance, or health insurance;
3. A suspension or removal . . . ;
4. Any examination, certification, or appointment; or
5. The classification of any position which does not result in the reduction in grade or pay of an employee.

When a prohibited personnel practice is involved, an employee must choose either the negotiated route or the route involving the Merit Systems Protection Board (see Chapters 2 and 8). When such a choice is available and an employee chooses the negotiated procedure, he may ask the MSPB to review the decision that is eventually reached. In cases of alleged discrimination, the employee may ask the Equal Employment Opportunity Commission to review a decision reached through the negotiated grievance procedure.

Most negotiated grievance procedures involve several steps, beginning with the employee meeting with his supervisor to discuss the complaint. The union shop steward, who is an employee in the unit, attends this meeting on behalf of the employee. In subsequent steps in the grievance procedure, the union may provide an attorney to defend the employee. If a satisfactory settlement is not reached at the first step, the case is appealed to the department head or, in large jurisdictions, to a bureau head and later to the department head. The last step prior to grievance arbitration is to appeal to a central administrative officer, such as a secretary of administration.

The grievance arbitrator, usually selected by each side alternately striking names from a list until only one remains, conducts a hearing on the case and normally must make a ruling within a specified time period. Where the language of an agreement is ambiguous, the arbitrator attempts to determine what has been the past practice in an agency and will attempt to devise a ruling in conformance with that practice. Where past practice offers little guidance, the arbitrator explores with the two sides the negotiations that led to the inclusion of the phrase in the contract. The powers of the arbitrator can be enormous. At the federal level, the FLRA can accept appeals on arbitration awards, but the Authority will not substitute its judgment for that of the arbitrator. Voiding such an award requires proof that it is contrary to statute or regulations. An award can be vacated if there is proof the arbitrator was biased or capricious or exceeded his authority.

Negotiated grievance procedures have posed problems for managers. Sometimes managers are not fully aware of contract provisions and take actions that prompt workers to file grievances under the negotiated procedure. Better understanding of the contract might have avoided many grievances. These procedures and collective bargaining in general may intimidate some managers. A manager may be reluctant to take appropriate action in order to avoid a possible confrontation that would ultimately result in his judgment being scrutinized by an arbitrator.

Impact of Collective Bargaining

Organized labor has had to fight hard for each power it has gained. At every point there have been attempts to exclude unions from the public sector. Yet, unions have won great powers that affect all aspects of government administration and not just personnel administration.

Involvement in wage determination has constituted one arena for conflict. The argument has been that wages should be nonnegotiable, in that they have direct bearing on total expenditures and ultimately on tax rates. Critics have insisted that employees should not be able to gouge taxpayers' wallets. Despite the argument, however, unions have won the right to bargain over wages in many state and local governments, although wages remain nonnegotiable at the federal level. Major wage gains undoubtedly have been won by some unions, and the mere threat of unionization surely has prompted major wage increases in some jurisdictions. Nevertheless, available evidence suggests that there is not a perfect relationship between unionization and labor costs. Public-sector salaries are in part influenced by private market salaries; local government employee wage rates are likely to be high in areas where private wages are high. Also, the wealth of a jurisdiction has been found to be associated with the level of public wage rates; relatively poor jurisdictions do not pay as well as wealthy jurisdictions regardless of unionization. Unions are necessarily sensitive to their political climates. Unions that seek wage demands that to taxpayers seem excessive may invite taxpayer revolts.[71]

---

[71] Victor E. Flango and Robert Dudley, "Who Supports Public Employee Strikes?" *Journal of Collective Negotiations in the Public Sector*, 7 (1978):1–9; Paul F. Gerhart, "Determinants of Bargaining Outcomes in Local Government Labor Negotiations," *Industrial and Labor Relations Review*, 29 (1976):331–351; Mark D. Karper and Daniel J. Meckstroth, "The Impact of Unionism on Public Wage Rates," *Public Personnel Management*, 5 (1976):343–346; Daniel J. B. Mitchell, "Collective Bargaining and Wage Determination in the Public Sector: Is Armageddon Really at Hand?" *Public Personnel Management*, 7 (1978):80–95; Gary A. Moore, "The Effect of Collective Bargaining on Internal Salary Structures in the Public Schools," *Industrial and Labor Relations Review*, 29 (1976):352–362; Steve W. Panyan, "Local Surveys as Community Indicators Showing Attitudes Toward Unions," *Public Personnel Management*, 5 (1976):368–372; Joan P.

Unions have had to fight for a right to participate in politics. Prior to being allowed to bargain with management, public-employee unions acted mainly as lobbyists seeking legislation for their benefit. Today organized labor is increasing its role in the electoral process. Unions have been active in lobbying for Hatch Act revisions, which would permit merit employees to become active in political campaigns (see Chapter 8). Public employee unions endorse candidates for office and sometimes run campaigns to defeat anti-union politicians at the polls. Campaign politics is perhaps keenest in local government elections, especially in jurisdictions that have worker residency requirements. If all municipal employees are required to live within the city, they can influence the outcome of a mayoral election. This is less likely in state and national elections. A local, state, or federal worker may not be particularly persuaded to vote for a presidential or gubernatorial candidate simply because of union support.[72]

A charge frequently made about collective bargaining is that it is antithetical to the merit principle.[73] Unions want to negotiate on how personnel decisions are made, while critics suggest much of the personnel process should be insulated from bargaining. A special committee of the International Personnel Management Association has suggested that most aspects of recruiting, testing, position classification, political activity regulations, and separation decisions should be nonbargainable.[74]

The case against unions on the merit issue is not as strong as it might seem.[75] In making an argument that unions are against merit, one surely cannot suggest that unions are for patronage; patronage is not simply the opposite of merit. Unions are one of the major opponents of patronage, since that system would threaten their members' job

---

Weitzman, "The Effect of Economic Restraints on Public Sector Collective Bargaining: The Lessons of New York City," *Employee Relations Law Journal*, 2 (1977):286–312; and Dennis C. Zuelke and Lloyd E. Frohreich, "The Impact of Comprehensive Collective Negotiations on Teachers' Salaries: Some Evidence from Wisconsin," *Journal of Collective Negotiations in the Public Sector*, 6 (1977):81–88.

[72] "Collective Bargaining and Politics in Public Employment," *UCLA Law Review*, 19 (1972):887–1083.

[73] Paul M. Camp and W. Richard Lomax, "Bilateralism and the Merit Principle," *Public Administration Review*, 28 (1968):132–137; David Lewin and Raymond D. Horton, "The Impact of Collective Bargaining on the Merit System in Government," *Arbitration Journal*, 30 (1975):199–211; Douglas I. McIntyre, "Merit Principles and Collective Bargaining: A Marriage or Divorce," *Public Administration Review*, 37 (1977):186–190; and Muriel M. Morse, "Shall We Bargain Away the Merit System?" *Public Personnel Review*, 24 (1963):239–243.

[74] "The Public's Interest in Personnel Administration," *IPMA News*, (December, 1977):9.

[75] Jerry Wurf, "Merit: A Union View," *Public Administration Review*, 34 (1974):431–434.

security.[76] Much of the issue centers on union endorsement of seniority as a factor in personnel decisions. Seniority is considered antithetical to merit, since the focus is on how long one has held a job and not how well one performs a job. Unions tend to prefer promotions, layoffs, and the like to be at least partially based on seniority. It should be noted that the seniority issue tends to clash with affirmative action, which itself has been criticized as antithetical to merit. Since the least senior workers often are minorities and women, these people are less likely to be promoted and more likely to be laid off when a seniority rule is used.[77]

Collective bargaining has been seen as increasing the number of personnel problems faced by administrators.[78] One should ask, however, whether the bargaining process created those problems or only facilitated their surfacing. Tensions between managers and their subordinates have always existed, and unions have been able to capitalize on those problems. Labor organizations have provided a strong voice for employees. From the line manager's perspective, few discretionary powers may seem to remain. The manager must not only abide by statutory requirements and civil service regulations but now must operate within the confines of a negotiated labor agreement. It is probable that some managers have become timid, fearful to take action that might lead to a union grievance. At the same time, collective bargaining may have been helpful to managers, in that agreements spell out what rights and obligations are assigned to each side. Managers now manage by contract, insisting that workers meet their obligations specified in the contract.

Unions can have positive and negative influences on worker performance. From the negative standpoint, unions are seen as needlessly driving a wedge between workers and their superiors, as encouraging confrontation rather than cooperation. Employees are encouraged to pledge allegiance to their union and not to the government that employs them.[79] Unions may serve to provide a defense or rationalization for poor performance. Employees may be encouraged to put less effort into their work, since management presumably is unconcerned about their welfare.

[76] June Weisberger, *Job Security and Public Employees*, 2d ed. (Ithaca, N.Y.: New York State School of Industrial and Labor Relations, Cornell University, 1973); and Joseph Adler and Robert E. Doherty, eds., *Employment Security in the Public Sector: A Symposium* (Ithaca, N.Y.: New York State School of Industrial and Labor Relations, Cornell University, 1974).

[77] Garry M. Whalen and Richard S. Rubin, "Labor Relations and Affirmative Action: A Tug-of-War," *Public Personnel Management*, 6 (1977):149–155.

[78] Ronald D. Merrel, "A Conceptual Model to Determine the Impact of Collective Bargaining on Management Practices," *Public Personnel Management*, 7 (1978):100–107.

[79] George E. Biles, "Allegiances of Unionized Public Employees Toward Employer and Union," *Public Personnel Management*, 3 (1974):165–169.

Indeed, managers are often instructed not to grant improvements in working conditions to their subordinates, because to do so is to relinquish a bargaining chip in subsequent collective bargaining negotiations. Labor organizations can increase worker dissatisfaction, in that the union itself seems to be another source of authority that dictates what employees may and may not do. Employees resent having to abide by union regulations as well as management regulations. Labor organizations are hierarchically structured and can discourage democratic decision-making among their members.[80]

On the positive side, unions can foster increased worker productivity by helping to develop improved methods of operation and by increasing worker motivation, although the counter view is that unions rarely are concerned with productivity improvement. Labor leaders in some cases have been instrumental in helping management deal with employee problems, such as habitual tardiness in coming to work. Labor-management committees have been used not only to deal with personnel matters but also to deal more generally with the operations of agencies.[81] Instead of being an opponent to innovation, unions can help facilitate changes that increase agency and worker productivity. Management can enlist organized labor's support in instituting motivational programs.[82] Nevertheless, there always will be the concern on labor's part that innovations not lead to layoffs.

While public employee unionism and collective bargaining have been emerging in the United States, developments that warrant attention have been occurring in Europe. European countries long have had powerful political parties that are tied with labor unions. Germany in recent years has received considerable attention because of its 1976 legislation establishing *Mitbestimmung*, or co-determination in all corporations

---

[80] Seymour M. Lipset, Martin Trow, and James Coleman, *Union Democracy: The Internal Politics of the International Typographical Union* (Garden City, N.Y.: Doubleday, 1962).

[81] Joseph M. Becker, *Shared Government in Employment Security: A Study of Advisory Councils* (New York: Columbia University Press, 1959); Anna C. Goldoff with David C. Tatage, "Joint Productivity Committees: Lessons of Recent Initiatives," *Public Administration Review*, 38 (1978):184–186; David C. Hershfield, "Barriers to Increased Labor Productivity," *Conference Board Record*, 13 (July, 1976):38–49; National Commission on Productivity and Work Quality, *Labor-Management Committees in the Public Sector: Experiences of Eight Committees* (Washington: Government Printing Office, 1975); Arthur A. Thompson, "Employee Participation in Decision Making: The TVA Experience," *Public Personnel Review*, 28 (1967):82–88; and Wayne E. Thompson, "Labor-Management Focus: Improving Government Productivity," *National Civic Review*, 64 (1975):335–338+.

[82] Albert A. Blum and Michael L. Moore with B. Parker Fairey, "The Effect of Motivational Programs on Collective Bargaining," *Personnel Journal*, 52 (1973):633–641; and Bernard J. White, "Union Response to the Humanization of Work: An Explanatory Proposition," *Human Resource Management*, 14 (Fall, 1975):2–9.

having more than 2,000 employees. The critical feature of co-determination is that employees have the same number of votes as stockholders on a corporation's board of supervisors, which is comparable to a board of directors in the U.S. The supervisory board sets corporate policy and selects a board of management to run the corporation.[83]

Employee representation on a German board of supervisors is divided in four ways. Unions are guaranteed two or three representatives, depending upon the size of the board, and these representatives need not be employees of the corporation. The remaining representatives must be employees, and are split proportionally on the basis of the mix of workers who are blue-collar, white-collar, and supervisory, with the last being guaranteed at least one seat. Assuming that the management representative is more likely to side with the stockholders than with organized labor, labor does not have absolute parity with the stockholders. The chairman of the board is likely to be a stockholder representative, given that unless two-thirds of the total board can agree on a chairman, then the stockholder representatives alone choose the chairman. In cases of tie votes, the chairman may cast two votes. Labor, on the other hand, has an important power in the selection of the management board. One of the three members of that board is the personnel director and a person cannot be chosen for that position without the approval of a majority of the employee representatives on the supervisory board; the same rule applies for removal of the personnel director.

Co-determination in Europe is largely a private-sector phenomenon, but there is increasing interest in extending it to the public sector. Whether that will occur is unknown, but for the moment, the European experiment in co-determination should stimulate thought in the U.S.; labor-management relations need not be exclusively structured in the collective bargaining mode. Unions in this country generally have not endorsed the European system; instead, they have defended collective bargaining as the more appropriate framework for labor-management relations.

---

[83] Klaus E. Agthe, "*Mitbestimmung:* Report on a Social Experiment," *Business Horizons*, 29 (February, 1977):5–14; J. Bautz Bonanno, "Employee Codetermination: Origins in Germany, Present Practice in Europe, and Applicability to the United States," *Harvard Journal of Legislation*, 14 (1977):947–1012; James N. Ellenberger, "The Realities of Co-determination," *American Federationist*, 84 (October, 1977):10–15; G. David Garson, ed., *Worker Self-Management in Industry: The West European Experience* (New York: Praeger, 1977); Michael Grunson and Wienand Meilicke, "The New Co-determination Law in Germany," *Business Lawyer*, 32 (1977):571–589; George H. Kuper, "Developments in the Quality of Working Life," *Labor Law Journal*, 28 (1977):752–762; T. D. Wall and J. A. Lischeron, *Worker Participation: A Critique of the Literature and Some Fresh Evidence* (London: McGraw-Hill, 1977); and John P. Windmuller, ed., "Industrial Democracy in International Perspective," *Annals*, 431 (1977):1–140.

SUMMARY

Despite the issue of governmental sovereignty, employee unions and collective bargaining have emerged as integral parts of public personnel systems. At the federal level, the largest unions include the American Federation of Government Employees and the National Federation of Federal Employees plus the American Postal Workers Unions and the National Association of Letter Carriers. The American Federation of State, County, and Municipal Employees and the National Education Association are major representatives of state and local workers. Unionism arose out of dissatisfaction with pay and working conditions plus a series of special factors peculiar to the 1960s. Labor-management relations are governed at the national level by legislation. States have used legislation, executive orders, and attorney general opinions to govern labor relations for both state and local employees.

Unit determination is essential before collective bargaining can commence. The main criterion is that employees have a community of interest. Special criteria pertain to various types of workers—supervisory, professional, and confidential. Once the unit is established, an election is held to determine whether collective bargaining is desired and what union will represent the employees. The federal government has more than 3,000 bargaining units, while small and medium-size cities have less than six. States differ widely on the number of bargaining units and the number of employees in each unit.

The bargaining process is complicated by who represents management, the scope of bargaining, and other factors. Sometimes the negotiated agreement must be submitted to the legislative body for approval as well as being submitted to the employees. Labor may have "meet and confer" rights, bargaining rights, or a combination of these. Some topics are mandatory items for bargaining, while others are only permissible or may be prohibited. In virtually every instance, there is a provision that management retain the right to manage. Wages are nonnegotiable at the federal level, but often are negotiable at the state and local levels. Bargaining strategies are developed by each side concerning what concessions they wish to win. Productivity bargaining has gained in popularity, but its future is uncertain.

The purpose of impasse procedures is to avert employee strikes. Mediation is usually the first step in an impasse procedure, followed by factfinding. Interest arbitration may follow, whereby management and labor are required to accept the award of an arbitrator or arbitration panel. Arbitration has been criticized as placing excessive powers in the hands of individuals who are not answerable to the electorate; arbitration decisions can make tax increases almost inevitable. Arbitration also may discourage the two sides from compromising, and for that reason final-offer arbitration is sometimes used. Regardless of general prohibitions against strikes, public workers increasingly have gone out on strike. Strikes have occurred most frequently in school districts. Some jurisdictions allow strikes when mediation and factfinding fail; when these strikes pose a threat to public health and safety, they can be halted by a court injunction.

Contract administration includes making budgetary adjustments to meet the higher personnel costs of a negotiated agreement and determining the precise meaning of various contract clauses. The latter involves a negotiated grievance procedure having several steps and usually ending with grievance arbitration.

Collective bargaining has had considerable effect upon the public sector. Employee wages have risen, although there is not a perfect relationship between wage gains and unionization. Unions have increased their role in political elections as well as continuing to lobby for favorable state and national legislation. Unions have been criticized as being opposed to the merit system, but that point is debatable. Patronage is opposed by unions, and they have supported some aspects of merit but at the same time have defended the use of seniority in personnel decisions. Collective bargaining has limited the powers of managers so that many unilateral actions can no longer be taken. Unions have had both positive and negative effects on workers. On the negative side, workers may have become alienated from management and may be discouraged from excelling in their work. On the positive side, unions occasionally have been instrumental in motivating workers and assisting in productivity improvement efforts. Finally, while public-sector labor-management relations have been undergoing great change in the United States, private-sector employees in Europe have been gaining co-determination rights that go far beyond traditional collective bargaining.

Chapter 14

Critique

Public personnel systems consist of numerous parts and relationships that frequently seem uncoordinated with each other and with the larger governmental system. This chapter provides a perspective on the problems that exist and possible future conditions that will influence personnel systems. The first section discusses the complaints that are frequently made about personnel systems. The second focuses upon the unresolved issues that are endemic not only to personnel administration but more generally to the governmental system. The third section considers the future of public personnel systems.

A NEGATIVE VIEW

Personnel administrators are dedicated to their work, perhaps being zealots for the advancement of the merit principle. The historical development of personnel systems, however, has tended to encourage an "us against them" outlook on government. In the early reform period, there was a real "them," namely persons who openly supported political patronage. Today, the "them" is not so apparent, since few persons would advocate a return to unlimited patronage throughout government. Personnelists, nevertheless, remain fearful that politicians and politically appointed executives, while pretending to support the merit principle, would embrace patronage if given the opportunity. There is a perceived need to be vigilant in watching for any administrative practice that might allow for political considerations in personnel matters.

The "us against them" outlook persists not only because of the historical development of the field but also because of organizational arrangements and contemporary pressures. Reformers were successful in creating independent civil service commissions, but that independence created a considerable degree of isolation. By insulating personnel from political pressures, reformers pushed this important function into a remote corner. Removed from the center of management, personnelists see themselves at best being ignored, and at worst, being attacked. Managers tend to consider personnelists as having no particular skills that could be helpful in improving agency operations; but personnel administrators hold the opposite view, that they have an extensive array of skills that, if they were only utilized, would facilitate more effective and efficient operations in government. Also, unions and collective bargaining are seen as constituting a new major force that could nullify the progress that has been achieved: "This is the greatest threat to the merit system that we face today."[1] The demand for affirmative action is another contemporary pressure that many personnel administrators have difficulty accepting.

Perhaps the most persistent line of attack that encourages the "us against them outlook" is the claim that personnel systems are dysfunctional. The conclusion reached in 1975 by the Study Committee on Policy Management Assistance for the U.S. Office of Management and Budget is typical:

> Civil service regulations, promulgated to guard against the ravages of unbridled patronage, limit the flexibility of policymakers and management in selecting and assigning personnel; thus needs determination and program development become futile because implementation is compromised.[2]

This is "the triumph of techniques over purpose."[3] By installing procedures for personnel actions, personnelists have hoped to produce systems based on merit, but critics contend that the procedures, better known as red tape, are not only superfluous but also harmful.

The field of personnel administration has been based primarily on the input side of government. The field of budgeting originally had a similar emphasis. Early budget systems stressed how dollars were being spent, with only limited concern about the consequences of those expenditures. Contemporary budget systems, however, attempt to link expenditures with program outcomes. Are people safer because of police expenditures, and do children read better because of educational expenditures? Personnel systems, in contrast, remain committed to the inputs. The assumption has been made that if tests are constructed appropriately and administered fairly, then the "right" people will be brought into govern-

---

[1] F. Arnold McDermott, "Merit Systems Under Fire," *Public Personnel Management*, 5 (1976):231.

[2] Study Committee on Policy Management Assistance, *Strengthening Public Management in the Intergovernmental System* (Washington: Government Printing Office, 1975), p. 23.

[3] Wallace S. Sayre, "The Triumph of Techniques over Purpose," *Public Administration Review*, 8 (1948):134–137.

ment. If performance appraisal systems are refined, then superior workers can be promoted and inferior workers can be removed.

Little attention has been paid to how workers influence the outcomes of governmental programs. The difficult problem entails analyzing the relationship of different types of workers in combination with supportive equipment and materials in producing governmental services that have measurable impacts. Program evaluation has gained wide acceptance in the 1970s, but evaluations tend to concentrate upon the relationships between total inputs, usually expressed in dollars, compared with program results. For example, police expenditures are analyzed in terms of their effects on crime rates. Personnel evaluation would take the additional step of relating the mix of personnel to program results. One group of researchers has suggested that it would be possible to compare crime rates by age group with the "type of personnel used for desk work."[4] The prospects for conducting such analyses are uncertain, as would be the results of the analyses, but the point here is that personnel administrators have largely ignored the impacts of personnel, preferring to concentrate on the processes or techniques of position classification, examination, performance appraisal, and the like.

The response of personnelists to these criticisms is to seek refinement in the techniques that are used. If the allegation is made that incompetents achieve high scores on civil service examinations while competent individuals are screened out, then the response is to redesign the test. If there are complaints that employees are not sufficiently protected from arbitrary disciplinary action, the response is to redesign the appeals system. If the appeals system is attacked for being exceedingly slow and for providing excessive protection to workers, the response again is to redesign the appeals system.

Skeptics suggest that refining techniques is fruitless and is likely to lead to more red tape. "Refinement" of procedures is viewed as making them more detailed and complicated. Once performance appraisal system has been "refined" it becomes a cumbersome device that places great burdens on the time of managers and ultimately is deemed by managers as no better than the appraisal system that was previously used. The prescription is:

> Fire the whole personnel department . . . The trouble with personnel experts is that they use gimmicks borrowed from manufacturing: inventories, replacement charts, recruiting, selecting, indoctrinating and training

---

[4] Selma J. Mushkin, Frank H. Sandifer, and Charles Warren, *Assessing Personnel Management: Objectives and Performance Indicators* (Washington: Public Services Laboratory, Georgetown University, 1977), p. 24.

machinery, job rotation, and appraisal programs. And this manufacturing of men is about as effective as Dr. Frankenstein was.[5]

Don't make the techniques better; instead, make government better by eliminating the techniques.

Personnel offices, like budgeting and planning offices, perform a staff and not a line function. Performance of a staff function often is a thankless task. Line managers can point to the accomplishments of their agencies. A highway department can justify itself by pointing to the redesigning of major intersections or the resurfacing of deteriorated roads. A mental health agency can claim great achievements in helping its clients deal with mental disorders. But what can be claimed by a personnel agency? Gauging the effectiveness of staff agencies is difficult, since they are facilitators rather than providers of governmental services. Personnel agencies attempt to get the "right" people into the "right" jobs, but if workers perform effectively, there is no obvious linkage between that effective performance and the work of the personnel office. Line managers can readily claim the success as theirs and that it was accomplished in spite of civil service regulations. Managers may view personnel offices as performing nonproductive functions, and, sometimes, counterproductive functions.

It is fashionable to attack personnel administration as being devoid of a governing theory or principle. Personnel administration has been seen as "a barren area for theoretical study" being mainly "the routine application of a practitioner's 'bag of tricks.'"[6] "There is an intellectual dryrot."[7] The merit principle has been the primary focus of personnel systems, but often the concept has been considered in a negative sense. Merit is perceived as keeping patronage out of government. The concept of merit was a useful focus for the reforms of the late 1800s and early 1900s, but, so say the critics, that idea is not sufficiently developed to provide guidance in meeting contemporary problems of administration. Even worse, many personnelists define "merit" as rigid adherence to procedures of their own design. Deviation from procedures becomes a "merit system violation," even though the "violation" may have had a positive effect on agency efficiency and effectiveness.

This is a harsh critique that personnelists, themselves, accept at least

---

[5] Robert Townsend, *Up the Organization: How to Stop the Corporation from Stifling People and Strangling Profits*, rev. ed. (Greenwich, Conn.: Fawcett Crest, 1971), pp. 126–127.

[6] Donald E. Klinger and John Nalbandian, "Personnel Management by Whose Objectives?" *Public Administration Review*, 38 (1978):366.

[7] H. Brinton Milward, "Politics, Personnel, and Public Policy," *Public Administration Review*, 38 (1978):393.

partially. The euphoria of the early reform years has gone. In the 1890s, reformists spoke glowingly of their cause:

> There are some among us who stood at the cradle of the Civil Service Reform movement. They remember the time when the practical politician looked upon the Civil Service Reformer as a visionary dreamer of singularly hopeless conceit—as little better than a harmless idiot who might be tolerated at large without the slightest danger to the existing order of things. When we remember that time, which does not lie very far behind us, and then contemplate the marvelous change that has since taken place, will the hope for the complete triumph of the cause we advocate still appear extravagantly sanguine?[8]

Today, many would consider such language embarrassing, empty rhetoric.

The second half of the 1970s has witnessed a resurgence of reform. Much attention has been directed at reorganization as one aspect of reform. Organization charts for personnel functions have been redrawn at the federal level, and some state and local governments can be expected to take similar action. Reorganization, however, should not be expected to eliminate the persistent criticisms of personnel systems. Reorganization alone can be a pointless exercise. "I was to learn that later in life we tend to meet any new situation by reorganizing, and a wonderful method it can be for creating the illusion of progress while producing confusion, inefficiency, and demoralization."[9] This is *not* to suggest that the federal reorganization effort is pointless, but to warn that reorganization is not a panacea.

Reform at the federal level has not been restricted to reorganization. Reforms have been aimed at encouraging the removal of nonproductive employees and rewarding productive employees with pay increases. These and other reforms have been incorporated into legislation, but reorganization and legislation, by themselves, will not recast the mode of personnel administration at the federal level. The same would be true for any state or local government that followed the federal government's lead. These changes need to be seen as creating a potential for redirecting personnel systems. Whether that potential will be realized will depend upon implementation efforts. In light of previous reform efforts, some skepticism is warranted concerning the likely effects of current reform initiatives.

---

[8] Carl Schurz, *The Spoils System* (Philadelphia: Altemus, 1896), p. 43.

[9] Attributed to Petronius Arbiter of Bithynia, ca. 66, *Public Administration Review*, 33 (1973):335. See also Rufus E. Miles, Jr., "Considerations for a President Bent on Reorganization," *Public Administration Review*, 37 (1977):155–162, and David S. Brown, "'Reforming' the Bureaucracy: Some Suggestions for the New President," *Public Administration Review*, 37 (1977):163–170.

UNRESOLVED ISSUES

Basic values that by themselves may seem unquestionably appropriate may collide with each other when applied to specific situations. The problem is that the *relative* importance of each value has not been determined, so that competition among values is characteristic of contemporary governmental systems. Personnel systems operate in an environment of uncertainty; they operate under conditions far beyond their control.

One of the most fundamental issues is the role of bureaucracy in a democracy.[10] "Bureaucracy is neither a system of government nor a collection of disagreeable men doing unnecessary things, but the personnel aspect of administration in all its ramifications and difficulties."[11] As society has grown and government has accepted greater responsibilities, bureaucracies have emerged to provide services. Bureaucracies have been seen as being essential to the survival of democracies. A different view, however, is that bureaucracies have become unwieldly organizations that are dehumanizing, defy anyone's control, and encourage inefficiency. Moreover, there has been a tendency for bureaucrats to aggrandize their role, actually setting themselves up as final arbiters of what is or is not good for the public.

Bureaucracies are characterized by red tape. Elaborate regulations are written that are unintelligible to the average citizen. The reasons for the "paper blizzard" are not difficult to discern. Regulations that prescribe procedures and forms that require extensive record keeping are imposed to set what is thought to be fair rules of the game. State and local governments, for example, complain about the information that must be supplied to federal agencies concerning equal opportunity, but those procedures were installed to discourage discriminatory practices and to encourage equal employment opportunities for minorities and women. Managers may complain about the red tape associated with dismissing employees, but those procedures have been established to protect workers against arbitrary dismissal. What is red tape to one person is not necessarily red tape to others. The employee who finds himself in a disciplinary situation is not likely to condemn the appeals procedure as mere red tape. In other words, all red tape has a purpose, and no matter how

---

[10] See Frederick C. Mosher, *Democracy and the Public Service* (New York: Oxford University Press, 1968) and Emmette S. Redford, *Democracy in the Administrative State* (New York: Oxford University Press, 1969).

[11] Carl J. Friedrich, "Responsible Government Service Under the American Constitution," in Carl J. Friedrich et al., *Problems of the American Public Service* (New York: McGraw-Hill, 1935), p. 28.

much one complains, red tape will continue to characterize government in general and personnel systems in particular.[12]

A problem stemming from red tape is that it can become counterproductive to the main objectives of the organization. Just as extensive air pollution controls reduce the efficiency of automobile engines, it is possible that extensive personnel controls and procedures can hinder agency efficiency. A police department eager to achieve racial balance in its work force may divert some of its limited resources away from the objective of controlling crime. Should a state government be advised to spend less on developing valid civil service tests and direct that money toward services that directly benefit the citizenry?

How political leadership is to control administrative processes is a related issue. The contention is made that those elected by the citizenry should have the power to govern, particularly that a chief executive should have control of the bureaucracy, including control of personnel. The 1962 Municipal Manpower Commission recommended: "The chief executive should be given clear-cut authority for personnel administration."[13] Allowing for chief executive control obviously arouses concern about politicizing personnel administration, a concern that always will be present.

The issue of political control is most sensitive in the higher levels of bureaucracy. Few people would openly contend that political considerations should enter into personnel actions concerning clerical workers and laborers. Where there are differing views is at high levels of administration, which necessarily involve questions of policy. In 1887, in a classic essay, Woodrow Wilson proposed a science of administration that would be largely divorced from politics.[14] That view of separating politics from administration is now considered unrealistic.

Between the partisan chief executive and mid-level merit employees are two types of officials for whom no clear-cut roles have been prescribed. One group consists of politically appointed executives—department secretaries, undersecretaries, assistant secretaries, and the like. Political executives often are amateur managers and have only limited support from the chief executive. Once political executives are

---

[12] Commission on Federal Paperwork, *Final Summary Report* (Washington: Government Printing Office, 1977); Herbert Kaufman, "The Direction of Organizational Evolution," *Public Administration Review*, 33 (1973):300–307; and Herbert Kaufman, *Red Tape: Its Origins, Uses, and Abuses* (Washington: Brookings Insitution, 1977).

[13] Municipal Manpower Commission, *Governmental Manpower for Tomorrow's Cities* (New York: McGraw-Hill, 1962), p. 106.

[14] Woodrow Wilson, "The Study of Administration," *Political Science Quarterly*, 2 (1887):197–222.

appointed, they are expected to carry out their responsibilities with little support from the chief executive and his immediate staff. Largely cut off from higher political authority, political executives must rely upon merit-appointed workers for information and advice and for performing the tasks of their agencies. Many political executives have felt trapped by their organizations; they have a sense of controlling their agencies in name only.[15]

The other group consists of career merit executives, who are one rung below the political executives. Career executives inevitably are involved in broad policy issues that have implications for partisan politics. A common recommendation has been that career merit executives should be afforded considerable job security while at the same time being responsive to political leadership. The idea of a career executive system with rank-in-the-person has been proposed many times, and President Carter's proposal for a Senior Executive Service was incorporated into the Civil Service Reform Act of 1978. Regardless of the specific proposals advanced for career executive systems, one fundamental issue remains: how are career executives to balance their professional judgments with the preferred policies of their immediate superiors and possibly differing preferred policies of the chief executive?

Special status for career executives is related to a more general issue, namely the extent to which the public service should consist of careerists. Encouraging careers in government is justified as helping workers, government, and the public. Career systems help individuals develop their potentials. A job is not just a job, but rather an opportunity for intellectual growth and the development of new skills. Career systems also are beneficial in that they supposedly increase governmental effectiveness and efficiency; the career worker is seen as being more productive than one who has been in government for only a short period. A competing value is that government jobs should be open to all qualified persons regardless of whether they are currently employed in government. Fostering careers can be an elitist approach to personnel administration. "Actually the career system verges on the closed system."[16]

The rights of executives and managers—both political appointees and those protected under a merit system—are another center of debate, particularly in relationship to subordinates. A common theme is that personnel systems have stripped managers of the power to manage. The Committee for Economic Development had taken this position, just prior to congressional passage of the Civil Service Reform Act:

---

[15] See Hugh Heclo, *A Government of Strangers: Executive Politics in Washington* (Washington: Brookings Institution, 1977).

[16] Paul P. Van Riper, *History of the United States Civil Service* (Evanston, Ill.: Row, Peterson, 1958), p. 554.

Perhaps the most serious charge that can be leveled at federal personnel administration under current conditions is that it is insufficiently oriented to support the management function. Under long established civil service restraints, department and agency heads are severely handicapped by their inability to deploy manpower in ways which put the right person in the right job, at the right time, for the right reason.[17]

Testing and selection procedures, such as the rule of three, limit managerial flexibility in personnel. Equal employment opportunity requirements and collective bargaining contracts further restrict managerial discretion. Managers are given official responsibility for directing their agencies to achieve expected results. However, such results only can be achieved through effective utilization of personnel, and the managers' powers in this respect are greatly circumscribed.

From the perspective of employees, managerial powers should be limited. Even when the vast majority of managers in government are dedicated to public service and are considerate of their subordinates, there may be some managers who would unfairly treat their workers should protective procedures not exist. Without appeal procedures on adverse action, for example, managers might feel unfettered in dismissing employees for inconsequential reasons. At the same time, these procedures do not guarantee fair treatment. Highly capable employees can be forced from their positions through reorganizations, transfers to different geographic locations, and being assigned undesirable tasks. Since the procedures do not guarantee equitable treatment, are they worth the costs that they impose on managers? Have merit systems provided excessive job security for workers so that firing incompetent workers is impossible? If this is the case, merit systems contribute to governmental inefficiency.[18]

There are other aspects to this issue of employee rights. One aspect involves participating in the political process. Government has precluded many of its workers from being active participants in partisan elections, but should acceptance of government employment require relinquishing this constitutionally protected right? To what extent should one's right to free speech be curtailed because of being a government employee? Is whistle blowing a healthy phenomenon or is it dangerous, in that it subverts the political administration chosen by the electorate? Do loyalty and security programs infringe on the right to privacy and foster timidity on the part of government employees?

---

[17] *Revitalizing the Federal Personnel System* (New York: Committee for Economic Development, 1978), p. 5.

[18] See David H. Rosenbloom, "Some Political Implications of the Drift Toward a Liberation of Federal Employees," *Public Administration Review*, 31 (1971):420–426 and David H. Rosenbloom, *Federal Service and the Constitution: The Development of the Public Employment Relationship* (Ithaca, N.Y.: Cornell University Press, 1971).

There is no universally accepted formula for motivating workers to increase efficiency and effectiveness. Part of the problem here is a substantive disagreement on what strategies are most likely to bring positive results. Should workers be given greater autonomy, as is encouraged by management by objectives and flexitime, or should more emphasis be given to group activities in which the manager is viewed as a leader and not the boss? Are workers motivated by being interested in the work they perform or in the financial rewards of work? Wage incentive systems, often considered in the past to have little bearing on worker performance, are regaining support by personnel reformists; while some see this as a reform, others regard it as a return to Theory X.[19]

Motivation also involves a value issue of what is fair play in dealing with workers. Are motivation schemes manipulative, in that the "right" strings are pulled on the marionette workers resulting in greater productivity? Labor unions have feared that efforts to improve worker motivation are intended to get more work from employees with no increase in pay.

A generally accepted value is that workers should have some role in determining how they perform their jobs. Motivation theories suggest that worker involvement leads to greater job satisfaction and improved performance. However, to what extent should workers be permitted to organize into labor unions and bargain with government over the conditions of work? To what extent are the various aspects of personnel systems appropriate subjects for collective bargaining? A traditional belief has been that bargaining is not totally compatible with merit.

Unresolved is the issue of how closely the public bureaucracy should represent the general population. Specifically, to what extent should personnel systems provide special procedures to increase the percentage of women, blacks, Hispanics, and other minorities in the public work force? Are policies intended to favor these groups a form of unacceptable reverse discrimination? Such favoritism would seem to conflict with the merit principle, in that skin color and sex have little bearing on how a worker performs a job.

Veterans are another group that has received special treatment. Veterans preference existed prior to the establishment of merit systems and has continued to be used even though the practice conflicts with the merit concept. The use of veterans preference is under increasing attack, but some form of preference is likely to continue.

Since the founding of this nation, a continuing problem has been determining the relative roles of the national, state, and local govern-

---

[19] Frederick C. Thayer, "The President's Management 'Reforms': Theory X Triumphant," *Public Administration Review*, 38 (1978):309–314.

ments. A continuous debate has focused upon whether the federal government has gained excessive powers. This problem of intergovernmental relations is apparent in the field of equal employment opportunity. State and local personnel systems must conform with federal requirements on affirmative action. Also, the federal government unsuccessfully sought to bring state and local employees under national work standards. There has been pressure for the federal government to adopt legislation that would set ground rules for labor-management relations at the state and local levels.

One aspect of the issue of intergovernmental relations involves federal grants for public employment. State and local governments have welcomed this financial assistance, but a problem has been that the federal program is designed to put people into jobs almost without regard to efficiency. This use of public employment as a means of economic stimulation can conflict with the merit principle.

An important societal value has been that citizens should be able to play some direct roles in government, even though ours is a representative form of democracy. When this value is applied to the field of personnel, it raises the issue of whether citizens should be involved in individual personnel actions. Should disciplinary proceedings include citizens, as in the case of citizen review boards? Should citizens be able to file legal suits not only against a government body but also against individual workers? How is the value of citizen rights to be balanced with the value of employee rights? Does allowing for citizen suits create timid government workers? Does protecting workers from suits make them indifferent to citizen needs? One study found that the longer an individual was employed by the federal government, the more likely that he held anti-democratic values.[20]

These unresolved issues are only some of the fundamental ones facing government and public personnel systems. They are not a complete catalog. The point is that these basic value questions have not been resolved, so that public personnel systems are expected to serve simultaneously a wide range of values that are not synchronized with each other. Attacking the personnel field as devoid of theory is unwarranted. The problem is not a lack of theory, but an overabundance of theories. Personnel administration cannot be governed by a coherent set of values when there is no societal consensus about the relative importance of fundamental values that affect the entire governmental system.[21] As long as the governmental system remains as it is, namely

[20] Bob L. Wynia, "Federal Bureaucrats' Attitudes toward a Democratic Ideology," *Public Administration Review*, 34 (1974):156–162.

[21] See Vincent Ostrom, *The Intellectual Crisis in American Public Administration*, rev. ed. (University: University of Alabama Press, 1974).

open or receptive to competing ideas and values, there will be no permanent resolution of this problem. Personnel systems must learn to cope with the ambiguity and not expect it to disappear.

THE FUTURE

Forecasting the future is not an easy assignment. It entails projecting what is likely to occur if present trends continue and then judging whether participants in the system are likely to alter their behavior and thereby change the direction of the projected trends. The process is highly susceptible to faulty extrapolations from current events. For instance, observers in the 1960s might have forecasted continuation of urban riots throughout the 1970s when, of course, that did not occur.[22]

A problem of forecasting is that it is difficult to predict the intensity of incentives for change. The air pollution resulting from increasing reliance on the automobile could have been projected, but until recent years there were insufficient incentives to adopt policies to combat pollution.[23] Similarly, the problem of energy supplies is acute, and despite the seemingly strong incentives involved, the political system has had great difficulty in adopting a comprehensive policy to deal with that problem.

Making a forecast for personnel administration could begin with forecasting societal and global changes and then attempting to relate those changes to personnel systems.[24] Will there be nuclear war? Will

---

[22] Herman Kahn and B. Bruce-Briggs, *Things to Come: Thinking About the Seventies and Eighties* (New York: Macmillan, 1972), pp. 162–163. See also Lewis Benton, ed., *Management for the Future* (New York: McGraw-Hill, 1978); J. Bronowski, *A Sense of the Future: Essays in Natural Philosophy* (Cambridge, Mass.: Massachusetts Institute of Technology Press, 1977); Harlan Cleveland, *The Future Executive* (New York: Harper and Row, 1972); Warren H. Fox, "Uncertain Future of Public Management," *Public Personnel Management*, 5 (1976):250–254; R. Buckminister Fuller, *Operating Manual for Spaceship Earth* (Carbondale: Southern Illinois University Press, 1969); Roger J. Goodman, "Change and the Public Personnel Manager," *Public Personnel Management*, 5 (1976):103–107; Walter A. Hahn and Dennis L. Little, eds.: "Public Administration in the Third Century," *Public Adminstration Review*, 36 (1976):577–613; Wallace S. Sayre and Frederick C. Mosher, *An Agenda for Research in Public Personnel Administration* (Washington: National Planning Association, 1959); Robert Theobald, *Beyond Despair: Directions for America's Third Century* (Washington: New Republic, 1976); Alvin Toffler, ed., *The Futurists* (New York: Random House, 1972); Franklin Tugwell, ed., *Search for Alternatives: Public Policy and the Study of the Future* (Cambridge, Mass.: Winthrop, 1973); and Dwight Waldo, ed., "Symposium on Organizations for the Future," *Public Administration Review*, 33 (1973):299–335.

[23] Joseph F. Coates, "Why Think about the Future: Some Administrative-Political Perspectives," *Public Administration Review*, 36 (1976):581.

[24] For possible projections, see Kahn and Bruce-Briggs, *Things to Come*, pp. 162–185; Coates, "Why Think about the Future," p. 581; and Walter A. Hahn and Kenneth F. Gordon, eds., *Assessing the Future and Policy Planning* (New York: Gordon and Breach, 1973).

extensive new oil reserves be located, and in what countries? Questions of this type are extraordinarily important but they cannot be addressed here; to open up those questions would start a new book, not end this one. Instead, the assumption made here is that there will be a general continuation of existing trends. This has been called a "surprise-free projection."[25]

In this surprise-free projection, the assumption can be made that the problems discussed in the preceding section will persist. There is no basis for assuming that the issue of political influence in personnel matters will subside. The familiar debates about the rights of a chief executive, agency managers, and employees will not fade. The pressure for equal employment opportunity and affirmative action will continue, along with increasing use of collective bargaining. As has been explained, these unresolved issues are fundamental ones that are not subject to "quickie" solutions.

Beyond those issues, there are economic forces that are likely to influence public personnel systems. Barring any radical redistribution of taxing powers and service provision responsibilities among the levels of government, budgets at the state and local levels may become tighter. While the federal government enjoys fiscal dividends, namely that revenues increase as the economy expands, state and local governments are less fortunate, since they rely largely on sales and property taxes rather than on a graduated income tax. Tight budgets are likely to mean a halt in the growth of public employment. Limiting growth may have the effect of blocking career advancement. When new jobs are being created, people in government have excellent opportunities for promotions, but when the size of the work force is stable, opportunities dwindle. For some jurisdictions tight budgets will lead to furloughing employees; that already has occurred in many central cities, some states, and in the U.S. Postal Service. The likely result of either a stable or declining work force is increasing worker demand for job security. This would stimulate further growth in collective bargaining as workers organize in the hope of protecting their jobs.

Another possible outgrowth of tight budgets would be increasing emphasis upon program evaluation and personnel evaluation. In other words, why fund programs and hire workers when only limited results are achieved? There may be incentives to find more cost-effective mixes of personnel. The general pressure for evaluation may encourage further developments in performance appraisal systems, but if these are used for weeding out less productive workers, the process will increase worker demands for job security.

---

[25] Kahn and Bruce-Briggs, *Things to Come*, pp. 39–40.

Tight budgets also may be an incentive for substituting machines for personnel. Labor costs in government have risen sharply, perhaps in part because of the increasing use of collective bargaining. As personnel costs rise, substitution of machines becomes more economically feasible. The conversion to greater use of machines, however, is limited by the nature of governmental services. Many government jobs cannot be handled by machines.

A different set of circumstances could occur because of other economic trends. The national economy has been in serious trouble throughout the 1970s, and one response has been to use state and local government employment as a means for economic stimulation. If this economic trend continues, public-service jobs financed by the federal government could become a permanent phenomenon, leading to substantial increases in government employment. Adoption of the original version of the Humphrey-Hawkins bill would have virtually guaranteed substantial expansion in public employment.

Another area of change is increasing complexity in governmental work. Patronage in the 1800s could be defended on the grounds that almost anyone could adequately perform the duties of government jobs. Today, government jobs are highly technical. Even many clerical jobs are technical, involving the use of complex office equipment, some of which is computer controlled. Of course, many nontechnical jobs will remain, at least until breakthroughs can be achieved in the way services are provided. Until the pothole-proof road can be built, there will be road crews and jobs that require little skill.

The increasingly technical nature of jobs creates problems. Recruiting people with the necessary skills may be difficult. Technical jobs may tend to keep minorities out of government. Increasingly technical jobs can be threatening to workers. Technological change makes workers' skills obsolete.[26] Some individuals will welcome the challenge of learning new skills, but others will not. There will be increasing emphasis on mid-career training, although present doubts about whether training has real payoffs will continue.

The increasing complexity of governmental work has been seen as a possible threat to democracy. The "administrative state," "professional state" or "technocracy" has already developed.[27] Many federal and state jobs require persons with college degrees in science and engineering. All

---

[26] David F. Linowes, *Strategies for Survival* (New York: American Management Association, 1973), pp. 71–72, and Alvin Toffler, *Future Shock* (New York: Bantam Books, 1971).

[27] Dwight Waldo, *The Administrative State: A Study of the Political Theory of American Public Administration* (New York: Ronald, 1948); Dwight Waldo, "The Administrative State Revisited," *Public Administration Review*, 25 (1965):5–30; Mosher, *Democracy and the Public Service*; and Kahn and Bruce-Briggs, *Things to Come*.

levels of government require persons with degrees in education, law, social work, and health. The Federalists were an elite of wealth, and today's elite consists of professionals. To what exent do professionals virtually dictate to the citizenry and their political leaders what policies and programs are to be adopted? To what extent is that practice likely to increase?

Technocracy challenges the traditional role of the manager as boss. Expertise has long been recognized as a source of power.[28] However, the gap may be widening between what managers know and what they need to know to take appropriate action. In other words, managers are likely to become increasingly dependent upon subordinate specialists. Authority based upon one's position in the hierarchy may be replaced by "sapiential authority," or authority based on knowledge.[29]

The increasing role of professionals in government has led to the suggestion that theory Y is likely to become the dominant approach to management. Professionals presumably resent hierarchical authority and perform best in situations that provide them with great autonomy.[30] Forecasts have been made that bureaucratic structures will become flatter, producing wider spans of control and consequently increased worker autonomy.[31] A nonhierarchical form of bureaucracy has been proposed.[32] Organizations of the future might consist of temporary groups, created to deal with specific problems and frequently restructured as the nature of the problems changed. Were that type of organization to emerge, there would be little need for position classification, pay plans, and other common aspects of personnel systems.

In contrast with this forecast of a fluid bureaucratic structure, a forecast could equally be made that rigidities will continue. The work ethic may be declining, so that Theory X is needed to keep worker performance from declining. A tradition of governmental systems has

---

[28] Robert Michels, *Political Parties: A Sociological Study of the Oligarchical Tendencies of Modern Democracy*, trans. by Eden and Cedar Paul (Glencoe, Ill.: Free Press, 1949). See also William G. Scott, "The Theory of Significant People," *Public Administration Review*, 33 (1973):308–313.

[29] Robert Theobald, *An Alternative Future for America II* (Chicago: Swallow, 1970), pp. 76–83. See also Victor A. Thompson, *Modern Organization: A General Theory* (New York: Knopf, 1961).

[30] George E. Berkley, *The Administrative Revolution: Notes on the Passing of Organization Man* (Englewood Cliffs, N.J.: Prentice-Hall, 1971), pp. 70–72.

[31] Richard L. Chapman and Frederic N. Cleveland, "The Changing Character of the Public Service and the Administrator of the 1980's," *Public Administration Review*, 33 (1973):358–366, and Richard L. Chapman and Frederic N. Cleveland, *Meeting the Needs of Tomorrow's Public Service: Guidelines for Professional Education in Public Administration* (Washington: National Academy of Public Administration, 1973).

[32] Neely Gardner, "The Non-Hierarchical Organization of the Future: Theory vs. Reality," *Public Administration Review*, 36 (1976):591–598, and Larry Kirkhart, "Toward a Theory of Public Administration," in Frank Marini, ed., *Toward a New Public Administration* (Scranton, Pa.: Chandler, 1979), pp. 127–164.

been to fix organizational structure, often establishing it by legislation. That tradition will be difficult to overcome. Fixed organizational arrangements provide a sense of holding agencies responsible for their actions, whereas a more fluid structure might encourage "buck passing." Corporations would seem more likely to move to fluid structures; when corporations are faced with declining profits, there has been considerable willingness to modify organizational configurations and reassign personnel. Reassigning personnel in government may be difficult because of the fear that such changes could be used for political advantage and would abuse the rights of employees.

Both fluid and rigid structures probably will exist in the future. Variety can be expected among and within governments. Not all state governments will operate alike, nor will all departments within a state government. Discovering where fluid structures are more effective than rigid ones, and vice versa, is a major task for the future.

CLOSING COMMENT

The early personnel reformers had a cause. They looked forward to the day "when a change of party in the national Administration will no longer present the barbarous spectacle of a spoils debauch, torturing the nostrils of our own people and disgracing the Republic in the eyes of civilized mankind."[33] The cause of eliminating patronage continues, but, as has been seen, there are many other values that influence public personnel systems. These values are not totally compatible with each other and reflect a lack of consensus about how government should operate. The future of public personnel systems is uncertain because the outcomes of the struggle over values is uncertain.

Since values vary throughout the society. it seems inappropriate to propose a single set of recommendations for future personnel systems. One model personnel system could not serve the varying needs of all jurisdictions. The federal government, for instance, has replaced the civil service commission model, but that model may still be an effective one for many state and local governments. Some jurisdictions may be able to loosen controls on political participation by government workers, whereas other jurisdictions that took such action would be inviting a return to political patronage.

The future obviously will bring change to public personnel systems, but what changes, and for what ends, are unclear. Condemning the practices of personnel administration can be great sport, but developing workable solutions to perceived problems is a formidable task.

---

[33] Schurz, *The Spoils System*, pp. 46–47.

A Research Guide to Personnel Literature

Aside from using the subject portion of a library's card catalogue, there are numerous sources that can be helpful in researching public personnel systems. This guide provides assistance in locating relevant materials. A traditional form of bibliography has not been included here because the preceding chapters are extensively footnoted. Bibliographies on selected topics in personnel administration are published periodically by the U.S. Office of Personnel Management.

There are both new and old general books on public personnel. These include: N. Joseph Cayer, *Public Personnel Administration in the United States* (New York: St. Martin's, 1975); William E. Mosher and J. Donald Kingsley, *Public Personnel Administration* (New York: Harper and Brothers, 1936), which is now in its 7th edition, authored by O. Glen Stahl (New York: Harper and Row, 1976); Felix A. Nigro and Lloyd G. Nigro, *The New Public Personnel Administration* (Itasca, Ill.: Peacock, 1976); Jay M. Shafritz et al., *Personnel Management in Government* (New York: Dekker, 1978); and William G. Torpey, *Public Personnel Management* (New York: Van Nostrand, 1953). Collections of articles include Robert T. Golembiewski and Michael Cohen, eds., *People in Public Service*, 2d ed. (Itasca, Ill.: Peacock, 1976) and Jay M. Shafritz, ed., *The Public Personnel World* (Chicago: International Personnel Management Association, 1977).

Several periodicals are of general use. *Public Personnel Management* (Washington: International Personnel Management Association) contains articles pertinent to all aspects of public personnel. The *Civil Service Journal* (U.S. Civil Service Commission/Office of Personnel Management) is geared specifically to federal personnel systems. More general periodicals that frequently contain articles on personnel include *Public Administration Review* (Washington: American Society for Public Administration), *State Government* (Lexington, Ky.: Council of

State Governments), *National Civic Review* (New York: National Municipal League), and *Public Management* (Washington: International City Management Association). Other periodicals are geared to specific aspects of personnel. Such periodicals include the *Journal of Applied Psychology, Organizational Behavior and Human Performance, Administrative Science Quarterly, Academy of Management Journal,* and *Labor Law Journal,* to name only a few. Perusing each of these journals to locate articles would be excessively time consuming. Therefore, the following indexes should be used: *Psychological Abstracts* (Washington: American Psychological Association); *Public Affairs Information Service Bulletin* (New York: Public Affairs Information Service); *Sage Public Administration Abstracts* (Beverly Hills, Calif.: Sage); *Social Sciences Citation Index* (Philadelphia: Institute for Scientific Information); and *Social Sciences Index* (New York: Wilson).

Several annual or biennial references on state and local governments contain chapters on personnel. Included are *The Book of the States* (Lexington, Ky.: Council of State Governments), issued every two years; *The Municipal Yearbook* (Washington: International City Management Association); and *The County Yearbook* (Washington: National Association of Counties).

Numerous federal government documents can provide important information. Two reference works that explain government documents are Laurence F. Schmeckebier and Roy B. Eastin's *Government Publications and Their Use,* 2d rev. ed. (Washington: Brookings, 1969) and Joe Morehead's *Introduction to United States Public Documents* (Littleton, Col.: Libraries Unlimited, 1975). *Public Employment,* compiled annually by the Census Bureau, is an excellent source for current data on workers at all levels of government. The U.S. Office of Personnel Management provides many useful reports. The Department of Labor and the General Accounting Office also issue useful reports. Several indexes are available for locating government reports. The indexes include the *Monthly Catalog of United States Government Publications* (Washington: Government Printing Office); *Index to U.S. Government Periodicals* (Chicago: Infordata International); and *Congressional Information Service Index* (Congressional Information Service). The *American Statistics Index* (Congressional Information Service) is useful for locating data contained in government documents. *Government Reports Announcements and Index* (National Technical Information Service, U.S. Department of Commerce) indexes many reports that have been prepared for federal agencies but are not published—they can be obtained in photocopy form.

This book has emphasized legal aspects of public personnel systems, because courts are assuming increasingly important roles in these systems. For the uninitiated legal research may seem frightening, but it need not. Three useful guides to legal research are *Basic Legal Research Techniques*, rev. 3d ed. (Charlottesville, Va.: Research Group, 1976); Morris L. Cohen, *Legal Research in a Nutshell*, 3d ed. (St. Paul: West, 1978); and J. Myron Jacobstein and Ray M. Mersky, *Ervin H. Pollack's Fundamentals of Legal Research*, 4th ed. (Mineola, N.Y.: Foundation Press, 1973). These books identify the main legal research tools and explain how to use them. For help on understanding legal terminology, consult Daniel Oran, *Law Dictionary for Non-Lawyers* (St. Paul: West, 1975), or Henry C. Black, *Black's Law Dictionary*, rev. 4th ed. (St. Paul: West, 1968).

If one is exploring a legal aspect of personnel for the first time, a place to begin is to find a summarization of the pertinent issues. Journal articles are helpful in this respect and identify leading court cases. To locate appropriate articles, use *Index to Legal Periodicals* (New York: Wilson). That index not only has subject entries but also court case entries; in other words, if a particular case is of interest, the index can be used to locate articles that interpret the case. *Corpus Juris Secundum* (St. Paul: West) is a massive legal encyclopedia that is updated annually.

Laws also need to be researched. U.S. laws are published in their original form in *United States Statutes at Large* (Washington: Government Printing Office). The Pendleton Act can be cited as 22 Stat. 403 (1883), with the first number being the volume and the second number the page. This is a common form of legal citation. The utility of *Statutes at Large* is limited because the original legislation may have been amended numerous times. Therefore, to locate the current governing legislation use the *United States Code* (Washington: Government Printing Office). The multi-volume reference codifies federal statutes; in other words, statutes are arranged by subject matter. An even more useful source is the *United States Code Annotated* (St. Paul: West), which follows the same format of the *U.S. Code* but in addition provides citations of court cases that interpret the pertinent legislation. Citations for the code follow a format similar to other legal citations. The title is abbreviated as "U.S.C.," for the code itself, or "U.S.C.A.," for the annotated code. One difference in citing the code is that section number is used rather than page number; the symbol "§" precedes the number. Similar reference works on state laws are available for each state.

Administrative agencies issue regulations that interpret the legislation being enforced. At the federal level, proposed regulations are published in the *Federal Register*, which is issued Monday through Friday. Once regulations are adopted, they are incorporated into the *Code of Federal Regulations*, cited as "C.F.R."

The federal government has three main levels of courts. District courts are the lowest level and their opinions are printed in *Federal Supplement* (St. Paul: West). Also in the *Federal Supplement*, cited as "F. Supp.," are U.S. Custom Court opinions. The next level is the circuit courts of appeal, and their opinions can be found in the *Federal Reporter* (St. Paul: West), cited as "F. 2d," with the "2d" for second series. The *Federal Reporter* also includes the opinions of the U.S. Court of Claims and the U.S. Court of Custom and Patent Appeals.

United States Supreme Court opinions are published in three series. The federal government prints *United States Reports*, which is cited as "U.S." This citation has been used throughout this book except for the most recent cases, where the "U.S." citation was not available. In those instances, the *Supreme Court Reporter* (St. Paul: West) has been used; those cases have "S.Ct." citations. The third source of Supreme Court opinions is the *United States Supreme Court Reports: Lawyer's Edition* (Rochester, N.Y.: Lawyers Co-operative); a case cited from the *Lawyer's Edition* would have a designation of "L. Ed. 2d." Both the *Supreme Court Reporter* and the *Lawyer's Edition* contain helpful research aids that are not included in the *United States Reports*.

Important state court decisions can be found through a series of regional reporters (St. Paul: West). The *Pacific Reporter*, for example, contains opinions from courts in Arizona, California, Colorado, and several other states. The *Atlantic Reporter* includes opinions from Maryland, New Jersey, Pennsylvania, and other states.

Several digests (St. Paul: West) compile court decisions by subject. *West's General Digest* is now in its fourth series. The *Eighth Decennial Digest* covers 1966 to 1976. Other digests are available for the regional reporters.

Keeping up to date in the legal field can be accomplished through several sources. Reading current articles from legal periodicals is helpful. If one wants to determine the current status of a court case that was decided a few years ago, *Shepard's Citations* (Colorado Springs: Shepard's) should be used. *Shepard's* indicates whether or not a lower court decision was appealed and it identifies other court opinions that have cited the case that is of interest. It also identifies court cases as they pertain to sections of the U.S. Code. *Shepard's Citations* are available for the regional reports mentioned above. *The Government Employee Relations Report* (Washington: Bureau of National Affairs) is issued weekly and is especially helpful in public-sector labor-management relations as well as other personnel-related topics. *United States Law Week* (Washington: Bureau of National Affairs) reports current court decisions.

Happy reading!

Index